THE

BIOGRAPHICAL RECORD

OF

ROCK ISLAND COUNTY,

ILLINOIS.

ILLUSTRATED.

"A people that take no pride in the noble achievements of remote ancestors will never achieve anything worthy to be remembered with pride by remote generations."—MACAULAY.

CHICAGO:
THE S. J. CLARKE PUBLISHING COMPANY.
1897.

"Biography is the only true history."
—EMERSON.

PREFACE.

THE greatest of English historians, MACAULAY, and one of the most brilliant writers of the present century, has said: "The history of a country is best told in a record of the lives of its people." In conformity with this idea, the BIOGRAPHICAL RECORD has been prepared. Instead of going to musty records, and taking therefrom dry statistical matter that can be appreciated but by few, our corps of writers have gone to the people, the men and women who have, by their enterprise and industry, brought these counties to a rank second to none among those comprising this great and noble State, and from their lips have the story of their life struggles. No more interesting or instructive matter could be presented to an intelligent public. In this volume will be found a record of many whose lives are worthy the imitation of coming generations. It tells how some, commencing life in poverty, by industry and economy have accumulated wealth. It tells how others, with limited advantages for securing an education, have become learned men and women, with an influence extending throughout the length and breadth of the land. It tells of men who have risen from the lower walks of life to eminence as statesmen, and whose names have become famous. It tells of those in every walk in life who have striven to succeed, and records how that success has usually crowned their efforts. It tells also of many, very many, who, not seeking the applause of the world, have pursued the "even tenor of their way," content to have it said of them, as Christ said of the woman performing a deed of mercy—"They have done what they could." It tells how many, in the pride and strength of young manhood, left the plow and the anvil, the lawyer's office and the counting-room, left every trade and profession, and at their country's call went forth valiantly "to do or die," and how through their efforts the Union was restored and peace once more reigned in the land. In the life of every man and of every woman is a lesson that should not be lost upon those who follow after.

Coming generations will appreciate this volume and preserve it as a sacred treasure, from the fact that it contains so much that would never find its way into public records, and which would otherwise be inaccessible. Great care has been taken in the compilation of the work, and every opportunity possible given to those represented to insure correctness in what has been written; and the publishers flatter themselves that they give to their readers a work with few errors of consequence. In addition to biographical sketches, portraits of a number of representative citizens are given.

The faces of some, and biographical sketches of many, will be missed in this volume. For this the publishers are not to blame. Not having a proper conception of the work, some refused to give the information necessary to compile a sketch, while others were indifferent. Occasionally some member of the family would oppose the enterprise, and on account of such opposition the support of the interested one would be withheld. In a few instances men never could be found, though repeated calls were made at their residence or place of business.

October, 1897.   THE S. J. CLARKE PUBLISHING CO.

J. M. Gould

BIOGRAPHICAL.

HON JOHN M GOULD, of Moline, Illinois, has for almost half a century been prominently identified with the interests of Rock Island county In every community there are those who are leaders of men Some lead by reason of that impetuous nature that brooks no delay and must be in the front Others because of that quiet dignity of character that commands the respect of all, and who steadily push on, doing everything in their power, not only to advance their individual interests, but that of the community in which they live, and who have a just regard for the rights of their fellow men Among the latter class there is no better representative than the subject of this sketch

John Maxfield Gould is a native of New Hampshire, born in Piermont, February 24, 1822, and is of the eighth generation from Zacheus Gould, a native of England, who settled in Massachusetts in 1620, and whose homestead yet remains in the family Amos Gould, the grandfather of our subject, was a native of Massachusetts, and in the American Revolution assisted the colonies in effecting their independence. In his later years a grateful country granted him a pension for his services in that struggle Soon after the close of the war he removed to New Hampshire, where his son, Amos Gould, Jr , the father of our subject, was born

Amos Gould, Jr , in early life learned the tanner and currier trade, but later engaged in agricultural pursuits, which occupation he followed throughout the remainder of his life He married Nancy H Bartlett, a native of New Hampshire and a daughter of Nathaniel Bartlett, also a soldier in the Revolutionary war, who fought seven years for American independence, and who likewise received a pension from the general government To Amos and Nancy H Gould ten children were born nine of whom grew to mature years, and all came west and settled in Rock Island and Henry counties, Illinois Of the ten seven are yet living In 1858 the parents joined their children, and were cared for by them in their declining years The father died in Moline in 1864, while his wife long survived him, dying in 1884 Both lie side by side in the beautiful Riverside cemetery, while their memories are cherished by their children and surviving friends

John M. Gould was the oldest of the family of children, and upon the old farm in the Granite State grew to manhood, his nature partaking somewhat of the character of its hills and mountains, on which he toiled year after year until past his majority He received a fair education, supplemented by two years' attendance in the academies of Canaan and Lyme, New Hampshire At nineteen, or after, he began teaching

1

three winters, working on the farm in the summer.

While the old hills were dear to his heart and the ties of kindred strong, the range of vision was too confining, and the possibilities too limited for one of his nature, and so he determined to come west, with the hope that he might better himself in life and be and do something worthy of his name Without capital, save willing hands and a stout heart, he set out, and in due season reached Grand Detour, Ogle county, Illinois, which at that time gave promise of a bright future   There he found employment as clerk in a general store, and for three years served in that position, receiving a thorough, practical business training, which has served him well through life

On the termination of his three years, Mr Gould was admitted as partner in the firm, and remained with it one year, when he sold out and came to Moline as partner and financial manager of the firm of Deere, Tate & Gould, manufacturers of plows This business was started by Mr Deere at Grand Detour in a small way, but needing the assistance of those with means and ability to look after the financial affairs of the concern, while he gave his attention to the manufacture, he formed the partnership with Messrs Tate & Gould, and the plant was removed to Moline. This was in 1848 From a modest beginning, and with limited capital, has grown one of the largest manufacturing concerns for the making of plows in the world, and the fame of the Deere plows is world wide

Mr. Gould acted as financial manager of this concern for nearly four years, when the firm was dissolved, Mr Deere succeeding to the entire business   Mr Gould then formed a partnership with D W a C

Dimock for the manufacture of woodenware, the first institution of the kind established in the west   It was conceived by our subject, who tried for years to interest some one and induce them to engage in the manufacture.   Land on the island was rented from the government and business began, which was carried on with great success for many years   In 1867 the government demanded the vacation of the island, and as their sawing had been done at the mill adjacent, they were compelled to make other arrangements   Accordingly they erected a sawmill and in 1868 commenced the manufacture and sale of lumber, in addition to that used for woodenware

At this time a stock company was formed to more successfully carry on the business, and Mr Dimock was elected president and Mr Gould, vice-president   In this latter office he served until 1886, when, on the death of Mr. Dimock, he was made president of the company, which position he still fills   In 1856 the plant of the woodenware manufactory was burned and was at once rebuilt, larger and better than ever   In June, 1875, their sawmill was struck by lightning and destroyed   In the first instance there was no insurance on the property, but in the latter case it was fully insured   Notwithstanding these and other drawbacks the business of the company continued to increase, until to-day it is one of the strongest lumber companies in the Mississippi valley   In 1890 the woodenware branch of the business was sold to a syndicate, who removed the machinery, since which time the entire business has been that of lumbering and the manufacture of paper pails   The company owns extensive tracts of pine lands in Wisconsin, and the lumber, after cutting of logs is rafted to

Moline, where it is manufactured into lumber The mills have a capacity of one hundred thirty thousand feet per day, and saw annually about thirty million feet Shingles and lath are also manufactured by the company.

In 1857, in the midst of the financial crisis of that period, Mr Gould, in company with D C Dimock and C P Ryder, established a bank in Moline under the firm name of Gould, Dimock & Company. This bank was personally managed by Mr Gould with good success until 1863, when it was incorporated and chartered as the First National Bank of Moline, with Mr Gould as cashier, which position he filled until 1867 The bank was organized with a paid up capital stock of fifty thousand dollars, which has been increased to one hundred and fifty thousand, with a large surplus On retiring as cashier, Mr Gould was elected president of the bank, which position he has continually held to the present time, a period of thirty years To his wise executive ability and clear judgment, much of the credit is due for its successful operation

It was for the purpose of giving more of his time to the milling and lumbering interests of the company that Mr Gould resigned as cashier of the bank This step was rendered necessary by the vastly increased business of the mill, and for years almost his undivided attention was given to it But a man of his active temperament could not be confined to any one line. His well-known business ability, recognized by every one, called his services into requisition in various ways In the organization of the Moline Water Power Company he took an active part, and has been its secretary since its conception In fact there has been few public or private enterprises organized in

which his advice or aid has not been invited He is a member of the Davenport & Rock Island Bridge & Railway Terminal Company, organized in 1888, at which time he was made a director For two years he has been serving as vice-president This company is now engaged in the construction of a new bridge across the river between Rock Island and Davenport, which will be one of the finest and best in the country

When Mr Gould came to Moline he kept the only set of double entry books in Rock Island county The system was a curiosity to many, and gave him quite a reputation as an expert book-keeper and accountant. His ability as a financier was also quickly recognized, and in all probability it was for this reason that he was elected county judge in 1853. That his selection was a wise one for the county is attested by the fact that when he was elected county orders were worth but fifty cents on the dollar, but before the expiration of his term they were worth one hundred cents on the dollar and have never since been below par In addition to the probate business, the county judge, with his two associates, at that time transacted all the business required of the present board of supervisors

Judge Gould has been twice married His first marriage, which event was celebrated August 13, 1848, was with Miss Alice Chase Moulton, a daughter of William Moulton, of Randolph, Vermont, and a second cousin of Secretary Chase, of Ohio Her death occurred a few weeks after their marriage. His second union was at Moline, Illinois, August 9, 1850, with Miss Hannah M Dimock, a native of Wellington, Connecticut, and a sister of De Witt C Dimock, who later became a partner of Mr Gould, a relation which terminated only in his death Mrs Gould was reared and educated in her native state, where she also taught school for a while before coming west On coming to Moline she again engaged in teaching, at a time when all the pupils in Moline district were accommodated in one small room To Judge and Mrs. Gould five children were born, three of whom are now living The oldest, Alice May, died in infancy. Frank W , now treasurer of the firm of Dimock, Gould & Company, married Marcia L Towndrow, and has one child. Fred G is shipping clerk for the same company He married Sarah Simpson and has three children Grace Eliza is the wife of S. M Hill, treasurer of the Moline Plow Company. John died in infancy. Mrs. Gould is a worthy member of the Baptist church of Moline, to which the Judge, although not a member, is a liberal contributor

Judge Gould was reared a Democrat, and on the ticket of that party was elected county judge, the only elective office he ever held It need not be inferred from this fact, however, that he could have been elected to other official positions, for the time has never been when he could not have had any office desired, but his business interests have been such that he could not serve Being strongly opposed to slavery and especially its extension into free territory, he naturally allied himself with the Republican party on its organization, and has since been identified with it He is a strong believer in the doctrine of protection and reciprocity, as well as of sound money, and therefore sees no reason for a change of political relation, especially as the Republican party stands square upon these questions For sixteen years he served as a member of the ... ...

ities, when he was removed by Governor Altgeld for political reasons His record in that position is a commendable one

Judge Gould has now been a resident of Moline for forty-nine long years, and is one of the few remaining of the honored old settlers of Rock Island county He has witnessed the growth and development of the state until it ranks third in population and wealth He has seen Moline grow from an insignificant village to be one of the first manufacturing cities of the state He has been one of the foremost in building up and advancing the interests of his adopted city, and has been identified with almost all of its institutions. Throughout Illinois and the western states generally he is well known, and as a man of superior business ability, of tried integrity and worth, he has the confidence and esteem of all, and none stand higher in the estimation of the people With such a record it is no wonder that Judge Gould is so highly honored

WILLIAM O BEAM, M D , a prominent and successful physician and surgeon of Moline, is one of the younger members of the medical fraternity, but he enjoys a large and lucrative practice, which many an older physician might well envy. His office is now located in rooms 1 and 2, in the Skinner Block, and is well equipped with all the appliances of the modern practitioner

The Doctor was born in Waltham, Tama county, Iowa, October 26, 1869, and is a son of Dr. William O and Hester Ann (Stewart) Beam, the former a native of Preble county, Ohio, born of German parents and the latter of Medina county, Ohio, of Irish ancestry Both accompanied their respective parents to Linn county, Iowa, at an early day, there met and married They were the parents of eight children, as follows Watson W , now a practicing physician of Rolfe, Iowa, Charles H , a druggist of Rolfe, Iowa, Hugh Atlee, clerk in his brother's drug store, Della J , wife of John A Owen, an undertaker of Toledo, Iowa, Jennie G , a teacher in Pocahontas county, Iowa, Frank L , wife of James H Charlton, a hustling stockman, William O , our subject, and Hattie L , wife of Charles E Fraser, cashier of the State Savings Bank of Rolfe, Iowa

From Linn county the family removed to Waltham, Tama county, where the father practiced his profession for some years In 1879 they removed to Dysart, in the same county, and later to Humboldt county, Iowa Dr Beam, Sr., was a physician of great skill, and had quite an extensive practice The country in which he lived being comparatively new, necessitated long drives to reach the afflicted His death occurred April 5, 1888, while his wife survived him some years, dying January 30, 1896

The subject of this sketch received his primary education in the public schools of Waltham and Dysart, Iowa, and later pursued his studies in an academy at Humboldt where he prepared himself for teaching At the early age of seventeen years he taught his first term of school in Humboldt county, Iowa, and for some years followed that profession as a means of livelihood, in his native state and in Rock Island county, Illinois While teaching in this county he formed the acquaintance with his future wife

It was never the aim of the Doctor to follow the teacher's profession as a life work It was only used as a stepping stone to that which in many respects takes prece-

dence of all others—the medical profession So in the fall of 1887 he began reading medicine in the office of Dr Samuel Thompson, of Toledo, Iowa, and one year later entered Rush Medical College, Chicago After attending lectures for two years in that institution, he passed a successful examination before the State Board of Medical Examiners of Iowa and at once commenced practice in Pocahontas county Later he spent one year in the College of Physicians and Surgeons, Chicago, from which he graduated April 13, 1893, ranking seventh in his class, and being one of sixteen on the roll of honor

In March, 1894, Dr Beam came to Moline with a view of making this his future home, and on the 25th of the following month was united in marriage to Miss Margaret L E Whiteside, a daughter of William and Elizabeth Whiteside, honored early settlers of Rock Island county One child graces this union—Margaret S , born in Moline, November 12, 1896

That the Doctor has made no mistake in the choice of a place in which to follow his profession, is attested by the large practice which he has acquired in the short space of three years His skill and ability, both as a physician and surgeon, are acknowledged not alone by the people, but by the medical fraternity as well, and he is to-day an honored member of the Illinois and Iowa Central District Medical Association, and of the Illinois and Iowa State Medical Societies In July, 1896, he was elected city physician of Moline, and so ably and satisfactorily did he discharge the duties of the position, that he was re-elected in July, 1897, and is the present incumbent

Fraternally Dr Beam is a member of Doric Lodge No. 319. A. F. & A M , of

Moline, and of Barrett Chapter, No 18, R. A M , of Rock Island, in both of which he takes special interest He is also a member of Manufacturer's Lodge, No. 485, I O O. F , of Moline, and of Moline Tent, No 164, K O T. M Politically the Doctor has always been an ardent supporter of Republican principles, but professional duties have prevented his taking that active part in political affairs that might reasonably be expected from one of his temperament

Having perfect confidence in the future of Moline Dr Beam has lately purchased a neat and attractive residence, No 524 Fourth avenue, where he may usually be found when not professionally or otherwise engaged The social qualities of both the Doctor and Mrs Beam have attracted a large circle of friends whom they delight to entertain in their pleasant home, and none stand higher in the social world or enjoy to a higher degree the respect and esteem of those who know them

ST ELMO MORGAN SALA, M. D In comparing the relative value to mankind of the various professions and pursuits, it is widely recognized that none is so important as the medical profession From the cradle to the grave human destiny is largely in the hands of the physician One of the ablest representatives of this noble calling in Rock Island is the gentleman whose name introduces this sketch.

The Doctor was born in Bloomington, Wisconsin, September 8, 1870, a son of Orlando P and Ina (Stewart) Sala, natives of Wisconsin and Iowa, respectively His paternal great-grandfather, Dr O J Sala, of Cincinnati, Ohio, was an own uncle of George Augustus Sala, the distinguished English

author. He married a daughter of Gen Morgan, of Revolutionary fame The paternal grandfather, Dr Eli Morgan Sala, was born in Ohio, and for a time practiced medicine in Rock Island, Illinois, but afterward removed to Beetown, Wisconsin, where he died in 1880, at the age of sixtysix He reared a family of seven children. W R Stewart, the maternal grandfather, was formerly a glassware merchant in Des Moines, Iowa, but is now living in Seattle, Washington, at the age of eighty-three years

Dr Orlando P Sala, the father of our subject, is still a practicing physician of Bloomington, Wisconsin, but the mother died in 1880 Both were formerly connected with the Baptist church, but the father is now a Congregationalist During the Civil war he manifested his loyalty by enlisting in the First Iowa Cavalry, and faithfully serving four years. After the death of his first wife he married Miss Alice Bowen, who is also now deceased. By the first union there were five children, but the only daughter died in infancy William O married Miss Edna Webb and resides in Davenport, where he is keeper of stock books for the Standard Oil Company Our subject is next in order of birth. Ono Polk is a practicing physician of Davenport Albert Franklin, the youngest, is a graduate of Augustana College of Rock Island, is employed by Hartz & Bahnsen Co , wholesale druggists, and also represents a Chicago house in gents furnishing goods at Rock Island

In the city of his birth, Dr Sala, of this review, was reared and acquired his literary education, graduating from the high school, after which he engaged in teaching at that place for one year He then entered the medical department of the State University of Iowa, but graduated at the Keokuk Medical College March 8, 1892 The following day he opened an office in Rock Island, where he has since successfully engaged in practice On the 28th of December of the same year Dr Sala led to the marriage altar Miss Mary Elizabeth, daughter of the late Ernest Krell and his wife, Elizabeth Mrs Sala is a member of the First Methodist church, of Rock Island, and, like her husband, occupies an enviable position in social circles.

The Doctor is a member of the Masonic order, the Sons of Veterans and the Mystic Workers of the World, and in connection with his profession also belongs to the American Public Health Association, the Illinois State Medical Society, the Illinois State Auxiliary Health Association, and the Iowa and Illinois Central District Medical Association He is secretary of the medical and surgical staff of St Anthony's Hospital, Rock Island, and is an honorary member of the adjunct staff of Mercy Hospital, Davenport He is also medical examiner for the following societies the Massachusetts Mutual, the Northwestern of Chicago, the Union Life Insurance Company of Omaha, and the Mystic Workers For three years he served as physician of the city poor of Rock Island, and in May, 1895, he was appointed city commissioner of health, a position which he is still acceptably filling His political support is given the men and measures of the Republican party, and he does all in his power to promote the interests or advance the general welfare of his adopted city and county The place he has won in the medical profession is accorded him in recognition of his skill and ability and his pleasant, genial manner has gained him a prominent position in the social world

BURTON F. PEEK Not by gift or purchase or by influence can one rise at the bar, but solely by merit must he gain his reputation, his ability winning him greatness and enabling him to pass on the highway of life many who perhaps had accomplished part of the journey ere he started out Among the younger members of the legal fraternity in Rock Island county who have already won for themselves a prominent place in the ranks of their professional brethren is the gentleman whose name introduces this sketch He is successfully engaged in practice at Moline, his office being in Rooms 1 and 2, Post Office Block

Mr Peek was born in Polo, Ogle county, Illinois, March 5, 1872, a son of Henry and Adeline (Chase) Peek The birth of the father occurred in Bethlehem, Vermont, in 1837, but when quite small he was brought by his parents to Ogle county, where he was reared upon a farm He early became interested in politics, and was elected sheriff of Ogle county, which position he faithfully filled for the long period of fourteen years, leaving office as he had entered it with the respect and confidence of all who knew him Since his retirement to private life he has been engaged in the grain business in Oregon, Illinois

Our subject was only about two years old when he accompanied his parents on their removal to Oregon, where his elementary education was obtained in the public schools At the age of fifteen he entered the office of J F Coe, of Barron, Wisconsin, where he read law for about six months, and then came to Moline to accept a position in the shops of Deere & Co. At the end of a few months he was given a position in the office, and for three years acceptably served as billing clerk

Going to Iowa City, Mr. Peek entered the University of Iowa, where he pursued his studies for one year, and then spent two years in the Harvard Law School, after which he was in the office of William Barge, of Dixon, Illinois, for a time, and in 1894 was admitted to the bar. In January of the following year he opened his office in Moline and is meeting with a well-deserved success in his chosen calling. His interests have ever been with the Republican party, but he took no active part in political affairs until the campaign of 1896, when he was called upon to address many assemblies in various parts of Rock Island county.

JOHN W POTTER, postmaster at Rock Island, and editor and publisher of the Rock Island Argus, it may well be said is a newspaper man by birth and adoption A native of Ireland, he was born in Skibbereen, county Cork, August 17, 1861, and is the son of John W and Josephine (Ryan) Potter, the former a native of Ireland, and the latter of Buffalo, New York, where their marriage occurred They were the parents of three children Osler F, John W and Marion E

John W Potter, Sr, was reared in his native country, and there learned the printer's trade He first came to America in 1853, and while working in Buffalo formed the acquaintance of Josephine Ryan, with whom he was united in marriage in 1856 Shortly after that event he returned with his young bride to his native country, where they remained until 1865

Believing the opportunities for material advancement greater in the new than in the old world, with his family he again came to the United States and in Buffalo, New

York, worked as a journeyman printer for a time and then came west, locating at Freeport, Illinois In 1867 he went to St. Louis, Missouri, where he remained four years, and then went to Bolivar, Missouri, and established the Bolivar Herald which he continued two years, with fair success

Disposing of the Herald, Mr Potter returned to Freeport and purchased an interest in the Freeport Bulletin, with which he was connected until his death, in 1885, at the age of fifty-one years His wife passed away five years previously, dying in 1880 Both were consistent members of the Episcopal church

John W. Potter, Sr., was a thorough newspaper man, and was truly wedded to his profession His boys he brought up in the same profession, his oldest son, Osler F., being connected with the Freeport Bulletin until 1895 In 1882 he came to Rock Island and purchased the Argus of Richardson & Powers, placing our subject in the office as general manager In 1877 he established the first daily paper in Freeport Politically he was a thorough Democrat, and through his newspapers wielded a large influence in his party throughout the State In 1880 he was a delegate to the Democratic National Convention in Cincinnati, which placed in nomination General Hancock for the Presidency

The paternal grandfather of our subject, also named John Potter, was a native of England He engaged in the publishing business in Ireland, being the founder of the West Cork Eagle, of Skibbereen, which he edited and published for many years and which is now continued by one of his sons His death occurred in Skibbereen in 1871 at an advanced age The maternal grandfather Ryan who was engaged in the shipping

J. W. POTTER.

business, died in New York State in middle life.

John W Potter, our subject, came with his parents to the United States when but four years of age He remained with them until he attained his majority, his literary education being confined to the public schools When but nine or ten years of age he commenced to learn the printer's trade in his father's office, and when but eleven years old had charge for a time of the mechanical department of the Bolivar Herald in his father's absence. He became a general job and all-around printer, learning the business in a thorough manner In the office of the Freeport Bulletin he made himself generally useful, and in 1880 established a department of the paper at Lena, in which he did the reportorial work

In August, 1882, on attaining his majority, he came to Rock Island and took the editorial and business management of the Rock Island Argus, daily and weekly, and on the death of his father became sole proprietor, continuing its publication to the present time The Argus, under his management, has become a most popular paper, and a recognized authority in Democratic circles A ready and fluent writer, and with a life-long experience in the trade, he endeavors to keep abreast with the times, making his influence felt in all honorable ways

On the 5th of March, 1889, Mr Potter was united in marriage with Miss Minnie E. Abbott, daughter of Fisher and Sarah (Whitman) Abbott, and by that union three children have been born—Marguerite F, John W and the baby Mrs Potter is a member of the Episcopal church, of which he is an attendant

Like his father, Mr Potter is a firm believer in Democratic principles Through President Cleveland he received the appointment as postmaster of Rock Island, a a position he has satisfactorily filled for more than four years Fraternally he is a member of the Knights of Pythias and Modern Woodmen of America, and beginning with 1888 he served for eight consecutive years as a member of the Democratic State Central Committee, representing the 11th Congressional District of Illinois, and has been a delegate to nearly all the State Conventions for the past ten years

DAVID HAWES, now serving as justice of the peace of Rock Island, has for three score years made his home in that city and is numbered among the pioneers who laid the foundation for its present prosperity and substantial progress He has been active in its development and has not only witnessed its splendid growth, but has ever borne his part in promoting those interests which have led to its advancement. Thus has he left the impress of his individuality upon the city and linked his name inseparably with its history

David Hawes is a native of the old Bay state, his birth having occurred in Hampshire county, October 19, 1809 He is descended from honored Revolutionary stock, his grandfather, John Hawes, having been one of the heroes who fought for the independence of the nation He was wounded at Ticonderoga, which necessitated his remaining in the hospital for a few days With this exception he was never ill a in his life, and died at the advanced age of ninety-three Harvey Hawes, father of our subject, was a farmer by occupation and spent his entire life in Massachusetts He married Ruth Pesoe, also a native of that state, and died at the age of seventy-two, while his wife passed away at the age of sixty They had five children, of whom David is the eldest, and, with the exception of his brother, Charles Wesley, he is the only one now living

Mr Hawes, of this review, acquired his early education in the common schools of Massachusetts, and afterward attended an academy, thus being well fitted for the practical duties of life Reared on the farm he early learned the business of growing fruit, grain and stock Before leaving the east he was married to Miss Julia M. Bocock In 1835 he made his way to the Mississippi valley, spent a year in St Louis, and in 1837 came to Rock Island, where he has since made his home In 1838 and 1839 he engaged in hotel keeping as proprietor of the Rock Island House, and subsequently carried on a grocery store for four years He was also in the United States service as gauger at Rock Island for many years and occupied other official positions wherein his worth, ability and honesty made him a valued officer and won him the commendation of all concerned His public career was above reproach and all his business dealings were conducted in the same straightforward, honorable way He has always carried forward to successful completion whatever he undertook

Mr. Hawes was called upon to mourn the loss of his first wife September 15, 1870 She died at the age of fifty-six years, and although she was the mother of eleven children, only two survived her Charles W., the elder, for five years has held the responsible position of head clerk for the Modern Woodmen of America, and is a man of excellent business qualifications He married Miss Jose͏ͅ ͏ ͏ ͏ ͏ ͏ ͏ ͏ ͏ ͏ ͏ who died leaving

three children—Catharine L , Josephine B and Charles W. He afterward wedded Miss Mary Fay, of Fulton, Illinois, and they have one child, John Marcus The second son, Frank B , is assistant head clerk for the Modern Woodmen of America He married Miss Elizabeth Rector, of Delavan, and has one son, David

Mr Hawes was the second time married December 17, 1872, when Mrs Susan Arnold became his wife She was born in Delaware county, New York, and is a daughter of Thomas J Hubbel, of Homesdale, Pennsylvania With her first husband she came from New York to Rock Island in March, 1868 Mr Arnold intended entering into business in this city, but died in July of the same year at the age of forty

Mr and Mrs Hawes are members of the Baptist church, with which he has been connected for over forty years During all that time until 1895 he served as deacon and trustee of the church and still holds the former position, but resigned the latter two years since Mrs Hawes is a lady of culture and refinement and like her husband takes a deep interest in the work of the church Socially he has affiliated with the Independent Order of Odd Fellows for nearly fifty years, has passed all the chairs, has several times been representative to the grand lodge of the state, and is a worthy exemplar of the teachings of that noble and benevolent order. His political support is given the Republican party. He has been a member of the city council two terms, was coroner twelve years, sheriff for two years and justice of the peace for sixteen years His public service is marked by the utmost fidelity to duty and over the record of his long and useful life there falls no shadow of wrong or suspicion of evil

JAMES McDOWELL MONTGOMERY, who was for a number of years one of the prominent and influential business men of Rock Island, and an honored member of the Masonic fraternity, passed to the unseen world on the 25th of January, 1894 He was born in Montour county, Pennsylvania, January 8, 1842, a son of Daniel and Margaret (Simington) Montgomery, also natives of the Keystone state, and he traced his ancestry back to the Revolutionary period, being a relative of General Montgomery, a noted officer of the Continental army. Both the paternal and maternal grandfather of our subject were natives of Pennsylvania.

Daniel Montgomery, the father, emigrated to Rock Island county, Illinois, at an early day and invested largely in lands, which he improved and cultivated, being a farmer by occupation He became one of the leading citizens of his community—a man highly respected by all who knew him He died in 1848, in middle life, but his wife still survives him and now lives with her son Daniel Both were consistent members of the Presbyterian church, in which he served as elder for some years In their family were four sons—Robert, now a resident of Edgington township, Rock Island county, his home being near Reynolds, Daniel, of the same township, John, of Aledo township, Mercer county, and James, of this review

Upon his father's farm in this county, our subject was reared to manhood, and obtained his early education in its district schools, but later was a student in Knox College, at Galesburg When the war broke out, however, he laid aside his text books and enlisted in the Eighty-ninth Illinois Volunteer Infantry—the famous Railroad Regiment, with which he participated

in the battles of Lawrenceburg, Perryville, Stone River and others On the 24th of May, 1863, he was discharged in order to enable him to accept a commission as second lieutenant in Company B, Sixty-fifth Illinois Infantry, where he rose to the rank of captain With his regiment he took part in various battles and campaigns until after the surrender of General Johnston, when hostilities ceased, and his services being no longer needed he was mustered out July 13, 1865

After the war Captain Montgomery was in business in Chicago for awhile, and then went to Andalusia, Rock Island county, where he engaged in the hardware, implement and grain business until 1871. Coming to Rock Island three years later, he became a member of the mercantile firm of Stewart & Montgomery, which connection continued until February 1, 1892, when he retired in order to devote his entire time to the Black Hawk Building & Loan Association He was elected president on its incorporation August 1, 1887, and held that position up to the time of his death The success which he achieved in business affairs attested his eminent and pronounced ability as financier

On the 8th of January, 1878, was celebrated the marriage of Captain Montgomery and Miss Mary Burrall, a daughter of Edward and Ann Caroline (Jack) Burrall, the former a native of Connecticut and the latter of Virginia, but both became early settlers of Rock Island county, Illinois (See sketch elsewhere in this volume) Our subject and his wife became the parents of two children—Annie and Charles

Endowed by nature with a sound judgment and an accurate, discriminating mind, Captain Montgomery feared not that laborious attention to the details of business so necessary to achieve success, and this essential quality was ever guided by a sense of moral right which would tolerate only those means that would bear the most rigid examination by a fairness of intention that neither sought nor required disguise He was a director of the Rock Island National Bank and at one time had charge of the Milan Paper Company The Black Hawk Building and Loan Association, which he did so much to advance, offered appropriate resolutions of respect and esteem at his death, showing their appreciation of his service, and the high regard in which he was held by its members He was serving his seventh year as worthy master of Trio Lodge, No 57, F. & A M , and was also steward of the grand lodge when called to his final rest Although quiet and unassuming, he was ever pleasant and genial in manner, and made hosts of warm friends who appreciated his sterling worth and many excellent traits of character.

G UST M FORD, who is doing a successful business as a confectioner at No 415 Fifteenth street, Moline, has justly won the proud American title of a self-made man He started out in life for himself at an early age and by industry, economy, perseverance and good management has steadily worked his way upward He was born in the central portion of Sweden, April 25, 1850, a son of L P and Anna (Britta) Carlson When he was thirteen years of age his parents came to America, making their way at once to Moline The father had about two hundred dollars in money, with which he purchased fifty-eight acres of land in school district 1   ·   · ·   · 1   had

miles east of the city There he carried on farming for a time, but in 1879 removed to Nebraska, where he spent his remaining days

Mr. Ford, of this review, had attended school in his native land for seven years before coming to America, and for a few months pursued his education in the public schools of Rock Island county After three months study here he was able to understand and speak the English tongue For two years he assisted his father in the development and cultivation of the home farm and then entered the employ of the Moline Plow Company, with which he remained for twenty years. He received only fifty cents per day in compensation for his services at first, but as he mastered the business and manifested his ability and trustworthiness he was steadily and consecutively promoted until his wages amounted to about twenty dollars per week At length after a connection of two decades with that company he resigned in 1887, and embarked in business on his own account, opening a confectionery store. In 1895 he removed to his present place of business, having erected the Ford building, and is now enjoying a large and constantly increasing patronage, from which he derives a good income

On the 28th of June, 1881, occurred the marriage of Mr Ford and Miss Emily Vinstrand, a native of Henry county, Illinois, and a daughter of Nels P Vinstrand, of Swedish birth They have three children, Gustave Almond, born March 17, 1885; Gladys, born March 9, 1891, and Alice Margaret, born April 19, 1897

Mr. Ford has always been a supporter of Republican principles since casting his first presidential vote for Grant in 1872 In 1   · he was elected assistant supervisor, serving three years in that capacity, and in 1893 was elected supervisor, to which position he has been re-elected, and is the present incumbent He has several times been delegate to the county conventions, and has twice been delegate to the district conventions He belongs to the Ancient Order of United Workmen, has filled all of its chairs, and has twice been its representative to the grand lodge He is a member of Swedish Olive Lodge, No. 583, I O O F, has occupied all of its official positions, and has also been its representative to the grand lodge, St George Lodge, No 28, K P., and Doric Lodge, F. & A M, both number him among their leading members As a citizen he is public-spirited and progressive, devoted to the best interests of the county, is esteemed in society circles, and in his business pursuits has gained a comfortable competence, while through his honorable dealing he has won the confidence and good will of all with whom he has been brought in contact

---

HON WILLIAM McENIRY, who is now representing the Rock Island district in the state legislature, is one of the eminent lawyers of western Illinois, and has won distinction by superior ability in his chosen profession In commercial life one may enter upon a business already established, but the lawyer must plead and win his first case and rise by his own merit and forensic power if he would take his place among the successful few. It is in this manner that Mr McEniry has won a position in the foremost rank of the legal representatives of Rock Island

William McEniry was born in the county which is still his home May 9, 1860, and is a son of William and Elizabeth (Coughlin) McEniry, natives of Ireland His father, a farmer by occupation, came to Illinois in 1841, and cast his lot with the pioneers of Moline, where he made his home until 1852 He then took up his residence upon a farm and devoted his energies to agricultural pursuits In 1846 he married MissCoughlin and they became parents of four sons and two daughters, who are yet living and two sons who died in infancy The father of this family was called to the home beyond February 18, 1874, at the age of fifty-seven years, but his wife still survives him at the age of seventy-seven years She is a devout member of the Catholic church, to which her husband also belonged

William McEniry, of this review, acquired his education in the schools of this county, pursued a commercial course in Prairie de Chien, Wisconsin, and a literary course in Notre Dame, Indiana Choosing the profession of law as a lifework he prepared for that vocation in the law department of Michigan University at Ann Arbor, where he was graduated in 1885 Soon after he opened an office in Rock Island, and his success was marked and immediate for he gave evidence of possessing the requisites needful to the able lawyer In 1887 he was elected city attorney and filled that position with fidelity and to the satisfaction of all concerned He has a keen, analytical mind, is a logical reasoner and forceful speaker, and has served as counsel in many important litigated interests

Mr McEniry is accounted one of the leaders of Democracy in Rock Island county, and has been very active and zealous in support of the men and measures of his party In the fall of 1896 he was elected to the State legislature running far ahead of his ticket, and is a valued member of the House, wherein he is serving on a number of important committees, including those on judiciary and appropriations   During the session of 1896-7 he took front rank among the legislators, and although of the minority party he succeeded in having passed each of the five bills only that he introduced, a record seldom equalled   Of his ability as a member the Inter-Ocean, of Chicago, spoke in the highest terms of praise

On the 15th of October, 1890, Mr Mc-Eniry was united in marriage to Miss Alice Cleary, a native of New Orleans, and a daughter of John Cleary, of the Crescent City.   They now have three interesting children—John, Bessie and William   Mr McEniry and his wife hold membership in the Catholic church and possess qualities which make them favorites in social circles   Their own home is noted for its hospitality   In the interests of the city Mr McEniry has labored, giving his support to all measures calculated to prove of public benefit   He was active in the work of securing a new court house, and the present fine structure stands as a monument to the enterprise and progressiveness of such men as himself   He was also instrumental in having the insane asylum located in the county   Mr McEniry is yet a young man, who has attained distinction at the bar and in politics, and the future undoubtedly holds in store for him still greater successes and higher honors

-- --

LEWIS D DUNN, M D , whose success as a physician and surgeon resulting from his pronounced skill and ability, has made him one of the foremost representatives of the medical profession in this section of the state, has practiced in Moline for

years   His life record is one of interest for it demonstrates the success that can be achieved by honorable effort and determined purpose   With no advantages of wealth or influence to aid him, a self-educated and self-made man, he stands to-day one of the foremost representatives in western Illinois of one of the noblest callings to which man can devote his energies

Dr Dunn was born in Hennepin, Putnam county, September 18, 1834, and is a son of Ferrel and Lydia (Fleming) Dunn, a descendant of Sir Thomas Fleming, who came to Virginia in 1617, renouncing estates and titles in Scotland to become a citizen of this country   The family is still prominent as it was in colonial days, numbering many statesman among its members, state Senator Solomon Fleming, an uncle of Dr Dunn's, and his cousin, Ex-Gov A Brooks Fleming of West Virginia, Gov. Fleming of Florida, and others.   His father was one of the rangers in the Black Hawk war and early became familiar with the varied experiences of frontier life   The Doctor's birth occurred in the little log fort near the Illinois river, but later his father entered land in Bureau county, where the family lived in the vicinity of what was then called Indian Town, a settlement of friendly Indians, now Tiskilwa. Shabbona, the chief, became quite attached to the Doctor and used frequently to entertain him at the Indian camp   In the neighborhood of his boyhood home, Dr Dunn remained until coming to Moline in 1875   He attended the district school and as he was not of robust health determined at an early age to study medicine   This he began while still in the public schools, his reading being directed by Dr S S Nichols   Later he spent a year in a seminary in Providence, where he made a special study of Latin necessary to fit him for a collegiate course ˙ At the age of eighteen he entered the University of Vermont, where he pursued his first term of lectures, but not having enough money to continue the course he was forced to leave the institution and engaged in clerking and in other work in order to gain money enough to enable him to continue his studies

In 1856 he entered Rush Medical College of Chicago, where he was graduated the following year. Returning to Tiskilwa, he there opened an office, and as his ability was demonstrated by success in his practice he secured a liberal patronage For eighteen years he remained at that place and enjoyed a large practice that came from all parts of the surrounding country This, however, necessitated long rides and much arduous night work, and in consequence he determined to remove to a city where his practice might be of a local character Accordingly he came to Moline and within a year had succeeded in securing a liberal share of the public support Before locating here he was appointed a member of the corps of local surgeons for the Rock Island Railroad Company and has ever since served in that capacity He has served on the staff of St Anthony's Hospital of Rock Island, was one year its president, and is now a member of the consulting staff In 1893 he was appointed by Governor Altgeld surgeon of the Illinois Naval Militia, with the rank of lieutenant, and now ranks as captain He is a member of the Association of Military Surgeons of Illinois, and Association of Military Surgeons of the United States He was a member of the first board of health of the city of Moline, acting in that capacity until the board was abolished While residing in Tiskilwa he was United States pension examiner for the district comprised in Bureau and

Stark counties. For twenty-six years he has been examining surgeon for the Connecticut Mutual Insurance Company, and occupies the same position with the following-named insurance companies—the Travellers Life and Accident, the Peru Mutual Life, Mutual Life of New York, Mutual Benefit Life of New Jersey, Home Life, Bankers Life of Des Moines, Bankers Life of St Paul, Ætna Life, Prudential Life of New Jersey, National Life of Vermont, Washington Life of New York, Phœnix Life of Hartford, Connecticut, and the Massachusetts Benefit Life Association The Doctor holds membership in the International Association of Railway Surgeons, belongs to the State Medical Society, to the Iowa and Illinois District Medical Association, and was a member of the American Medical Association He belongs to the Alumni Association of Rush Medical College, was its president in 1889, attends nearly all of its meetings and keeps in close touch with the hospital work He has ever been an earnest student of his profession, constantly reading, studying and thinking along new lines, and his progress in his profession has therefore been marked and continuous

While a resident of Tiskilwa he was married to Miss Julia Mills, a descendant of the Cleveland family, one of the oldest families of New England From them she inherited a literary taste that has distinguished other members of the Cleveland family, notably Edmund Clarence Stedman, Bishop Arthur Cleveland Cove, of New York, and many of the best known writers of the country.

She is a charter member of the Illinois Woman's Press Association, and founded the Board of Associated Charities of Moline thirteen years ago, of which she is and al-

ways has been a prominent officer   She is
president of the Illinois Equal Suffrage Association, and is a well known member of various
philanthropic, reform and charitable and
patriotic societies, and is well known as a
club woman throughout the State   She is
the author of "The Days We Celebrate,"
a manual extensively used by the Daughters
of the American Revolution

Her literary work, which has been more
of a recreation than a pursuit, consists of
contributions mostly for the Youth's Companion, Frank Leslie's publications, various
temperance publications, and the Arena

Three children were born to the Doctor
and his wife, Clara Mabel, Marian Douglass
and Lewis Mills   Lewis died in infancy
and Marian closed a singularly amiable and
beautiful life at the age of twenty-six

Clara, the only remaining daughter, has
decided talents in the direction of painting,
literature and music, though she also possesses strong domestic tastes   She has
done some fine work in water-color painting, and exhibited her work at several art
exhibitions

The members of this family are recognized leaders in cultured society circles and
their home is noted for its hospitality

The Doctor was reared in the faith of
the Democracy and voted that ticket until
1860, when he became a Republican, and
was allied with the interests of that party
until 1896, when he became a champion of
the free silver cause   For eight years he has
served as alderman of Moline, being elected
one year as an independent candidate   His
service in the city council has been conscientious and of much benefit to Moline, for he
is progressive and enterprising and has the
best interests of the city at heart   Soon
after loca   ιοι ιἑ ψ - ιι ιλ ιὶ ιιι ιιιἱ ι

of the library board, and for many years
acted as its president. He belongs to Doric
Lodge, No 319, F. & A M , of Moline,
having been made a Mason in Sharon Lodge
of Tiskilwa   He and his wife and daughter
all belong to the Unitarian church, and
throughout the community they are held in
the highest regard by a large circle of
friends

GEORGE H EDWARDS, of Moline,
has for more than sixty years been a
resident of this section of the state, and is
numbered among its honored and prominent pioneers, who has not only witnessed
the development and improvement of the
locality with which he is identified, but is
also actively connected therewith   Determined purpose, keen discrimination and untiring industry have been the salient points
in his business career, while fidelity to every
duty of citizenship has marked his private
life   He needs no introduction to the pres
ent generation, for he is widely and favorably known in Rock Island county, and it is
to future generations that we dedicate this
history of one who has been prominent in
the substantial advancement of the county
for more than half a century

Mr Edwards was born in Windham
county, Vermont, and in 1835 came to Rock
Island county with his father, William Edwards, who purchased the land now occupied
by East Moline   There were but slight improvements upon the place and our subject
assisted in the cultivation of the farm during his minority in the intervals between the
school terms   He acquired a good practical
education in Moline and when a young man
went with his brother to Galena, Illinois,
where he began to learn the trade of car-

GEO. H. EDWARDS.

MRS MARIA EDWARDS.

riage painting Upon his father's death he returned home to settle up the estate, and in connection with his brother, Herbert R Edwards, took charge of the old homestead and carried on the farm for a number of years He then resumed painting in Chicago, and in 1855 went to Greenfield, Massachusetts, where he followed the same business through the summer In the autumn he returned to Moline and accepted a position with the firm of Dimock & Gould Subsequently he turned his attention to house painting, and in 1856 he went to Minneapolis, but after one season there passed again came to Moline, where he engaged in painting for several years In 1858 he resumed the operation of the home farm and was thus identified with agricultural interests for seven years He then purchased a farm near Orion, Henry county, which he successfully conducted for seven years, when he sold the property and in 1875 returned to Moline, where he has since made his home At a later day he purchased a farm in Henry county for his son and lived thereon for a year, but with this exception has maintained his residence continuously in Moline since 1875 His business interests were well conducted and brought to him a handsome income, so that he has been enabled to lay aside all business cares with the exception of the superintendence of his investments The Edwards brothers laid out the first addition to Moline on the tract of land which their father had purchased, and now all the old farm, including one hundred and seventy acres, is within the corporate limits of the city. The brothers platted two additions and sold other portions of the place. Mr Edwards of this review has been a stockholder in the Moline National Bank almost from its organization has long served as a

2

director, and for five years has been vice-president He is also a director of the Savings Bank and is engaged in loaning money

Mr Edwards was married in Moline, March 4, 1857, to Miss Maria M Waterman, a native of New York, born June 14, 1836, and a daughter of John and Emeline (Shepard) Waterman, natives of New York and Connecticut, respectively Her parents became pioneer settlers of Moline and she was reared and educated in the Twin Cities For many years she was a consistent and conscientious member of the Congregational church, though while residing in Henry county she held membership with the Lutheran church, there being no organization of Congregationalists In the work of the church she was always quite active until compelled to retire on account of ill-health She was a superior business woman, and while her husband spent the summer of 1875 in Colorado on account of his health she managed the farm, giving personal attention to every detail She had platted two additions to the city of Moline, known as the Maria Edwards first and Maria Edwards second addition to Moline The first was recorded April 30, 1886, and the latter June 19, 1893 In the sale of the property she took almost the entire charge of the business and successfully placed upon the market and disposed of valuable lots Her only child, Milton F. Edwards, was educated in Moline and Davenport, and for some years engaged in agricultural pursuits In early life he also learned the tinner's trade and followed that business for some time He wedded Mary Harper, of Weston township, Henry county, Illinois, a lady of good education and many excellent qualities They have three children—Milton F, Jr, Genevieve Gretchen and an infant In the fall of

1896 Milton F Edwards and his family went to California, but in the spring of 1897 moved to Colorado Springs, Colorado, where they are living at present.

In the fall of 1881 the family went to California, spending the succeeding winter in visiting the many points of interest and beauty in that state Having abundance of means, they did not hesitate to gratify their tastes by travel and recreation. For several years, however, Mrs. Edwards was in ill-health, and when the summons came, December 14, 1895, to "come up higher" she was ready to go. Her death was sincerely mourned, not alone by a loving husband and son, but by all who knew her

The subject of this review, George H Edwards, has been a stanch Republican in politics since the organization of the party, has served as a delegate to numerous county conventions and was assessor of Moline township. He has been a member of the Congregational church in this city since 1875, and is deeply interested in all that pertains to the moral, educational or material advancement of the community He has witnessed almost the entire growth of Rock Island county, has seen its wild lands transformed into good homes and farms and has ever borne his part in the work of public improvement.

LOUIS P YOUNGREN eminently deserves classification among those purely self-made men of Moline who have distinguished themselves for their ability to master the opposing forces of life and to wrest from fate a large measure of success and an honorable name He is now superintendent of the Peterson & Youngren organ factory, one of the important business enterprises of the city, and his home is at 728 Fifth avenue

A native of Sweden, Mr. Youngren was born in Horna Ohus Taken, province of Christianstadt, August 10, 1832, and was reared and educated there. His paternal grandfather was a soldier in the Swedish-Russian war Upon the home farm our subject early became familiar with agricultural pursuits, which he afterward followed to some extent and also learned the painter's trade, at which he worked for some years before coming to the New World

In 1864 Mr. Youngren boarded a sailing vessel at Gottenburg bound for Quebec, Canada, near which place they became stranded on the island of Antecosta, but finally reached their destination after a voyage of nine weeks Our subject then proceeded to Montreal and by the lakes to Chicago, whence he went to Chestertown and South Bend, Indiana, but the following year came to Illinois. After about three weeks spent in painting in Galesburg, he worked on a farm during March and April, and in July, 1865, took up his residence in Moline, where he has since made his home The same year he secured employment with the Rock Island Plow Company and also painted the Swedish Lutheran church He was then with Deere & Company for fifteen years, serving as foreman of the paint shop for twelve years of the time, and when work was slack would work at other occupations. In 1881 he became interested in the manufacture of organs, and the following year bought stock in the company, with which he is still connected The stock company later sold out to Peterson & Youngren and since 1888 he has served as superintendent. They have the reputation of manufacturing a superior organ and are now doing a large and profitable business Mr Youngren is also a stockholder in the Moline Manufacturing Company of East Moline—one of the largest brick manufactories in this section of the state

In 1868, in Moline was celebrated the marriage of Mr Youngren and Miss Sophia Peterson, who was born in Sweden and came to the United States when three years old They have become the parents of the following children —Berdena, wife of Alfred Lawson, a real estate and insurance agent of Sioux City, Iowa, Oscar, who belongs to the Moline fire department, Alben, an engineer in the organ factory; Hilda and Hannah, at home, Reuben, Linneas and Karl, all in school, and Anna, who died at the age of thirteen months

Politically, Mr Youngren is a stalwart Republican, believing in protection and sound money, but has never aspired to office, although he served as alderman of the city for one term In their church relations he and his family are Lutherans He is a man of scrupulous honor, his integrity is above question, and his straightforward course has won him the confidence and high regard of all with whom he has come in contact.

ROBERT STOCKHOUSE, general freight and ticket agent of the Rock Island & Peoria Railroad at Rock Island, Illinois, while in heart and soul an American citizen, is yet of foreign birth, and of the nobility of Prussia He was born in Cologne, Germany, August 14, 1840, and is the son of Philip and Elizabeth (Herman) Stockhouse, both natives of Prussia, and the parents of five children, of whom three are now living Robert, Joseph and Maria

Philip Stockhouse was a man of note in his native country, holding a commission as notary public under the King of Prussia, and having served one year in the German army His death occurred in 1851 at the age of about forty-five years, thus passing away in the prime of life His wife long survived him, dying January 6, 1897, at the age of eighty-one years They were both devout and worthy members of the Catholic church

The paternal grandfather of our subject, Jodokos Stockhouse, was a collector of customs, as were also his great-grandfather and and great-great-grandfather Jodokos Stockhouse served in that office over fifty years, and lived to a very old age, while the great-grandfather lived to be one hundred and ten years old The latter was a fine marksman and had an eye like an eagle The maternal grandfather, William Herman, was for many years a merchant in Cologne, but in later years lived retired on the interest of his money, dying at the age of eighty-seven years A street in Cologne was named in his honor

Robert Stockhouse grew to manhood in his native city, and received his literary education in the University of the Jesuits In 1859, when nineteen years of age, he crossed the ocean, and for four years resided in the city of Hamilton, Ontario, Canada, where he served as assistant city clerk In 1863 he removed to Springfield, Illinois, where he had an uncle living, and became an accountant in the general office of the "Great Western Railroad of Illinois of 1859," and was there two years In 1866 he became assistant secretary of the state, under Sharon Tyndale, when Oglesby was governor. However, he remained in this position but two years and then went to Oil City, Pennsylvania, where he had charge of the oil wells of his uncle's In the latter part of 1869 he returned to Springfield and re-engaged in the railroad business in the local freight office of the Toledo, Wabash & Western Railroad One year later he was appointed agent, at Beardstown, of the Rockford, Rock Island & St. Louis Railroad, now the Chicago, Burlington & Quincy In 1874 he came to Rock Island as agent for the same company Two years later he severed his connection with that road, and became contracting agent for the Rock Island & Peoria Railroad at Davenport, Iowa In 1878 he was appointed agent for the same company at Peoria, Illinois, and in 1880 he was made joint agent of the Chicago, Rock Island & Pacific and the Rock Island & Peoria Railroads Proving faithful and reliable in every position, he was made cashier and paymaster of the Rock Island & Peoria Railroad in 1882, and in 1884 was promoted to the position of general freight and passenger agent of the same road, which position he still holds, the duties of which office he discharges in a most satisfactory manner

While residing in Springfield, Mr Stockhouse was united in marriage, in 1866, with Miss Clara Louisa Hild, daughter of Michael and Maria Eva Hild, by whom he had two children, Eliza, who died in infancy, and Charles Philip, now claim clerk for the Rock Island & Peoria Railroad For more than thirty years Mr and Mrs Stockhouse lived in that perfect love and confidence of those truly wedded, when death claimed the loved wife and affectionate mother February 13, 1897 She was a devout member of the Catholic church and died in that faith Her remains were interred in the consecrated grounds of the Catholi l i l   Spiritual Illinois   A

woman of refinement and lovely disposition, her death is mourned not alone by the lonely husband and son, but by all who knew her in this life Since her death Mr Stockhouse has made his home at the Harper House, Rock Island.

Politically, Mr Stockhouse is a Republican, with which party he has been identified since he became a naturalized citizen The principles of the party are such as meet his just conceptions of what is best for the general welfare of the country, and while he does not take that active interest shown by others of more leisure, he gives his time and means as he can spare them Religiously, he is also a Catholic, being reared and well grounded in the faith of that body Kindhearted and affable, he has the bearing of a gentleman and is highly esteemed in the community and his circle of friends and acquaintances is very large He is a fine type of character and is justly proud of his ancestors, a trait of character commended by the great historian, Macaulay, who says that one who takes no pride in his ancestry will in all probability never do anything worthy of remembrance by his posterity. To the great body of German-Americans this country owes a debt of gratitude, and none are more worthy than Robert Stockhouse, the subject of this brief sketch

THOMAS J MEDILL, JR., Mayor of Rock Island, is a representative of the best type of American progress His active identification with the interests of Rock Island has been most beneficial to the city and he has left the impress of his individuality upon its substantial development He is never a follower but is a recognized leader in all works of public improvement and to-day his name stands high on the roll of Rock Island's honored and eminent men

A native of Rock Island county, he was born in Milan, March 16, 1859, and belongs to one of the oldest families in this section of the state His maternal grandfather, William Dickson, came from Erie county, Pennsylvania, to Rock Island county in 1837, and located at what is now known as Sears In 1845 he laid out the town of Milan, formerly called Camden Mills, and was a very important factor in the pioneer development of the locality The parents of our subject, Thomas J and Eliza A (Dickson) Medill, still reside in Milan The father was born in the north of Ireland, and the mother in Erie county, Pennsylvania They had a family of nine children, two of whom are now deceased

Mr Medill, of this review, the fifth in order of birth, acquired his education in the public schools of Milan, and in his youth learned the paper maker's trade, which he followed for seven years in his native town He then went to the south with a company engaged in putting in the Holly system of water works in various cities in Texas In 1885 he returned, taking up his residence in Rock Island, where he engaged in the real estate business for two years, dealing in western lands In 1889 he became one of the organizers of the Black Hawk Homestead Building & Loan Association, of which he has served as secretary and director from the beginning, the president being H D Mack, division freight agent of the Chicago, Burlington & Quincy Railroad The business of this company is conducted on a safe, conservative basis and has assumed extensive proportions. This is an age of organized and united effort and the most successful operations are conducted through co-operation It is this which has made the building and loan associations of the country such a potent element in substantial improvement and progress and as one of the prime movers in such an enterprise, he is not only adding to his individual prosperity but at the same time is advancing the interests of the city with which he is connected

Mr Medill is a man of resourceful ability, whose efforts have by no means been confined to one line, but have reached out in many directions, benefiting both himself and his fellow townsmen He was one of the organizers and for two years the secretary of the Citizens Improvement Association, which largely advanced the welfare of Rock Island In 1893 he was elected mayor of the city for a two-years' term, and proved a most capable and efficient officer, administering the affairs of his office along broad and comprehensive lines. During his incumbency many splendid improvements were made, including the extension of the water works, electric light and drainage systems, the building of twelve miles of sidewalk and the construction of five miles of street paving He was re-elected in 1897 by a majority of two hundred and ninety-five votes, which was certainly complimentary, when it is considered that McKinley carried the city by nine hundred and twenty-seven votes He holds the responsible position of president of the board of trustees for the Illinois Western Hospital for the Insane, which is located at Watertown, this county. His associates on the board are John R Eden, of Sullivan, Illinois, and Hon. W Selden Gale, of Galesburg, all being appointed by Governor Altgeld in September 1895 After a spirited and protracted contest of three months Mr Medill succeeded in locating the hospital in Watertown, the citizens of the county donating for the purpose three hundred and eighty-four acres of land, valued at forty thousand dollars

Mr Medill is a supporter of the Democracy and was tendered the nomination of his party for secretary of state in June, 1896, but declined the honor He is a prominent and valued member of the Masonic Lodge of Rock Island, of which he has been Worshipful Master for several terms, and is a member of the National Union, the Modern Woodmen of America and the Knights of the Globe. His demeanor is marked by courtesy and culture In manner he is genial and social, and it would be difficult to find a citizen of Rock Island who has more friends than Thomas J Medill

---

CHESTER C WATERS, one of the influential and leading citizens now living a retired life at No 526 Sixteenth street, is a native of New York, born in Oneida county, July 30, 1824, and is a son of Abner H. and Adaline (Law) Waters His boyhood and youth were spent upon a farm, while his education was obtained in the common schools, and at the age of eighteen he began learning the carpenter's and joiner's trade, serving a three-years' apprenticeship and receiving the first year thirty-five dollars and board, the following year forty-five dollars and the privilege of attending school three months in Augusta, New York, and the third year seventy dollars and three months schooling For a time he then worked as a journeyman in New Hartford, Connecticut, and on his return home was married January 1 1847 to Miss Maria

Mansfield, also a native of Oneida county, New York, with whom he had become acquainted while serving his apprenticeship She was a daughter of David Mansfield, and by a good education had qualified herself for a teacher.

After his marriage Mr. Walters located in Westmoreland, Oneida county, where he was employed as a pattern maker in a foundry for thirteen years and the following decade was engaged in bridge and house building at Englewood, Bergen county, New Jersey. He also served as railroad station agent at that place for a year and a half, and in his undertakings met with excellent success There his wife died in 1869, leaving five children who are still living, namely Charles, who is now serving his twelfth year as post office inspector at Denver, Colorado, is married and has three children; George M, a mechanic of Moline, is married and has one child, Annette is the wife of Nelson Powell, of Lee Center, Oneida county, New York, and they have three daughters, Joseph M, a bookkeeper living in Clinton, Iowa, is married and has three children; and Gertrude is the wife of Ansel O Cole, of Lyons, Iowa

Selling out his business in Englewood, New Jersey, Mr Waters traveled over Ohio, Indiana, Illinois, Wisconsin and Iowa in settling up an estate At Marengo, Illinois, he met and married Mrs Ann S Buxton, in 1869, and the same year located at Moline, where he has since made his home He embarked in the hardware business, but during the five years of his connection therewith he lost heavily, and subsequently accepted a position in the pattern department of the Union Malleable Iron Company, where he remained for seven years, but has now laid aside all business cares.

On attaining his majority Mr Waters gave his support to the men and measures of the Whig party, and since voting for John C. Fremont in 1856 has been a stalwart Republican For a term and a half he creditably served as alderman in Moline and was the nominee of his party for mayor, and although he made no effort to secure his election, he was only defeated by forty votes For twelve years his name was placed on the ticket for assessor and with two exceptions was always elected, the latter defeat being in 1895 He has always taken an active and prominent part in political affairs, has served as a delegate to county conventions and has done much to insure the success of his party. With the Congregational church of Moline he holds membership, and socially is a third degree Mason, belonging to Doric Lodge, No 319, F & A M, and is a charter member of Moline Camp, No. 38, M. W A, in which he has served as venerable consul and which he has twice represented in the head camp After a pure, honorable and useful life, actuated by unselfish motives, prompted by patriotism and guided by truth and justice, he may rest assured that the people of his county are not unmindful of him who has devoted himself to their interests

---

ANDREW G ANDERSON, manager and treasurer of the Lutheran Augustana Book Concern, whose success in business and sterling worth numbers him among the valued citizens of Rock Island, comes from that land that has furnished to America so many of her best citizens, the kingdom of Sweden There he was born on the 4th of December, 1857, and comes of farming ancestry. Both his maternal and paternal grandfathers were agriculturists, and continued to till the soil throughout the period of their active lives Both have long since passed away The parents of our subject, Olof and Anna Christine (Olsson) Anderson, were also natives of Sweden, and the father followed farming there until 1870, when he crossed the Atlantic to America and took up his residence in Red Wing, Minnesota For some time he worked in a sawmill, but is now living retired there Both he and his wife are consistent members of the Lutheran church. Their family numbered seven children, five of whom are now living Andrew G, John, Christine, wife of C G. Thulin, of Moline, Illinois; Clara, who is bookkeeper for the firm of McCabe Brothers of Rock Island, and Olof P

Andrew G Anderson, whose name forms the caption of this article, acquired his early education in the land of his birth, and continued his studies in Red Wing, Minnesota, after his emigration to America Throughout his entire business career he has been engaged in printing and publishing, his initial experience being gained in the office of the "Luthersk Kyrkotidning," a paper published at the Argus office in Red Wing He began his labors there in 1873 and the following year on the removal of the "Augustana" from Chicago to Rock Island he came to this place, continuing as an employe in the office of that journal for some time. When his first employer, A C F. De Remee, sold out he continued with his successors, and became a member of the firm of Wistrand, Thulin and Anderson in the conduct of a job office in Moline for two years On the expiration of that period the firm sold out to the publishing board of the Augustana Synod, their present building at the corner of Thirty-eighth street and Seventh avenue was erected and the establishment was moved to the present location Mr Anderson continued as foreman of the printing department until 1889, when he was elected by the board to take entire charge of the whole institution as manager and treasurer, which offices he has held ever since They publish works of authority for the Swedish Lutheran church in the United States, also the Augustana, which is the weekly official organ of the Evangelical Lutheran Augustana Synod, and is published in the Swedish language, the Augustana Journal, printed in English, a semi-monthly, the Olive Leaf, in English, and Barnens Tidning, Sunday-school papers in Swedish, beside many books and tracts, of which they have gotten out a large catalogue They also import books and do their binding in addition to the composition work on their books Their printing and binding is done in the highest style of the art, according to the most modern and improved methods, and on their pay roll are forty-eight names This is regarded as one of the most important industrial concerns in Rock Island, and the success which attends the enterprise is largely due to the careful management and superior business and executive ability of Mr Anderson

On the 26th of October, 1880, Mr Anderson was united in marriage to Miss Hilda L Lindstrom, a daughter of Johan P and Anna Lindstrom They have five children, two sons and three daughters Anna V E , Paul A , deceased, Alvin G J , Agnes, deceased, and Laura Their pleasant home, located at No 3908 Eighth avenue, Rock Island, is noted for the gracious hospitality which pervades it, and it is a favorite resort especially

of the city Mr. and Mrs Anderson are valued members of the Zion Lutheran church, of Rock Island, take a very active part in its work, and Mr Anderson, who has been deacon for two terms, is now serving as superintendent of the Sunday-school His political support is given the Republican party His character has always been one of great sincerity and firmness. His integrity is unquestioned Careful, painstaking, exact and conscientious he has prospered deservingly from year to year By reason of his success, his unblemished character, his just and liberal life and the universal esteem which he here enjoys Mr Anderson may well be called one of the foremost citizens of Rock Island

---

WILLIAM KERNS —" We build the ladder by which we rise " is an axiom certainly applicable to this gentleman, whose history is one of earnest labor and well directed effort—effort that has overcome all obstacles and enabled him to utilize the difficulties in his path as stepping-stones to something higher He has also left upon the city of Moline—which has long been his home—an impress as beneficial as it is ineffaceable Few men have done more for the city than he in the promotion of its commercial activity and substantial improvement, and no man claims less credit for his acts He is a perfect type of a noble American citizen, and manliness, patriotism, sincerity and friendship are instinctively associated with his name

Mr Kerns, who is now practically living retired, at his pleasant home at No 1930 Sixth avenue, was born in East Marlborough, Chester county, Pennsylvania, July 4, 1820 He traces his paternal ancestry back to the

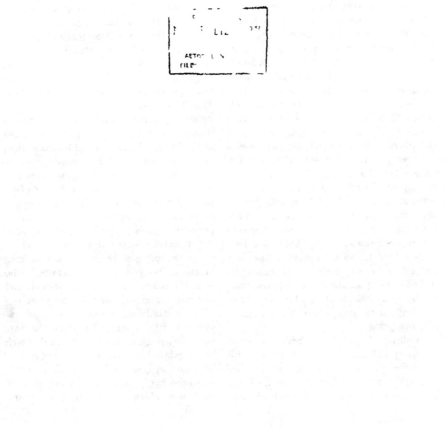

Emerald Isle, whence his great-grandfather, Thomas Kerns, who was born in Tyrone, Ireland, came to America about 1740 He took up his residence in New Garden, Chester county, Pennsylvania, where he married a lady of Quaker faith, and for many years the family was connected with that religious sect He had a family of four children of whom William Kerns, the grandfather of our subject, was the third He was born in New Garden, and afterward removed to a farm in East Marlborough, a Quaker settlement in which for many years there was no church save of that one denomination In this township Simon Kerns and William, our subject, were both born The natal day of the father was July 16, 1791, and he was the ninth in order of birth in a family of eleven children. He married Elizabeth Ocheltree, a lady of Scotch descent, whose family name at an earlier date was probably spelled Ochilthree She was born in New Castle county, Delaware, January 1, 1797, was liberally educated and was a member of the Presbyterian church until after her marriage, when she became identified with the Society of Friends and was a devout believer in the doctrines of their church until her death. In 1834 Mr. Simon Kerns went with his family across the mountains to Salem, Columbiana county, Ohio, and purchased land in Salem township, the first real estate he ever owned There he carried on farming for about twelve years, when on the 29th of September, 1846, he died of apoplexy, at the comparatively early age of fifty-five years

William Kerns, of this review—named for his grandfather—was fortunate in his home surroundings, having the cultured and Christian training of honored parents His education was acquired in the schools near

his home and at one time he attended school with Bayard Taylor He pursued his lessons in a log school house and there laid the foundation for the practical mental training which he received and which has so well fitted him for the responsible duties of life He was the elder son and the first child in a family of six children, and in consequence his labors were largely given to the work of developing and improving the home farm He carried on agricultural pursuits in Columbiana county, Ohio, until thirty-three years of age. when, thinking he might have better opportunities for advancement in business life in a western district, he started for Iowa He drove through with a team and carriage to Tipton, that state, intending to locate there, but finding that he could secure employment he came to Moline, arriving in this city on the 10th of December, 1853 Here he engaged in teaming from Moline to different points in Iowa, and also helped to deliver ties on seven miles of the west end of the Chicago & Rock Island Railroad, then almost completed He scorned no labor that would yield him an honest living and give him a start to reach the higher plane to which his ambition pointed. When spring came he found that he had not only supported his family, but had also saved eighty dollars as the results of the winter's work

In the spring of 1854 he began working at the carpenter's trade His father, who was a mechanic as well as a farmer, and had manufactured the first threshing machine in East Marlboro, Pennsylvania, had instructed him in the use of tools and he was, therefore, prepared for the new work which he began He followed that occupation with fair success until the panic of 1857, when the hard times made it very difficult for him to obtain work In the meantime his mother had come to make her home with him, and he manfully struggled to support his family until the success which ultimately crowns honest and persevering effort came to him   In 1854 he bought a lot and built a little house thereon.   From 1858 until 1861 he was clerk of the village of Moline, and in the latter year was appointed by President Lincoln as postmaster of the city, an office he held continuously, with the exception of twenty-two months during the early part of Johnson's administration, until August, 1869   His deposition came through some wiley intriguing on the part of opponents, but he laid his case before the authorities and, when the facts were learned, was re-instated in office.

In 1867, while still serving as postmaster, Mr. Kerns was given charge of the legal business of the Moline Plow Company, which he represented in Washington, D C., and in some very important suits heard in the Illinois and federal courts, involving hundreds of thousands of dollars,—a majority of these being for alleged infringement of trademarks and patents.   During the period in which Mr Kerns had charge of this business, the Moline Plow Company and others for which he was acting, never had a decree against them   He also did collecting for the company and other important service.   In 1881 he disposed of his stock in the corporation and retired from its affairs.   He did not, however, remain idle. He was made executor and trustee of the estate of R K. Swan, of the Moline Plow Company, who died in 1878, and until October 15, 1890, he devoted himself to the management of that estate, and did it so well that it paid over one hundred and fifty thousand dollars, whereas, when Mr Kerns assumed the management it was doubted very much whether

as large an amount as sixty thousand dollars would be realized

Mr. Kerns is a man of resourceful ability, capable of controlling extensive and varied interests, and his efforts have been by no means confined to one line alone   In 1873 he secured a franchise for the purpose of putting in a gas plant in Moline, organized a company, and in 1874 this scheme was carried forward to successful completion.   He was made secretary and superintendent of the company, and for five years conducted the enterprise, the investment proving a profitable one   It is a fact that while the gas plants at Rock Island and Davenport both failed when they were first started, the Moline works were successful from the beginning

Mr Kerns also served on the state board of equalization by appointment of Governor Cullom, and was a faithful officer, but since that time he has declined to act in an official capacity.   He has materially aided in building up the city with which he has so long been connected, not alone by the promotion of commercial activity through the channels of legitimate business, but by advancing money to many of his friends, thus enabling them to erect homes, and practically giving them their own time in which to repay.   In this fact he takes a pride that is as commendable as it is just.

In early life Mr Kerns gave his political support to the Democratic party and from the time slavery became a prominent issue was a Freesoiler.   He indorsed the Buffalo platform in 1848, voted for Van Buren and Adams that year and in 1852 cast his ballot for John P. Hale.   From the organization of the Republican party he has been a stalwart advocate of its principles and has supported all its presidential candidates except in 1872, when he voted for Horace Greeley As every true American citizen should do, he manifests a deep interest in political affairs and keeps well informed on the issues of the day

The home ties and relations of Mr. Kerns have ever been of the most pleasant character, and he is never happier than when with his wife and children he is entertaining his friends by his own fireside. He was married May 17, 1842, to Miss Beulah Shinn, who was born near his boyhood's home in Ohio, where her people had located in 1810, removing to the Buckeye state from New Jersey She is a daughter of William B and Elizabeth (Jones) Shinn Four children were born to Mr and Mrs. Kerns George H , the eldest, became a soldier in Company H, Nineteenth Illinois Volunteer Infantry He was born March 2, 1843, and was lost in the battle of Stone River, December 31, 1862, being buried in one of the " unknown graves" which marked so many battlefields Simon A , born January 25, 1847, is now the efficient superintendent of the Rock Island plow shops He was married May 14, 1868, to Miss Clara Martin, of Muscatine, Iowa, and with their one son, George M., they reside in Rock Island Anson, born April 6, 1850, died at Massillon, Ohio, on the 4th of October, 1853, while the family were en route to the west He was buried at Salem, Ohio, but later his remains were removed to the cemetery at Moline Charles S , born in Moline, October 22, 1858, obtained his literary education in the public schools of this city, and was graduated from Eastman's Business College, Poughkeepsie, New York He married Elizabeth M Vernon, of Mount Cuba, Delaware, June 6, 1889, and they have three children, Vernon, Arthur and Beulah He

is teller in the First National Bank, of Moline, where he has been employed for fourteen years

With his own hand William Kerns has shaped his destiny. The common testimony of him is that he is a man of remarkable sagacity, a quality of the human mind that we can scarcely overestimate in business and many relations of life, a man who is careful, prudent and honest, a man therefore not by chance, but by the due exercise of his own good qualities His honesty is the root of honor, which is one and the same thing, something sweeter, nobler and more far-reaching than square dealing He possesses in a marked degree unselfishness, and eagerness and willingness to see that all men have opportunities and a desire to favor all.

CAPTAIN JAMES McBURNEY, who, after the labors of a long and busy life, is spending his later years in ease and retirement in the city of Moline, his residence being at 1204 Fourteenth street, is a native of Ireland, born in County Armaugh, August 24, 1819 His parents, John and Jane (Reed) McBurney, were born, reared and married in Scotland His grandfather, James McBurney, also born in Scotland, served as justice of the peace in the old country

During his boyhood and youth our subject was provided with fair school advantages, and learned the carpenter's and joiner's trade in Ireland and England, serving a five-years' apprenticeship In 1848 he emigrated to the United States, leaving Liverpool on the Clipper, a sailing vessel, bound for Boston After about a month spent in that city he began work at the carpenter's trade and also attended the Mechanic's Institute In 1850 he came to Illinois, first locating in Jacksonville, where he secured work on the insane asylum, and remained there about ten months, but in 1851 went, by way of New York, to California At that city he took passage on the steamer Nicaragua, crossed the Isthmus, and by steamer proceeded up the Pacific to San Francisco In Sonora, California, he engaged in contracting and building, and erected the first court house in Tuolumne county. During his residence there of about four years he erected many good buildings, and met with success financially, but at the end of that time returned east by the same route, arriving in New York in the spring of 1855

On again coming to Illinois, Captain McBurney purchased a farm in Bowling township, Rock Island county, where he had his first experience in agricultural pursuits, which for ten years he successfully followed, improving one of the best farms in the township Renting his place in 1863, he removed to Moline, where he engaged in the livery business for seven years, and then, in partnership with Mr McBride, had a steamboat built at a cost of eight thousand dollars It was used as a ferry running between Dimock & Gould's dock, Moline, and Gilbert, Iowa, and our subject served as captain until 1876, when he sold the boat, which was taken to St Charles, Missouri. He has since practically lived retired, only looking after his property, as he had invested in and erected several residences in Moline In this way he has done much toward building up the city and advancing its welfare

The Captain has been twice married In Rock Island county, in 1856, he wedded Miss Helen L⸱ ⸱ ⸱ ⸱ ⸱ ⸱ ⸱ ⸱ ⸱ ⸱ ⸱ who

was one of the best musicians in the county, a fine singer and a composer as well Her death occurred in 1880, and two years later Captain McBurney married Miss Julia Campbell, who was born, reared and educated in New York, and, as a young lady, came to Davenport, Iowa, where she gave her hand in marriage to our subject

In 1852 the Captain cast his first vote for Franklin Pierce, and has since supported the Democratic party on state and national questions, but at local elections, where no issue is involved, he votes independent of party ties, supporting the man whom he considers best qualified to fill the office For himself, he has never cared for official honors He was reared a Presbyterian, and, with a few others, erected the first Presbyterian church in Bowling township, but now attends the Episcopal church, with his wife, and contributes to its support A man of exemplary habits and sterling worth, he has the confidence of the entire community, and he and his wife hold a high social position, and their many friends will be pleased to read this brief record of their lives

THOMAS CAMPBELL, a well-known and prominent agriculturist now living at the head of Elm street, Rock Island, was born in County Down, Ireland, January 8, 1842, a son of John and Margaret (McQuoid) Campbell, also natives of the Emerald Isle. The paternal grandfather, Thomas Campbell, was of Scotch descent Both he and the maternal grandfather, Robert McQuoid, were farmers by occupation, and died in Ireland when well advanced in years

In 1850 the parents of our subject, with their family, crossed the Atlantic to America, landing at New Orleans after a voyage of seven weeks and three days, and then coming up the Mississippi on a steamboat to St Louis Being ill with ship fever they remained in that city for a short time, and there the mother died The father then brought his children to Rock Island county, Illinois, and located on the William Carr farm on Rock river, where his death occurred in 1857, when he had reached the age of fifty-one years There were three children beside our subject, the others being Mary, now the wife of Robert Retherford, of Audubon county, Iowa, Margaret, deceased, and Robert a resident of Drury township, Rock Island county

Owing to the death of his parents, Thomas Campbell was reared by Mr and Mrs John A Boyer, of this county, who had no children and tenderly cared for him as if he had been their own He was provided with good district and common-school advantages and upon their farm early became familiar with the duties which fall to the lot of the agriculturist On attaining to man's estate he rented the place, which he operated until the death of his benefactors when the property was willed to him and children Mrs. Boyer preceded her husband to the other world about six years. On the death of the latter he gave his farm, improvements and ten thousand dollars to Mr Campbell and his family, each member being mentioned in the will, and our subject and E E Parmenter were appointed executors Mr Boyer was one of the pioneers of Rock Island county, and was widely and favorably known

Loyal to the interests of his adopted land, Mr Campbell enlisted August 9, 1862, in Company I, One Hundred and Twenty-Sixth Illinois Volunteer Infantry, but was discharged on the 17th of October, of the same year

as he was accidentally shot in the knee joint by a comrade while guarding sutlers' tents in Chicago This wound has made him a permanent cripple, and since the war he accidentally broke the same knee Through it all he is a happy man, believing that the hand of God was in it to call him back from the world

On the 7th of September, 1864, Mr Campbell was united in marriage with Miss Mary J , a daughter of John and Mary (Johnson) Carson, and they now have seven children, namely John T , Ada B , Samuel M , Charles C , Mary Alice, Albert H and William R , all at home with the exception of the two eldest. John T. married Miss Margaret James and has one child, Mary Alice Ada B is now the wife of John G Huntoon, superintendent of the street railways of the three cities, and they have two children—Frank C and Jay G

As an ardent Republican, Mr Campbell has taken a prominent and active part in political affairs, and has been called upon to fill a number of responsible public positions For eight consecutive years he represented the South Rock Island township on the board of supervisors, being first elected in 1881, and for the last two years he served as chairman He was a member of the school board for the long period of eighteen years and was then succeeded by his son Samuel, who served for six years In November, 1890, he was elected county treasurer for four years, and filled that important position with credit to himself and to the satisfaction of the public Twice he has been the candidate of his party before the convention for representative in the Illinois legislature, but was defeated in the nomination When elected county treasurer there were only three on his ticket that were victorious, thus showing his popularity and the confidence his fellow citizens repose in him He is now the honored president of the Rock Island County Farmers' Institute, is a member of John Buford Post, No 243, G. A R , and Charley Hawes Camp, No. 1550, M W. A. He and his estimable wife and all their children are members of the First Baptist church of Rock Island, in which he is now serving as deacon and as a member of the board of trustees Coming here at an early day he has witnessed almost the entire growth and development of the county and has cheerfully born his part in promoting those enterprises calculated to advance the general welfare or benefit the community

FRANK P LEWIS has since 1872 been connected with the business interests of Rock Island county, and is an honored representative of its trade circles A well-spent life has won for him the confidence and good will of all with whom he has been brought in contact, and his interest in and labors for the development of Rock Island and Moline have made him a valued citizen.

Mr Lewis is a native of the Granite state, his birth having occurred at Claremont, in Sullivan county, October 5, 1850 He is descended from honored New England ancestry who in colonial days came from England and took up their residence in Connecticut. His grandfather was born in the Nutmeg state and became one of the early settlers of Sullivan county, New Hampshire. His father, John H Lewis, was born in New Hampshire, February 28, 1808, was reared in Sullivan county, and acquired a good education there. He served an apprenticeship to the millwright's trade in Hartford,

Connecticut, and also followed that pursuit in New Haven. He afterward returned to New Hampshire, where he carried on business along that line throughout his entire life He also owned and operated a farm, whereon he reared his family He was married in Sullivan county to Amanda L Nason, a native of Vermont, and a sister of C O Nason, of Moline Mr Lewis died in August, 1883, at the age of seventy-six years He was a Democrat in politics and an earnest advocate of the measures of the party, but never aspired to political honors His wife, who survived him for a number of years, passed away December 19, 1895, and was laid by the side of her husband in the West Claremont cemetery, where a substantial monument marks their last resting place Their family numbered three sons and a daughter, who reached mature years and became heads of families The oldest, James N , is a Pullman car conductor and resides in St Louis, Edward C is engaged in the express business in Claremont, New Hampshire, and Charlotte M is the wife of Fred Waite, of Windsor, Vermont

Frank P Lewis, the youngest of this family, was reared to manhood in his native city and supplemented his primary education, acquired in the common schools, by a course in the Stephens high school. He afterward learned the millwright's trade under the direction of his father and followed it for a time in Claremont In 1874 he removed to Moline and joined his uncle, C. O. Nason, in August The following year he entered the employ of Deere & Company in the wood work department and remained with that mammoth concern for about twenty years, serving as a contractor during the last ten years of his connection therewith He resigned in September, 1894, in order to accept the position of government gauger for the fifth district of Illinois, to which position he was appointed by President Cleveland on the 22nd of May of that year He is now occupying that position and is a most capable and efficient officer, discharging his duties with marked fidelity

Mr Lewis returned to Claremont, where he married July 13, 1874, to Miss Adella E Ingals, who was born in Boston, Massachusetts, and is a daughter of Francis J and Orilla H (Slade) Ingals. Her father removed to Alstead, New Hampshire, and later to Claremont, where he reared and educated his children, two daughters and a son, the eldest of whom was Mrs. Lewis The others are Julia, wife of Aaron King, of Claremont, New Hampshire, and Herman F., who died at the age of eleven years. The father of this family died in Claremont, in May, 1894, at the age of sixty-three, and was laid to rest by the side of his wife who died May 1, 1888, and was buried in the Claremont cemetery. Mr. and Mrs Lewis have two sons—Walter H , who completed the high school course of Moline in 1896, and is now in the employ of Deere & Company, and Francis Herbert, who is still in school.

Politically, Mr Lewis is a stanch Democrat and an active worker in local political circles. He served as alderman for one term and was re-elected but resigned in order to accept his government position He has been a delegate to many county conventions and does all in his power to promote the growth and insure the success of his party. Socially he is a valued member of the Knights of Pythias Lodge of Moline and the Modern Woodmen Both he and his wife are members of the Unitarian church and occupy a prominent position in social circles where true worth and intelligence are received as the passports into good society

FRANK D PAUL, M D , has attained distinction in the medical profession by reason of a skill and ability that ranks him above the average practitioner He is now one of the leading physicians and surgeons of Rock Island and stands pre-eminent among the representatives of the medical fraternity in northwestern Illinois.

A native of Maine, the Doctor was born March 17, 1862, in Piscataquis county, and is a son of Daniel and Mary (Hobart) Paul, whose birth also occurred in that state On both sides of the house have been a number of able representatives of the medical profession, including the Doctor's grandfather, Daniel Hobart To the same family belongs Vice-President Hobart. The Pauls are of Scotch and English extraction William Paul and Daniel Hobart, the great-grandfathers of our subject, both aided the colonies in their struggle for independence during the Revolutionary war The grandfather, William Paul, Jr , was a very noted man in Maine, where he successfully followed school teaching, and in an early day was an ardent Democrat He was in favor of liberating the slaves by purchasing them, but was opposed to the war. His son, Joseph Paul, was also a teacher in early life, but later became a very noted physician of Havanna, Illinois, where he died in 1895.

Until 1875, Daniel Paul, our subject's father, followed agricultural pursuits in Maine, and for about twenty years served as postmaster of South Solon. Being one of the most prominent and influential citizens of his community, he was called upon to fill the office of selectman, or town commissioner, for many years, and also served as a member of the school board He was faithful in the discharge of every trust reposed in him, whether public or private, and had the respect and confidence of a wide circle of friends and acquaintances He died December 7, 1886, aged sixty-six years, but his wife is still living at the old home in Maine, at the age of seventy-four She is a consistent member of the Baptist church

Dr Paul, of this review, is the youngest in the family of seven children, of whom four are still living (1) George is a commission merchant in Boston, Massachusetts (2) Dr. Newell had just entered upon the practice of medicine in Webster City, Iowa, when he was attacked by typhoid fever and died in 1870, at the age of twenty-two years (3) Martha, a young lady of pleasing address and fine literary ability, died at the age of nineteen years (4) Dr Cyrus Almon is a prominent physician and surgeon engaged in practice in Solon, Maine (5) Willard A is a graduate of Hahnemann Medical College of Chicago He came to Illinois as a practitioner in 1879, but is now a professor in the Boston School of Homeopathy, being assistant to the chair of gynecology and holding three clinics a week in that institution He is a surgeon of considerable notoriety, does a large general practice, and makes a specialty of the diseases of the eye and ear He was born in Piscataquis county, Maine, and married Miss Jennie Stevens, of that state (6) Edward died when quite young All of the children were born in the Pine Tree state

Dr. Frank D Paul pursued his early studies in the common schools of North Anson, Maine, and in Kents Hill Seminary and at other place and after completing his literary

erary education, he began reading medicine with his brother Willard A , then a practicing physician of Rock Island, but now of Boston, Massachusetts Subsequently he attended lectures at the State University of Iowa, where he graduated with the class of 1886, and at once began practice in Cambridge, Illinois, but in 1892 returned to Rock Island and for a time was in partnership with his brother He is a prominent representative of the Homeopathic school, keeps well posted on the important discoveries and progress made in both the science of medicine and surgery, and to-day enjoys a large and lucrative practice. He is an examiner for a number of insurance companies and beneficiary orders, and is a member of the State Homeopathic Association The Doctor also belongs to the Masonic Order, and in politics is identified with the Republican party In 1886, four years after coming to this state, he was united in marriage to Miss Almeda F Andrews, also a native of Maine, and a daughter of Austin Andrews Their home is blessed by the presence of two children—Mary and Daniel The Doctor is a member of the Central Presbyterian church of Rock Island, while his wife belongs to the Unitarian church of Moline.

CAPTAIN THOMAS J ROBINSON, president of the Rock Island National Bank and president of the Rock Island & Davenport Ferry Company, is a man who deservedly ranks high in the esteem of his fellow citizens for his work's sake Few enterprises have been established in Rock Island in the past forty-four years in which he has not been more or less interested in a financial way or in moral support He was born

in the town of Hope, now Appleton, Maine, July 28, 1818, and is the only surviving one of a family of five sons and two daughters born to John and Polly (Dillaway) Robinson, who were also natives of Maine His paternal grandfather was a native of Massachusetts of English descent, and by occupation was a farmer In a very early day he moved to Maine and there passed the remainder of his days John Robinson also died in Maine in 1827 at the age of fifty-six years, while his wife preceded him to their heavenly home two or three years The maternal grandfather, Samuel Dillaway, also an agriculturist, was a native of Massachusetts of French descent

As Stephen A Douglas said of Vermont, so it can be said of Maine, it is good state to be born in Its citizens seem to partake of the rugged nature of its hills, and are almost always men and women of sterling worth and solid character But the old hills are not always inviting to the aspiring youth and many emigrate at an early date, settle upon the broad prairies of the west, and give their best energies to the building up of the new country, giving it some of the solidity of the old.

In 1838, when twenty years of age, our subject determined to cast his fortunes with the great west, and hearing of the broad prairies and productive soil of Illinois, felt that should be the place for his future home Accordingly he set out, making the journey principally by water, and was thirty days in coming from his old home to Whitehall, Greene county, where he first located and remained two years He then went south and was a clerk on a steamboat, plying between New Orleans and Nashville, for nearly two years Whether he became a little homesick or not we find him returning to

Maine, where he remained one year, and was then glad to get back to Illinois He came back by the Great Lakes, landing in Chicago, when that city had but nine thousand inhabitants, and with no great promise for the future This was in June, 1843, at which time he could have bought the land where the Grand Pacific Hotel now stands, on the corner of Clark and Jackson streets, for fifty dollars

From Chicago, Mr Robinson went by stage to Joliet and La Salle, and at the latter place took a boat for Apple Creek Landing Going back to the vicinity of Whitehall he taught school for two years, and during the succeeding four or five years was engaged as deputy in the office of the county treasurer and county clerk of Greene county He then purchased a farm on Rock river, near Hillsdale, and lived there nearly two years Selling the farm, he removed to Port Byron, Rock Island county, and engaged in merchandising and milling In the former he was the junior partner of Temple, Dickerson & Company, and in the latter junior of the firm of Temple, Dorrance & Company He remained at Port Byron for about five years, meeting with fair success in both lines of business

Closing out his interests at Port Byron, Mr. Robinson, in 1853, came to Rock Island and took charge of the ferry between that city and Davenport, with which he has since been connected either as master of the vessel or president of the company As already stated, from that date to the present he has been actively and closely identified with almost every business interest of the city He was one of the organizers of the Rock Island Stove Company, and was its president a number of years During that time he became one of the organizers

3

of the Rock Island Glass Company, and was vice-president for some years He also helped organize the Rock Island Quilt Manufacturing Company and the Rock Island Watch Company, and in the latter served as president several years In the organization of the Rock Island & Moline Railway Company, he materially assisted, in fact, he was one of its originators, and served for some years as its secretary In 1871 he was the prime mover in the organization of the Rock Island National Bank, and has ever since been its president Much of the credit is due him for the successful operation of that bank, which is regarded as one of the strongest and most conservative in this section While most of his business interests are with Rock Island, he has some investments elsewhere, and is now a director in the North Wisconsin Lumber Company, of Hayward, Wisconsin

On the 15th of January, 1846, Captain Robinson was united in marriage with Miss Amy Ann Henderson, daughter of James and Mary (White) Henderson They were married at Whitehall Two children came to bless their union—J Frank and John The latter died when two and a half years old J Frank is the present efficient cashier of the Rock Island National Bank, and who married Miss Mary Rhoads

After a happy married life of almost fifty years, Mrs Captain Robinson was called to her reward in 1895, at the age of seventy-three years She was a consistent member of the Methodist Episcopal church, and with a loving trust in her Heavenly Father, feared not the summons to "come up higher" While her death is deeply mourned by her companion, yet he is not as one th t t c t h kn w th t sh

has just gone before, and in the sweet bye and bye they will meet never more to part.

Captain Robinson is also a member of the Methodist Episcopal church and is a member of the board of trustees of the church in Rock Island In the work of the church he takes a lively interest, and in all its various departments contributes of his means Fraternally he is a Mason, a member of the blue lodge and of Everett Commandery, No 18, K T Originally he was in politics a Whig, but on the dissolution of that party, and because of the fact that he was opposed to the institution of slavery, he became a Republican, with which party he has since been identified In his younger days he took an active part in political affairs, but of late years he has given his undivided attention to his business interests For two terms, beginning in 1849, he served as associate justice, and for some years was a member of the county board of supervisors, serving as chairman of the board during the dark days of the Civil war

Since 1864 Captain Robinson has occupied a pleasant home at No. 613 Twentieth street, and its hospitable doors have ever been open to his many friends and acquaintances A genial and affable gentleman, he is highly esteemed in the community, being recognized as one of its leading and substantial citizens, one having at all times the interest of his adopted city and county at heart, and one who never hesitates to do that which in his judgment will bring prosperity.

DANIEL M SECHLER is the president and founder of the Sechler Carriage Company, of Moline, one of the most extensive industries of the county, and has won a distinctive place in commercial circles An eminent writer has said that far greater credit and gratitude is due to the man who each week pays over his counters one hundred employes than to him who commands a company on the field of battle The former places within the reach of his workmen the means of livelihood that enables him to maintain his family and become a self-respecting citizen This Mr. Sechler does as the head of the important industry which he controls, and Moline numbers him among its prominent and influential citizens

Mr Sechler was born in Danville, Pennsylvania, March 4, 1818, and comes of a family that, in the days of the persecution of John Huss and his followers, were forced to flee from Austria They took up their abode in Holland, and from the latter country the great-grandfather of our subject came to America. He located in Pennsylvania, where occurred the birth of John Sechler, the grandfather, and the parents of our subject, Rudolph and Susan (Douty) Sechler, who were also natives of that state

In the city of his birth Daniel M. Sechler spent his boyhood, and supplemented his early education, acquired in the common schools, by a few terms' attendance at an academy there When nineteen years of age he began learning the carriagemaker's trade at Port Deposit, Maryland, where he remained for three years, receiving not a cent in compensation for his services He afterward worked under instruction at Newark, New Jersey, for a year and a half, and when twenty-two years of age embarked in business at Milton, Pennsylvania, as the junior member of the firm of Ball & Sechler, a partnership that was maintained until Mr. Ball's death Mr Sechler then continued the business alone for three

years, turning out from fifty to seventy-five carriages each year He then sold, and in 1844 removed to Wooster, Ohio, where he lived retired from business for a time His next place of residence was in Ironton, Lawrence county, Ohio, where he took charge of the pattern department in a large machine shop, remaining there until 1868. He then removed to Cincinnati, where he opened a wholesale and retail iron store as agent for a rolling mill company of Pomeroy, Ohio, and continued in charge until 1867, when he became a partner in Swift's Iron and Steel Works at Newport, Kentucky, but continued his residence in Cincinnati until 1869 He then became interested in the manufacture of pig iron in Montgomery county, Tennessee, conducting the enterprise until 1877, when he engaged in the manufacture of carriages in Cincinnati, under the firm name of Sechler & Company, for ten years. After selling out he and his wife made a trip to Europe, spending five months abroad, visiting many points of beauty and historic interest in England, Ireland, Scotland, France, Switzerland, Italy, Austria, Germany, Belgium and the battlefield of Waterloo

It was Mr. Sechler's intention on his return to put aside all business cares, but his life has been one of great activity, and indolence and idleness are utterly foreign to his nature, so that he could not content himself without some business interests and in 1888 established the plant of the Sechler Carriage Company This has a floor surface of over two acres, and a capacity of more than ten thousand carriages annually They employ over one hundred and forty men when running in full force

On the 19th of January, 1841, in Milton, Pennsylvania Mr Sechler married Pamela

Mackey, a native of Berks county, Pennsylvania, and a daughter of Thomas S. and Catherine (Angstadt) Mackey They have one son, Thomas Mackey Sechler, who was born in Milton, Pennsylvania, October 25, 1841, and attended the public schools of that place and of Ironton. He also pursued his studies in Cincinnati, where he entered the senior class of the Hughes high school, and was graduated in 1860 The same fall he joined the sophomore class at Marietta, Ohio, where he was graduated with third honors July 2nd, 1863. Sixteen days later he enlisted as a member of Company K, Ohio Heavy Artillery, but the regiment was mostly engaged in infantry service He went to the front as second lieutenant under commission of Governor Tod, and by Governor Brough was commissioned first lieutenant He spent the first eight months of his service in Kentucky, and afterward in Tennessee, where he participated in many skirmishes. After nearly two years at the front he resigned in June, 1865 Returning to Cincinnati he pursued a course in a commercial college and then served as his father's bookkeeper until the business was closed out in that city, after which he was with him in the iron manufactory in Tennessee, and is now his partner in Moline.

Thomas M Sechler was married in Ironton, Ohio, June 7, 1866, the lady of his choice being Juliet A McCullough She was born in West Union, Adams county, Ohio, and is a daughter of Addison and Eliza (Wilson) McCullough. One child, Mary Addie, has been born to them, and is now the wife of Howard O Edmonds, of Chicago

Mr. Sechler, of this review, cast his first presidential vote for William Henry Harrison in 1840, and supported the Whig party until 1856, when he voted for Fremont, since which time he has affiliated with the Republican party on questions of national importance His son is also a Republican and is a member of the Congregational church of Moline. He is a Knight Templar Mason, holding membership in Doric Lodge, No. 319, and in Everett Commandery, No 18 He also belongs to Graham Post, No 312, G A. R., of Moline, and to the Loyal Legion of Cincinnati Both father and son are men of excellent business ability and executive force, of keen discrimination and resolute purpose and in the conduct of their business interests have met with splendid success

---

CHARLES J LARKIN is a leading contractor and builder of Rock Island, of whose skill many notable examples are to be seen at various points in this region. Thoroughly reliable in all things, the quality of his work is a convincing test of his own personal worth, and the same admirable trait is shown in his conscientious discharge of the duties of different positions of trust and responsibility to which he has been chosen in business and political life

The birth of Mr Larkin occurred September 13, 1852, in Schenectady, New York, but at the age of four years he was brought to Rock Island by his parents, Michael and Mary (Smith) Larkin, natives of Ireland, the former from Galway, the latter from Athboy, County Meath Of their five children, three are still living—Charles J., John W and Mary. The paternal grandfather, Patrick Larkin, was a herder in Ireland, where he died in old age In his family were seven sons and three daughters The maternal grandfather, Peter Smith, also departed this life on the Emerald Isle when well advanced in years By trade the father of our subject was a blacksmith, and later in his active life he assisted his son Charles J in contract work On coming to the United States he located in Schenectady, New York, but in 1856 came to Rock Island, where he spent his remaining days, dying in 1893, at the age of seventy-five years Six months later his wife was also called to her reward at the age of seventy-four. Both were devout members of the Catholic church and respected by all who knew them

After graduating from the public schools of Rock Island, Charles J Larkin learned the stone cutter's trade, and at the early age of twenty years began contract work He has built many of the most important buildings in Davenport, Rock Island and Moline and has done considerable work in other cities, including the erection of the Cathedral in Des Moines, Iowa He built the United States post office building at Davenport, at a cost of about eighty thousand dollars, did the stone work on the court house in that city, and has built all but two of the public school buildings of Rock Island

One of his most important works is the new court house at Rock Island, which will for years stand as a monument to his architectural skill and ability In June, 1895, he took the contract for its erection the architects being Gunn & Curtis, of Kansas City, Missouri, and in March, 1897, it was completed and ready for use It would be a credit to any county and is a high testimonial of Mr Larkin's excellent ability The building is of Roman style of architecture, one hundred and seventy-two by ninety feet, four stories in height, with a dome one hundred and fifty feet high, and contains sixty rooms furnished in the most modern and approved style It is heated throughout with the Sturtevant fan system of steam heat, such as is used in the Stock Exchange of Chicago, and requires an extra engine house, which is connected with the building by a tunnel It has an electric elevator, and is lighted by gas and electricity, the fixtures being put in by E. Baggot, of Chicago The inside is frescoed and finished very artistically, W Andrew, of Clinton, Iowa, doing the former work The wood work is of quarter oak, the floors of the rooms of maple, while the halls and corridors are of Mosaic and the wainscoting of pink Tennessee marble The vaults are furnished with the latest improved metallic cases, manufactured by the Fenton Metallic Company, of Jamestown, New York, and the wood furniture, which matches the finish in the rooms, was manufactured by the Moline Furniture Company. The stairs are of iron, electroplated, with slate treads. The building itself is constructed of buff Bedford stone, of Indiana, and the covering of the cornice, dome and pavillion is of copper. The roof is also of that metal It is practically fire-proof

Mr Larkin was married October 20, 1873, to Miss Annie T Ford, a daughter of William and Ann (Broderick) Ford, of Sheffield, Illinois, and they now have four sons and four daughters, namely May, Kathryne, Leo, Harry, Annie, Hattie, Charles J and Willard, all at home The family is one of prominence in social circles, and its members are all connected with the Catholic church Mr Larkin is domestic in his tastes, preferring the quiet of home life to other enjoyments His residence is at No 556 Elm street

In his political affiliations he is a Republican, and he has represented the fifth ward in the city council for six years He has also been a director of the public library for ten or twelve years, and has ever taken an active and prominent part in public affairs, being interested in the Hennepin canal, now in course of construction, and serving as a delegate to Washington in the interest of the canal Not confining his attention alone to contracting and building, he has become a director in the Home Building and Loan Association, and is also a stockholder in the Peaslee Shoe Company A genial, pleasant gentleman, he is deservedly popular among the people and has hosts of warm friends in Rock Island and other places

---

ERIC OKERBERG, a retired capitalist of Moline, whose residence in Rock Island county connects the pioneer epoch with the present development, was born in Sweden, July 21, 1821, and spent the days of his boyhood and youth there. His education was obtained mostly through his own exertions in his leisure hours, his school privileges being limited In his youth he served a five years' apprenticeship to the jeweler's trade in Sundsvall, and afterward remained there for eight years working at the business which he had mastered He also learned the trade of watch and clock making and has kept apace with the wonderful progress that has been achieved along these lines He now has in his home office a large, old-fashioned regulator which runs for thirty days without winding, one of the heirlooms of the past

Learning of the advantages offered by the New World, Mr Okerberg determined to try his fortune in America and took passage on the Swedish ship vessel Spline

which weighed anchor on the 11th of June, 1850, and reached its destination in August, after a voyage of six weeks One severe storm occurred during the passage, occasioning much fright among the women and children On reaching the United States our subject at once proceeded westward by way of Albany and the canal to Buffalo, whence he took a lake vessel for Chicago, and thence continued on his way by canal to La Salle. He walked from there to Victoria, Knox county, Illinois, where he spent the succeeding winter In the spring of 1851 he came to Rock Island, went to Minnesota, in the summer, and in August of that year returned to Moline. A month later he took up his residence in Rock Island, where he arrived with a cash capital of four dollars, and after purchasing a watch sign he had only eighty cents remaining He possessed, however, a resolute, enterprising spirit, and began the work of cleaning and repairing watches and clocks He soon built up a good trade and continued in business there for three and a half years.

In 1855 Mr Okerberg once more settled in Moline, purchasing a lot on Third avenue, whereon he erected the first business house on that street. For fifteen years he remained at that place and then sold the lot and shop, after which he erected his present residence on the bluff and a store room on Third avenue, where the post office now stands That was his business location for several years, but at length he sold out to C H. Deere and erected a fine three-story brick block on the opposite corner This is one of the finest business houses in the city. Carrying a large and complete line of jewelry he commanded a liberal share of the public patronage until 1891, when he retired from active business, although he still owns the stock The store is now managed by his son, and in addition to his property he owns considerable real estate in Moline

Mr Okerberg was married in this city January 7, 1853, to Johanna Peterson, a native of Sweden, who came to America in 1852. They have a family of seven children—Emma, wife of August Elmgreen, of Moline, Matilda, wife of John Buford, of Moline, Eric O , who now conducts the jewelry business, Jennie, wife of Andrew W Anderson, of Moline, Rosa, wife of Charles P Heine, who for thirteen years has held a responsible position in the recorder's office of Chicago, Frank Oscar, a jeweler and watch maker, who is engaged in business in Sherrard, and Nellie, at home

Mr. Okerberg is a man of independent views, who on questions of politics exercises the right of forming his own opinions and of supporting those interests which he believes calculated for the best government During the days of the war he supported the Republican party, afterward he voted for Peter Cooper, and in 1896 voted the Republican ticket, and may be said to be independent He served as trustee of the village before the organization of the city of Moline, has been alderman one term, and city treasurer two years, but has never sought nor desired public office He is, however, deeply interested in the welfare of city and state, and is ever mindful of his duties of citizenship, never neglecting any interest that can prove of benefit to the public He has been an important factor in the development and growth of Moline, and has witnessed its transformation from a small village into one of the leading manufacturing centers of the state He is a man of great sincerity and firmness of character

and his integrity is proverbial Business successes have come to him as the reward of honorable dealing and well directed efforts and his prosperity and unblemished career have secured him a place among the leading residents of his adopted county

GEORGE W GAMBLE, now serving his third term as circuit clerk of Rock Island county, Illinois, is a most popular official, and ranks among the leading and most influential citizens of the county He was born in Allegheny county, Pennsylvania, December 18, 1848, and is a son of John and Isabella (Alexander) Gamble, the former a native of England and the latter of the north of Ireland Of their ten children, nine are yet living—Hugh A , Charles J , George W , Philip R , Mary, wife of A R Schadt, Elizabeth, wife of William Cubbison, Henry, William, David A , and Ida, wife of Willis Hancox Of these Hugh A was a soldier in the late war and was wounded in the battle of the Wilderness

John Gamble, the father, was a farmer in Mercer county, Pennsylvania, and died there in 1875, at the age of about sixty-three years. His wife died some years later Both were members of the Methodist church, and died in that faith The paternal grandfather, Charles Gamble, was a native of England, who settled in Mercer county, Pennsylvania, when his son John was a small boy He died there when about eighty years of age He had two sons and two daughters By occupation he was a farmer The maternal grandfather, John Alexander, was a native of the north of Ireland Religiously he was of the United Presbyterian faith, and on coming to America located in Washington, Iowa, where many of that belief are located, and where his death occurred when about eighty years old.

The subject of this sketch was reared upon his father's farm, where he remained until he was seventeen years old, when he began learning the printer's trade at Greenville, Pennsylvania, which he followed nine years His education was obtained in the public schools, but his nine years training in a printing office—the "poor man's college" —fitted him in a special manner for the active duties of life In 1874 he came to Moline, Illinois, and went into the grocery business, in which line he continued for three years, and then became billing clerk for the Chicago, Rock Island & Pacific Railroad in its freight office at Moline He remained there until December, 1884, when he was appointed deputy circuit clerk, and served in that position about four years So well did he discharge the duties of the office, thus proving his ability, that he was nominated for the office of circuit clerk in the fall of 1888, and triumphantly elected He was re-elected in 1892 and again in 1896, each time by an increased majority, thus proving his popularity.

On the 15th of October, 1874, at Adrian, Michigan, Mr Gamble married Miss Huldah A. Lutton, daughter of Peter Lutton, by whom he has three daughters—Madge A , Etta G. and Ruth E , all yet under the parental roof Their home is at No 2306 Sixth avenue, Moline

Mr and Mrs. Gamble are members of the Congregational church and are active workers in that body Fraternally he is a member of the Knights of Pythias, Modern Woodmen of America, the Ancient Order of United Workmen, Knights of the Globe and Court of Honor Politically, he is a Republican, with which party he has been identified since attaining his majority, and in whose principles and policy he has the utmost faith Especially is this true as regards protection and reciprocity

---

W H. EDWARDS, who is living retired in Moline, claims descent from some of the oldest families of America. From the rock-ribbed country of Wales there came to this country, in the seventeenth century, representatives of the name, who founded the family in America. The great-grandfather of our subject, William Edwards, was born in Coventry, Connecticut, in 1741, and married Temperance Huntington, an English lady. Their son, Benatha Edwards, was born in Coventry, May 5, 1772, and his son, William Edwards, the father of our subject, was born in Guilford, Windham county, near Brattleboro, Vermont, July 18, 1795. He married Huldah Bangs, who was born in Montague, Massachusetts, December 31, 1798, a daughter of John Bangs Their marriage was celebrated January 28, 1823, at Bernardston, Massachusetts Three years after the landing of the Pilgrims at Plymouth Rock, Edward Bangs, who was born in Colchester, England, in 1592, came to Massachusetts His son, Captain Jonathan Bangs, was born at Plymouth in 1640 Captain Samuel Bangs was born July 12, 1680, in Harwich, Massachusetts, and his son, Nathan Bangs, was born in 1736, while John Bangs, the grandfather of our subject, was born June 21, 1764 He was one of the heroes of the Revolution His daughter, Mrs Huldah Edwards, died at Moline, Illinois, February 21, 1885.

Mr Edwards, the father of our subject, died in Moline, July 3, 1848 He removed

W. H. EDWARDS.

from Vermont to Illinois in 1834, and the following year located in Moline Three of his brothers had come to this state in 1827, and he joined them in Greene county, coming to Rock Island county in 1835 Here he purchased of Huntington Wells a claim of one hundred and seventy-three acres, which is now within the corporation limits of Moline. There he cultivated and improved a good farm, and the old farm residence, which was erected in 1838, is still standing on the place, the city having grown up around it His first home was a cabin, 12 x 16 feet In this little dwelling lived a family of seven persons, and many strangers were entertained there while looking for land in this neighborhood Their first neighbors lived about a mile from their home, near the present site of the Moline water works Mr Edwards died in 1848, but lived to see in embryo the future cities of Davenport, Rock Island and Moline.

William H Edwards, of this review, is the eldest of the family of four sons Herbert R died November 21, 1874, George H. is still living in Moline; and Charles T resides in Galesburg Our subject was born in Guilford, Vermont, October 14, 1823, and was, therefore, twelve years of age when the family removed to this county His education was acquired in private schools of Rock Island, and after completing his studies he learned the carriage maker's trade, which he followed in that city until 1863, with the exception of two years spent in Galena, in 1847 and 1848 He then became superintendent of the wood department of the Moline Plow Company, in which capacity he served continuously and acceptably until 1883, discharging his duties with a promptness and fidelity that won him the unqualified confidence of his em-

ployers In 1884 and 1885 he engaged in merchandising in Cedar Rapids, but in the latter year sold out and returned to Moline, where he has since lived retired

Mr Edwards was married in Davenport, Iowa, April 3, 1844, to Miss Caroline Fleming, a native of Morgantown, Pennsylvania, who had located in Davenport in 1840, her father being Isaac Fleming They were twenty-one and sixteen years of age respectively at the time of their marriage and for forty-one years they traveled life's journey together, until separated by death July 8, 1885, the wife being called to the home beyond They had six children Nettie H., the eldest, became the wife of Dr J B Davison, and died in 1893 Edwin A and Clarence W died in childhood Ella is the wife of James Magill, of Moline William M. is with the firm of Barnard & Leas Fred L. is in the employ of the Chicago & Rock Island Railroad Company. There are also eleven grandchildren Mr. Edwards was again married November 21, 1888, in Moline, his second union being with Mary E Davison, a native of Westmoreland county, Pennsylvania.

From the organization of the party until 1892 Mr Edwards was a Republican, but since the latter date has voted with the Prohibition party About 1846 he was elected constable and for some years served on the school board, and was assessor of his township in 1869, but he has never sought political preferment, desiring rather to give his attention to his business interests For about ten years he was trustee of the Moline cemetery, and for many years he has been a member of the Congregational church, being one of its most active and influential workers He served as deacon for more than a quarter of a century was superintendent of the

Sunday-school for about ten years, and was leader of the choir for six years

Few men have longer been identified with the interests of Rock Island county than Mr Edwards He came here when much of the land was a dense wilderness or a swampy district, and has seen it develop into richly cultivated farms, while two large and thriving cities have sprung up, together with a number of enterprising towns The work of progress has been carried steadily forward, bringing with it all the improvements of civilization until to-day the county ranks among the foremost in this great commonwealth Mr Edwards has ever borne his part in the work of improvement and his name occupies a conspicuous place on the roll of Rock Island county's honored pioneers.

FRANK L NATT, a wide-awake, progressive business man of Moline, is a successful dealer in hard and soft coal and coke, carrying on operations at the corner of Third avenue and Eleventh street Like many of the best citizens of Rock Island county, he is a Scandinavian by birth He was born in Sweden, February 13, 1863, a son of Andrew and Mary Natt His father, who was a laborer in that country, was born September 29, 1836, and crossed the Atlantic to America in 1868, leaving his family in the old world until he should be able to earn money enough to send for them The following year the mother, with her two sons, our subject and an older brother, arrived here

Making his home in Moline, Andrew Natt worked on the government dam during the winter and spring, while in the summer he went north and worked as a harvest

hand at three dollars and a half per day In 1870 the family removed to Keokuk, Iowa, where they conducted a boarding house for the men working on the government canal and were very successful in this enterprise The following year they engaged in the same business at La Grange, Missouri, boarding the railroad men, and then for the same length of time they carried on a boarding house in West Quincy, Missouri Returning to La Grange they resided there until 1872, when they opened a boarding house in New Canton, and later engaged in the same business at Hull until the fall of 1881 when they returned to Moline. The mother had died March 20, 1881, in Hull, where her remains were interred

Our subject had attended school at the various places where the family had made their home, and had thus acquired a good practical education, which well fits him for the responsible duties of business life. On his return to Moline he obtained a position with a wagon company, and in 1883 entered the office of H Woodworth as clerk, serving in that capacity for four years His father then furnished him the money to start his present business, and for two years he carried on operations under the firm style of A Natt & Son, but at the end of that time was able to purchase his father's interest and has since been alone in business

In Moline, on the 5th of December, 1894, was celebrated the marriage of Mr Natt and Miss Jennie May Richardson, who was born in Orion, Illinois, June 4, 1878, and is a daughter of Vance and Malissa (Snyder) Richardson, of Scotch-Irish and German ancestry, respectively

The father of our subject is a member of the Swedish Lutheran church, and in politics is a Republican, but has never cared for the honors or emoluments of public office Mr Natt, of this review, cast his first vote for John P St John, the Prohibition candidate, but later has given his allegiance to the Republican party In religious belief he is a Baptist, and socially is a member of Abe Lincoln Camp, No 153, M. W A , and King Philip Tribe, No 94, I O R M Public-spirited to a great degree, he takes a deep interest in every measure which is calculated to benefit the community, or to accrue to the good of society in general, and as a business man his straightforward dealings and honorable course have gained for him the confidence and respect of all with whom he has come in contact.

GEORGE E LAMBERT.--Honored and respected by all, there is no man in Rock Island who has a higher standing in commercial circles than Mr Lambert This is due not only to the prosperity he has attained but more to the straightforward and commendable business methods he has pursued He is now manager and treasurer of the Twin City Ice Company, and his steadfast purpose, keen discrimination and sound judgment have brought him success.

A native of Brookville, Massachusetts, he was born on the 12th day of March, 1852, and is descended from English ancestry. His parents Abraham H and Emily F (Hersey) Lambert, are natives of the Bay State, and have three children now living— Annie H , wife of Bernard McGuire, of Salida, Colorado, George E and Abraham The parents are members of the Baptist church and are most highly esteemed citizens of Rock Island, where for the long period of forty years they have made their home The maternal grandfather of our subject, Elijah Hersey, came to the west about 1856, but after four years returned to Westboro, Massachusetts, where he carried on farming Subsequently, however, he became a permanent resident of Rock Island, where he died in 1894, at the advanced age of eighty-eight years

George E Lambert was but five years of age when, with his parents, he became a resident of this city He acquired his preliminary education in its public schools and afterward entered the Davenport Business College, where he was trained for a business experience He then joined his father, who was in the ice trade and continued with him as an employe for several years. Subsequently he was admitted to a partnership in the business and after his father's retirement in 1874, on the incorporation of the company, he became manager and treasurer, a position which he has since filled most acceptably Under his able administration the business has become one of the important industries of the city, with an extensive trade which is constantly increasing, and in addition to the interests in Rock Island the company has ice plants in Moline, Watertown and Havanna, Illinois

The marriage of Mr. Lambert and Miss Mary Graham, daughter of Robert Graham, was celebrated September 13, 1877 She died April 17, 1891, leaving a son, Harry, while her second son, Russell, died in infancy On the 11th of May, 1892, Mr Lambert was joined in wedlock to Miss Clara Fider, daughter of Augustus G and Eliza (Jack) Fider They have one son, Silas A Mrs Lambert is a member of the Episcopal church, and is a lady of culture, who has made her hospitable home a favorite resort with a large circle of friends

Mr Lambert supports the Republican party by his influence and ballot He served for two years as city treasurer, but has never been an office-seeker, preferring to devote his attention to his business interests His life history most happily illustrates what may be attained by faithful and continued effort in carrying out an honest purpose, and integrity, activity and energy have been the crowning points in his career

WILLIAM A. NOURSE, of Moline, is a gentleman who has retained a personal association with the affairs of Rock Island county for more than half a century and his ancestral line traces back to the colonial epoch in American annals His life has been one of honest endeavor and due success has not been denied him. A man of unswerving integrity and honor, who has a perfect appreciation of the higher ethics of life, he has gained and retained the confidence and respect of his fellow men and is distinctively one of the leading citizens of Moline, with whose interests he has been identified for fifty-one years

Mr Nourse is a native of the Empire state, born in Wolcott, Wayne county, February 9, 1820 His grandfather, Timothy Nourse, was of Welsh descent His father, William Mason Nourse, was born in Massachusetts and grew to manhood in that state, obtaining a good education in its public schools He afterward engaged in teaching, both in Massachusetts and in New York He was married in Waterville, of the latter state, to Miss Sarah Candee, a native of Harwinton, Connecticut, and afterward located in Wolcott, Wayne county, New York, where he engaged in merchandising for a number of years, and also

carried on a distillery For some years he was a resident of Lyons, N Y., and in 1838 emigrated westward, taking up his residence in Peoria, Illinois, where he engaged in the manufacture of fanning mills, continuing in active business there until his death in 1848 His wife survived him for a number of years and was a second time married By her first union she had three sons—William A , Alonzo and Horatio G

In 1846 William A and Alonzo Nourse came to Moline and engaged in the manufacture of fanning mills, building up an extensive and profitable business They had at one time the largest manufactory in the town, and Alonzo carried on the enterprise for ten years, but the partnership was dissolved at the end of six years They had also opened a small mercantile establishment on locating here and constantly enlarged their stock in order to meet the growing demand of the trade until their business had assumed a considerable magnitude On the dissolution of the partnership our subject continued in charge of the mercantile interest and was at one time the owner of the largest store in three cities He continued in business until 1857 and for two or three years thereafter gave his attention to the settling up of his affairs, collecting debts, etc He then engaged in working for the Universal Clothes Wringer Manufactory, and later turned his attention exclusively to the nursery business, which he conducted on the bluffs at Sixteenth street, which he had previously began He began operations on a small scale, but constantly increased his stock until the volume of his business exceeded that of any other in Rock Island or adjoining counties He also established a greenhouse and engaged in the cultivation of ornamental plants and flowers

His extensive business brought to him a handsome income and he conducted the enterprise until 1882 For several years before his retirement to private life he engaged in magnetic healing and was very successful in that work

From time to time Mr. Nourse made judicious investments in real estate, and was the owner of much valuable property here, a portion of which he still retains He is a man of excellent business capacity, of keen foresight, great energy and sound judgment, and in the exercise of his natural and acquired abilities has won a handsome competence which now enables him to live retired He has never sought or desired political preferment, but before the war was an antislavery man, and since voting for Fremont in 1856 has supported every presidential candidate of the Republican party

Mr Nourse was married in 1844 in Peoria, Illinois, to Sarah Frances Pettengill, a native of Franklin, New Hampshire, who was reared and educated in Illinois, whither she came with her father, Benjamin Pettengill, a pioneer of Alton, this state He established a sawmill there and carried on business until his death. To Mr and Mrs Nourse were born two children—Allen C , who died at the age of fourteen years, and Mary Frances, wife of John H Porter, president of the Porter Printing Company, of Moline The mother of this family was killed by the fall of a windmill in 1881. In the spring of 1888 Mr Nourse was again married, his second union being with Mrs Laura A Sunderlin, a native of New York, and a daughter of Dr. A and Rovey (Chapin) Barney, who were born in Allegany county, New York Mrs Nourse was educated in Independence and Alfred University, and for six years was engaged in teaching. She

was married in 1855 in Pennsylvania to Samuel Sunderlin and removed westward to Indiana, and later to Iowa, where Mr Sunderlin died, leaving three children—Floyd L , a lawyer, editor and publisher, of Delmar Junction, Iowa, Gertrude, wife of Curtis B Jones, a merchant of Redfield, Iowa, and Estella Fifield, widow of F J Fifield, who was a photographer of Cedar Rapids, Iowa Mrs Nourse is a lady of superior intellectual ability and is the author of two volumes of poetry and prose Two of her long poems, "Lyrics of Life ' and "Pencilings of Immortality," show especial poetic merit and deep thought

Fifty-one years have passed since Mr Nourse came to Moline, years in which he has witnessed almost the entire growth and development of the city He has seen the introduction of business enterprises and industries, the building of schools, the promotion of social interests, and in all these has borne a very active and important part, doing all in his power to advance the welfare of the city

---

HENRY CARSE is extensively engaged in the manufacture of soda water and bottled drinks, as a member of the firm of Carse & Ohlweiler, and in business circles he is one of the most prominent and respected of Rock Island's representatives The invariable law of destiny accords to tireless energy, industry and ability a successful career, and these elements are essential characteristics of Mr Carse Prosperity with him has been self-acquired, and to-day he enjoys the reward of his painstaking and conscientious work

Mr. Carse is a native of the Emerald Isle He was born near the city of Belfast, and in 1848 came to America with his parents, John and Mary Carse, who took up their residence in Pittsburg, Pennsylvania, where the father died   The mother became a resident of Rock Island and died there in 1882

Mr Carse, of this review, obtained his education in the schools of Pittsburg, and in 1868 located in Rock Island   In his youth he learned the bottling business and for forty years has been engaged in that line He has been associated with his present partner for a quarter of a century, and the firm is one of the oldest and best known in the west   They do a very extensive business, employing about fourteen hands, and their goods are shipped to all parts of the state   These include soda water and all kinds of temperate drinks.   In volume and importance their trade has steadily grown and their house enjoys a most enviable reputation for reliability as well as for the excellence of its goods   In the prosecution of his business there is manifest one of the most sterling traits of Mr Carse's character —his desire to carry forward to the highest perfection attainable anything that he undertakes   Not content with mediocrity in any line, he has given deep and earnest thought to the improvement of his business, and his splendid inventive genius has been brought into use in the manufacture of a number of very useful devices used in the bottling works   He is the inventor of the economical air valve for letting the air out of the bottle while it is being filled   He also invented the safety screen, which is placed around the bottle while filling to prevent breaking and protect the employe   This has proved a very useful device, is extensively used and is now manufactured by the house of John Matthews of New York

Mr Carse's latest invention, which was perfected in 1892, is called the Carse continuous operator   He sold the patent on this and it is now being manufactured by the Hartt Manufacturing Company of Chicago Mr Carse also has a number of other inventions which he uses in the business that he has not yet patented

In 1870 was celebrated the marriage of our subject and Miss Mary Wright, daughter of Robert H. Wright, of Rock Island They have seven children   Mary Belle is the wife of Henry Treeman, proprietor of the largest meat market in the city and also of a branch store.   Catherine C is the wife William Pratt, who is employed in the Rock Island arsenal, and they have one son, Henry C   Elizabeth is the wife of Joseph Shearer, of Rock Island, who was secretary of the Peasley Shoe Company, of this city John W , William R , Gertrude F. and Alice B complete the family.

In his political affiliations Mr Carse has always been a stanch Republican, is a member of the Lincoln Club of Rock Island, and was a delegate to the Republican state convention, where he gave a very active and earnest support to McKinley and Hobart. His interest in politics is deep and sincere, and he has informed himself thoroughly on the issues which are now before the people of the nation.   In the spring of 1897 he was the nominee of his party for the office of mayor of Rock Island   Prominent in Masonic circles, he has attained the Knight Templar degree of the York Rite and the thirty-second degree of the Scottish Rite He holds membership in the blue lodge, chapter and commandery, was proclaimed a sublime prince of the Royal Secret in the Consistory, and is a Noble of the Ancient Arabic Order of the Mystic Shrine   Both

Mr and Mrs Carse hold membership in the Central Presbyterian church of Rock Island and are promoters of all interests which tend to uplift humanity. They hold an enviable position in social circles, have many warm friends and receive the high regard of all who know them.

WILLIAM WHITESIDE The natural advantages of this section attracted at an early day a superior class of settlers, thrifty, industrious, progressive and law-abiding, whose influence gave permanent direction to the development of the locality Among the worthy pioneers of Rock Island county Mr. Whiteside holds a prominent place, and the results of the labor and self-denial of the early settlers is manifest in the comfortable homes and fertile, well-arranged farms which are now to be seen on every side For many years our subject was one of the leading agriculturists of Zuma township, but is now living retired at No 2403 Sixth avenue, Moline.

Mr. Whiteside was born in Lancastershire, England, June 6, 1826, a son of Nicolas and Mary (Wright) Whiteside, and was reared upon a farm until thirteen years of age, when he began learning the baker's trade in Liverpool During his three years apprenticeship he received his board, clothing and a little pocket money, and was later employed at that work in the same city On the 14th of March, 1851, he led to the marriage altar Miss Elizabeth Robinson, also a native of Lancastershire, and a daughter of William and Sarah (Stoker) Robinson. Like her husband she had received a good common-school education

In 1853, Mr and Mrs Whiteside took passage on the Constellation, an American vessel, leaving Liverpool June 3, and after seven weeks spent upon the Atlantic arrived safely in New York, where they remained but a few days Their eldest child, Sarah, died and was buried in that city They then proceeded to Illinois, traveling by stage from Peru to Rock Island county, where Mr Whiteside had another brother living

At this time the cash capital of our subject consisted of about seventy-five dollars, which he invested in thirty-five acres of land in Zuma township, but he located in Moline, where he worked at his trade until he could finish paying for his land. He then turned his attention to agricultural pursuits, and soon sold his first purchase and bought one hundred and twenty acres, to which he added from time to time until he owned six hundred and forty acres in one body He successfully engaged in farming until 1894 when he removed to Moline and has since lived retired, enjoying a rest which he so richly deserves His success illustrates in no uncertain manner what it is possible to accomplish when perseverance and determination form the keynote to a man's character A true and earnest Christian, he has always taken an active part in church and Sunday school work, serving as superintendent of the latter organization for over twenty years For thirty years he was a Methodist, but now holds membership in the Congregational church He has always been a Republican since casting his first vote for Abraham Lincoln, and for three terms filled the office of supervisor with credit to himself and to the satisfaction of his constituents

Nine children have been born to Mr and Mrs. Whiteside since taking up their residence in Rock Island county, and all are still living here, seven making their homes in Zuma township   The family is one in which the parents may take a just pride as they have grown up to be honored and respected citizens   Bessie is now the wife of Alonzo Dunbar, of Zuma township, and they have nine children, William H , a merchant of Joslyn, is married and has two children, Joseph W is now clerking for his brother William; Frederick J , a general hardware merchant of Joslyn, is married and has three children, Robert is serving as deputy county treasurer; Christopher C., a farmer of Zuma township, is married and has one child, Dr Charles E , of Moline, is mentioned more fully below; Roland N is married and engaged in agricultural pursuits in Zuma township, and Margaret L is the wife of W O Beam, M D , of Moline, by whom she has one child

OLOF OLSSON, D D   The history of the world shows that the highest civilization has been reached by those countries where education and Christianity go hand in hand   The best development can never be reached when attention is given to either the moral or the mental nature to the neglect of the other   Recognizing, therefore, the necessity of symmetrical development of all the powers and forces with which man is endowed, the Lutheran denomination has founded in the Mississippi valley, upon this principle, a school which ranks among the best institutions of learning in the great west and to-day at the head of Augustana College and Theological Seminary of Rock Island stands Dr Olof Olsson, whose noble life and character have been an inspiration to all with whom he has come in contact, while he has carried forward the work of Christianity and education

Dr Olsson was born in Karlskoga, Vermland, Sweden, March 31, 1841, a son of Olof and Brita (Johnson) Olsson, who were also natives of the same country   In 1869 they crossed the Atlantic to America, locating in Kansas, near the town of Lindsborg, before McPherson county had been organized Both the paternal and maternal grandfathers of Dr Olsson were farmers of Sweden and spent their entire lives in that land, the latter, Jonas Monsson, dying at the age of fifty-four years   After locating in Kansas Olof Olsson, Sr , was identified with the agricultural interests of that state until called to the home beyond in 1878, at the age of eighty-three years   His wife survived him until 1893 and passed away at the age of eighty-seven   Both were members of the Lutheran church.   Two children survive them—Dr Olof and Carl, the latter a farmer of Lindsborg, Kansas.

Dr Olsson was fortunate in his youth in having the surroundings of a Christian home and the careful guidance of worthy parents His more advanced studies were begun in Stockholm, Sweden, in 1858.   He spent the year of 1859-60 in study in Leipsic, Germany, and was graduated at Upsala, on the 22d of January, 1861.   Determining to devote his life to the ministry, he then began the study of theology and after the completion of the prescribed course in December, 1863, was ordained on the 15th of the same month in the Cathedral at Upsala Through the succeeding six months he served as assistant pastor in the bishopric of Karlstad, and for two and a half years was superintendent of a large common school, at the same time serving as pastor of the largest mining district in Sweden   Subse-

REV. O. OLSSON.

quently he accepted a pastorate in eastern Vermland

His residence in America dates from 1869, when in response to a call from the Augustana synod he came to the United States with a colony of pioneers, who located in a then unimproved district of central Kansas He remained there as missionary and pastor of the congregation at Lindsborg, McPherson county, for some time, and was called to represent his county in the state legislature in 1871, serving for two terms He was the first Swedish Lutheran minister in that locality and for seven years untiringly prosecuted his labors there

At the annual meeting of Augustana synod in 1875, Dr Olsson was elected to a professorship in Augustana College and Theological Seminary, but declined the position. The following year, however, on the same call being extended him, he removed to Rock Island in the autumn of 1876 and entered upon his duties as a member of the faculty of the institution, of which he is now president. In 1879 he made a five-months' tour through England, Germany and Bohemia, gaining that broader culture and knowledge which only travel can bring. In 1888 he resigned his position in Augustana College and for a time labored in the interests of Bethany College of Kansas In the spring of 1889 he again visited Europe returning to America in the summer of 1890, after which he became pastor of the congregation in Woodhull, Illinois, in the autumn of that year. In April, 1891, he was called by the board of directors to the presidency of Augustana College and Theological Seminary as the successor of Dr. T N Hasselquist, deceased, and subsequently in the same year was unanimously elected to this position by the synod. In addition to his duties as president was added that of instructor in theology, and he occupies at present the chair of catechetics, homiletics and pastoral theology The college has an annual enrollment of more than five hundred students.

In 1892 the degree of doctor of divinity was conferred upon President Olsson by the board of directors of Augustana College and in 1893 he was made an honorary doctor of philosophy of the University of Upsala His first literary venture was the publication of a religious periodical in Kansas Since that time he has contributed largely to the church papers of the Augustana synod. He has for many years rendered valuable assistance in making collections for the payment of the college debt, and with this end in view has published a paper entitled Skolvannen He is the author of a volume called "At the Cross," of which four editions have been published in this country and one in Sweden From his pen came "Greeting from Abroad," which has been translated into the Norwegian language and published by the Luther Society of Christiana, "The Christian Hope," "To Rome and Home Again," besides numerous pamphlets published by the Lutheran Augustana Book Concern These include "The Reformation and Socinianism" and "The Reformation of the Eighteenth Century," two very valuable treatises

On the 22d of December, 1864, Dr. Olsson married Miss Anna Johnson, daughter of John and Maria Johnson, but after twenty-three years of happy married life was called upon to mourn the loss of his wife, who died March 18, 1887. He has four children Anna, Maria, Lydia and Johannes

The Doctor is a Republican in his political views, but his ministerial and educational duties have left him no time for political work

WILLIAM EAMES BROOKS, deceased, was for many years a leading citizen of Rock Island His history touched the pioneer epoch in the annals of the state of Illinois and his days were an integral part of that indissoluble chain which linked the early formative period with that of latter day progress and prosperity The strength and courage of those who became pioneers of the west and voluntarily resigned their claims to the conveniences and comforts of the older sections of the Union, can scarcely be realized by those who are in the full enjoyment of the privileges which these pioneers provided by undergoing the pioneer experiences With the development of the county for half a century Mr. Brooks was prominently identified, ever bearing his part in the work of substantial advancement

A native of Northumberland, New Hampshire, born July 5, 1819, he was a son of William and Harriet (Eames) Brooks The Brooks family was one of early identification with New England, and the maternal grandfather, Thomas Eames, was born in New Hampshire, and served as a soldier in the war of 1812, and for many years conducted a farm and a hotel, his entire life being passed in the Granite state William Brooks, father of our subject, was born in Boston, Massachusetts, and his wife was a native of New Hampshire In 1835 he left his home in Northumberland and with his family came direct to Rock Island, where he arrived on the 15th of November Here he purchased a tract of land, now lying within the city limits, and suc-

cessfully carried on agricultural pursuits until his death. He was born December 3, 1783, and died April 23, 1864. In his family were three children who reached mature years—William E , of this review, Jeanette, wife of S W McMasters, and George, who died at the age of thirty-nine years

William E Brooks was a youth of sixteen when he came with the family to Illinois He was reared to manhood in Rock Island, and for a short period was employed in a clerical position in one of the stores of the city, but later returned to the farm, which is now in one of the finest residence portions of Rock Island Owing to the excellent improvements made upon the place and to the extension of the city limits beyond the bounds of their property the Brooks farm became very valuable   Mr. Brooks gave the greater part of his attention to its development and made it one of the model farms of Illinois He was a man of energy, enterprise and progressiveness and kept fully up with all improvements and the advances of civilization

On the 27th of December, 1852, Mr Brooks was united in marriage to Miss Eliza Mary Drane, daughter of Alexander G. and Sarah (Caufield) Drane She was born in St Johns, Canada, and removed with her parents to Aurora, Illinois, where they spent their remaining days Her father was a harness maker, and was born in Louisville, Kentucky His parents were natives of the Emerald Isle, but afterward returned to that land, but subsequently again came to the New World, locating in Montreal, Canada, where they both died Mr and Mrs Brooks became the parents of six sons and two daughters, but lost three children— George, Freddie and Mary, who died in childhood William and Charles E are still living upon the homestead and manage the property Harry G married Miss Phœbe Beardsley and is proprietor of a meat market Mattie is also with her mother, and Josh R is associated with his brothers in the management of the family estate

Mr. Brooks gave his political support to the Republican party and served his township and city in the offices of supervisor and alderman He died December 29, 1885, at the age of sixty-six years and five months, respected by all who knew him His life was quietly passed in the faithful performance of every duty which fell to his lot He was honorable and straightforward in all relations, and by his sterling worth commanded the unqualified respect of those with whom he was brought in contact His family still reside in Rock Island and their home is the center of a cultured society circle

CHARLES EDWARD WHITESIDE, M D, an eminent physician and surgeon of Moline, whose office is located in rooms 15 and 16 Skinner Block, is a native of Rock Island county, his birth occurring in Zuma township Upon the home farm the days of his boyhood and youth were passed and in the schools of the neighborhood he acquired his literary education Under the direction of Dr J W Morgan he began the study of medicine and later attended the College of Physicians and Surgeons of Chicago, where he graduated with the class of 1894. After six months spent in a private sanitarium at Lake Geneva, Wisconsin, where he gained much practical knowledge, he opened an office in Moline and has since successfully engaged in practice By his skillful treatment of cases he has

gained an enviable reputation and receives a liberal share of the public patronage

During his stay in Chicago, the Doctor was with Dr. Adolph Gehrmann, in the College of Physicians and Surgeons, who at that time was head of the milk inspection of that city, and as his assistant Dr Whiteside gained much practical as well as theoretical knowledge of his chosen profession He is now a member of the Illinois and Iowa Medical Association, and is medical examiner for Abe Lincoln Camp, No. 153, M W A, of which he is a member Like his father and brother, he is identified with the Republican party, and has served as a delegate to various conventions of his party

ALBERT M BEAL, M D, a leading representative of the medical fraternity of Rock Island county, is successfully engaged in practice in Moline, with office at 316 Sixteenth street One of the most exacting of all the higher lines of occupation to which a man may lend his energies is that of the physician A most scrupulous preliminary training is demanded, and a nicety of judgment but little understood by the laity Then again the profession brings its devotees into almost constant association with the sadder side of life—that of pain and suffering—so that a mind capable of great self-control and a heart responsive and sympathetic are essential attributes of him who would essay the practice of the healing art Thus when professional success is attained in any instance it may be taken as certain that such measure of success has been thoroughly merited

The Doctor is a native of Rock Island county, born October 31 1 in Zuma township, and is a son of Daniel N and Betsey (Spencer) Beal. Upon his father's farm he spent the days of his boyhood, and besides attending the country schools, he was also a student in the schools of Port Byron and Rock Island At the early age of seventeen he began teaching at what is now Barstow, and later entered Western College of Iowa, where he completed the classical course and graduated with the class of 1876, receiving the degree of A B The following year he was principal of the Hampton (Illinois) schools In 1879 he received the degree of A M from his alma mater, and after the removal of the college to Toledo, Iowa, in the same year, he was called to the chair of physics and chemistry, in which capacity he served for twelve years. In the meantime, however, he had spent one year in study at Dartmouth College Previously he had read law and was admitted to the bar in 1879, and from 1876 until 1879 was employed as assistant by the president of the Moline Water Power Company.

In 1890 Dr Beal began a regular course of lectures in the College of Physicians and Surgeons at Des Moines, and at the same time delivered a course of lectures in the schools on chemistry and medical Latin During the years 1891 and 1892 he served as president of his alma mater with the understanding that he was to still carry on his studies, and in 1894 he graduated at the College of Physicians and Surgeons and began practice in Toledo, Iowa, but in December of the same year located in Moline, where he has already succeeded in building up a large and lucrative practice

At Andalusia, Illinois, Dr. Beal was married October 31, 1876, to Miss Etta Thompson, of that place, a daughter of Henry S and Mary (Buffum) Thompson

She died November 11, 1880, leaving one daughter—Mamie, who was born in Moline October 18, 1878, and is a graduate of the high school of Toledo, Iowa. The Doctor was again married January 1, 1884, his second union being with Miss Carrie E Middlekauff, of Polo, Illinois, who is a native of Ogle county, and a daughter of Daniel and Elizabeth (Jones) Middlekauff They had five children—Etta Grace, born in Toledo, Iowa, February 15, 1885, Daniel Middlekauff, who was born in the same city August 21, 1886, Althea, born in Toledo, October 15, 1888, Albert Milton, who was born in Toledo and died in Des Moines March 19, 1892, when a year old, and Walter Hubert, born September 12, 1894, in Toledo.

Like his father, the Doctor has always been a Republican in politics, casting his first presidential vote for Rutherford B Hayes in 1876, and he has taken quite an active and prominent part in political affairs While a resident of Toledo he served as mayor for three successive terms, during which time he succeeded in putting in one of the best system of water works now in use, and also revised and drafted the laws for that city He resigned the position on his removal to Des Moines He was elected the first clerk of South Moline and acceptably discharged the duties of that office. A man of deep research and careful investigation he to-day occupies an enviable position among his professional brethren, and has written many valuable articles which were read before leading medical societies and others which were published in medical journals In 1897 he delivered the doctorate address before the graduating class of the College of Physicians and Surgeons at Des Moines · Prominence as a physician and surgeon comes through merit alone, and the high position which Dr Beal has attained attests his superiority He is a valued member of the Iowa and Illinois Central District Medical Association and also the Illinois State Medical Association and affiliates with the Knights of Pythias fraternity, and Camp No 38, Modern Woodmen of America, while he is examining physician for Bell K Camp, Royal Neighbors and the Northwestern Life Insurance Company of Chicago and the New York Life At the age of sixteen he joined the United Brethren church, served as superintendent of the Sunday school in Toledo for for some time, but since his return to Moline in 1894 he has become identified with the First Congregational church

FRANCIS M SINNET —High on the roll of Rock Island's most eminent and honored citizens is found the name of this gentleman, whose prominence in the business and public affairs of the city has made him deserving of the regard and gratitude of all who are interested in its welfare The prosperity of a community depends upon its business activity and he who advances this is a factor in the growth and substantial development of the city with which he is connected It is impossible to measure the far-reaching effects of any enterprise, but it is well known that Mr Sinnet has been active in carrying on many business interests which have greatly benefited his town and county

He comes of a family both honorable and honored His grandfather, James Sinnet, was a native of Ireland, and wedded Mary Isham, probably of English descent They became early residents of New England Alanson Sinnet, father of our sub-

ject, was prominently identified with the history of Rock Island for many years. He was born in Massachusetts, August 15, 1801, and for a number of years engaged in agricultural pursuits in Licking county, Ohio, developing his farm from its primitive condition In June, 1857, he allied his interests with those of Rock Island, and was prominent in commercial circles as a dealer in ice He was also well known in real estate circles, and laid out Sinnet's addition to the city In his early manhood he married Miss Julia Webster, a native of East Poultney, Vermont, and a representative of the same family to which Daniel Webster belonged They became the parents of seven children, four of whom are living— James W , of Carthage, Missouri, Georgiana, wife of G W Heck, of Rock Island; Francis M , and Laura, wife of I P Wilson The mother of this family, who was long a sincere member of the Baptist church, died February 11, 1868, at the age of sixty-eight years Mr Sinnet was afterward again married, his second union being with Miss Pauline E Williams, a relative of United States Senator Rawlins They were married at Rock Island, November 11, 1871

Mr Sinnet died in December, 1885, at the age of eighty-four years He was a member of the Baptist church from boyhood, and his life was noble and upright His political support was early given to the Whig party, and on the organization of the Republican party he joined its ranks, affiliating therewith until his death Political office was frequently tendered him but he always declined such honors His duties as a private citizen, however, were most faithfully performed, and he was a liberal supporter of all measures which were calculated to promote the general welfare. He was the prime mover in the organization of the first street railway company of Rock Island, and his name is inseparably linked with many of the enterprises of the city, industrial, educational and moral His own educational privileges were those afforded by the common schools Realizing how powerful is knowledge in the affairs of life, he became one of the foremost patrons of an academy of learning established in the village where he spent his boyhood and youth He became one of the founders of Granville College of Ohio, and at different times subscribed to it one thousand dollars. For twenty-two years he was a trustee of that institution, and throughout that period was also a member of the executive committee Through the legitimate channels of business he accumulated a handsome competency He died as he had lived, honored and respected by all, and the influence of his life remained as a blessed benediction to those who knew him

Francis M Sinnet spent his boyhood and youth on his father's farm near Granville, Ohio The latter had begun life there as a cattle raiser, but after a few years turned his attention to sheep raising, and was one of the three largest sheep raisers in the county The son assisted his father in his business there, and in 1856, when the property was sold, he came with his parents to Rock Island, where he has since made his home. He taught school for several terms and afterward began dealing in ice, which business he has since successfully followed For more than twenty-five years he was engaged in the retail trade, but now conducts a wholesale business In connection with his father he purchased fifty-five acres of land and laid out Sinnet's addition to the city He has dealt more or less in

real estate throughout the years of his residence here and now owns some valuable realty.

On the 17th of December, 1861, occurred the marriage of Mr. Sinnet and Miss Jennie, daughter of Charles and Mary (Hollinger) McLaughlin, natives of Blairsville, Pennsylvania, as is Mrs. Sinnet. They have had three children—Jesse K , wife of Ralph E Taliaferro, by whom she has one child, Francis Sinnet, Julia M., wife of Ennis Spauling, by whom she has two children, Bessie and Kingman, and Mary Florence, who died in 1873, at the age of three years and eight months Mrs. Sinnet is a member of the Broadway Presbyterian church Mr Sinnet is a charter member of the Immanuel Baptist church of Rock Island, is trustee and deacon and has been superintendent of the Sunday school for many years

Advocating the principles of the Republican party since its formation he cast his first vote for Salmon P Chase for governor of Ohio in 1856 He has just completed a nine years service as supervisor, was alderman of the seventh ward four years, and a member of the school board for nine years, serving as its president for one year He was one of the first to advocate the building of the new court house in Rock Island and it was largely through his instrumentality that the present fine structure was secured, he serving as a member of the building committee He is a man to whom the most envious can scarcely grudge success, so well has he earned it and so admirably does he use it He is kind, unaffected and approachable and always ready to aid and relieve the suffering and distressed His integrity stands as an unquestioned fact and he has ever been guided by a sense of moral right that would bear the most rigid investigation.

CAPTAIN CHARLES REESE —Prominent among business men of Moline is this gentleman, who though now living retired, was for many years closely identified with the business interests of the city, while for forty-one years his name has been inseparably connected with the development and advancement of the city He is a man of keen discrimination and sound judgment and his executive ability and excellent management have brought to him a high degree of success. Few men in the county are more widely known and the circle of his friends is so extensive that we feel assured that this record of his life will prove of interest to many of our readers

Mr Reese was born in Holstein, Germany, April 2, 1832, and was educated in the schools of the Fatherland, but all his knowledge of English has been self-acquired. In 1849 and 1850 he was with the artillery forces of the German army in service in the war between Prussia and Denmark After receiving his discharge he was for two years an attache of the household of Baron Sidlitz, who was at the head of the royal family of Holstein When twenty-one years of age he was informed that he must report for duty in the regular army, but securing a leave of absence he emigrated to the new world in 1856, taking passage at Bremen on a sailing vessel bound for New York After three months spent on the ocean, during which they encountered some severe storms and were driven far out of their course, anchor was dropped in the New York harbor in the month of August.

Landing in this country Captain Reese at once made his way to Moline, where lived some friends whom he had known in the fatherland Here he began keeping a boarding house and continued in that line

of business until September 22, 1861, when feeling that his country needed his services, he joined Company E of the Second Iowa Cavalry, which was organized at Davenport He was made sergeant six months later and then drill master, and in 1864 he veteranized, continuing at the front until the close of the war He participated in the battles of New Madrid, Shiloh, Iuka, and the battle of Corinth, where the Second Iowa Cavalry in seven minutes had fifty-five men and one hundred and five horses killed He also participated in the engagements at Tupelo, Coffeyville, West Point, the second battle of Corinth and a number of others of lesser importance, making sixty-two in all He was wounded in the face at the battle of Iuka, and still carries the scars which indicate his honorable defense of the old flag during the most trying period in our country's history. He was honorably discharged at Selma, Alabama, during the latter part of the war.

On returning home, Capt Reese erected the Reese House, now the Peal's Hotel, and engaged in the hotel business This was the first good hotel erected in Moline, and for a number of years our subject continued as its host, enjoying a liberal support from the traveling public He then erected a fine business block and engaged in the confectionery and tobacco trade, continuing in that enterprise until the spring of 1897 when he sold out and now lives retired, enjoying the rest which he has well earned and richly deserves

Captain Reese was married in Moline in 1869 to Mary Neiman, a lady of German birth, who was reared and educated in the Fatherland They had three children, but one died at the age of three years, and another at the age of five Henry C , the third child, is now chief of the fire department of Moline. He is a man of good education and a tinner by trade. He is married and has two children, Julia and Charles II Mr Reese lost his wife January 20, 1893, and many friends mourned her death

In politics the Captain and his son are both stanch Republicans He has never been an aspirant for official honors, but was elected and served as city collector and has several times been a delegate to the conventions of his party The success tha crowned his business career is the legitimate outcome of his own industrious efforts He started out in life a poor boy but steadily worked his way upward, resolutely overcoming the obstacles and difficulties in the path to success A manly purpose and honorable dealing, combined with unflinching fidelity to duty have been the marked characteristics of his career and have brought him the high regard of many friends.

OTTO J SALA, of Rock Island, is a western man by birth, training and interest, and possesses the spirit of enterprise and progress which dominates this section of the country and has led to its splendid development He is numbered among the wide-awake and enterprising citizens of this county and by his own unaided efforts he has attained an enviable success in business life

Mr Sala was born in Missouri, near Ashley, on the 7th of February, 1854, and is of German lineage. His grandfather, Jacob Sala, was a native of the Fatherland, and died in West Point, Iowa, in 1861, at the age of eighty-three He was a book binder by trade and reared a large family. The parents of our subject were Eli M and Susan (Shellenbarger) Sala, the former a native of Canton, Ohio, and the latter of Switzerland The father was a physician and successfully practiced his profession in Iowa and Wisconsin for more than forty years. He died in Beetown, Wisconsin, at the age of sixty-two, and his wife passed away in 1873 at the age of forty. Both were members of the Baptist church and their well-spent lives won them the high regard of all They had seven children, namely: Frank, Orlando P , E Quince, Mary, wife of H. C. Boggess, of Rock Island, Otto J., Ada, wife of John Burns, of Beetown, Wisconsin, and Mattie, wife of Richard O Campbell, of Dubuque, Iowa

During his early childhood Otto J Sala was taken by his parents to West Point, Iowa where he remained until sixteen years of age, acquiring his elementary education there He afterward lived in Bloomington, Wisconsin, for a number of years, and when his school days were over learned the tinsmith's trade, which he followed for about fourteen years. In 1874 he took up his residence in Moline, which has been his home the greater part of the time since About 1888 he established a meat market and grocery store in Moline, which he conducted with success for five years For the past two years he has operated a farm three and a half miles southwest of Taylor Ridge, and in the spring of 1897 he purchased his present grocery store in Rock Island of Thomas Smart Here he carries a full line of staple and fancy groceries and receives from the public a liberal patronage, owing to his honorable business methods and his courteous treatment of his patrons He also handles baled hay, straw, chopped feed and flour, and is conducting a successful business, being a valuable addition to the commercial circles of Rock Island

On the 13th of January, 1885, Mr Sala was united in marriage to Miss Jennie M Thede, daughter of Christian and Laura (Herbst) Thede They have one child, Mamie. Mrs Sala's parents are natives of Germany—the former of Rendsburg, the latter of Berlin Her father was a blacksmith, and, coming to America in 1853, located in Pontiac, Michigan In 1855 he took up his residence in Rock Island, where he made his home until 1866, since which time he and his wife have lived in Aledo. They are United Presbyterians in religious faith. Their family numbered six sons and six daughters, namely, William, a shoe merchant of Moline, Christian, a blacksmith and carriage dealer of Aledo, Illinois, Charles; Henry, Frederick, of Rock Island, Lena, wife of Ashley Debord, of Aledo, Jennie M, wife of our subject, Amelia, wife of Robert Dooman, of Reynolds, Illinois, Laura, a dressmaker of Trinidad, Colorado, Mamie, of Aledo, Illinois, and two now deceased The paternal grandfather of Mrs. Sala, a blacksmith by trade, died in Pontiac, Michigan, when about forty-eight years of age He had three sons and one daughter. The maternal grandfather, Mark Herbst, was a shoemaker of Berlin, Germany, occupied one house in that city for sixty years, and died at the advanced age of ninety-seven.

Mr. Sala belongs to the Modern Woodmen of America, and he and his wife hold membership in the Royal Neighbors fraternity. Politically he is a Republican, but aside from taking an intelligent passing interest in party issues and voting to support the principles in which he believes, he is not active in political work, giving his entire time and attention to his business interests His property has been acquired through his own efforts, and by worthy means he has attained to a high position in business circles, where he is known and respected for his sterling worth and many excellent qualities.

ROBINSON NYE, who is now living retired in his pleasant home at 1821 Sixth avenue, Moline, was for many years one of the leading contractors and builders of the city His name was a synonym for honorable business dealing, he faithfully fulfilled his part of every contract, and has always been mentioned as one of the invaluable citizens of Rock Island county, where he is also numbered among the honored pioneers, dating his residence here from October, 1854

A native of the old Pine Tree state, Mr. Nye was born in Fairfield, Somerset county, August 7, 1827, and is a worthy representative of the old and prominent New England families, his ancestors, who were of English origin, having located in Massachusetts prior to the Revolutionary war. In Sandwich, that state, his father, Elisha Nye, was born, and in early life became a pioneer of Somerset county, Maine, where, in the midst of the wilderness, he developed a farm. There Joseph Nye, the father of our subject, was born and grew to manhood. He wedded Mary Freeman, also a native of Somerset county, and a daughter of Barnabas Freeman, who had removed from Cape Cod, Massachusetts, to Maine during its pioneer days The parents never left their native country, the father dying there in 1865 at the age of seventy-five years, and the mother in 1881 at the age of eighty-six years

In the family of this worthy couple were

six sons and three daughters, all of whom reached mature years, and but one is now deceased They are as follows Sophronia, wife of Elihu Lawrence, of Fairfield, Maine, Joseph, who still resides on the old home farm in that state, Lemuel, who died in 1892, Robinson, of this review, James F, who is operating his grandfather Nye's old farm in Maine, John W, who is engaged in the real estate business in San Francisco, California, Mary F, who is residing with her brother on the old homestead, Daniel F, who is also at the old home place, and Rebecca, wife of A B Green, a business man of Waterville, Maine.

The boyhood and youth of our subject were spent under the parental roof, and he was provided with fair common-school advantages For three years he served an apprenticeship to the carpenter's and joiner's trade, and then worked as a journeyman for several years in the east On coming west in 1854 he spent a night in Davenport, but the next day recrossed the river and located in Moline, where he has since made his home Here he began contracting and building on his own account and continued operations until about 1890, since which time he has lived retired Many of the finest residences in the city stand as monuments to his architectural skill and ability

Mr Nye has been twice married, his first union being at Brownsville, Maine, in October, 1850, with Miss Susan Sheldon Thomas, daughter of Jonah Thomas, also a native of Maine One child was born to them, but died in infancy Mrs Nye came with her husband to Moline, and here died in August, 1856 She was an exemplary member of the Congregational church, and died in the full assurance of faith The second marriage of Mr Nye was at Moline

January 1, 1861, with Miss Thirza Ann Judson Merryman, also a native of Maine, who was brought to the Mississippi Valley when a child of six years and was reared in Mercer county, Illinois Her father, Timothy Merryman, was a pioneer of that county, where he opened up a farm and operated the first saw-mill, but in 1852 came to Moline, where Mrs Nye was mostly educated She was for some time a successful teacher in the Moline schools during early life By her marriage she has become the mother of four children—Mary Elizabeth, now the wife of J H McEniry, of Minneapolis, Robert, who graduated as mining engineer at the school of mines at Golden, Colorado, in June, 1897, Wilfrid Curtis, who is in the employ of Dimock, Gould & Company, of Moline, and Carl Merryman, who graduated as civil engineer at the State University, Champaign, Illinois, with the class of 1897.

Originally Mr Nye was an old-line Whig, but voted for Fremont in 1856 and has since been a pronounced Republican He and his wife are both active and earnest members of the First Congregational church of Moline, and cheerfully give their support to all objects tending to promote the moral, educational or material welfare of the city and county They are the center of friends and acquaintances who appreciate their sterling worth and many excellent traits of character and who have for them the highest regard

EZRA WILCHER, the efficient superintendent of the city water works of Rock Island, is a representative of one of the honored pioneer families of the county, and though yet in the prime of life, he forms the link in the chain that unites the frontier development with the latter-day progress and advancement, having for a half century resided in this section of the state In the work of transformation which has advanced the county to its present high state of improvement he has ever borne his part as a loyal, faithful citizen, and is now ranked among the wide-awake and reliable business men of Rock Island.

The Wilcher family is of English descent, and the grandfather of our subject, Josiah Wilcher, was a native of Kentucky He served in the war of 1812, and in civil life acted as justice of the peace He had a family of seven sons and three daughters and lived to the age of eighty-seven years His son, Patrick Henry Wilcher, was born in Kentucky, and in Illinois married Martha Perdue, daughter of James Perdue, a native of Virginia and a farmer by occupation. He became one of the pioneers of Warren county, Illinois, where he died at an advanced age Patrick II Wilcher is a farmer by occupation, and in 1845 came to Rock Island county, where he long followed that pursuit For the past few years he has resided in Murray, Iowa His wife died in April, 1866, at the age of forty-two, in the faith of the Christian church, of which he is also a member They had ten sons and two daughters, and nine are now living, as follows Ezra, Horace, Truman, Henry, Sarah, wife of Frank Young, of Topeka, Kansas, John, Cassie, wife of William Kimball, of Carbondale, Kansas, James, and Grant

Brought to Rock Island county during his infancy, Ezra Wilcher acquired his education in the schools of Hampton, and when eighteen years of age began learning the blacksmith's trade He also became an engineer and for twenty-eight years has followed one or the other of those pursuits

His business career was interrupted by several months' service in the Civil war, in 1865, as a member of Company B, Ninth Illinois Cavalry.

On his return from the scene of conflict, Mr. Wilcher again engaged in the blacksmith business in Hampton, where he remained until 1885, when he removed to Rock Island, and accepted the position of engineer for the Rock Island & Milan Street Railway Company He afterward became superintendent and continued with that company for five years, when he accepted his present position as superintendent and engineer of the city water works His thorough and accurate understanding of all machinery, his reliability and his splendid business qualifications make him very efficient in this position and render his services most satisfactory

On the 28th of December, 1865, Mr Wilcher was joined in wedlock to Miss Mary Ann Skinner, daughter of Orrin and Betsey (Benson) Skinner, the former a native of Vermont and the latter of Chautauqua county, New York They were among the first to establish a home in Rock Island county, and lived upon a farm near Pleasant Valley, in Hampton township, which had been entered by his father from the government He was at one time president of the Old Settlers' Association His death occurred December 4, 1896, when he had reached the age of seventy-six years, and his wife passed away on the 9th of January of the same year

Mr and Mrs Wilcher have a family of three children Mary Alice, wife of Robert Trenneman, of Moline, by whom she has three children, Lucy, Robert W and Charles E , Phil Sheridan, who married Miss Alice Hill, of Rock Island, and has one child living, Frank E , and Morris Henry, at home. Mr and Mrs Wilcher hold membership in the Methodist church and are members of the Order of the Eastern Star, while Mr Wilcher still maintains his relation with the Blue Lodge of the Masonic fraternity. He belongs to the Modern Woodmen of America, John Buford Post, No. 243, G A R , and gives his political support to the Republican party

– – – – —

JOHN SWANSON, one of the self-made men of Moline, has shown in his successful career that he has the ability to plan wisely and execute with energy, a combination which, when possessed by men in any walk of life, never fail to effect notable results Under the firm name of J Swanson & Co., he carries on business at the corner of Twelfth street and Fifth avenue, as a dealer in groceries, flour, feed, queensware, glassware, lamps, etc , and by honorable dealing has built up an excellent trade

A native of Sweden, Mr. Swanson was born December 18, 1850, near Rogberga, in Smoland precinct or county, but when four years old removed with his parents, Swan and Anna Kathrina Johnson to Rangedala, where he remained until his emigration to the new world at the age of seventeen He was reared upon a farm and was provided with very meager advantages for securing an education

In October, 1868, Mr Swanson took passage on a westward bound vessel, which was twelve days in crossing the Atlantic, and after landing it was ten days later before he reached Moline, his destination Here he began work as a day laborer upon the streets and was later employed as a

farm hand Two years after his arrival he had saved enough to send for a younger brother—Charles Victor, now a resident of Moline, and together during the following decade they saved enough to send for their mother and the other children After two years of work here our subject secured a position of teamster with the Plow Company and remained in their employ four years, after which began delivery for a grocery firm, who soon recognized his worth and promoted him With that company he remained for eight years, and then in partnership with F. A Landee, he began business for himself on a small scale This connection is still continued, and in 1893 Mr. Landee erected the building which they now occupy They carry a large and complete stock of everything found in their line and from the beginning their trade has constantly increased until it has now assumed extensive proportions.

Mr Swanson was married January 25, 1872, to Miss Caroline Lund, of Moline, who is also a native of Sweden, and they now have three children—Anna M , Carl Oscar, who is a graduate of the business college of Davenport, Iowa, and is now clerking in his father's store, and Florence Alvina As a Republican, Mr Swanson cast his first presidential vote for General Grant in 1872, and he has served his fellow citizens as a member of the board of education for eight years He is a conscientious, earnest Christian gentleman, a faithful member of the Swedish Baptist church, in which he has served as deacon for many years, and was one of the organizers of the Sunday school, of which he has since been superintendent, a period of twenty-four years In all the relations of life he has been true and faithful to every trust reposed in him, and has the confidence and respect of all with whom he has come in contact

---

HENRY S CASE, who is now living a retired life in Rock Island, is one of the native sons of the city, and this volume would be incomplete without the record of his life. During the greater part of the time for sixty-four years he has been identified with its interests, has been an active factor in its development, a promoter of many of its enterprises and a citizen of worth whose loyalty to the public welfare is above question

Mr. Case was born November 11, 1833, and there flows in his veins the blood of Scotch-Irish ancestry   The family, however, was early founded on American soil, and its representatives were actors in those events which go to form the history of the nation   His grandfather, Louden Case, a native of Vermont, was in the military service of the country in the war of the Revolution, and for years engaged in hotel keeping in the Green Mountain state, but died in Rock Island at an advanced age

The father of our subject, Jonah H Case, was born in Vermont, April 15, 1797, and on arriving at years of maturity married Julia Spencer, who was born in the same state, November 27, 1799.   Her father, Calvin Spencer, a native of Vermont, was also in the military service, but during the greater part of his life followed the quiet and peaceful pursuits of the farm. Removing to the West he located in Valley City, Iowa, where his death occurred at about the age of seventy-five years   Jonah H Case was also an agriculturist and became one of the honored pioneers who

braved the hardships and dangers of frontier life to establish a home in the West and aid in the development of this splendid commonwealth   In 1826 he located in Morgan county, Illinois, and three years later took up his abode in Rock Island county   The forests stood in their primitive grandeur, the broad prairies of Northern Illinois were still unturned by the plow and the state was offering its many resources and advantages to those who dared to meet the trials of frontier life   This section was still the home of a large number of Indians and for a time Mr Case lived in the wigwam of Black Hawk, there being only one house in the neighborhood.   Judge Spencer and Judge Pence also shared the hospitalities of that noted chieftain, for whom Mr. Case always retained a warm regard   Although obliged at a later date to fight against his tribe, he said that Black Hawk was never of a quarrelsome disposition, but was peaceably inclined and wished to live amicably among the white people, that he had a high sense of honor and fairness, and asked for nothing more nor less than justice

Jonah H Case began his life in Rock Island county by operating a half section of land which George Davenport had purchased for him   He later engaged in the manufacture of brick and made the brick for the old court house, which was erected at a cost of eleven thousand dollars, and was then the finest building of the kind in the state   It stood for many years as the seat of justice, but in the spring of the present year, 1897, it was torn down, a handsome structure having been erected in its place at a cost of one hundred and seventy thousand dollars   Mr Case and his brother-in-law laid out what is called Spencer & Case's addition to the city   He was a man of good business ability, devoted to the interests of his adopted home, and for many years was one of the most honored citizens of Rock Island. He died at the age of sixty-six and his wife survived him but a short time. Both were members of the Baptist church, and then many excellent characteristics and their sterling worth won them the highest regard of all

Henry S Case was one of their six children and is now the only living representative of the family He was reared on his father's farm amid the wild scenes of the frontier, and obtained his education in the old-time subscription schools At the age of nineteen, attracted by the discovery of gold on the Pacific slope, he went to California, where for four years he engaged in mining In the fall of 1856 he returned to Illinois, and with the exception of a short period spent in Henry county, he has made his home in Rock Island continuously since His time and attention for twenty years were devoted to agricultural pursuits and to the manufacture of brick His business interests were conducted with the strictest regard to commercial ethics and his honesty in all transactions was above question. Earnest purpose, close application, industry and sound judgment were the salient points in his career and won him success For twenty years he continued his dual occupation and then, with the capital he had acquired through his own labors, he retired to private life to spend his remaining years in the enjoyment of the fruits of his former toil, and in the pursuit of those interests which afforded him pleasure This has included many efforts for the best development and advancement of the city Throughout his entire life he has been most loyal to his native town, and has done much to promote

its growth and progress, withholding his support from no enterprise calculated to advance its material, social, moral or educational welfare.

In 1856 Mr Case was united in marriage to Miss Mary Frost, who died about 1863, leaving one daughter, Mary, now the wife of Robert McEcron, of Omaha, Nebraska One son, Anson, died in infancy Mr Case was again married, his second union being with Miss Jane E Hanna, daughter of James and Susan (Bockus) Hanna Her death occurred in 1893 She was a member of the Methodist church, and her loss was deeply felt by many friends, as well as her immediate family Three children were born by this union, two sons and one daughter Harry died in infancy, and Charles at the age of twenty-two Edith, the daughter, is living with her father

In his political views Mr Case is a Republican. He served as school director for twelve years, justice of the peace eight years and supervisor eight terms, discharging his duties in a most prompt, faithful and commendable manner He is a man of great modesty, pleasant and unassuming in demeanor, kind-hearted and affable He possesses those qualities which everywhere command respect and denote the high-minded, noble-spirited gentleman As one of the pioneers of Rock Island, he has witnessed almost its entire development He is public-spirited, proud of his country and its achievements, and Rock Island numbers him among its most honored and respected citizens

---

HON HENRY A AINSWORTH, president of the Moline National Bank, and president of the Williams & White Com-

H. A. AINSWORTH.

pany, manufacturers of steam hammers and other special tools, is classed among the truly representative citizens of Moline, and dates his residence there since 1870 He is a native of Vermont, born in Williamstown, September 28, 1833 His father, Calvin Ainsworth, was also a native of Vermont, born in Brookfield, but in early life moved to Williamstown, where for fifty years he was a general merchant, well and favorably known in all that section of the country. He married Miss Laura Lynde, a native of Vermont, whose father, Cornelius Lynde, was the first circuit judge of Orange county, that state The Ainsworth family was of English descent, the first of the name coming from England in the seventeenth century and locating in Chelsea, Massachusetts The Lyndes are also of English descent, having settled in this country prior to the Revolutionary war, several of the name taking part in that struggle.

The subject of this sketch grew to manhood in his native village, and in the district schools received his primary education which was supplemented by attendance at two academies In 1853, at the age of twenty years, he left home and came west, locating in Geneseo, Henry county, Illinois, where he engaged in general merchandising on his own account In this line he continued eight years, then sold out and for a few years was engaged in the hardware and agricultural implement trade in the same place. In both lines he met with good success.

In 1870 Mr Ainsworth came to Moline and secured an interest in the manufactory of Williams & White One year later the business was incorporated and Mr Ainsworth was elected secretary of the company, a position he held for seven years, when purchasing about three-fourths of its capital

stock, he was elected president, a position he still retains Under his general management the business has attained mammoth proportions, and is one of the leading industries of Moline Soon after coming to Moline he took stock in the Moline National Bank, and also in the Moline Savings Bank and for some years served as director and vice-president of both institutions His ability as a financier and good executive ability, were recognized by his associates, and in 1894 he was elected president of the former institution, a position he is well qualified to fill On his election as president of the Moline National Bank, he resigned the vice-presidency of the Moline Savings Bank, but was retained in its directory

On the 28th of July, 1858, Mr Ainsworth was married at Ashland, Ohio, to Miss Sarah Andrews, a native of Ohio, and a sister of Mr Andrews, then president of Kenyon College After a happy married life of thirty-three years, Mrs Ainsworth was called to her reward, dying in a hospital at Chicago, leaving two children—Harry and Mary The former is a graduate of Oberlin College, and of the law department of Harvard University He is a man of exceptionally good business ability and is now secretary of the William & White Company Mary is also a graduate of Oberlin College and is a woman of rare attainments At present she is making a tour in Europe Mrs Ainsworth was a sincere and honest Christian woman, one who delighted in the service of the master, and when the summons came she was ready to go, having that perfect confidence and trust in the Blessed Redeemer and the life beyond the grave

For his second wife Mr Ainsworth wedded Miss Sarah F Anderson, June 30, 1896 She was born in Bucyrus, Ohio, moved to

Geneseo, Illinois, in early life, and was a graduate of Rockford Female College A teacher of recognized ability, a woman of grace and refinement, and of good executive ability, she was called to the presidency of her alma mater, and for six years occupied that position She was still serving as such when her marriage with Mr Ainsworth occurred In February, 1896, Beloit College conferred on her the degree of M. A , a degree worthily bestowed

Mr Ainsworth has always taken a commendable interest in public affairs, though never to the neglect of his business interests He believes it the duty of every American citizen to keep posted and act intelligently upon all questions affecting the people, and in pursuance of that idea he carefully reads the current literature of the day and attends the public speaking as his time will admit. The conventions of his party he also attends, more frequently as a delegate than otherwise Politically he is a strong Republican Attaining his majority the year in which the birth of that party occurred, he gave adhesion to its principles, and has never deviated therefrom

While a residence of Geneseo Mr Ainsworth was elected a member of the board of village trustees, and was the youngest member of that body. For six years he was a member of the state board of equalization, and was state senator from the Moline district from 1882 to 1886 He was later appointed by Governor Fifer president of the state board of labor statistics, which office he resigned when Altgeld was elected governor In every position filled, he discharged its duties faithfully and well and to the satisfaction of all interested

Religiously Mr Ainsworth and family are members of the First Congregational church of Moline, and in the work of the church he has always manifested an interest, being among its most liberal contributors Fraternally he is a Royal Arch Mason, a member of both the blue lodge and chapter at Moline. In the former body he is now past master. As a citizen he has ever taken a lively interest in every enterprise calculated to build up his adopted city and county, and few men have a wider circle of friends and acquaintances throughout the state

WILLIAM JACKSON is one of the leading attorneys of Rock Island, where he has successfully practiced law for more than a third of a century. He is a man of splendid intellectual endowments, having that strong mental grasp which enables him readily to discover the points in a case and to present them with telling force before court or jury. His reasoning is logical, his arguments forcible and convincing, and he has won distinction as an able representative of the legal fraternity

Mr. Jackson is a native of Liverpool, England, born August 14, 1834, and is a son of William and Ann (Pott) Jackson, the former originally a farmer by occupation Our subject obtained his education in his native city, after which he was apprenticed to a grocer for a period of five years Before that time expired, however, he became imbued with a desire to try his fortune in the New World, having heard excellent accounts of its advantages and opportunities from relatives who lived in New York and Illinois Therefore he relinquished his position after three years of service, took passage on a westward-bound ocean vessel and on the third of July, 1851, landed in New York City.

Mr Jackson remained in New York only a short time and then started for Illinois, arriving in Rock Island county in August of the same year He at once sought and obtained employment, serving in various minor capacities in different stores and factories of Moline, but continually working his way upward He continued to reside in Moline until 1862, and during the latter part of his residence there devoted himself to the study and practice of law He pursued his studies in the office and under the direction of H L. Smith, and afterward with the firm of Graham & Webster, being admitted to the bar in 1860 Entering into partnership with James Chapman under the firm name of Chapman & Jackson that connection was continued until May, 1862, when Mr Jackson removed to Rock Island.

He was alone in practice until January 1, 1864, when he became associated with E. D Sweeney, under the firm style of Sweeney & Jackson They soon rose in prominence and continued to occupy a leading position in the legal field until August, 1883, at which time Mr. Jackson was compelled to retire from active practice, owing to nervous prostration. He then rested from all business care until May, 1885, when he once more entered the field of jurisprudence, practicing alone until March, 1890, when he admitted to partnership Elmore W. Hurst, forming the firm of Jackson & Hurst, which is the acknowledged peer of any law firm in the city. Their practice is general, and they have been connected with the most important litigated interests of the county during the seven years of their partnership Hardly a case of prominence has been tried in Rock Island during the past

third of a century that has not found Mr. Jackson as counsel either for the plaintiff or defendant

A marked characteristic of all his appearances in court is the thoroughness with which his cases are prepared. Although possessing quick perceptive faculties and working with facility and ease, he studies every case closely and carefully, and his dignified and courteous demeanor commands alike the respect of the court and the esteem of his associates at the bar

Mr Jackson was married May 21, 1863, to Miss Jennie E Sammis, of Moline. They have two daughters—Carrie, wife of Dr. J M Barth, and Hattie, wife of Dr George M Babcock. The parents are members of the Methodist church, and take a deep interest in all that pertains to the higher development of mankind Mr. Jackson, who is a stanch Republican in politics, served as township collector of Moline in 1859 and 1860, and was appointed postmaster of Rock Island by President Grant in 1873, serving in that position for three years In 1880 he was alternate delegate to the Chicago National convention, which nominated Garfield for the presidency But while he has taken a deep interest in political issues and the success of his party, he much prefers to labor for the election of his friends than for his own political advancement in the line of political honors. As president of the Citizens Improvement Association of Rock Island for three years, and as park commissioner, Mr Jackson has performed splendid service in beautifying the city. Spencer Square, which he, as park commissioner, laid out, is one of the prettiest and most ornamental parks in the west, and stands as a monument to his skill and public spirit. Without solicitation, or even knowledge on his part, he was appointed by Governor Tanner, in the spring of 1897, as one of the board of managers of the reformatory at Pontiac, a position which he is well qualified to fill and which is an honor worthily bestowed

HENRY P. STAPLEY, although a young man, occupies the responsible position of manager for the Western Union Telegraph Company at Rock Island His career is typical of the progressiveness of the West and demonstrates what can be accomplished by perseverance, close application and ready adaptability of surrounding opportunities to the worthy ambition of achieving an honorable success in business

Mr Stapley was born in Lincoln, Nebraska, February 5, 1868, and is a son of Frederick and Elizabeth (Foster) Stapley, the former born in England, the latter in Canada The paternal grandfather died in England at an advanced age and the maternal grandfather followed agricultural pursuits in Canada until his death Frederick Stapley made farming his life work and for many years was identified with the agricultural interests of Piatt county, Illinois He was a soldier of the Civil war, and served for eleven months with the Ninety-second Illinois Volunteer Infantry, being honorably discharged on account of sunstroke His family numbered three children—Lydia, wife of Calvin Williamson, Henry P., and William R , who is living in Piatt county, near Monticello.

Henry P Stapley was reared in Piatt county, where he early became familiar with the labors that fall to the lot of the agriculturists Having acquired his elementary education in the public schools he afterward completed a course in the McKee business college in Champaign, Illinois, and was graduated, accepting a position as teacher in that school in the business course Taste and inclination then led him to take up the study of telegraphy and after preparing for his chosen vocation in Champaign, he was assigned to duty as telegraph operator for the Western Union Telegraph Company at Excelsior Springs, Missouri Later he was promoted to the managership at Vinton, Iowa, and in September, 1895, came to Rock Island, as manager for the company at this point His selection for this responsible position came somewhat in the nature of a surprise, as it is an almost universal rule of the company to appoint to such places as Rock Island men who have long been in its service and who have been thoroughly tried. With but three years' experience he was appointed over the heads of many who had served in minor positions for a decade or more, and who would have been highly gratified to have been assigned to such an important point But Mr Stapley is thoroughly competent to discharge the duties devolving upon him, having attained a high degree of proficiency in telegraphy. He is a young man of great energy, firmness of purpose and laudible ambition and undoubtedly the future holds in store for him still greater success, He is an affable and courteous gentleman, popular in social circles, and a valued adherent of the cause of Republicanism

STILLMAN LOVEJOY, who passed from this life January 16, 1897, was for many years identified with the business interests of Moline He was born on the 1st of May, 1834, in Winchendon, Massachusetts, about sixty miles from Boston, and was a son of Elisha Lovejoy, a cooper by trade He was also a second cousin of Owen Lovejoy, who became so famous in the anti-slavery troubles

When a young man our subject learned the painter's trade and after coming to Moline in 1853 began painting tubs for the firm of Dimock & Gould, whose factory was then located on the Island With them he remained for about eighteen years In the meantime he was married September 2, 1857, the lady of his choice being Miss Mary A. Hilt, of Moline, who was born in Carroll county, Ohio, and had come with her parents to Illinois They became the parents of six children as follows

George A , the oldest, was born August 24, 1858, in Moline, received a fair common-school education, and in July, 1876, in connection with his father opened up a meat market at the corner of Fifth avenue and Twenty-third street, where the latter had purchased an acre of land In 1894 he sold out to his son, Charles Owen, and the business has since been successfully conducted by the two brothers. George A was married in Rock Island, December 31, 1879, to Miss Lottie McDaniel, a native of that city, and to them have been born four children —George Stephen, born in Moline, January 21, 1881, Clifford, who died in infancy, Fay Edna; and Stillman The second and third child of our subject died in childhood Ida Belle is the wife of William Evans, foreman in the blacksmith shop of the Moline Plow Company, and they have one daughter, Grace   Mary Dell and Charles Owen are still with their mother, and the latter is the junior member of the firm of Lovejoy Brothers

In early life Stillman Lovejoy gave his

allegiance to the Whig party, and later was an ardent supporter of Republican principles, but cared nothing for official honors He was a charter member of the Modern Woodmen of America, and when a young man joined the Baptist church but later in life became an Adventist He was a man of excellent principles and a blameless life, and thoroughly enjoyed the esteem and respect of the entire community, and died mourned by a large circle of friends and acquaintances.

Like his father, George A Lovejoy is a pronounced Republican in politics, casting his first vote for James A Garfield in 1880, and in 1891 he was elected alderman from the seventh ward, serving in that capacity for four years. He was made chairman of the ground and building committee, and was also a member of other important committees, including that on fire, water and light. During his incumbency he was instrumental in securing the fire alarm system now in use and the Nineteenth street storm drain, also established the grades for the streets, and took part in the famous struggle with the railroads to make them grade their tracks on a level with the streets, in which the city was successful He is a charter member of the local camp of the Modern Woodmen of America, and also of the Home Forum, of which his wife is also a member. She is connected with the First Baptist church of Moline, and like her husband is held in high regard by all who know her

ADOLPH J RIESS, a successful druggist of Rock Island, is one of the native sons of the city, born July 18, 1867 He belongs to one of the honored pioneer families whose identification with the interests of the county have been of material benefit thereto   His father, George Riess, was a native of Germany, and in his youth learned the carpenter's trade.   He came to America in the '40s and in 1849 took up his residence in Rock Island, then a small western town With the development of the city from that period to the present, he has been prominently associated   In the line of his trade he has been active in its upbuilding and has erected many of the large and substantial structures here   In other works tending to advance the general welfare he has also borne his part, and is a public-spirited, progressive men, numbered among the valued residents of Rock Island

George Riess was united in marriage to Lena Geertz, also a native of Germany Her mother is one of three survivors of a family of eight children and is now living with Mrs. Riess at the very advanced age of ninety-four years, her mental and physical powers being well preserved   Mr Riess has reached the age of sixty-nine years and his wife of sixty-five   He was one of the first members of the German Lutheran church in Rock Island, and aided in the erection of the first little house of worship.   In 1866 they built a church on the corner of Twentieth street and Fifth avenue, which was torn down in order to erect on the same site the finest church in the three cities He is one of the oldest and still one of the most efficient church workers connected with that congregation, having indeed been active in the promotion of its interests

Mr and Mrs Riess have a family of eight children, namely   Bertha, wife of George Gumtow, a carpenter, residing at 1309 Sixth avenue, by whom she has four children, Lena, Etta, Carl and Bertha, Minnie is t'   [' ~ .

farmer, residing in Blue Island, Illinois, by whom she has three children, Albert, Alma and Martha, Albert C , a postal clerk of Chicago, who married Minnie Johnston and has two children, Florence and Alexander, Charles E , a druggist of New York, who married Emily Marquette and has two children, George and Byron, Adolph J , of this review, Eliza, at home, Herman W , who is now hospital steward in the United States barracks at Washington, D C , and Ernest A , a railroad employe, living at home

Adolph J Riess, whose name introduces this review, obtained his education in the schools of Rock Island and of Chicago, living with his brother Charles during his stay in the latter city   Determining to engage in the line of business to which he now devotes his energies, he pursued a thorough course in pharmacy and is well versed in the use of drugs and medicine   He now owns a good store at the corner of Fourth avenue and Twenty-third street, where he keeps in stock a full line of everything found in a first-class establishment of the kind, including drugs, oils, toilet preparations, perfumes, etc   He has built up an excellent trade and his courteous treatment of his customers and his honorable dealing insures to him a continuance of this liberal patronage

Mr Reiss was married on Christmas day of 1894 to Miss Louisa Clark, of Chicago, who was born December 25, 1870, and is of Welsh extraction   They have one child, Bessie, who is the joy and pride of the household   They attend the German Lutheran church and occupy a prominent position in social circles   Mr Riess affiliates with the Republican party, but has never :   . . 1 ' . J , ' u ent, his time and attention being taken up by his business interests, in which he is meeting with a splendid success, of which he is truly deserving

---

JOHN M HOLT —The commercial history of Rock Island county would be very incomplete and unsatisfactory without a personal and somewhat extended mention of those whose lives are interwoven so closely with the industrial and financial development of the state When a man or a select number of men have set in motion the occult machinery of business, which materializes into a thousand forms of practical utility, or where they have carved out a fortune or a name from the common possibilities, open for competition to all, there is a public desire which should be gratified to examine the elements of mind and the circumstances by which such results have been achieved The study of biography yields in point of interest and profit to no other on account of the many lessons that may be gleaned therefrom and profitably followed

The life of Mr Holt is an illustration of this, he possesses splendid business qualifications and a determined purpose which resolutely and honorably meets all obstacles and overcomes them He is now the oldest grocer in years of continuous business activity in Moline, and is one of the honored early settlers of the city

He was born in Erie county, New York, February 21, 1844 His father, Arnold Holt, was born and reared in Vermont and was first married there, his second wife being Hannah Millington, a native of the Green Mountain state, whom he wedded in 1842 in Colden, Erie county, New York,

He was a tanner and currier by trade and located at Colden, New York, where he opened a large tan yard and carried on business for some years In 1855 he removed to a farm in Moline township, Rock Island county, and spent his remaining days here, his death occurring in the fall of 1864 He held several local offices in New York, and was a man of sterling worth His wife still survives and is now living with a daughter in What Cheer, Iowa The Holt family is of English ancestry, and was founded in the new world in the early part of the seventeenth century by Nicholas Holt The family has been represented in every war in which the country has been involved, including the many Indian wars of early days, the Revolutionary war, and the war of 1812 Arnold Holt was a lieutenant in the Vermont militia stationed at Bennington, Vermont, in his early manhood

When a lad of eleven years, John M Holt accompanied his parents to Rock Island county, and obtained his education in the schools of this place and in Buffalo, New York In his youth he learned the printer's trade, which he followed for five years in Moline, but when his country became involved in civil war he left the case and went in the defense of the Union, enlisting December 1, 1861, as a member of Company H, Eighth Kansas Infantry The company was formed of Illinois men, but was attached to the Kansas regiment and joined the Army of the Cumberland Mr Holt served for three years, participating in many hotly-contested engagements, including the battle of Perryville and Chattanooga, where the regiment lost sixty per cent of its members, Missionary Ridge, Orchard Knob, the Knoxville campaign, the siege and capture of Atlanta, and the battles of Jonesboro, Lovejoy Station and Franklin, Tennessee. Mr. Holt was in every battle and skirmish of his regiment, loyally defending the old flag and the cause it represented, and on the 5th of December, 1864, was honorably discharged Soon afterward, however, he returned to his old corps and acted as sutler's clerk of Eightieth Illinois Volunteers, until the close of the war. His interest in military affairs has never abated, and in 1877 he joined the state militia, serving for five years as sergeant of a Moline company By Colonel William Clendenin he was appointed quartermaster of the Sixth regiment, in which capacity he has served for fifteen years With his command he was called out to aid in quelling the disturbance caused by the strikers at East St Louis, where he remained for fifteen days, was also similarly engaged in the Spring Valley strike, and for twenty-one days was in Chicago in military service during the strike there in 1894

At the close of the Civil war Mr. Holt returned to Moline and in June, 1865, embarked in the grocery business with his brother, D. A. Holt, with whom he was thus connected for four years During the last year of this time he was also collector and constable for the city and township. In 1870 he established a grocery store at the corner of Fifth avenue and Twelfth street in partnership with W D Benham, and for three years they carried on an extensive and profitable business They then sold out, rented the store and through the succeeding year Mr Holt engaged in clerking About 1874 he resumed business on his own account at the old stand, and after a year and a half admitted to partnership S L Wilson, who remained with him seven

and a half years, when he bought out Mr. Wilson's interest. For a year and a half he remained alone and then sold the store. Not long after this he embarked in the flour, feed and fruit business as a commission merchant on Third avenue, where he remained for three years

On the expiration of that period Mr. Holt turned his attention from private business to public duties, becoming postmaster of Moline, to which position he was appointed May 1, 1890, by President Harrison He acceptably and efficiently served in that capacity until July, 1894. His next venture in the business world was in the painting trade He took contracts for this work and employed a number of men In January, 1897, he formed a partnership with Charles Savage and again embarked in the grocery business on Fifteenth street His long experience in this line has given him an accurate knowledge of the desires of the public, and his courteous treatment of his patrons, combined with honorable dealing, has secured to him an extensive trade

In Moline, July 12, 1877, was celebrated the marriage of Mr Holt and Miss Maria W Hitchcock, a daughter of Rev A B. Hitchcock She was born in Davenport, Iowa, but was educated in Moline, and before her marriage successfully engaged in teaching. By their union have been born three children—Mabel D , George E , a student in the high school, and Niel Allen Mr Holt and his wife are active members of the Congregational church, and their home is the center of a cultured society circle He is a valued member of the Masonic fraternity, affiliating with Doric Lodge, No 319, A F & A M , and Barrett Chapter, No 18, R. A M He is also a member of the Modern Woodmen, the Grand Army

Post, and the Home Forum, a beneficent organization In politics he is a stanch Republican, earnestly upholding the principles of that party on account of his firm belief that they will best promote the welfare of the nation A man of exemplary habits and upright character, he receives and merits the confidence and good will of all whom he meets and his friends throughout the county are many.

--- ---

REV CONRAD EMIL LINDBERG, D D., is one of the most eminent theologians of the Lutheran church in the United States and ranks among the foremost educators of the country His life has been devoted to those pursuits which advance civilization and lift man to a higher and nobler plane In the interests of humanity he labors earnestly and as he is comparatively a young man there is probably a long career of usefulness still before him He is now professor of systematic theology, liturgics and church policy, and instructs also in other subjects such as Hebrew, Greek, etc , in Augustana College of Rock Island.

Dr. Lindberg was born at Jonkoping, Sweden, June 9, 1852, and in the college of his native city his preparatory studies were completed He was for some time tutor in a high school and began preaching before he was eighteen years of age. His humanitarian principles and his broad and comprehensive views of life led him to enter a field where his services would benefit his fellowmen, and his career, carried out along this line, has been a noble one In 1871 he entered Augustana College, where the following year he completed the theological course In harmony with the wish of the synod he entered the Theological Seminary at Phila-

delphia in 1873, and continued his studies therein until his graduation in 1876, although he was ordained to the ministry in 1874 He was tendered the pastorate of the Swedish church in Minneapolis in 1876 but declined, preferring to thoroughly fit himself for his chosen vocation by the prosecution of his studies in Philadelphia In 1879 he accepted the pastorate of the Gustavus Adolphus church in New York City, where he labored with unusually great success and built a beautiful church For ten years he was president of the New York conference and was the recognized leader of the Swedish Lutheran church in the east

The labors of Dr Lindberg have been varied, yet all have been along the line of development and progress In 1890 he was unanimously elected to a professorship in Augustana College and Seminary of Rock Island, and the same year entered upon the duties of his office. He has since been connected with that institution as one of its most able and learned instructors After the death of Dr Hasselquist he became chairman of the theological faculty. He uses both the Swedish and English languages as medium of instruction, and the subjects of his teaching include dogmatics, ethics, liturgics, church polity, theological encyclopedia, hermaneutics and the Hebrew and Greek languages In 1893 the degree of Doctor of Divinity was conferred upon him by Muhlenberg College of Allentown, Pa , the leading collegiate institute of the Lutheran church in the east.

Dr Lindberg has contributed largely to church literature and his writings are forceful, fluent and profound. He was co-editor of the Nad och Sanning, a religious journal published in Chicago, and for a number of years was co-editor of the Augustana Observer, an English paper published in New York He has made many valuable contributions in both Swedish and English to various other papers. He has published two books called "Studies on the first three chapters of Revelation" and "Concerning Baptism" In 1897 he wrote a syllabus on church polity and has now in preparation a work on dogmatics, which will be published in 1898

In 1894 Dr Lindberg erected one of the finest residences in Rock Island, built in modern style of architecture, it is beautifully furnished and in its adornment is indicated the refined and æsthetic taste of the owner With the Doctor lives his mother, who is now over seventy years of age A student of the political conditions of the country he always votes with the Republican party on questions of national importance, but at local elections, where no issue is involved, often disregards party ties He is a man of scholarly attainments and broad culture, of pleasant, genial manner, easy of approach and has the warm regard of all with whom he comes in contact

SAMUEL CRAIG PLUMMER, M D, has for half a century been one of the most prominent physicians of Rock Island. The world has little use for the misanthrope The universal truth of brotherhood is widely recognized; also that he serves God best who best serves his fellowmen There is no profession or line of business that calls for greater self-sacrifice or more devoted attention than the medical profession, and the successful physician is he, who through love of his fellow-men gives his time and attention to the relief of human suffering Dr. Plummer i ⁙ of the ablest representatives

of this noble calling, and to-day, besides his large general practice, he is serving as president of the staff of St Anthony's Hospital, and is surgeon for the Chicago, Rock Island & Pacific and Rock Island & Peoria Railroads He was also the honored surgeon of the Thirteenth Illinois Infantry during the dark days of the Civil war.

The Doctor was born April 10, 1821, at Salem Cross Roads, Westmoreland county, Pennsylvania, and is of English descent, one or two branches of the family still being found in Middlesex, England The founder of the family in America, Francis Plummer, who was by occupation a linen weaver, crossed the Atlantic in 1633, and settled at Newbury, in the Colony of Massachusetts Bay, which in 1776 became the state of Massachusetts In the old records of that state, he is declared to have been made a freeman the year after his arrival in New England, which signifies that he was a voter by reason of his membership in the Puritan church, which alone in those times qualified a man for citizenship in the colony He had left his old home at Woolwich, near London, England, with his wife Ruth, and several children, including two sons, Samuel and Joseph, and his descendants have become prominent in the public affairs of this country, being well represented in the colonial legislature of Massachusetts, and in later years having furnished a governor to New Hampshire, and five members to Congress

Dr Plummer's ancestors have also been well represented in the wars of this country John Plummer, the grandson of the patriarch, Francis, became a soldier from Dorchester, Massachusetts, and was killed by the Indians while defending Hatfield, that state, on the 28th of August, 1675 The Doctor's

DR. S. C. PLUMMER.

paternal great-grandfather served on General Braddock's staff, and was with that commander at the time of his defeat in 1755, at Braddock's Field, now a part of the city of Pittsburg, Pennsylvania The maternal grandfather was a soldier of the war of 1812

At an early day the family was founded in Western Pennsylvania, and in Westmoreland county the Doctor's parents, John B and Elizabeth (Craig) Plummer, were both born There our subject passed the days of his boyhood and youth and obtained his early education in the common schools After attending the preparatory department of the Western Reserve College, of Ohio, for one year, he returned to Greenville, Pennsylvania, and for two years was a student in the academy at that place. Under Dr H. D. La Cossett he then studied medicine for three years, and also attended lectures at the Cleveland Medical College, of Ohio, from which he subsequently graduated He received the *Ad cundem* degree from the Western Reserve University at Cleveland, and for thirteen years previous to entering the army, he successfully engaged in practice in Rock Island, Illinois Thus it will be seen that by long, patient and thorough study and subsequent practice, Dr. Plummer brought to his new position as army surgeon the full equipment and rich furnishment which were necessary to that position and its collateral possibilities His military record is best given in the words of his old friend and comrade, Asa B Munn, historian of Company I, Thirteenth Illinois Infantry

"Samuel Craig Plummer, M D , surgeon of the Thirteenth Illinois, enlisted at Rock Island, April 16, 1861, and mustered with the regiment at Dixon, Illinois, on May 24, 1861, with the rank of major On entering the army he was forty years old, light complexion, blue eyes, dark brown hair, five feet, nine and one-half inches tall, weighed one hundred sixty pounds and was by profession a physician Being the ranking surgeon in the volunteer army—as he believed —together with his social qualities, and his great executive abilities and devoted patriotism, he was conspicuously well fitted to fill the important and honorable position to which, early in the service, he was called, and whether a regimental surgeon, medical director of the army of the Eastern District of Arkansas, surgeon-in-chief First Division of the Fifth Army Corps, or medical director of the Fifteenth Army Corps, he honored the service as much as these various grades of service honored him While these higher grades of service were enjoyable to him—as he says—it bringing him into close and intimate association with many of our most prominent generals and commanding officers in all departments of the service, his fealty to his old regiment never faltered.

"As characteristic of the fealty to his comrades of his old regiment, and his hatred of shams and the fuss and feathers of high-graded red tape, it will be both pertinent and proper here to relate that on the day that Col Wyman fell at Chickasaw Bayou, Dr Plummer, being a medical director, and with his operating table in the woods, somewhat back and to the southwest of Lake Plantation, and near General Sherman's headquarters, was notified that Colonel Wyman was shot The Doctor dropped everything, mounted his horse, and without asking leave hastened, with such speed as the nature of the country would allow, away to the right to where our regiment was in line of battle, immediately to the left of General

Morgan L Smith's second division, and was hotly engaged   The ranking surgeon was immediately informed of Dr Plummer's action, and started a mounted messenger in hot pursuit with orders for the Doctor to return immediately to his post of duty, which, on overtaking the Doctor, the messenger delivered, and received the reply that the Doctor's colonel had been shot and he was going to him   The messenger called the attention of the Doctor to the fact that the order was imperative   This raised the Doctor's ire to its highest executive pitch, and he sent back a plump refusal to obey the order, together with a message couched in language of such scorn and contempt as enraged the ranking surgeon to that degree that he at once preferred charges against the Doctor, but on being brought before General Sherman, his explanation caused the General to dismiss the case with something less than a reprimand, and scarcely more than a suggestion that henceforth his language should be somewhat more carefully considered when communicating with his superior officer.

" It seems unjust and certainly unfortunate that such eminent services as were rendered his country by Dr Plummer do not carry with them promotion in rank such as is received by commanders of troops in the field   Measured by the actual value of important services rendered, the unsurpassed, if approached, sanitary condition of his regiment during its full term of service, and his eminent ability in many higher positions, as a surgeon, fully entitled him to have carried home with him the stars of a major general   Dr O P S Plummer, a brother of the subject of this sketch, was for a few months assistant surgeon of our regiment "

On being mustered out, Dr Plummer returned to his family in Rock Island, and resumed the practice of his profession   On the 17th of October, 1844, he had married Miss Julia Hayes, of Burg Hill, Ohio, who died October 6, 1872   There were five children born to that union, namely   Emma, now the widow of G W Darrow, by whom she had one son, Samuel P ; Clara, at home, Elizabeth, wife of George M Loosley, by whom she has three children, Helen, Frederick and George; Frederick H , who married Miss Anna Hale, of Junction City, Kansas, and is now confidential accountant for Kilpatrick Brothers & Collins, heavy contractors of Beatrice, Nebraska, and Samuel C , a physician and surgeon of Chicago   On the 9th of June, 1874, the Doctor was again married, his second union being with Sarah Moore Dawson, of Wilmington, Pennsylvania, and they occupy a pleasant home at 709 Twentieth street.

Dr Plummer has witnessed almost the entire growth of Rock Island, as on locating there almost fifty years ago, the place contained but six hundred inhabitants, and he has borne a prominent part in its development, giving his support to all measures for good to the community   Through all these years he has successfully engaged in active practice, has served as county physician, and was a member of the board of health of Rock Island for some years   He is now the honored president of the Rock Island Medical Society, and is a prominent member of the Iowa and Illinois Central District Medical Associations, the State Medical Society and the American Medical Association   He has held some very important positions in the State Medical Society, being at one time the first vice-president

During the siege of Vicksburg, Dr Plummer lost the hearing of his right ear by the explosion of a shell at the assault on the 22nd of May, 1863, but otherwise, with the grizzled hair and white beard of his seventy-six years, he is remarkably well preserved, and attends to the duties of surgeon for two important railroad companies besides a large home practice. Politically he is a Republican, and socially a member of the Masonic fraternity. As he is still interested in the boys that wore the blue, he belongs to the Society of the Army of the Tennessee, the Grand Army of the Republic, and the Military Order of the Loyal Legion, and periodically attends the meetings of the latter organization at Chicago, but he never misses the annual re-union of his old regiment at Dixon, Illinois. The latch-string of his home always hangs outside, and his pill box is invitingly open to every surviving member of the Thirteenth Illinois, who all hope that he will be spared to them for many years yet to come. The Doctor, his wife and family all hold membership in the Broadway Presbyterian church, in which he is now serving his second term as elder, and in social circles they occupy a prominent position. His acquaintanceship is an extended one and his friendships many. Well may succeeding generations pay a tribute of honor to his noble name and to the memory of his noble deeds.

SWAN TROPP, president of the Moline Stone Company, has the reputation of a strictly first-class business man, reliable and energetic, and is a citizen of whom Moline may be justly proud. His office is situated at No 252 Second street, while his residence is at 131 Third avenue. Although a foreigner by birth he possesses the progressive spirit so characteristic of the inhabitants of the New World and has met with remarkable success in his undertakings.

Mr Tropp was born in Smoland, Sweden, November 7, 1842, a son of Andrew and Mary Tropp. The father was a member of the Swedish army until receiving a severe injury which disabled him for further military service, after which he drew a pension. He died about 1876, at the age of fifty years. The boyhood of our subject was spent in a small village in his native land, where he attended school to a limited extent, but at an early age began working upon a farm and also assisted his father in quarrying stone. After reaching the age of eighteen he was allowed to keep his wages, but as he saw but little chance for rapid advancement in that country, he resolved to come to America, where he had been told better opportunities were afforded industrious and enterprising young men. Accordingly, in 1868, at the age of twenty-five, he started for the United States, landing in New York after a voyage of fifteen days. As he had an uncle living in Rockford, Illinois, he went to that place where he remained for two years and a half, working upon a farm and in a flouring mill.

In that city Mr. Tropp was married December 26, 1871, to Miss Christina Larson, also a native of Sweden, and soon afterward removed to Moline, where he engaged in teaming. Here his wife died in 1876, leaving three children, namely. Dora, now the wife of Emil Carlson, of Moline, by whom she has one daughter, Ruby, Helma, and Lida, the wife of Merton Smith, of Moline. Mr Tropp was again married June 28, 1878, his second union being with Miss Sophia Lindstrand, who was also born in Sweden, and by whom he has six children

—Esther, Alma, Hugo, Elsie, Rute and Regina

Mr Tropp continued to follow teaming in Moline for six years, and then embarked in the stone business, with which he has since been connected, but he has not confined his attention to one line of endeavor Subsequently he became connected with the Moline Ice Company, of which he is still serving as manager, was for some time a partner in the Twin City Coal Company, of which he is now the sole proprietor, and is also interested in the sand business as a member of the firm of Tropp, Darling & Company Since voting for Hayes in 1876 he has been identified with the Republican party, and religiously is a faithful member of the Swedish Lutheran church. He is a gentleman who started out in life with nothing but his own indomitable energy, and his accumulation of this world's goods is attributable to his good judgment in business affairs, his perseverance and industry.

REV S P A LINDAHL.—The stamp designating true nobility of character must ever find its ineffable tracery on the brow of one who sets himself apart from the " madding crowd's ignoble strife " and dedicates his life to the uplifting of his fellowmen A more than superficial investigation is demanded when one essays to determine the mental struggle and the spirit of unselfish devotion that must animate the man that must give all that he has and all that he hopes to be to service in the great vineyard of life, seeking reward only in that realm " where moth and rust do not corrupt and where thieves do not break through and steal " Our subject, who is now serving as editor of the Augustana, the official organ of the Augustana Synod, has devoted the years of his manhood to the work of the ministry.

Mr Lindahl was born November 8, 1843, in Christala, Sweden, of which country his parents, Olof and Stina Erson, were also natives, and there spent their entire lives The father, a farmer by occupation, died in 1854, at the age of fifty-two years, and the mother passed away in 1878, at the age of seventy-seven Both were earnest, consistent members of the Lutheran church The paternal grandfather of our subject, who lived to be over eighty years of age, was a soldier and participated in the war which ended in the battle of Leipsic and when Norway was conquered He had nine children Eric Ericson and wife, the maternal grandparents, died in Sweden when well advanced in years

There were six children born to the parents of our subject—Stina Lisa, now the wife of Mauritz Anderson, of Sweden; Nils E Lindahl, who recently died in Kansas, Mary Catharine, wife of Andrew Nelson, of McPherson, Kansas; Carl J Lindahl, of Branford, Kansas, Anna Charlotte, widow of Eric Ericson, of Clyde, Kansas, and Rev. Sven Peter August, of this review

Upon a farm in his native land Rev. Lindahl was reared, and there prepared for college in the common schools Resolved to seek a home in the New World, he crossed the Atlantic, landing in New York on the 3d of September, 1865. He came at once to Illinois, and the same year entered Augustana College at Paxton, from which institution he graduated in 1869 Soon afterward he was ordained to the ministry of the Lutheran church in Moline, and first had charge of the congregation at Woodhull, Illinois, where he remained for one year In

1870 and 1871 he served as a traveling missionary in Iowa, Nebraska, Kansas, Missouri and Dakota, and the following two years was assistant pastor of Immanuel church, Chicago. He had charge of the First Lutheran church of Galesburg from November, 1873, until 1885, and was then pastor of the church at Altoona, Illinois, from 1886 until 1891 In the latter year he accepted his present position as editor of the Augustana In 1894 he was honored by his alma mater, receiving the degree of D. D

On the 20th of May, 1875, Rev Lindahl was united in marriage with Miss Clara Anderson, of Galesburg, who died in 1877, and he was again married July 1, 1885, his second union being with Miss Hannah Johnson, of the same city, a daughter of Olof and Ingred Johnson. They now have one daughter, Alberta Christina The family occupy a pleasant home at No 1010 Thirty-eighth street, Rock Island.

Mr. Lindahl gives his political support to the Republican party For the long period of eighteen years he has been a member of the board of directors of Augustana College, and is now serving as its president. He is also president of the Scandinavian Mutual Aid Association of Galesburg, and there is hardly a position in the synod he has not filled, being president three years and secretary seven Long and faithfully he has labored for the Master's interests and no more earnest, truer Christian can be found

---

REV NILS FORSANDER, D. D , professor of historical theology in Augustana College, Rock Island, was born in Gladsax, Skane, Sweden, September 11, 1846, and is a son of A. Person and Ellen Person His father has long been a successful educator and is still living in Skane, but his wife died during the childhood of our subject She had four children, two of whom still survive Nils and John, the latter a teacher in the public schools of Skane The grandfather, P Fors, was in the military service of his country throughout his entire life The maternal grandfather, P. Person, was a farmer by occupation and died in Sweden at a very advanced age

Nils Forsander began his education in the public college at Lund, but was subsequently graduated at a private college in the same city During the summer of 1870 he first met Dr T N. Hasselquist, who was then at the head of Augustana College and was spending the summer in Sweden With that gentleman Mr Forsander came to America, arriving in Paxton, Illinois, in September, 1870 There he completed his theological studies, and also, during the illness of Professor A J. Lindstron, took charge of his classes in Latin and Greek during the spring term of 1871 In the year 1872 he was engaged as assistant pastor and teacher with Rev J Swenson, of Andover, Illinois, and in 1873 was ordained to the ministry of the Lutheran church Filled with the noble purpose of devoting his life to the uplifting of his fellow men and bringing to them a knowledge of Christianity, he entered upon his pastoral work in Aledo and spent the two succeeding years in that place and in Sagetown and Raritan, Illinois During the latter part of this period he was secretary of the Illinois conference

Removing to Iowa Mr Forsander spent five and a half years as pastor of the Lutheran congregation in Kossuth and nine and a half years had charge of the Bethesda congregation in Page county During this period he served at different times as secre-

tary and vice-president of the Iowa conference and was secretary of Augustana synod
for four years　In the fall of 1889 he was
tendered and accepted the position of assistant professor in the Theological Seminary
in Rock Island, and in 1890 he was made
regular professor, in which capacity he has
since continued to lecture on church history,
symbolics, isagogics, exegesis and apologet-
ics.　He is a man of strong mental powers,
of keen analytical mind, logical in his de-
ductions and clear in expounding to others
the truths he has gleaned in his wide and
varied investigation.　He has made many
valuable contributions to church literature,
is the author of a number of treatises and
essays which have been published in the Augustana, Bethania, Hamvannen and Lutersk
Kvartalskrift, also the author of several
treatises on church history　The degree of
Doctor of Divinity was conferred upon him
by Augustana College in 1896.

On the 6th of January, 1875, the Rev.
Forsander was united in marriage to Miss
Charlotte Ahlgren, who like her husband is
a consistent member of the Lutheran church
and is to him an able assistant in his work
He is a man of thoughtful mein and earnest
purpose, of unfaltering devotion to duty,
counting no personal sacrifice too great that
will advance the cause of Christianity　His
kindly, and charitable spirit has endeared
him to all who know him and his circle of
friends in Rock Island and among the
students of Augustana College is extensive.

EDWARD CORYN, junior member of
the well-known grocery firm of Rank &
Coryn, whose place of business is at 1317
Fifteenth street Moline is a native of Bel-

gium, his birth occurring near Ghent, on
the 2nd of November, 1857.　He was provided with excellent school privileges, being
educated in both the Flemish and French
languages, and on laying aside his text
books he assisted in the work of the home
farm until the family concluded to come to
America

In 1880, the parents, Leonard and Catherine (Schatteman) Coryn, and their three
sons, August, Edward and Charles, took
passage on board a westward-bound vessel,
which was twenty-three days upon the water,
having been delayed by severe storms　It
was reported that the ship was lost and
those on board never expected to again see
land, but finally reached the harbor of New
York in safety although the vessel was
greatly disabled.　The father made his
home in Moline until called to the world beyond in 1890, but the mother is still living.

Our subject was not long in becoming
familiar with the English language, and
began his business career here as an employe
in a sawmill, after which he worked in a
private family for several years.　In 1892
he formed his present connection with Mr
Rank, and has since successfully engaged in
the grocery trade, doing a large and profitable business　In politics he was first a
Democrat, later a Republican, and at the
present time is again supporting the men
and measures of the Democratic party.　In
1896 he was chosen to represent the sixth
ward of Moline in the city council, and is
now chairman of the street and alley committee, and a member of the committees on
building and ground, and paving　As a
public-spirited, progressive citizen, he has
done much to advance the interests of his
adopted county and is recognized as one of
the representative business men of Moline.

At the age of fourteen he was confirmed by the Bishop of Ghent in the Holy Catholic church, and still adheres to that faith

EMIL PETERSON, of the firm of Horst & Peterson, contractors and builders, of Rock Island, needs no special introduction to the readers of this volume, for he is widely known in business circles. The world instinctively pays deference to the man whose success has been worthily achieved and who has acquired a high reputation in his chosen calling and such a man is found in Mr Peterson He stands to-day an example of what can be accomplished through determined and resolute purpose and honorable effort, and Rock Island may well be proud to number him among her citizens

The kingdom of Sweden has furnished to this county many of its best citizens, and in that country, in Orebro, Mr Peterson first saw the light of day, November 21, 1858. His paternal grandfather, Peter Peterson, made farming his life work and died in Sweden in middle age. The maternal grandfather, Nils Nilson, was also a farmer of Sweden, and never left the land of his nativity The parents of our subject, Peter and Stina Maria (Nilson) Person, were also natives of that land, and to agricultural pursuits the father devoted his energies until called to the home beyond in 1880, at the age of sixty-eight years His wife still survives him and is now living with her son, Rev. John Ehrick Holzt, in Madrid, Iowa She is a member of the Lutheran church, to which her husband also belonged They had a family of four children—Per Robert, who is living in Finland, Emil, John Erick,

and Anna, widow of Carl Carlso, of St Paul, Minnesota

Mr Peterson, of this review, attended the common schools of Sweden, and when about sixteen years of age began learning the carpenter's trade, which he has made his life work In 1882 he determined to seek a home in America, hoping thereby to benefit his financial condition Crossing the Atlantic he took up his residence in Kansas, and, realizing the value of a good education in the practical affairs of life, he attended Bethany College for two winters In 1882 he came to Rock Island and in 1892 entered into partnership with Henry W Horst, as contractors and builders They soon demonstrated their ability to rank among the leaders in their line and as they gave evidence of their skill their patronage increased until they now have a large and profitable business They have erected many of the fine business houses and residences in this city, including Tremann's meat market and the home of Mr Rosenfield on Twentieth street. They employ a competent force of workmen, and their faithfulness to their contracts, their straightforward methods and uniform courtesy has won them a liberal patronage and the respect of the entire community

On the 17th of September, 1889, Mr Peterson married Miss Maggie Miller, daughter of John J and Margaret Miller They have two children—Inez Elenora and Ethel Elizabeth Mr and Mrs Peterson are members of the Lutheran church, and he is serving as its president They reside in a beautiful residence which he erected in 1894 and their home is noted for its warm-hearted hospitality In politics Mr. Peterson is a Republican, supporting by his ballot the men and measures of that party He has never had occasion to regret his determination to make his home in the land of the free, for success has crowned his efforts and his upright life has gained for him a large circle of friends

JOHN W WARR —America owes much of her progress and advancement to a position foremost among the nations of the world to her newspapers, and in no line has the incidental broadening out of the sphere of usefulness been more marked than in this line of journalism   Rock Island county has enlisted in its newspaper field some of its strong intellects—men of broad mental grasp, cosmopolitan ideas and notable business sagacity   Prominent among these is Mr Warr, who is editor of the Practical Age, and is also engaged in a general publishing business at the corner of Third avenue and Seventeenth street, Moline

A native of Ohio, he was born near Cleveland, August 17, 1844, and is a son of William and Mary (Earle) Warr   While the father was a mason by trade and followed that business in Cleveland, he lived on a farm outside of the city, and there our subject spent the greater part of his boyhood, attending the country schools until fourteen years of age   After clerking in a country store for a time, he entered Baldwin University at Berea, Ohio, where he was pursuing his studies when President Lincoln issued his first call for troops to put down the rebellion   He offered his services at this time but was rejected on account of his youth, and in June, 1862, enlisted as a private in Company G, Eighty-seventh Ohio Volunteer Infantry   Being at Harper's Ferry at the time of its surrender, he was taken prisoner and sent home on parole,

and in the fall of 1862 was honorably discharged   Returning to Baldwin University, he engaged in teaching and also continued his studies there for about two years

On the 17th of January, 1865, in Cleveland, Ohio, Mr Warr was united in marriage to Miss Harriet M Smith, and they have become the parents of five children—Bertha, who was born in Deerfield, Michigan, where her mother was spending the summer while their home was near Louisville, Kentucky, Percival, who was born in Jeffersonville, Indiana, and graduated at the Burlington Business College in the class of 1897, Wilbur, born in Moline, Archie and Norman

After his marriage, Mr Warr removed to Louisville, Kentucky, to take charge of a business college, and remained there as general manager and teacher for about ten years   Coming to Moline in 1878 he was made cashier of the Moline Plow Company, with which he was connected for eight years, and in the meantime established the Western Plowman, at first an advertising medium for the plow company, but finally developed into a regular paper, which he purchased on leaving the company and successfully published until 1896   While in the service of the Moline Plow Company, he started the Moline Building, Savings & Loan Association, of which he has since served as secretary. There grew up along with the paper some other publications which he still carries on with good success.

In his political adherence Mr Warr is stanchly in line with the principles advocated by the Republican party, to the cause of which he lends his active support   His first vote was cast for General Grant in 1868   For two terms he acceptably served on the board of aldermen of Moline, representing the fifth ward, and in 1891 was the candidate on the citizens' ticket for mayor, and received the largest vote ever polled for an anti-license nominee Always a friend of the cause of education, he was for several terms a most efficient member of the school board, and was instrumental in securing the erection of school house No 2, and the Grant school house He has also been president of the board of trustees of Moline township, of which he has been a member for six years, and has cheerfully given his support to all enterprises calculated to promote the interests of his town and county or advance the general welfare Whether in public or private life he is always a courteous, genial gentleman, well deserving the high regard in which he is held In early life Mr Warr attended the Methodist church, but being quite liberal in his views he united with the Unitarian church, becoming one of the charter members of the church in Moline, of which he has for some time been a trustee Fraternally, he is an honored member of Graham Post, No 312, G A R , and he attended the National Reunion at Louisville in 1895.

FRANK E ROBBINS, the well-known engineer in charge of the government bridge at Rock Island, was born in Connellsville, Pennsylvania, February 27, 1855, a son of John and Anna (Keepers) Robbins, also natives of the Keystone state The paternal grandfather, Aaron Robbins, a successful bricklayer and contractor, was born in Pennsylvania of English parentage, and served his country as a soldier in the war of 1812 He died at the ripe old age of eighty-six years Charles Keepers, the maternal grandfather, was also a native of

Pennsylvania and of German origin He was one of the prominent and wealthy citizens of his community and conducted a hotel for some time He died in early life The father of our subject, who was a contractor by occupation, is also deceased, having passed away in Connellsville. Pennsylvania, in 1875, at the age of seventy-five years, but the mother is still living at the age of eighty. Both were faithful members of the Christian church and were held in the highest regard by all who knew them

This worthy couple were the parents of ten children, six sons and four daughters, of whom five are still living, namely. Catherine, widow of Charles Carrington, Sarah, wife of Samuel Freeman, Carrie, wife of John Furtney, Lindley, and Frank E The oldest son, Ephraim, was captain of a company of Pennsylvania volunteers during the Civil war, and laid down his life on the altar of his country, being killed in battle Another son, Joseph, was also in the volunteer service, and was for some time incarcerated in Andersonville prison

Until eighteen years of age Frank E. Robbins remained in his native city and acquired his education in its public schools At fifteen he began learning the machinist's trade, which he successfully followed until 1880 Coming West in the spring of 1873 he first located at Rock Island, but a few weeks later went to Aurora to enter the service of the Chicago, Burlington & Quincy railroad as a machinist, and later removed to Jackson, Michigan, where he served as foreman in the machine shops of the Michigan Central railroad At the request of his wife's parents he returned to Rock Island, but after spending a short time here, he went to Beardstown, Illinois, where he was foreman of the St Louis list of the

Chicago, Burlington & Quincy machine shops In the spring of 1880, however, he again came to Rock Island as Mrs Robbins' mother had died and her father wished her to be near him For some time our subject then served as a member of the engineer corps of the United States army, but in 1885 was compelled to resign his position on account of ill health and for a few months did nothing On his recovery he accepted the position of manager of the Arc Scale Works, and in 1886 was made engineer on the government railroad bridge across the Mississippi river at Rock Island In May, 1892, he was promoted to engineer in charge, and has since acceptably filled that responsible position, having his office on the island at the new bridge, which is free and considered the finest across the Mississippi He has nineteen men under his charge ordinarily and sometimes more

On the 25th of May, 1874, was celebrated the marriage of Mr Robbins and Miss Emma Reaugh, who was descended from good old Revolutionary stock and was a daughter of George and Mary (Williams) Reaugh She was a devout member of the Methodist Episcopal church, which she joined at the early age of thirteen years, and was also an active and faithful member of the local Woman's Christian Temperance Union On the 21st of November, 1896, she departed this life, her death resulting from an attack of typhoid fever, which eventually required an operation to be performed, through which she passed all right, but later a relapse came and she soon died She was the mother of four children—Edgar, Lucia, Blanche, and one who died in infancy

Mr Robbins is also a Methodist in religious belief and in politics is independent

Socially he affiliates with the Independent Order of Odd Fellows, the Modern Woodmen of America, and the Knights of the Globe He has a pleasant home at 735 Twenty-second street, and is a man whose genial temperament, sound judgment and well-proved integrity have brought him the esteem and friendship of a host of acquaintances far and near. Having always taken an active and commendable interest in educational affairs, in July, 1892, he was elected a member of the school board of Rock Island, and two years later was made president of the board, in which capacity he is still serving to the satisfaction of all concerned

WILLIAM RINCK, one of the leading grocerymen and influential citizens of Rock Island, doing business at 1420 Seventh avenue, was born March 11, 1839, near Wehsel, on the Rhine, in Prussia, Germany, and his parents, Garrett and Catharina (Uppeg) Rinck spent their entire lives in that country The paternal grandfather, Johann Rinck, a potter by trade, died there when quite advanced in years, and his wife when nearly one hundred The maternal grandfather, a foundryman, died in Germany in middle life During early manhood the father of our subject followed school teaching, but later devoted his time and attention to agricultural pursuits He passed away at the age of ninety-two, and the mother, who survived him some years, died at the age of ninety-one

Of the six children born to this worthy couple William is the only one now living. In the Fatherland he was reared and educated until sixteen years of age, when he resolved to try his fortunes in the New

World, where he believed better opportunities were afforded ambitious, industrious and energetic young men Accordingly he came to this country in 1856, locating first in Davenport, Iowa, where he learned the shoemaker's trade, but the following year came to Rock Island

In 1858 Mr Rinck went to St Louis, where he continued to work at his trade until 1861, when he enlisted for three months in Company B, Second Missouri Infantry, and on the expiration of that term he re-enlisted for three years in Company F, Twelfth Missouri Infantry, as a private He participated in many hotly-contested battles, including those of Pea Ridge, Helena, Jackson, Lookout Mountain, Missionary Ridge, Ringgold and those of the Atlanta campaign The last engagement in which he took part was at Jonesboro, from whence the regiment started back to St Louis, where Mr Rinck was honorably discharged after three years and two months of faithful service He was slightly wounded at the battles of Resaca and Vicksburg, but was always found at his post of duty, gallantly defending the old flag and the cause it represented

On receiving his discharge, Mr Rinck rented a piece of land near Davenport, Iowa, where he engaged in farming for one year, and then again turned his attention to shoemaking Since the fall of 1865 he has made his home in Rock Island, where he continued to work at his trade for eight years, and then embarked in the grocery business, in which he is still successfully engaged

On the 7th of May, 1866, Mr Rinck was united in marriage to Miss Catharina Cordes, a daughter of William and Anna (Wallas) Cordes, and to them have been born eleven children, five sons and six daughters, of whom ten are still living, namely Frederick, who married Lula Bliss, Catharina and Mary, at home, William, deceased, Benjamin, who married Bertha Zude and has one child, John, who married Edith Gordon and has two children; Anna, at home, Henry, who married Florence Dillman, and Dora, Matilda and Elizabeth, all at home. The family reside in the same building in which the store is located

In religious faith both Mr and Mrs Rinck are Lutherans, and in his social relation he affiliates with the Independent Order of Odd Fellows, the Ancient Order of United Workmen, and Buford Post, No 243, G A R, of Rock Island He is an ardent Republican in politics and on that ticket was elected county supervisor from Rock Island township, a position he is now filling for the third term with credit to himself and to the satisfaction of all concerned. As a representative business man and prominent citizen of Rock Island, he takes a deep and commendable interest in public affairs and gives his support to all worthy enterprises calculated to promote the general welfare

---

REV. HENRY L BULLEN, who is now living retired in Moline, is a scholarly gentleman of splendid intellectual attainments, who, through the pioneer epoch of Illinois, was prominently engaged in ministerial work as a representative of the Congregational church He has made his home in this state since 1849 and has been closely identified with the interests of Rock Island county.

Mr. Bullen was born in East Midway, Massachusetts, August 17, 1820, and is a son of Lewis Bullen, a native of the same state The family is of English origin and was planted on American soil in 1641 by Samuel Bullen, who in that year crossed the Atlantic and located in Dedham, Massachusetts. Representatives of the name served in the war of the Revolution, and the grandfather of our subject, Judson Bullen, who held the rank of first lieutenant, was enrolled as a soldier of the American army April 19, 1775, the day on which the war was inaugurated by the hostilities at Lexington. Captain Lewis Bullen, the father, was reared to manhood in the Bay state and married Esther Grout, a native of Massachusetts, and a daughter of Elias Grout, who belonged to one of the old families and owned a large estate there   Captain Bullen held a commission and commanded a cavalry company of the State Militia   He made farming his life work and continued his residence in the state of his nativity until his death, which occurred in August, 1865   His wife passed away in 1835   They had two sons who reached mature years, the younger, John Bailey Bullen, now living a retired life in Melbourne, Australia.

In the history of Rock Island county specific mention should be made of Rev. Henry L Bullen, who has borne an important part in molding the destiny of this locality, leaving the impress of his strong individuality upon the community.   Spending his youth in Massachusetts, he was afforded excellent educational opportunities, which he eagerly improved, gaining an extensive knowledge to fit him for life's duties   He attended the Franklin Academy, of Massachusetts, was a student in the Western Reserve College, of Ohio, and was graduated in Dartmouth College with the class of 1842   Having thus acquired broad information in the classics, languages and sciences, he entered the An

dover Theological Seminary to study of man's relations to his fellowmen and his duty to his Creator   Fitting himself for the ministry he was licensed to preach and went to Georgia   Through the three succeeding years he devoted his energies to teaching in the schools of Macon and Eatonton, Georgia, and then accepted a position as teacher in Holliston, Massachusetts, where he remained two years   In 1849 he came to Illinois to accept the pastorate of the Congregational church of Port Byron   He was afterward called to the chair of mathematics in Iowa College of Davenport, serving in that capacity for eight years, when he removed to Durant, Iowa, where he was ordained as minister of the Congregational church, and labored with the people of that society for eight years   In 1871 he returned to Rock Island county, and has since made his home in Moline, where he is engaged in loaning money, thus encouraging the industries of the city and proving an important factor in its commercial life.

Mr Bullen has been twice married   In Millidgeville, Georgia, November 28, 1844, he wedded Mary Farrington, daughter of Nathaniel Farrington, of Walden, Vermont She was born and educated in the Green Mountain state, is a lady of superior culture and an accomplished music teacher   She died in Durant, Iowa, in 1866, leaving two children—Mary E., who formerly engaged in teaching in Moline, and John L , who was educated in the State University and is now farming near Elreno, Oklahoma   Rev. Bullen was again married October 9, 1867, his second union being with Laura E. Day, who was born, reared and educated in Denmark, Iowa, a daughter of Kellogg Day, of Ohio   They have two children—Laura Day and Henry Webster   The former, a graduate of the high school of Moline and for some years a successful teacher, is now the wife of W E Clark, of this city The son is yet a student in the high school

Mr Bullen is a Prohibitionist in principle and practice and does all in his power to insure the acceptance of the tenets promulgated by that party. He has long been deeply interested in educational work and during his five years incumbency on the school board of Moline did much to advance its interests here He and his family are members of the Congregational church and are foremost in all church and benevolent work, being active factors in the spiritual advancement of the community Mr Bullen has given the greater part of his life to the intellectual and moral development of his fellow men, and his own fidelity to duty, his uprightness in all relations, his kindliness and his breadth of spirit have won him the highest regard of all with whom he has come in contact

A BRAHAM H LAMBERT —In this enlightened age, when men of energy, industry and merit are rapidly pushing their way to the front, those who, by their individual efforts, have won fame and fortune, may properly claim recognition Years ago, when the west was entering upon its era of growth and development and Illinois was laying its foundation for future prosperity, there came thither from all parts of the country men of sturdy independence and with determination to succeed that justly entitles them to representation in the history of the great west Among this class is numbered Mr. Lambert, who, after an active and useful business life, is now enjoy-

ing a well-earned retirement from labor in his pleasant home in Rock Island

Mr Lambert was born in Dorchester, now Boston, Massachusetts, May 22, 1813, and is the only survivor of a family of nine children, whose parents were Paul and Patience (Howe) Lambert The family was early founded in America, and the paternal grandfather was a resident of Maine Paul Lambert was born in the Pine Tree state, became a carpenter and went to the south to erect some buildings, his death there occurring when fifty-two years of age. He had served as an officer in enforcing the Puritan laws, and was a man of considerable local prominence His wife, a faithful member of the Presbyterian church, was born in Dorchester, now Boston, Massachusetts, and reached the advanced age of eighty-six years. Her father, Abraham Howe, at one time owned nearly all the southern portion of Boston, but sold it for a small consideration

Abraham E Lambert, of this review, was reared in what was then called Dodgester, but now forms a part of "The Hub" He received a common-school education and at the age of sixteen began to learn the trade of carriage making, blacksmithing and horseshoeing, which he followed for many years, conducting business along that line in Brookline, Massachusetts In 1857 he came to the west, taking up his residence in Rock Island, where for a number of years he was accounted one of the leading representatives of the business interests of the city He embarked in the ice business and dealt in that commodity until 1874, since which time he has lived retired, occupying a beautiful residence at 749 Thirtieth street.

Mr Lambert was married to Miss Emily Frances daughter of Elijah and Emily

(Whitney) Hersey   Four children were born of this union—George E.; Abraham Howe, Anna, wife of Bernard McGuire, and Sophia, who died at the age of three years   The family has long been one of prominence in the community where their circle of friends is extensive

Mr Lambert is a Republican in politics and manifests an intelligent interest not only in the political questions which affect the country but also in all matters pertaining to the general welfare   His life has not been marked by events of thrilling interest, but contains its lessons of earnest purpose well carried out, of honorable endeavor and successful accomplishment   Such a career wins the respect of the multitude and Mr Lambert is regarded as a worthy and highly esteemed citizen of Rock Island

GEORGE LOUGHEAD EYSTER, M D , devotes his life to one of the noblest callings to which man has ever given his attention, the relief of human suffering He is a practitioner of the regular school, and by reason of his superior natural gifts, his close study of his profession and his deep and conscientious interest in his work he has steadily risen to a position of prominence in his chosen calling

He was born in Chambersburg, Pennsylvania, May 14, 1853, and is a son of William F and Lucretia (Gibson) Eyster, the former a native of Pennsylvania, and the latter of Vermont   The Eyster family is of German origin and was early founded in the Keystone state   The grandfather, General Jacob Eyster, followed merchandising in his earlier years in Gettysburg, Pennsylvania He was one of the most prominent and influential citizens of the state   served in the

Pennsylvania senate for four years, and was afterward surveyor general of the state for many years   He reared a large family, and died at the age of seventy-six   The maternal grandfather of the Doctor was Nathaniel Gibson, who removed from his home in Middlebury, Vermont, to Philadelphia.   In the former place he conducted a retail dry goods store, but wishing to enlarge his field of operations removed to Philadelphia, where he carried on an extensive business as a wholesale dealer   At the time of his death he had reached the advanced age of ninety-three

William F Eyster was for many years a clergyman of the Lutheran church, and also engaged in educational work, serving as president of the Hagerstown Female Seminary of Maryland for a long period   In 1876 he came to Rock Island and accepted the professorship of English literature in Augustana College, occupying that chair for ten years   He has since lived in Crete, Nebraska, and is now retired from active life, save that he occasionally fills the pulpit of some church   He and his wife had four children, two sons and two daughters— Frances, wife of John C Snively, of Crete, Nebraska, George L , William L , and Alice M , who resides with her parents in Crete

The Doctor is fortunate in having back of him an honored ancestry long connected with the higher walks of life   His character was formed in a cultured Christian home and educational advantages of a superior order were afforded him   He attended the private schools and an academy in Hagerstown, Maryland, where he was reared, and subsequently became a student in Pennsylvania College, graduating therein with the class of 1871   He then entered the medical department of the University of Pennsylvania, where he was graduated in 1874, and through the following year he practiced his chosen profession in Nebraska In 1876 he came to Rock Island, and soon won a place among the foremost representatives of the medical fraternity here His practice is general and his extensive patronage comes from among the best class of Rock Island's citizens. He is now a member of the staff of St Anthony's hospital, was county physician for about ten years, and commissioner of health for the city for about six years He is a member of the American Medical Association, the American Public Health Association, the Illinois State Medical Society, and the Iowa and Illinois Central District Medical Association

The Doctor holds membership in the Masonic Lodge and with the Knights of Pythias and Modern Woodmen of America, and is a valued representative of these orders By his ballot he supports the men and measures of the Republican party. He and his wife hold membership in the Episcopal church The Doctor was married on the 17th of February, 1876, to Miss Fannie P. Wright, a daughter of John K Wright, of Philadelphia They move in the best circles of society and their pleasant home is noted for its charming hospitality

A LBERT MALCOLM PARKER is a leading representative of the industrial interests of Rock Island, and one of the prominent young business men of the city Enterprise and energy are among his marked characteristics and have brought to him a merited success in his undertakings He is well known in business circles as the proprietor of Parker's Steam Laundry, and as his interests are conducted with regard to the strictest ethics of commercial life he has the confidence and good will of all

Mr Parker was born in Cassopolis, Michigan, October 31, 1866, a son of Nathan and Rachel (Jacobs) Parker, natives of Ohio The paternal grandfather, Haynes Parker, was born in New York, and was a Christian preacher He had a large family of fourteen children, and died in Michigan when more than ninety years of age The maternal grandfather, Jacob Jacobs, was a native of Germany, became one of the early settlers of Ohio, and afterward removed to Michigan The father of our subject was a farmer by occupation and in the pioneer days of Michigan took up his residence in Cass county, near Cassopolis, where he died in 1874, at the age of fifty-five years, having survived his wife six years Both were members of the Christian church They had a family of eight children, of whom seven are living, namely George S, Hannah M, wife of William Barnhart, of Rock Island, Joseph H; Nancy, wife of W L Pollock, of Cassopolis, Michigan, Byron W, of Summerville, Michigan, Lydia J and Albert M

Mr Parker, whose name introduces this review, was reared upon his father's farm in Michigan and attended the district schools. He was left fatherless when eight years of age, after which he went to Iowa to live with his sister Hannah and continued his education in the public schools there, being graduated at the high school of Muscatine Later he pursued a commercial course in Eastman's Business College, Poughkeepsie, New York, where he was graduated in 1887. Thus well equipped by educational training for the practical duties of life, he entered upon his business career purchasing a laundry plant in Muscatine, where he carried on operations along that line until 1893 He then sold that property, having in 1890 purchased his present laundry in Rock Island, which he has since conducted, doing an excellent business, furnishing employment to twelve hands His laundry is supplied with the latest improved machinery and equipments, and the excellent work which is done, together with his honorable dealing, has secured him a liberal patronage which is constantly increasing

On the 29th of October, 1890, was celebrated the marriage of Mr Parker and Miss Florence I Coates, daughter of Jason B. Coates. They have one daughter, Helen I, and lost a son, Malcolm J Their pleasant home, located at No 736 Seventeenth street, is noted for its hospitality Mr. and Mrs Parker are members of the Christian church, and he is serving as a member of its board of deacons and has been clerk of the church since 1894 He is also one of the directors of the Y M C A, of Rock Island. His political support is given to the Republican party Genial in disposition, modest in demeanor, faithful to all duties of citizenship, Mr Parker is highly esteemed throughout the community, wherein he has a large circle of friends

THOMAS P LAFLIN, who for forty-seven years has been a resident of Rock Island county, is now proprietor of one of the leading livery and feed stables in the county seat He was born near Taylor Ridge, on the 27th of May, 1850 The family was founded in America at an early day by the grandfather, Parley Laflin, a native of Massachusetts. He removed to New York where for many years he en-

gaged in the lumber business He had two sons and died in middle life Benedict Laflin, the father of our subject, was born in Massachusetts, and married Miss Eliza Phares, a native of Hamilton, Ohio, and a daughter of Thomas F Phares, who at his death was in his eighty-eighth year In the early '40s Benedict Laflin came to Illinois and pre-empted a farm in Edgington township, Rock Island county, where he lived for many years, engaged in agricultural pursuits For the past two years he and his wife have resided in Sears, Illinois They have had four sons—Thomas P., Charles, Clarence, who died at the age of two years, and Frank S

Thomas P Laflin spent the days of his boyhood and youth in Rock Island county, and supplemented his early educational training of the district schools by study in the public schools of Moline Later he was a student in Bryant & Stratton's Business College of Davenport, and thus equipped for life's practical duties he then returned to the farm For many years he gave his attention to agricultural pursuits and the neat and thrifty appearance of his place gave evidence of his careful supervision and progressive methods In 1894 he came to Rock Island, where he purchased ground and built his livery barn He has one of the best equipped stables in this section of the state, keeping on hand a large number of horses and many fine carriages of all descriptions His patronage comes from among the best class of citizens and has now assumed large proportions He has built up this business from a small beginning, securing the liberal support of the public by his straightforward dealing, his efforts to please and his courteous treatment of all.

On the 4th of January, 1871, Mr Laflin

T. P. LAFLIN.

MRS. T. P. LAFLIN AND DAUGHTER.

married Miss Emily Cropper, daughter of Edward Cropper, and they now have a family of five children—Clarence, Cora, Geneveive, Ben and Martha, all living at home. Mrs Laflin is a member of the Methodist Episcopal church In his political views Mr Laflin is a Republican, and socially is connected with the Modern Woodmen of America In addition to his other property he owns a fine fruit farm of forty acres, and by his own efforts he has risen to a position of affluence. He has traveled quite extensively through the United States, gaining that knowledge and culture which only travel can bring In manner he is genial, in disposition social, and throughout the county in which he has spent his entire life has a host of warm friends

ELMER E. MORGAN is unquestionably one of the strong and most influential business men whose lives have become an essential part of the history of Moline and Rock Island county Tireless energy, keen perception, honesty of purpose, genius for devising and executing the right thing at the right time, joined to every-day common sense, guided by resistless will power, are the chief characteristics of the man As an extensive real estate dealer, abstract, loan and collection agent, the places that he occupies in business circles are in the front rank. His office is in the Skinner block, Moline

Mr Morgan was born just across the river from Moline, in De Witt, Iowa, September 13, 1861, and is a son of Isaac F Morgan, whose birth occurred at Dayton, Ohio, July 4, 1830 The paternal grandfather, Isaac Morgan, Sr., was born in Kentucky, in 1789, was a soldier in the war of

1812, and was a descendant of General Morgan, of Revolutionary fame He married a South Carolina lady of German parentage, and became a pioneer of Ohio, erecting the first slab house in Dayton. About 1836 he emigrated to Davenport, Iowa, and settled on a farm near that city.

At that place Isaac F. Morgan grew to manhood and married Miss Sarah E Williams, who was born, reared and educated in Tennessee, and successfully engaged in teaching in early life In 1849 her father started for California with a number of others, but died of cholera while en route After his marriage Mr Morgan located in De Witt, where he engaged in merchandising for a number of years, afterward was interested in the hotel business, and still later successfully engaged in agricultural pursuits His first wife died in 1864, and some years later he married again

Elmer E. Morgan spent the days of his boyhood and youth in Iowa, remaining upon his father's farm until he had attained his majority His early school privileges were rather meagre, so that he is almost wholly self-educated by reading and study since reaching manhood Coming to Moline, in 1884, he began reading law with William A Mease and soon afterward embarked in the collection business, which he still continues, his being the oldest collection agency in this part of the state At the present time he is also interested in the abstract and loan business and is an extensive dealer in real estate

In his political views Mr Morgan is a stanch Republican, but has never cared for official honors, preferring to devote his entire time and attention to his business interests He was one of the founders of the Unitarian church of Moline of which he is an active member, and belongs to a number of civic societies, including Doric Lodge, F & A M , the Eastern Star, the Elks, Knights of Pythias, Select Knights, Modern Woodmen, and Home Forum   Of the last named he was appointed secretary in 1895, and has since written hundreds of applications for that popular order   He has traveled quite extensively through the United States and Europe   In 1896 he traveled through France, Holland and the British Isles on a bicycle, and in the same way spent six weeks in the Rocky Mountains, New Mexico and Texas, and has thus gained that culture and knowledge which only travel can bring Always a courteous, genial gentleman, he well deserves the high regard in which he is held

JOHN THOMPSON, a well-known locomotive engineer, who has now been a trusted employe of the Chicago, Rock Island & Pacific Railroad for many years, makes his home at 537 Twenty-third street, Rock Island   He was born in Greenock, Scotland, September 24, 1847, a son of William H and Jeannette (Corbet) Thompson, also natives of Scotland   The former was the youngest in a family of twelve children, whose father, John Thompson, a foundryman, died in Scotland in middle life. The maternal grandfather of our subject, was a tailor by trade, and also died in middle life in Glasgow, Scotland

In his native land William H Thompson learned the molder's trade, and on coming to America in 1848, worked in foundries in New York City, Jersey City and Cincinnati for about a year, but in the spring of 1849 came to Moline, where he was employed for ever   He then went to Quincy

and later to St Louis, but in 1856 returned to Rock Island, where he established a foundry for the manufacture of steam engines and machinery of all kinds   It is still in successful operation, and with the exception of four years spent in Chicago, Mr Thompson has since made his home in Rock Island, but for the past five years has lived retired from active business

The mother of our subject, who was a consistent member of the Presbyterian church, died in St Louis, in 1853   She had six children, three sons and three daughters, of whom four are now living   David C , of Rock Island, Ellen, wife of Robert Pelton, of Davenport, Iowa, Mary, wife of John Eggleston, of Denver, Colorado, and John   After the death of his first wife, William H Thompson married Mis Jeannette Smith, widow of William Smith, and a daughter of Captain Foster, a sea captain, who lost his life in the burning of the steamer Lexington between New York and Boston

Since 1856 Mr. Thompson, of this review, has made his home in Rock Island, where he obtained his education in the public schools   At the age of fourteen he began learning the machinist's trade, at which he worked for the Chicago, Rock Island & Pacific Railroad Company for a number of years, and has for the past fourteen years run a locomotive on that line.

On the 22nd of February, 1872, Mr Thompson led to the marriage altar Miss Mary Jane Johnston, a daughter of William and Mary Johnston, and to them have been born five children, as follows   Matilda Frances, William Alexander, David C , John David, and one who died in infancy   Mr. and Mrs Thompson are connected with the First Baptist church of Rock Island, and have many warm friends and acquaintances throughout the city. Fraternally he affiliates with the Ancient Order of United Workmen and the Brotherhood of Locomotive Engineers, and politically is identified with the Democratic party On first coming to Rock Island the property which he now occupies was just as the Indians had left it, and in its vicinity no streets had yet been laid out He has watched with interest the growth and development of the city and has done all within his power to advance its interests

JACOB STOFFT, who has for fourteen years been a faithful and trusted employe of Deere & Company, of Moline, is a native of Illinois, born in Chicago, February 7, 1854, and a son of George M Stofft, whose birth occurred September 12, 1820, in Germany, where he grew to manhood On coming to America in 1848, he located in New York City, where he married Anna Marie Metzger, also a native of the Fatherland There he continued to work at the cabinet maker's trade for some years, but in 1853 removed to Chicago, where he continued to work at his trade for a few years, then went to Naperville, Illinois, to take charge of a furniture store for other parties There he continued to reside until 1869, when he removed to Galesburg and was in the employ of the Chicago, Burlington & Quincy Railroad Company, manufacturing passenger coaches, until 1891, since which time he has lived retired

Our subject is the third in order of birth in the family of four sons, all of whom reached years of maturity, and the others are as follows· Charles, a passenger conductor on the Chicago, Burlington & Quincy Railroad, residing in Burlington, and running to Quincy, George M , of Chicago, who is a locomotive engineer on the Wisconsin Central Railroad; and William, a jeweler and engraver residing in Galesburg

Jacob Stofft acquired his education in the public schools of Naperville and Galesburg, and in the latter city learned the machinist's trade, serving a three years apprenticeship in the same shop where he continued to work for five years more On the 3d of May, 1879, he came to Moline and secured a position with Barnard & Leas Company, but three months later began working for William White & Company, with whom he remained for three years, having charge of the night force for one winter He entered the employ of Deere & Company June 26, 1883, and is still one of their valued assistants although he is interested in other enterprises. On the 1st of April, 1893, as a member of the firm of Stofft & Company, he embarked in the sprinkling business by putting three wagons on the road, and has since bought the interests of his partners and is now doing a successful and fairly remunerative business

In Davenport, Iowa, Mr. Stofft was married May 16, 1878, the lady of his choice being Miss Catherine G Watson, who was born, reared and educated in that city, and is a daughter of F W Watson, who for years conducted a hotel there Three children graced this union—W. W , who is now driving one of the sprinkling wagons, F R and Rose E M , who are both attending school The wife and mother is a consistent member of the Second Congregational church, and while not a member of any religious denomination, Mr Stofft attends the same church, to which he contributes liberally, and is inclined to its teachings

Mr Stofft possesses considerable musical talent, and was for a number of years a member of the Waste Opera Band of Galesburg, with which he became connected in 1876. This was a stock company, of which he was president, and they played at various places in this section of the state, at one time forming a concert troupe, which gave entertainments in a number of towns Since coming to Moline, Mr Stofft helped to organize the Deere Cornet Band, which for many years played at many state fairs throughout the country, including those held at St Paul, Minneapolis, Des Moines and even as far as Dallas, Texas, and won a number of premiums Our subject served as business manager, but the company was disbanded a few years ago

In his political views Mr Stofft has always been a Republican, casting his first presidential ballot for Rutherford B Hayes, but he has never aspired to office Socially, he is a member of St George Lodge, No 28, K P , in which he has passed all the chairs and is past chancellor, and also served as district deputy for one year He affiliates with the Modern Woodmen Camp, No 38, and was formerly a member of the Ancient Order of United Workman, filling all the chairs in the local lodge of that order For several years he also served in the volunteer fire department of Moline Wherever known he is held in the highest esteem and since coming to Moline has made a host of warm friends who fully appreciate his sterling worth

---

SWAN OLSON Like many other residents within the bounds of Rock Island county who started out in life with naught but an almost utter of determination and in-defatigable industry, and who have succeeded through their own diligence, energy and economy, we classify the gentleman whose name stands at the head of this sketch Since 1869 he has been a resident of Moline, and for the past nine years has successfully engaged in merchant tailoring on his own account, now doing business at 620 Fifteenth street

Mr Olson first opened his eyes to the light December 23, 1846, in Christianstadt, Sweden, where he grew to manhood and was provided with fair common-school advantages After serving a three years' apprenticeship to the tailor's trade, he worked as a journeyman for five years in his native land. Peter Hokanson, with whom he learned the trade, is now working in his, Mr Olson's, shop in Moline, having come to the New World in 1865

It was in 1869 that our subject crossed the Atlantic to join his father, Olof Swanson, in Moline, and here he worked at his trade, first on the board and then nine years as a cutter for J A Johnson At the end of that time, however, he purchased a stock of goods and began business on his own account in connection with his brother Olof Olson, but the partnership only lasted five years, the brother going to Oregon at that time His work being satisfactory and first class in every particular, Mr Olson has built up an extensive trade and is meeting with a well deserved success

On the 5th of January, 1872, in Moline, Mr Olson led to the marriage altar Miss Betsy Johnson, also a native of Sweden, where she was reared and educated The children born to them are as follows Charles, who is now working with his father, Anna, at home Selma who is also in the shop with his father, Minnie, Livia, Swan and Agnes, all attending school, and three who died in infancy

Mr Olson gives his political support to the men and measures of the Republican party, but takes no active part in public affairs, his time being fully occupied by his business interests. He and his family are all active members of the Swedish Methodist Episcopal church, and for five years he has now served as superintendent of the Sunday school. He was former connected with the United Workman Lodge and is now a member of the Bankers' Life Insurance Company of Des Moines Both as a business man and citizen he stands high in the estimation of his fellowmen and has the respect of all who know him

---

JOHN F ROSENFIELD, a leading and representative business man of Rock Island, is a member of the well-known firm of Rosenfield Brothers, plumbers and gasfitters, whose shop is located at No 1609 Third avenue He is a native of the city, his birth occurring September 18, 1860, and is a son of Henry and Letitia (Haley) Rosenfield, natives of Prussia and Ireland, respectively The paternal grandfather, Joseph Rosenfield, was born in Westphalia, Prussia, was a carpenter by trade, and on coming to America located in Gettysburg, Pennsylvania, where he spent his remaining days, dying at the age of eighty-one In his family were two sons and one daughter John Haley, the maternal grandfather, came from the Emerald Isle to Davenport, Iowa, but later located in Rock Island, where his death occurred at the advanced age of ninety-two years

It was in 1845 that Henry Rosenfield, the father of our subject emigrated to America, and for a number of years he also lived in Gettysburg, but in 1855 took up his residence in Davenport, and four years later came to Rock Island, where he is still living, an honored and respected citizen of the community He and his estimable wife are both communicants of the Catholic church Eight children have been born to them—Henry, John, Sarah, Joseph, Thomas, Mary, Lottie and Albert

After attending the public schools of his native city for some time John Rosenfield took a course in the Davenport Business College, and began his business career as a saw filer and hammerer in a sawmill, where he was employed until 1892, when in partnership with his brother, Thomas, he established his present business Industrious, enterprising men, they have met with excellent success in this undertaking, their fair and honorable dealing gaining for them a liberal share of the public patronage and the confidence and esteem of all with whom they come in contact

In April, 1888, was celebrated the marriage of Mr Rosenfield and Miss Katie L Cass, a daughter of Patrick and Mary Cass, and they now have four attractive children—Grace, Gertrude, Harry and Charley In 1891 Mr Rosenfield erected his beautiful residence at 825 Twenty-fourth street, the culture and artistic taste of its occupants being reflected in its appointments, while a gracious hospitality adds a charm to its material comforts Our subject and his wife are both members of the Catholic church, while socially he affiliates with the Modern Woodmen of America, and politically is identified with the Democratic party He is deservedly popular with all classes of citizens, and has been elected supervisor from Rock Island As a business man he also stands in the front rank, is systematic and practical, and the work which the firm of Rosenfield Brothers turn out is first-class in every respect.

BENEDICT LAFLIN, now living a retired life in the village of Sears, has been a resident of Rock Island county for almost three score years, having located in Edgington township in 1840, the year of the great "hard cider campaign" in which Harrison and Tyler—"Tippecanoe and Tyler, too"—were the Whig candidates for president and vice-president. He comes of good old Scotch and Irish ancestry and has inherited many of the traits of each. His paternal grandfather was of Irish birth and his paternal grandmother of Scotch. They lived and died in Massachusetts at a ripe old age. The maternal grandfather also died in that state.

Parley Laflin, the father of our subject, was a native of Massachusetts, from which state he emigrated to Gennessee Valley, New York, where he engaged in the hotel business, and also run a saw and grist mill and a tub and pail factory. He first married Miss Esther Benedict, who died in 1835, leaving two children, Benedict and Charles. The latter died near Taylor Ridge, Rock Island county, June 9, 1888, at the age of sixty-eight years. For his second wife Parley Laflin married Mrs. Mary Harrington, widow of Asa Harrington, by whom he had four children, Catherine, George, Lewis and Joseph.

Parley Laflin came to Rock Island county in 1840, and located in Edgington township, where he purchased one hundred and sixty acres of wild land and at once commenced its development. For a time, however, he lost his cattle which he drove to the Chicago markets, this being before the advent of railroads. He then engaged in general farming, which he followed until his death in May, 1850, at the age of about fifty-eight years. Religiously, he was a Universalist.

Benedict Laflin was born in Massachusetts, February 9, 1825, and there spent a portion of his boyhood, going from thence to New York, and later to Ohio. In 1840, when but fifteen years of age, in company with his brother Charles, he came to Rock Island county and they subsequently located on farms near their father. His first purchase was of eighty acres on which he erected a dwelling and there lived until his removal to Sears in March, 1895.

The educational advantages of our subject were meager, indeed, his first school days being spent in Chautauqua county, New York, where he attended the common schools for a time. In Ohio he had about the same privileges. But his life was one of toil. The hoe and the ax were implements the use of which he was early made acquainted. On coming to Illinois they followed the Indian trails for many miles, wagon roads not having been located. They waded swamps and for some years constructed their own roads. Farms had to be developed, houses erected, orchards planted, and all this required work, hard work.

Realizing "that it was not good for man to live alone," Mr. Laflin was united in marriage, October 24, 1848, with Miss Eliza Ann Phares, daughter of Thomas F. and Martha (Douglass) Phares, the former a native of New Jersey, of Scotch ancestry, born in 1802, and the latter of Pennsylvania, of Irish parentage, born in 1805. In their family were six children—William W., Eliza A., Thomas, Martha R., Susan and

Mary M   They came to Illinois in 1839, locating in Mercer county, where the mother died August 17, 1845, at the age of forty years.   Mr Phares again married, his second union being with Mrs Elizabeth Mc-Duff   By this union were six children· Ruth Applegate, Catherine Beath, Charles, Albert, Carl, Ellen, and two who died in infancy   Thomas F Phares died at Atlantic, Iowa, January 25, 1890, when almost eighty-eight years old   The paternal grandmother of Mrs Laflin was named Stewart, and is supposed to be of English descent   She had a brother who was a very rich merchant in the West Indies   Her grandfather Douglass was in the war of 1812

To Mr and Mrs Laflin four children have been born· Thomas P married Emma A   Cropper and they have five children, Charles E married Jessie Bopes and they have one daughter, Edna, Clarence died at the age of two years, Frank, the youngest, lives with his parents

Since the organization of the party Mr Laflin has been a thorough and consistent Republican   A firm believer in the doctrine of protection, with a royal good will he cast his vote for its great exponent in 1896, William McKinley   Other and more aspiring persons might fill the offices, while he would be content to exercise the privilege of casting his ballot for the party of his choice, and when that was done he would feel content.   As a citizen he was ever ready to aid in all measures that would advance the interests of his adopted county and State, so far as lay within his power   As a friend and neighbor, there were none better   His home was ever open to all   His good wife has been to him a help-meet indeed   Quick of mind, active in body, she seconded him in all his efforts for their mutual welfare,

and to-day as they journey pleasantly together along the pathway of life, and near its end, they can feel their life has not been in vain, that while never making a great stir in this busy world they have done what they could

---

CHARLES H PERRIN, one of the active and enterprising business men of Moline, holds the responsible position of purchasing agent for the Moline Plow Company, and makes his home in that city at No 528 Twentieth street   On the 16th of March, 1845, he was born in Webster, Worcester county, Massachusetts, a son of H A and Augusta (Freeman) Perrin, also natives of the Bay state   The father, who was born in the village of Holland in 1813, was a merchant and baker by occupation, carrying on a wholesale business in Webster for a number of years   In 1855, with his family, he came to Henry county, Illinois, locating near Geneseo, where he had his first experience in agricultural pursuits   He opened up and developed a valuable farm, which he cultivated for a number of years and then removed to Wyanet, Bureau county, where he spent his last years in retirement, dying there July 14, 1896, at the advanced age of eighty-three   The death of his wife occurred in 1872, and they now sleep side by side in Oakwood cemetery at Geneseo, where a neat and substantial monument marks their last resting place   In their family were three children, who are all married and heads of families   Ambrose D is a business man of Wyanet, Illinois, and Myra E is the wife of William Arnold, of Rock Island

Charles H Perrin, who completes the family, accompanied his parents on their removal to Illinois and was reared in Henry county, where he assisted in improving and cultivating the home farm, remaining under the parental roof until he had attained his majority He was provided with excellent educational advantages, being for some time a student in the Geneseo Academy, and in early life successfully engaged in teaching during the winter season, while through the summer months he assisted in the work of the farm As a clerk in a store in Geneseo, he received a thorough and practical business training, and on coming to Moline March 14, 1875, he secured a position in the shops of Deere & Company A few weeks later he was prevailed upon to accept a position in the office as assistant buyer and three years later was made purchasing agent for that extensive manufacturing enterprise, which responsible position he acceptably filled for eighteen years In 1893 he accepted a like position with the Moline Plow Company, where he has since remained

In Geneseo, March 16, 1869, was celebrated the marriage of Mr. Perrin and Miss Z Augusta Baxter, who was born in Sharon, Whiteside county, Illinois, but was reared in Geneseo Her father, Captain John Baxter, for many years sailed the high seas, and later became a pioneer settler of Illinois Mr and Mrs Perrin have three children—Ida B , now the wife of Charles J Dunn, a business man of Moline, and Charles H and Andrew Crawford, who are both students in the Moline schools

Mr Perrin is a stanch Republican, following in the political foot-steps of his father, who was originally an old-line Whig Our subject has taken quite an active part in local affairs, has been a delegate to numerous conventions of his party, has served on seve al impe ii ant con mitt rs, and h is

been the efficient alderman from his ward for the past six years He is a director in the Moline Building & Loan Association and is a man of superior business ability, whose success in life is due entirely to his own well directed efforts Although not members of any religious denomination, he and his wife attend the Congregational church and contribute to its support In manner Mr Perrin is social and genial He is the center of a circle of friends who honor and esteem him for his many manly virtues and genuine worth

AUGUSTANA COLLEGE and THEO-LOGICAL SEMINARY is one of the leading institutions of learning of the Lutheran denomination in America Its history embraces a story of zeal, sacrifice and untiring devotion that is always inspiring and in many instances both beautiful and pathetic It was not until about 1845 that the Scandinavian countries sent many of their children to the United States, but about that time there came from the peninsula many representatives who located in Illinois, Iowa, Wisconsin and Minnesota They were a religious people, mainly identified with the Lutheran church, and congregations were soon formed among them for worship after their particular belief. At the organization of the Evangelical Lutheran synod of northern Illinois in 1851 there were several Scandinavian pastors present and by 1860 their number had so increased that they constituted about one half of the synod This organization, together with other Lutheran bodies in the west, established a school known as the Illinois State University at Springfield for the speci d purpose of educating Lutheran

AUGUSTANA COLLEGE AND THEOLOGICAL SEMINARY.

ministers   At the meeting of the synod in 1855 a Scandinavian professorship was established and to this chair Rev L P Esbjorn was elected, but in 1860 he resigned, owing to some differences between the Scandinavian and American members concerning the doctrinal basis   This led to the withdrawal of the Scandinavians from the synod and the establishment of a theological seminary of their own.   This act gave birth to Augustana College and Theological Seminary, which was temporarily located in Chicago, but removed to Paxton, Illinois, in 1863, and to Rock Island, in 1875   It had both a preparatory and theological department, but the courses of study were not definitely arranged for some time   The institution was incorporated under the general laws of Illinois in 1863 as Augustana College and Seminary, and in 1865 was granted a charter by the legislature, which was amended by a supplementary act in 1869, since which time the institution has been known by its present name

The courses of instruction in the theological seminary were gradually made to embrace three years, and in 1890 the university plan was adopted and the instruction was arranged in distinct and independent courses, at first fourteen in number, and in 1892 increased to eighteen   The college proper now includes ten departments, namely   Swedish, English and Philosophy, Latin, Greek, Modern Languages, Christianity, History and Political Science, Biology and Geology, Physics and Chemistry, and Mathematics and Astronomy

The college has entered upon an era of prosperity and is an excellently equipped institution, its various departments being under the care of most able and skilled educators   Its general faculty consist of two,

O Olsson, D D , Ph D , president; A W Williamson, Ph D , secretary, and all the permanent professors of the special faculties   Of the theological faculty Dr Olsson has charge of catechetics, homiletics, pastoral theology and Hebrew, Nils Forsander, D D , of church history, symbolics, isagogics and Greek, and Conrad E Lindberg, D. D , of dogmatics, liturgics, church polity, Greek and Hebrew   The church faculty, with Dr Olsson as president, consists of Dr C O Granere, professor of Latin and literature, A O Bersell, Ph D , professor of Greek and literature, A W Williamson, Ph. D , professor of mathematics and astronomy, C W Foss, A M , professor of history and political science, C L Esbjorn, A M , modern languages, E F Bartholomew, D D , English literature and philosophy, J A Udden, A M , natural history and geology, V O Peterson, A M., physics and chemistry, P M Lindberg, A M . Christianity, E A Zetterstrand, Swedish language and literature   The conservatory of music has the following faculty   A D Bodfors, B M , organ, piano, harmony and director of chorus, Alma Larson, B M., piano, C F Toennigss, string and wind instruments, and leader of orchestra, Mrs. Edla Lund, voice, piano and organ   The professors in the business college are J. Edwin Gustus, M Accts , who has charge of bookkeeping, business practice, commercial law and penmanship, J A Bexell, B S , bookkeeping, arithmetic and civics, and Mrs Edith Wilkins-Gustus, stenography and type-writing   The art school is under the direction of Miss Mae Munro, and the physical culture department under E A Edlen, M D   Augustana college has a most beautiful location

The body, its one of twenty-six acres of land in Rock Island, a fine gymnasium and two college buildings, which are filled up most completely with every facility for advancing educational interests In addition to these buildings, there are two frame dwelling houses on 35th street and a double brick building on 38th street, the western half of which is occupied by the president and the eastern half is used as a Ladies' Hall   The present excellent condition of the college is the outcome of the earnest, patient and devoted labor of representatives of the Swedish Lutheran Church It is an educational institution, of which the denomination may well be proud, its faculty consists of cultured men and women, well fitted for their especial duties, and the institution is a credit not only to its founders and to those who are now active in promoting its work, but also to the city of Rock Island

COLONEL EDWARD KITTILSEN, who resides at No 1301 Fifteen and a half street, Moline, has spent his entire life in that city, his birth occurring there July 19, 1854. His father, Andrew Kittilsen, a native of Norway, on coming to the new world when a young man located in Moline, where he married Frederica Johnson, a lady of Swedish birth   By trade he was a cooper

After attending the public schools of Moline for some time, the Colonel completed his education by a course in Frey's Commercial College, of Rock Island   After laying aside his text books he clerked in a grocery store for a while and later learned the moulder's trade, but at the age of twenty embarked in the ice business in which he was successfully engaged

until the spring of 1880, when the high waters of the Mississippi ruined his ice and ice-house, causing a heavy loss.   Previously he had formed a partnership in the dry goods and grocery business but became dissatisfied and sold his interest.   In 1880 he entered the police force, two years later was made deputy marshal, and in 1883 was promoted from deputy marshal to chief of police, which position he has now acceptably filled for fourteen years   By virtue of his office he is also chief of the health department

Joining the state militia in 1875, Mr Kittilsen was elected corporal, later was advanced to sergeant, and subsequently major sergeant of the Fourteenth Battalion, and after its consolidation with the Sixth Regiment continued to hold that rank   While the battalion was at East St Louis during the strike of 1876, he was advanced to major on the field, and in 1893 was commissioned lieutenant-colonel of the Sixth Regiment, which rank he still holds

On the 17th of September, 1884, in Moline, was celebrated the marriage of Colonel Kittilsen and Miss Carilla Stewart, who was born March 4, 1859, in Hamilton, Canada, where she was reared and educated   Her parents are James and Mary (Graham) Stewart   The Colonel and Mrs Kittilsen have four children—Myrtle L , Arthur E and William W , all attending the public schools, and John Andrew, at home   With the family reside the Colonel's father and mother, now aged respectively eighty and seventysix years

Politically our subject is a stanch Republican, and socially is a member of Moline Lodge, No. 153, I O O F , the Knights of Pythias fraternity the Modern Woodmen of America and the Select Knights of

America, while his wife holds membership in the Baptist church at Moline He is one of the most public-spirited and progressive men of the city, has been prominently identified with its growth and prosperity, and is recognized as one of the representative and leading citizens He is deservedly popular in both military and civic circles and as a public official has won the commendation of the entire community

HON JOHN MORRIS, deceased.—No state in the union can boast of a more heroic band of pioneers than Illinois In their intelligence, capability and genius they were far above the pioneers of the eastern states and in their daring and heroism they were equal to the Missouri and California argonauts Their earnest labors have resulted in establishing one of the foremost commonwealths in America, the possibilities of which are far greater than those possessed by any of her sister states, and though they are fast passing away their memory will forever remain green among those who loved them and appreciated their efforts

The name of John Morris was closely associated with the growth and material development of Rock Island county and in all the relations of life he commanded the respect and confidence of those with whom he was brought in contact. He was born in Fayette, Madison county, Ohio, on the 6th of May, 1823, a son of William and Sarah (Allen) Morris, the former a native of the Buckeye state, the latter of Pennsylvania They had a family of nine children, but only one is now living, William M, who makes his home in Asheville, North Carolina The father was a farmer and cattle dealer and removed from Ohio to Illinois

in 1853, taking up his residence in Buffalo Prairie township, Rock Island county, where he purchased four hundred acres of land He continued the cultivation of that farm for many years, but spent his last days in Andalusia, where he died in 1876, at the age of seventy-three years His wife passed away in 1881, and was buried on the seventy-seventh anniversary of her birth

On his father's farm in Madison county, Ohio, John Morris spent the days of his youth, and in the public schools of the neighborhood acquired a good practical English education. He remained at home until he had attained his majority and then began buying and selling cattle on his own account He followed that business in the state of his nativity until 1848 when he came to Rock Island, here continuing the same pursuit until 1850, when he also took up farming. In 1852 he removed to his farm about ten miles south of the city and soon placed his land under a high state of cultivation, the rich and fertile fields yielding to him a good return for the labor he bestowed upon them In his pastures were found good grades of stock which he raised for the market and his business interests were conducted with an energy and wisdom that brought to him a high degree of success

On the 29th of April, 1850, Mr Morris was united in marriage to Miss Abby L. Gardner, a daughter of John V and Sarah (Spear) Gardner, of Ohio They had no children of their own, but their generosity and kindness prompted them to take into their home and heart two little girls, namely· Lizzie Catharine Eckhardt, now the wife of Robert Crampton, and Maud Morris Montgomery, a niece of Mr Morris Mrs Morris was descended from an old and honored family of Massachusetts Her grandfather, Richard Gardner, was born in the Bay state, but his parents were natives of Ireland By occupation he was a farmer The maternal grandfather was also a native of Massachusetts, and his parents were born in Scotland Both John V and Sarah (Spear) Gardner were born in Massachusetts The former was a farmer and merchant in early life, but in his later years his time was mostly given to the discharge of some official duty for which he was chosen by his fellow citizens For many years he was justice of the peace and his fidelity to duty in that office was most marked His family numbered four sons and five daughters, four of whom are now living, namely Reuben F , Abby L , Caroline A , wife of Orman C Holden; and Sarah Felicia, wife of Urial G Nourse Mr Gardner died April 6, 1879, at the age of ninety years and eight months His wife was called to the home beyond February 19, 1838, at the age of forty-three years. They were members of the Disciples church at the time of her death, but Mr Gardner afterward became a member of the Universalist church He was married a second time, the lady of his choice being Margaret Beatty, by whom he had three children, two now living—George D , and Estella F , wife of A M Chase

Mrs Morris came to Illinois with her sister, Mrs Julia A E Price, wife of Nathan Price, and located in Knox county in 1846 She was married in Galesburg, April 29, 1850 From that time she has made her home in Rock Island county   Mr Morris continued his farming operations until August, 1862, when he put aside the pursuits of civil life to enter his country's service, enlisting as a member of Company I the Illinois

captain   He served for three years and his meritorious conduct on the field of battle won him promotion to the rank of major He ever loyally followed the old flag, and in August, 1865, after the close of the war, was honorably discharged   He never received a furlough during the entire time, but after he had been at the front for eighteen months Mrs Morris visited him at Duvall's Bluff, Arkansas

Mr Morris always took a deep and commendable interest in the affairs that tended to promote the welfare of his county and his fellow citizens appreciating his worth and ability frequently called him to public office, where he served with the same fidelity that marked his course on southern battle fields, when he defended the nation's starry banner For a number of years he filled the office of supervisor, and in 1871 2 represented his district in the Illinois General Assembly In early life he was a member of the Odd Fellows Society, but afterward ceased to attend its meetings In his later years he belonged to the Presbyterian church, of which his wife also became a member He died December 8, 1874, at the age of fifty-one years, and his death was deeply mourned by many friends He lived a quiet and unassuming life, but his fidelity to all that was honorable, his faithful fulfillment of every trust reposed in him and his earnest efforts to promote the best welfare of his adopted county made him a valued citizen and won him the high regard of all with whom he was brought in contact

Mrs Morris still survives her husband In 1876 she removed to the city of Rock Island, and erected a comfortable residence at No 1018 Second avenue. She is a well preserved lady a very pleasant and cordial hospitality and is a fine conversationalist

She is widely known among the most prominent people of the county and the circle of her friends is very extensive She is well informed on all matters of general interest and her memory of early days and times is remarkable

JOHN SIEGRIST, who has been actively engaged in the ice business in Rock Island for many years, is one of the honored native sons of the city, and his life is a verification of the fact that the inevitable law of destiny accords a tireless energy, industry and ability a successful career A community depends upon commercial activity, its welfare is due to this, and the promoters of legitimate and extensive business enterprises may well be termed its benefactors Prominent in the business circles of his native city stands Mr Siegrist He was born October 14, 1843, a son of John and Ann (McBratney) Siegrist, the former a native of Alsace, France, and the latter of Belfast, Ireland They had a family of four children, two of whom are now living—Philip and John The father was a teamster and came to America about 1832 He located in Warren, Pennsylvania, and by way of the lakes came to Illinois in 1834 Here he was employed on the construction of the old branch of the Illinois and Michigan canal, working on the lower lock He afterward returned to Chicago and engaged in hauling water from the lake, thus supplying the Tremont house He afterward returned to Warren, Pennsylvania, where he remained for about five years, during which time he married Miss McBratney, who had come to America in 1829, landing at New York, whence she removed to Philadelphia and thence to Pittsburg Her father McVaughet

McBratney, was a farmer and died in Ireland at an advanced age

In the spring of 1841 John Siegrist, Sr , came to Rock Island, by way of the Alleghany, Ohio and Mississippi rivers and began teaming with oxen He hauled lumber for the Rock river bridges and did general heavy hauling He helped haul the first locomotive across the Mississippi river on the ice, at the foot of Twentieth street His death occurred in September, 1877, at the age of sixty-seven years, and his wife passed away on the 1st of August, 1890, when nearly eighty-six years of age She was a member of the United Presbyterian church Mr Siegrist was a soldier of the Civil war in the one-hundred-days service For ten or fifteen years prior to his death his energies were devoted to the grain trade His father, Philip Siegrist, owned a farm near Warren, Pennsylvania, and died there at the age of eighty-four years

Reared in Rock Island, John Siegrist has witnessed almost the entire growth of the city and has borne his part in the work of advancement and progress He attended the first public school in the city, and was one of the first Sunday-school scholars in the United Presbyterian church When his literary training was ended he entered upon his business career as a hand in a saw mill, and learned that business in connection with filing, following the dual occupation until 1877, when he abandoned it in order to engage in the ice business For fifteen years his brother was in partnership with him, but he is now alone He has a large trade and the excellent quality of the ice which he puts up, his fair and honest dealing and his earnest desire to please his customers insures him a continuance of this liberal patronage He is now directed

labors, his earnest purpose and his unflagging industry have brought to him success, and he is now one of the substantial citizens of Rock Island. On the 25th of November, 1885, Mr Siegrist was united in marriage to Miss Ella De Voe, a daughter of Anthony and Corinda (Shipman) De Voe, of New York Her father followed the moulder's trade in the Empire state for many years, but in 1879 came to Rock Island, where he and his wife have since made their home His father was William De Voe, a native of Holland, and a farmer by occupation. His family numbered eleven children The maternal grandfather of Mrs Siegrist was David Shipman, a native of New York, in which state he spent his entire life, dying at an advanced age To Mr and Mrs Siegrist have been born two sons, Harry and George Socially, our subject is a Knight Templar Mason, belonging to Everts Commandery, No 18 K T In his political views he is a Democrat, but the honors or emoluments of office have never had for him a greater attraction than his business interests His life history exhibits a long and virtuous career of private industry, performed with moderation and crowned with success

— — —

COLONEL DAVID O REID, of Moline, has been a resident of Rock Island county for forty-one years

A native of Pennsylvania, Mr Reid was born in the city of Harrisburg, June 1, 1834 His father, Robert Finley Reid, was a native of Ireland, and when a young man left the Emerald Isle for the new world, taking up his residence in Harrisburg, where he was united in m̄·iii⁻: ·⁻ M̄·⁻ S ⁍ O ꞌꞌ native of P̄·ı·⁻ ·⁻ ꞌ·ıı꜒ 1 ꞌꞌ·,·꜒ ꜒ ıı꜒ꜜ [꜒ı

father, David Ogle, was born in the Keystone state, and came of a family of Welsh origin that was founded in Delaware in the seventeenth century by two brothers who came from Wales to the colonies Mr Reid was a boot and shoemaker by trade and for some time followed that pursuit in Harrisburg He afterward removed to Indianapolis, Indiana, and there spent the last years of his life, dying in 1843 His attention was there given to the boot and shoe business and was one of the pioneer merchants of that city. After the death of her husband Mrs Reid returned to Harrisburg where she reared her family She died about 1854, leaving four sons and a daughter Jane married Jacob M Barr, of Harrisburg, but is now a widow and resides in Cheboygan, Michigan David O is the second of the family John is now living a retired life in Chicago James enlisted in the Fifty-fifth Pennsylvania Infantry, was captured at Richmond, and died in Andersonville prison Robert, who completes the family, is now living in Oklahoma

Colonel Reid, of this review, obtained his education in Harrisburg, and learned the tinsmith's trade, at which he served a four years' apprenticeship and then worked as a journeyman In 1856 he made his way westward to the Mississippi Valley and took up his residence in Rock Island, where he entered into partnership in the hardware business as a member of the firm of Swiler & Reid, which partnership was dissolved through Mr Reid's enlistment

In June, 1861, he donned the blue as a member of Company H, Forty-fifth Illinois Infantry, and went to the front, where he remained until the close of the war He re-·ıı⁰·ˢ⁻ 1 ·⁻ ·1·ı ıı ıı꜒1 ꞏꞏ ⁻ ꞏıomoted to ꞏꞏ꜒ı ·ıı⁰ ˢ⁻ ꞏꞏꞏ ıı W·ꞏꞏ̄ ꞏꞏˢ⁻ ⁻egıment he participated in all the engagements of the Army of the Tennessee from the attack on Fort Henry, to the surrender of Johnston at Raleigh, North Carolina, with the exception of the siege of Vicksburg At the battle of Raymond, Mississippi, he was shot in the right leg just above the knee and was captured, but was soon afterward paroled His wound, however, disabled him for duty for several months After being exchanged he rejoined his command, with which he continued until the close of the war, when he was mustered out at Louisville, Kentucky, in June, 1865 His military record is an honorable one.

Returning to Rock Island, Mr Reid worked at his trade until 1868, when he was appointed city clerk, filling that position through the following year He then removed to Moline, and forming the partnership of Spencer & Reid has since been actively engaged in business on his own account

In February, 1861, in Rock Island, was celebrated the marriage of the Colonel and Miss Amanda Louis Webster, a native of Beaver county, Pennsylvania, and a daughter of John B Webster, a pioneer merchant of Rock Island, who located in that city in 1853 They have seven children living—Caroline, wife of Fabian Lawson, of Moline, Sarah, wife of George E Evans, of White Bear, Minnesota, Robert F , a mechanic, at home, Frances, a member of the class of 1898 in the Moline high school, William M , also a student in the high school, and Arthur Webster, who is pursuing his studies in Moline. Mrs Reid is a member of the Methodist Episcopal church, and the Colonel is a Unitarian in belief

In ante bellum days he was an opponent of slavery, and when the Republican party

was formed to prevent its further extension he joined its ranks and has since been one of its advocates He is also a believer in free silver In 1869 he was elected county treasurer and by re-election served in that office for four years He has served as delegate to numerous county conventions and for eight years served on the governor's staff with the rank of colonel In 1858 he took the initiatory degree of Entered Apprentice in Rock Island Lodge, F & A M , was afterward raised to the sublime degree of a Master Mason, and for three terms served as worshipful master of Doric Lodge of Moline He belongs to the Grand Army of the Republic, in which he has served for two terms as commander, and is a prominent worker in the Ancient Order of United Workmen, taking a very active part in its advancement and for several years serving as chairman of the finance committee of the state In society, business and military circles he has ever won the highest esteem by his devotion to duty and sterling worth, and Colonel Reid is numbered among the most prominent citizens of Moline

---

HERMAN C W SCHUBERT —It is astonishing to witness the success of young men who have emigrated to America without capital and from a position of comparative obscurity worked their way upward to a position of prominence The readiness with which they adapt themselves to circumstances and take advantage of opportunities offered brings to them success and wins them a place among the leading business men of the communities in which they reside Prominent among this class is Mr Schubert f Rock Island the well-known manager of the Variety Wood Works

He was born in Armenruh, Germany, May 5, 1860, a son of Johann Gottlieb and Johanna (Schroether) Schubert, who spent their entire lives in the Fatherland, as did also the grandparents of our subject The father died in 1881, at the age of seventy-two, and the mother in 1873, at the age of sixty The former served some time as a soldier in the regular army They were members of the Protestant Evangelical church, and were the parents of four children, three of whom still survive—Caroline, wife of William Breiter, of South Rock Island, Henrietta, wife of Herman Maiwald, of Rock Island, and Herman C W

The common schools of his native land afforded our subject his educational privileges, and at the age of fourteen he began learning the cabinet maker's trade, which he has made his life work In 1884 he bade adieu to friends and home and sailed for America, taking up his residence in Rock Island, Illinois, where for seven years he worked for the Rock Island Lumber & Manufacturing Company, being foreman of the carpenter department three years, and general superintendent of the factory during the last year He then started in business for himself, conducting a cabinet shop for about a year, and at the end of that time aided in establishing the Variety Wood Works, of which he became one of the stockholders, and has since been general manager The firm does all kinds of interior hard wood finishing and also manufactures store and office fixtures, employing from eighteen to twenty hands They put in the hard wood finishings in the elegant new · · · h · · · u l t l u Rock Isl u l · · l u l th post

office and other fine buildings in the same city Their work is first-class in every particular and gives the utmost satisfaction

Mr Schubert was married July 25, 1888, to Miss Augusta Hoffman, a daughter of Johann and Wilhelmina (Hoffman) Hoffman, and to them have been born four children—Paul, Annette, Martha and Henry They have a pleasant home at 916 Seventh avenue, Rock Island, where hospitality always reigns supreme In politics Mr Schubert is independent, and in his social relations is a member of the Modern Woodmen of America He deserves great credit for the remarkable success he has achieved in the business world, and well merits the confidence and esteem which is so freely accorded him by all with whom he comes in contact

---

LE RAY HOSKINS, who is now living retired in the village of Stewartsville, was for many years actively identified with the agricultural interests of Rock Island county The common-place duties of life, trivial though they may seem to the casual observer, demand for their proper fulfillment the same admirable qualities of character which in a higher degree and under other circumstances attract universal notice and approbation However it may seem to the superficial mind, our rural communities furnish an excellent field for the development of the traits which go to making of good citizens and one purpose of this work is the preservation of records which show the innate worth and dignity of such a life

The birth of Mr Hoskins occurred November 14, 1828, near the city of Boston, M · · l· tt f whi h ·t t· his parents, W· ·ht and P·ttn ·Dim·ck H·skins, were also natives Both grandfathers were soldiers in the Continental army during the Revolutionary war, contributing their share in the efforts of the Colonies to throw off the yoke of British oppression In 1831 the parents of our subject removed to Delaware county, New York, which was then an almost unbroken wilderness and there the father cleared and developed a fine farm of two hundred acres, becoming one of the prosperous and most highly respected agriculturists of his community He died there March 1, 1861, at the ripe old age of seventy-two years, and his wife passed away March 16, 1863, both being interred in the home cemetery Our subject is the youngest and only survivor in their family of seven children, four sons and three daughters, of whom three died in early life

Mr Hoskins, of this review, obtained a very limited education in the public schools of Delaware county, New York, as his time was principally occupied in assisting his father in the arduous task of clearing and cultivating a new farm Remaining under the parental roof, he cared for his parents during their declining years, and at his death succeeded to the old homestead, which was a valuable place under a high state of cultivation and improved with excellent buildings. He paid off the last of the indebtedness and there continued to reside until his emigration to Illinois

On the 10th of May, 1851, Mr Hoskins was united in marriage to Miss Elizabeth Beach, a native of Delaware county, and a daughter of Jeremiah and Julia (Barnes) Beach In 1865 he sold his old home farm and came to Rock Island county, where he purchased two hundred and forty acres of bottom lands on Rock river His first home was a small residence which he occupied

while opening up his farm, but this was later replaced by a large substantial dwelling Good barns and other outbuildings were also erected and the place was converted into one of the most desirable farms of Moline township From time to time he added to the original purchase until he is now the owner of nearly four hundred acres of rich and arable land, where in connection with general farming he engaged in dairying for a number of years Meeting with excellent success in his undertaking he is now enabled to lay aside all business cares and is enjoying a well earned rest at his pleasant home in Stewartsville, where he located in the fall of 1893

Mr Hoskins lost his first wife, who died in Rock Island county, October 2, 1866, leaving three children—Gelany, now the wife of Alvin Harrold, a carpenter and joiner of Moline, Gero, who is married and has five children, and is now engaged in farming and dairying upon the old home farm in Moline township, and Delinda, wife of Charles Darling, also a farmer of Moline township, who makes a specialty of dairying and the raising of small fruits Returning to New York, Mr Hoskins was again married, September 1, 1869, to Mrs Lucy A Paul, a cousin of his former wife She was born, reared and educated in Delaware county, where her father, Luman Beach, made his home, and in early life she engaged in teaching In 1858 she gave her hand in marriage to Mr Paul, of Delaware county, who died in 1861 Her early home adjoined that upon which our subject was reared Two children were born to them, but Walter L died at the age of two years Jennie A is now the wife of George Kingsbury, of Rock Island

Mr H . . . . e Moline

Baptist church, and while not a member of any religious denomination, our subject attends that church and contributes to its support Since its organization he has been identified with the Republican party, but has never cared for the honors or emoluments of public office, preferring to devote his entire time and attention to his family and his business interests In many respects his life is well worthy of emulation He is strictly temperate, never using tobacco or intoxicating drinks in any form In those finer traits of character which combine to form that which we term friendship, which endear and attach man to man in bonds which nothing but the stain of dishonor can sever, which triumph and shine brightest in the hour of adversity, in those qualities he is royally endowed

WILLIAM ROTH —The study of biography, says Carlyle, is the most universally pleasant and profitable of all studies It yields in point of interest to no other, because it shows how success is achieved, how fame is won, and points out the way for others to follow A study of biography shows that certain effects produce certain results, that the majority of American citizens who have risen to a high position owe their success to unbounded energy, resolute purpose, untiring labor and keen discrimination Of this truth the life of Mr Roth is an exemplification, and to-day he stands prominently among the leading and wealthy citizens of Rock Island, the architect and builder of his own fortune

William Roth was born in Caton, St Gallen, Switzerland, December 25, 1852. His father Jacob Roth, grandson of Jacob Roth, Sr

Switzerland at an advanced age Jacob Roth, Jr , was married in that country to Regula Hilbertzhauser, also a native of the same land He followed farming and engaged in real estate dealing His death occurred in Switzerland in 1868 at the age of forty-five years, after which his widow came to the United States, and died in Rock Island in 1889, at the age of sixty-nine. They were members of the Presbyterian church Mr. Roth served as a soldier of his native land in 1847 Their family numbered thirteen children, of whom seven are now living—John H , of St Joseph, Missouri, William, Susanna, wife of Louis Ritzler, of Rock Island, Wilhelmina, wife of Jacob Mason, of New Boston, Illinois, Frederick, of St Joseph, Missouri, Eliza wife of Frank Fogel, of Rock Island, and George F , also of Rock Island

William Roth obtained his education in the common schools and remained in the land of his nativity until eighteen years of age, when he crossed the Atlantic to America He took up his residence in Rock Island in 1871 and entered the employ of Thomas Murdock, a contractor and builder Later he worked in the arsenal on the island, and next was employed by J & M Rosenfield In 1872 he accepted a position in the lumber yard of Weyerhauser & Denkman, with which firm he has since been connected Showing a disposition and willingness to work, and proving most faithful to every interest and trust committed to his care, he was promoted from one position to another, and for the past fifteen years has been a general salesman, having entire superintendence of both the Rock Island and Davenport yards

The efforts of Mr Roth have not been in his chosen to this enterprise He is a man of resourceful ability and has been the leading factor in various concerns which have not only added to his individual prosperity but have advanced the general welfare of the community He is now secretary and one of the largest stockholders in the Variety Wood Works Company, which manufactures all kinds of fancy wood work for interior trimmings and ornamentations for state rooms, mantels and other fine wood decorations This company did the inside wood work in the new post office and court house in Rock Island and received the contracts for the wood work in most of the fine residences in Rock Island They also did the finishing in the Munro house This company was organized in 1892 and is now one of the most important industrial concerns in the city In addition to his other interests Mr Roth has served as a director of the Black Hawk Building and Loan Association since its organization He is also dealing in real estate and has both valuable country and city property, including extensive acreage in Minnesota, also near South Rock Island and several fine lots in the city

Mr Roth was married on the 14th of March, 1882, to Miss Mary Wespe, and they have three children—Bertha Lilly May, George William and Walter Frederick Their home, located at No 908 Fourth avenue, is one of the beautiful residences of the city, a large modern brick, with handsome surroundings and tasteful interior decorations One of its most charming features, however, is the hospitality for which this home is noted, Mr and Mrs Roth occupying a prominent position in social circles He is a valued member of the Masonic fraternity, also the Grutth Verein, a mutual benefit and benevolent society formed among his countrymen. He has served as abbi-

man of the first ward for two years, but does not ally himself with any political party, viewing the issues of the day in the same broad and comprehensive way that marks his business career His life illustrates the possibilities open to young men and the success that is possible of accomplishment through meritorious, honorable and well directed effort

HON GEORGE W. VINTON —While the disposition to do honor to those who have served well their race or their nation is prevalent among all enlightened people and is of great value every where and under all forms of government, it should be particularly fostered in this country, where no man is born to public office or to public honor or comes to it by inheritance, but where all men are equal before the law, where the race for distinction is over the road of public usefulness and is opened to every one who chooses to enter, however humble or obscure he may be, and where the adventitious circumstances of family and wealth count, in the vast majority of cases, for little or nothing According to the true democratic doctrine they should never count for anything at all In honoring those who have served well the republic, the people do credit to themselves and thus also supply a powerful stimulus to honorable ambition for the public good Among the leading and influential citizens of Moline is numbered Mr Vinton, who has for many years been prominently identified with the public interests of this section

He was born under the shadows of the Green mountains in Middlebury, Vermont, December 5, 1834, and is a son of John A Vinton who was a prominent figure the war of 1812, and for his services received a land warrant, which our subject located in Minnesota At the age of fifteen he graduated at the Randolph Academy of his native state, being a classmate of Judge Adams, late supreme judge of Iowa, and before coming west engaged in teaching for six terms In 1855, he went to the territory of Minnesota, where he learned the carpenter's trade, but in the fall of the same year came to Moline and took the contract to build the Riverside Academy He then entered the employ of his uncle, John Deere, and remained with the firm until 1885, traveling from ocean to ocean in establishing agencies and general business For fifteen years he was also a stockholder and director and rendered valuable service in building up the business In 1875 he removed to Burlington, Iowa, where he erected the Buffington Wheel Company's works, and was interested in the business for some time While a resident of that city he served as alderman for four years, during which time the city hall was built, but in 1887 he returned to Moline

For a number of years, Mr Vinton was one of the leading Republicans of the state, and on that ticket was at one time the candidate for lieutenant governor, but when Horace Greeley ran for president he became identified with the Democratic party, with which he has since affiliated He assisted in incorporating the city of Moline, was for many years chairman of the old town board, and was also president of the school board, his successor being S W Wheelock For four years he was chairman of the county Democratic committee, and in 1892 was elected to the legislature by a majority of seven tl   l   i ', ,i ii   li , , u l always l   ,   ,   , ,   ,   l,   Durlin

his service in that body he was chairman of the committees on public charities, state institutions and militia, and introduced a bill for the establishment of an insane hospital west of the Illinois river, which has since been located in Rock Island county He also introduced the bill appropriating one million dollars to the World's Fair, nine hundred fifty thousand to be devoted to the general expenses and fifty thousand to the woman's building The state board of agriculture made him manager of the Illinois building during the exposition, and since his return home he has been appointed deputy collector of internal revenue for the Peoria district, which position he is still acceptably filling He is an ardent admirer of Grover Cleveland, and is a recognized leader in the local Democracy Fraternally he is connected with the Masonic Order and the Knights of Pythias His career has been such as to gain for him the confidence and esteem of all who know him.

CARL BERNHARDI, M D , has attained prestige as a representative member of the medical fraternity in Rock Island, and is now enjoying a large and lucrative practice He was born in the eastern part of Prussia, on the 10th of September, 1843, and spent the first sixteen years of his life in the land of his birth He obtained his education in the schools of Germany, completing his course in the Berlin University He then took up the study of medicine in Berlin, followed it in other places of the German empire, and for two years engaged in practice in that country

In 1869 Dr Bernhardi determined to   l   in the new world and came to America taking up his residence in St

Louis   Soon afterward, however, he removed to Rock Island, where he has engaged in the practice continuously since. He is a close student of his profession, and does all in his power to advance himself in his chosen calling   He has a broad and thorough understanding of the science of medicine and the best methods of applying it to the needs of the human system   He has a large general practice, and since the opening of the Rock Island Sanitarium in 1893, has been connected with that institution.   No physician who engages in practice there stands higher than he either professionally or socially   He is also medical examiner for a number of medical insurance companies, and both the profession and the public accord to him a foremost place in the medical fraternity

On the 10th of October, 1873, was celebrated the marriage of Dr Bernhardi and Miss Zoe Olshausen, a daughter of Dr J J Olshausen, then of Davenport, but formerly of St Louis, where Mrs Bernhardi was born   By her marriage she has four children, three daughters and a son   The Doctor is a public-spirited and progressive citizen who takes a deep interest in the welfare and progress of Rock Island   He was for many years a member of the school board and did much to advance the cause of education here   By his right of franchise he supports the Republican party   Socially he is a prominent Mason, belonging to the blue lodge, chapter and commandery

---

HENRY T MOSS, one of the most active and enterprising business men of Moline, has successfully engaged in the clothing trade here since 1887   He was born on the 17th of D   18   in

Louis, Missouri, and is a son of B H Moss, a native of Germany, born October 26, 1832   On crossing the Atlantic in 1845 the father located in St Louis, where he was united in marriage with Miss Catherine Otten, a German lady   In that city he engaged in the clothing business for a number of years, but in 1857 removed to Davenport, Iowa, becoming one of the first merchants of that place, which was then a small village   He first embarked in the grocery trade and merchant tailoring business, and subsequently engaged in the clothing trade   As the city grew and his trade proportionately increased, he enlarged his stock to meet the growing demand   He built up an immense trade and for many years was one of the leading and most successful business men of Davenport, where his death occurred October 23, 1895   Seven years previously his sons, Frank, George, John and Henry T , had become associated with him in business, and in 1887 they established a branch house in Moline, of which our subject took charge   The partnership continued until 1893 when Henry T bought out his brothers' interests and has since been sole owner and proprietor   He carries a large and complete stock of clothing, gents furnishing goods, etc , does an extensive business, and has established an enviable reputation for good goods and fair dealing

Mr Moss spent his boyhood and youth in Davenport, where he attended the parochial schools and later Bryant & Stratton Business College   During early life he also spent much time in his father's store, where he received a thorough, practical business training, and continued to remain in the Davenport establishment until coming to Moline, to take charge of the business   s united in marriage to Miss Kate Reagan, who was born, reared and educated in Davenport, and they now have a little daughter, Bessie, who is attending kindergarten

Mr Moss is identified with no political party, but casts his ballot independently, endeavoring to support the best man for the position   He cares nothing for the honors or emoluments of public office, preferring to give his exclusive time to his extensive business interests   Self-reliance, conscientiousness, energy, honesty—these are the traits of character that insure the great success, and to these may be attributed the success that has crowned the efforts of Mr Moss

HARRY P SIMPSON, the well-known city editor of the Argus, Rock Island, Illinois, is a native of Iowa, born in Davenport, July 6, 1863, and is a son of Joseph S and Eliza A (Purcell) Simpson, the former a native of Missouri, and the latter of South Carolina

The paternal grandfather of our subject, Dr Robert Simpson, was a pioneer physician in St Louis, Missouri, and was one of the first sheriffs of St Louis county The maternal grandfather, Edward Purcell, was a lawyer in South Carolina and Connecticut, and the son of a Revolutionary soldier

Joseph S Simpson, the father, moved to Buffalo, Iowa, in 1852, and there engaged in farming, but in 1858 changed his residence to Davenport, where he engaged in general merchandising for many years   He was reared a Catholic   His wife is a member of the Protestant Episcopal church His death occurred in 1885 at the age of seventy-one years   His widow still makes her home in Davenport

Harry P Simpson grew to manhood in his native city, and there received his education in the public and high schools While yet in the high school, he showed a decided taste for literary work, and served as reporter for the Saturday Afternoon People, a weekly society paper   His work on that sheet attracting the attention of the Davenport Gazette, after a six months engagement, he was offered a position on the reportorial staff of the Gazette, and represented that paper in Rock Island and Moline   A little later he was made city editor of the Gazette and served that paper two years   He then became city editor of the Davenport Herald, continuing with that paper until the spring of 1855 when he came to Rock Island, took the position of city editor of the Argus, daily and weekly, where he still remains

On the 20th of August, 1884, Mr Simpson was united in marriage with Miss Ella P Skiles, daughter of H M G and Eliza J (McKissen) Skiles, by which union there are two children—Mary E and Dorothy B

Religiously Mr and Mrs Simpson are members of the Episcopal church   Fraternally he is a member of the Fraternal Tribunes, Modern Woodmen and National Union   As city editor of the Argus he is best known, and it is probable that his personal acquaintance in the three cities of Rock Island, Moline and Davenport is equal to that of any other one man   Under his management the local department of the Argus is superior to that of most papers published in cities of equal size with that of Rock Island   Ever alert to gather and sift local news, but little of importance misses his watchful eye   In the advocacy of measures for the best interests of his city and county he never halts, but does all in his power, and in so doing has contributed to making the Argus almost indispensable to people of both city and county

---

GEORGE DOWNING, Sr, who has for many years been prominently identified with the industrial interests of Rock Island as a foundryman and molder, was born in Coal Brookdale, Shropshire, England, July 29, 1829, and is a son of Joseph and Elizabeth (Powell) Downing, the former a native of England and the latter of Wales The maternal grandfather spent his entire life in Wales, but George Downing, the paternal grandfather, died in England at the advanced age of eighty-six years He was a carpenter by trade and had a family of eight children, of whom Joseph was the only son He became a carpenter and continued to follow that occupation in his native land until called to his final rest at the age of seventy years His estimable wife, who was a Methodist in religious belief, survived him some years, dying at the age of eighty-two In their family were six children, five sons and one daughter, of whom four are still living—George, James, John and Thomas

Mr Downing, of this review, grew to manhood in England, receiving his education in the common schools, and at the age of fourteen began learning the trade of a molder, at which he has since worked either for himself or others Before leaving his native land he was married in 1843 to Miss Jane York, a daughter of Richard and Mary York, and to them were born five sons and one daughter, as follows Mary, who first wedded Conrad Smith, by whom she had three children n w living nd f r h

death married Thomas Manual, by whom she also has three children, Joseph, who married Ellen Beechler and has three children, George, who married Martha McCord and has six children, John, who married Laura Krise and has five sons and one daughter, James, who married Rebecca Lawler and has three children, and Thomas, who married Florence Bostock and has three children Mrs Downing, who was a consistent member of the Methodist church, passed away in January, 1893, at the age of sixty-eight years

Crossing the Atlantic, Mr Downing took up his residence in Rock Island in 1857, and the following year erected a foundry, which he subsequently sold He was then employed as foreman by Mr Buford for ten years, but at the end of that time built another foundry in company with his sons, Joseph, George and John, and until recently was a member of the firm He has sold his interest to his sons, but still continues to work at his trade, of which he is a thorough master

On the 2nd of May, 1897, Mr Downing was again married, his second union being with Mrs Eliza Cox, widow of Noah Cox, and a daughter of William and Mary (Bold) York, her father being a brother of the first Mrs Downing s father Until her second marriage she made her home in England—her native land—and on coming to this country was met in Chicago by Mr Downing and was there married By her first husband she had nine children, eight sons and one daughter—William York, who married Emily Deeken and has three children, Noah Thomas, deceased, Alfred Crighton, who married Phœbe Bishop, George Henry, who married Edith Doling

Frances Mary, wife of Thomas William Swan, by whom she has three children, and two who died in infancy

Mr Downing is independent in politics, and in religious belief is an Episcopalian, while his wife is a member of the Wesleyan Methodist church   In early life they became acquainted, and as both are genial, happy-hearted people we predict for them a happy married life   Mrs Downing has a round, sweet face, not marred by wrinkles, and has the usual ruddy complexion characteristic of the English   Her hair is jet black and her eyes as bright and clear as usually found in the young   Her voice is soft and musical and her manner, easy, graceful and gentle   Mr Downing has always been popular among his fellowmen for his good nature and kindly manner as well as for his industrious habits and business capacity

E DWARD BURRALL, deceased —It is an important duty to honor and perpetuate, as far as is possible, the memory of the eminent citizen—one who by his blameless and honorable life and distinguished career reflected credit not only upon his city and state, but also upon the whole country   Through such memorials as this at hand the individual and the character of his services are kept in remembrance, and the importance of those services acknowledged   His example, in whatever field his work may have been done, thus stands as an object lesson to those who come after him, and though dead he still speaks   Long after all recollection of his personality shall have faded from the minds of men, the less perishable record may tell the story of his life and commend his example for imitation

Mr Burrall, who was for many years prominently identified with the business interests of Rock Island county, was born April 13, 1815, in Canaan, Connecticut, of which state his parents, Edward and Lucy (Hunt) Burrall, were also natives   They had three children—Edward, of this review, Dr. George W., and Mrs Lucy Crane, now a resident of Beloit, Wisconsin   In early life the father was a merchant, but later turned his attention to banking   His last years were spent in Beloit, Wisconsin   The paternal grandfather aided the colonies in their struggle for independence during the Revolutionary war

Our subject was reared at Stockbridge, Connecticut, and was a schoolmate of Cyrus W Field, who laid the first Atlantic cable   After leaving home he clerked in a store at Troy, New York, but in 1836 came to Mercer county, Illinois, to engage in farming as his father had offered him four eighty-acre tracts there if he would cultivate and improve them.   He continued to follow agricultural pursuits until 1849, when he was stricken with the gold fever, and rented his land, going to California, where he engaged in mining for about nineteen months   On his return to Illinois he spent a short time in Henry county, and then purchased a store in Edgington, Rock Island county, where he successfully engaged in merchandising until 1859   In that year he came to the city of Rock Island and carried on the same business until the spring of 1865, when he sold out   He accumulated considerable property, was one of the organizers of the quilt factory, was a stockholder in the Rock Island Stove Manufactory and

EDWARD BURRALL.

the watch factory, and a director in the Rock Island National Bank . He also owned several farms in Henry county and had a wide reputation as a most capable financier Straightforward and honorable in all his dealings, energetic and progressive, his remarkable success in business affairs was certainly well deserved

On the 13th of June, 1843, Mr Burrall was united in marriage with Miss Ann Caroline Jack, daughter of Captain Charles and Ann (Robertson) Jack, both natives of Scotland, the former of Aberdeen and the latter of Edinboro Five children graced this union, two sons and three daughters, namely Charles E , now a resident of Chicago, Arthur, of Rock Island, Mis Mary Montgomery, Grace Caroline, wife of George P Frysinger, of Rock Island, and Alice, wife of Manuel M Briggs, of the same city

Although not members of any religious denomination, Mr. and Mrs. Burrall attended the Episcopal Church He was a Knight Templar Mason, belonging to the Evert Commandery, and was a stanch Democrat in politics At one time he served as justice of the peace in Mercer county, and was postmaster of Edgington for several years As a public-spirited, progressive citizen, he took an active interest in the affairs of his community, did all in his power to advance the general welfare, and was the founder of the Library Association in Rock Island On the 26th of April, 1876, he departed this life at the age of sixty years and thirteen days, but his estimable wife still survives, and like her husband is beloved by all who know her

Captain Charles Jack, the father of Mrs Burrall, was a finely educated man, having completed a collegiate course at the early age of sixteen years But in the British army, he was commissioned lieutenant at the battle of Waterloo when only seventeen His father was for sixty years connected with King's College of Old Aberdeen, Scotland, serving as professor for the first twenty years, and later as principal of that noted institution He died at the advanced age of ninety years

Of a roving disposition, Captain Jack traveled extensively, and previous to his marriage made a trip to South America to aid the people in one of their wars, but became disgusted with their patriotism and returned home on the next ship Crossing the Atlantic to the United States, he became a pioneer of Illinois, settling in Ottawa in the summer of 1831, and erecting the first house at that place It stood for many years but was finally burned down Afterward he lived at the head of Peoria Lake, at the place called Rome, where he also built the first house, but in 1835 he removed to Knoxville, Knox county, conducting a store at that place for a short time On selling out, he turned his attention to farming, but in 1838 took up his residence in New Boston, Mercer county, where he erected the largest house, but not the first. After conducting a store at that place for four years, he located in Henry county, and again devoted his attention to farming. Later he followed the same pursuit in Texas, where at one time he owned over ten thousand acres of land During his residence there he made two trips to Kentucky and Illinois, besides various other long journeys, traveling on horseback and carrying his effects in saddle bags He died at St Louis, Missouri, in August, 1867, at the age of seventy years, and was buried in the cemetery at Rock Island He was an Episcopalian in faith, while his wife who died in 1874,

8

aged eighty years, was a consistent member of the Scotch Presbyterian church   They enjoyed the respect and esteem of all who knew them

- - -

DANIEL N BEAL, now living a retired life at No 2529 Sixth avenue, Moline, is a pioneer of 1834, and to-day is one of the oldest living settlers in Rock Island county, with a personal knowledge of its entire history, and having a personal acquaintance with nearly all who have been instrumental in giving the county of his adoption its high rank among its sister counties of the great state of Illinois   He is a native of the grand old state of Vermont, born in Beacham, Caledonia county, February 15, 1815, and is a son of Samuel and Rachel (Wells) Beal, both of whom were natives of Massachusetts, of English descent.

The family name, in the beginning, was doubtless spelled Beale, but in the course of time the final letter was dropped as being superfluous, and for generations it has been spelled as at present   Samuel Beal was a farmer by occupation, and followed that calling during his entire life, his death occurring in his adopted state in 1820   His widow subsequently married James Lindsay and died in 1845

Our subject was but five years of age when his father died   His mother feeling her inability to keep the family together, he was taken by Leonard Johnson, a brother of the noted Oliver Johnson, of anti-slavery fame, and by him reared as one of the family, though not formally adopted   On the farm of Mr Johnson he remained until he passed his nineteenth year, and from the time physically able to handle a hoe or hold a plow, he did his share of far ... work, while he

attending school three months in the year. He considered the schools of his neighborhood very good for that early day, and therein laid the foundation for the knowledge afterward acquired by reading and contact with men.

"Vermont," said the lamented Stephen A Douglas, ' is a good state to be born in if you only emigrate early enough "   Although our subject had not heard such a statement made, yet he realized its truthfulness at an early period in life, and securing the consent of Mr Johnson, his foster parent, when but nineteen years of age, accompanied by his next younger brother, he set out for what was then the far west Two uncles and an aunt had settled in Rock Island county, and to that place he directed his steps with the hope of its being indeed an Eldorado to him   By river and canal he went to Buffalo, New York, from which place he took a steamer on the lakes for Detroit, Michigan   From Detroit he came by foot to Rock Island county, landing here in October, 1834, with fifty cents as cash capital with which to begin life in a new and strange country

In the early day money was an almost unknown commodity   Land was plenty, and of wild game there was an abundance. People cared nothing for the fashions, in fact didn t know the meaning of the word, at least as commonly accepted   With flax and wool cloth could be made, and linsey-woolsey and blue or butternut jeans was good enough for any one.   For two years Mr Beal worked at what he could find to do, and for some months was employed in mining coal   He assisted in mining and loading the first steamboat that ever took on board a cargo of Rock Island coal   This

Back east there was a bright-eyed maiden whose heart had been touched by the sturdy lad ere he left for the west   Back to the old home he went in the summer of 1836, and on the 18th of September of that year a marriage ceremony was performed that united the destinies of Daniel N Beal and Betsy Spencer, a daughter of Samuel and Betsy (Currier) Spencer, the father a native of New Hampshire and mother of Massachusetts   By this union four children were born, who lived to maturity   Lucius Wells, the eldest, has been twice married, and by his first union has two children   He is a farmer, but is now living retired in Cherokee, Iowa, and for several years served as auditor of Cherokee county   He enlisted in the One Hundred and Twenty-sixth Illinois Volunteer Infantry and was commissioned captain September 4, 1862, was promoted lieutenant-colonel on August 12, 1864, and colonel May 11, 1865   He first went out under Colonel Graham to Kansas, but later was sent to Lexington, Missouri, where he was captured and sent home on parole   After being exchanged he enlisted in the One Hundred Twenty-sixth regiment   Samuel Spencer is a farmer residing in Zuma township, where he was born and reared   He is married and has five daughters and one son   Albert M. is a prominent physician of whom mention is made elsewhere in this volume   Eunice C, the only daughter, married Fred Cooper and resides in Moline   They have four children

Immediately after their marriage Mr and Mrs Beal came to Rock Island county where he made claim to one hundred and sixty acres of government land on section 18, Zuma township, which he entered as soon as it came into market   A finer location could hardly be found in Rock

Island county, the farm being upon an eminence and could be plainly seen for many miles around   The traditional log. cabin was at once erected in which the family lived for nine years, when a more pretentious frame house was built   What with clearing and breaking, setting out of orchards, and otherwise improving the place, the time rapidly passed, while children came to brighten the home

Mr Beal returned to the county in time to cast his first presidential vote in November, 1836, for William Henry Harrison, who was defeated that year, but four years later was triumphantly elected, the campaign resulting in his election being in many respects the most exciting in the history of the country.   "Tippecanoe and Tyler, too," was the battle cry of the Whigs, and, what with log cabins, coons, hard cider and the inevitable campaign song, it was, indeed, lively   Mr Beal continued to act and vote with the Whig party until its dissolution, in 1852, when General Scott was defeated for the presidency

New issues were now being formed and the slavery question was the all-absorbing one.   In 1854 the Republican party sprang into existence and to that organization Mr. Beal transferred his allegiance, and with which he has since continued to act.   As a Republican, but more especially as a good, reliable and honorable citizen, he was elected to almost every official position in his township, including road commissioner, assessor, school director, school trustee and township supervisor, serving upon the county board for a number of years   No charge of boodle ever attached to him, as he was honest and upright in every position to which he was called

both   Mr and Mrs B l were con-

nected for many years with the United
Brethren church, in Zuma township, and
did much for the Master's cause   The
golden rule of the Son of Man has been with
him a ruling principle in life

In 1875, feeling need of rest, he rented
his farm, built a neat and comfortable home,
No 2529 Sixth avenue, to which he removed
with his family and there resided nine years,
when he again returned to his farm and took
up its active management   Two years later
a most important event occurred in the life
of himself and estimable wife—the celebration of their golden wedding, September 18,
1886   Friends to the number of over one
hundred gathered at their hospitable home
and spent some hours in social converse, relating stories of pioneer life and, last, but not
least, partaking of the refreshments so
abundantly provided   A gold watch and
chain, and a gold-headed cane were presented to Mr Beal, and a gold watch and
other useful and ornamental articles to Mrs
Beal   Time passed all too rapidly, and when
the hour came to part it was with the sincere wish that the worthy couple might live
to celebrate their diamond wedding   While
that time has not yet arrived, their sixtieth
anniversary was remembered pleasantly by
a number of their friends

The infirmities of age creeping upon this
worthy couple, in 1893 they sold the old
farm, though still retaining one hundred
acres of another tract, and again removed
to their home in Moline, where they patiently wait the summons to "come up higher "
Their third son, Dr Albert M Beal, resides
near them and tenderly looks after their
welfare, while they enjoy life as best they
can   More than four score years have
passed over the heads of each, and more
than si...

spent in Rock Island county   On their
settlement here Zuma township had but six
families, the county but a few hundred inhabitants, the thriving city of Rock Island
was but in name, Moline was unknown
How great the change, and blessed are the
men and women by whose toils all these
have been brought about, and among those
who have done their full share in the development of the county it is a pleasure to record
the names of Daniel N and Betsy Beal

HIRAM DARLING —The career of him
whose name heads this review illustrates most forcibly the possibilities that are
open to a young man who possesses sterling
business qualifications   It proves that
neither wealth nor social position, nor the
assistance of influential friends at the outset
of his career are necessary to place him on
the road to success   It also proves that
ambition, perseverance, steadfast purpose
and indefatigable industry, combined with
sound business principles, will be rewarded,
and that true success follows individual effort only   Mr Darling has gained recognition and prestige as one of the influential
and representative business men of Moline,
but is now practically living a retired life, enjoying the fruits of his former toil

A native of Vermont, he began his
earthly career in Caledonia county, October
2, 1827, and on both sides is descended from
honored ancestry of English origin   His
paternal grandfather, Moses Darling, a native of New Hampshire, joined the Colonial
army during the Revolutionary war, and participated in the battle of Bunker Hill, together with a number of other important
H...   ...   a pension

in recognition of his services At the close of the war he removed with his family to Vermont In the same struggle the maternal grandfather, Eli Bickford, also took an active part Both grandfathers were born in New Hampshire, where their respective families were founded at an early day

Although a native of New Hampshire, David Darling, the father of our subject, was reared in the Green Mountain state, where he wedded Mary Bickford He became an extensive farmer and prominent citizen of Caledonia county, where he held various local positions of honor and trust There he and his wife died, the latter surviving her husband a few years. In their family were nine children, of whom two are still living Hon Ezra F is now living retired in West Derby, Vermont, Calista and Harriet both died unmarried, Laura married and reared a family, but is now deceased, Alfred, one of the substantial farmers and honored early settlers of Rock Island county, died leaving a family who still reside here, Hiram is next in order of birth, Alanson, and Horace who operated the old homestead until his death

After attending the common schools for some time, Hiram Darling pursued his studies for several terms in the Phillips Academy at Danville, Vermont, and then successfully engaged in teaching in his native state for a few terms Subsequently he had charge of a fruit farm at South Reading, Massachusetts, for five years, but in April, 1856, emigrated to Rock Island county, Illinois, where in partnership with his brother Alfred he operated rented land for a few years They then purchased a small tract of land, to which they added from time to time as their financial i   '   ' ' '
continued v   p   ui   i ili i y   ii

for ten years, when the property was divided Our subject's place adjoined the cities of Moline and Rock Island, and there he successfully engaged in the culture of small fruits for many years He also owns sixty-five acres in South Moline, and is connected with a number of important business enterprises in the city On the organization of the Moline Savings Bank, he became a stockholder and director, and is now serving as vice-president, and is also a stockholder and director in the Moline National Bank He has just completed an elegant and commodious residence at No 1812 Sixth avenue, Moline, where he is now living retired, surrounded by all the comforts and many of the luxuries of life

In Mendota, Illinois, Mr Darling was married August 12, 1863, to Roena Festella Guy, who was born, reared and educated in New York, and was for some time a successful teacher in the schools of Mendota. She died August 6, 1889, leaving three children— William Alfred, a resident of Rock Island, is a graduate of the public schools of that city and also of the Iowa State University and is now a civil engineer by profession. He is married and has a family Harriet Calista, a graduate of Oberlin College, taught school at Port Byron for one year, and died March 16, 1894 Guy H has also been well educated and is still with his father At Ottawa, Illinois, Mr Darling was again married February 14, 1895, his second union being with Maria Amelia Guy, a sister of his first wife She is also a native of New York, but when a child was brought to Illinois by her father, George Guy, who located at Paw Paw and later at Mendota, where he resided for many years ''   '   '' ' blic life,
ons He

departed this life in 1894, and his wife many years previous, having died in 1861

Since the formation of the party, Mr Darling has been an ardent Republican, but has never taken a very active part in political affairs, preferring to devote his time and attention to his business interests Being a warm friend of our public school system he has served as a member of the school board Both he and his wife belong to the Congregational church of Moline and do all in their power to promote the moral educational and material welfare of the community During the forty-two years of his residence here, Mr Darling has borne an important part in the upbuilding and progress of the county and deserves to be numbered among its honored and valued citizens His sterling worth and many excellent traits of character are justly appreciated by a large circle of friends and acquaintances

---

CHARLES F HEMENWAY, cashier of the Moline National Bank, came to Moline, Illinois, a lad of nine years, with his parents, Luke and Jane E (Marsh) Hemenway He was born in Grand Detour, Ogle county, Illinois, November 1, 1846, and there commenced his education in the common schools, which he also attended in Moline until he was fourteen years of age He then left home and went to Lansing, Iowa, where he was employed in the postoffice until August, 1862

For more than sixteen months the war for the Union had now been in progress In that time the northern army had suffered several severe defeats and to the minds of many it seemed as if the south would prevail and the grand American union would be dissolv

nal sides young Hemenway came of good stock, both sides serving their country faithfully and well in the Revolutionary war. That union, cemented by the blood of his forefathers, must not be dissolved Although less than sixteen years of age, he offered his services and was accepted as a private in Company B, Twenty-seventh Iowa Volunteer Infantry, and, with his regiment, marched to the front, and was in the battle of Little Rock, resulting in the capture of that city.

Soon after his enlistment young Hemenway was detailed as clerk to General Hurlbert, of the Sixteenth Army Corps, at headquarters, where he had charge of the private correspondence When the Sixteenth Army Corps was divided he was assigned as clerk at the headquarters of the department of the Mississippi As such he served with satisfaction to his superior officers until the close of the war, when he was discharged, in May, 1864, at Vicksburg, Mississippi

Returning to Moline, Mr Hemenway at once secured employment as clerk and bookkeeper in the First National Bank, of which Judge J M Gould was then cashier. With this bank he remained until 1869, when he was elected assistant cashier of the Manufacturers' Bank, a state institution, then organized In this capacity he served until 1872, when the bank was merged into the Moline National Bank, when the same position was offered him, and in which he served until 1875, when he was promoted cashier, a position which he has filled with honor and credit to himself and the company, and to the satisfaction of the patrons of the bank.

On the 4th of November, 1869, Mr Hemenway was united in marriage to Miss Mary E Harold, a native of Rock Island (Harold and Nancy

Harold, who were numbered among the early settlers of 1840   At Moline she grew to womanhood and in its public schools received her education   By this union five children have been born, four of whom are living—Martha J, Frances B, Harold and Joseph C   The deceased one is Clara T, who died in infancy

Mr Hemenway is a member of the Unitarian church, while his wife and oldest daughter are members of the Congregational church   He contributes of his means to the support of both churches   Fraternally he is a member of R H Graham Post, No 312, G A R, and is treasurer of the Moline Club, and one of the directors of the Moline Art Association, in which he takes great interest

As a business man, Mr Hemenway ranks among the best in Rock Island county On the organization of the Manufacturers' Bank, he became one of its stockholders, and has since increased his holdings, his interest, however, being transferred to the Moline National Bank   In the Moline State Savings Bank he is also a large stockholder and has been its cashier from the start   He has also business interests outside of the bank, being secretary and treasurer of the Guffin Clay Manufacturing Co, manufacturers of brick and tile, and secretary and treasurer of the Christy Coal Company He is also the owner of the Opera House building, which is a credit to the city of Moline

As might reasonably be expected Mr Hemenway is a strong Republican, with which party he has been identified since attaining his majority   While taking a lively interest in politics, he never does it to the neglect of business, and the honors conferred by office holding, he never cared for   As a

man of the city one term he discharged his duties faithfully, and as city treasurer several terms he handled its money carefully and conscientiously   For some years he was a member of the board of education of Moline, and served on the finance committee   During the campaign of 1896 he favored sound money, and was an advocate of the distinctive principles of the Republican party, protection and reciprocity.   As a citizen he is highly esteemed by those who know him

———

CARL T ACHTERMANN —Prominent among the energetic, enterprising and successful business men of Rock Island is the subject of this sketch, who is now proprietor of the C. O D steam laundry, located at No 1808 Third avenue   He was born in Holle, Hildeseim, Germany, August 13, 1854, and his parents, Anton and Sophia (Borgars) Achtermann, were natives of the same country, where they spent their entire lives, the father dying in 1873, at the age of seventy-three years, and the mother in 1868   In religious belief they were Lutherans   Their children were Christian, Mary, wife of Julius Gurlich, of St Louis, Missouri, Amelia, wife of Carl Illis, of Hildeseim, Germany, Augusta, wife of William Busse, of Germany, Carl T, of this sketch, and William, of Denver, Colorado   The grandparents of our subject never left Germany, where the paternal grandfather followed farming and reared his small family, and where the maternal grandfather engaged in the butcher business.

In the public schools of Germany, Carl T Achtermann acquired his education, and at the age of fourteen commenced learning the trade. ally followed both in Germany and after coming to America It was in 1881 that he crossed the Atlantic and first located in St. Louis, where he spent three years For over seven years he then made his home in Madison, Wisconsin, where he conducted a dying establishment, and was later in Sheboygan, Wisconsin, until coming to Rock Island in 1891 Here he purchased the C O D steam laundry, which he has since successfully carried on, employing quite a force of hands and turning out first class work

On the 8th of September, 1886, Mr Achtermann was united in marriage to Miss Emma Jeska, and to them have been born three children Robert, Norma and Herman His home as well as his place of business is on Third avenue between Eighteenth and Nineteenth streets His political support is given the Democratic party, in the success of which he takes a deep interest, while socially he is connected with the Home Forum and the Modern Woodmen of America A man of keen perception, of great sagacity and of unbounded enterprise, he has met with a well deserved success in his undertakings, and is to-day numbered among the leading and substantial business men of Rock Island

SAMUEL W ODELL, the well-known city attorney of Moline, is one of the ablest lawyers practicing at the Rock Island county bar, having that mental grasp which enables him easily to discover the intricate points in a case A man of sound judgment, he manages his cases with masterly skill and tact, and is regarded as one of the best jury advocates in Moline He is a logical reasoner, and has a ready command of English

Mr Odell is a native son of Rock Island county, born at Hampton in November, 1864. His father, John P. Odell, was born, reared and educated in Ohio, where he married Miss Sarah Nelson, of Guernsey He was a mechanic and active member and local preacher of the Methodist Episcopal church in Hampton, Illinois, whence he removed to Scott county, Iowa, and later resided in Kansas for a few years In 1879, however, he returned to Rock Island county, this time locating in Port Byron

Our subject pursued his studies in the public schools and also in the academy of Port Byron, graduating therefrom in 1884 Later he taught for a time in the academy Entering the Bloomington Law School, he graduated from that institute in 1887, and practiced law one year at Port Byron, and also acted as editor of the Port Byron Globe. He removed to Moline in 1890, where he entered the office of Browning & Entrikin, and remained with them two years In March, 1892, he opened an office of his own, and is now practicing at No 418 Sixteenth street

In Port Byron Mr. Odell was married December 20, 1888, to Miss Clara Morgan, who was reared and educated in that city, though born in Cordova, Illinois Her father, Dr J W Morgan, is now a prominent physician of Moline Mr and Mrs Odell have two children, Samuel Morgan and Donald A

Mr. Odell is a man of considerable literary ability, and has written and published four different works, including the "Lives and Campaigns of Generals U. S Grant and Robert E Lee," a subscription book He also compiled the Moline City Ordinances in 1892 His books include two juvenile . . . . In Method-

S. W. ODELL.

1st Book Concern, of Cincinnati, and have had a fair sale Mr Odell has spent almost his entire life in Rock Island county, has become widely and favorably known in professional, social and church circles, and in the spring of 1897 was elected city attorney of Moline Thoroughness characterizes all his efforts, and he conducts all his business with a strict regard to a high standard of professional ethics In the First Methodist Episcopal church of Moline both he and his wife hold membership, and take an active and prominent part in its work.

ROBERT CRAMPTON, who follows farming and stock raising on section 10, Bowling township, is one of the worthy sons that the Emerald Isle has furnished to this country. He was born in Ireland, in 1845, and is a son of Robert and Anna (Rudd) Crampton, both of whom were natives of the same country The grandparents spent their entire lives in that land. The parents came to America in 1850, and after two years passed in New York, removed westward to Moline, Illinois A year later they moved to Rock Island, where they lived four years Mr Crampton engaged in bookkeeping, both in Moline and Rock Island He afterward purchased one hundred and twenty acres of land in Bowling township, and to this added a tract of eighty acres, which he improved, making his home thereon for some years Afterward, however, he erected a residence in Milan, which continued to be the home of himself and wife until their deaths He passed away in 1891, at the age of ninety-one years, and his wife died at the age of seventy-five Both were members of the Method st church

class leader They had a family of eight children, six of whom are now living, namely Richard, Henry, of Reno, Nevada, Emily, wife of Frank Tindall, Robert, Charles, of Farnam, Nebraska, and Anna, wife of James Betty

When a child of five years Robert Crampton was brought to America by his parents. The voyage across the Atlantic was made in a sailing vessel, which after six weeks dropped anchor in the harbor of New York He came with the family to the west, and for a time attended school in Rock Island, but removed to the farm when his father turned his attention to agricultural pursuits He continued under the parental roof until he had attained his majority, and started out in business for himself by buying cattle He afterward purchased one hundred and sixty acres of land in Bowling township, and is now the owner of a valuable tract of two hundred and forty acres Much of this is under a high state of cultivation and yields to the owner a rich return for his labor He is also quite extensively engaged in stock raising, making a specialty of short horn cattle

On the 7th of October, 1876, Mr Crampton married Miss Lizzie Morris, and to them have been born five children, namely John Morris, Alford William, Mary Truesdale, Faith Anna, and Carl Eckhardt Mrs Crampton is a native of Germany, born in Frankfort, November 17, 1850, and a daughter of Ferdinand and Barbara Eckhardt, both of whom are also natives of Germany They came with their family to the new world in 1851 and settled in Cincinnati, Ohio, where they remained three years, and then came to Rock Island county, locating on a farm in Buffalo Prairie township Of their family of nine children all are now grown and heads of families Mrs Crampton was the youngest of the nine Soon after the family settled in Buffalo Prairie township, she was taken by John and Abbie Morris and reared by them as their own daughter, taking the name of Morris Mr Morris was a successful farmer, stock buyer and dealer and operated a farm near the Eckhardts

Mr and Mrs Crampton are members of the Presbyterian church, in which Mr Crampton is serving as elder His political support is given the Republican party, but he has never sought or desired official honors, preferring to give his attention to his business interests, in which he is meeting with signal success His life demonstrates the fact that labor and usefulness are the highway to honor

---

JOHN A MUNRO – There are no rules for building characters, there is no rule for achieving success The man who can rise from the ranks to a position of eminence is he who can see and utilize the opportunities that surround his path The essential conditions of human life are ever the same, the surroundings of individuals differ but slightly, and when one man passes another on the highway to reach the goal of prosperity before others who perhaps started out before him it is because he has the power to use advantages which probably encompass the whole human race To-day among the business men of Rock Island stands Mr Munro, who for years has been at the head of one of the industrial concerns of the city of Moline, and by his perseverance, well directed efforts and honorable dealing has worked hi

Mr Munro was born in Davenport, Iowa, September 24, 1858, a son of Robert and Isabel (Ewen) Munro, natives of Scotland The paternal grandfather, Robert Munro, engaged in running a stage line and died in Scotland in middle life. The father of our subject was a blacksmith by trade, and on coming to America located in New York, but for the past forty years has lived in Davenport, Iowa, carrying on business there His wife also still survives, and both are consistent members of the Presbyterian church They have a family of eight children, as follows Robert H , John A , David William, Walter, Mary, wife of Robert Bryson, of Indianapolis, Jennie and Caroline

John A Munro was reared in his native city, acquired his education in its public schools, and at the age of fifteen years began learning the blacksmith's trade under the direction of his father with whom he worked for seven years In 1881 he came to Moline and has since conducted a general blacksmithing and carriage making shop on his own account Straightforward dealing and excellence of workmanship have secured to him a very liberal patronage, from which he derives a good income

On the 11th of March, 1896, Mr Munro married Mrs Telitha A Kay, daughter of Samuel and Eliza (Wheeler) Bowles Her father came to Rock Island county in 1835, at which time the city was called Stevenson At different times he purchased tracts of land, and at one time was the owner of an entire section He lived upon his first purchase until his death, and was a very prominent and influential citizen of the community By his fellow townsmen he was elected to various offices of honor and trust in the township, including those of super-
h I r ish He w is a member

of the Universalist church, and his wife held membership in the Methodist church Mr Bowles passed away December 6, 1893, at the age of eighty-three years, and his wife departed this life March 30, 1886, in her fifty-eighth year The paternal grandfather of Mrs Munro was Samuel Bowles, a native of Virginia and of German descent He followed farming as a life occupation, reared a family of eleven children, and passed from this life at an advanced age The maternal grandfather, James Wheeler, who died in middle life, was a native of Kentucky, and also devoted his energies to agricultural pursuits

Mrs Munro was reared on her father's farm near Moline, attended the public schools of that city, and afterward was a student in the academy of the Immaculate Conception in Davenport. She is a lady of culture and refinement and presides with gracious hospitality over her charming home By her first marriage she had one son, John Alfred, and one daughter, Edith Eliza, who is now a student in the academy in Davenport, and who possesses superior artistic talent

Mr Munro gives his political support to the Republican party, but has never sought office, preferring to devote his energies to his business, in which he has met with fair success. In 1896-7 Mr and Mrs Munro erected at No 2920 Fifth avenue one of the finest residences in the city It is built in a modern style of architecture, substantial and at the same time adorned in a most pleasing and tasteful manner It contains nine rooms on each floor, with three bath rooms and one bathing pool The finest woods have been used in finishing the rooms, every article for any purpose has been added until the interior is a marvel of beauty In the furnishings of the house everything that good taste could suggest and wealth could procure has been obtained and the harmony and beauty of this home makes it one of the finest residences in Rock Island

JOHN H THORNTON, now living retired in the city of Moline, was one of the brave boys in blue who devoted the opening years of their manhood to the defense of our country from the internal foe who sought her dismemberment, and was later for many years connected with the military service, as a soldier of the regular army, being retired on his own application May 24, 1894 Whether on the field of battle or in camp he did his duty nobly and unflinchingly, and is now enjoying a well-earned rest in his pleasant home at Park Ridge, Moline

The birth of our subject occurred June 24, 1847, in Ireland, but the following year he was brought by his parents to this country. His father, Patrick Thornton, located in Philadelphia, Pennsylvania, where the son passed the days of his boyhood and youth, receiving but limited educational privileges, but he has become a well-informed man by reading and study since reaching maturity.

On the 24th of July, 1862, when only fifteen years of age, Mr Thornton joined Company B, Twenty-ninth Pennsylvania Volunteer Infantry, which belonged to what was known as the White Star Division, Twelfth Army Corps Under General Mc-Clellan he participated in all the engagements around Richmond, and later took part in the battle of Antietam where he abdomen,

which disabled him for some time   After
being confined in the hospital for six weeks
he rejoined his regiment at Aqua creek, and
later took part in the battles of Fredericksburg Chancellorsville and Gettysburg, being
again wounded by a gun shot in the face at
the last-named engagement   He still carries the scar made by that honorable wound
in defense of the old flag and the cause it
represented   He was also in the battles of
Lookout Mountain, Missionary Ridge and
those of the Atlanta campaign, participating
in seven very important engagements, besides a great many skirmishes and lesser
fights   The war having ended he was honorably discharged July 26, 1865, but on the
14th of the following February he re-enlisted in the regular army and was sent
south to the Carolinas to assist in preserving
order during the trying days of the recon-
struction period   After three years spent
in the south he was again discharged, but
April 25, 1870, joined the Ordnance Corps
of the United States Army and came west
to the arsenal at Rock Island, where, as
sergeant, he was on duty for twenty-four
years, having charge of the grounds — a
most pleasant position   He was subject to
being called into the active service at any
time, and is now required to report monthly
to the war department at Washington,
District of Columbia

At the arsenal Mr Thornton was married September 17, 1885, to Miss Martha J
Montgomery, daughter of A E Montgomery head guard on the island and one
of the early settlers of Illinois   They began their domestic life at the army quarters
on the island, where they continued to live
until Mr Thornton retired May 24, 1894,
since which time they have made their
home in M

United Presbyterian church, and have the
respect and esteem of all who know them

In politics Mr Thornton is a stanch Republican, and since his retirement to private
life has taken an active and prominent part
in public affairs   In 1897 he was elected
supervisor of South Moline, and is also serving as overseer of the poor and president of
the school board of his district. Fraternally
he is a member of the Grand Army of the Republic, the Home Forum, is one of the oldest members of the Ancient Order of
United Workmen in the state, and also belongs to the Select Knights of America, of
which he has been commander two terms,
and is now grand lodge deputy   He is a
popular, genial gentleman, whose friends
are many, and no man in Rock Island
county is more deserving the high regard in
which he is uniformly held than John H
Thornton, whose public and private career
has been above reproach

FRANK M SHINSTROM, a leading agriculturist of section 16, Black Hawk
township, is a man of great energy and perseverance, and has effected many improvements upon his farm since taking possession
He is recognized as a valued member of the
community, a man possessing excellent
judgment, and giving his support and encouragement to those enterprises calculated
for the general welfare

Mr Shinstrom was born in Linn, Henry
county, Illinois, February 6, 1849, and is a
son of Magnus and Mary (Wahlberg) Shinstrom, natives of Sweden, where the grandparents spent their entire lives   The parents crossed the Atlantic in 1848 and took
up their residence first in Henry county,
        l   l   Il   l ll   l his trade

of shoemaking until 1850, when he sold out and came to Rock Island county, and in March, 1852, located where the son now resides. Here he purchased forty acres on Big Island in Black Hawk township, and at once began to clear and improve his place He died there February 6, 1891, at the age of sixty-nine years, and his wife passed away June 23, 1890, at the age of eighty They were faithful members of the Methodist church, and their sterling worth and many excellencies of character gained for them many friends In his native land the father had been a member of the militia, and in this country acceptably served in various local offices in Black Hawk township In the family were only two children, the other being Matilda, now the wife of John P Anderson, of Oakland, Nebraska

At the age of one year Frank M Shinstrom was brought by his father to Rock Island county, and has since resided upon his present farm After the death of his parents he purchased his sister's share in the old homestead, which contains one hundred and seventy acres, and is now successfully operating the same He is a wide-awake, progressive business man, a thorough and systematic farmer and the success that has come to him is certainly well deserved.

Mr Shinstrom was married September 26, 1878, to Miss Sarah Vanderveer, by whom he had six children, five sons and one daughter, namely Delilah Rebecca, who died of membranous croup in February, 1882, Llewellyn, Herman Elmer and John Lester, who all died of diphtheria in October, 1887, and Clayton and Ralph, who are the only ones now living

Mrs. Shinstrom is a native of Ohio, where she spent the first six years of her life, coming to Illinois in 18... her ...

parents, John and Delilah Aiken, Vanderveer, natives of Warren and Darke counties, Ohio, respectively. Benjamin Vandeveer, the grandfather, was born in New Jersey, where he married Jane Vandeveer, and they became the parents of a large family of children At an early day they emigrated to Ohio and both died on the old homestead there when well advanced in years In his native state John Vanderveer followed the blacksmith's trade, but on coming to Illinois in 1856 purchased two hundred and fifty acres of land in Andalusia township, Rock Island county, and devoted his time and attention to the improvement and cultivation of his property He became the owner of over three hundred acres of valuable land and continued to engage in agricultural pursuits until 1891, when he rented his place to his son Elmer E , who still conducts it The father died November 14, 1892, but the mother is still living in the village of Andalusia He held various township offices of honor and trust and both were connected with the Baptist church In the family of this worthy couple were thirteen children, seven of whom are still living— Benjamin, Sarah J , wife of our subject, Mary, wife of Warren Conner, of Fairfield, Iowa, John H , Lydia Margaret, wife of Reuben P. Roth, of Andalusia, Illinois, William Ira, Elmer E , and Frank L

Mr and Mrs Shinstrom are earnest, conscientious Christians, the former holding membership in the Methodist church and the latter in the Baptist Socially he is connected with the Knights of Pythias and Court of Honor, and politically has always been identified with the Republican party Since 1878 he has most efficiently filled the office of school director, and has been clerk ... for forty-seven years he has been a resident of Rock Island county, and since 1852 has lived on his present farm on Big Island, where he has one of the most desirable places in this section of the state He is a philosophical and practical man, always looking on the bright side of life, and he and his wife are industrious, intelligent people, highly esteemed by their neighbors and many friends. Their religion has certainly had much to do with moulding their character, and they prove their faith by their good works Mr Shinstrom's father was also a devout Christian, and was one of the organizers and charter members of the Milan Methodist Episcopal church, having resided in that village for one year

ADOLPH WECKEL, a well-known agriculturist of Section 7, South Moline township, is an honored pioneer of Rock Island county, dating his residence here from 1841 The difference between the past and present can scarcely be realized, even by those who were active participants in the development of the county The present generation can have no conception of what was required by the early settlers in transforming the wild land into the well settled and highly cultivated county which we to day see In the work of transformation our subject has borne an important part

Mr Weckel comes from over the sea, his birth occurring in Baden, Germany, December 18, 1822, and there he grew to manhood and attended school, acquiring an excellent education, and becoming proficient in German, French and English languages At the age of nineteen he left

Rotterdam for Havre, France, and there took passage on a sailing vessel bound for New Orleans, where he arrived after a stormy voyage of forty-eight days, which at that time was considered a quick passage They encountered severe weather on the Gulf of Mexico, and during a storm which lasted three days and three nights the sails were carried away Coming up the Mississippi to St Louis the vessel encountered a tornado at Cairo Accompanied by his sister Catherine and twenty-seven other relatives, Mr Weckel crossed the river from St Louis on the ice, and proceeded on foot to Springfield, Illinois, but before reaching their destination they were overtaken by a terrible hailstorm Finally after nine days they reached that city, where our subject remained during the winter, and the following spring came to Moline, but after a month spent here, he returned to Springfield, where he lived with Philip Casn, also a German, for some time

In 1844, however, Mr Weckel located permanently in Rock Island county, and he and Joseph D Taylor built a brick house opposite the court house in the city of Rock Island. He purchased ten acres of his present farm in 1848 and in 1853 built his first residence upon the place From time to time he added to his land until he owned two hundred and twenty-five acres, which he placed under a high state of cultivation and improved with substantial buildings, which stand as monuments to his thrift and enterprise On coming to the United States his brother Adam had furnished him the means to pay his passage, and here he began life empty-handed, his capital consisting of only a pair of willing hands and a determination to succeed, but he has steadily worked his way upward overcoming the difficulties in his path, until to-day he is one of the substantial citizens of the county

On the 29th of April, 1847, in Illinois City, Mr Weckel was married to Miss Catherine Hensel, who was also born and reared in Germany, and they became the parents of eight children, four of whom died in early childhood Those living are. John, who is mentioned more fully below, Louis, a merchant of Rock Island, Rosa, wife of John Wiess, of the same city, and Eva Cecelia, wife of John Balinger, of Rock Island

As a Democrat, Mr Weckel cast his first presidential vote for James K Polk in 1844, but in 1856 he supported John C Fremont, after which he again gave his allegiance to the Democratic party However, he now votes independent of party ties, supporting the man whom he considers best qualified to fill the office Taking a deep interest in educational affairs, he has served for many years as a member of the school board, and he has also filled the office of commissioner of highways He is a public-spirited, progressive citizen, and has done much to advance the welfare of his adopted county His well-spent life has gained for him the confidence and esteem of all who know him, and he enjoys the friendship of a large circle of acquaintances, who appreciate his sterling worth

John Weckel, the oldest son of our subject, lives on section 6, South Moline township, and is one of the active and enterprising agriculturists of the community He is a native of Rock Island county, born April 8, 1848, and in the schools of his childhood home he was educated Remaining under the parental roof for some time after he had reached man's estate, he assisted his father in the cultivation and improvement of the home farm. In Rock Island county Miller in 1878

was married June 18, 1878, the lady of his choice being Miss Theresa Wolz, who was born in Winona, that state, of German parentage, and they began their domestic life upon his present farm, which now comprises eighty-five acres and is improved with a comfortable residence and good barns and outbuildings. He also operated his father's farm for some years and with him engaged in the dairy business for seven years, and subsequently alone for fifteen years Stock-dealing has also claimed his attention, and in his undertaking he has met with a well-deserved success

At state and national elections Mr Weckel supports the men and measures of the Democratic party, but on local affairs votes independently, and he takes quite an active interest in political matters, serving as a delegate to county and congressional conventions and as chairman of his township committee For twelve years he was trustee of schools in his district, and has been highway commissioner, but has never aspired to official distinction He is a charter member of both the Home Forum and the Modern Woodmen of America, joining the latter lodge in 1887, and he has served as a director in the Forum He is a wide-awake, progressive citizen, and, like his father, is held in high regard by all who know him Mr and Mrs Weckel have two daughters—Clara E , at home, and Ada L., who is attending the Moline schools

JOHN A WILSON, who resides on section 27, Rural township, occupies a prominent place in agricultural circles His home is a beautiful residence of fourteen rooms, built in modern style of architecture niences of the present day Good barns and outbuild-ings indicate his careful consideration for his stock, and the well tilled fields attest his en-terprise and capable management Success has come to him, not as the result of for-tunate circumstances, but as the outgrowth of honorable purpose well directed, and of energy and industry controlled by sound judgment

Mr Wilson was born in the township which is still his home, May 14, 1851 His parents, John M and Alma (Sayre) Wilson, were natives of Ohio The paternal grand-father, Robert F Wilson, was born in Ken-tucky and at an early day removed to the Buckeye state, where he reared a large family His business was that of farming, which pursuit he followed until his death, which occurred in Ohio, at the age of fifty-three years The maternal grandfather of our subject was also an Ohio farmer who died in the prime of life John M Wilson always gave his attention to agricultural pur-suits After his marriage he resided for a time in Logan county, Ohio, whence he re-moved to Rock Island county, Illinois, in October, 1840, locating in Rural township, where he and his wife spent their remaining days He purchased forty acres of land of the government at a dollar and a quarter per acre, and by additional purchase from time to time extended the boundaries of his farm until it comprised five hundred and thirty acres, which yielded to him a good in-come in return for the care and labor he bestowed upon it

While successfully managing his business interests Mr Wilson ever found time to faithfully perform his duties of citizenship and his service in the public interest was very beneficial He acceptably filled the offices of supervisor, justice of the peace

and assessor, and for six years was county judge, resigning that position shortly before his death on account of ill health He pre-sided over the court with a fairness and im-partiality that won him the commendation of all fair-minded citizens In his early life he was a Democrat, but at the time of the war became identified with the Republican party and was a stanch advocate of the Union cause He was instrumental in se-curing the passage of a bill by the board of supervisors for the relief of the soldiers' widows, wives and children and thus won the gratitude of many of the boys in blue upon the field He died April 1, 1871, at the age of fifty-three years, and the com-munity thereby suffered the loss of one of its best citizens Both he and his wife were members of the Methodist church and took a very active part in its work After his death Mrs Wilson united with the Presby-terian church Her death occurred October 13, 1893, at the age of seventy-six years

Our subject is the only survivor in their family of four children He was reared on his father's farm and began his education in the district schools of the neighborhood, supplementing his early privileges by a course in a private school in Orion He lived with his father until the latter's death and then assumed the management of the old homestead, caring for his mother until she, too, passed away He then came into possession of the farm property, now com-prising four hundred and ninety acres of land which is under a high state of cultiva-tion and improved with all the accessories and conveniences of a model farm of the nineteenth century He is extensively en-gaged in stock raising and feeds much of his grain His business interests are well managed and his keen discrimination, enterprise and perseverance bring to him a rich return for his labors. In addition to his farming operations he is vice-president of the Sherrard Banking Company of Sherrard

On the 19th of December, 1872, Mr Wilson was united in marriage to Miss Jennie Scott, a daughter of Archibald and Elizabeth (McCandless) Scott, of Henry county, Illinois Six children have been born to them, two sons and four daughters —Arthur M , who is now teaching in Ford county, Alma E., who taught for one year in Bowling township, and is now a teacher in South Heights school in South Rock Island, Harry S , Jennie S , now the wife of H W Bailey, a native of Rural township, but now of Keswick, Iowa, Maude E , and Mabel A , at home. All of the children have been students in the State Normal School of Normal, Illinois, and the home is one of culture and refinement, while the members of the family hold an enviable position in social circles. Mrs. Wilson is a member of the Beulah Presbyterian church, in which she has served as organist since she was fourteen years of age. She possesses much musical ability, and this talent has been inherited by her children The sons are now members of the State University Cornet Band of Normal

Mr Wilson belongs to Sherman Lodge, No 535, F & A M , and is clerk of Rural Camp, No. 186, M W A He also belongs to the Knights of the Globe. Both he and his wife belong to the Home Forum, the Court of Honor and Royal Neighbors, and Mrs Wilson is a member of the Order of the Eastern Star Mr Wilson gave his political support to the Republican party until 1876, but has since voted with the Democracy and - in , , , , , , , of , silver For twelve , , , ,

supervisor of Rural township and has acted upon some of the most important committees, during which time he has materially advanced the interests of the community He was also constable and commissioner of highways for several terms and has been school director for five years, his efforts in behalf of the cause of education being very effective and beneficial. He is public-spirited in an eminent degree and has always done much in behalf of the general welfare of his community His memory goes back to the time when the county was almost a wilderness, touching the pioneer epoch in the history of western Illinois Through the years which have since come and gone he has not only watched its progress and development but has borne his part therein His genial temperament, sound judgment and well proved integrity have gained him the esteem and friendship of a host of acquaintances

CYRUS D GORDON, senior member of the firm of Gordon & Bowman, real estate and loan agents, is one of the most widely known and deservedly popular citizens of Rock Island county. He is a native of Pennsylvania, born in Venango county, February 23, 1842, and is the son of Alexander and Elizabeth (Wilson) Gordon, both of whom were also natives of the Keystone state Of their eight children, six sons and two daughters, four sons are now living—James P , John W , Cyrus D and Samuel H The father was by occupation a farmer and followed that calling his entire life

Leaving his old Pennsylvania home, Al- , , , , , family to cated in

9

Rural township, where he improved a fine farm and successfully engaged in agricultural pursuits He was a man universally esteemed and lived in peace with his neighbors, while enjoying the love and filial regard of each of his children His death occurred in 1873, at the age of seventy-three years For years he was a ruling elder in the Presbyterian church, of which body his wife was also a member She survived him some years, dying at the age of eighty-two

The paternal grandfather of our subject, James Gordon, was a soldier in the Revolutionary war, a patriot who did his duty faithfully and well, and died revered by all with whom he came in contact He was also a farmer, and in his old age came to Rock Island county and here passed to his reward in 1844 at the age of eighty-eight years His wife also died here at the age of eighty-nine The maternal grandfather, James Wilson, was a native of Scotland, who came to this country when quite young, locating in Pennsylvania, where he married a native of that state and there spent the remainder of his life, dying at the age of eighty-five

Cyrus D Gordon was reared on the home farm in Rural township, Rock Island county, and in the district schools received his education In common with other farmer boys he was early trained to work, and in boyhood and youth did his part in the cultivation of the soil The outdoor life served to develop his physical being, and gave him that strength and general good health that served him so well in early manhood In his youth the slavery question was the all-absorbing theme that agitated both men and women, young and old alike The Soul

that political control of the country so long enjoyed, determined to extend slavery into all the territories of the Union The freemen of the North objected, and war was the result

Mr Gordon was an interested observer of the signs of the times, and his patriotic blood was stirred within him as each succeeding step was taken by the impulsive leaders of the South to dismember the Union Early in the struggle he determined to enlist and became a member of the Forty-fifth Illinois Volunteer Infantry, November 13, 1861 With his regiment, as brave and courageous as any serving during that awful four years of fratricidal war, he marched to the front and did his duty manfully and well, although he was " only a private " Among the principal engagements in which he participated were those of Fort Henry, Fort Donelson, Shiloh, Jackson, Iuka and Vicksburg In addition to these he was in numerous small engagements and skirmishes At Fort Donelson and Pittsburg Landing he was slightly wounded, and yet bears upon his body the marks of the enemy's bullets By reason of a surgeon's certificate of disability he was discharged December 13, 1863 Two of Mr Gordon's brothers were also in the service and it may be said here for the consideration of the admirers of the old soldier, that while these three boys were in the service a draft was issued that not one of the Gordon family was subject to and their father subscribed $450 to hire substitutes, the greater part of which was paid by the boys out of their pay, $13 per month

Returning home, Mr Gordon engaged in farming one year and then went to Pennsylvania, where the succeeding twelve i . . part in the il business with gratifying success While in that business he was for a time vice-president of the Grease City Bank, which did a very extensive business He then came back to Rock Island county and until 1887 was engaged in agricultural pursuits From the farm he removed to Rock Island city and engaged in the hotel business It was while here that he acquired the title "Dad," by which he is known near and far, from the kind and fatherly manner with which he treated all None were allowed to leave his door hungry, the price being an after consideration, and many pleasing stories are yet told how he cared for boys that were away from home and friends. Were he to travel in any direction near or far at nearly every station he would be greeted with that friendly "Hello, Dad"

While still engaged in the hotel business he was elected sheriff of the county and served four years, discharging the duties of the office in a most acceptable manner

On the completion of his official term as sheriff, Mr. Gordon formed a partnership with E H Bowman and opened a real estate and loan office, and in the business of the office they have been quite successful, handling a large amount of real estate and making large and extensive loans, principally on real estate security Before engaging in this business, however, Mr Gordon had been interested in gold mining, and is at present treasurer and general manager of the Rock Island Gold Mining Company; treasurer of the Spring Gulch Gold Mining Company, treasurer and general manager of the Black Lion Gold Mining Company, treasurer and general manager of the Sue-Ole Gold Mining Company, and is one of the principal owners of each of these mine l w ll a s f s f

his business interests are indeed quite extensive

Soon after returning from the war, Mr Gordon on the 4th of January, 1864, was united in marriage with Miss Zilpah A Livingston, a daughter of Hugh and Elizabeth (Smith) Livingston, the former a native of Pennsylvania, and the latter of England Of their four children, Emma Frances married Edwin Wright, by whom she has four children Reta, Marion, Edgar G. and Pauline, Marion Edith is the wife of John Rinck, deputy county clerk of Rock Island county, and they have one child, John Cyrus, and Susan Estella and Viola Wright yet reside with their parents.

Religiously, Mr Gordon is a Presbyterian, of which body his wife is also a member, and in the work of the church as well as in all moral and social reforms both are alike interested Politically, he is a free silver Democrat, but his business interests prevent his taking a very active part in political affairs. Fraternally he is a Mason, with the rank of Knight Templar, being a member of Evert Commandery, No. 18, K. T He is also a member of the Grand Army of the Republic, Union Veterans' Union, Modern Woodmen of America, Court of Honor, and Knights of the Globe

Mr. and Mrs Gordon reside in a pleasant home at No 1411 Fourth avenue, Rock Island, and also have a mountain home on Ute creek, Clear Creek county, Colorado They are popular and highly esteemed wherever known, and Mr Gordon represents one of the old families of the county, where he has made his home since one year old, save the time spent in the oil regions Few men are better known in Rock Island county and none stand higher in the esteem of their fellow of refined tastes and lovely disposition, one who delights in doing good as the opportunity is afforded her In her the poor have always a friend, and the Master an obedient and willing follower To one and all Mr and Mrs Gordon give this wholesome advice

"Do all the good you can
Keep good company or none at all
Be virtuous and you will be happy
Where sinners entice thee consent thou not "

JOHN J PRYCE, of Coal Valley, is identified with two of the most important industries of the county, farming and mining In the latter connection his interests contribute not only to his individual prosperity, but also advance the general prosperity of the community by promoting commercial activity. He occupies a foremost place among the honorable and representative business men of this locality, his straightforward dealing and honesty of purpose commending him to the confidence and good will of all with whom he is brought in contact

Mr Pryce was born in the northern part of Wales, August 15, 1839 His parents were also natives of the same country, his father devoting his life to the work of the Presbyterian ministry

In 1869, John J Pryce crossed the Atlantic, and made his home in Coal Valley township, Rock Island county, where he has resided ever since The remarkable industry and thrift of himself and his family have enabled him to acquire a good competence which he has invested in a farm of one hundred and seventy-five acres and in coal mines He employs from forty to fifty men in the mines A determination to succeed, and that by honorable methods, has characterized hi

enterprise and good management have brought him prosperity.

On the 2nd of May, 1862, Mr Pryce was united in marriage with Miss Margaret Morris in their native land They have eight children, two sons and six daughters, John Morris, Mary, Richard Morris, Annie, Margaret, Helen, Ida and Fanny, and the family circle remains yet unbroken John is now foreman of the mines. Richard manages the farm. Mary, Helen, Ida and Fanny are teachers Annie and Margaret are at home. The family belongs to the Presbyterian church It is intelligent and occupies a high position in social circles

Mr Pryce holds membership in the Odd Fellows Society and the Ancient Order of United Workmen His political support is given to the Republican party, and he has served as school director and road commissioner for six years each As a citizen, he meets every requirement and manifests a commendable interest in everything that is calculated to promote the county's welfare in any line In private life he is sympathetic and generous, extending a helping hand to the poor and needy, and always willing to help those who help themselves This wins for him the friendship of all classes

ALBERT F. VINTON —The records of the lives of our forefathers are of interest to the modern citizen, not alone for their historical value but also for the inspiration and example they afford, yet we need not look to the past. Although surroundings may differ, the essential conditions of human life are ever the same, and a man can learn from the success of those around him if he will heed the obvious les-
·· · ·t us·l in their history Turn to

the life record of Mr Vinton, study carefully the plans and methods he has followed, and then you will learn of managerial ability seldom equaled. He is a man of keen perception, great sagacity and unbounded enterprises, and for almost a third of a century was prominently identified with the business interests of Moline, but has now laid aside business cares, and is practically living a retired life

Mr Vinton was born in Granville, Addison county, Vermont, May 27, 1840, a son of John Vinton, whose birth occurred September 2, 1793, in Brantree, Massachusetts, where he grew to manhood, and married Charlotte Lamb, a native of the same state, born in Spencer, Massachusetts, August 26, 1792 Later John Vinton removed to Vermont, where he engaged in farming and stock-raising until called from this life in 1870 He was a drummer in the war of 1812, and later in life drew a pension His wife survived him and passed away in 1881 Our subject is the youngest of their ten children, seven sons and three daughters, all of whom reached man and womanhood They were as follows Charles L., who died in Vermont at the age of thirty-nine, William L , who died in the same state in 1896, at the age of seventy-four, Henry, who also died in Vermont, in 1889, at the age of fifty-four years, Mrs Charlotte Jane Dimick, who died at Montpelier, Vermont, in June, 1897, at the age of seventy-two years, Hon Geo W , who was a member of the General Assembly in 1891, is still living in Moline, John A , Augustus F , Mrs H E Flint and Mrs Lenora L Jewett, all living in Vermont

Albert F Vinton completed his literary education in th b h l d R i j and Rochest r, N q t l t

the home farm until coming to Moline in 1863, when he entered the employ of his uncle, John Deere, as shipping clerk, remaining as such three years He was then a traveling salesman for Deere & Company until 1874, his route being in Iowa and Wisconsin, but in 1875 helped to organize the Plow Company of Davenport, Iowa, of which he was made secretary and treasurer, and was one of the stockholders and general agent until 1883 Disposing of his interest in the business, he spent the following two years in Colorado and Georgia for the benefit of his wife's health

Mr Vinton was married in Moline, in 1870, to Miss Cherrie Pennell, who was born, reared and educated in Canandaigua, New York, and was a daughter of Horace Pennell She died in 1885, and on the 18th of September, 1890, Mr. Vinton was again married at Waukegan, Illinois, his second union being with Miss Tee Crockett, a native of Kentucky, where she spent her early life Her father, William D Crockett, was a lineal descendant of old David Crockett, for whom he was named In ante bellum days he owned a large plantation and many slaves, but in 1868 came to Rock Island county, Illinois, where he engaged in farming and breeding fine horses. Later he removed to Waukegan, where his death occurred in 1891, and where his wife is still living

In 1888 Mr Vinton bought a third interest in the Union Malleable Iron Company, which soon built up a large, profitable and satisfactory business, and to him much of the success of the enterprise was due He continued to serve as vice-president and business manager until 1894, when the

engaged in any business He is a stock-holder and director of the First National Bank of Moline, and is now serving on the loan committee

Politically, Mr Vinton has always been identified with the Democratic party and has taken an active and prominent part in public affairs In 1891 he was elected a member of the county board of supervisors, was re-elected in 1893, 1895 and 1897, and was instrumental in securing the erection of the handsome new court house which now adorns Rock Island county He has been a delegate to many of the county and state conventions of his party, and has done all in his power to insure its success His estimable wife is a member of the Christian church of Rock Island, and to that denomination and to others he contributes liberally. Fraternally he is a Master Mason The career of Mr Vinton has ever been such as to warrant the trust and confidence of the business world, for he has ever conducted all transactions on the strictest principles of honor and integrity His devotion to the public good is unquestioned and arises from a sincere interest in the welfare of his fellow men

— —

EDMOND G JAMIESON is a member of the Jamieson Coal Company, and for nine years has been prominent in the development of this industry in Rock Island county His rating is high as a business man and by the exercise of energy, keen discrimination and perseverance he has achieved prosperity in his undertakings

A native of Derbyshire, England, Mr Jamieson was born August 25, 1861 His grandfather, Gilbert Jamieson, was numbered amo

Island county, where he located in 1842 Purchasing eighty acres of raw land he developed a farm and reared his family thereon He was a man of prominence and held a number of local positions of honor and trust He was born in the highlands of Scotland, but afterward removed to the lowlands and thence went to England when a young man, engaging there in merchandising He handled teas, silks and fine goods and did an extensive business He was married in England and continued his residence there until his emigration to the United States in 1842.

William Jamieson, the father of our subject, was a native of Derbyshire, and came with his parents to Rock Island county, being reared and educated in Moline township He then returned to England where he married Ann Crocker, also a native of Derbyshire, and with his bride returned to Illinois. For a few years he gave his attention to farming on the old homestead and then again went to England with his family, remaining abroad for several years Once more he came to Illinois, and spent his remaining days as a farmer of Rock Island county, his death occurring in April, 1870 His widow still survives and is now living with her son, Walter S Jamieson, in Shawnee county, Kansas The family numbered eight children and since the father's death there has never but once been a physician called to the house The children are Anna B, wife of E. F Gabbey, of Colorado, Edmond G., of this review, Walter S, A Fergus, of Rossville, Kansas, Stanton L, of Geneva, Wisconsin, Harry Wallace, of Kansas, Arthur Bruce and John W., who are living in Roseville, Kansas

Mr Jamieson, of this review, was reared to manhood on the old homestead and his education was acquired in the common schools, was supplemented by about three years' study in the Moline schools In 1879 he went with his brother to Shawnee county, Kansas, and purchased two hundred and forty acres of land That year he broke one hundred acres which he planted in wheat and then returned to Rock Island county for his mother and her family He spent two years in Colorado and visited Leadville, the Rocky Mountains and other sections of the west On returning once more to Rock Island county, he began farming on the old homestead and successfully followed that pursuit for six years, when he turned his attention to the development of the coal interests, opening up a mine upon his place There is an excellent vein of coal from three to four feet in thickness and produces an excellent quality of this mineral The first shaft was sunk in 1888 by our subject, who began operations on a small scale, but when it was seen that the business would prove a profitable investment the Jamieson Coal Company was incorporated and in 1892 the present shaft was sunk The annual output is now about one hundred thousand bushels, and the enterprise yields to the stockholders a good income

Mr. Jamieson was married in Rossville, Kansas, January 26, 1881, to Sarah D McAdams, a native of Indiana, and to them have been born five children—Nellie A , Harry G., Stewart C , Frank S. and Reuben

In his political affiliations, Mr Jamieson was formerly a Republican, but is now a free-silver Democrat, and voted for W. J Bryan in 1896 He has filled the offices of township collector, constable, justice of the peace, road supervisor and school director, and is a w.rth fr. u l f th. .1. .

tion, doing all in his power for its advancement He has served as a delegate to two county conventions, and meets fully every obligation that devolves upon him as a man and a citizen Socially he is connected with the Modern Woodmen of America During his long residence in Rock Island county, his well spent life, marked by the utmost fidelity to duty, has gained him the high regard of a large circle of friends, and his well directed business efforts have won him a deserved success

---

CAPTAIN J C CAMERON is one of the most widely known citizens of Rock Island Long has been the period of his identification with the city and his life is closely interwoven with its history Through more than half a century he has witnessed its growth and development The many changes which have come with the passing of the years have wrought a wonderful transformation in this region and of the progress made Captain Cameron has not been an idle spectator, but has ever cheerfully borne his part in the work of public improvement His circle of acquaintances is indeed extensive and all entertain for him the highest regard

Captain Cameron was born near Newcastle, Pennsylvania, April 4, 1823, and is of Scotch lineage His grandfather, Allen Cameron, was a native of the land of hills and heather, and came to America during the war of the Revolution. He had a large family and died in Pennsylvania in middle life. Joseph Cox was a native of Pennsylvania and spent his entire life in that state, where he died at an advanced age He was a soldier in the war of 1812 These two

ron, Jr ,

and Margaret Cox, respectively Born and reared in the Keystone state they became man and wife and reared a family of nine children, of whom Captain Cameron is one The others are James, Robert, deceased; La Fayette, Elizabeth, wife of Robert Mc-Connehay, Jane, Bazaleel and Bartley The father of this family was a blacksmith by trade, but during the greater part of his life followed farming He died in Pennsylvania in the spring of 1845, at the age of forty-seven years, and his wife, who survived him until 1881, passed away at the age of eighty-three Both were members of the Presbyterian church

Captain Cameron spent the years of his minority in his native state, and attended the select and common schools of his neighborhood He was reared on a farm, early becoming familiar with all the duties which fall to the lot of the agriculturist Thinking the advantages of the West superior to those of the more thickly settled East, he came to Illinois in 1844, locating in Rock Island where he has since made his home. He was living here at the time of the killing of Davenport in 1845, and is familiar with many of the historic events which form the annals of this region

Captain Cameron gave his time and energies to millwright work on coming to the west and later turned his attention to bridge building, after which he secured employment in a boat yard He is probably best known to Rock Island citizens, however, as the genial and popular ferryman, who for thirty-six years was engaged in ferrying boats belonging to one company He was also engaged in steamboating on the Mississippi between St Louis and Galena for a time His life has been a busy and useful one and the success that has come to him in the re-

ward of his meritorious and well directed efforts

In 1845 Captain Cameron was united in marriage to Miss Lucinda Wakefield, daughter of Thomas Wakefield She died in 1882 and is survived by seven of a family of fourteen children, namely Allen, Margarettean, Medora, La Fayette, Joseph, William, and Lincoln For his second wife the Captain chose Miss Clara Hardy, and they had five children, of whom three are living—Elmer, Esther and Florence Mrs Cameron is a member of the Baptist church The Captain is a member of the Odd Fellows society He voted with the Republican party from the time of its organization until 1896, and for two years was a member of the city council His genial manner and kindly disposition, his uniform courtesy and his high personal worth has won him a circle of friends that is limited only by the circle of his acquaintances

SAMUEL M ZEIGLER —Among the leading and representative agriculturists of Rock Island county, stalwart and sturdy tillers of the soil, there is none who stands a more prominent figure than the gentleman of whom this notice is written His fine farm is pleasantly located on section 8, Moline township, adjoining the city limits of Moline, but he is now practically living retired, leaving its active management to other hands He has made his home in this section since the 18th of April, 1849, and deserves a prominent place among the honored pioneers of the locality

Mr Zeigler was born July 25, 1822, in Cumberland county, Pennsylvania, a son of Charles and Sarah (Minich) Zeigler, both born in the same county of German parent-

age   The Zeigler and Minich families came to America on the same vessel and settled in the same neighborhood in Cumberland county, Pennsylvania, but the Minichs later sold their property there and removed to Franklin county, the same state   The birth of Philip Zeigler, the paternal grandfather of our subject, occurred in the Fatherland, but at the age of twelve years he was brought by his parents to the New World, becoming a resident of Pennsylvania when it was almost an unbroken wilderness   He assisted in the cultivation and improvement of a farm, and became one of the well-to-do and prosperous agriculturists of Cumberland county.   The mother of our subject was one of a family of nine girls and in early life she often assisted in the work of the fields   The father dying when Samuel M was only a year and a half old, Mrs Zeigler was again married, but she, too, passed away at the early age of thirty years.

After the death of his father our subject went to live with his paternal grandfather, remaining there until nine years of age, when he returned to his mother in Franklin county and made his home there until her death   In the meantime, however, he ran away, but just before reaching the home of his grandfather in Cumberland county, he was caught and taken back   With his stepfather he remained for awhile, was later with an uncle, and subsequently spent three years with a farmer, during which time he was allowed to attend the public schools, where he acquired a good practical education   At the age of fourteen he went to live with another uncle, who had been appointed his guardian, and remained upon his farm for four years, after which he worked for other farmers until attaining his majority.

On the 23d of May, 1844, Mr Zeigler was married in Cumberland county, Pennsylvania, to Miss Catherine Bender, who was born in Lancaster county, Pennsylvania, but was reared in Cumberland county, where her father became a substantial farmer.   After his marriage our subject located on the old homestead, where he followed agricultural pursuits until 1847, and the following year came west to look up a location   He purchased one hundred and fifty acres of his present farm in Moline township, Rock Island county, which was partially improved, the bottom land being under cultivation, as it was one of the first farms to be settled in the county   In the spring of 1849 he brought his family here, and after spending a year in Rock Island, he located upon his farm, which he has converted into one of the most highly cultivated tracts of the county   He has sold some of the place which is now included in Prospect Park, and the remainder he has improved with good and substantial buildings

To Mr and Mrs Zeigler were born six children, but four are now deceased   Charles J married and removed to Creston, Iowa, where he engaged in business and there his death occurred   William Harvey died in childhood   Mrs Martha Matilda McClure is a widow residing in Davenport   Kate Elizabeth is the wife of A S Gunn, a resident of Chicago   Clara Janet married William C Wilson, and Albert S was also married, but both are now deceased

Since voting for Abraham Lincoln in 1860, Mr Zeigler has supported every presidential nominee of the Republican party, but at local elections generally votes independent of party ties, supporting the man whom he thinks best qualified to fill local po-

sitions of honor and trust, including those
of commissioner of highways, supervisor,
and school director, which he filled for
thirty consecutive years, during which time
he did much to improve the grade of schools
in his district   In 1845 he joined the Independent Order of Odd Fellows in Pennsylvania, but at present is connected with no
lodge   For almost half a century he has
been identified with the growth and development of this region and has been an important factor in bringing about its present
prosperity   His business dealings are
characterized by fairness and strict honesty,
and he and his amiable wife have won for
themselves an enviable place in the regard
of others in the community

JOSEPH BOLLINGER —Among the influential members of the farming community of Rock Island county and one of its
leading and prosperous citizens, is the gentleman whose name heads this sketch   He
is entirely a self-made man in the truest
sense of the word, having been the architect
of his own fortune and has achieved success
through his indomitable energy and perseverance

Mr Bollinger was born in the village of
Bodenheim, Germany, March 17, 1827, and
in that country his parents, George and
Anna (Trunk) Bollinger, spent their entire
lives, the former dying when over sixty
years of age and the latter some years afterward   Both were communicants of the
Catholic church and most estimable people
The father operated a small farm in his native land   The paternal grandfather died
in Germany at a ripe old age, and the maternal grandfather passed away when his
children were all young

Our subject is the youngest in a family
of seven children, and with the exception of
himself all are now deceased   In the common schools of the fatherland he acquired a
fair education and remained in that country
until he had attained the age of twenty-two,
crossing the Atlantic to the United States in
1849   From that fall until the following May
or June he remained in Michigan, but since
the spring of 1850 has made his home in Rock
Island county, where he was first employed
in sawing hickory wood in the city of Rock
Island   Later he worked in a brickyard for
a short time and afterward engaged in
steamboating, but was obliged to give up
the latter on account of chills and fever
from which he suffered   He next worked
at gardening or whatever he could find to
do   In 1854 he purchased twenty acres of
his present farm on section 7, Rock Island
township, and has since devoted his energies to agricultural pursuits   He now has a
beautiful and productive farm of eighty
acres three miles from the court house, and
improved with excellent buildings, including
a fine brick house erected in 1858.

On the 20th of April, 1854, Mr Bollinger was united in marriage to Miss Sophia,
daughter of Paul and Catharine Anthony,
who the year previous had brought their
family to America   They had only two
children, the other being Jacob, who still
makes his home in Rock Island   The father, who was an agriculturist, became the
owner of the farm in South Rock Island township now owned and occupied by our subject   Upon this place Mr Anthony died at
the age of sixty-nine and his wife at the age
of seventy-one   Lawrence and Anna Maria
(Jacobson) Anthony, the paternal grandparents of Mrs Bollinger, had a family of
three sons Paul, John and Philip, who all

came to Rock Island to live, but are now deceased. The grandfather died in Germany, but his wife passed her last years in Rock Island, where she died at the age of eighty.

Seven children blessed the union of Mr and Mrs Bollinger, namely Kate, who became the wife of Orin Andrews and died at the age of twenty-seven years, George, who married Sophia Stewart, and has two daughters, Florence and Katie, Jacob, who died at the age of twenty, Joseph and William, who are still single, John, who married Eva Wegel and has one daughter, Mabel, and Mathias, who married Eugenia Poiriot

In political sentiments Mr Bollinger is a Democrat, and he and his wife are devout members of the Catholic church They have witnessed almost the entire development of this section of the state and have been important factors in its growth and prosperity Together they have labored earnestly and persistently, overcoming the trials and difficulties incident to pioneer life, and through their own unaided efforts have secured a comfortable competence Their pleasant, social, kindly manner has won for them many friends and they have the respect and esteem of all who know them.

WILLIAM KEENE CROCKETT, who resides upon a fine farm of four hundred acres, section 28, Coal Valley township, is a well-known and highly respected citizen, one who thoroughly understands his calling, and whose ability as a farmer and worth as a citizen is acknowledged by all He was born in Scott county, Kentucky, February 10, 1857, and is a son of Colonel William D and Eliza (Ware) Crockett, both of whom were natives of Kentucky

Colonel W D Crockett was one of the most polished men, a gentleman of the old school, kind-hearted and polite under all circumstances, one whom to know was to admire, and whose friends were many, and limited only to those who had in any manner formed his acquaintance In early life he followed mercantile pursuits for a time, but almost his entire life was spent in farming, stock breeding and raising He came to Rock Island county from Kentucky in 1868 and purchased a farm of three hundred twenty acres in Coal Valley township, to which he subsequently added eighty acres, and which comprises the excellent farm of our subject

In 1883 he rented the farm to his son, William K., and removed to Waukegan, Lake county, where he engaged in the breeding of fine horses, a business in which he was quite successful Among the most noted bred by him was "Lulu," which he sold for twenty thousand dollars, and "Judge Hayes," which he sold for five thousand dollars

Colonel Crockett was married three times, his first union being with Miss Anna Graves, by whom he had three children, Thomas, Mattie and Charles. His second wife was Eliza Ware By this union there were six children, four of whom are yet living —Sallie Tee, now the wife of A F Vinton, of Moline, Fannie W , now the wife of B J. Perrin, of Waukegan, Illinois, Phil M and William Keene The third wife was Mrs Laura Perrin, widow of Nelson Perrin, of Waukegan She yet resides in that city, and religiously is a Presbyterian

Colonel Crockett died in Waukegan in 1892 at the age of seventy-three years For many years he was a member of the Christian church and died in the faith His second wife was also a member of that body. Politically, the Colonel was a Democrat of the most orthodox faith, and fraternally was a Mason.

David Crockett, the paternal grandfather, followed farming in Kentucky. He reared a large family, the descendants of whom are now widely scattered. The maternal grandfather was John Ware, a native of Kentucky.

William Keene Crockett was eleven years of age when he came with his parents to Rock Island county. His literary education was begun in the public schools of his native state and completed in the schools of Rock Island. Later he attended Bryant & Stratton's Business College, Davenport, Iowa. His boyhood and youth were spent upon his father's farm, but on leaving business college he entered the notion store of Field & Bro., Rock Island, where he remained two years. Returning to the farm he followed agricultural pursuits one year and then went to Maryville, Missouri, where he lived seven years, about five years of which time engaged in handling driving and trotting horses.

Renting the old homestead of his father in Coal Valley township, he commenced general farming, which occupation he has followed ever since. After the death of his father he purchased the interest of the other heirs, except that of Mrs. Vinton, of Moline. Since returning to the old farm he has given considerable attention to the raising of Durham cattle and Hambletonian horses, and is now the owner of "Star Hambletonian," with a record of 2 23¼.

On the 11th day of October, 1881, Mr. Crockett was united in marriage with Miss Emma Glenn, daughter of George and Susan Glenn b... ... ...

Clara, Phil and Bert. Mrs. Crockett, who was a native of Athens, Illinois, died May 13, 1892. She was a consistent member of the Methodist Episcopal church, a woman of most excellent traits of character, an affectionate wife and loving mother.

Mr. Crockett is a member of the Christian church at Rock Island. Politically he is a Democrat. Never an office-seeker, and averse to holding official positions, nevertheless he has served eight years as school director, a position well qualified to fill for the reason of his deep interest in the public schools.

JOSEPH KING, a prosperous and substantial farmer and dairyman of South Moline township, residing on section 22, is a native of Bavaria, Germany, born January 15, 1850, and the same year was brought to America by his parents, Peter and Margaret (Zentgraf) King, who were born, reared and married in that country. By occupation the father was a linen weaver and also a farmer. On his arrival in the United States, he located in Pennsylvania where he remained two years and then came to Rock Island, Illinois, reaching here in May, 1852, and spent the first season in the city, working at brick making. He then purchased forty acres of land in South Moline township, which he at once began to clear and improve, but at the end of five years sold that place and purchased the farm now owned and operated by his sons, Charles and Chris. It comprises two hundred acres, which he placed under a high state of cultivation, and there he reared his family and made his home until called to the world beyond in the fall of 1887. His ... ... dying in January, 1892, and was buried by his side in Calvary cemetery, Rock Island

In the family of this worthy couple were eleven children, who in order of birth are as follows   John A , who is now engaged in farming near Dallas, Texas, Joseph, of this sketch, Leonard, a farmer of Cedar county, Iowa, Mary and Theresa, twins, the former the wife of John Vogel, of Rapid City, Illinois, and the latter the deceased wife of William Mock, of Henry county, Illinois, Amanda, who is the present wife of William Mock, and now lives in Davenport, Iowa, Clara, deceased wife of Mike Streckfus, of Salina, Kansas; and Charles and Chris, who own and operate the old homestead

Joseph King spent his boyhood and youth in much the usual manner of farmer lads, aiding his father in the development and cultivation of the old homestead, and attending the district schools when his services were not needed at home   He was married in the city of Rock Island, February 6, 1877, to Miss Mary Vogele, a daughter of Ferdinand Vogele, a native of Boaden, Germany, and a pioneer merchant of Rock Island, where he continued to engage in business until his death May 1, 1878   His wife is still living and resides in that city

Of her family of nine children, five are still living—Mary, wife of our subject, Mrs Frances Klatt, a widow lady living in Rock Island, Ferdinand P , who is engaged in the hardware business in the same city, Ida, widow of John Demoulin, of St Louis, Missouri, and Anna, wife of John McCaffery, of Galesburg, Illinois

Mrs King was born and reared in Rock Island, and began her education, which was completed by a course in the Sisters' Academy of Davenport   By her marriage to

our subject she has become the mother of seven sons and two daughters, namely Ferdinand P , Joseph F , Charlotta M , Leo C , Louis J and Robert W , who are all attending school, and Marie F , Raymond A and Peter M , at home

Previous to his marriage Mr King had removed to Rock Island, where for ten years he was connected with the Western Brewery, and leaving that concern he removed to Moline, and there engaged in the hotel business until May 1, 1882, when he was burned out   In September following he removed to a farm adjoining the one on which he now resides, and on selling that place removed to his present farm in South Moline township, where he has seventy-five acres of well improved and valuable land   The well tilled fields and neat and thrifty appearance of the place testify to his skill and ability as an agriculturist, and he is meeting with a well-deserved success in his undertakings, In 1894, he embarked in the dairy business, the first day selling only three quarts of milk, but his trade has constantly increased, and he now supplies about one hundred customers

Politically, Mr King is a stanch Democrat, and during the campaign of 1896 was an earnest advocate of the free coinage of silver   He cares nothing for official distinction, but being a strong friend of our public school system, he has efficiently served as a member of the school board for six years Socially he belongs to the Modern Woodmen of America, and religiously both he and his wife are members of the Moline Catholic church   For almost half a century Mr King has been actively identified with the growth and development of the county, and well remembers the first dry goods and gro-
                                           hich has

now grown to be one of the most flourishing manufacture towns in this great commonwealth Through his own efforts he has succeeded in accumulating a comfortable competence, and is recognized as one of the most reliable and valued citizens of his township

JOHN TINDALL, whose home is on section 11, Bowling township, has been identified with Rock Island county for sixty-one years, and has contributed to its material progress and prosperity to an extent equaled by but few of his contemporaries He early had the sagacity and prescience to discern the eminence which the future had in store for his great and growing country, and acting in accordance with the dictates of his faith and judgment he has reaped, in the fullness of time, the generous benefits which are the just recompense of indomitable industry, spotless integrity and marvelous enterprise

Mr Tindall first opened his eyes to the light of day July 21, 1815, in Worcester county, Maryland, and is a son of Elijah and Margaret (Wiley) Tindall, who were born, reared and educated in Virginia Our subject is the only one now living in their family of seven children, five sons and two daughters The paternal grandfather, an Episcopal clergyman, on coming from England located in Worcester county, Maryland, where he erected a house of brick brought from England, and for over a century that building stood, a landmark of early pioneer days The maternal grandfather was a sea captain, and was lost at sea when Mrs Tindall was quite young

Near Snow Hill in Worcester county, Maryland

milling and coopering throughout his entire life, dying at that place in 1826, when about sixty years of age His widow came west with our subject in 1836 and located in Rock Island, but died at the home of her youngest son, Samuel, in Bowling township, in 1844, at the age of seventy years Both were devout Methodists and no better man or woman lived than this worthy couple, who had the respect and esteem of all who knew them The father was a man of good education, and his house was a stopping place for all ministers and circuit riders in those early days

In the old fashioned subscription schools of his native county, John Tindall, of this review, received his education, and was reared to habits of industry In 1836, at the age of twenty years, he came west with his mother and during the first summer spent here, he helped to make the brick for the old court house in Rock Island The next year he operated twenty acres of rented land south of the city, and in connection with farming also engaged in teaming In 1838 he located upon his present farm in Bowling township, where he had entered two hundred acres of wild land on coming to the county, and this place has now been his home for the long period of fifty-nine years He has successfully followed general farming and stock raising, and as his financial resources have increased, he has added to his landed possessions until he now has about twelve hundred acres of the richest and most productive land in the county

On the 31st of March, 1836, Mr. Tindall was joined in wedlock to Miss Elizabeth, daughter of Josiah Cropper, and they became the parents of thirteen children, ten sons and three daughters, including two sets of twins, namely Harriet, Frank, Edward, Harriet, Frank, Samuel and Joseph (twins), Winn, Margaret, Henry, Atlas, and Abraham and Lincoln (twins)   Harriet and Frank, the first of those names, both died in infancy,   Samuel married Louisa Bridgeford, by whom he had six children, five now living—Albert, Lizzie, Laura, Nancy and Arthur—and he died at the age of fortyfour, leaving a widow, who now makes her home in Black Hawk township, four miles east of Milan   Joseph married Maggie Shaunnessy, by whom he had two daughters, Mary and Kittie, and after her death he wedded Rebecca Bridgeford, by whom he had six children, five still living—Mila, Myrtle, John, Estey and Joseph   Winn, who conducts a livery stable in Rock Island, is not married.   Margaret became the wife of John H. Gilmore, of Milan, and died leaving three children—May, Nina and George   Henry is a traveling salesman   Atlas carries on the home farm   Abraham and Lincoln both died in infancy

Mr Tindall has been called upon to mourn the loss of his worthy wife, who passed away in 1876, at the age of sixtyone years   She was an earnest member of the Methodist church, to which he also belongs and was beloved by all who knew her for her many excellencies of character   Mr Tindall gives his political support to the men and measures of the Republican party, but has never taken a very active part in political affairs, preferring to give his undivided attention to his extensive business interests.   As a man he is looked upon by the community as one who can be trusted, who "breaks no promise, serves no private end, who gains no office, but who has lost no friend "   The success that he has achieved in the field would a' ''

just reward of earnest, persistent toil, guided by sound judgment and excellent business ability

THOMAS R. LEES is a general merchant of Coal Valley, and in that town was born on the 11th of August, 1861, his parents being Thomas and Jane (Mills) Lees, natives of Lancastershire, England, who are mentioned at length on another page of this volume.   The father is still living, one of the highly respected citizens and honored pioneers of Coal Valley   On the homestead farm our subject spent the days of his boyhood and youth, at work, at play or in attendance at the district schools   He assisted in the cultivation of the home farm during the summer season and pursued his studies through the winter months   Later he supplemented his early educational privileges by a course in Knox College, Galesburg, Illinois.

When Mr. Lees laid aside his text books to take up the more serious duties of life and learn in the school of experience the lessons of deeper meaning, he determined to try his fortune in the west and going to Colorado was for three years employed in the silver mines there   In 1885 he returned to Rock Island county, and assumed the management of the old home farm while his father made a visit to England   He carried on agricultural pursuits for about two or three years and then turned his attention to merchandising, purchasing the interest of the senior partner in the firm of Gus Krapp & Son   Thus becoming a partner of G B Krapp, business has since been continued under the style of Krapp & Lees   They carry a large stock of general merchandise, farm implements, etc , and enjoy an ever

On the 6th of April, 1889, Mr Lees was united in marriage to Miss Matilda, daughter of Gustav Krapp, and three children now grace their union —John, Gertrude and Dena

Mr Lees is a Master Mason, the present master of his lodge, and he and his wife are members of the Eastern Star He also belongs to the Modern Woodmen of America He exercises his right of franchise in support of the men and measures of the Democracy, and for two years has held the office of town clerk, while for one year he was collector In 1893 he was elected to the office of supervisor, and so promptly and faithfully discharged his duties that he was re-elected in 1895 and again in 1897 He has strict regard for the ethics of commercial life, a true conception of the duties of citizenship, and is ever actuated by an honest purpose to meet fully the obligations that rest upon him in both public and private life

B YRON JORDAN —Among the leading and influential farmers of Rural township who thoroughly understand their business and pursue the vocation of their chosen calling in a methodical and workmanlike manner is the subject of this biography He resides on section 36, and his farm which at first comprised only one hundred acres, now contains within its borders three hundred and six acres of fertile and well-improved land

Mr Jordan is a native son of Illinois his birth occurring in Mercer county, June 11, 1842 His parents were Captain John A and Rachel Metzler) Jordan, natives of Maine and Coshocton, Ohio, respectively. The pat---

was also born in the old Pine Tree state, and in 1833 emigrated to Ohio, where he died in middle life, two weeks after his arrival Of his fourteen children seven of them became seafaring men The Jordan family was originally from Ireland, and was founded in this country sometime during the seventeenth century. Peter Metzler, the maternal grandfather of our subject, was a native of Pennsylvania, and of German descent By trade he was a millwright, but after coming to Richland Grove, Illinois, in 1836, he followed farming until his death in 1875, when eighty-five years of age

John A Jordan, with his twin brother, Thomas J, came to Mercer county, Illinois, November 9, 1839, locating at Richland Grove, where he was married and all of his children were born—Byron, of this review, Edwin T., now a resident of Montezuma, Iowa, William H., a government clerk living in Rock Island, and Olive M, who died at the age of seventeen years while at Abingdon, Illinois In the spring of 1856 the father sold his farm of one hundred and sixty acres in Mercer county, and came to Rock Island county, where he purchased a like amount in Rural township, then called Coal Valley As his financial resources increased he added to his landed possession until at one time he owned four hundred and twenty acres of which one hundred and sixty were located in Iowa During the Civil war he was commissioned captain of Company A, Thirty-seventh Illinois Volunteer Infantry, but after five months of service was stricken with paralysis which ultimately caused his death He died in 1886 at the age of sixty-seven years, while at work in the fields on his farm in Rural township His widow is still living at the age of sev-
.. f . l i w .k h home in

BYRON JORDAN.

Orion Both were active and prominent members of the Methodist church, and he attended seveial conferences Being a Free-soiler in early life he joined the Republican party on its organization and ever afterwaid was one of its most earnest advocates For several terms he creditably filled the office of justice of the peace, and was supervisor one term, discharging the duties of that office with the same fidelity and promptness which marked his entire career. As an earnest Christian gentleman and upright, honorable business man, he gained the confidence and esteem of all who knew him

The first fourteen years of his life our subject passed in Mercer county, was then a resident of Rock Island county from 1856 until 1867, but the following decade was spent in Henry county, Illinois, after which he returned to Rock Island county, and located on the farm now known as the White Pond farm, making his home here ever since The common schools afforded his early educational privileges, but after his return from the army he attended the Western high school for a time Throughout his entire business career he has successfully followed agricultural pursuits

In 1862 Mr Jordan laid aside his text books and joined Company C, One Hundred and Second Illinois Volunteer Infantry, with which he continued to serve for almost three years, being honorably discharged in June, 1865, at the close of the war, when his services were no longer needed. He participated in the battle of Resaca, and was with Sherman on the celebrated march to the sea, was all through the Carolina campaign, and proceeded with his regiment to Washington, after having taken part in twenty engagements On his enlistment he was ma ꞏ ꞏ ꞏ ꞏ
10

later commissioned second lieutenant, and during the last year of his service commanded his company

Captain Jordan was married November 17, 1867, to Miss Mary Anna, daughter of William and Elizabeth K (Trego) Blackfan, and four children bless their union— Rolland B , Elmer H , Samuel Lester, deceased and Erwin B The oldest son, who is a carpenter by trade, married Miss Linnie Davis, who died when their daughter Edith was only twelve days old, and he afterward wedded Miss Sophia Davenport, of the same place The other sons are single and reside at home

On attaining his majority Mr Jordan became a Republican, but for the past few years has supported the men and measures of the Prohibition party, and has served as county chairman He has been a delegate to numerous state conventions of his party, and in 1896 attended as a delegate the national Prohibition convention at Pittsburg In 1894 he ran as the Prohibition candidate for State Senator in the 23d senatorial district and received a fair vote He and his wife are faithful members of the Methodist church, in which he is now filling the position of class leader, steward, trustee and teacher in the Sunday school Twice he has been a lay delegate to the Central Illinois Methodist Episcopal Conference, first when held in Macomb and later in Peoria He is now president of the Rock Island Camp Meeting Association and was a member of its executive committee a number of years He is a kind-hearted, conscientious man, who has the confidence and good will of a large circle of friends and acquaintances At present he is serving as president of the Osco and ꞏ ꞏ ꞏ mpany

Upon his farm is a beautiful grove of sugar maples, cedars, white pine, walnuts and a great variety of other trees, which are nicely trimmed and afford lovely grounds for picnics Mr Jordan very generously allows the grounds to be used for that purpose He set out the trees and has watched with interest their growth, until to-day they form one of the loveliest groves in this section of the State

G EORGE SCHERER, prominent among the thrifty and industrious farmers of South Rock Island township, is one of its most prosperous and energetic men, who from a humble beginning in life has accumulated a handsome property He not only commenced without means, but was obliged to battle with the elements of a foreign soil and the customs of a strange country, as he is of German birth and parentage He was born in Hesse-Darmstadt, July 20, 1829, and lost his mother during his infancy His father, Jacob Scherer, a weaver by trade, died about 1837, at the age of seventy years He was a Lutheran in religious faith

Upon a farm in Germany George Scherer passed the days of his boyhood and youth, and in that country acquired a fair common-school education and learned the weaver's trade. In 1850, at the age of twenty, he bade good-by to friends and native land and sailed for America, stopping first in St Louis for about two months as the river was frozen over and he could not proceed, but on the 10th of April of that year, he arrived in Rock Island He was variously employed in a brick-yard, on a farm, at railroading, or at anything by which he could ea··· ····· ·· ····· ···· ·· ·· ···

years he engaged in teaming and then rented the farm on which he now resides for one year It contained at that time one hundred acres, of which he purchased five acres, and has kept adding to it from time to time until he now has one hundred and six acres of the most productive land in the county This valuable farm is pleasantly located only two and a half miles from the court house in Rock Island, and is improved with excellent buildings, including a substantial residence erected in 1877 Mr Scherer devotes the principal part of his attention to gardening

On the 15th of April, 1858, was consummated the marriage of Mr Scherer and Miss Maggie Brockman, a daughter of Frederick and Maggie (Wagner) Brockman, and to them were born eleven children, six sons and five daughters Johnnie, who died in infancy, Maggie, wife of Henry Reithel, by whom she has four children, Maggie, Henry, George and Ernst, Jacob, who married Barbara Schneider and has four children, George, Walter, Johnnie and Frieda, George, who married Maggie Hammer and has two children, Mary and Katie, Christina, wife of James Kerr, by whom she has one daughter, Clara, Gertrude, Kate, Philip and Fred, who are all at home, Johnnie, who died at the age of five years, and Mary, at home The wife and mother, who was a consistent member of the Lutheran church, died in December, 1886, when in her forty-eighth year Politically Mr. Scherer is an ardent Republican, and religiously, he, too, is a member of the Lutheran church. For the long period of forty-seven years he has been a resident of Rock Island county and has been prominently identified with its agricultural interests Although he started out in life for himself with no capital or influential friends to aid him, he has steadily overcome the obstacles and difficulties in his path by industry, perseverance and good management, and is to-day numbered among the well-to-do and most reliable citizens of his township

WILLIAM H CROPPER, a well-known and prominent agriculturist residing on section 1, Bowling township, was born on his present farm, April 19, 1857, and belongs to one of the oldest and most honored pioneer families of Rock Island county His paternal grandfather, Josiah Cropper, was born in Maryland of English descent, was a farmer by occupation and served as a soldier in the war of 1812 He died when well advanced in years The maternal grandfather, Mr Peckenpaugh, also an agriculturist, was of German lineage At a very early day he emigrated to Rock Island county, where he died at an old age In his family were four daughters and one son

The parents of our subject were Edward and Mary (Peckenpaugh) Cropper, the former a native of Maryland, and the latter of Indiana In early life the father was a sailor, but on coming to Rock Island county, he located in Bowling township, where he entered forty acres of land and devoted his energies to farming As his financial resources increased, he extended the boundaries of his place until it comprised two hundred and eighteen acres of highly improved and valuable land, upon which he made his home until 1885, when he removed to Milan and spent his remaining days in retirement, dying September 10, 1886, at the age of eighty-four. His wife had long preceded him to the other world, her death having occurred in 1874 In religion both

they were Methodists and their sterling worth and pleasant, social manners won for them a host of warm friends

In the family of this worthy couple were nine children, but only five are now living, namely Martha E , wife of David Adams, of Milan, Illinois, Julia A , wife of David Bowen, of Waterbury, Connecticut, Emily E , wife of Thomas P Laflin, of Rock Island, Hettie A , wife of David Hoover, of Wayne, Nebraska, and William H

The subject of this sketch has spent his entire life upon his present farm, and in the district schools of the neighborhood acquired his early education, which was supplemented by a course in the Davenport Business College His father gave him the old homestead and he has met with excellent success in its operation, being a most thorough and skillful farmer and successful stock raiser

Mr Cropper was married March 2, 1885, the lady of his choice being Miss Anna M Koch, daughter of John and Dorothea (Litscher) Koch, natives of Switzerland, in whose family were ten children, nine yet living—Anna Magdalena, wife of our subject, Margaretta, widow of George Carder; Dorothea, wife of Henry Gude, Leonard, now a resident of Arizona, John, Lena, Christian, Bernard A , and Henry J. The father is a successful machinist, gunsmith and bicycle dealer in Rock Island, and his sons, John, Christian and Bernard, are associated with him in business Leonard Koch, Mrs Cropper's paternal grandfather, was also born in Switzerland, was a carpenter by trade, and spent his last years in Davenport, Iowa, where he died a few days before he reached the age of eighty years In his family were six children The maternal
 . . a native

THE BIOGRAPHICAL RECORD

of Switzerland, and in 1856 became a farmer of Scott county, Iowa, where he continued to actively engage in agricultural pursuits until a few years previous to his death, which occurred in Davenport in 1892, when he was seventy years of age

Three children have come to bless the union of Mr and Mrs Cropper, as follows Dorothea E , Bernard E and Audra May Fraternally Mr Cropper affiliates with the Modern Woodmen of America and the Knights of Pythias, while politically he is identified with the Republican party, and has been called upon to serve as school director and road commissioner for three years each As a public-spirited and progressive citizen, he has done much to advance the interests of his township and county, gives his support to all worthy enterprises for the public good, and justly deserves to be numbered among the valued and useful members of society He has a host of warm personal friends who appreciate his sterling worth

JOHN W STEWART, M D is one of the most prominent business men of Rock Island Young men in the past have often been deterred from devoting themselves to a business life because of the widespread impression that such a life yields no opportunity for the display of genius The time, however, has gone by when, other things being equal, the business man must take a secondary place to the lawyer, the doctor, the minister or the editor In fact, as a rule, let the business man be equally equipped by education and natural endowment and you will find him to-day in every community exerting a wider influence and wielding a larger share of power in every capacity treading other walks of life The "men of affairs" have come to be in a large degree the men upon whom the country leans The subject of this sketch is pre-eminently a "man of affairs," and is now conducting a wholesale business, dealing in shelf and heavy hardware, blacksmith's and machinist's supplies

Dr Stewart was born in Frederick county, Maryland, January 21, 1844, and is a representative of an old and honored family of that state. His grandfather, John Stewart, was there born and was identified with its business interests as a farmer and merchant In the days of slavery he owned a number of negroes, but when twenty-eight years of age he set them at liberty He was of Scotch-Irish descent, and died at the age of eighty-eight Six of his children reached mature years, one of whom was Dr Alexander Stewart, of Shippensburg, Pennsylvania Our subject is also a cousin of Judge Stewart, a prominent jurist of Chambersburg, Pennsylvania. His father, John S Stewart, was born in Maryland and married Margaret B Witherow, a daughter of John Witherow, of Scotch-Irish ancestry He was born in Maryland, and made farming his life work The parents of our subject had but two children The elder is Rosa J , widow of James C Annan, of Emmetsburg, Maryland, who was a son of Dr Andrew Annan, a prominent abolitionist, who on the morning of the battle of Gettysburg drove over the scene of the conflict with General Reynolds, who was killed later in the day, and whose monument now stands at the entrance of the Gettysburg cemetery. Dr. Annan died in Emmetsburg, Maryland, at the advanced age of ninety-two The father of our subject died in

was a member of the Presbyterian church and died in the faith Mrs Stewart afterward became the wife of Rev Robert S Grier, who served as pastor of one church for fifty-two years She is now a widow for the second time A devoted member of the Presbyterian church, she has spent a long life in the Master's service

Dr Stewart, of this review, was reared in his native county, and after attending the schools of Emmetsburg pursued his studies in Tuscarora Academy of Pennsylvania, and was graduated at LaFayette College, of Easton, Pennsylvania He then studied medicine, was graduated at the University of Pennsylvania with the class of 1867, and engaged in practice in Dayton, Ohio, and at the Soldiers Home. He was the physician at the latter place until September, 1869, when he came to Rock Island, and succeeded to the hardware business formerly owned by Harper & Co , who were his brothers-in-law His time and attention has since been devoted to mercantile pursuits For eighteen years he was associated in partnership with Captain James M Montgomery, but since 1892 has been alone in business He is in the wholesale trade and carries a large stock of shelf and heavy hardware, blacksmith's and machinist s supplies, and takes large contracts for furnishing goods in his line The house is represented by several traveling salesmen and his business has assumed extensive proportions Dr Stewart is a man of keen discrimination, sound judgment and great enterprise and his business methods commend him to the confidence and support of all He is also a director in the Rock Island Building & Loan Association, and has been an active factor in many interests in th   d   d the elfare of his adop i

On the 5th of December, 1867, Dr Stewart married Miss Rosa B McLean, daughter of William and Nancy (Johnston) McLean, natives of Pennsylvania, the former born in Adams county, near Gettysburg, the latter near Shippensburg, Cumberland county James McLean, the paternal grandfather, was born in Adams county, of Scotch-Irish parentage, and was a descendant of William McLean, who located in that locality in 1732, the first of the name to establish a home there He wedded Mary Reed, and had four children He died in middle life, his wife surviving him a number of years He was a relative of the McLean who surveyed the Mason and Dixon Line, and other representatives of his family were prominent in the war of the Revolution George Johnston, the maternal grandfather of Mrs Stewart, was also born in Pennsylvania, and was of Scotch-Irish descent He made farming his life work and accumulated a handsome property He married Margaret Edmiston, a cousin of General Joe Johnston, and they had twelve children

Mr McLean, father of Mrs Stewart, engaged in the manufacture of leather at various points in eastern Pennsylvania and was an extensive land owner He and his wife held membership with the Presbyterian church at Shippensburg, and he served as its treasurer for many years His death occurred in Shippensburg December 22, 1892, in his eighty-fifth year, and his wife passed away in 1880, aged seventy-three years They had eight children, of whom three are now living—Margaret Reed, wife of J R McAllister, of Pittsburg, Rosa B , wife of our subject, and Florence Edith, wife of George C Coughlin, of Norristown, Pennsyl-   cy, wife of

Lieutenant William Harper, who served in the late war, Mary C , wife of George H Stewart, of Shippensburg, Pennsylvania, James E , a graduate of Princeton College, who was collector at the port of Chicago during the time of the great fire there, and at one time a partner of Orville Grant, of Chicago, in the leather business He was a man of much prominence and superior ability, and at the time of his death was president of a bank in Shippensburg George, a corporal of the One Hundred and Thirtieth Pennsylvania Infantry, was wounded at the battle of Fredericksburg in 1862, and died in Harewood Hospital, Washington, nine days later, but was buried at Shippensburg Sarah E died in infancy

Mrs Stewart is a graduate of Oakland Institute of Pennsylvania By her marriage she has become the mother of four sons and four daughters Florence A is a graduate of the art department in Wilson College, Pennsylvania William McLean is a graduate of Augustana College and is now traveling in the interests of the house Alexander is a graduate of the law department of Michigan University, Ann Arbor, Michigan Margaret completed the regular course and was graduated from Wilson College, Pennsylvania John S , a graduate of the Rock Island High School, is now associated with his father in business Nancy J , who is a graduate of the Rock Island High School, Rosabel and James E are at home Dr and Mrs Stewart have provided their children with excellent educational advantages and their home is the center of a cultured society circle They reside in a commodious residence, which was erected by the Doctor in 1871, at the corner of Nineteenth street and Eighth avenue He is president of the board of t   [   ]   [   ]

sity Association, and he and his wife are prominent members of the Broadway Presbyterian church, in which he has served as elder and Sunday school superintendent since the organization of the church By his ballot he supports the Republican party, but otherwise is not actively interested in political affairs Mrs Stewart advocates the principles of the Prohibition party He is a man of broad general information and culture, of superior intellectual endowments, of much force of character, and possesses in a large degree those qualities which indicate the high minded man and which throughout the world command respect and regard.

JOHN RUDY —The splendid farm owned by this gentleman on section 35, South Moline township, is a standing monument to his industry, perseverance and good management He comes under the category of self-made men, having come to this country with no capital, and has succeeded only by the exercise of his steady, plodding labors He was born on the 15th of February, 1827, in Baden, Germany, where he grew to manhood and was provided with good school advantages He also served a three years' apprenticeship to the stone mason's trade, but never followed it, as he preferred agricultural pursuits

At Havre, France, Mr Rudy took passage on a sailing vessel bound for America, and after twenty-eight days spent upon the Atlantic, arrived safely in New York, April 28, 1852, but the passage had been a stormy one He proceeded at once to Montgomery county, Pennsylvania, where his brother had located two years previous, and on a farm in Philadelphia worked until November,

1854, when he determined to try his fortune in the west

In Philadelphia, he was married September 26, 1853, to Miss Catherine Walch, also a native of Baden, Germany, who had come to America on the same vessel with her future husband and went with him to Philadelphia, where she found employment and continued to work until her marriage They have become the parents of six children, as follows Elizabeth, now the widow of Jacob Carb, John H , who is married and resides in South Dakota, William C , who is married and also lives in the same state, Catherine Susanna, wife of Thomas Sweney, of Tacoma, Washington, Emma Helena, wife of John Fur, of Rock Island county, and Charles Frederick, who is now operating the home farm for his father

On the 9th of December, 1854, Mr Rudy arrived in Rock Island county among entire strangers, and until the following March rented a house of Abram Hartzell in South Moline township He then removed to a little log cabin, and until the fall of 1855, he and his wife worked for fifteen dollars per month They then located upon the place now owned and occupied by Joseph King, but in the spring of 1856 removed to the Henry Miller farm, on which Mr Rudy worked by the day In the spring of the following year he went to Whiteside county, Illinois, where he raised three crops, and then returned to the Joseph King farm In the spring of 1860 he rented Peter King's farm, which he operated for four years, and spent the following three years on Mr Britton's place In November, 1866, he purchased a tract of forty-five and a half acres of timber land in South Moline township, about two acres of which had been cleared and a small house on it which in it L it

further development and cultivation he at once turned his attention and now has one of the best and most highly improved farms in the locality In 1882 he built his present comfortable residence, which is surrounded by good and substantial outbuildings and well tilled fields, which indicate his careful management and industrious habits The success that he has achieved is due entirely to his own well directed efforts and those of his estimable wife, who has indeed proved a true helpmeet to him and patiently shared with him the hardships and trials of their early married life

Mr Rudy is a stalwart Democrat in politics, and as he is not an advocate of free silver, he supported General Palmer at the presidential election of 1896 He and his wife were reared in the faith of the Lutheran church, to which they still adhere, and their upright, Christian lives have won for them the confidence and respect of all with whom they have come in contact Mr Rudy has had no occasion to regret his emigration to America, as here he has met with success financially and found a pleasant home He has become a loyal and patriotic citizen of his adopted country, and wherever known is held in high regard

---

GUSTAV B KRAPP, senior member of the firm of Krapp & Lees, general merchants of Coal Valley is one of the most progressive and energetic young business men of Rock Island county He was born in the village where he still resides, on the 15th of August, 1867, a son of Gustav J and Mary (Miller) Krapp, natives of Prussia, Germany The paternal grandfather died in that country in middle life, leaving two ... ed again, having by the second union ten children, all of whom are now deceased John Miller, the maternal grandfather, came to the new world and is now living in Coal Valley at the ripe old age of eighty-two years His wife died a few months since In his family were six children

About 1862 the father of our subject crossed the Atlantic and has since been a resident of Coal Valley, where for many years he engaged in coal mining, but is now living retired, enjoying a well earned rest, free from all the cares and responsibilities of business life With the Lutheran church he and his wife hold membership, and have the respect and esteem of all who know them Gustav B is the oldest in their family of nine children, the others being as follows Matilda, now the wife of T R Lees, John, Frederick, William, Sarah, Alvina, Louis, and Nettie

In the common schools of Coal Valley, Mr Krapp, of this review, obtained his education, and he began his business career by working in a brickyard for a number of years In 1889 he and his father opened a general store and together carried on business for a year and a half, when the latter sold his interest to F R Lees The firm has since been Krapp & Lees, and by fair and honorable dealing they have succeeded in building up an excellent trade, receiving from the public a liberal patronage They carry a full and complete line of general merchandise, including dry goods, groceries, lumber, grain and farm implements

On the 18th of October 1893, was celebrated the marriage of Mr Krapp and Miss Mary I Lembke, daughter of William and Elizabeth (Rodenbaugh) Lembke Two children grace their union William L and Earl Henr '   " " '

member of the Modern Woodmen of America, is a Master Mason, and both he and his wife belong to the Eastern Star As a Democrat he takes quite an active and prominent part in local political affairs, and for seven years has most creditably served as village clerk Public-spirited and progressive, he gives a liberal support to all worthy enterprises calculated to advance the general welfare or promote the material interests of the community, and wherever known is held in high regard

—

AUGUST V ESTERDAHL, an undertaker and dealer in artists' supplies at No 1216 Fifth avenue, Moline, is but a comparatively recent acquisition to the goodly array of progressive business men of that thriving city, but his ability, enterprise and upright methods have already established for him an enviable reputation. Although he is still a young man his popularity is established on a firm basis—that of his own well-tested merit

Mr Esterdahl was born in Kalmer Lan, Sweden, July 26, 1861, a son of Charles E and Christina (Peterson) Esterdahl, who came to America in 1866 and located in Marshall county, Illinois, where the father purchased land and followed farming for many years, but is now living retired in the village of Varna He has reached the age of sixty-seven and his wife sixty-six In much the usual manner of farmer boys our subject spent the days of his boyhood and youth, aiding in the cultivation of the fields and acquired his education in the district schools

Until twenty-two years of age Mr Esterdahl remained under the parental roof '   ' F   a 0, 1884, to Miss Anna J Johnson, of Moline, who is also a native of Sweden They now have three children—Minnie Victoria, born in Varna, February 24, 1885, Elmer Theodore, born in the same place in May, 1886, and Lydia Esther, born in Moline, in January, 1892

For one year after his marriage, Mr Esterdahl carried on agricultural pursuits, and then removed to Varna, where he engaged in wagon and plow repairing and also in building, being a natural mechanic Coming to Moline one year later, he followed carpentering and contracting until 1891, when he embarked in his present business, and in this undertaking he has met with excellent success In his political affiliations he is a Republican, casting his first vote for James G Blaine in 1884, and in religious belief is a Lutheran, belonging to the Swedish church, of which he is now serving as trustee For thirteen years he served as organist of the church at Varna

J EROME W. CALDWELL, one of the leading and representative agriculturists of Rock Island county, now residing on section 16, Rural township, was born in that township on the 25th of January, 1861, and is a son of William and Lydia (Wilson) Caldwell, natives of Butler and Greene counties, Ohio, respectively Robert Caldwell, the paternal grandfather, was born in New Jersey and was probably of Scotch descent On leaving his native state he emigrated to Ohio, but spent his last days in Indiana, becoming one of its earliest settlers There he followed farming and reared his large family of thirteen children The maternal grandfather of our subject was an honored judge   in k i l   i

and died in Rural township when about the age of sixty years

William Caldwell, father of our subject, was the tenth in order of birth in his father's family, and was born in Butler county, Ohio, December 4, 1813 During his boyhood and youth he attended the common schools and also learned the cooper's trade, which he successfully followed for fifteen years On coming to Rock Island county, Illinois, in the spring of 1851, he purchased one hundred and fifty-seven acres in the southwest corner of Rural township, and continued to operate the same for a number of years In 1864, however, he bought forty acres in Mercer county, Illinois, upon which he made his home until 1883, when he purchased the present farm of our subject known as the James Donaldson farm. Although he started out in life for himself with nothing but his indomitable energy, he succeeded in accumulating a handsome property by industry, perseverance and good management, and at one time owned six hundred and sixty-five acres in Rock Island county, and two hundred and forty acres in Mercer county His word was always regarded as good as his bond, and he had the confidence and respect of all with whom he came in contact either in business or social life. He indeed deserves mention among the prominent and representative citizens of the county and should find a place in the history of men of business and enterprise, whose force of character, sterling integrity and control of circumstances have contributed in such an eminent degree to the solidity and progress of this section of the state His life was manly, his actions sincere, his manner unaffected and his example well worthy of emulation His political support was   i   j l   he was called to various local offices of honor and trust

In Rural township, William Caldwell was married June 3, 1860, to Mrs Lydia (Wilson) Halley, a daughter of William and Rachel (Mills) Wilson, and widow of Henry Halley, by whom she had five children— Mary C , Robert C , Hannah M Isaac N and William H Two children graced her second union—Jerome W , of this sketch, and Frank H , now a resident of Milan, Rock Island county The father died in December, 1885, at the age of seventy-three years, and the mother, who was a consistent member of the Baptist church, passed away August 16, 1884, at the age of sixty-six

In 1864 Jerome W.Caldwell was taken by his parents to Mercer county, Illinois, where he attended the district schools and continued to make his home until the return of the family to Rock Island county in 1883 He never left the parental roof and after his father's death came into possession of the old homestead, now owning four hundred and fifty-nine acres of excellent farming land constituting one of the most desirable places in Rural township In connection with general farming he is also interested in stock raising and has met with a well deserved success in his undertakings

On the 29th of June, 1892, Mr Caldwell led to the marriage altar Miss Mary D , daughter of William P and Martha J Davis Wynes, and they now have a little son, William Raymond Politically, Mr Caldwell is a stanch Republican, and has most efficiently served as school director for the last decade He has also served as a member of the county central committee two terms Fraternally he is a member of Milan Lodge No ___ I O Rural Camp

No 186, M W A , Valley Lodge, No. 547, F & A M , and both he and his wife belong to Valley Chapter Eastern Star and the Royal Neighbors, while she is a consistent member of the German Evangelical church In social circles they occupy an enviable position, and wherever known are held in the highest regard, their friends being numerous throughout the community

ROBERT J HUTCHINSON, one of the most energetic and enterprising farmers of Rock Island county, was born on the 18th of June, 1862, on his present farm on section 21, Bowling township, and is a son of William and Margaret (Ramsey) Hutchinson, natives of Ireland The paternal grandfather, Robert Hutchinson, brought his family to America in 1845 and located in Bowling township, where he purchased land and carried on farming until called from this life at an old age In his family were six sons and three daughters George Ramsey, the maternal grandfather, also left the Emerald Isle, and is still living in Rural township, Rock Island county, at the remarkable age of ninety-eight years He is a native of County Fermanagh, Ireland, always followed agricultural pursuits throughout his active business life and reared a large family

Like the other members of his family, William Hutchinson came to the United States in 1845, and took up his residence in Bowling township, Rock Island county, Illinois, where for several years he worked as a farm hand at ten or twelve dollars per month Being economical and industrious he managed to save some money, and finally was able to purchase one hundred and sixty acres of land which he cultivated and improved until his death in 1876, when about forty-eight years of age He took an active and prominent part in public affairs, was called upon to serve in various township offices, and was one of the most useful and valued citizens of the community. His wife died about 1868. Both were members of the Episcopal church and were highly respected by all who knew them

To this worthy couple were born three children, but our subject is the only one now living With the exception of about four years his entire life has been passed upon the old homestead, where he still continues to reside, and his farm, which comprises three hundred and twenty acres of valuable land, he has placed under a high state of cultivation and improved with good and substantial buildings, which stand as monuments to his thrift and industry

On the 9th of November, 1882, Mr Hutchinson was united in marriage to Miss Matilda, daughter of Robert W and Rachel (Johnston) Johnston, and they now have three interesting children—Elizabeth Sadie, Margaret Jane Louisa and James Edward The parents hold membership in the Episcopal church, and Mr Hutchinson belongs to the Modern Woodmen of America, the Society of Loyal Orangemen and the Republican party Public and private charities receive his support and no deserving object is ever refused his aid He is a man of even temperament, calm and self-poised, of refined character, and all who know him esteem him highly for his genuine worth.

PETER FREDERICK MAAK, a successful gardener and dairyman of South Rock Island township, is a native of John

stein, Germany, born September 23, 1838, and is a son of Peter and Dorothea (Miller) Maak, who spent their entire lives in the fatherland, the former dying at the age of seventy-eight and the latter some years later The father was a soldier in the German army, was a common laborer by occupation, and was a Lutheran in religious belief, as was also his wife. Of the four children born to them our subject is the only one now living His paternal grandfather, who was quite a small man, engaged in farming, and died when between the ages of fifty and sixty years The maternal grandfather also died in Germany when about sixty, leaving a large family

During his boyhood and youth Mr Maak, whose name introduces this sketch, attended the public schools of his native land and later served for several years in the German army He was married October 12, 1867, to Miss Margaret, daughter of Hans and Dorothea (Jens) Wehrend, who never left the old country The father, who was a hard-working, energetic man, passed away at the ripe old age of seventy-two years, and his wife was forty-three at the time of her death Five of their seven children are now living, namely: Dietrich, John, Margaret, Katie and Doris Hans Wehrend, the paternal grandfather of Mrs Maak, died in Germany at an advanced age and left a large estate The maternal grandfather also spent his entire life in that country and lived to an old age

To Mr and Mrs Maak have been born four children, three sons and one daughter, as follows Delos, now a resident of West Side, Crawford county, Iowa, who married Annie Schuldorf and has one son, Arthur Grover, William and August, who are still . . . e of John

Erbs, of South Park, and they have two sons, William and Martin

In 1867 Mr and Mrs Maak came to America, and spent the first two years in Iowa, near Davenport, but with that exception have made their home in Rock Island county, living for a time near the Rock river For about two years our subject worked for Mr Carr and was later employed in the brickyard of Henry Case for four years He then purchased ten acres of his present farm, to which he has added from time to time as his financial resources have increased until he now has sixty acres of highly improved land He has erected a good dwelling, barns and other outbuildings, and the neat and thrifty appearance of his place testifies to his skill and ability in his chosen calling For the past sixteen years he has devoted his attention principally to gardening and also does a large dairy business, commencing with five cows, but now has sixteen

In political sentiment Mr Maak is a Democrat, and in religious belief he and his wife are both Lutherans Together they have labored earnestly and persistently until they have secured a comfortable competence and have secured the respect and esteem of all with whom they have come in contact

— — —

LOUIS HENRY REID KARWATH, who is engaged in the drug business at 712 Eighteenth avenue, Moline, was born across the river in Davenport, Iowa, August 1, 1868, a son of Henry and Julia A (Belken) Karwath, who are still honored residents of that city The birth of the father occurred in Austria, November 1, 1839, but at the

came alone to America, making his home for a few years with a maternal uncle at Baraboo, Wisconsin He then went south on a raft and landed at St Louis, but not finding employment in that city, he returned to Davenport and was hired by a farmer of Scott county, with whom he remained until the outbreak of the Civil war Feeling that his adopted country needed his services, he enlisted at the first call for troops, becoming a private of Company E, Twentieth Iowa Volunteer Infantry, but he was later made corporal, and subsequently promoted to the rank of second lieutenant For over three years he followed the stars and stripes on southern battlefields and was stricken with swamp fever, which nearly terminated his life

The war having ended and his services no longer needed, Henry Karwath removed to Davenport, where for twenty-three years he successfully engaged in the manufacture of boots and shoes He is an ardent Republican in politics and acceptably served as alderman of the city for one term, but refused a renomination Under Mayors Henry and Thompson he filled the office of marshal to the entire satisfaction of the public Although reared a Catholic, he now holds membership in the Episcopal church, and fraternally he belongs to the Knights of Pythias, and the Ancient Order of United Workman, of which he is past master

In Davenport, on the 22d of July, 1867, was celebrated the marriage of Henry Karwath and Miss Julia A Belken, who was born and reared in that city, and they became the parents of seven children, three sons and four daughters, of whom our subject is the oldest, the others being Minerva T, Carrie and Arthur, who all died in infancy John, Annie, Theresa also died at the age of nineteen years and five months, Lucilva Cecelia, born in Davenport, November 21, 1882; and Alonzo Henry, born in the same city, April 2, 1887

On reaching a sufficient age, Mr Karwath, of this review, entered the public schools of Davenport, where he pursued his studies until reaching the ninth grade, and then took a course in a business college of that city At the early age of seven years he began work, and for some time clerked in a drug store in his native city, taking charge of the store at the age of sixteen Two years later he passed the examination for an assistant pharmacist, and when twenty-six came to Moline and started in business for himself at his present stand, being competent for registration and so licensed By his energy, perseverance and fine business ability he has met with a well deserved success, and to-day enjoys the reward of his painstaking and conscientious work Systematic and methodical, his sagacity, keen discrimination and sound judgment have made him one of the leading business men of Moline.

In his native city Mr Karwath was married March 10, 1892, the lady of his choice being Miss Winifred Henrietta Metzger, a native of Davenport and a daughter of Dietrich and Amanda (Littig) Metzger They now have two interesting little sons—Louis Grant, born in Davenport, April 7, 1893, and Leon Henry Theodoric, born at No 712 Twelfth avenue, Moline, August 2, 1895

In 1892 Mr Kawath cast his first presidential vote for Benjamin Harrison and is unswerving in his allegiance to Republican principles On his party ticket he was elected alderman from the Fifth ward in 1897, is he of his town of his public

and fuel committee, and is a member of the committees on ordinance and sewers He is a member of Columbia Lodge, No 33, K P , of Davenport, Joe Hooker Camp, Sons of Veterans, in which he has served as quartermaster sergeant and second lieutenant, Moline Tent, No 164, K O T M , Trinity Lodge, No 208, A F & A M , of Davenport, and both he and his wife belong to the Eastern Star in Moline They also hold membership in the Davenport Cathedral Episcopal church and in social circles occupy a most enviable position

---

JACOB SIMMON, one of the self-made men and progressive agriculturalists of Rock Island county, now owns a very valuable property, all of which he has accumulated by his own perseverance and industry His fine farm is pleasantly located on section 5, Rural township, and in its operation he has met with excellent success

Mr Simmon was born in Weisenheim, Weinpalz, Germany, in 1820, a son of Peter and Catharine (Kranwis) Simmon, who were also natives of that country The paternal grandfather died there when past the age of forty, leaving six children, two of whom were soldiers under Napoleon The maternal grandfather also died in Germany in middle life. In his native land the father followed the occupation of farming, and continued that pursuit after coming to the new world in 1831 He spent the first nine years in Coshocton county, Ohio, then was a resident of Tuscarawas county, that state, for the same length of time, and in 1849 came to Rock Island county, Illinois, settling in Rural township, where he purchased one hundred and sixty acres of ... nade that place his home until his death at the age of eighty-three years His wife had died the year previous aged seventy He was a Lutheran in religious belief, while she held membership in the Presbyterian church

In the family of this worthy couple were twelve children of whom nine are yet living, the oldest being seventy-eight and the youngest sixty years of age. In order of birth they are as follows Philip, Jacob, Mrs Louisa Dieffenbach, Christoph, Charles, Catharine, wife of Lewis Wilson; Henry J , Elizabeth, wife of Perry Cheney, and Maria

The subject of this sketch was eleven years of age when he crossed the Atlantic with his parents, remaining with them until 1848 when he left home and came to Illinois For nine years he drove a dray in Rock Island, and then entered a tract of land in Rural township, which he afterward sold, purchasing one hundred and seventy-five acres elsewhere His present farm comprises fifty-seven acres, but besides this he owns other tracts, aggregating three hundred and fifty-four acres of most productive and well improved land His energies are now devoted to general farming and stock raising with results which cannot fail but prove satisfactory

In 1872 Mr. Simmon was united in marriage to Miss Rosetta Engel, by whom he had eight children, seven sons and one daughter — Peter, Eva, Jacob, Christian, Philip and three who died in early childhood Those living are still at home and prove a great comfort and help to their parents, as they are affectionate and obedient children Mr and Mrs Simmon hold membership in the Presbyterian church, and in politics he is identified with the Democratic pa⸱⸱ ⸱⸱ ⸱⸱ ⸱⸱ ⸱⸱ ⸱⸱ ⸱⸱

drafted but hired a substitute Although his cash capital consisted of about one hundred dollars on his arrival in Illinois, he has by hard work, economy and good management secured a comfortable competence, which has enabled him to obtain the comforts and luxuries which go to make life worth the living His social, genial manner and many excellent qualities have won for him the high regard of many friends and acquaintances

JOHN PERRY WALDRON.—There is particular satisfaction in reverting to the life history of the honored and venerable gentleman whose name initiates this review, for his life of more than four score years has been one of ceaseless activity in which the good of others has ever been uppermost in his mind For many years he was actively identified with the business interests of Bureau county, but is now living retired in the city of Rock Island, enjoying the competence secured by former years of toil. His home is at the corner of Sixteenth street and Third avenue

Mr Waldron is a native of the Empire state, his birth occurring in the town of Steuben, Oneida county, March 8, 1816, and is a son of Joseph and Martha (Perry) Waldron, the former a native of New York City, and the latter of Carnarven, Wales Of the eight children born to them, the youngest four are still living—Ephraim G , a resident of Alden, Erie county, New York, John Perry, of this review, Margaret, who first wedded Stanley Bostwick, and after his death Mr Jones, of Erie county, New York, and Jane, widow of Henry Shaw, of Amboy, Illinois One daughter, Mrs Ann E Fowler, died in the spring of 1897, at the age of eighty-eight The father, who was born September 28, 1784, spent the greater part of his life in Albany, New York, where he died December 24, 1839 He was a very wealthy man and for many years served as captain of a company of New York militia His wife was born February 1, 1787, and died September 6, 1871, at the advanced age of eighty-four years and seven months In religious belief he was a Baptist, and although she had been reared in the Presbyterian faith, she also became a Baptist

The paternal grandfather of our subject, David Van Waldron, was a native of Holland, and on coming to America located in New York City, where he served as captain of the watch during the Irish rebellion He was very large and stout, and was a farmer by occupation John Perry, the maternal grandfather, was born in Wales and came to the new world about 1765 He settled on a farm in New York, where he died when well advanced in years.

In the county of his nativity, Mr Waldron, of this sketch, spent the days of his boyhood and youth and acquired his early education there, but later was a student in an institute at Brockport, New York In Oneida county he learned the carriage-maker's trade, and for many years followed carriage painting in that state In 1840 he left Oneida county and removed to Erie county, New York, and in 1854 came west and took up his residence in Dover township, Bureau county, Illinois, six miles from Princeton, where he followed painting for some years, painting the first house in the village of Malden Having accumulated a sufficient amount of this world's goods, he came to Rock Island in 1881 and has since lived retired

forts and conveniences which make life worth the living

On the 6th of October, 1847, Mr Waldron married Miss Melinda Bowman, a daughter of Dr Peleg and Theodosia (Bidwell) Bowman, of Akron, Erie county, New York, and they became the parents of two children—John Perry, now forty-nine years of age, who is still living in Monument, Colorado, and Maria, now the wife of Dr C B Kinyon, of Rock Island

While a resident of Bureau county, Mr. Waldron served as constable, and was a member of the board of village trustees in Dover Politically he is a stanch Republican, and religiously is a faithful and consistent member of the Christian church There is an old age that is a benediction to all that come in contact with it, that gives out its rich stores of learning and experience, and grows stronger intellectually and spiritually as the years pass Such is the life of Mr. Waldron, an encouragement to his associates and an example well worthy of emulation to the young

THOMAS HUTCHINSON has lived for half a century in Bowling township, Rock Island county, and now makes his home on section 13 His life has been one of industry and honest endeavor, and the success he has achieved is due entirely to his own efforts He was born in county Fermanagh, Ireland, in January, 1822, a son of Robert and Bessie (Lipton) Hutchinson, also natives of the same county His paternal grandfather, Thomas Hutchinson, was a farmer, and died on the Emerald Isle at an advanced age He had a family of three sons and two daughters followed farming, and spent his entire life in Ireland Robert Hutchinson, the father, bade adieu to his native land in 1847, and crossing the Atlantic to America, took up his residence in Rock Island county, Illinois He purchased eighty acres of land in Bowling township, and transformed it into a good farm, the boundaries of which he afterward extended by the purchase of an additional forty acres, constituting the home place of our subject There he spent his remaining days, passing away in 1853, at the age of seventy years His wife long survived him, and died at the advanced age of ninety-three Both were members of the Episcopal church They had a family of six sons and three daughters, of whom the following are now living—Thomas, Bessie, widow of Robert Hicks, Robert, Mary, James, and Alice, wife of John Johnston

Thomas Hutchinson, of this review, was reared in his native land, in the usual manner of farmer lads, and acquired his education in the common schools When twenty-five years of age he came to the United States with his parents and in 1847 purchased eighty acres of land in Bowling township at one dollar and a quarter per acre This property he still owns His landed possessions, however, now aggregate two hundred acres He broke and fenced his land himself, and in those pioneer days worked from early morning until late at night in order to place his fields under cultivation Industry has ever been one of his chief characteristics, and by his honest toil, his perseverance and good management he has overcome all obstacles and difficulties in his path and worked his way steadily upward to success

Mr Hutchinson was united in marriage to Miss S   "   to   f G

Ramsey, of Rural township, who is now ninety-eight years of age Her mother was Mrs Jane (Hutchinson) Ramsey Ten children, seven sons and three daughters, were born to our subject and his wife, namely Robert, deceased, married Frances Petty, and they had a son, Alford George married Alice Johnston, and they had three children, Marion, Florence and Clarence. Bessie Jane died at the age of fifteen years Margaret died in infancy William is at home Thomas married the widow of his brother Robert and lives in Dale, Iowa Annie is the wife of Wilson W Long, of Rural township, by whom she has one son, Ralph W James and Samuel are at home, and Joseph died in infancy The parents are members of the Episcopal church, and they have the high regard of a large circle of friends In his political views he is a Republican, and for two years served as school director. He has witnessed almost the entire growth and development of his adopted county, has seen its wild lands transformed into beautiful homes and farms and the work of progress carried forward until the county of to-day bears little resemblance to that of a half century ago He has ever borne his part in the work of improvement as a public-spirited citizen, and well deserves representation in this volume

C B KINYON, M D , the oldest medical practitioner of the homeopathic school in Rock Island, is accounted one of the eminent physicians of the state, nor is his reputation limited by the confines of Illinois Superior skill and ability have enabled him to rise above the ranks of the   and among the successful few and

DR. C. B. KINYON.

MRS C B KINYON.

has made his opinions in medical circles of great importance One of the most pleasing considerations in this connection is that his success has come to him entirely through his own efforts, and is a tribute to his merit and peculiar fitness for his chosen vocation

Dr Kinyon was born in Walworth county, Wisconsin, January 6, 1851 His parents, James N. and Mary A (Benedict) Kinyon, were natives of New York, the former born in Steuben county, the latter in Otsego county In 1840 they located in Wisconsin The father is still living, but lost his eyesight fifty-seven years ago However, he has always been an industrious, energetic man, and in his earlier years devoted his energies to farming Seven years ago he removed from Wisconsin to Normal, Illinois, to make his home with his daughter, Mrs Henry McCormick, whose husband is vice-president of the State Normal University, and professor of geography and history

Dr Kinyon is the fourth in order of birth in a family of seven children, six of whom are yet living, but the youngest died in infancy He obtained his education in the State Normal University of Illinois, graduating therefrom in 1876, and began his medical studies in the University of Michigan at Ann Arbor, taking a full course during the session of 1876-7 He is a graduate of the Chicago Homeopathic College of the class of 1878, and in that year began practice in Rock Island, where he has since remained, enjoying a large and lucrative business He is serving as medical examiner for about eight of the old and reliable insurance companies and was a member of the United States pension board during the Harrison administration He h   ... .

11

member of the City Board of Health, performing these duties in connection with his extensive private practice He has ever been a close and earnest student of his profession and by extensive reading and study of the medical journals and publications he has kept abreast with the theories and improvement of the time, and has also been a leader in the advancement, for he has carried forward his investigations along original lines and has made some important discoveries His contributions to the medical literature of the country have been very valuable and extensive During the past year he published five different papers on professional subjects, and has prepared and read fourteen different papers before the American Institute of Homeopathy—the oldest national medical association in the United States, in which he has held a membership for sixteen years For ten successive years he has been a member of the board of censors He was president of the Illinois State Homeopathic Society in 1887, and is now serving his fourth term as president of the Rock River Institute of Homeopathy

On the 25th of April, 1878, Dr Kinyon was united in marriage to Miss Maria Waldron, daughter of John P. and Melinda Waldron, who are living with our subject Mr Waldron is a wheelwright and cabinet maker by trade, but is now retired from business life He is a direct descendant of Baron Von Waldron, one of the original patentees of Harlem Flats, New York Mrs Kinyon has only one brother, Perry Waldron, who is interested in silver mining in Colorado The Doctor and his wife have two children—Howard, born April 19, 1880, and Melinda, born August 8, 1886

In p u Ju t   .   p in the

Methodist Episcopal church and Dr Kinyon was serving as trustee and a member of the building committee at the time of the erection of the present house of worship. He has been a member of the board of education He holds membership in a number of civic societies, including the Masonic Lodge, Independent Order of Odd Fellows, the American Order of United Workmen and the Uniformed Rank of Knights of Pythias. In politics he is an ardent Republican but has made all these interests minor considerations in comparison with his profession He feels a deep love for his chosen calling and never content with mediocrity he has availed himself of every opportunity for perfecting himself in his work, until to day he stands among the foremost representatives of his calling in Illinois

Without solicitation on his part, Dr Kinyon was elected to the chairs of obstetrics and gynacology in the homeopathic medical department of Michigan University at Ann Arbor There were over a score of applicants for the vacant chairs in the institution, but the Doctor was the unanimous choice of the existing faculty This is certainly an honor worthily bestowed, for Dr Kinyon has for some years been an authority on obstetrics, and while he is very modest in his claims the medical fraternity appreciate his ability and true worth

The homeopathic department of Michigan University is equipped with splendid buildings, libraries and hospitals, and its faculty is composed of eight men of high standing in their profession The new member of the faculty is well equipped in every respect for the important position to which he has been called In his leaving Rock Island loses one of its most eminent physicians, an ' ' -   '   .   ' ' ' f \

practice, which has been constantly growing. But in his new field he will have larger opportunities for greater usefulness, and the best wishes of patrons and friends go with him

CHARLES C STONE, who resides in South Moline township, Rock Island county, is one of the leading horticulturists in this section of the state The cultivation and improvement of fruit is comparatively a new art and Mr. Stone is a leader in this movement, his labors having done much in producing improvement in fruit in size, quality and flavor, and also in producing new varieties As a business man he is highly respected, his straightforward methods commending him to the confidence and good will of all

Born in Elmira, New York, November 5, 1840, he is a son of Charles H. Stone, a native of the same state, and of English parentage The father was reared to manhood there, and married Marmary B Howe, also of English descent In 1843 he removed from Ithaca, New York, to Chicago, and as a master mechanic was employed by the Chicago, Galena & Union Railroad Company building the first depot on their line and all the others along that road as far west as Galena After eight years' residence in Chicago, he removed to Geneva, Kane county, Illinois, but continued in the employ of the railroad company for three years thereafter He then turned his attention to contracting and building, which he followed in Geneva Aurora and other northern cities. He was one of a family of thirteen sons and six daughters, all of whom reached mature years One brother was a _neral and another a colonel in the Confederate army, and another brother was H O Stone, a wealthy real estate dealer of Chicago The father of our subject served for two years and four months in the Union army as a member of Company H, Forty-sixth Illinois Infantry, and was then discharged on account of disability In 1868 he went to Milwaukee, Wisconsin, on a business trip, and died while in that city

Charles C Stone, of this review, was principally reared in Geneva, Illinois, where he received good school privileges In 1857 he ran away from home and crossed the plains with a freighting train, which left Omaha, Nebraska, under command of Captain John L Creighton As they neared the crossing of Green river, called Rawlings Springs, they were attacked by a band of three hundred Indians and Mr Stone was struck by three arrows, one striking him in the chin, another in the knee and a third behind the ear This disabled him for several days A number of the train were killed, and nine of the Indians lost their lives

Mr Stone continued with the freighting train until February, 1861, when he returned to his home in Geneva, there remaining until the war On hearing of the attack on Fort Sumter, with two companions he started for Chicago, and on the 14th of April enlisted in the three months service as a private He was at Springfield, Birds Point and Cape Girardeau, Missouri, and then returned home, where he remained for a few weeks In August, 1861, at Dixon, he joined Company H, Forty-sixth Illinois Infantry, and was promoted to the rank of sergeant, participating in the engagements of Fort Donelson, Shiloh, the siege of Corinth, Memphis the siege of Vicksburg and the second battle of Jackson He was

ward veteranized and was granted a furlough, on the expiration of which he rejoined his command and participated in the siege of Mobile and other engagements in that district On the 18th of February, 1866, he was mustered out at Baton Rouge, was paid off at Springfield, Illinois, and then returned to his home

Mr Stone continued in Geneva until 1871, after which he engaged in railroading, contracting and ditching in Oregon, California, New Mexico, Nevada, Idaho and Texas In the last named state he was stricken with yellow fever and after seven months illness was so reduced that he weighed only sixty-seven pounds This led him to return to the north in 1872, and he located in Ogle county, Illinois, where he regained his health and strength and advanced his weight to one hundred and eighty-four pounds. Through one summer he worked in a stone quarry and then turned his attention to farming, which he followed three years In 1874 he came to Rock Island county, and located at Stewartsville, where he secured employment in the Deere shops He was married there, on the 21st of December, of that year, to Eliza Yothers, a native of Centre county, Pennsylvania, who had come to the west to visit her sister

Mr Stone worked for fourteen months as a common laborer and then secured a position in the blacksmith shop, continuing in the employ of the Deere Company for eight years In the meantime he purchased three lots and a residence in Stewartsville, which he traded for ten acres of land in South Moline township, locating thereon in the spring of 1884 In the summer he built a house and planted some fruit, and each year has set out more He now owns acres are principally devoted to the raising of cherries plums, raspberries and strawberries, but he also has a good apple orchard and some fine varieties of peaches and pears He has many varieties of blackberries and has produced several new and distinct varieties of strawberries, including some of the largest and best ever grown in any country He has a knowledge of horticulture surpassed by few and his scientific methods of fruit growing have brought to him handsome returns. He is now one of the most extensive fruit growers in this part of the state and no finer fruit farm can be found in western Illinois

The family of Mr and Mrs Stone numbered six children, three of whom are living—Theresa Gertrude, Charles Milton and Susan Etta Elsie Agnes died at the age of ten years, and two died in early childhood The mother of this family is a member of the Methodist Episcopal church and a most estimable lady

Mr Stone belongs to Graham Post, No 312, G A R , of Moline, and in politics is a Republican He was a faithful follower of the old flag throughout the long years of the Civil war, and is as true to his duties of citizenship in times of peace Success has crowned his well directed efforts in business and he has gained prestige in his chosen calling

THOMAS LEES — There is always an element of interest attaching to the history of the development of city, county or state from its early beginning to its present advancement, and in tracing the part that the pioneer settlers have borne in its continued progress and improvement Mr Lees is nu   t   ly merchants

of Rock Island county, dating his residence here from 1852 At that time there was no railroad in the county and many of its thriving towns and villages had not sprung into existence Much of the land was still wild, awaiting the awakening touch of the farmer when it would respond with rich fertility Mr Lees' labors in improving the county have been more especially along the lines of developing its mining and agricultural interests, and in this way he has contributed not a little to the general prosperity

Born in Lancastershire, England, October 20, 1825, he is a son of Robert and Betty (Dronsfield) Lees, also natives of England His paternal grandfather was Thomas Lees, a farmer, who spent his entire life in England and died when about eighty years of age He had two sons and a daughter The maternal grandfather was George Dronsfield who reared a large family and provided for their support by following the weaver's trade. He died at an advanced age Robert Lees was a stone and brick layer and died in England at the age of seventy-five His wife survived him four years and passed away at the age of seventy-eight They had five children, four sons and a daughter

The gentleman whose name introduces this review was reared in the mining districts of Lancastershire In 1847 he married Miss Jane Mills, daughter of John and Ann (Jones) Mills and the following year crossed the Atlantic to America, locating first near Pittsburg, Pennsylvania He afterward went to Steubenville, Ohio, where he spent four years, and in April, 1852, he came to Rock Island county, Illinois A few weeks later, however, he went to Peoria, but in the same year returned to Rock Island county, and worked in the mines at Coal Valley for some time There were only two log houses in the place at the time of his arrival, but it grew to be a prosperous and thriving town, although in later years its population has decreas'd owing to the coal mines at that point being exhausted Mr. Lees purchased forty acres of land in partnership with John Bailey and paid for it in coal He mined coal from his own land, hauling it to Rock Island, Moline and Milan, and also supplied many of the farmers in the vicinity His persistent labor and well directed efforts continually added to his financial resources and at different times he has purchased land He now has two hundred acres in his home farm, and a half interest in a one-hundred-and-sixty-acre tract on section 25 and on section 26 He successfully followed general farming and stock raising until 1893, when he rented his place, and is now resting from the more arduous duties of a business career He has never had occasion to regret his emigration to America for here he has found prosperity, a pleasant home and many friends He has twice visited his native land, and the first time—in the winter of 1868—had a very stormy voyage, but on his second visit in the summer of 1885, it was very pleasant

During his first absence Mr Lees received news of the death of his wife, who passed away January 25, 1868 They had a family of ten children, seven of whom are now living Elizabeth became the wife of Matthew G Bedford, but died some years ago, leaving several children, three of whom are now living—Stella, Gertrude and Thomas L John M married Ann Wooley and they have four children living—Jane ┆ ┆ ┆

Jerry H married Elizabeth Wooley, and has five children--Selina, Ellen, James, Frederick and Waldo Joseph D wedded Mary Ann Stevens, and they have a daughter, Winifred Thomas R married Tillie Krapp, and they have three children—Gertrude, John and Dena Mary A is engaged in teaching in the state of Washington Selina Alice is the wife of James Glenn and has one child Emma J is engaged in teaching and lives at home Two of this family died in infancy There is also an adopted daughter, Betty A , a young lady at home.

Mr Lees is a Master Mason and in politics has always been a stalwart Democrat He has been called to public office, wherein he has discharged his duties with marked fidelity and ability, having served as supervisor for two terms, as assessor for several terms, justice of the peace one term and collector and member of the school board for several terms Honorable in his business dealings, active and energetic in the prosecution of his interests he has won a comfortable competence and is to-day numbered among the substantial citizens of the community, but more prized by him is the regard in which he is held by his many friends by reason of his well spent life

---

GEORGE M LUKEN, who resides on section 18, South Rock Island township, is a native of Louisville, Kentucky He was born on the 26th of January, 1837, and is a son of Samuel S and Mary B (Bills) Luken, the former a native of Pennsylvania, and the latter of Tennessee His grandfather, Joel Luken, was also born in the K ┆ ┆ ┆ ┆ ┆ its ancestry back to the first settlement of Germantown, now Philadelphia They were connected with the Quakers Joel Luken was at one time a prominent merchant of Philadelphia He had a son who was owner and captain of a trading vessel, engaged in trade with China This son was supposed to have been murdered for the proceeds of a cargo, and the loss of this money so crippled the grandfather financially that he was obliged to abandon his business in the east and came to Illinois, where he turned his attention to farming He died at the home of his son in Wabash county in 1846, when seventy-nine years of age The maternal grandfather of our subject was a resident of Marshall county, Tennessee, and there continued to make his home until his demise, after which his family removed to Illinois, in 1824, located in Lawrence county, where his widow married again After the death of her second husband she and her sons removed to Hazel Green, Wisconsin, where her remaining days were passed Her sons worked in the lead mines of Galena, which were near their home

When twelve years of age Samuel S Lukens the father, accompanied his parents to Lawrence county, Illinois, where the grandfather purchased land and developed a farm The prairie and township in which he lived were named in his honor Upon that farm Samuel Luken grew to manhood and soon after his marriage removed to Louisville, Kentucky, whence he came to Rock Island in 1838 He afterward removed to Wabash county, where, in 1846, he was elected to the state legislature. In 1850 he was elected sheriff of the county, and while filling that position died, in the fall of 1851, at the age of thirty-nine years His widow -- ' ' until January 27

1897 They had eight children, two of whom are now living George M and Emma L , wife of Scott Jackson, who is now living near DesMoines, in Warren county, Iowa Mrs Luken was a member of the Christian church, Mr Luken of the Universalist He was at one time editor of the Mt Carmel Register for two or three years, and took quite an active interest in politics, being a recognized leader in the ranks of the Whig party His widow became the wife of Ephraim D Turner, and reared three of his youngest children born of his first marriage

When a child of four years George M Luken accompanied his father on his removal to Wabash county. In 1848 he began learning the printer's trade which he followed until 1865 In the winter of 1855–6 he was employed on the Chicago Times, and in the following winter was employed on job work in the office of Hays & Thompson Going to Davenport he secured a position in the office of the Gazette through the winter of 1857 -8, and in the latter year returned to Mt Carmel, where he entered the employ of Colonel Theodore S Bowers on the Register, in which office he continued until the spring of 1859 Going then to Memphis, Tennessee, he next secured a position as foreman of the Bulletin and in 1860 was president of the Printers' Typographical Union He was arrested by a "vigilance committee" two weeks after Fort Sumter was fired upon and ordered to return to the north For six months he remained in Cairo and reported the battle of Belmont, sending it to the Chicago Times one day ahead of any other reporter on the field. In the fall of 1861 he went to St Louis, where he was employed on the Democrat until the spring of 186- when on the establishment of the

Union he was made its first foreman   The Union is now called the Post-Dispatch   He continued in charge until 1864, when he went to St Joseph, Missouri, thence to Chicago, and in 1865 came to Rock Island

While in St Louis Mr Luken was president of the Printers' Union and in 1863 was elected a delegate to the National Convention of the Union, which met in Cleveland, where he was elected first vice-president of the organization   He presided at the opening of the National Typographical Union Convention, in Louisville in 1864   From 1865 until 1876 he engaged in farming and then purchased a fourth interest in the Rock Island Union, acting as its business manager for two years when he sold out and returned to the farm, since devoting his attention to agricultural pursuits in the operation of a valuable tract of land of two hundred and twenty-four acres belonging to his wife

Mr. Luken was married February 4, 1864, the lady of his choice being Eliza J Carr, a daughter of William and Eliza J (Tureman) Carr, the former a native of Ohio and the latter of Cass county, Illinois They were among the early settlers of Rock Island   Her father came to the county in 1825, but did not make a permanent location until 1830, when he settled in South Rock Island   He built one of the first houses on Rock river in what is now known as South Rock Island township and carried on agricultural pursuits and also run a ferry across Rock river known as Carr's ferry He was a soldier in the Black Hawk war and had a brother, Peter, who served as a colonel in that war   He held membership in the Universalist church   His first wife died when Mrs Luken was only a week old and he afterward married Mrs Mayhew, widow of Z A Mayhew, who was murdered and

the first man to meet death by violence in the county   Mrs Luken was reared on the farm where she now lives and where her entire life has been passed with the exception of four years spent in Rock Island   Her father died May 3, 1869, at the age of sixty-eight years and five months   His father was John Carr, a native of New Jersey, of Scotch descent   The family name was originally spelled with a K, but he changed the initial letter to C   The maternal grandfather of Mrs Luken was George Tureman, a native of Kentucky   Mrs Luken is a highly cultured lady, who in 1856 attended the Ladies' College in Davenport and the following year was a student in the high school in Moline   In that year she went to Galesburg, where she entered Lombard University, pursuing her studies in that institution until 1860

Four children have been born to Mr and Mrs Luken, namely   Myra, who died in infancy, Nellie S , William C and Lura Nellie is the wife of Alan D Welch, of Rock Island, and they have two living children, Raymond Kenneth and Jean Lillian The other children are at home and aid their parents in making the Luken household one of the most hospitable in the entire neighborhood   Mr. Luken is a Master Mason, belonging to Trio Lodge, No 57, of Rock Island   He is also an honorary member of the Twin City Printers' Union.   In politics he is a Democrat and has served his township as assessor for three terms   He and his wife are of a happy, genial temperament, and are kind and hospitable people who have the faculty of making their guests feel at ease   Their friends throughout the county are many and by all they are highly esteemed for their many excellencies of

JAMES F ROBINSON, who for nearly a quarter of a century has occupied the responsible position of cashier of the Rock Island National Bank, is a native of Rock Island county, born on a farm near Hillsdale, February 27, 1849, and is a son of Captain Thomas J and Amy Ann (Henderson) Robinson, a sketch of whom appears elsewhere in this volume Shortly after his birth his parents removed to Port Byron, and in 1853 to the city of Rock Island, which has since been the home of the family

In this city our subject grew to manhood and in its public schools received his primary education Desirous of obtaining a more thorough education he later entered Northwestern University, Evanston, Illinois, where he pursued the classical course, graduating from that institution in June, 1872 After receiving his diploma he returned home, and early in the fall of the same year entered the employ of the Rock Island National Bank as clerk, and in November following he was elected by the directors cashier and has since continued in that position

On the 29th of October, 1889, Mr Robinson was united in marriage with Miss Mary E Rhoads, of Pekin, Illinois, daughter of Samuel and Martha (Burnett) Rhoads Her father was a native of Selinsgrove, Pa , who settled in Pekin about 1840 He was a thoroughly loyal man and showed his devotion to his country by serving in the Mexican war and later in the war for the Union In Pekin he engaged for years in the mercantile trade, and was well-known throughout Tazewell county. His death occurred in September, 1888

Fraternally Mr Robinson is a Mason, holding membership in Trio Lodge, No 59, Barrett C'   ''   '' R \ M   and

Everts Commandery, No 18, K T He is also a member of the Ancient Order of United Workmen, Knights of Pythias, Knights of the Globe, and Fraternal Tribune, in each of which he has been somewhat active Religiously he is a member of the First Methodist church, Rock Island, of which his wife is also a member. In the work of the church he is also quite active, serving on the official board as steward for some years At present he is assistant superintendent of the Sunday school, and in that work manifests the same interest and zeal as in other duties As organist of the church Mrs Robinson has served some years to the satisfaction of all, as she is a musician of more than ordinary ability

Born in the exciting times in which slavery was the all-absorbing question, and having instilled in him the rights of all men, white or black, he naturally became a Republican, and with that party he has affiliated since casting his first presidential vote for Gen U. S Grant, in 1872 In the principles of that party he has the utmost confidence, believing as they are adopted and enforced by the people the country will be the more prosperous Protection, reciprocity and sound money are the watchwords that should guide all alike who have the best interests of the people at heart

While a politician in the best sense of the term Mr Robinson has never aspired to official position The honors of office he is willing that others should enjoy The only official positions held by him have been city treasurer and treasurer of the Board of Education of Rock Island, neither of which can be said to be a political office

It is as a business man, however, that Mr Robinson is best known A full quarter

JAMES F. ROBINSON

of a century he has been connected with the Rock Island National Bank, and in that time has been brought in contact and associated with the leading business men in all parts of the country, and his acquaintance is quite extensive. While conservative in the management of the bank's interests, he is accommodating at all times, and more than one man in Rock Island county will acknowledge that his present good financial standing is due to the timely aid rendered him while in need.

As a citizen he takes a commendable interest in every enterprise calculated to advance the welfare of his native county, and has been associated more or less in the greater number of manufacturing establishments, while at all times advocating such improvements as will enhance the wealth and beauty of the city. Socially he and his estimable wife hold a foremost place in the city.

DAVID SEARS.—On the pages of Illinois history the name of this gentleman stands conspicuously forth as one of the prominent pioneers who opened up civilization much of Rock Island county. A military commander leading his troops forth to battle is deserving of great credit, but how much more are the thanks of a grateful public due the man who leads the hosts of workmen to daily toil, giving them the means of sustaining instead of destroying life. This Mr Sears has done. His father was the founder of the city of Moline, and in Rock Island county his entire life has been passed. From the time that he became interested in business concerns he has done much to promote the advancement

activity of the county and his labors have been of material benefit to the community.

Born in Moline, March 22. 1838, he is a son of David B and Delilah (Caldwell) Sears, the former a native of New York, the latter of Kentucky. His paternal grandfather, Joseph Sears, was a native of New Hampshire and was of English lineage. By occupation he was a farmer and trader, and died in Mississippi in middle life. His family numbered five children. At the time of the war of 1812 the family were living in Ohio, and one of the sons was drowned in the Ohio river, while fleeing from the Indians. The maternal grandfather of Mr Sears was a native of Scotland and having emigrated to America became a farmer in Kentucky. He was a stanch Presbyterian in religious belief.

David B Sears, the father of our subject, was one of the honored pioneers who opened up northwestern Illinois to the advancement of civilization. He came to the state in 1821 locating in Gallatin county, where he made his home until coming to Rock Island county in 1837, having purchased property in Moline the previous year. In southern Illinois he followed farming, stock raising and pork packing. He was one of the first "prospectors" who found their way to the upper Mississippi valley and located permanently in Black Hawk's domain. He was born in Lima, Livingston county, New York, in April, 1804, and after a long, honorable and useful life, passed away, January 22, 1884. When he was seven years of age his parents removed to the Scioto valley in Ohio, where they lived during the war of 1812, and their lives being imperilled by the Indians, they were finally obliged to leave home and enlist at the fort, and their flight took them across the Scioto river and in making the passage the boat was capsized and two of David's sisters and a brother were drowned The family afterward removed to Cincinnati, and in 1814 located in Switzerland county, Indiana, whence they removed to the Wabash valley in 1818 In 1822, at the age of eighteen, David B Sears married Miss Melinda Stokes, of Shawneetown, Illinois, and began his domestic life near that place on a farm of eight hundred acres, which he operated through the fourteen succeeding years, making annual trips to New Orleans by flatboats, to dispose of his produce Having a desire to visit the upper Mississippi he left home in 1836 and directed his steps to this point Not a building then stood on the site of Moline Around him stretched a lovely scene and his quick eye noted the superior advantages for the location and development of large manufacturing interests It is said that he was instrumental in establishing and developing more industrial enterprises, particularly in the line of milling throughout this section of the country, than any other one man.

In 1837, in company with J W. Spencer, Calvin Ainsworth and Spencer H White, David B Sears began the building of the first dam across the river between the island of Rock Island and the Illinois shore He helped to lay out the town of Moline and built the first flouring mill, the first foundry and the first sawmill there In the fall of 1841, in connection with the gentlemen previously mentioned he erected a two-story sawmill and placed on the upper floor two run of burrs for the accommodation of the neighboring farmers, the nearest flouring mill at that time being one hundred miles distant In 1843 Mr Sears fitted up a big four-- - - '' -- - -t f thirty thou-

sand dollars, every article of machinery being the best that could then be obtained He controlled the mill until 1848, shipping its products to Saint Louis and other markets on the lower Mississippi About the time the large mill was commenced, Mr Sears, in company with Charles Atkinson, laid out the town of Moline and its "Island City sub-division," which consisted of a tract of fifty-seven acres on the upper end of Rock Island, which was then held as a military reserve After three winters spent in Washington and much laborious effort, he secured the right from congress to enter this land at a dollar and a quarter per acre, the privilege being granted him in consideration of the benefits to navigation which had accrued from the building of the dam on the Illinois side of the Island In 1843 Mr Sears established a foundry, erected a store and put up other buildings in Moline In 1845 he built a three-run flour mill on Benham's Island, a narrow strip of land lying contiguous to Rock Island, thereby developing a water-power between the two islands, He constructed a steamboat landing below the mill, erected a house and other buildings on the main island, and when in 1865, the government took possession of the island for the purpose of establishing a national arsenal and armory, all the commission awarded him for his property and improvements was one hundred and forty-five thousand one hundred and seventy-five dollars He contracted for the development of the water-power and for the construction of water-works throughout Illinois, Iowa, Kansas and Missouri, and laid out the boundary line between Iowa and Minnesota, but all the time made his home in Moline Many other business interests occupied his attention until 1861 when he entered the army as quartermaster of the Twenty-seventh Illinois Infantry, and later was promoted post commissary, serving until the close of the war He was taken prisoner at Resaca, but was exchanged within a few days

In 1867 David B Sears, again prominently connected with the business interests of this county, built a mill of three hundred barrels capacity at Sears His costliest work was the development of the water power of the Rock river In 1870 he built a mill at Cleveland, Illinois, one at Linden in 1873, and one in Tama City, Iowa, in 1875, two years after this dug a canal, built a dam and otherwise improved the water power at Ottumwa, Iowa. In 1880 he constructed water works at Red Oak, Iowa, and the following year one at Joplin, Missouri His last work was the building of a beautiful home on a bluff overlooking his town and commanding a magnificent view of the Mississippi and Rock river valleys

By his first marriage Mr. Sears had a family of five children, but only one is now living,—Sarah, widow of L W Eastman By his second wife, the mother of our subject, he had seven children, four sons and three daughters, and four are now living, as follows David, William, George W and Jeannette The mother of this family passed away in 1863, at the age of fifty years, and Mr. Sears afterward wedded Mrs Sales, who still survives him His death occurred in 1889, at the age of eighty years, and the community lost one of its most valued citizens, the impress of whose individuality is left upon the development and the life of the county in a way that will ever make him honored while the county cherishes the memory of its family He

was a man of sterling principles honest in all his dealings, liberal to an extreme He was a strong advocate of temperance, and both he and the mother of our subject were members of the Congregational church Among all classes his friends were numbered Honored by all, loved by those who knew him most intimately, his life is well worthy of emulation and on the pages of history his name shines with a glory that time cannot efface

David Sears, whose name introduces this memoir, is the oldest native son of Moline and he fully sustains the honor of one of the most prominent and influential families of the Mississippi valley He was reared in Moline, acquired his education in its public schools, and when a boy learned the sawyer's trade in his father's sawmill. Later he learned the business of manufacturing flour and was thus engaged until 1889, when his mill was destroyed by fire He then established a mill in Moline and is also interested in a farm in Minnesota His business affairs have been of an extensive and varied character, and his sound judgment, unflagging industry and undaunted determination have enabled him to carry these forward to a successful conclusion He took a contract on the Hennepin canal and excavated the lock pit and a part of the canal trunk above Milan, which was mostly rock work This he completed in 1894, and the following year he built his flouring mill in Moline In 1896 he erected the Rock Island pottery near his home at Sears station and manufactures general stoneware, employing a number of men

On the 15th of March, 1858, Mr Sears was united in marriage to Miss Marion Stimson, a daughter of Lovett and Harriett ...ther, John

Stimson, was a native of Massachusetts, born of English parentage and was one of the heroes of the Revolution   He reared a large family and lived to an old age   The maternal grandfather of Mrs Sears enlisted for service in the war of 1812, and died in battle. He had three children, Mrs Stimson, Mrs Clarissa Cooley and Chauncey Crane, who lived to be over eighty years of age and was drowned in the Des Moines river, together with a daughter and granddaughter, while crossing that stream in a wagon   He had a grandmother who was a centenarian

Mrs Sears' father, Lovett Stimson, was a soldier in the war of 1812   He was a shoemaker by trade but in later life gave his attention to farming   He was born in Boston, Massachusetts, and his wife was a native of Utica, New York   When he was fifteen years of age he entered the army as a drummer boy, and twice joined the service as a substitute for others. After attaining his majority he removed to Illinois where he followed his trade for a time   He also bought a farm and successfully carried on agricultural pursuits   Just before the Civil war he removed to Rock Island, where he lived retired from business cares until his death, which occurred in 1866, at the age of seventy years   His wife died in Ohio at the age of forty-four   Both were members of the Universalist church   They had twelve children, six of whom are now living   Abner, Laura, wife of Byron Van Alstine, Robert, Marian, wife of David Sears, Harriet, wife of Hiram Coles, and Catherine M , wife of William Sears

Five children have been born of the union of our subject and his wife, two sons and three daughters   Lila, wife of S K Field, of M   '   '   '   r   Hugh

R , a cattle dealer of northwestern Nebraska, Harriet D , who is living with her brother Hugh, John D , who married Lulu Barnett, and with their daughter, Marian M , resides at Sears, and Vesta, who is now attending school   The family is one of prominence in the community and the circle of friends is very extensive

Mr Sears is a Master Mason and also belongs to the Ancient Order of United Workmen   In politics he is a stalwart Republican, but has never sought or desired office, preferring to devote his attention to his business interests in which he has met with signal success   He has witnessed almost the entire growth and development of the county, has seen Rock Island and Moline transferred from villages into thriving cities, has seen towns spring up and wild lands transformed into beautiful homes and farms   In the work of progress and improvement he has ever borne his part, carrying forward the labors of his father   His life, honorable in every relation, commends him to the confidence and regard of all, and in his native county he ranks among the best and most highly respected citizens. He now occupies one of the most beautiful homes of the county, located in Sears, and forming the center of a cultured society circle

WILLIAM SEARS, whose family name at once suggests the history of progress and advancement in Rock Island county, was born in Moline, on the 18th of November, 1840, and is a son of David B Sears and a brother of David Sears, whose sketches are given above   Reared in his native city, his boyhood days were spent in the usual manner of lads of that period. He pursued his education in the public schools of Moline and later spent a year as a student in Davenport, Iowa In his youth he worked in his father's mill and not only learned that business but also mastered the trade of dressing stone. He was thus engaged from 1860 until 1864, during which period his father was in the army Upon the latter's return the firm of D B Sears & Sons was formed and continued in existence until 1872, when the brothers bought out the father and carried on business under the firm style of D B Sears' Sons until 1889, when the mill was destroyed by fire. Since that time various enterprises have claimed the attention of William Sears In 1891 he built an ice house in Sears and conducted that business for a year, and in 1892 operated a stone quarry on the island near the town In 1893 he worked for the government as a foreman on the canal and in 1896 was street commissioner of Sears

In January, 1864, was celebrated the marriage of William Sears and Miss Catherine M. Stimson, a daughter of Lovett Stimson Four children have been born of their union, namely: Will, who married Miss Patterson, by whom he has two children, is living in Carney, Nebraska, where he is foreman of a large ranch owned by W. D Watts Ernest was drowned at the age of two and a half years Chauncey Barton is a telegraph operator and Benjamin L is living at home

Mr Sears is a valued member of the Odd Fellows fraternity and exercises his right of franchise in support of the men and measures of the Republican party In 1867 he took up his residence in the town of Sears and in 1871 erected his pleasant residence Widely known throughout the community, he is held in the highest regard He possesses many excellent traits of char-

ter, is true to all the duties and obligations of life and merits the respect which is tendered him by all classes

---

NELS JOHN ERICKSON, a well-known agriculturist residing on section 4, South Moline township, was born in Sweden, June 4, 1825, and was reared in that county, receiving a fair common-school education At the age of sixteen he began learning the blacksmith's trade, and during his five years apprenticeship received no wages After mastering the trade, he lived in Stockholm for two years, and in 1851 sailed for America Landing in New York, he proceeded at once to Chicago and by canal and river to St Louis, where he was stricken with cholera

In 1852 Mr Erickson arrived in Moline, where for four years he worked for Mr. Deere, and was then in the employ of the Moline Plow Company for several years In the meantime he was married and purchased a lot in that city, erecting thereon a house which continued to be his home for some time Subsequently he bought forty acres of his present farm, which at that time was all wild land, but to its improvement and cultivation he devoted his time and attention until it was converted into one of the best farms of the locality He also extended its boundaries until it contained over one hundred acres, but has since given a portion to his children. He is a wide-awake, progressive farmer and has met with a well deserved success in his undertakings

In November, 1853, was consummated the marriage of Mr Erickson and Miss Anna Nelson, also a native of Sweden, who   merica in

1851, but her father died two weeks after their arrival and her mother a year later Mrs Erickson then came to Moline, where she gave her hand in marriage to our subject Nine children have been born to them, of whom two died in infancy The others are Matilda, who married Olof Olson and died leaving two children, one still living, Emma, wife of S Bengblom, of Walnut Grove, Minnesota, by whom she has four children, Albert, who is married and lives in South Moline township, Rock Island county, Amelia, who died at the age of twenty-six years; Nathaniel, who is married and with his wife and two children lives near his father, Christina, who died in infancy, John, who died at the age of twenty-five, Frank, who died at the age of fourteen months, and Ellen, who died at the age of seventeen years

Although an ardent Republican in politics, Mr Erickson has never cared for the honors or emoluments of public office He and his wife are charter members of the Swedish Lutheran church of South Moline and contributed liberally toward the erection of the house of worship They are widely and favorably known and have a host of warm friends throughout their adopted county.

NATHAN ERICKSON, a progressive and energetic farmer residing on section 9, South Moline township, was born on the 9th of April, 1865, on the old homestead in South Moline, where he was reared During his boyhood he assisted his father in labors of the farm and attended the district schools Later he supplemented the knowledge there acquired by a two years course in the city schools of Moline He remained under the

which was celebrated in South Moline, October 22, 1891, Miss Hulda Burgston becoming his wife She is a native of Sweden, but when a child of only two years was brought to America by her father, G A Burgston, who located in Moline, where he engaged in wagon-making They now have two bright, interesting children—Eleanora and Rosella.

Previous to his marriage Mr Erickson had purchased his present place of thirty-five acres on Section 9, South Moline township and erected a neat and substantial residence, where he began house-keeping. In connection with general farming, for two years he also engaged in the dairy business, but now gives his entire time and attention to his farming interests, in which he is meeting with a well deserved success. Besides the cultivation of his own land, he also operates a tract of one hundred acres, which he rents, and is recognized as one of the most enterprising, energetic and successful farmers of the community

With the Swedish Lutheran church, at Moline, Mr and Mrs Erickson hold membership, and politically he is identified with the Republican party For two years he most capably served as road overseer, and has also been an efficient member of the school board, doing all in his power to promote the cause of education, and advance the grade of schools in his district He is a public-spirited citizen, widely and favorably known

LAFAYETTE METZLER, who is successfully following farming on section 27, Rural township, where he owns and operates two hundred acres of valuable land, was born in Mercer county, Illinois, near Swedona, December 5, 1847 His father, Peter Metzler, was a native of Westmoreland county, Pennsylvania, and his grandfather, John Metzler, was also born in that state The latter came to Illinois in 1843, and died in this state when about eighty-six years of age, having survived his wife for several years They had a large family

John Metzler came to this state about 1843, and for some time engaged in the milling business in Richland Grove township, Mercer county He afterward purchased land and now has one hundred acres, constituting one of the well improved and valuable farms of the community His wife bore the maiden name of Sarah Cowley, and was a native of Maryland, in which state her father, Branson Cowley, was also born At an early day he removed to Illinois, but soon afterward removed to Pike county, Missouri, making his home near Frankfort, where he died at an advanced age. Mrs. Metzler passed away August 14, 1895, at the age of seventy-two years She was a member of the Methodist church, and Mr. Metzler holds membership in the United Brethren church His political support has always been given to the Democratic party In the family were six children, five of whom are now living, namely. Elizabeth, wife of John L. Reeves, Lafayette, Branson, Jennie, Hester Ann, wife of Wesley Rhodenbaugh, and Abraham, who died in early childhood.

Lafayette Metzler was reared on the old home farm in Mercer county, remaining under the parental roof until he had attained his majority To the district schools of the neighborhood he is indebted for his educational privileges. He continued his residence in his native county until 1880, when he came to Rock Island county and located in Rural township In 1880 he purch [illegible]

his present farm, comprising two hundred and one acres of rich land under a high state of cultivation, and improved with good buildings He is a progressive and enterprising agriculturist whose well-directed efforts have brought to him success in his business affairs   ʻ,

On the 24th of February, 1876, Mr Metzler married Miss Alma Cheney, daughter of William C and Emily (Sayre) Cheney Her parents removed from Quincy, Ohio, to Rock Island county, in 1845, and located in Rural township, two miles from the present home of our subject, and there Mrs Metzler was born Her father was a farmer and improved two hundred and twenty-five acres of land in Rural township, continuing its cultivation until his death, which occurred May 19, 1894, at the age of seventy-five years His wife died on the old homestead, October 8, 1886, at the age of seventy-two They were members of the Methodist church and were highly respected people Their family numbered six children, four of whom are now living Mary Ellen, wife of Edwin McCartney, Hannah M , wife of Robert Coffee, of Hardin county, Iowa, Alanson P , and Mrs Alma Metzler The other two, Vincent Sayre and Francis Owen, died in early childhood The grandfather of Mrs Metzler died in Ohio, and her grandmother died in Rural township, Rock Island county

To our subject and his wife have been born two sons Jesse Roland and Perrin L Mr Metzler is a member of the Modern Woodmen of America and gives his political support to the Democracy He is now serving as road commissioner and school director and has filled the former office for six years and the latter for ten years He is deeply interested in all that pertains to the welfare [illegible]   ty and is numbered among the public-spirited citizens whose support is ever given to worthy measures for the public good

KRAMER, BLEUER & COMPANY is the name of a firm engaged in printing, lithographing and book-binding at No 1508 Second avenue, Rock Island. In May, 1888, Henry Kramer and Charles Bleuer formed a partnership under the name of Kramer & Bleuer and at first only engaged in book-binding, but in 1893 added a job and book-printing department and now do all kinds of commercial and book printing and the manufacture of blank books The company assumed its present name in 1893, on the admission of Charles Kramer, a nephew of the senior partner, to membership Their extensive trade has been secured through enterprise and indomitable energy of the proprietors,—the product of the fertile brain, the ready hand and the superior directing powers of the owners, who are most progressive, industrious and far-sighted young men

Henry Kramer was born in Philadelphia, Pennsylvania, February 6, 1860, a son of John Peter and Marie Kramer, the former a native of Germany, born in Hesse Darmstadt in 1818 and the latter of Hesse Darmstadt, born in 1820 The father was a weaver and designer of all kinds of patterns for his work, which he successfully followed in Philadelphia until 1867, when he came to Rock Island, where he still makes his home He served as a soldier in the German army before coming to America and was a Lutheran in religious belief, as was also the mother of our subject, who died in 1865 In their family were five children, four sons and one daughter but the latter

is now deceased. The sons are Adam, George F , George L and Henry. The paternal grandfather, George Wilhelm Kramer, was born in Hesse Damstadt in 1783, and died in 1858 at the age of seventy-five years

At the age of seven years Henry Kramer was brought by his father to Rock Island, where he completed the prescribed course in the public schools, and after his graduation worked at cigar making for one year He then learned book binding at which he was employed until becoming connected with his present business He is a Master Mason and also belongs to the Eastern Star and to the Order of Fraternal Tribunes, while politically he is a Democrat He makes his home with his father at 817 Fourteen and a half street

Charles Bleuer, whose birth occurred in Rock Island, February 18, 1865, is a son of John and Anna (Taylor) Bleuer, natives of Switzerland, in whose family were thirteen children, eleven sons and two daughters, namely John; Elizabeth, now the wife of Philip Bladle, Jacob, Nicholas, William, Mary, widow of Adam Peterson, Frank, Charles, Edward, Benjamin, Albert, Henry, and one who died in infancy The father, a carpenter and contractor by occupation, came to the new world about 1840 and spent two years in New York, whence he removed to Iowa, but as the climate did not agree with his health he came to Rock Island and was for more than forty-five years identified with its interests, dying here in December, 1891, at the age of seventy years He was a consistent member of the Lutheran church to which his widow also belongs In his native land he was a member of the regular army for a time The grandfathers of our subject both died in Switzerland, the maternal grandfather passing away when Mrs Bleuer was quite young, but his wife crossed the Atlantic and spent her last days in Rock Island, where she died at the age of eighty

Charles Bleuer was reared in Rock Island and obtained his education in its public schools At the age of fourteen he began work in a brickyard and continued to follow that occupation for four years, after which he was employed in a cracker bakery for two years He then learned bookbinding which he has since followed, becoming a member of the firm of Kramer, Bleuer & Company in May, 1888, as before stated On the 26th of June, 1888, he led to the marriage altar Miss May, daughter of John and Anna Bartha, and to them have been born three children—Charles, Gertrude and Arthur Mrs Bleuer is a member of the Catholic church, while our subject belongs to the Modern Woodmen of America, and in politics is a Democrat He is now serving as alderman from the fourth ward and is one of the most popular and influential members of the council He and his nine brothers are all excellent musicians and years ago organized a cornet band, which each would join as soon as they were old enough Benjamin is now the leader and Charles has been connected with it for eighteen years Theirs is one of the leading orchestras of the city and furnishes music for many parties, entertainments, etc Mr Bleuer, of this review, lives at No 733 Seventeenth street, where he erected his dwelling in 1888

Charles Kramer, also a native of Rock Island, was born on the 15th of January, 1872 and is a son of Adam and Christina (Stuelmil) [   ]   [   ]
phia, Pe [   ]   [   ]   [   ]

Rock Island For almost four years the father was a member of the Union army during the Civil war, participated in many hard fought battles, and was injured while in the service He is a printer by trade and is the present foreman in the Rock Island Union office He is a member of the Broadway Presbyterian church, to which his estimable wife also belonged Her death occurred in 1891 when in her thirty-sixth year Seven children were born to them—Louise, wife of Adolphus Dunlap, Charles, Katie, wife of Fred Garnett, Carrie, Daisy and Elsie

When quite small Charles Kramer was taken by his parents to Des Moines, Iowa, where he lived for a number of years and acquired the greater part of his education in its public schools, but graduated from the Rock Island high school At the age of eighteen he commenced learning the printer's trade, which he has successfully followed ever since, being actively connected with that department of his present business He is also a member of the Broadway Presbyterian church, and is an ardent Republican in politics

WALTER J ENTRIKIN, a leading attorney and counselor at law, of Moline, whose office is located at No 316 Sixteenth street, was born on the 8th of February, 1846, in Salem, Columbiana county, Ohio, and belongs to a family of Scotch-Irish origin, which has for several generations resided in this country Brinton Entrikin, father of our subject, was born in Chester county, Pennsylvania December 8, [   ] the grand- emoval to

12

Columbiana county, Ohio, where he engaged in farming. He was there married to Miss Eliza Jane McCracken, who was born in that county in 1814. In connection with the operation of his farm the father also worked at the plasterer's trade in the Buckeye state until 1861, when he brought his family to Henry county, Illinois, and located on a farm which he purchased two and a half miles from Geneseo.

The early education of our subject was obtained in the country schools of the celebrated school district of Water Valley, where the Republican party had its birth. After coming to Illinois he pursued his studies in the high schools of Geneseo, where he acquired a knowledge of Greek and Latin, and in 1865 entered the college at Oberlin, Ohio, from which institution he graduated August 4, 1870. He had previously determined to fit himself for the legal profession, and during his vacations had taught school in the home district and read law in the office of Wait & Moderwell, of Geneseo. In April, 1871, he entered the office of John T Browning, of Moline, and on the 12th of October, of that year, was admitted to the bar, being the last one admitted under the old law, which permitted an examination by the circuit court. He remained in the office of his preceptor until January 1, 1873, after which he was alone in practice for one year and then formed a partnership with W K Moore. On the 1st of July, 1876, he became connected with Mr Browning and that partnership lasted until January 1, 1894. Since that time he has continued in the law without a partner.

On the 18th of August, 1870, in Moline, was celebrated the marriage of Mr Entrikin and Miss Julia A Chamberlin, who was born in I . . . .

educated in Derby, that state, and came with her parents to Moline in 1861. Five children have been born to them: Eva Mary completed the prescribed course at the Augustana Conservatory of Music, later took a two years' post graduate course at Oberlin, Ohio, and is now a most successful music teacher. William B , a graduate of the Moline High School, is now a student in the Chicago College of Law, and lives in Chicago. He married Bertha C Farris, of Moline. Fred C is also a law student and is engaged in the insurance, real estate and collection business. Roy J was engaged in the plumbing business for two years, but is now a law student in his father's office. Ada L , who completes the family, is also a graduate of the Moline High School, is also a law student in his office.

Mr Entrikin holds and merits a place among the representative legal practitioners and citizens of Moline; and the story of his life, while not dramatic in action, is such a one as offers a typical example of that alert American spirit which has enabled many an individual to rise from obscurity to a position of influence and renown solely through native talent, indomitable perseverance and singleness of purpose. In making the record of such a life contemporary biography exercises a most consistent and important function. From 1884 until 1888 Mr Entrikin most creditably served as state's attorney, was city attorney in 1873 and 1874, and again in 1881 and 1882. Reared as a Republican he cast his first vote for General Grant in 1868, and has since been an ardent supporter of that party. He is a prominent and active member of the First Congregational church, of which he has been trustee for twenty years and superintendent of the Sunday school district of long period. Fraternally he belongs to the Modern Woodmen of America, the Ancient Order of United Workmen and the Order of Chosen Friends

ALBERT FLEMMING is the efficient and well-known manager of the Flemming Furniture Company, doing business at 1614 Second avenue, Rock Island. His record is that of an enterprising business man, who has followed the beaten paths of earnest, honest endeavor until he has reached the goal of prosperity.

Mr Flemming was born in Davenport, Iowa, a son of Peter Flemming, a native of Germany. The family numbered seven children, three sons and four daughters, of whom four are now living. Albert Flemming was reared in his native city, and acquired his education in its public schools. In early life he learned the barber's trade, which he followed for some years. In 1882 he removed to Rock Island and engaged in that line of business on his own account, owning at different times four shops. He continued business as a barber until 1892, when he sold out and engaged in the furniture trade as a member of the firm of Kohn & Flemming, a partnership that was continued for three years

Mr Flemming then sold out and again engaged in the barber's business, which he followed until 1896. In that year he established his present business under the name of the Flemming Furniture Company. He carries a large and well-assorted stock of modern furniture and is meeting with success in his undertakings. His business methods are honorable and commend him to the public confidence and his earnest desire to please his customers has brought to him a liberal patronage. H

awake and progressive business man and his success is well merited. As his capital has increased he has invested in real estate and has erected three houses in the town

Mr Flemming was united in marriage to Miss Louisa Buncher, a daughter of Matles and Christina Buncher. Three children have been born to them,—Louisa, Roy and Albert J. They occupy a pleasant home, 726 Seventeenth street, and have many friends in the community. In his political affiliations Mr Flemming has always been a Republican

DANIEL MONTGOMERY.—The time has come in the history of the world when the path of labor and usefulness is indicated as the highway to honor. Biography has brought to the attention of mankind the fact that it is the men in the industrial and commercial pursuits of life to whom is due more largely the development and prosperity of town, county and state. Those distinguished in military service, statecraft, in science or in letters play an important part in the public life, but it is now a recognized fact that the stability of a country and its substantial growth is due to the citizens who are the workers in trade and agricultural circles

It is of this class that Mr Montgomery is a representative, and among the reliable and prominent farmers and grain dealers of Rock Island county he is numbered. He resides on section 26, Edgington township, and was born in that township, January 8, 1840. His parents were Daniel and Margaret (Simington) Montgomery, natives of Pennsylvania. His grandfather, John Montgomery, was born in Danville, Pennsylvania, and died in the prime of life. He had a family of sons and daughters, one of whom, John, was the first Presbyterian minister in Rock Island county   The maternal grandparents of our subject were Robert and Elizabeth (Jacoby) Simington, who had a family of nine children who reached mature years, but for the past nine years Mrs Margaret Montgomery has been the only survivor   Her father was a farmer and was one of the heroes who fought for American independence in the war of the Revolution   He was of Irish lineage, the youngest of his father's family, and died at the age of eighty-four years   His wife passed away at the age of seventy-five   Both were consistent members of the Presbyterian church and Mr Simington served as elder   His life was one of industry and of the highest respectability   His mother had two cousins who were very prominent in the ministry of the Presbyterian church in Philadelphia.

Daniel Montgomery, Sr , father of our subject, was reared to manhood in Pennsylvania and operated a flouring and woolen mill in the east   He came to Illinois in 1836 and located on section 26, Edgington township, Rock Island county, where he entered a large tract of land   There was no family living within four miles of the place and the whole region was wild and unimproved, but with characteristic energy he began the development of his land and transformed it into a fine farm   He died on the old homestead in 1849, at the age of forty-five years   His widow still survives him and is now living with her son Daniel, at the age of eighty-eight years, her birth having occurred in Columbia county, Pennsylvania, August 11, 1809   Both were members of the Presbyterian church and Mr Montgomery served as elder in the Edgington church, of which he was o.   He was alway-

a prominent and influential citizen of the community and his death was deeply lamented   His wife is the only charter member of the Edgington church now surviving, and this was the first church of the denomination in Rock Island county   Mrs Montgomery has been a resident of the county for sixty-one years, eighteen years being spent in Black Hawk township and the remainder of the time on the old homestead with the exception of two years passed in Rock Island when her children were attending school there   She has therefore witnessed almost the entire growth and development of this region, and her Christian influence and kindly spirit have left their impress upon all with whom she has come in contact   By her marriage she became the mother of four sons   Robert, John, Daniel and Captain James, the last named now deceased

Daniel Montgomery, whose name introduces this review, was reared in his native township and obtained his education in the primary district schools   At one time school was conducted in his father's house   Later he attended the public school of Rock Island and subsequently Knox College, of Galesburg, after which he returned to the home farm, which he has since operated in connection with his brother Robert, each owning four hundred and forty acres of land   Their brother John is now a farmer of Mercer county   Our subject carries on general farming and stock raising and in the management of his business interest, and by his industry and enterprise has accumulated a handsome property   In 1881 he erected a fine residence and has otherwise improved his property with all the accessories and conveniences of the model farm of the nineteenth century   Although living on a farm he and his brother have extensively engaged in buying and shipping grain at Reynolds in partnership with Martin Schoomaker, and the company buy nearly all the grain that is shipped from the surrounding country, operating two elevators in Reynolds They thus afford a market for the farmers and at the same time add to their prosperity by the capable management of their business interests in this direction

On the 3d of January, 1871, Mr Montgomery was united in marriage to Martha A , daughter of Henry Hulbert and Martha (Jingles) Parks Three sons and five daughters have been born to them, namely Walter L , who is engaged in stock dealing in Chamberlain, South Dakota, Mary W , Ella P and Sarah S , at home, Harriet, John P and Charles, all deceased, and Martha P , also at home

The parents are members of the Presbyterian church, in which Mr Montgomery is now serving as elder In his political views he is a Republican and has served as school director for about twenty years, in which capacity he has materially advanced educational interests in the community He is a kind-hearted gentleman, ever ready to help those who are willing to help themselves, exercises a broad influence for the betterment of humanity, gives his co-operation to all movements for public good and is a genial gentleman, very popular with a host of friends He represents one of the oldest families of the county and wears worthily the untarnished family name.

L OUIS F KERNS, justice of the peace and police magistrate, of Moline, needs no special introduction in in the this work would be incomplete without a

record of his life He is one of the honored early settlers of the city, where he has made his home since 1854, and for many years he was prominently identified with its industrial interests, but now devotes his entire time and attention to the discharge of his official duties.

Mr Kerns was born in Delaware county, Pennsylvania, and is a son of John Kerns, who was born in Chester county, the same state, and was a non-commissioned officer in the war of 1812 The father married Miss Esther Williamson, a native of Delaware county, who belonged to an old Quaker family He was a mechanic and also an agriculturist, and on his removal to Columbiana county, Ohio, in 1835, located upon a farm, where he spent his remaining days, dying in 1871, at the advanced age of ninety years. His wife only survived him about six months, her death occurring at the age of eighty-seven All of their children, three sons and four daughters, reached years of maturity, and two sons and one daughter are still living

When a lad of seven years, Louis F Kerns accompanied his parents on their emigration to Ohio, where he assisted his father in the arduous task of opening up and developing a new farm Although his early educational privileges were limited, he has become a well informed man by reading, study and observation, since reaching man's estate At the age of seventeen he began learning the blacksmith's trade, and after serving a three years' apprenticeship worked as a journeyman in various states Soon after locating in Moline in 1854, he opened a wagon and blacksmith shop, and continued to engage in business here for thirty-five

In 1854 s was married in 1864, the lady of his choice being Miss Elizabeth B Entrikin, who was born in Ohio and reared in Columbiana county, that state Four children blessed this union, namely Dr E L , a leading physician of Moline, Jennie M , at home, Mary G , wife of James Hewson, a business man of Moline, and Florence G , who is prepaiing herself for a teacher in the Moline Training School The wife and mother was called to her final rest, March 4, 1886, and her remains were interred in Riverside cemetery

In early life Mr Kerns was a Jacksonian Democrat, but on its organization he became identified with the Republican party, voting foi John C Fremont in 1856, and while still claiming to be a Republican of the Abraham Lincoln school does not take an active part in modein politics Four times elected to seive his waid in the city council, elected magistrate in 1890 and now serving on his second term

---

F RANK ECKARD, assistant chief of police of Rock Island, is one of Ohio's native sons who entered upon the scene of life's activities in Tiffin, that state, December 18, 1862 His parents were William and Nellie Eckard His father, a carpenter by trade, located in Ohio at an early day and about 1866 iemoved to Illinois, locating in Geneseo, where he made his home for some years He afterward took up his residence in Cambridge, where he contiaued for some time, and then came to Rock Island, wheie he remained for about ten years He died here in December, 1891, at the age of fifty-six, and his wife passed away in 1877 at the age of thirty-six years She hel   'he M th dest

church, and Mr Eckard attended its services with her They were people of the highest respectability and won the esteem of a large circle of friends Their family numbered five children, three sons and two daughters, of whom four are now living, as follows Mary, wife of Andrew Oake, of Cambridge, Illinois, Charley, of Peoria, Frank, of this review, and Eva, who is living in Chicago

Frank Eckard was a child of only four years, when he accompanied his parents on their removal to Illinois He acquired the greater part of his education in Cambridge, this state For sixteen years he has lived in Rock Island, and after coming to this city he learned the carpenter's trade, which he followed continuously until entering upon his official service Being a good workman he never lacked for employment and evidences of his handiwork may be seen in many of the fine residences and substantial buildings of the city In the spring of 1897 he was appointed assistant chief of police and in the discharge of his duties has manifested a most commendable fidelity to the trust reposed in him and to the law interests of the city.

On the 15th of October, 1891, was celebrated the marriage of Mr Eckard and Miss Flora Eaton Their home is now blessed by the presence of a little daughter, Pearl Mr Eckard is a member of the Modern Woodmen of America, the Court of Honor and the Carpenters' Union, and of the last named has several times been president He exercises his right of franchise in support of the men and measures of the Democratic party He is a genial, pleasant man, popular with a large circle of friends and discharges his official duties in a manner   with   and justice.

ERNEST OTTO FISCHER is a leading representative of the industrial interests of Moline, being engaged in the marble business as a member of the firm of Devore & Fischer, at the corner of Seventh avenue and Fifteenth street He started out in life with no capital save a strong determination to win success by honorable effort, and throughout his career he has adhered most strictly to the ethics of commercial life He has worked his way steadily upward by industry, perseverance and capable management, and well merits the prosperity that has come to him

Mr Fischer was born in Hessen, Germany, June 23, 1865, and during his early boyhood came to America with his parents, Edward and Mary (Machatany) Fischer, who located in Ottawa, Illinois He was reared to manhood there, obtaining a good education in the common schools At the age of sixteen he began to learn the art of wood engraving, and after a year commenced learning the granite and marble business, which he has thoroughly mastered He worked at that trade in Ottawa for a time and then went to Chicago, where he was engaged in making crayon portraits for a few months Returning then to Ottawa, he continued in the marble business there until 1891, when he went to Henry, Illinois, and began business on his own account as a partner of Charles K Devore In 1896 they removed to Moline, where they are now well established in trade The work which they turn out is of a very superior quality, and the firm has a most enviable reputation for reliability These two characteristics of their business have secured to them a very liberal patronage, which is constantly increasing

Mr. Fischer was married in Ottawa, April

28, 1890, to Jennie E Shields, who was born in Pennsylvania and removed to Ottawa during her early girlhood They have one child, Carl Alexander, who was born in Ottawa Mr Fischer is a member of the Knights of Pythias lodge of Henry, in which he has filled several offices He cast his first presidential vote for Harrison in 1888, and is a warm adherent of Republican principles A wide-awake and enterprising young business man, he possesses that energy and force of character which always accomplishes what it undertakes, and Moline is glad to number him among the representatives of her commercial interests

PHILIP J MILLER, ex-chief of police of Rock Island, began his earthly career April 5, 1848, in Germany, but in 1853 was brought to America by his parents, Joseph and Christina (Clauder) Miller, who located in Rock Island, where the father was for many years a successful gardener He spent the last twenty years of his life in retirement, and died in 1894 at the ripe old age of seventy-eight He was widely and favorably known, and was a faithful member of the Presbyterian church, while his wife was a Lutheran in faith Her death occurred in 1891, when in her seventy-fourth year Of their fourteen children, Jacob, Catherine, Fisher and Philip J are still living and make their home in Rock Island

In the common schools of the city our subject acquired his education, and began life for himself as a sawyer in Weyerhauser & Denkman's lumber yard Since 1876, however, he has been connected with the police service For one year he was deputy marshal under Mayor W P Butler

[ ] Perkins two

years, marshal under Mayor Harry Carse three years, served in the same office for two years under Major J. Z Mott, was deputy sheriff for John M Redicker for two years, and for Sharp Silvis two years, the following four years was marshal under Mayor William McCombie, was then collector of tolls for Thomas Murdock for a year, and is now serving his second year as policeman under Frank B Knox Prompt and faithful in the discharge of his duties, he has proved a most efficient officer, and has won the confidence and respect of the entire community

On the 19th of February, 1869, was celebrated the marriage of Mr Miller and Miss Annie L Van Meter, daughter of David J Van Meter, of Mercer county, Illinois, and to them were born three children —Joseph, who married Emily ———, and is employed as bookkeeper by the Illinois Steel Company, of Chicago, Carrie, wife of William A Strell, of Chicago, and David J, who is connected with Parker's Laundry, of Rock Island The wife and mother, who was a consistent member of the Methodist Episcopal church, departed this life in April, 1894, at the age of forty-six years

Socially, Mr Miller is identified with the Knights of Pythias fraternity, the Home Forum, the Modern Woodmen of America, and the Court of Honor, while his political support is ever given the men and measures of the Republican party Although of foreign birth, he possesses the true American spirit of enterprise, and his love for his adopted country has been manifest by the faithful performance of all public duties His repeated calls to office and his long continuance in the same testifies to his faithfulness, and he stands deservedly high in the estimation

DANIEL GORDON, whose name is ineffaceably stamped on the history of Rock Island county, has led a life of practical usefulness and honor that has won for him the highest regard of all with whom he has been brought in contact He is now living retired in Moline enjoying a rest which is certainly well merited. Fifty-four years ago he came to Rock Island county, joining that band of heroic pioneers who paved the way to civilization and transformed the wild region into beautiful homes and farms

Mr Gordon was born in Wayne county, Michigan, on a farm near Dearbornville, February 7, 1822, and there remained until thirteen years of age, during which time he attended the common schools

His father, Amos Gordon, was born in Hopkinton, New Hampshire, December 4, 1791, and married Amy Bucklin, who was born in Cayuga county, New York, June 3, 1803, the marriage taking place in Michigan Mrs Gordon's father, William Bucklin, removed to the Wolverine state before the war of 1812 The paternal grandfather of our subject removed from New Hampshire to Ohio, became a captain of militia and joined the Fifth Regiment of United States troops, in which he served for two and a half years He was discharged in Detroit and located in Michigan The father of our subject lived to a very advanced age, passing away May 1, 1890 His wife died October 10, 1896, and they were buried in what is known as the Old cemetery in Moline Their family numbered eight children, seven of whom grew to mature years, while three are yet living

In the spring of 1835 the family, with a team and covered wagon, drove across the country to Chicago, but found the land there so marshy and wet that after a few months they went to Plato township where the fa-

DANIEL GORDON.

ther built a log house and made a claim In a short time, however, he sold out and removed to Henry county, purchasing a farm on the edge of the military tract near where Geneseo now stands He built a log cabin and sawmill there and remained until 1843. when he removed to Moline and purchased a town lot on what is now Third avenue In the fall of 1844, accompanied by our subject, he went to the pineries in Wisconsin and engaged in the manufacture of shingles He there secured a lot of lumber, which, with the shingles, he rafted down the river From this lumber he constructed a house, and the old home which he erected is still standing and is yet occupied

Daniel Gordon obtained his education in the schools of Henry county, and attended an academy at intervals for about three years, but his privileges were somewhat meager While yet a boy he began assisting Mr Seymour, the first county surveyor of Henry county, carrying the chain and flag and doing other such work After coming to Moline he engaged in teaching school through several winters, but in the spring of 1850 he was appointed deputy surveyor of Scott county, Iowa, by the surveyor of that county, who wished to go to California in search of gold and had to secure some one to take his place It was in this way that Mr Gordon engaged in laying out some of the additions to Davenport and in surveying some of the farms of that locality, but there was not enough work to make the business profitable, and he was obliged to resume school teaching In the spring of 1852 he was appointed to a position with a party that was to survey the state lin '   I   M
which w r

The chief of the party was Colonel Andrew Talcott, of Richmond, Virginia, who became chief of ordnance for the Confederate States of America during the Rebellion The chief chain man in the party was Eugene W Crittenden, son of Senator Crittenden, of Kentucky, and others were a son of Senator McDuffey, of South Carolina, and a son of Senator Jones, of Iowa, the last named being the tent-mate of our subject

On that trip Mr Gordon was detailed with Captain Marsh to go on an exploration and survey, and after their return they went as far west as the Sioux river Mr Gordon was appointed chief of one of the mound parties and completed the state line, returning home in the fall With the money earned in that way he purchased ten acres of land where he now lives, paying two hundred dollars in gold for the same This adjoined a forty-acre tract which he had purchased in 1849 Mr Gordon was next employed to go to western Iowa to aid in the subdivision of twelve townships in Sac and Ida counties, spending the fall of 1852 there Returning to Moline he began to improve his farm and at intervals continued surveying In 1869 when the water power was to be improved he was employed as assistant engineer under Peter A Dey, a railroad civil engineer He has been prominently connected with the interests of Moline and has ever given his support to all measures calculated to prove of public benefit He added to his farm until he owned over one hundred acres, a portion of which was afterward divided into town lots and sold He has also bought and sold other real estate and in his business interests ac-   competence, which

At the first presidential election which occurred after he had attained his majority Mr Gordon was in the lumber woods of Wisconsin and in consequence did not get to vote He was an abolitionist and supported James G Birney and John P Hale In 1856 he voted for John C Fremont, and has since been a stalwart Republican He was the first clerk of the village of Moline, was afterward trustee, in 1860 was elected assessor and for several years filled that position In the fall of 1859 he was elected county surveyor and with the exception of six years held that office continuously until 1888 His father having then become helpless, and Mr Gordon being the only one of the children unmarried he returned home in order to take care of his parents, and resigned his position For several years he has been a member of the board of county supervisors was elected justice of the peace in May, 1897, and is now school trustee In his youth he became a member of the Congregational church and he and most of the other members of the family became charter members of the church in Moline His life has been an honorable and upright one, undimmed by shadow of wrong and characterized by the utmost fidelity to duty in all relations of a public or private character His friends are not alone from one class but are numbered among the young and the old, the rich and the poor

ROBERT SIMINGTON MONTGOMERY, who resides on section 26, Edgington township, is one of Rock Island county's pioneers, and in tracing the development and progress of this section of the state we find that he and his family have been imp . . . .

vancement, their labors being of incalculable benefit in the promotion of varied interests, educational, social, moral and material It is but, therefore, a matter of justice that the life record of this gentleman finds a place in the history of the county, which, were the sketch omitted, would be incomplete

Mr Montgomery was born in Danville, Pennsylvania, March 30, 1836, and is a son of Daniel and Margaret (Simington) Montgomery, who were also natives of the Keystone state In the year of his birth they came to Rock Island county and the father entered four hundred and forty acres He also had a section of land adjoining this tract on the south, which he bought of an uncle, and owned several other farms, together with a tract of land near Joliet which he entered from the government and upon which he intended to settle, but he changed his mind and continued to make his residence in Edgington township until his death His life record is given at some length in connection with the sketch of Daniel Montgomery, Jr, on another page of this work

Robert S Montgomery has spent his entire life on the old family homestead, where as a boy he played in the fields, and later assisted in their cultivation and improvement As the years went by he assumed his share of the farm work, and throughout his entire life he has known no other home than the farmstead whereon he was reared He and his brother Daniel came into possession of this property, although each own four hundred and forty acres in their own right The enterprise and progressive spirit of our subject are indicated by the fine appearance of his fields and by the substantial and modern improvements upon his place In his youth he attended the district school of the neighborhood and later pursued a collegiate course at Macomb, Illinois, after which he returned to the work of the farm which he has since continued, with the exception of the short period of his military service in the Civil war, followed by a year spent in the oil regions of Pennsylvania

Mr Montgomery responded to his country's call for troops to aid in the preservation of the Union and joined the boys in blue of Company B, Sixty-fifth Illinois Volunteer Infantry He raised this company, was commissioned its captain and served in that capacity until the close of the war He was three times wounded, first at Lexington, then in front of Atlanta by a piece of shell and again in front of Columbus, Tennessee He participated in the Atlanta campaign, where he was under fire for several weeks, was in the siege of Knoxville and the Tennessee campaign With his company he was taken prisoner at Harper's Ferry, but was paroled on the field and sent to Camp Douglas, Chicago, where he remained until exchanged, when he went to Kentucky. He was ever a brave and loyal soldier, who loyally performed every duty devolving upon him and faithfully followed the old flag until the restoration of peace Having spent the summer of 1865 in Pennsylvania, he then returned to the work of the farm and has since been prominently connected with the agricultural interests of the county

On the 23d of June, 1869 Mr Montgomery was united in marriage to Miss Jane Titterington, a daughter of James and Eleanor (Beall) Titterington, early settlers of Rock Island county Nine children have graced this union, four sons and five daughters Alexander Boyd, Elizabeth Simington, Ann Beall, Margaret J, Eleanor Ruth, Louisa Reed Daniel T, James Howard and Thon ╷ ╷ T

worthy members of the Presbyterian church, and Mr Montgomery is now serving as elder He is a Master Mason and exemplifies in his life the benevolent and helpful spirit of that fraternity His political support is given the Republican party, and he warmly espouses its principles He has served as supervisor two terms and for a number of years held the office of school director He manifests a deep and commendable interest in all that pertains to the public welfare, is an influential and leading citizen and his name is synonymous with honorable business dealing and integrity in all the relations of life

PHILLIP SIMMON, now living retired at 1907 Fourth avenue, Rock Island, began his earthly career October 10, 1818, in Meisenheim, Germany, and is a son of Peter Henry and Catharine Eva (Crawfius) Simmon, also natives of the fatherland, where the father engaged in farming and teaming In the spring of 1833, with his family, he crossed the Atlantic to America, and first located in Bedford county, Pennsylvania, when he removed to Tuscarawas county, Ohio, spending about nine years in each place In 1850 he emigrated to Rock Island county, Illinois, and two years later located upon a farm in Rural township, where he continued to make his home until called to his final rest He was born in 1793 and died at the age of eighty-three, surviving his wife, who was born in 1795, one year Both were consistent Christian people, the former a member of the Lutheran church and the latter of the Presbyterian church There was an old fort at their home in Germany, and before leaving his ╷ ╷╷ ╷ ╷ 'he home guaids Nine of the children of the family are still living, the oldest being our subject, who is seventy-nine, and the youngest sixty The paternal grandfather, a tanner by trade, reared a family of four sons and three daughters He died in middle life The maternal grandfather served for some time in the Germany army and died in his native land

At the age of fifteen years Philip Simmon accompanied his parents on their emigration to the United States He had attended the public schools of his native land, also pursued his studies for a short time while living in Pennsylvania, and, after his marriage, went to night school in Rock Island, as he saw how essential to a successful business career was a good education He was reared as a farmer boy, but after coming to this state worked at various employments, and for a number of years followed draying, but has now laid aside business cares and enjoys a well-earned rest

On the 19th of March, 1843, was celebrated the marriage of Mr Simmon and Miss Anna Catharine Miller, daughter of Frederick Miller, and they became the parents of four children—Johnnie and Alexander, who died in infancy, Eliza, who married John Fleener and had four children, Harry, George, Tillie and Willie, and George Henry, who married Ingy Robley, and had three children, two now living, Lillie Viola and Peter Canna The wife and mother, who was a faithful member of the Presbyterian church, died in 1852

Mr Simmon was again married April 16, 1853, his second union being with Miss Cornelia Jane, daughter of John and Louisa Hitchcock, and to them were born six children, of whom two died in infancy Peter Canna,

has been in the employ of the Deering Company of Moline, married Anna Richards, and now has two daughters—Gertrude and Anna May Harrison B, teller in the People's Bank of Rock Island, married Emma Dindinger Maria E is the wife of William A Darling, the present county surveyor of Rock Island county, and they have two children—Philip Hiram and Harriet C Matilda is at home, keeping house for her father, as the mother died September 26, 1892, when almost sixty years of age She was an active member of the Methodist church, and her father was a Methodist minister

Mr Simmons belongs to the Lutheran church, is an ardent Democrat in politics, for one term served as alderman, and was street commissioner of Rock Island for two years He erected a brick house on Fourth avenue, which was the first on the block where he now lives, and his present dwelling, which is a frame structure, was built by him in 1866 Being endowed with many virtues, and a genial, hospitable manner, he receives the respect and confidence of the entire community, and his circle of friends is only limited by his circle of acquaintances

---

CHARLES A LARSON, who is successfully engaged in general farming and stock-raising on section 9, South Moline township, was born April 12, 1861, on the farm adjoining where he now lives, and is the only son of John E and Anna C (Young) Larson, who were born, reared and married in Sweden In 1854 they emigrated to the new world and first settled in the city of Moline, Illinois, where they spent seven years The father later operated land in the . . . time, after which he purchased the place where his son is now living, and here spent his remaining days, dying October 22, 1872, at the age of forty-eight years and six months His wife survived him many years, passing away April 18, 1895, and now sleeps by his side in Rock River View cemetery, where a neat monument marks their last resting place

Upon his present homestead, Charles A Larson was reared to habits of thrift and industry, becoming a thorough and skillful farmer, and in district schools of the neighborhood he obtained a good literary education After his father's death he took charge of the farm, his mother remaining with him during her declining years, and he has manifested good business and executive ability in its management The place comprises one hundred and twenty-three and a half acres of valuable land, which he has placed under a high state of cultivation and improved with good buildings, including a substantial residence, and a large basement barn and other outbuildings In connection with general farming he is meeting with excellent success as a breeder, dealer and shipper of Poland China hogs and Holstein cattle, having some very fine specimens of these animals upon his place

Mr Larson cast his first presidential vote for James G Blaine, but has since been an ardent Democrat, and has taken quite an active and prominent part in local politics In 1897 he was elected township clerk, and has efficiently served as highway commissioner and school director, having always been a warm friend of our public school system He is also secretary and treasurer of the Rock River View cemetery, and whatever position he has been called upon to fill, he has ever discharged the duties of the same in a most prompt and capable manner, thus winning the commendation and respect of the entire community

JAMES M HUTCHINSON, who is now serving as supervisor of Rural township, and makes his home on section 22, is a representative of America's enterprising and progressive citizens, who by his own efforts has steadily worked his way upward to success He was born in Fayette county, Pennsylvania, April 25, 1843, and is a son of Samuel K and Rosanna (Hogan) Hutchinson His grandfather, Isaac Hutchinson, was born in New Jersey, of English parentage, being descended from James Hutchinson, who emigrated from England about 1740 and took up his residence near Trenton New Jersey At a reunion of the family, held in Trenton on Thursday, August 13, 1885, there were four hundred of his descendants present The old house where the reunion was held was completed August 12, 1785, and was built by James Hutchinson, whose wife laid the first and last brick The old building is still standing

In early life Isaac Hutchinson our subject's grandfather, removed to Pennsylvania, walking the entire distance, and built the first mills at the foot of the Alleghany mountains on Redstone creek, three miles south of Uniontown, as by trade he was a millwright Later he purchased a large tract of land and erected a good mill of his own, successfully operating the same until his death, which occurred at the advanced age of eighty-nine years He cast his first presidential vote for General Washington In Pennsylvania he had married and became the father of nine sons and one daughter

The maternal grandfather of our subject

was John Hagan, who was born and reared in Ireland and came to America when a young man, locating in Baltimore He had a contract on the old National road and built a section of it from Baltimore into Ohio He made considerable money and afterward purchased a large tract of land near Uniontown, Pennsylvania, where he engaged in farming until his death, which occurred at the age of eighty years He had a family of three sons and seven daughters

Samuel K Hutchinson, the father of our subject, was a native of Fayette county, Pennsylvania, where he followed farming throughout his entire life, his death occurring in South Union township, in 1882, at the age of sixty-eight years He was a member of the Baptist church, held various township offices and gave his political support to the Republican party His wife still survives him at the age of seventy years, and is a member of the Cumberland Presbyterian church They had a family of five sons and two daughters, and six of the number are yet living, namely John C , James M , Isaac, Mary Margaret, who became the wife of Harvey Sutton, and after his death married James Robinson, being a second time a widow, Albert, Elizabeth, wife of Charles Brownfield, and William, deceased

James M Hutchinson was born on the farm of his grandfather, John Hagan, and was there reared to manhood His education was acquired in the district schools, and when eighteen years of age he entered his country's service, enlisting in 1861 as a member of Company A, First West Virginia Cavalry, being mustered in as a Virginian That was the first cavalry company sworn into the United States service for the Civil war He served three years and four months and was l　　　　　　　in the r

12, 1864, having participated in the battles of Carney Fox Ferry, the charge of Withville, the second battle of Bull Run, Antietam, South Mountain and many skirmishes At various times he was under the command of General Rosecrans, General Cox, General Crook and General Hancock

When his military service was ended Mr Hutchinson returned to the home farm, where he remained for about two years and then went to Iowa, spending five years in that state and in Dakota at the Yankton agency, when there were but eight white men in the place Returning to Pennsylvania, he was married there and continued his residence in his native state for seven years He came to Illinois in August, 1876, and soon afterward located in Rural township, Rock Island county, where he rented land for twelve years He then purchased eighty acres of his present farm and has since added to it a tract of forty acres He successfully carries on general farming and stock raising, making a specialty of the raising of horses, and has one horse, Charley Negus, with a record of 2 25¼.

On the 31st of December, 1872, Mr Hutchinson was united in marriage to Miss Sarah G Summers, a daughter of John and Sarah (Ross) Summers, natives of Pennsylvania Five children have been born to them, three sons and two daughters—Edward Earl, who is a conductor on the street car line in Rock Island, Albert Jesse, Samuel Guy, Mary Ruth and Rhoda Ross, all at home

Mr Hutchinson is a pronounced Republican in politics, and his fellow citizens, recognizing his worth and ability, have called him to several official positions of honor and trust For four years each he served as township collector and assessor, and in the spring of 1897 was elected supervisor, the duties of which office he is now faithfully discharging Socially he belongs to Trego Post, No 334, G A R , Sherman Lodge, No 535, F & A M , the Modern Woodmen of America, and he and his wife are both members of the Royal Neighbors In religious belief she is a Baptist Courteous, genial, well informed, alert and enterprising, Mr Hutchinson stands to-day one of the leading representative men of his township—a man who is a power in his community.

WILLIAM BAKER is one of the enterprising and progressive young men of Rock Island This is his native city, his birth having occurred on the 3d of December, 1864 His parents, H B and Frederica Louise (Libb) Baker, were natives of New York and Sweden, respectively, and are still residents of Minnesota. The father is a stonemason by trade, and for many years has been employed as foreman of construction work on railroads Their family numbered four children—Emma, a dressmaker living in Rock Island, William, of this sketch, George, and Lucy M , wife of B L Wilson, of Rock Island

Mr. Baker, of this review, obtained his education in the public schools of his native city and then learned the carpenter's trade He was afterward employed in the wood working department of the plow shops here for fourteen years, and then embarked in business on his own account as a commission merchant, dealing in butter, eggs and poultry He also traveled in the interest of the Rock Island Plow Company in 1893 and 1894 His resolute purpose and unbending will

success in his undertakings, and his abilities will no doubt secure for him still greater prosperity in the future

Mr Baker is regarded as one of the representative young Republicans of Rock Island and is very active and influential in the work of the party He has served as a member of the ward and county central committees, was one of the original members of the Lincoln club of Rock Island, of which he formerly served as vice-president, and in 1896 was assistant sergeant-at-arms at the Republican national convention in St Louis He strongly believes in reciprocity, the protection of American industries, and in a money standard that will be received for its face value throughout the world, and is indefatigable in his efforts to promote the cause of Republicanism

On the 23d of April, 1891, Mr Baker married Miss Nellie O'Neal, a daughter of Timothy O'Neal, of Rock Island Her father was born in Ireland, her mother in New York, and in 1876 they came to this city, where Mr O'Neal is still living at the age of seventy-two years His wife died in 1882, at the age of forty-nine They were both members of the Catholic church, and Mrs Baker was reared in that faith She is the third in a family of seven children, the others being William, of Rock Island, a moulder by trade, who wedded Mary Meanor and has two children, Louis and Edna, John, who died at the age of twenty-eight years, Joseph, who is connected with a hotel in Buffalo, New York, Fred, a glass gatherer residing in Fairmont, Indiana, Mary, who lives in Seneca Falls, New York, and Emma who died at the age of two years

Mr Baker holds membership in the Odd Fellows Society has filled all the chairs in the local lodge and is now past grand He has represented the Red Men in their Great Council in Chicago in 1893 Prominent in social, business and political circles, he is a young man of sterling worth, of undoubted honesty in all business relations, and in every walk of life commands the confidence and respect of those who know him

JAMES TAYLOR — In the annals of Rock Island county's pioneers this gentleman deserves honorable mention Fifty-five years have passed since he located within its borders and the history of its development is very familiar to him for he has not only been an eye witness of its changes, but has also been an important factor in its progress and improvement His name is closely associated with its early history and his valuable counsel and the activities of his useful manhood have been of great moment in the material advancement of his county and state Taylor Ridge was named in his honor and through this means his memory will be perpetuated long after he has passed away

Mr Taylor was born in the historic town of Forrest, Scotland, November 6, 1814 His paternal grardfather, John Taylor, was a cooper by trade and spent his entire life in Scotland, where he reared a large family, and died at the age of eighty years He was a son of James Taylor, also a cooper by trade, who died in 1828, at the age of ninety-six. The father of our subject, John Taylor, Jr, learned the tailor's trade He married Jeannette Roy, also a native of Scotland and a daughter of John Roy, who followed the tailor s trade in that land, where he died at the age of seventy-eight In

to America, locating at Taylor Ridge, then called Pleasant Ridge, where he made his home until 1859, when he returned to the land of his nativity He died in Birmingham, England, about 1878, when more than eighty years of age His wife passed away several years previous They were both members of the Presbyterian church.

Of their family of ten children our subject was the oldest and is the only one now living His boyhood days were spent in the land of hills and heather, and in attendance at the common schools he acquired a practical English education He learned the tailor's trade during his youth and followed it as a means of livelihood until coming to Rock Island On crossing the Atlantic he located in Quebec, Canada, where he remained for a year and a half He then started for Illinois, making the trip from Lockland, Ohio, by team, and on the 4th of July, 1842, he arrived in Rock Island He found here a wild and unimproved region and took up his residence in Edgington township, where there were no white settlements for miles around Coyotes and wolves made the night hideous with their howlings and the Indians were his neighbors, but he had a firm faith in the development of the county, owing to its rich fertility and excellent natural advantages, and cheerfully bore his part in the work of improvement and progress His first home was three miles north of Taylor Ridge There he remained for a year, after which he took up his residence at Pleasant Ridge, and the name was changed in his honor He bought one hundred and sixty acres of land at a dollar and a half per acre, and from time to time added to this until his landed possessions aggregated two thousand acres He has . . . . en a quarter

JAMES TAYLOR.

section of land, or its equivalent in value Farming has been his life work, and with great energy and perseverance he prosecuted his labors until 1889, when he laid aside the cares of business life and is now living retired

Mr Taylor was married May 8, 1836, to Miss Elspet Malcolm, who was born in Scotland, January 19, 1816, and was a daughter of John and Ann (Harvey) Malcolm Two children were born of this union Ann and John The former is now the wife of John Frey, of Eldora, Iowa, and they have five children Clarence, Roy, James, Mary and Emma Mrs Elspet Taylor, who was a faithful member of the Presbyterian church, died in Lockland, Hamilton county, Ohio, September 23, 1839.

On the 20th of April, 1840, Mr Taylor was again married, the lady of his choice being Miss Rachel Ann Van Camp, who was born March 13, 1817, in Somerset county, New Jersey, and was a daughter of Tunis and Catherine (Smith) Van Camp The children born of this marriage were as follows (1) William Roy is deceased (2) James P. married Ellen Hatten, by whom he had three children—Charlie and Cora, twins, and Ella For his second wife he chose Jessie Douglas, of Canada, and the children born to them are Margaret, Helen and an infant (3) Catherine Ellen became the wife of Preston Ball and died in 1889, leaving a family of children (4) Louise married Hibbard Moore and both are now deceased Their children are Gilpin, Grace, Horace, Hibbard Stuart, Leonard and Louise (5) Samuel C , a resident of Edgington township, married Eliza Bruner and has five children—Harriet, James Bruce, Glen, Fay and Thadeus (6) John C married Henrietta Davis and has two children—

13

Hartley and Blanche They made their home in Malvern, Iowa (7) Jeannette E is the wife of Horace W Fowler, of Huron, South Dakota, and their children are Roy, Irma, Flora, Ruth and Horace (8) Flora M died at the age of twenty-two, and (9) Martha G died of scarlet fever when three years old Mrs Taylor, the mother of these children, was called to her final rest February 25, 1892, at the age of seventyfive years She held membership in the Presbyterian church, to which Mr Taylor also belongs

Politically he has always been a stanch Democrat, and has been called upon to serve in a number of responsible positions, the duties of which he most capably and faithfully discharged For six terms he served as supervisor and was chairman of the board four terms, being elected by a Republican board, which fact plainly indicates his fidelity to duty and the confidence and trust reposed in him In a Republican township, he was also elected assessor for seventeen years, was school director for many years, and served as postmaster at Taylor Ridge from 1845 until 1862, after the election of President Lincoln

An honored and prominent pioneer of the county, Mr. Taylor was elected president of the Old Settlers Association in 1877, and has ever taken an active interest in the organization In the early days he experienced all the hardships and privations of frontier life, and during a terrible storm in the month of June, 1844, fearing that his log cabin would be blown down, as the roof had already blown off, he opened the door and taking his little daughter Ann by the hand started out They were blown up the road three-quarters of a mile before they were able to stop and were considerably cut and bruised by the hail stones On their return they found the house flooded but the family quite safe. As a citizen Mr Taylor meets every requirement and manifests a commendable interest in everything that is calculated to promote the general welfare. In private life he is sympathetic and generous, extending a helping hand to the poor and needy and always ready to aid those less fortunate than himself.

RUFUS A. SMITH is a man of sterling worth and reliability, who in public and private life has ever commanded the respect and esteem of those with whom he has been brought in contact. He is now engaged in the real estate business in Moline, and is rated as one of her leading men. He comes from the far-off Pine Tree state, his birth having occurred in Farmington, Franklin county, August 24, 1836, a son of Benjamin M and Elizabeth (Allen) Smith. He resided on the farm where his birth occurred until fourteen years of age, and then accepted a clerkship in a store in Farmington, where he remained from 1852 until 1856. In the latter year he removed to Adams county, Illinois, where he was employed as a farm hand for six months. In October of the same year he went to Henry county, Illinois, where he engaged in farming through the summer months and in teaching in the winter season following that profession until 1861.

Mr Smith then purchased land in Henry county and made a home for his bride. He was married on the 15th of January of that year to Hattie F. Hanna, a daughter of John P and Nancy (Dockery) Hanna. They began th... ...

county, but after nine months sold that place, removing to Colona in April, 1862. Mr Smith there engaged in speculating in timber land and in carrying on a store until 1864, when he became agent for the Rock Island Railroad Company at that point, also for the Chicago, Burlington & Quincy Railroad, and at the same time was express agent. He was agent for the railroad companies from 1864 to 1887 and never lost a day in all that time. In 1864 he was appointed postmaster at Colona, and held that position continuously until 1883. As school treasurer he served for many years while a resident of Colona, and for four terms was elected supervisor.

In 1883 Mr Smith removed his family to Moline, although he still continued his business interests in Colona until 1887. Here he has since engaged in the real estate business and owns extensive tracts of land in Nebraska. He is a man of excellent business and executive ability and his able management and honorable dealing have secured to him a well merited success. His fellow townsmen of Moline have also called him to public office. For six years he served as supervisor and for three years was chairman of the county board. He has been a staunch Republican since casting his first Presidential vote for Abraham Lincoln in 1860, and has been a delegate to various party conventions.

Mr and Mrs Smith have a family of four children - Benjamin M, a prominent lawyer of Chicago, who is now assistant state's attorney, is married and has one child, Frances. Harry A, a railroad engineer, was born the day of Lincoln's death. Etta T and Hattie A are at home with their parents. The family is one of ... ...county, and their circle of friends is extensive, while their home is noted for its warm-hearted hospitality

CAPTAIN OTIS E McGINLEY, the genial and popular captain of the F C A Denkman, a steamer plying between Rock Island and Stillwater, Minnesota, has resided in the former city for the past sixteen years, his home being now at 528 Twentieth street He is a native of Illinois, born in Albany, October 17, 1857, and is a son of John and Charlotte (Aldrich) McGinley, natives of Ohio and Geneseo, Illinois, respectively The paternal grandfather was born in Pennsylvania, but at an early day emigrated to Ohio, where he reared his large family and died at a ripe old age Columbus Aldrich, the maternal grandfather, was a typical New Englander, born in Rhode Island, and was a farmer by occupation His death occurred when about eighty years of age.

When Illinois was still on the western frontier John McGinley, our subject's father, located in Albany, later he removed to Louisiana, Missouri, where he spent two years, and finally settled permanently in Clinton, Iowa, where he is still living Throughout his active life he was engaged in the sawmill business, but for the past six years has lived retired, enjoying the fruits of his former toil His estimable wife was called to her final rest in 1881 Both were Universalists in religious belief and highly respected by all who knew them For three years during the dark days of the Civil war the father aided in the defense of the Union, and was wounded in the service of his country The seven children in his family are as follows Mary, wife of Charles Mace, of Chicago Otis E Addison John

Kettie, wife of Willis Roberts, who lives near Pink Prairie, Illinois, Nettie, wife of Mr McHenry, of the same place and Claude

The first thirteen years of his life Captain McGinley spent near Geneseo, Illinois, and then accompanied his parents on their removal to Clinton, Iowa, where he grew to manhood, pursuing his studies in the schools of both places Early in life he began working in the sawmill with his father, but on attaining his majority commenced steamboating on the Mississippi, to which he has since devoted his energies, being captain of the F C A Denkman for the past five years

On the 22d of November, 1883, Captain McGinley led to the marriage altar Miss Jennie Conwell, a daughter of Hugh and Mary (Gartland) Conwell They now have two interesting children—Charlotte and Thomas Mrs McGinley is a member of the Catholic church, and a most estimable lady Politically the Captain has always been identified with the Democratic party, and socially affiliates with the Knights of Pythias and Modern Woodmen of America He is a pleasant, genial gentleman, of high social qualities, and is very popular, having a most extensive circle of friends and acquaintances who esteem him highly for his genuine worth

CHARLES K DEVORE is one of the more recent additions to the business circles of Moline, yet has already attained a prominent place there and his popularity is well deserved, as in him are embraced the characteristics of an unbending integrity, unabating energy and industry that never flags

Mr Devore was born in Woodford county, Illinois, near Eureka, April 15, 1859, and is a son of Jackson N and Hannah (Woods) Devore He was only four years of age when his parents removed to Bloomington, where his father followed the brick mason's trade Reared to manhood there he acquired a fair common-school education and at the age of sixteen began to learn the marble cutter s trade, serving a three-years apprenticeship During the first year he received fifty cents per day, the second one dollar per day, and the third one dollar and a half He afterward worked in Lincoln, Illinois, for three months, then worked at piece work in Springfield Missouri, making good wages in that way Subsequently he returned to his old home in Bloomington, afterward spent one summer in Kansas and thence went to Colorado, where he was employed on a ranch in the San Luis Valley He afterward went to Pueblo, thence to Bloomington, spent a few months in Clinton, Illinois, two months in Louisville, Kentucky, and a few months in Dayton, Ohio, followed by a residence of eight years in Ottawa, Illinois During all this time he worked at his trade gaining therein an efficiency that would be hard to excel. In 1892 he went to Henry, Illinois, where he engaged in business on his own account for four years, and in 1896 removed to Moline, where, in partnership with E O Fischer, he established the granite and marble works now run under the firm name of Devore & Fischer This firm commands a liberal share of the public patronage A thorough understanding of their business enables them to so direct their employes as to obtain the best results from their work and their marble and granite cutting is most artistic and finishe

ters of business has gained them the public confidence and goodwill and they well merit the success which is attending their efforts

Mr Devore was married in Ottawa, Illinois, March 11, 1891, the lady of his choice being Miss Rosa Funk, of that city Their union has been blessed with three interesting children—Rosa Myrtle, born in Ottawa, Paul, born in Henry; and Anna Marie, born in Moline

Mr Devore cast his first presidential vote for James A Garfield in 1880, but is independent in politics He is a member of the Odd Fellows Society, of Ottawa, the Knights of Pythias fraternity, of Moline, and in both organizations has filled all the chairs He is a man of sterling worth, true to all the duties of public and private life, a progressive and public-spirited citizen and a gentleman whom to know is to respect

---

JAMES JOHNSTON was for some time chief of the fire department of Rock Island, a very important position, the duties of which he discharged with marked fidelity and ability With the growth of the city, as business and population becomes more congested, the danger of fire in consequence increases, but under the careful supervision and constant watchfulness of an efficient chief a safety is assured which is not maintained in a smaller town with an illy-equipped fire department While Mr Johnston was chief of the department the city authorities reposed the utmost confidence in him—a confidence which he fully merited

He is one of Rock Island's native sons, his birth having occurred here on the 31st of October, 1849 His paternal grandfather Thomas Johnston was a native of

Ireland, and there followed the weaver's trade until his death, which occurred at an advanced age The parents of our subject were William A and Mary (Cain) Johnston, natives of Londerry, Ireland The former was a shoemaker by trade, and came to America when sixteen years of age, locating in Philadelphia, Pennsylvania He afterward removed to St Louis, where he married Miss Cain, daughter of James Cain, who died in Ireland, after which she came alone to America She lived for a time in Philadelphia and then removed to St Louis In the spring of 1849 Mr Johnston brought his family to Rock Island and here carried on shoemaking until within a short time of his death He died in 1893, at the age of seventy-three years He served as township supervisor at one time, and was a most loyal and faithful citizen He was one of the founders of the Presbyterian church and took a very active part in its work His wife also belongs to the same church She is still living, and resides at the old home on Ninth street They had a family of thirteen children, eight of whom are now living, namely James, Matilda, wife of R M Sweeney, of Wichita, Kansas, Mary Jane, wife of John Thompson, of Rock Island, Sarah, Kate, wife of O M Gunnell, of Paxton, Iowa, William, Emma and Robert

Reared in Rock Island James Johnston attended the public schools and after his graduation from high school pursued a course in bookkeeping in Bryant & Stratton's Business College, in Davenport He then spent one season on a farm, after which he began learning the tinner's trade in Rock Island, and for twenty-eight years followed that pursuit He was first with the firm of Don & Elliott, and after Mr Elliott withdrew two ⟨illegible⟩

Mr Don as foreman of the shop for twenty-five years He then worked in Moline for two years, after which he was appointed chief of the fire department His business record is without a blemish, his long continued service with one house well indicating his fidelity, his efficiency in his work and his honesty under all circumstances

For ten years Mr Johnston was chief of the old volunteer fire department, and for a few months was a member of the department on pay, following its organization in 1891 In April, 1895, he was appointed chief by the mayor of Rock Island, and confirmed by the city council and occupied that position until the present city administration came in power He had under his charge three hose stations, a hook and ladder company, a number of chemical fire extinguishers and thirteen men who were regularly employed and one extra hand

On the 6th of September, 1876, Mr Johnston was united in marriage to Miss Kate F Smith, a daughter of Michael Smith Her father was one of the pioneer settlers of Rock Island, and died February 26, 1897, at the age of seventy-four years His wife is still living at the age of seventy-three Ten children have been born to Mr and Mrs Johnston, eight sons and two daughters, but four of the sons are now deceased, namely George C Harry D Edwin and John T , three of the four dying within eight days The living children are Mary, Charles C , Grace, James T Joseph and Raymond

Mr. Johnston is a member of the Presbyterian church, and his wife is a communicant of the Roman Catholic church In his political views he is a stanch Republican and for twenty years has been a worthy ⟨illegible⟩ resents one of the old and honored families of the city and well deserves mention among the leading and faithful citizens of the community He is ever true and loyal to the trust reposed in him, and has so lived as to win and merit the confidence and regard of all with whom business or social relations have brought him in contact

---

JOSIAH G HECK is one of the prominent pioneers and leading and representative business men of Rock Island county, where he has made his home since the 15th of May, 1844 He now resides near Prospect Park and successfully carries on farming, dairying and the ice business In Harrison county, Ohio, he first opened his eyes to the light, May 18, 1840, a son of John and Sarah (Widle) Heck, natives of Pennsylvania, where their marriage was celebrated The paternal grandfather, Philip Heck, was of German descent, and belonged to a family that was early established in the United States

John Heck, father of our subject, was born September 10, 1786, and for several years after reaching manhood carried on agricultural pursuits in his native state, but in 1833 emigrated to Harrison county, Ohio, becoming one of its pioneer settlers After spending eleven years there, however, he started for Illinois, coming down the Ohio and up the Mississippi to Rock Island, where he arrived May 15, 1844 Fifty years later the family celebrated the anniversary of their arrival here, in which four generations participated The county at that time was one vast wilderness and swamp and deer and other wild game were found i

chased a tract of forty acres of wild land, to which he later added ten acres, and at once began the improvement and cultivation of his place, making it his home until his death August 6, 1878, at the advanced age of ninety-two years His estimable wife passed away in 1881 and lies buried by his side in Rock River View cemetery, where a substantial monument marks their last resting place

Josiah G Heck of this review, is the youngest in the family of thirteen children, the others being as follows Elizabeth became the wife of Josiah Gamble but both are now deceased Philip married a Miss Frick, whose people were early settlers of Rock Island county, and he later moved to Iowa, but subsequently returned to Moline where he lived retired for some years before his death His remains were interred at West Liberty, that state Mary Ann wedded James Bayles, a pioneer of Rock Island county, who followed the river, and both are now deceased Sarah married John Gamble, and both have passed away John died in Rock Island county, in 1849 William married, but he and his wife are both dead and are buried in Hartsell cemetery Rachel is the widow of John Willis and resides in Creston, Iowa Margaret became the wife of J F Shoffer, and at their deaths they were also buried in Hartsell cemetery George is married and lives in Rock Island J F is a resident of Moline Of this large family only the three youngest sons and one sister now survive

Our subject was but four years of age when brought by his parents to Rock Island county, where he grew to manhood amid the primitive scenes of frontier life He afforded good educational advantages and ... W ... college when the Civil war broke out On the 5th of October, 1864, he joined Company C, Sixty-sixth Illinois Volunteer Infantry for one year, or during the war, and was a private under command of Captain Thomas W Rush and Colonel Andrew K Campbell The regiment was assigned to the Second Brigade, Second Division, Sixteenth Army Corps, Army of the Tennessee, and participated in the following engagements Mt Zion, Missouri, Fort Henry, Tennessee, Fort Donelson, Shiloh, Corinth, Iuka, Mississippi, Tuscumbia, Alabama Danville, Hatchie's Run, Resaca, Rome, Dallas, Kenesaw Mountain, the Atlanta campaign, Jonesboro, Lovejoy Station, with Sherman on the memorable march to the sea, Savannah Congaree Creek, and many other battles and skirmishes of less importance Mr Heck was always found in the thickest of the fight and patiently endured all the hardships and privations of army life, but was taken ill and confined in the hospital at Evansville, Indiana, from January to April 1865 He was honorably discharged at Quincy on the 10th of June of that year, as the war was over and his services were no longer needed

Mr Heck then returned to his home and cared for his father and mother during their declining years He was married in Moline May 11, 1881, to Miss Dora E Cornwall, who was born in Fayette county, Iowa, and is a daughter of George W and Araminta (Crawford) Cornwall, natives of Canada, who resided for a number of years on Pelee Island, in Lake Erie In 1864 her parents came to Rock Island county, where she was reared and educated One daughter graces this union—Elzarik S After his marriage Mr Heck located on his present farm, and in connect

cessfully engaged in the ice and dairy business, which he has found quite profitable

Being a strong temperance man, Mr Heck's sympathies are with the Prohibition party, but he often votes independent of party ties, supporting the man whom he considers the best qualified to fill the office He has served as a delegate to numerous conventions, and takes quite an active and influential part in public affairs His fellow citizens, appreciating his worth and ability have often called him to public office, and it is needless to say his duties were always most promptly and faithfully discharged He has been justice of the peace seven years collector two years, overseer of highways, a member of the school board for several years, and has been township trustee for almost twelve years He belongs to the Home Forum Lodge of Stewartsville, and he and his wife are consistent members of the United Brethren church Their exemplary Christian lives and well tried integrity have gained for them the esteem and respect of a large circle of friends and acquaintances, and they certainly deserve honorable mention among the leading citizens and honored pioneers of Rock Island county

OSCAR HAKELIER, whose studio is at No 1722 Second avenue, is a photographer of wide experience and stands at the head of his profession in Rock Island His patrons include the best class of people in the city and his work is of the latest and most approved style His birth occurred in Paris, France, but when only three years old he was taken by his parents to Germany, where his father died when he was still a small child At the age of ten years he then traveled in Russia and Siberia with a Swedish gentleman by the name of Jacobson, who was an optician and later a photographer. With him our subject learned his profession.

On his return from Siberia, Mr. Hakelier went to Sweden, and later to Paris, where he remained until the outbreak of the Franco-Prussian war in 1871, when he came to America and spent the first three months in New York City. Later he worked at photography in Memphis, Louisville, St. Louis and other cities, but for the past nine years has conducted a gallery in Rock Island and from the public receives a liberal patronage.

Mr. Hakelier was married in June, 1875, to Miss Louisa Olson, by whom he has two sons—Rudolph and Alfred. The parents are both earnest members of the Broadway Presbyterian church, and socially Mr. Hakelier belongs to Trio Lodge, No. 57, F. & A. M., the Modern Woodmen of America and the Home Forum. In his political affiliations he is a Republican. In 1889 he erected his pleasant residence at 2416 Eighth avenue and there hospitality reigns supreme. His life illustrates what can be accomplished through industry, perseverance, good management and a determination to succeed, as he started out in life for himself with no capital or influential friends to aid him, and is a self educated as well as a self-made man.

D R. ISAIAH B. SOUDERS, a well-known and popular veterinary surgeon of Rock Island, whose office is at Laflin's livery stables, was born in Perry county, Pennsylvania, January 4, 1848, a son of Martin and Elizabeth (Sidel) Souders, also natives

Perry county. The paternal grandfather, Henry Souders, was born in Pennsylvania of German ancestry, was a farmer by occupation, and served as a soldier in the war of 1812. He died at the age of eighty-five in the faith of the German Reformed church, of which he had long been a member. Jacob Sidel, the maternal grandfather of the Doctor, was also born in Pennsylvania, of German descent, and throughout life engaged in farming, distilling and milling. He was always regarded as a model man, being quite religious.

Martin Souders, the Doctor's father, spent his entire life upon one farm in Perry county, of one hundred and sixty acres, which he cleared, cultivated and improved with good buildings, making it a most desirable home. He died upon that place in 1887, at the age of sixty-eight, and his wife passed away in 1889 at the same age. Both were earnest members of the Evangelical church and stood high in the community where they had so long made their home. The father was called upon to fill various township offices of honor and trust. In their family were five sons and one daughter, of whom four are yet living: David, Susan, wife of George Ensminger of Perry county, Pennsylvania, William A., and I. B.

The Doctor was reared on his father's farm near Bloomfield, Pennsylvania, and obtained his primary education in the district schools. Later he attended college at New Berlin, Pennsylvania, and after eight years spent upon the home farm began the study of medicine and horse anatomy in the Pennsylvania College at Philadelphia. In 1877 he began the practice of his chosen profession in Union county, Pennsylvania, where he remained seven years, and then went to Cedar county, Iowa, where he en-gaged in farming and also in practice until 1892 Since that time he has been a resident of Rock Island, and now enjoys a large and lucrative practice

On the 22nd of June, 1869, Dr Souders was united in marriage to Miss Sarah A Gebhart, a daughter of Leonard and Ellen (Rank) Gebhart, and to them have been born six children, five sons and one daughter, namely Charles, John, Wallace, Eddie, who died in his eighth year, Blanche and Ralph All are single and reside with their parents The Doctor and his wife are consistent members of the Methodist Protestant church, and are held in high regard by all who know them They also belong to the Home Forum, and in politics he is an ardent Republican He has met with a well deserved success in his profession, and is a mild-mannered, genial gentleman, having a kind word for everyone

WILLIAM B FONES, of the firm of Fones & Erickson, dealers in hard and soft coal and feed of all kinds, is one of the self-made men of Moline He started out in life for himself with no capital, save the enterprising and industrious nature which has been the keynote of his success By perseverance and good management he has worked his way steadily upward and in the fields of trade has garnered a good harvest

Mr Fones was born in Buffalo, New York, August 9, 1848, a son of William and Catherine Fones He remained in his native city until sixteen years of age, when with his parents he removed to Geneseo, Illinois, completing his education in the public schools there His father conducted a meat market fi

ended his business career His wife survived him several years and departed this life in Geneseo in 1874

When about seventeen years of age William B Fones began learning the painter's trade, serving a three-years apprenticeship He became an expert workman and was able to command good wages from the start He followed that trade until the spring of 1872, and then accepted a position as fireman on an engine on the Chicago, Rock Island & Pacific Railroad, but did not continue long in that position, his fidelity winning him constant promotion until at the end of four years he was given charge of the round house in Rock Island, and served in that capacity for four years In 1879 he turned his attention to farming in Scott county, Iowa, and for three years was identified with its agricultural interests, during which time he met with a high degree of success, although he had never had any experience as a farmer previous to that time In March, 1882, he came to Moline, and purchased a livery barn, which he conducted until 1895, when he sold out and began dealing in hard and soft coal and feed of all kinds The firm of Fones & Erickson enjoys a large and constantly increasing trade for their business methods have won them a high reputation for reliability and secured for them a liberal patronage

Mr Fones was married in Rock Island, February 23, 1876, to Miss Mollie E Buckey, who was born at Harpers Ferry Virginia, and is a daughter of John and Susan Buckey They have a large circle of friends in Moline, and their home is noted for its hospitality Mr Fones is independent in politics He voted for Cooper, Garfield and Bryan, and always supports the candidates office regardless of party affiliations He has served as city alderman from the second ward for eight years, was one of the originators of the fire department company and was chairman of the fire commission He takes a deep interest in all that pertains to the public welfare, is a progressive and substantial citizen, and withholds his support from no measure calculated for the public good

FRANK L HODGDON, whose home is at 3112 Ninth avenue, Rock Island, has for over a quarter of a century been one of the most trusted employes of the Chicago Rock Island & Pacific Railroad He was born March 27, 1849, in Barnstead, New Hampshire, of which state his parents, Charles and Marian (York) Hodgdon, were also natives The paternal ancestors of our subject came to this country from England at the time the tea was thrown overboard in Boston harbor and for many generations they have resided in New England There his grandfather engaged in farming and died at an old age He had four sons and three daughters The maternal grandfather, also of English descent, devoted his entire life to agricultural pursuits in New Hampshire

On the old homestead at Barnstead, New Hampshire, the father of our subject continued to live until called to his final rest in 1861, at the age of sixty-five years His estimable wife long survived him, dying in 1885, at the age of seventy-three They were earnest, consistent Christian people, and in early life the father took quite a prominent part in military affairs, serving as captain of a company of militia He also held various township offices of honor and trust

In tl

fourteen children, seven sons and seven daughters, of whom eight are still living—Samuel, George, Frank L , Betsy, wife of George Hobbs, of Pittsfield, New Hampshire. Mary, wife of John Dudley, of Concord, New Hampshire, Mattie Abby, widow of Moses Hobbs, of Davenport, Iowa, and Linda, wife of Adelbert Whittier of Barnstead

Frank L Hodgdon attended the schools of Barnstead during his boyhood, but at the age of thirteen years he left home and went to New York, where he began life for himself in a logging camp in the Adirondack mountains, remaining there one winter In 1870 he came west to Davenport, where he made his home for seven years, since which time he has resided in Rock Island In the fall of 1870 he entered the employ of the Chicago, Rock Island & Pacific Railroad as fireman, serving as such until July 15 1872, when he was promoted to engineer He ran a freight train until 1890, since which time he has had charge of a passenger engine

On the 27th of November, 1876, occurred the marriage of Mr Hodgdon and Miss Kate, daughter of Patrick Kehoe, and they have become the parents of six children, three sons and three daughters—Alda, Walter Lewis, Frank Lester and Charles Arthur, both deceased Maggie Loretta and Una Albina All are still at home with the exception of Alda, who married M C O Harra, now of Bloomfield Nebraska, and has one child, Charles Francis The family occupy a pleasant home at 3112 Ninth avenue, which was erected by Mr Hodgdon in 1880 His wife is a devout member of the Catholic church, and fraternally he belongs to the Brotherhood of Locomotive Engineers and the Ancient Order of United Workmen

given the

men and measures of the Democratic party
He is known as one of the most careful
engineers on the road and the fact that he
has for over a quarter of a century been connected with it, testifies to his ability and
faithfulness His social, genial nature has
made him an entertaining companion, and
he is a stanch and loyal friend, fond of good
fellowship and devoted to those who have
his confidence

J HENRY EFFLANDT was born in
Holstein, Germany, May 15, 1855, and
is a son of Christian and Katherine (Plain-
beck) Efflandt His father, who was a veterinary surgeon, died when our subject was
only seven years of age The latter remained at home until seventeen, during
which time he secured a fair common-school
education He then started for America in
1872, and soon after landing in New York
continued his journey across the country to
Moline, where lived his married sister, Mrs
Kathrina Schacht In this city he secured
employment and during the first two years
managed to save up a small capital He
had but twelve dollars and seventy cents on
his arrival In 1874 he commenced working in a meat market, working for others
until 1878, when he began operations on his
own account He conducted a shop at
Sixth avenue and Nineteenth street until
1883, and then removed to No 1618 Fifteenth street, where he carried on business
for ten years, after which he sold out and
purchased his present property at No 165
Fourth avenue He here owns a good store
building that it is fitted up with all the accessories for carrying on a first-class market,
and he enjoys there a good business His
trade has s

directed efforts have resulted in bringing to
him an excellent income

Mr Efflandt was married in Moline November 18, 1877, to Johanna Wind, who
was born in Schlesswig, Germany, a daughter of Lawrence and Tina (Jenson) Wind
They now have eight children—William
who was born in Moline May 20, 1878, is a
graduate of the Augustana Business College
of the class of 1897, Helen, born October
23, 1884, Clara born October 2, 1886,
Julius, born October 15, 1888, George, born
December 21, 1890, Otto, born December
20, 1892, Stella, born December 8, 1894,
and Herbert, born February 14, 1887, are
all at home

Mr Efflandt is independent in politics,
voting for the man whom he thinks best
fitted for the office He supported Garfield
in 1880, Cleveland in 1884, and Bryan in
1896 He is a prominent and popular member of the Turners Society, in which he
has served as trustee and treasurer

HERMAN F LAGE, the efficient and
well-known engineer of the Moline
water works is a native son of Germany
He was born in Holstein, January 9, 1853,
his parents being Henry and Helena (Brockman) Lage His father, who was born
February 21, 1828, is still living, but the
mother died many years ago, Our subject
was reared in a country town, where he attended school until sixteen years of age
after which he began learning the carpenter s trade under the direction of his father,
with whom he worked for four years He
then bade adieu to friends and native land
and sailed from Hamburg on a vessel which
eleven days later dropped anchor in the har-

Mr Lage soon afterward came to Moline and entered upon his business career here at carpenter work, but soon accepted a position as millwright in a paper factory, where he remained twelve years He severed that connection in order to become engineer at the Moline water works, where he has remained eleven years His faithful performance of every duty, his thorough understanding of his work and his promptness in its discharge has made him a most trusted employe of the city and won him the regard of all with whom he has come in contact

Mr Lage was happily married April 27, 1872, to Miss Johanna Rolfs, a native of Holstein, Germany, who had been one of his friends in youth and who crossed the Atlantic in the same vessel in which he made the voyage They were married soon after their arrival in Moline and their union has been blessed with five children—Augusta, born September 5, 1872, Minnie, who was born June 12, 1876, and is the wife of Frank Michael, of Davenport, by whom she has one child, Karl Henry, born March 20, 1878, Tina, born January 23, 1880. and Karl, born June 18, 1890

Mr Lage voted for Garfield in 1880, supported Cleveland in 1884, and Bryan in 1896 It will thus be seen that he is a man of independent views who exercises his right of franchise as he sees fit He is a member of Camp No 38 M W A , and his sterling worth and true manly qualities have won him the esteem of his brethren of the fraternity

In the spring of 1889 Mr Lage erected a large two-story building at 132 Fourth avenue, for business purposes and residence, and has placed therein a stock of dry goods and notions the store being conducted by his wife an

MARTIN SCHOONMAKER —Prominent among the energetic, far-seeing and successful business men of Rock Island county is the subject of this sketch, who is now an extensive grain dealer of Reynolds and president of the Reynolds Bank His life history most happily illustrates what may be attained by faithful and continued effort in carrying out an honest purpose Integrity, activity and energy having been the crowning points of his success and his connection with various business enterprises and industries have been a decided advantage to this section of the county, promoting its material welfare in no uncertain manner.

Mr Schoonmaker was born in Greene county, New York, October 21, 1835, a son of Christian and Sylvia (Maraquat) Schoonmaker, also natives of the Empire state The paternal grandfather was born in Germany, and on coming to the new world spent his remaining years in New York, where he reared a large family. Peter Maraquat, the maternal grandfather, was a native of Dutchess county, a farmer by occupation, and died at the advanced age of ninety-four years Throughout his active business life the father of our subject engaged in agricultural pursuits in New York, and held various local offices of honor and trust in his county, including that of supervisor. He died there in 1876, at the age of sixty-seven years, and his wife, who long survived him, passed away in 1894, at the age of seventy-eight Both were devout members of the Methodist church and were widely and favorably known In their family were four sons and one daughter, namely Martin, Mary, wife of Willis Finch, of Catskill, New York, George, of Cawker City Kansas Charles who died but his his service in the Civil war, and

Walter, who lives on the old homestead at Cairo, New York

On the old home farm in the Empire state, Martin Schoonmaker was reared in much the usual manner of farmer boys, pursuing his studies in the local schools and assisting in the labors of the fields In 1856 he came to Rock Island county, Illinois, and for several years worked as a farm hand by the month in Edgington township, where he later operated rented land for some time His first purchase consisted of eighty acres of partially improved land in the same township, which he afterward traded for another eighty-acre tract, and this in turn he sold, buying another farm of the same size Finally he purchased one hundred and four acres one mile east of Edgington For six years previous he had conducted a general store and implement business in Milan and Edgington and engaged in shipping stock in Edgington He later embarked in merchandising in Reynolds, and in 1880 he began buying and selling grain, being alone in that business until 1892, when he formed a partnership with Robert and Daniel Montgomery, and together they have since carried on operations They have a large elevator and buy nearly all the grain raised in this section of the county On the 18th of June, 1888, Mr Schoonmaker also opened a bank called the Reynolds Bank, which he still conducts, and is also agent for six fire and tornado insurance companies As a grain dealer, however, he does the largest business, handling from one hundred and forty to one hundred and forty-five thousand bushels of oats in a season, in addition to a large quantity of corn and other grain

Mr Schoonmaker was married in 1860 to Miss I ' ¹ ' ' '

Mary (Myers) Boltinghouse, but she died in July, 1871 In religious belief she was a Baptist On the 28th of February, 1876, he led to the marriage altar Miss Jennie C Smith, a daughter of James R and Martha Smith, and to them have been born two sons and three daughters - Elizabeth, Lura, Martin, Fay, Walter, who died at the age of nineteen months, and one who died in infancy The wife and mother is a most estimable lady and a faithful member of the Presbyterian church

Politically Mr. Schoonmaker has always been a Democrat until 1896, when he supported the Republican party For eight years he was an efficient member of the board of supervisors, during which time the new court house was erected and he assisted in selling the bonds Although a Democrat, he was appointed postmaster of Edgington, under President Grant, and for four years served in that office For twelve years he has been notary public, and is now a member of the board of village trustees in Reynolds His public as well as his private duties have ever been faithfully discharged, winning for him the commendation of the entire community Without the aid or influence of wealth he has risen to a position among the most prominent and successful men of the county, and his native genius and acquired ability are the stepping stones on which he has mounted

ANDREW ETZEL, a worthy representative of one of the honored pioneer families of Rock Island, was for some years on the police force, and from 1895 to 1897 served as marshal and chief of police He is a man who has ever been found in the ' ' ' ' ' ' devoted to their country's best interests and to the welfare of their fellowmen, in private life and in official positions always laboring for others with an unselfish devotion that well entitles him to the respect which is so freely given him and to a place among the honored and valued residents of Rock Island

Mr Etzel was born in the city where he still continues to reside, on the 22nd of May, 1850, and is a son of George and Margaret (Striffler) Etzel, natives of Bavaria, Germany, who came to America in 1847, first stopping in St Louis, but the following year located in Rock Island, where the father first worked as a blacksmith and later as a teamster He died in 1886 at the age of sixty-seven years, and his wife passed away November 11, 1894, at the age of seventy-four For six years he served as a soldier in the regular army of his native land, and was a consistent member of the Lutheran church, to which his wife also belonged They had a family of seven children, four still living—George L, Andrew, Peter and Charles The grandparents of our subject spent their entire lives in the fatherland, where the maternal grandfather worked as a blacksmith

During his boyhood Andrew Etzel attended the public schools of Rock Island, and at the early age of twelve years commenced working in a sawmill, following that business continuously until he had attained the age of twenty-three He next worked as ship calker and carpenter in the shipyard, and in 1880 was first appointed to a position on the police force, where he most acceptably served for five years For a short time he was then employed as fireman at the water works, later was assistant health inspector, and subsequently engaged in teaming

served as guard at the government arsenal, and when that post was disbanded returned to the police force, with which he was connected until the spring of 1897, most efficiently serving as chief of police for the last two years He was a terror to all evildoers, and the law-abiding citizens had the utmost confidence in his ability to preserve order

On the 4th of February, 1874, was performed a wedding ceremony which united the destinies of Mr Etzel and Miss Rose Imhoff, a daughter of Nicholas and Martha (Blau Imhoff, and ten children bless their union, five sons and five daughters, namely Emma Josephine, Elnora, Lavine, Lucy, George, Robert, Arthur, William and Clarence All are still with their parents except Emma, who died at the age of seven years Socially, Mr Etzel affiliates with the Modern Woodmen of America, and politically is identified with the Republican party

ANDREW DONALDSON —The subject of this sketch stands second to none among the prosperous and substantial farmers of Rural township, whose record it has been deemed wise to preserve in this manner for the perusal of coming generations As a judicious tiller of the soil he has met with excellent success, and as a man and citizen he holds a good position among his neighbors His life has been one of unabated industry, and his fine farm on section 14 is one of the most attractive and desirable places in Rural township

A native of Washington county, Pennsylvania, Mr Donaldson was born near Midway, March 2, 1831, and his parents, Richard and Catharine (Ritchie) Donaldson, ... -tate Of their seven children, five are still living, namely Ann Eliza, James Andrew, Richard and Catharine H The father, a successful farmer, died in Washington county, Pennsylvania, in 1879 when past the age of eighty years, and the mother of our subject was called to her final rest in 1845, when about fifty-three years of age Both were earnest and consistent members of the Presbyterian church, in which the father served as elder for over half a century

James Donaldson, the paternal grandfather of our subject, was born in Chester county, Pennsylvania, of Scotch-Irish ancestry, was a farmer by occupation, and died in that state when well advanced in years, leaving a large family of children, among whom was Richard, John, Andrew and Thomas, the latter serving as a soldier in the war of 1812 The maternal grandfather, Andrew Ritchie, was also a native of Pennsylvania and of Scotch-Irish descent Agricultural pursuits claimed his attention, and he died at the age of eighty and was laid to rest at Cross Creek, Pennsylvania Four or five of his brothers aided in the defense of their country during the war of the Revolution Richard Donaldson, a brother of James, was also a soldier in the Revolutionary war

In the district schools of his native county, Andrew Donaldson conned his lessons, the building being of the most primitive character, made of logs and supplied with slab seats Until he had reached manhood he remained upon his father's farm, but in 1851 his brother James came to Rock Island county, Illinois, and selected a couple of farms in Rural township, which the father purchased They comprised nine hundred and sixty acres, which was divided equally between J

still owns his portion together with a tract of thirty acres of timber land, making in all five hundred and ten acres of valuable land By persistent and well directed labors he has placed it under a high state of cultivation, has made many excellent improvements, including an elegant residence, barns and granaries to match, and has successfully engaged in both farming and stock raising

On the 4th of July 1865, was solemnized the marriage of Mr Donaldson and Miss Ellen M, daughter of John Titterington, and to them have been born two sons and six daughters Mary E, Clara B, Annie E, Richard, Susan, Andrew, Maudie P, who died in 1890 aged seven years, and Catharine H Those living are all at home with the exception of Mary E, who is now the wife of R W Battersby, of Whatcome, Washington, and has one son, Donald R

In his political affiliations, Mr Donaldson is a Democrat, and socially is identified with Coal Valley Lodge, No 547 F & A M He has served as supervisor and assessor for a number of years, and for the long period of thirty years has been a member of the school board He has seen almost the complete development of this region, having made his home here since 1853, almost all the land being then in its primitive condition and only worth two dollars per acre Industrious, progressive and public-spirited, he has been an important factor in bringing about the wonderful transformation that has since taken place aiding in converting the wild land into valuable and productive farms As a strong Democrat, he believes that the free coinage of silver would materially benefit this country, and is opposed to the principles of protection as advocated by the politicians He is well informed on the current events of the day, votes intelligently on all questions, and as a genial, hospitable gentleman well deserves the high regard in which he is uniformly held His estimable wife is a member of the Presbyterian church

SAMUEL HEAGY, deceased, was for many years one of the leading and influential citizens of Rock Island county His life was well spent, and in business circles he commanded the confidence and respect of all who knew him Born in Taneytown, Maryland, on the 20th of April, 1838, he was reared to manhood there His father died before his birth, and his mother when he was six years of age, so that he was thus early thrown upon the mercies of the world. He was taken into the home of a man who was not a relative and lived with him until the age of sixteen years, when he went to Baltimore, securing a clerkship in a wholesale notion house, where he was employed until 1857 In that year he came to Illinois, taking up his residence in Hampton For a number of years he was employed as a clerk in the store of Mr Black About that time he met and married Miss Henrietta Birchard, whose home was in Scott county, Iowa, just across the river She was born there, a daughter of Jabez Avery and Lydia (Chamberlain) Birchard Her father was born in Massachusetts, and with his parents removed to Pennsylvania, where he became acquainted with Miss Chamberlain, who was born in Vermont, August 7, 1804, and during her girlhood went to Silver Lake, Susquehanna county, Pennsylvania After their marriage Mr and Mrs Birchard removed to Scott county, Iowa, in 1836, and were [illegible]

of that locality, taking an active part in its development and progress Mr Birchard became the owner of one of the finest farms in Scott county, and was one of the wealthy agriculturists of that community, being a very enterprising, progressive and successful business man He died October 21, 1871, and his wife passed away July 17, 1881 They were people of the highest respectability, held in the highest regard by all who knew them, and their friends were many

After an acquaintance of about five years, Mr Heagy and Miss Birchard were married at her home in Scott county, April 20, 1863, the ceremony being performed by Rev H A Batherst They began their domestic life in Hampton in the home in which Mrs. Heagy is still living. One son was born of this union—Morris S , who was born March 7, 1866 He is a graduate of Port Byron Academy, and on the 1st of January, 1890, married Miss Theo Black He is now living in Rock Island, where he holds a responsible clerical position in the office of the government engineer

Samuel Heagy began business for himself in 1864, in Hampton, as a dealer in dry goods and groceries, and in 1868, after engaging in the coal business, admitted A R Stoddard to a partnership Prosperity attended the enterprise from the beginning and their patronage steadily increased until the volume of their business had assumed extensive proportions In 1871 they embarked in a new field of endeavor by opening the first coal mine north of Rock Island at a little village known as Happy Hollow This town sprang up around the mines, which were profitably worked for a number of years, but after a time the supply of coal [illegible] that the mine ceased to be

SAMUEL HEAGY.

profitable, and when the company were obliged to cut wages the miners went out on a strike With these disadvantages to contend against, the business was finally suspended before Mr Heagy's death He was a man of excellent business sagacity, progressive and enterprising, and his well-directed efforts brought to him a richly-merited success He was systematic and methodical and had the strictest regard for the ethics of business life

Mr Heagy always gave his political support to the Democracy, was frequently called upon to serve as delegate to the party conventions, filled the office of village trustee, and was school treasurer of his township for more than twenty years He belonged to the Masonic fraternity, and was a charter member of the Ancient Order of United Workmen and the Modern Woodmen of America He died January 28, 1896, and was laid to rest in Oakdale cemetery of Davenport. His life demonstrated most fully the truth of the saying that there is no royal road to success, but that enterprise, industry and perseverance can overcome all obstacles and ultimately attain the goal of prosperity His career was such as to command uniform respect, and his death was a loss to the entire community His wife still survives him and is now living in Hampton, where she has a large circle of friends

J N HARDY, secretary of the Moline Art Association, is a recognized leader in art circles in this city He was born in Attica, New York, February 13, 1847, and is a son of Joseph and Anna J (Norton) Hardy His father was born in Birmingham, England, about 1819, and engaged in the manuf(...

14

manhood he emigrated to New York, and was married in Attica, to Miss Norton, who was born in Dublin, Ireland, of English parentage, but was reared in the Empire state The father followed the printer's trade in Buffalo, New York, until our subject was a year and a half old, when he removed with his family to Dodge county, Wisconsin, locating on a farm

J N Hardy attended the district schools there until seventeen years of age, when he was sent to Waterloo Academy, where he pursued his studies for one year, after which he spent two years in Wayland University, of Beaver Dam In order to earn the money with which to meet the expenses of this course he engaged in teaching When twenty-two years of age he went to New York to attend the American Phrenological Institute, by which he was granted a diploma the following year In West Virginia he engaged in teaching near Parkersburg for a time and also delivered lectures on phrenology until 1873, when he came to Rock Island, where he followed both teaching and lecturing until 1877. Possessing superior mechanical genius he then began the manufacture of fencing and archery goods which he continued until 1880 For a time he did a large business, selling twenty-two thousand dollars worth of goods, but the demand finally fell off and as a result he abandoned that trade

For the past seventeen years Mr Hardy devoted his time and attention to the fine arts From his boyhood his love for the beautiful has been one of his most marked characteristics and he early evinced artistic talents, which, however, remained undeveloped until he went to New York City Since 1882 he has spent a considerable portion of each year in Chicago in study He opened a studio in Rock Island, which he conducted until 1891, when he removed to Moline. The following year he conceived the idea of forming a stock company for the promotion of art interests and for the purpose of building an art institute, in which exhibitions might be made and lectures and instruction given   This work was carried forward to successful completion, and Mr Hardy has been secretary of the association from the beginning   It is the leading art center of Moline and has been an important factor in promoting a cultured taste among the citizens.   Mr Hardy spent a considerable time in the study of the works of art at the World's Fair   He possesses much taste and talent in this direction and has produced many creditable works   His mechanical genius is also very evident and is now being put to the practical test in the manufacture of violins

In 1868 Mr Hardy cast his first presidential vote for Grant and has since been an ardent advocate of Republican principles He belongs to the Universalist church, to Trio Lodge, No 57, F & A M , and also to the Independent Order of Odd Fellows He moves in the highest circles of society and is a gentleman of broad culture and scholarly attainments, who commands the respect of all with whom he comes in contact

FOSTER ARMSTRONG — There are men in every community whose lives though quiet and unpretentious exert a beneficial influence that is strongly felt.   Their strength of character is such as to leave its impress upon those with whom they come in contact   Of this class Mr Armstrong is a represen ative   He has spent his entire

life in Bowling township, Rock Island county, and his stanchest friends are among those who have known him from boyhood This fact plainly indicates an honorable career, and there is no one in the county who more justly merits the respect of young and old, rich and poor, than this gentleman

Born in Bowling township, February 24, 1853, Mr Armstrong is a son of Christopher and Mary Ann (Foster) Armstrong, who were natives of County Fermanagh, Ireland   The family originated in Scotland, but the grandfather, Maxwell Armstrong, died in Ireland, where for many years he had followed farming   The maternal grandfather was also an agriculturist of the Emerald Isle and there spent his entire life. It was in the year 1850 that Christopher Armstrong crossed the Atlantic to America and located in Bowling township, Rock Island county   He first purchased one hundred and twenty acres of land, to which he added from time to time until his possessions aggregated five hundred and sixty acres This he improved and finally divided among his children   He died in September, 1889, at the age of seventy-six years, but his wife survived him until March, 1897, passing away at the age of eighty-two   Both were members of the Methodist church, and politically he was numbered among the supporters of Republican principles.

Mr and Mrs Christopher Armstrong were the parents of nine children, namely Thomas, Robert, deceased, Archibald, Margaret, wife of George Allelly, of Montezuma, Iowa, Christopher, Jane, wife of Francis W Johnston, of Omaha, Nebraska, William John, Foster, and Elizabeth, wife of Christopher Frederickson

Identified with the business and public interests of Rock Island county throughout his entire life, it is but just that Mr Armstrong be accorded representation in this volume In his youth he went to the district school each morning through the winter season, and there conned his lessons until he had mastered the branches of a practical English education In the summer months he assisted in the labor and cultivation of the home farm, remaining under the parental roof until twenty-two years of age, when his father gave him eighty acres of land and he started out in life for himself. Industry and enterprise have characterized his entire business career and success has attended his well directed efforts As his financial resources have increased he has added to his farm until he now owns four hundred and forty acres of as fine land as can be found in the county In connection with general farming he raises horses, cattle, hogs and sheep, and in the management of his business interests he has not only gained a comfortable competence but has also won the respect of all with which he has been brought in contact by his honorable business methods

On the 7th of December, 1876, Mr Armstrong was united in marriage to Miss Mary L Sweeney, a daughter of Moses T Sweeney Her mother died when she was very young, and she was reared by David Little, by whose name she was known. Mr and Mrs Armstrong became the parents of six sons and four daughters, as follows Robert Morton, Christopher Lawrence, Thomas Parks, Mary Foster, Margaret Elizabeth, Sarah Lucinda, James Harbison Seyler, Frances, and David Little and William, who are both deceased Mrs Armstrong has carefully reared her family, and has been to her husband a faithful companion and helpmeet during the twen-

years of their married life They both hold membership in the Methodist church, and he is now serving as a member of the board of trustees

Mr Armstrong also belongs to the Orangemen, and to the Masonic fraternity In politics he is a Republican, and for thirteen years has efficiently served as school director, greatly advancing the cause of education He served as collector for two terms and also as supervisor for two terms While in the latter office he was a member of the bond committee, and aided in negotiating a loan of one hundred and twenty-five thousand dollars He was chairman of the finance committee, served on other important committees and was a member of the board during almost the entire time of the building of the court house He is a man of substantial character, quiet and unpretentious, but a loyal, progressive citizen who co-operates in all that is calculated to promote the interests of township, county or state His private life and his public career are alike commendable and above reproach

ANDREW E EHMER is one of the prominent young men of Rock Island, a leader in church and musical circles The business interests of the city are also well represented by him, and whether in public or private life, he is always a courteous, genial gentleman, well deserving the high regard in which he is held He is now one of the leading dealers in marble and granite monuments, statuary, etc , in the city, his place of business being at 225 Eighteenth street

Mr Ehmer began his earthly career

a son of Andrew and Maria (Biers) Ehmer, also natives of Germany, in whose family were nine children Those still living are Frank, Barbara, wife of John Jones, of Wurtemburg, Anna, wife of John Meenan, of Camden, New Jersey, Joseph, of Chicago, Pauline, and Andrew E , of this review The father, who was a dealer in shoes, died in his native land in 1882, at the age of sixty-nine years, having survived his wife for many years, her death occurring in 1871 He served as a soldier in the German army The paternal grandfather was a shoe maker and dealer in Germany, where he died at the age of sixty-eight, leaving five children The maternal grandfather conducted a hotel and also run a stage line in the fatherland

Our subject was provided with excellent school privileges, having attended a high school and college in Germany In 1886, at the age of sixteen years, he sailed for America, and on reaching the shores of this country located at Lanark, Illinois, where he learned the trade of marble cutting, at which he worked as a journeyman there and elsewhere, for five years After two years spent in Lanark, he went to Milwaukee, Wisconsin, where he worked for one season in a wholesale granite and marble house He was then for a number of months in the employ of Reible & Son at Maysville, Wisconsin, after which he returned to Lanark, but one year later went to Fulton, Whiteside county, Illinois, where he worked for E L Passmore for a year At the end of that period he came to Rock Island and opened a shop of his own in partnership with W H Caldwell, who sold his interest a year later to Joseph W Ehmer, a brother of our s '   "
ducted fo   of

Ehmer & Ehmer, but since that time Andrew E Ehmer has been alone

In 1895 he purchased his present place of business, No 225 Eighteenth street, remodeled the building and fitted it up expressly for the display of his stock of marble, finished and in the rough, and also for a workshop in the rear. It is well lighted and well suited to his business, the location being at the same time a good one

He does all kinds of marble and granite work, and by fair and honorable dealing, as well as good workmanship, has built up an excellent trade which is constantly increasing

In his political affiliations, Mr Ehmer is a Republican, and in his social relations is a member of Rock Island Lodge, No 18, I O O F , the Knights of the Globe and the Home Forum He is an active and prominent member of the Methodist Episcopal church, is a member of the choir, and has been a teacher in the Sunday school for a number of years He is also a member of the official board of the church and of the board of directors of the Young Men's Christian Association His life is exemplary in all respects, and he has ever supported those interests which are calculated to uplift and benefit humanity, while his own high moral worth is deserving of the highest commendation

JOHN PRICE ODELL, a retired mechanic, living in Hampton Village, was born in Belmont county, Ohio, October 27, 1824, and is a son of Stephen and Eleanor (Price) Odell His father was a native of Connecticut and was of English descent He and the was born in Maryland, and their marriage was celebrated in Ohio, whither they had removed with their parents in childhood

Our subject was reared to manhood in the Buckeye state, obtained a fair education in the common schools and learned the brick layer's trade with his father He resided in Ohio until 1858, at which time he came to Rock Island county and turned his attention to farming Shortly afterward he purchased a small farm in Canoe Creek township, and followed his trade in connection with the cultivation of his land After a few years, however, he removed to Hampton and later took up his residence in Henry county, Illinois, but when he had been there about a year his house was destroyed in a cyclone, and he returned to Hampton A few years later he again went to Henry county and on returning to Rock Island county took up his residence in Watertown, whence he removed to Scott county, Iowa, where he purchased land and carried on farming until his removal to Cloud county, Kansas A year was there passed, and he then established a home in Port Byron, Illinois, where he followed his trade for twelve years He afterward spent a few years in Moline and then took up his residence in Hampton Village, where he is now living a retired life, having acquired a competence that enables him to put aside business cares

Mr Odell was married in Ohio, December 10, 1846, to Miss Sarah Nelson, a native of West Virginia, who had lived in Guernsey, Ohio, from the time she was six months old Nine children have been born of this union Mary E., who was born in Ohio, is the wife of Manuel Smith, of Hampton, and has five children, Thomas W , who was born in Ohio, and now resides in Washington, is married and has five children, Robert Nelson, born in Illinois and now living in

Stewartsville, has five children, Stephen F is at home, Cornelia Jane is the wife of Daniel Fullmer, of Scott county, Iowa, and has two children, Samuel W is a prominent lawyer, John Price, who graduated at the Port Byron Academy and also in the Northwestern University of Evanston, Illinois, is now teaching in the high school of Moline, Illinois

On the 10th of December, 1896, Mr. and Mrs Odell celebrated their fiftieth wedding anniversary, on which occasion four children, ten grandchildren and one great-grandchild were present They now have nineteen grandchildren and two great-grandchildren This worthy couple, who are people of the highest respectability, and have the warm regard of all with whom they come in contact, have long been members of the Methodist Episcopal church, and in his political affiliations Mr Odell is a Republican

E L MARSTON, M D , a leading physician and surgeon of Buffalo Prairie, was born in West Gardiner, Kennebec county, Maine, on the 13th of April, 1860 More than two centuries before the Marston family had been planted on American soil by Robert Marston, a native of England, who crossed the briny deep in 1634 and took up his residence with the Salem colony in Massachusetts The family has been represented by patriots in the colonial and Revolutionary wars and the grandfather of our subject, Captain David Marston, was a soldier in the war of 1812 and captain of a militia company The Doctor's father, G A Marston, was born and reared in Maine and in early life followed the profession of teaching, but afterward turned his

attention to farming He married Catherine Burr, a native of Litchfield, Maine, and
in 1869 removed to Illinois, locating in
Rock Island county, where he purchased land
and spent his remaining years as a successful
farmer He held several local positions of
honor and trust, including those of supervisor and justice of the peace, and discharged
his duties with marked fidelity His death
occurred in July, 1883 His first wife died
in Maine in 1862, and he afterward married
again, his second wife still surviving him

The Doctor is the youngest of a family
of six children, five of whom grew to mature
years, while four are still living and are now
heads of families These are Freeman B ,
a farmer of Mercer county, Mary E , wife
of R B Platte, of Buffalo Prairie, Herbert,
an agriculturist of Mercer county, and the
Doctor One brother, Carroll B , died in
California, at the age of twenty-seven years

Dr Marston was reared and educated in
Rock Island county, and for about five
years successfully engaged in teaching in
the public schools of his locality Determining to make the practice of medicine his life
work he studied under the direction of Dr
Stewart, of the village of Reynolds, and pursued his first course of lectures in 1886, at
the Rush Medical College The following
year he re-entered the same college and was
graduated with the class of 1888. He also
took special work and had the privileges of
the hospitals, so that he was particularly
well fitted for his chosen vocation

Locating in Marston, Mercer county, he
practiced there for three years, and also engaged in merchandising and served as postmaster of the village In 1890 he came to
Buffalo Prairie, where he has now been engaged in active practice for seven years He
receives a   patronage from the town

and surrounding country, many of his patrons living in the northern part of Mercer
county He has a broad and comprehensive knowledge of the science of medicine
and in his practice has given evidence of a
skill and ability that has brought to him an
excellent business which is constantly increasing He is a close student of medical
journals and thus keeps fully abreast with
the times in the advancement that is continually being made in his calling

The Doctor was married in Buffalo
Prairie township, April 24, 1884, to Miss
Adaline Volkel, a native of the county, and
a daughter of George and Mary Volkel
Her father was a soldier of the Union army
and died in the service. The Doctor and
his wife have five children Carroll G ,
Elmo V , Catherine M , Frances E and
Alice M , and the family circle yet remains
unbroken by the hand of death

Dr Marston is a Master Mason of Illinois
City Lodge, No 679, A F & A M , and in
his political views is a stanch Democrat, his
last vote having been cast for W. J Bryan
and the free silver platform in 1896 In
manner he is pleasant, genial and kindly
and his presence in the sick room is a source
of encouragement He ranks high with the
profession as well as the public and is
rapidly winning a foremost place in the
ranks of Rock Island county's leading medical practitioners

ANDREW P BRANDT, proprietor of
one of the leading photograph galleries
in Moline, was born near Ramfall, Ostergotland, Sweden, on the 20th of April,
1857, and is a son of Johan and Stina Car-
rin (Alstedt) Brandt His father was a
soldier in the Swedish army for thirty-two

years, and was stationed at his own home village except when called out by the government for active duty In 1862 he was retired upon a pension, and engaged in hunting, fishing and fruit growing, having a large orchard of his own

Our subject during his boyhood assisted his father in those pursuits and attended the public schools until fourteen years of age He remained at home until nineteen years of age, when he went to Stockholm, where he was employed as an iron molder for three years He was reared amid one of the picturesque regions of his native land, famed for its beautiful lakes, mountains and valleys At the age of twenty-two, however, he bade adieu to home and friends and sailed for America, May 2, 1879, landing at New York May 18th, after a voyage of six days, from Liverpool For two years he resided in Clarinda, Iowa, devoting his attention to agricultural pursuits He afterward worked at the iron molder's trade in Clarinda and attended school for three months in order to master the English language He next went to New York, where he spent one year at work in an iron foundry

Mr Brandt had a two-fold purpose in going to the eastern metropolis While crossing the Atlantic he had become acquainted with Miss Mary White, an English lady, who was born in Corfew, Greece, August 15, 1860 Her father was Sergeant John White, a paymaster in the English service, who married Esther Nolan, who was of Irish lineage He was killed at Hong Kong, China, by the caving in of an embankment, when Mrs Brandt was about ten years of age Mrs White with her daughter Mary then returned from China to her people in Rathdowney, Ireland, where

she died two years later The daughter then continued to make her home with an aunt until eighteen years of age, when she sailed for the new world on the vessel City of Berlin, on which Mr Brandt had taken passage He noticed her among the other girls on deck, and though neither could speak the other's language but very little, they became acquainted and exchanged addresses Miss White remained in New York, while Mr Brandt continued on his way to the west, but they maintained a correspondence until his return to New York, where their marriage was celebrated September 11, 1882. They have three children Emil Carl, born September 2, 1883, Esther Mary, born October 29, 1884, and Elroy, born December 20, 1896 All are natives of Moline

Mr and Mrs Brandt remained in New York until April 18, 1883, and then came to Moline, where he secured employment in the Deere & Company plow works, as machine woodworker, where he remained thirteen years During his leisure hours he began the study of photography He is a true artist by nature, and it had long been his desire to master the art of making photographs In April, 1895, he opened a studio and now has one of the well appointed establishments in the city, supplied with the latest improved appliances He follows the most modern methods and his work is always artistic and pleasing, so that he is enabled to command a liberal share of the public patronage

Mr Brandt was reared in the Lutheran church and his wife in the Catholic church, but both are now members of Christian Science, by which Mrs Brandt was healed He belongs to the Knights of Maccabees, and Camp No 38, Modern Woodmen of

America, in which he has filled a number of offices. Mrs. Brandt is a member of "The Ladies of Maccabees," Hive No 119, Moline.

JAMES B TITTERINGTON —Among the agriculturists of Rock Island county who have attained success from a financial point of view, is the gentleman whose name heads this sketch. He is one of the largest land-owners and most progressive and energetic farmers and stock-holders in this section of the county, and is a complete master of the calling which he is following. His sterling integrity and honorable, upright manhood fully entitle him to the position which he holds in the estimation of the people of the community.

On the old homestead on section 12, Buffalo Prairie township, where he still continues to reside, Mr Titterington was born May 30, 1843, and is a worthy representative of one of the most honored pioneer families of the county. His father, James Titterington, was born in 1809, in Yorkshire, England, and when a lad of about twelve years came to the new world with his father, Thomas Titterington, who first located in Ross county, Ohio, where he resided for a few years. In 1838 he came to Rock Island county, Illinois, where he made his home with his children until his death. Four of his sons, John, James, Moses and Charles, had located here, where they reared families of their own, but only the last named is now living at the ripe old age of eighty-six years.

In his native land James Titterington, Sr, began his education and while a resident of Ross county, Ohio, continued his studies for a time. There he married Lena Beall, a native of that county, of which her father, William L

coming to this state Mr Titterington entered one hundred and sixty acres of land, where our subject now resides, and at once commenced to clearing and improve his place, making his home in a little log cabin he erected thereon. Later he bought more land until his farm contained two hundred acres, which he improved with good and substantial buildings, including a comfortable frame residence. He became one of the most prosperous and well-to-do farmers of his community, as well as one of its most highly respected citizens. He died upon the old homestead in 1876, and his wife, who long survived him, passed away in 1893, and now sleeps by his side in the Edgington cemetery, where a neat and substantial monument has been erected to their memory.

In the family of this worthy couple were three sons and three daughters, namely Mrs David Bopes, who died in Mercer county, Illinois, Jane, now the wife of R S Montgomery, of Rock Island, Mary E, who died at the age of fourteen years, William T, a resident of Rock Island county, James B, of this sketch, and Thomas, who died in childhood.

James B Titterington was reared in much the usual manner of farmer boys, early becoming familiar with the labors of the farm, and conning his lessons in the district schools of the neighborhood. After the death of his parents he purchased the interests of the other heirs in the old homestead, to which he has added until he now has three hundred and sixty acres of as fine land as can be found anywhere in the county. Being a thorough and systematic agriculturist, he has met with excellent success in the management of his farm, and is also

JAMES B. TITTERINGTON.

dealer in cattle and hogs, being one of the most successful stockmen of the county

Politically, Mr Titterington is a life-long Republican, and has supported every presidential nominee of his party since casting his first vote for "Honest Old Abe" in 1864 He has served as a delegate to many county and district conventions, and is a recognized leader in local politics For three years he filled the office of highway commissioner and was a member of the county board of supervisors for two terms As a neighbor, friend and citizen he is held in the highest regard

---

HENRY CLARK —Go into any village, town or city in this great Northwest of ours, seek out the men who are leaders in spirit, thought and action, learn the history of their lives, and you will find there is usually a striking similarity which leads to the inevitable conclusion that like conditions produce like results The story usually begins, "Born in New England, parents in rather limited circumstances, self-made, etc " Now this fact, for fact it is, illustrates most aptly one of the salient features of our American civilization There is an opportunity offered here under our emblem of liberty for every human being to work out and develop the best there is in him

To this honored class belongs Mr Clark, who is agent for the Steam Packet Acme Line, and a leading resident of Hampton, Illinois He was born May 11, 1828, in New Boston, New Hampshire, a son of Henry and Nancy (Clark) Clark, and was reared on the old home farm He supplemented his common-school education by a thorough academic course, and is a well read and cultured gentleman At the age of twenty

he went to Medford, Massachusetts, where he served a three-years' apprenticeship to the carpenter's trade, receiving the wages of sixteen dollars per month and board, and later worked as a journeyman for some time

In 1852 Mr Clark removed to Chelsea, the same state, where he was married on the 20th of October of that year to Miss Julia Melvina Taylor, a native of Medford whose father was a large ship builder and owner He had removed from Medford to Chelsea to enlarge his facilities for ship building, and our subject was in his employ from 1852 until 1862, with the exception of a short time spent in the Boston Navy Yard at Charlestown, where he helped to build the Merrimac

On the 8th of August, 1862, Mr Clark enlisted for three years in Company C, Thirty-fifth Massachusetts Volunteer Infantry, and within nine weeks had taken part in two important battles South Mountain, September 14, and Antietam, September 17 During the latter engagement he was wounded in both legs, and still carries a bullet in his right limb above the knee The same ball had broken the bone just above the ankle in the right leg He was in the front rank, kneeling while firing, and had just turned to reload when struck After being sent home, he was furloughed from time to time, until February, 1863, when he was honorably discharged on account of his wounds

As soon as he had sufficiently recovered, Mr Clark again secured a position in the Boston navy yard where he worked until the spring of 1867, when he emigrated to Illinois, and took up his residence in Hampton For about five years he owned and operated a farm of one hundred and sixty acres, and for the following year conducted a drug store in Monmouth, but not liking the business as it took him away from home, he sold out and embarked in merchandising in Hampton with Mr. Baker, a partnership which was continued for ten years In 1888 he was appointed postmaster and most acceptably discharged the duties of that office for four years In the meantime he had become agent for the steam packet line, with which he has since been connected.

Mr Clark's first wife died in Chelsea, Massachusetts, November 26, 1866, and was laid to rest in Woodlawn cemetery There were two children born of this union —Caroline Martha, now the wife of Arthur S Wells, of Chicago, by whom she has three children, and Harriet Dart, wife of William D Taylor, of Howard, Kansas Mr Clark was again married, his second union being with Miss Nancy J Denison, of Hampton, where the wedding was performed July 30, 1868 She was born in Pennsylvania, and had come to Illinois in 1840 with her parents, William and Margaret (Johnson) Denison, who settled in Rock Island county

Mr. Clark was reared a Whig and cast his first vote for General Scott in 1852, but four years later on the organization of the Republican party cast his ballot for Fremont and has since been an ardent supporter of the latter party He served as president of the village board and was re-elected to that position, but resigned during his second term He is an honored member of William McDonald Post, No 595, G A R , of which he is past commander and at present chaplain His parents were Presbyterians, but on coming to Hampton he joined the Congregational church, and has been deacon since 1868 · k · he n remem-

ber he has been a Sunday-school worker and for many years has served as superintendent He is a pleasant, genial gentleman, of high social qualities and is very popular, having an extensive circle of friends and acquaintances who esteem him highly for his genuine worth

---

WILLIAM DRURY is one of Rock Island county's substantial citizens and honored pioneers, whose residence here dates from 1847 In the years which have since come and gone, he has borne his part in the work of improvement and development and belongs to the valued class of early settlers to whose labors is largely due the present prosperity and substantial growth of the county His has been a well spent life, winning to him the confidence and regard of all with whom he has been brought in contact and it is with pleasure that we present to our readers this record of his career, knowing that it will prove of interest to his friends

Mr. Drury was born in Madison county, Indiana, December 20, 1828. His father. Isaac Drury, was born in Pennsylvania, December 16, 1799, and was a son of William Drury, who was a native of Maryland, and was of English lineage. The family were identified with the Quaker society In 1801 William Drury removed with his family to Ohio and in 1811 to Indiana, taking up his residence in Wayne county on land now included within the corporation limits of Richmond Isaac Drury was reared to manhood in that state, and was married there to Hannah Reese, a native of Pennsylvania, and a daughter of Thomas Reese, of Washington county, Pennsylvania, where he and his wife spent their entire lives. During her girlhood Mrs Drury accompanied an uncle to the Hoosier state In 1834 Mr Drury removed with his family to what is now Mercer county, Illinois, and opened up a farm, whereon he made his home for some years In 1847 he came to this county, and purchased eighty acres of land on section 33, Buffalo Prairie township, to which he afterward added a tract of one hundred and sixty acres He built a house and barn and continued to farm that place until 1854, when he sold out and removed to Missouri, locating in Putnam county, near Unionville, where he purchased a farm and spent his remaining days He was a member of the Thirty-seventh Iowa Graybeards during the Civil war and served until honorably discharged on account of disability He died in 1875 and his wife passed away in 1879, both being interred in the cemetery of Unionville, Missouri, where a substantial monument marks their last resting place

Mr and Mrs Drury had a family of five sons and four daughters, all of whom reached mature years Isaiah took up his residence near Lake Charles, Louisiana, where he made his home until his death, William is the second of the family, Cecelia is the deceased wife of David Duffield, Sarah J is the deceased wife of James L Robins, of Putnam county, Missouri, Jesse R. is a farmer of Putnam county, Paris also follows farming there, James M is an agriculturist of Harrison county, Missouri, Emily is the deceased wife of Mathew Boner, Vashti is the wife of Jesse B Campbell, of Unionville, Missouri

William Drury was reared to manhood in Illinois and obtained his education in the common schools In 1850, attracted by the discovery of gold in California, he crossed the plains leaving home with a train on the 6th of April, crossing the Missouri river at Omaha, and reaching his destination in September. He spent the winter and spring in the mines and returned by way of the Panama route to New Orleans and thence up the river to Rock Island county After his return he purchased eighty acres of raw prairie land and twenty acres of timber land, and locating on the former began transforming it into rich and productive fields Several years later he sold that property and removed to Unionville, Missouri, where he purchased an interest in a store and engaged in merchandising until after receiving his appointment to the office of deputy sheriff, when on account of the demands his official duties made upon his time, he sold his store He served as deputy sheriff of Putnam county, Missouri, three years

In 1860 Mr Drury again came to Rock Island county and located upon a part of the farm which he now owns He has since added to this place and his landed possessions aggregated five hundred and fifty acres at one time, but he has since generously divided with the children and retains possession of only two hundred and eighty acres He has upon his farm a pleasant residence, substantial barns and outbuildings, the latest improved machinery known to progressive farming, and all the accessories and conveniences of the model farm of the nineteenth century His property is valuable and productive and the return therefrom materially increases his financial resources

On the 1st of September, 1883, Mr Drury wedded Mary Kistler, a native of Pennsylvania, who came to Illinois in 1839 with her father John Kistler, one of the first settlers on Buffalo Prairie township Mrs Drury was therefore reared and educated in the same neighborhood with her husband They have four children Perry I who is engaged in the cultivation of rice near Lake Charles, Louisiana, John K, a farmer of Buffalo Prairie township, Jessie M, wife of C W Bramhall, cf Welsh, Louisiana, and Logan, who operates the old homestead

Mr Druin is a stanch Republican and formerly took a very active part in local political affairs He served as township clerk and in 1868 was elected sheriff of Rock Island county for a term of two years He made his home in the city of Rock Island during that time, and discharged his duties with marked fidelity and ability He has served for two or three terms as town supervisor and as a member of the county board, and for twenty consecutive years filled the office of town treasurer, being the present incumbent His official service is above reproach and was creditable alike to himself and his constituents He is a warm friend of the cause of education and has done all in his power for the good of the schools He belongs to Illinois City Lodge, No 679, A F & A M, and has served as its secretary He has resided in Rock Island county for nearly half a century, and has been an important factor in transforming it from a wilderness and swampy region into beautiful homes and farms He has ever been active in the work of improvement, and has withheld his support of no worthy object calculated to promote the public good His business career has been crowned with success, for it has been characterized by those qualities which always bring prosperity— industry, perseverance and good management He now has a handsome competence which supplies him with all the comforts a

and has largely put aside the care of business For a number of years he and his estimable wife, who has indeed proved a helpmeet, have spent their winters in Welsh, Louisiana Ease and comfort are surely their rightful portion, and their prosperity is so well merited that it places them above envy Their circle of friends is very extensive, and they have the warm regard of all.

WARREN HUNTER, M D, a successful physician and surgeon of Hampton, Illinois, traces his ancestry back to one of the most honored and distinguished families of Scotland, whose early home was near the city of Ayr In 1656, however, John Hunter, his great-great-grandfather, removed to the North of Ireland, settling in County Londonderry, where he built a large stone mansion, which is still in the possession of some of his descendants It is located in the town of Ballygruba and descended to the Doctor's great-grandfather, Henry Hunter, who, like the other members of the family, was extensively engaged in the manufacture of linen He married Miss Nancy Kennedy, whose family had lived near the Hunters in Scotland, and had come to Ireland at the same time and settled in the same town. Henry Hunter was the youngest of three sons, the others being John and Matthew The oldest had a son, also named John, who with his uncle Matthew came to America and located on a farm in South Carolina He became a member of the continental congress, was judge of the supreme court of South Carolina, and was a wealthy planter of that state One of his brothers crossed the At-
lanti t the can his chil took up his res-

idence in Boston, Massachusetts His sister Nancy married John Kennedy, of Ballygruba, Ireland, and is the Miss Nancy Hunter who won the prize and diploma offered by the Royal Musical Society of Edinburg for the best singer in the kingdom

Henry Hunter, the Doctor's great-grandfather, was born in 1725 and before the French and Indian war came to America, where he engaged in business with his nephew, Henry, in Boston On his vessel, the former carried soldiers to Quebec at the time it was captured by General Wolfe Under the old elm on Boston common, he was married to Miss Sarah Wyer, of Londonderry, Ireland, who died four years later and was buried in the cemetery there In 1760 he was again married to a lady by the name of Wyer, of Londonderry, New Hampshire, and later located in Bristol, Maine His vessel was at one time captured by a British fleet, but as the commander was an old schoolmate of Captain Hunter's in the north of Ireland, he gave back the vessel and also gave him a paper which prevented its re-capture The Captain had a family of six sons and two daughters, among whom were John, James and David, who became residents of Strong, Franklin county, Maine

The last named, David Hunter, was the Doctor's grandfather, and was the founder of the old homestead at Strong, Maine, known as Maple Wood Farm, where he died May 7, 1871, at the advanced age of ninety-eight years, his birth having occurred in 1773 In 1796 he married Eleanor Fossett, of Bristol, Maine, and she survived him for a time, dying at the age of ninety-four

From the earliest period the Hunter family has been eminent, upright and been strict adhe

ter faith They were Puritans, believing and living up to the principles of liberty of conscience, and were ready to meet every call of duty The successes of Cromwell was what led them to leave their old home in Scotland and go to Ireland, and the influence of a pious ancestry shone through the life of David Hunter, who, like Jacob of old, emigrated to a new country with scarcely more than a staff in his hand He was a frugal, hard working man, and during his boyhood when on trips to Boston with his father, he would save the seeds of the fruit bought to eat and would plant them on his return home. He lived to enjoy the fruit raised in this way From the virgin forests he hewed out a home, built the first frame house in Strong, and owned the first carriage ever taken to that place He became one of the original members of the Congregational church there and always took an active part in all church work He was survived by over seventy descendants, not one of whom used intoxicants or tobacco in any form

Dr Hunter, of this review, was born in Strong township, Franklin county, Maine, October 18, 1833, and is a son of David F and Lydia A (Belcher) Hunter, also natives of the Pine Tree state The father was born on Maple Wood farm, in 1802, was educated in the common schools and throughout life followed agricultural pursuits, owning a farm about a mile west of the old homestead His place is also in the possession of the family Originally he was an old-line Whig in politics, later became a Republican, and was a Congregationalist in religious belief In early life he was captain in the state militia and held various local offices He survived his wife for 'eceased

This worthy couple became the parents of ten children, whom they provided with good educational privileges, thus well fitting them for the practical and responsible duties of life Samuel Belcher, the oldest, is a graduate of the Jefferson Medical College of Philadelphia, and is successfully engaged in practice in Machias, Maine. In 1896 he was the honored president of the State Medical Association. He is married and has two daughters Sarah, who is a graduate of the Woman's Medical College, and is now associated with her father in practice, and Anna, at home Our subject is the second of the family Eliza A is the wife of Albert Stoddard, of Hampton, Illinois Rose A is the wife of Alden J Blither, of Seattle, Washington, and has four children Evelina B married John Harvey Conant and lives in Strong, Maine, adjoining the old homestead William Henry, who resides on his father s old farm, is married and has two children Nellie is the wife of Otis M Moore, of Seattle, Washington. David is married and is engaged in the printing business in Minneapolis, Minnesota. Hiram Andrew, a farmer of Phillips, Maine, died leaving four children Supply Belcher is married and carries on farming in the Pine Tree state, at Farmington.

Dr. Hunter, whose name introduces this sketch, attended the common schools and was later a student in the Farmington Academy, where he prepared for college At the age of nineteen he left home and began teaching, which profession he followed for four years during the fall and winter, while in the spring he attended school At the end of that time he obtained a position as clerk in ~ ~~~~~~~ ~~~~ ~~ R '~ ~~~ Cutter in Farming   M   ~ ~~ ~ ~~ th stud\

of medicine with his brother, who was already engaged in practice at Steuben, Maine In 1862 he was made assistant surgeon of the Sixteenth Maine Infantry, but was obliged to resign at the end of four months on account of physical disability. During his service he had discharged the duties of regimental surgeon and would have been promoted to that position had his health permitted

In Steuben, he was married April 9, 1861, to Miss Harriet Melvina Toothacre, of Phillips, Maine, who died Saturday, May 31, 1884, leaving two children—Charles Warren, a graduate of Rush Medical College, who is married and is engaged in practice in Victoria, Knox county, Illinois, and Nettie E , at home with her father

For one year after his return from the war, Dr Hunter engaged in practice in Steuben, and in 1865 removed to Cherryfield, Maine, where he remained for five years After a short time spent in Phillips, Maine, he returned to the old home in Strong, where he lived for ten years and in 1879 came to Hampton, Illinois, where he soon succeeded in building up a large and lucrative practice For many years while a resident of Maine, he was a member of the board of pension examiners, and has also served as examiner for insurance societies. He is a member of the American, the State and the County Medical Association, and has held various offices in the same. Since the age of eighteen years the Doctor has been a faithful member of the Congregational church, is an earnest, conscientious Christian gentleman, and has been for many years trustee of his church. While living in Cherryfield, Maine, he joined the Masonic order, the Blue Mountain Lodge, and is still a member of the fraternity He has filled all the offices in the United Workmen Lodge of Port Byron, and is a charter member of Laurel Lodge, No 30, M W A , in which he has also filled all the chairs. In 1856 he supported General Fremont for the presidency and has since been an ardent Republican, has been a delegate to numerous conventions, but has never cared for official honors, preferring to devote his entire time and attention to his extensive practice Constant study and close application to the details of his profession have made him one of the most prominent and successful physicians of Rock Island county, and as a gentleman he also occupies an enviable position in the regard of his fellow-citizens

WILMOT S WARNER, of Moline, is engaged in the real estate and insurance business, and the integral elements of success in any business—industry, perseverance and sagacity—are numbered among his chief characteristics One of Illinois' native sons, he was born in Henry county, February 22, 1859 His parents, W W and Olive (Washburn) Warner, are still living in that county, the father being now seventy years of age He removed from Massachusetts to Illinois about 1853 and located in Henry county, where he was married. In connection with general farming he has carried on business as a grain and stock dealer

Mr. Warner, of this review, spent his boyhood days amid the green fields and meadows of the home farm and acquired his early education in the country schools, supplementing it by study in the graded schools of Colona At the age of eighteen he began teaching, and followed that profession four years, after which he enter 1 th i t l

service, learning telegraphy in Moline. He afterward went to northern Minnesota, and was stationed at various points on the Northern Pacific Railroad Subsequently he entered the employ of the Rock Island Railroad Company, in the construction department and while thus engaged was located at different times in Nebraska, Kansas, Indian Territory and Colorado His next service was as train dispatcher at Goodland, Kansas, and on leaving the company in 1891, he returned to Moline, where he embarked in business as a real estate and insurance agent. He has an excellent knowledge of the value of realty and his sagacity and keen discrimination in business affairs, have made him quite successful in this enterprise

In Henry county, on the 30th of January, 1883, was celebrated the marriage of Mr Warner and Miss Fannie Wood, who was born on a farm in that county, and is a daughter of Wellington and Ellen (Bradford) Wood Two children were born of this union, but one died in infancy The remaining daughter is Eva Lenore, who was born in Goodland, Kansas, in November, 1888

In politics Mr Warner is a Republican, having supported that party since casting his first presidential vote for Garfield in 1880 He has always taken quite an active part in political affairs, and while in Dawson, Minnesota, served as city clerk for three years, at Bluffton, that state, was justice of the peace two years, and was a member of the city council in Goodland, Kansas, for three years At that place he was also vice-president of the Sherman County State Bank, which position he resigned on his return to Moline. By the county board of super-

pointed justice of the peace of Moline in February, 1897, and is now acceptably filling that position, discharging his duties with a fairness and impartiality most commendable   He served as a delegate to the district and state conventions in Minnesota and to the county and district conventions in Kansas   He and his wife are members of the Congregational church of Moline, and socially he is connected with the Odd Fellows' Society and the Modern Woodmen of America   Prompt and faithful in the discharge of his public duties and true to every trust he is both widely and favorably known in business and social circles of Moline

FRANCIS BLACK, a well-known merchant and prominent citizen of Hampton, has for the long period of fifty-six years been connected with the history of this county, and few, if any, have done more for its upbuilding   He has been a champion of every movement designed to promote the general welfare, a supporter of every enterprise for the public good, and has materially aided in the advancement of all social, industrial, educational and moral interests

Mr Black was born February 20, 1815, in Barre, Worcester county, Massachusetts, and is a son of Hon Archibald Black, a native of the same state, as was also the grandfather, Captain John Black, who commanded a company of minutemen at the battle of Bunker Hill   The great-grandfather, Marmaduke Black, was a native of Scotland, whence he came to America about 1731   In the state of his nativity, Hon Archibald Black grew to manhood and married Miss Sophia Caldwell, also a native of Barre Massachusetts and a daughter of Set

originally from the north of Ireland or Scotland and were Protestant in religious belief   The founder of the family in the new world was William Caldwell, who crossed the broad Atlantic and became a resident of Massachusetts as early as 1684   After his marriage Archibald Black located on a farm in Barre, where he reared his family and spent his remaining days   He was one of the leading and influential citizens of the community and was called upon to serve in a number of official positions of honor and trust, including those of sheriff and representative to the state legislature   In his family were three children, two sons and one daughter, but our subject is the only one now living

The common schools of his native state afforded Francis Black his educational privileges, and he began his business career as a clerk in a country store at the age of thirteen   When twenty he started for New York, and from there proceeded to Chicago, where he arrived in 1836, and for about five years engaged in the auction and commission business   In November, 1841, he first set foot in Hampton, Illinois, which at that time was the second best town in Rock Island county, and at once established a store, which he conducted alone for some time   Later he admitted S L Bretton to a partnership in the business and together they carried on operations for several years, during which time his present store building was erected   Mr Bretton sold his interest to his son-in-law, Milton Cropster, who was a member of the firm during the year 1858, but since that time Mr Black has been alone in business   He is one of the oldest merchants in the county, and from the public has always received a liberal patronage, he having by upright and honorable business methods gaining him the confidence of all with whom he came in contact

In 1847, in Hampton, occurred the marriage of Mr Black and Miss Charlotte C Burton, a native of Maine, who died in 1861, leaving one son, Charles C , who is married and is a leading attorney of Kansas City, Missouri There was also another son, Archibald L , who died in infancy On the 9th of October, 1862, Mr Black was again married, his second union being with Miss Philena Luce, who was born and reared in the Pine Tree state, and when a young lady came to Rock Island county Four children blessed this union, namely Sophia, now the wife of William Conant, of Iowa City, Francis C , who died in infancy, Theodosia, wife of Morris Hoay, of Rock Island, and Walter L., who is clerking in his father's store Though not members of any religious denomination the parents attend the Congregational church and give an earnest support to all objects which they believe calculated to benefit the community or advance the welfare of their fellowmen

Since the organization of the party Mr Black has been a stalwart Republican, and was originally a Whig Although he has never cared for political honors he has most creditably served in a number of official positions, being postmaster at different times and serving in all several years When he was first appointed to that position, only two mails were received at Hampton each week and these were brought by wagon He has also been treasurer of both the village board and the school board for many years, and has faithfully discharged every duty devolving upon him, whether public or private He has witnessed almost the entire growth and development of the county and has ever borne a prominent

part in promoting its welfare, doing all in his power to advance its interests To-day he is not more honored on account of the enviable position which he occupies in business circles than on account of the many kindly deeds of his life, which have ever been quietly and unostentatiously performed

ALEXANDER DUNBAR —In the career of this gentleman we find an excellent example for young men just embarking in the field of active life, of what may be accomplished by a man beginning poor, but honest, prudent and industrious He is now a leading farmer and stock raiser residing on section 13, Zuma township, where he owns a fine farm of eighty acres adjoining the village of Joslin, and also has two other well improved tracts of sixty and forty acres respectively

A native of Ohio, Mr Dunbar was born in Trumbull county, December 17, 1827, and is a son of Matthew Dunbar, who was born and reared in Ireland, and as a young man came to the United States, locating in Trumbull county, Ohio, where he met and married Miss Susan Campbell, a native of that county Her father, George Campbell, was one of the earliest settlers of Trumbull county, where he purchased seven hundred acres of land and in the midst of the wilderness developed a farm and raised his family of fourteen children Matthew Dunbar worked at his trade of marble cutting in his adopted county until his death, which occurred in 1830 during early manhood. His widow reared their family and afterward became the wife of John Reed, who subsequently became a resident of Zuma township, Rock Island county, Illinois She passed away at the home of our subject

After the death of his father, Alexander Dunbar went to live with an uncle, Abner C Finton, of Trumbull county, with whom he remained until reaching man's estate He was provided with very limited school privileges, and during his youth learned the blacksmith's trade, which he followed in his native county for about five years previous to coming to Illinois in 1852 Near the village of Zuma he built a small shop and began work at his trade and some years later purchased the eighty-acre tract upon which he now resides In connection with work at his trade, he commenced to transform the raw land into highly cultivated fields and now has one of the best and most highly improved farms of the Zuma township As he prospered in his undertaking he bought sixty acres on the Rock River bottom and another forty-acre tract adjoining the village of Joslin both of which are now under a high state of cultivation

In Youngstown, Ohio, Mr Dunbar was married in 1849, the lady of his choice being Miss Elizabeth Miller, a native of that city and a daughter of Joseph Miller, who removed from Pennsylvania to Trumbull county, Ohio, during pioneer days There were twelve children born of this union who reached mature years, namely Alonzo, a farmer of Zuma township, Eveline, wife of Isaac Struble, of Keokuk county, Iowa, Melissa and Marilla, twins, the former of whom died in childhood, and the latter now the wife of Joseph Parks, who is connected with the Great Northern Railroad and resides in Rothsay, Minnesota, Jane, wife of Marion Walker, of Zuma township, Joseph, an agriculturist of Tilden, Madison county, Nebraska, Olive, wife of Charles Beck, of Wichita, Kansas, Samantha, wife of Jacob Graham 1 k and h dad county Iowa

Anna Eliza, wife of Ed McFadden, of Ottumwa, Iowa, Agnes E , wife of Albert Michaels, of the same place, Lois, wife of William Gilpin, of Coal Valley, Rock Island county, Florence, wife of William E Miller, a teacher in the Davenport Business College, and Mary E , who died at the age of twenty-four years

On the organization of the Republican party Mr Dunbar joined its ranks, voting for Fremont in 1856, but being a strong temperance man, he now supports the men and measures of the Prohibition party Feeling the need of a better education, as his own school privileges were limited, he has taken an active interest in educational affairs, and has for almost a third of a century been a most efficient member of the school board of his district Although a quiet, unassuming man, he makes many friends and has the happy faculty of easily retaining them During the Civil war he manifested his loyalty to his country by enlisting in Company A, One Hundred and Fifty-sixth Illinois Volunteer Infantry, and served about eight or nine months and was honorably discharged Rock Island has reason to number him among her valued and honored citizens

L N LARSON is the possessor of a comfortable property which enables him now to live in retirement from active business cares. He was for many years an enterprising, progressive and sagacious business man whose well directed efforts brought to him rich returns He came to America in 1863 with little capital and started out to overcome the difficulties and obstacles in the path to prosperity His hopes have been realized and in their happy fulfillment he sees the fitting reward of his earnest toil

Mr Larson was born in the southern part of Sweden, November 6, 1829, and is a son of Lars and Elsa (Polson) Nelson His boyhood days were spent on a farm and so continually did he labor that he was denied all educational privileges He attended day school for only two weeks and acquired his education by study alone at night When twenty-one years of age he began working in a distillery, where he was employed for thirteen years He then determined to seek a home in America and crossing the Atlantic in 1863 arrived in Moline on the 15th of June Entering the employ of Deere & Company he was for more than eighteen years connected with that factory as one of its most faithful and trusted workmen Failing health at length forced his retirement.

Before leaving his native land Mr Larson was united in marriage on the 20th of July, 1858, to Miss Peta Nellie Anderson, and to them have been born three children— Lars W , born in Sweden, September 21, 1860. pursued the greater part of a high school course in Moline, afterward spent five years as a student in Augustana College, and later pursued a business course in Davenport He is now a successful photographer of Moline Anna and Hannah, twins, were born November 2, 1862 The latter died three months after the arrival of the family in America The former is a graduate of the Moline high school of the class of 1880

Mr Larson votes with the Republican party, but has never sought or desired political preferment He is a prominent member of the Swedish Lutheran church, has served as trustee and contributed quite largely in proportion to his means to the

erection of their house of worship He gives a generous support to all measures calculated to prove of public benefit and is deeply interested in the welfare and advancement of his adopted city

DAVID S ADAMS is an honored veteran of the Civil war and a prominent representative of the agricultural interests of Zuma township, Rock Island, his fine farm of ninety-two acres being pleasantly located on section 12, adjoining the village of Joslin. He was born on the 23d of July, 1835, in Warden Creek township, Berks county, Pennsylvania, and is a worthy representative of one of the leading pioneer families of that locality His paternal grandfather was a native of Germany, and on his emigration to this country took up his residence in Mulltown, Berks county, Pennsylvania, where he reared his family and engaged in the undertaking business

Anthony Adams, father of our subject, was born in that county in January, 1871, and on attaining man's estate married Elizabeth Shopwell, a native of the same neighborhood and a daughter of Mr Shopwell, who was one of the first settlers of that county, and a soldier of the Revolutionary war, receiving for his services a pension and a land warrant After his marriage Mr Adams continued to reside on the old homestead farm and, like his father, followed the undertaking business in Mulltown, where he died in 1875 Our subject was the eighth in order of birth in his family of nine children, all of whom reached years of maturity, but only three are now living, the others being Miss Sarah Adams and Mrs Maria Hefner who still resides in Berks county

At the age of sixteen David S Adams

left home and first located in Circleville, Ohio, where for five years he worked at the bricklayer's trade, which he had previously learned, being all this time in the employ of William Lavan, who proved a true friend to him. During the winter season, when work was slack at his trade, he found employment on a farm. On the 17th of September, 1856, he arrived in Zuma township, Rock Island county, Illinois, having come to this locality with James Clarke, who made his home here until his death. For four or five years our subject worked as a farm hand by the month.

On the 26th of December, 1862, Mr Adams was joined in wedlock to Miss Sarah Clarke, who was born reared and educated in Circleville, Ohio, and was a daughter of James Clarke. Our subject then purchased a farm of eighty acres on which he now resides, but only one-half of the amount had been broken and a small house erected thereon. To its further development and cultivation he at once devoted his attention, has since erected a neat and substantial residence, good barns and other outbuildings, and has bought a tract of fifteen acres adjoining and thirty acres on Rock river, on section 24, Zuma township, all rich and arable land.

In 1864 Mr Adams laid aside all personal interests and joined Company A, One Hundred and Fifty-sixth Illinois Volunteer Infantry, which was assigned to the Second Army Corps of the Cumberland. Going south to Nashville, Tennessee, he faithfully served until the close of the war, when he was mustered out and returned home.

To Mr and Mrs Adams were born three sons and two daughters, namely James, who is married and engaged in farming in Zuma to   who is-

sists his father in carrying on the home farm, William Mason, who was engaged in business in Barstow, Illinois, and died June 9, 1897, Laura, wife of Benjamin Brooks Osborn, of Osborn Station, Rock Island county, and Mary, wife of Frank Talby, of Zuma township. The wife and mother was called to her final rest October 7, 1883, and her remains were interred in Henry county cemetery. Mr Adams was again married March, 1886, his second union being with Miss Mary Jane Shively, a native of Zuma township, and a daughter of Jacob Shively, an early settler of Rock Island county, now deceased.

In his political affiliations Mr. Adams has been a stanch Republican since casting his first ballot for Abraham Lincoln in 1860, and has supported every presidential nominee of the party since that time. For twenty-one consecutive years he has been a member of the school board, and has been trustee for three years, but has never cared for the honors or emoluments of political office. Through his own exertions he has attained an honorable position and marked prestige among the representative farmers of Rock Island county, and with signal consistency it may be said that he is the architect of his own fortune and one whose success amply justifies the application of the somewhat hackneyed but most expressive title, "a self-made man."

SAMUEL DEVINNEY WAINWRIGHT, who follows farming and stock-raising on section 12, Hampton township, is the owner of one hundred and eighty-five acres of rich and arable land, and the neat and thrifty appearance of the place well indicates the progressive and enterprising spirit of the owner, who is accounted one of the leading agriculturists of the county. He was born in Indiana county, Pennsylvania, December 7, 1833, and is a son of Isaac and Rachel (Devinney) Wainwright, the former a native of Derbyshire, England He was about fourteen years of age when, with his father, Samuel Wainwright, he came to America, locating in Indiana county, where he met and married Miss Devinney He was a farmer and also leased land and engaged in farming.

Mr Wainwright, of this review, obtained a common-school education, and when about fourteen years of age began working in the coal mines, but during the greater part of his youth his attention was given to the work of the farm In 1851 he sold out and with his father went by canal to Pittsburg, by steamer to St Louis and then up the river to Hampton The father intended to rent land but could secure no farm that season, and after remaining for a time in Rock Island he purchased ninety acres, a tract which adjoins our subject's farm on the north It was heavily timbered and had to be cleared before the work of cultivation could be begun The father afterward purchased another ninety acres, making a farm of one hundred and eighty acres, and on this place coal was found He died in December, 1886, at the age of eighty-one years In his family were four sons and four daughters who grew to maturity John, a carpenter of Fulton, Illinois, who has one child, Sarah, who became the wife of Isaac Monk and died in Shenandoah, Iowa, in 1876, leaving four daughters; Rachel, twin sister of our subject, now living in Omaha, Nebraska, Isaac, who died in Rock Island county about 1883, Elizabeth, who is the widow of Jo____ ____ ____ ____ ____ ____

Nebraska, with her four daughters, Rebecca, wife of Andrew P Anderson, of Iowa, by whom she has four children, George, who lives on the old homestead and has two children, Mary, who died in Pennsylvania at the age of five years

Samuel D Wainwright assisted in the cultivation and development of the home farm and remained with his father until thirty-two years of age For his services he was deeded eighty acres of the land in Zuma township, which he traded for his present home, locating thereon in 1865 He afterward purchased other land and now has a valuable farm of one hundred eighty-five acres under a high state of cultivation, improved with good buildings, supplied with excellent machinery, and giving evidence of the enterprise of the owner by its neat and thrifty appearance

Mr Wainwright was married March 30, 1865, to Clarinda Burchard Smith, who was born and reared in Scott county, Iowa, a daughter of Ira F and Nancy (Hoffman) Smith, both representatives of old Pennsylvania families Seven children graced this union: Ida Belle, who died suddenly a few days before her twentieth birthday and was buried in Port Byron cemetery; Ira F, who married Ella Crompton, by whom he has two daughters, and lives on a farm in Zuma township, George Elmer, who married Lula Leslie and resides in Scott county, Iowa, Frank N, who married Bessie Warren, by whom he has three children and lives in Zuma township, Samuel D and Isaac, at home, and Dwight, born November 10, 1888

Mr Wainwright cast his first presidential vote for Buchanan, and has always been a Democrat. He has been called to serve in ____ ____ ____ ____ ____ ____ it, was highway commissioner six years, supervisor one year, has frequently been a delegate to county conventions He is now agent for the Farmers' Mutual Insurance Company of Rock Island, which was organized in Coe and Zuma townships A valued member of the Methodist Episcopal church, he is now serving on its board of trustees For fourteen years he has been a member of the Ancient Order of United Workmen, has filled all of its offices, and was its representative in the grand lodge at Chicago

CHARLES WILLIAM LUNDAHL, the well-known bookkeeper and teller of the Peoples Savings Bank of Moline, was born in Rock Island, June 24, 1856, a son of Nels and Eva (Lundahl) Lundahl, natives of Denmark and Sweden respectively They came to America in 1853 and were married at Rock Island the following year. Our subject is the oldest of their children In the public schools of Rock Island he began his education, and after the removal of the family to Moline in 1866 continued his studies until sixteen years of age when he laid aside his text books to accept a position as delivery boy in a grocery and feed store

In 1873 Mr Lundahl entered the ticket department of the Moline office of the Chicago, Rock Island & Pacific and the Milwauke & St Paul Railroads, and also became connected with the United States Express Company, remaining with them for ten years He then became bookkeeper and teller in the First National Bank of Moline, and since the organization of the Peoples Savings Bank has held his present position, ' ' ' " (' Jr his most effic He . o u : t

business ability, enterprising and progressive, and not only has the respect and confidence of the officials of the bank but its patrons as well

On the 2d of August, 1876, Mr Lundahl was united in marriage to Miss Mary Johnson, a native of Sweden, and a daughter of Jonas and Johanna Johnson. She received a good common-school education and is a lady of culture and refinement Four children grace this union, namely Charles Wallace, who was born March 28, 1878, and graduated from the commercial department of Augustana College in 1896, Arvid, born January 14, 1880, Alfred Albert, born April 7, 1883, and Robert Harrison, born October 31, 1888

Since casting his first presidential vote for General Garfield in 1880, Mr Lundahl has been an ardent Republican in politics, and he has most acceptably served as city treasurer of Moline for two terms He also received the nomination for mayor on the citizens ticket, and has been a delegate to a number of county conventions of his party He attends and supports the Swedish Lutheran church, of which his wife is a faithful member, and he affiliates with the Knights of the Globe being a charter member of General Rodman Garrison, No 84, in which he has filled all the chairs In all the relations of life he has been true and faithful to every trust reposed in him, and his devotion to the public good is unquestioned, arising as it does from a sincere interest in the welfare of his fellow men

ORVILLE I ADDITON, whose home is on section 30, Cordova township, is well known as a successful farmer through his twenty years of faithful and efficient

service, and his work will not readily be forgotten by the many who have been helped
by him in the steep and sometimes weary
path of knowledge   Born in Leeds, An-
droscoggin county, Maine, August 31, 1855,
he is a son of Isaiah B and Eliza Ann (Jen-
nings) Additon, and is a representative of one
of the oldest families of this county   His
ancestors came from England and located
at Duxbury, Massachusetts, previous to the
year 1640   They spelled the name Arddaton, which mode was continued during the
residence of the family at Duxbury. Thomas
Arddaton, a soldier of the Revolutionary
war, was the father of Thomas Arddaton,
Jr , the first of the family to emigrate to
Leeds, Maine, where the name was changed
to its present form   Although they were
not members of the Society of Friends,
Thomas Arddaton and his wife, Bethiah, located on Quaker Ridge, where they reared
their family, including Thomas Additon, the
grandfather of our subject   He married
Anna Beals, daughter of Isaiah Beals, and
they became the parents of five children,
of whom Isaiah Beals Additon, our subject s
father, was the oldest   He was a well-edu-
cated man and successfully taught twenty-
six terms of school in connection with the
operation of his farm   For many generations the family has given its support to the
Democratic party, and although his party
was in the minority, Isaiah B Additon was
made chairman of the board of selectmen
for eighteen years, and when nominated for
reprsentative to the state legislature received
a very flattering vote, although the district
was strongly Republican   In 1860 he was
census enumerator, and was one of the most
prominent and influential men of his community

Upon th L f   M   \ 1 1

this review, spent the days of his boyhood
and youth and attended the country schools
until about fifteen years of age, when he
entered Monmouth Academy, where he
pursued his studies for two years   At the
age of eighteen he began teaching a country school in his home district, in which way
he earned the money to pay his expenses
while attending Westbrook Seminary, where
he graduated in 1876 with high honors,
grading over ninety-nine on his average
He next had charge of high schools in various places in Maine, including the townships of Greene, Leeds and Turner in An-
droscoggin county

While still a resident of the Pine Tree
state, Mr. Additon was married November
5, 1878, to Lucy A Benner, of Lewiston,
Maine, who was born in Monmouth, and is
a daughter of Ensign W and Sarah F
(Loomis) Benner   He had also been a student in the Monmouth Academy, and had
successfully followed the teacher's profession   Mr and Mrs Additon have three
children, Forrest O , born in Auburn, Maine,
December 9, 1879, Henrietta, born in Utica,
LaSalle county, Illinois, May 14, 1887,
and Flora L , born at the present home of
the family in Cordova township, Rock Isl-
and county, May 30, 1897

With the hope of bettering his financial
condition Mr Additon came west in 1881,
and within a week after his arrival in Rock
Island county secured a position as teacher
in the Pleasant Valley school, where he
taught for two years   He was then principal of the graded schools at Stewartsville
for the same length of time, after which he
accepted a similar position in St Mary's,
St Genevieve county, Missouri, but at the
end of a year was obliged to resign on ac-
f f l   l l l   D   to his

father's farm in Maine, he spent the time there until fall, and then taught the high school at that place. Returning to Illinois he was made principal of the schools at Plattville, Kendall county, but resigned at the end of a year and a half to accept a better position in Utica, LaSalle county, where he remained for four years. He then came to Cordova to take the place of C. B. Marshall, who was principal of the Cordova village schools and had been elected county superintendent. After holding that position for three years Mr. Additon was principal of the schools of Princeton, Iowa, for one year, and in 1895 traveled for the Central School Supply House, selling supplies throughout Kentucky and Illinois. The next year he was a teacher in his home district, and in 1897 was again elected principal of the Cordova village schools, a position he is now acceptably filling. His wife also taught with him for two years in Cordova. In 1893 he purchased thirteen acres of land in Cordova township, pleasantly located on the banks of the Mississippi, where he has a fine residence and is successfully engaged in fruit raising.

Like his father and grandfather, Mr. Additon is a Universalist in religious belief, and is a staunch Democrat in politics. He is a genial, courteous gentleman, a pleasant, entertaining companion, and has many warm and admiring friends among all classes of men. He stands deservedly high among the successful educators of Rock Island county, and wherever known is held in high regard.

GEORGE H. McKINLEY, postmaster of Moline, has been an almost life-long resident of the city, coming to the place with his parents when but

of but six years. He is a native of Wisconsin, born in Whitewater, May 28, 1856. He traces his ancestry in this country to his great-grandfather, David McKinley, who was a native of Ireland, but who came to the United States prior to the Revolutionary war, a boy of twelve years of age, locating in Pennsylvania. David McKinley had four sons, William, James, Stephen and John. When but twenty-one years of age he enlisted in the war for independence and did his full share in throwing off the yoke of British oppression.

James McKinley, the grandfather of our subject, was a native of Pennsylvania, and there married. His son, James McKinley, the father of our subject, was born in Columbia county, Pennsylvania, but removed with his parents to Ohio at a very early day, and there grew to manhood. In his youth he learned the moulder's trade, which occupation he followed almost his entire life. While yet residing in Ohio he married and soon after moved to Mayville, Wisconsin, and later to Whitewater, in the same state. His wife dying, he subsequently married Mrs. Marian McGill, a widow lady, whose maiden name was Wooden.

From Whitewater, Wisconsin, James McKinley moved with his family to Cedar Rapids, Iowa, but only remained there a short time, when he removed to Davenport, in the same state. In 1862 he removed to Moline, Illinois, where he accepted the position of foreman in the foundry of Deere & Co., a position which he acceptably filled for fifteen years, when he resigned and lived retired until his death, which occurred May 22, 1882, at the age of seventy years. His wife survives him and is yet residing in Moline.

James McKinley was a man of fine

ability, and while he followed a trade very confining in its nature, he did not neglect his social and religious duties For years he was a prominent member of the Odd Fellows society, and filled all the chairs in his local lodge A licensed local preacher of the Methodist Episcopal church, he labored in word and doctrine as the opportunity was given him His heart was in the cause and he dearly loved to work for the Master. His death was mourned by a large circle of friends and acquaintances, and was a loss to the community The father of President McKinley was an own brother, and, therefore, the president is a first cousin of our subject

George H McKinley was a lad of six years when he came with his parents to Moline, and here his entire life has since been passed He was one of a family of five children of James and Marian McKinley Of these children, Charles grew to manhood, married, located in Lousiana, Missouri, but later returned to Moline where his death occurred April 8, 1897 Milton R is married and is a foreman in the Moline Plow Company's works George H is next in order of birth Eva is the wife of Joseph Bierce, of Moline Carrie is the wife of Charles T. Morey, a paymaster in the employ of Deere & Co

George H McKinley received his education in the Moline public schools, and early in life commenced to learn the moulder's trade in the shops of Deere & Co , but later entered the employ of the Barnard & Leas Manufacturing Co , where he remained until 1887 when he engaged with the Moline Plow Co In 1893 he was made foreman of the foundry and continued to faithfully discharge the duties of that responsible position until

resigned to take charge of the Moline post-office, having been commissioned as postmaster by his illustrious cousin, William McKinley, President of the United States

At Mt Pleasant, Iowa, September 28, 1876, Mr McKinley was united in marriage with Miss Hester A Ferries, a native of Canada, and a daughter of Willett Ferries, also a native of that country In her early childhood she was brought by her parents to Illinois, and later went with them to Carthage, Missouri In Illinois and Missouri she received a fair education and grew to womanhood Her father now resides in Fruithurst, Alabama By this union six children have been born—James B , George H , Jr , Agnes, Charles W , Anna Hester and Mabel Edna, all of whom yet remain at home

The McKinley family is noted for its strong advocacy of Republican principles In this respect George H McKinley has never departed from the faith of his fathers. Born at a time the Republican party was being formed, and when the country was at white heat over the slavery question, his first recollections are of witnessing the departure of the boys in blue as they marched to the front, and hearing the beating of the drum and the music of the fife as the young and active men of the land were summoned to their country's defense But the war had been ended many years before he cast his first presidential ballot, which was in 1880, when he voted for that grand Christian statesman, James A Garfield, who from the tow path of a canal wended his way onward and upward until he reached the pinnacle of an American's fame, the presidential chair From that time our subject has been an humble worker in the ranks of his party but has been honored by his fellow citizens with various local positions, which he has filled with credit to himself and all concerned For two years he served upon the county board of supervisors from Moline, making a valuable member He was also for some time a member of the literary board of Moline, but which, of course, is not a political office His interest in good literature secured him this appointment

In the campaign of 1896, resulting in the election of William McKinley as president, he took an active interest, and during the time served as president of the Moline Republican Club A firm believer in protection and reciprocity, and also of a sound and stable currency, he worked with and among his associates to the end that all might see the light as he saw it, and that his influence was felt is attested by the vote in Moline and the surrounding country The work in this campaign commended him to his fellow Republicans, and especially with those who were his fellow workmen in the factories of Moline By their solicitation he was induced to apply for the position of postmaster of the city Although others were applicants, among whom was one of the most popular and self-sacrificing workers in the party, he was duly commissioned and took possession of the office October 1, 1897 That he will make a faithful and popular postmaster is attested by his past life

Fraternally Mr McKinley is a Master Mason and is in 1897 junior warden of Doric Lodge, No 319 He is also a member of the Modern Woodmen of America and for seven years was venerable consul of Abe Lincoln Camp at Moline As a testimonial of ⟨illegible⟩ by his assoc ⟨illegible⟩

sented by them with an ebony gold-headed cane

As a citizen Mr McKinley enjoys the confidence and good will of all Modest and unassuming in manner he goes on the even tenor of his way doing his duty faithfully and well In everything that may add to the growth and prosperity of his adopted city, he takes a lively and commendable interest As already intimated, his fellow workmen in the various manufacturing institutions of the city believe in him and stand by him For some years he was president of the Iron Moulders Union, and is personally known to nearly every workman In social circles, he and his estimable wife are deservedly popular

JOHN W SNITZER is one of the courteous gentlemen in the post office department of Rock Island, and for about four years has been at the head of the carrier service, one of the most trustworthy and capable officials in the office He was born in Rock Island, August 1, 1872, and is very popular among the many friends who have known him from boyhood

Mr Snitzer is a son of John Snitzer, a native of Germany, who came to the new world when fourteen years of age and spent most of his time in the south up to the inauguration of the Civil war. He was a fine mechanic and early in the struggle he entered the government service, being stationed at various places where he did mechanical work until hostilities had ceased In 1871 he came to Rock Island with Colonel Flagler, who had been transferred from Augusta Island, Georgia, to this place to take charge of the arsenal The Colonel ⟨illegible⟩ Mr Snitzer the position of master mechanic on the island and he continued to serve as foreman for a quarter of a century, when his career was ended by death He was married in Augusta, Georgia, to Caroline Dressel, a native of Germany, who was reared and educated in Georgia They had three sons: Frederick, John W and W H are living in Rock Island The father was a prominent member of the Odd Fellows society and at his death, which occurred July 11, 1897, his lodge took charge of the funeral obsequies

John W Snitzer has spent his entire life in the city of his nativity and acquired the greater part of his education in the public school, but pursued a commercial course in the Davenport Business College On completing his studies he accepted a position in the employ of the United States government on the island, where he served in different capacities until 1893, when he was appointed to a position in the postoffice by Postmaster Patten He was placed in charge of the carrier service and has since served in that capacity with marked ability and fidelity Every trust reposed in him is faithfully performed and he meets fully every obligation resting upon him He is very courteous, affable and pleasant in manner and is very popular with the patrons of the office and those with whom his business relations bring him in contact

REUBEN G HOLLISTER, living retired upon his farm on section 18, Coe township, near Port Byron, is a worthy representative of one of the most prominent pioneer families of Rock Island county, and came here in July, 1836 For many years he was actively identified with its busin·

While struggling with the primitive soil and bringing about the improvements which he has reason to view with satisfaction, he also watched with the deepest interest the growth and development of the county, and in the establishment of one of its most valuable farms has contributed his quota to its progress and prosperity

A native son of Illinois, Mr Hollister was born in Joliet, December 23, 1835 His grandfather, Isaac Hollister, a native of Connecticut, was a soldier of the militia in the Revolutionary war, and was a sea captain in early life, trading in the West Indies In 1810, he removed to Washington county, New York, where he spent his remaining days upon a farm

Isaac Hollister, Jr, our subject's father, was born in Glastonbury, Connecticut, February 2, 1795, but grew to manhood in Washington county, New York, and at Troy, that state, married Miss Martha De Wolf, a native of Massachusetts, and a daughter of Abel DeWolf After their marriage they resided in Granville, New York, until 1833, when they started westward, first stopping in Joliet, Illinois, where Mr Hollister worked at the carpenter's trade for a few years The year 1836 witnessed his arrival in Rock Island county, and in Coe township he took up a claim of one hundred and sixty acres of timberland on section 17, and a like amount of prairie land on section 20 However, he only entered eighty acres of each He continued to work at his trade for a time and built the first frame house in Port Byron, but crippling his right hand a year after his arrival he was obliged to give up carpentering, and then turned his attention to agricultural pursuits He spent his last days in Port Byron, where he died · age of ninety years His wife passed away in February, 1891, and was laid by his side in Port Byron cemetery Our subject is the second in order of birth in their family of four children, the others being as follows William W , a resident of Decatur county, Kansas, Edwin H , who is living in the same county, and Mrs James Bell, also of the Sunflower state

Reuben G Hollister is principally self-educated, as he had little opportunity of attending school during his childhood, but his training in farm work was not so meagre and he became a thorough and skillful agriculturist After his father's removal to Port Byron he took charge of the farm and business in connection with his brother Edwin and together they carried on operations for several years After the father's death our subject succeeded to a part of the estate and purchased the remainder, and is still living on the old homestead where almost his entire life has been passed He owns two hundred and twenty acres of valuable land improved and with good and substantial buildings

On the 15th of August, 1861, Mr Hollister enlisted in Company D, Twelfth Illinois Volunteer Infantry, which was assigned to the Army of the Tennessee, and joined the regiment at Bird's Point He participated in the battles of Fort Henry, Fort Donelson and Shiloh, and was wounded in the left arm at the last engagement He was granted a furlough and returned home, but was later discharged while in the hospital at Keokuk, August 16, 1862, as he was unfit for active service He has never fully recovered the use of his arm

On the 12th of October, 1864, in Port Byron, was ꞏ ꞏ ꞏ ꞏ ꞏ ꞏ ꞏ Mr Hollister and ꞏ ꞏ ꞏ ꞏ ꞏ ꞏ ꞏ tive of a na-

tive of Kentucky and a daughter of German Trent She died December 9, 1894, leaving three children, two still living—Effie M , wife of Charles H Torpin, of Oakdale, Nebraska, and George H , who is married and carries on the home farm for his father Frank G , the older son, married and located in Buffalo Prairie township, Rock Island county He was accidently killed by a runaway team in Rock Island, in March, 1896

Politically, Mr Hollister has been identified with the Republican party since casting his first vote for Abraham Lincoln in 1860, and has capably served his fellow-citizens in the capacity of overseer of highways town collector two terms, and in other positions of honor and trust He is a prominent member of the Grand Army Post of Port Byron, and wherever known is held in high regard His loyalty as a citizen and his devotion to his country's interests have ever been among his marked characteristics, and the community is fortunate that numbers him among its citizens

MATTHEW ROBISON —As a representative of the intelligent and hardy pioneers who opened up Rock Island county for settlement and have since taken a conspicuous part in developing it, we are pleased to place in this volume a brief sketch of the life of the gentleman whose name introduces this notice He has a pleasant home on section 31, Andalusia township, and is successfully engaged in agricultural pursuits

A native of Illinois, Mr. Robison was born in Warren county, November 10, 1831, and is the only one now living of the three children born to James and Nancy (McAfee)

Robison, natives of Ohio His paternal grandfather, who was of Scotch descent, and a farmer by occupation, spent his entire life in the Buckeye state, where he reared his family of four sons and four daughters

During his early life James Robison followed blacksmithing, but later devoted his energies to farming When this state was still on the western frontier he became a resident of Warren county, and in 1833 removed to Rock Island county, becoming the first settler of Edgington township, where he entered one hundred and twenty acres of land, now owned by J L Harris At that time it required fifteen days to go to mill, having to travel by ox team to a little watermill in Warren county, and owing to the rush he would have to wait sometimes for several days before he could get his grist ground The early settlers hauled much of their wheat to Chicago, where they were often unable to get cash, and would return with salt, which they sold to their neighbors When going to mill Mr Robison was compelled to leave his wife and young children alone, and the Indians were still numerous in this region and sometimes very troublesome. He, himself, was never afraid of them and would often punish their offenses with a raw-hide They would set fire to the prairie grass in order to secure the deer concealed in it, and would thus endanger the lives and property of the settlers Mr Robison continued to improve and cultivate his farm until his death, which occurred in 1848, when about sixty years of age His wife had passed away two years previous. Both were earnest and consistent members of the Presbyterian church, and wherever known were held in the highest regard

Our

when brought by his parents to Rock Island county, and has since made his home in Edgington and Andalusia townships, covering a period of sixty-four years In the primitive log school-house of pioneer days, he conned his lessons, the school being conducted on the subscription plan and taught by a lady After his father's death he and his brother Robert became the owners of the old homestead, which they operated for a number of years, and then traded for a farm, which they later divided To his portion, comprising fifty-nine acres, Matthew Robison has added until he now has two hundred twenty acres, lying in Andalusia, Edgington and Buffalo Prairie townships With the exception of fifty acres it is all under a high state of cultivation and well improved with good and substantial buildings. In connection with general farming, he has operated a threshing machine almost every year since ten years of age, also has a separator run by horse power, and was the first to bring a machine of that kind into the district, operating the same during the fall and winter seasons for a number of years

On the 31st of December, 1857, Mr Robison was united in marriage to Miss Sidney Robins, a daughter of David Robins, of Illinois City, their wedding being celebrated at the residence of Lorenzo Parmenter Four children were born to them as follows: James, who married Mary Snell, and with their eight children lives near Grinnell, Iowa, Rachel Alice, wife of Ora Sherwood, of Edgington, Illinois, by whom she has two children, Elias S , who married Rosa Sedan, and also lives near Grinnell, Iowa, and Alonzo M , who was a twin brother of Elias S , and died in infancy The wife and mother, who was a member of the Baptist ... three weeks after the birth of the twins Mr Robison was again married October 26, 1869 his second union being with Miss Caroline M, daughter of Samuel and Mary Sloan, and to them was born a son, William H, who married Alice Roberts and has two children They live on the old homestead

In politics Mr Robison casts his vote for the candidates of the Republican party, and, although he has never taken a very active part in public affairs, he conscientiously performs his duties as a good citizen, and has creditably filled a number of township offices Socially he affiliates with Andalusia Lodge, No 516, A F & A M, and religiously he and his wife are members of the Presbyterian church and are people of high consideration in social circles of their community Mr Robison is a keen, practical man, well gifted with mental and physical vigor, and on the rolls of Rock Island county s honored pioneers, his name should be among the foremost

JASPER FORSYTH —In time to come this volume will acquire added value as a repository of records whose historical significance will then be fully appreciated, but readers will doubtless peruse with special interest the stories of the gallant service in that great struggle which settled once for all that this nation is, in truth, " one and indivisible It has often been said that the letters sent home during the war by the soldiers of all grades would make, if published, a better history of the war than has yet been given and the suggestive views of the conflict in the individual experiences contained in this book certainly give new color to many historic scene.

Among

Forsyth, who is now successfully engaged in farming and stock raising on section 17, Cordova township, Rock Island county He was born in Muskingum county, Ohio, October 31, 1842, a son of John and Lucy (Hayden) Forsyth In the Buckeye state the father followed farming, but after his emigration to Scott county, Iowa, in 1854, he erected the first sawmill in Princeton and engaged in the manufacture of lumber throughout the remainder of his life Our subject was the fifth in order of birth in his family of seven sons, of whom five served their country in the Civil war Jariel, the oldest, now a resident of Cass county, Nebraska, was not in the army Jacob was a member of the Twentieth Iowa Infantry, and served for three years William, also a member of an Iowa regiment, was in the service about a year John enlisted as a private in the same company as our subject, and was mustered out at the close of the war with the rank of lieutenant Luther was a member of the Twenty-first Iowa Infantry, and served as private until hostilities ceased None were wounded, captured or killed, but were always found at their post of duty, valiantly fighting for the old flag and the cause it represented

Jasper Forsyth was fourteen years of age when he accompanied the family on their removal to Scott county, Iowa, and was provided with a good common-school eduation In October, 1861, he enlisted at Princeton, Iowa, in Company E, Thirteenth Iowa Volunteer Infantry, as a private for three years' service, was sworn in on the 28th of that month, was soon afterward sent to Davenport and then to Benton Barracks, St Louis At Jefferson City, Missouri, the regiment was attached to a

see soon

after the battle of Fort Donelson Our subject's first engagement was at Shiloh, where he was in the thickest of the fight and had a chance to run for his life, which he improved In that engagement he was under the command of Dick Oglesby He took part in all the battles of his regiment including those of Corinth and Bolivar, Tennessee, after which, with the Fourth Iowa Infantry, they became a part of Crocker's Iowa Brigade, Fourth Division, Third Brigade, Seventeenth Corps, Army of the Tennessee After the battle of Corinth, Mr Forsyth was in the hospital at Jefferson Barracks for a few weeks but rejoined his regiment just before the siege of Vicksburg, in which he participated, and was later in the battles of Iuka and Atlanta He was on detached service at corps headquarters during the Atlanta campaign, and was in that city when his time expired and he was mustered out November 1, 1864

Returning to his home in Scott county, Iowa, Mr Forsyth enlisted in a different service and for life under a commanding officer with whom he is still serving, as on the 27th of December, 1864, he was united in marriage to Miss Josephine Rathbun, of Cordova, Illinois, where she was born May 10, 1840, a daughter of Ami R and Sarah A (Whiting) Rathbun, who were born, reared and married in Steuben county, New York, and emigrated to Illinois about 1834 or 1835 In the common schools of her native village Mrs Forsyth obtained a good education By her marriage to our subject she has become the mother of five children Dexter, born in Port Byron township, Rock Island county, November 4, 1865, married Electa Hull, by whom he has three children, Laura, Benjamin and Daisy, and lives on a farm in C

Port Byron township, March 3, 1870, married Junnie Simpson and resides in Cordova township, Millie, born in Princeton, Scott county, Iowa, August 6, 1874, is the wife of James Gunn, of Cordova township, and has two children, Bessie and Johnnie, Luther, born on the home farm in Cordova township, March 6, 1877, is still under the parental roof, and William, born July 6, 1879, is also at home

In February, 1865, Mr Forsyth located on a farm in Port Byron township, where he remained until the following fall, when he purchased forty acres of land in Cordova township, which continued to be his home for five years Selling out in 1870, he moved to Cass county, Nebraska, but after a short time spent there, on account of failing health he returned to Princeton, Iowa, where he lived for three years He then purchased forty acres of his present farm in Cordova township, Rock Island county, upon which not a tree was standing and all the improvements were of an inferior order He has added to his land until he now has a fine farm of one hundred and twenty acres, has erected good and substantial buildings thereon, and made many other excellent improvements which add to its value and attractive appearance

Since casting his first vote for General Grant in 1868, Mr Forsyth has been an ardent Republican, has served as school director thirteen years, pathmaster and highway commissioner several years and four years was supervisor He was one of the most popular and capable members of the county board, served on nearly all of the committees at different times, and was chairman of the miscellaneous committee two or three terms He is a charter member of

Albany, is also a charter member of Burr Oak Camp, No 33, M W A, and belongs to Riverside Lodge, K P, of Cordova In times of peace as well as on southern battlefields he is a loyal and devoted citizen, faithfully discharging every trust reposed in him, and his friends are many throughout the county.

STEPHEN BRAYTON, who resides on section 17, Buffalo Prairie township, is the possessor of a handsome farm property which now enables him to spend his years in the pleasurable enjoyment of his accumulations The record of his life, previous to 1892, is that of an active, enterprising, methodical and sagacious business man, who bent his energies to the honorable acquirement of a comfortable competence for himself He started out in life with no capital, but has steadily overcome the difficulties and obstacles in his path to prosperity His youthful dreams have been realized and in their happy fulfillment he sees the fitting reward of his earnest toil

Mr Brayton was born on the old homestead where he still resides, November 24, 1836, and is a son of Stephen Brayton, who was born in Lower Canada, June 1, 1807 At the age of ten years he accompanied his father, Gideon Brayton, to Ohio, later to Michigan, Indiana, and finally to Illinois, becoming one of the pioneers of this state Stephen Brayton, Sr, made his way through Chicago, then containing only a few log houses, and located near Rockford. He was married in Ohio to Catherine Coleman, a native of Pennsylvania, and in 1836 he removed to Rock Island county with his family He first ̶ ̶ ̶ ̶ ̶ ̶ ̶ ̶ ̶ ̶ ̶ ̶ ̶ ̶ ̶ ̶ of fifty acres and ̶ ̶ ̶ ̶ ̶ ̶ ̶ ̶ ̶ an additional

eighty, which he cleared and developed, transforming the wild land into a fine farm upon which he reared his family In the meantime he entered a claim in Iowa, but afterward sold it, making his home in Rock Island county His death occurred in May, 1882, but his widow still survives him and resides on the old homestead with her son The family numbered six sons and four daughters Mary J, wife of B F Brown, of Dallas county, Iowa, Joseph, who was a soldier of Company H, Forty-fifth Illinois Infantry, and died at Shiloh, Stephen B, of this sketch, William, of Logan, Harrison county, Iowa, who served in Company B, One Hundred and Twenty-sixth Illinois Infantry until the close of the war, Coleman, who was first lieutenant of Company K, One Hundred and Fortieth Illinois Infantry, Gideon, a member of Company B, One Hundred and Twenty-sixth Illinois Infantry until the close of the war, John, now a resident of this county, Lucy Ann, deceased wife of B F Brown, Elizabeth, wife of James T Sedam, a farmer on the old Brayton homestead

The subject of this sketch was reared to manhood on the farm and in the intervals of farm labor attended the common schools of the neighborhood To his father he gave the benefit of his services until twenty-five years of age, when feeling that his duty to his country was paramount to any other he enlisted in September, 1861, as a member of Company H, Forty-fifth Illinois Infantry, in which he served until discharged on account of disability in 1863 He participated in the battles of Fort Henry and Fort Donelson, Medan Station, Thompson Hill, Raymond, Jackson, Champion Hill, Black River and the siege of Vicksburg and in the last named was wounded, his right hand being

shot off, June 26, at the time of the blow-
ing up of the fort He was then taken to
the hospital at Memphis, Tennessee, where
three amputations were performed upon his
arm Later he was sent to Jefferson Barracks, St Louis, and about three months
later, November, 1863, was honorably discharged and returned home

Mr Brayton continued on the farm for
about a year and then entered the Soldiers'
School, in Fulton, where he remained for
two years On completing his studies he
went to Harrison county, Iowa, where in
connection with B F Brown, he engaged
in buying and shipping stock for two years
He then returned to the old homestead,
where he spent two years, after which he
went to Minburn, Dallas county, Iowa,
where he entered into partnership with his
brother in the hardware business For
eight years they carried on operations along
that line and then sold their store and stock,
removing to Persia, Iowa, where they carried on a hardware business for nine years,
when Stephen Brayton sold out to his
brother and returned to the old homestead
in Rock Island county In the meantime
he had made a trip to Nebraska, where he
took up both a homestead and tree claim,
residing thereon long enough to obtain possession of the same While there he helped
to organize the township in which he lived
and was its first delegate to the county convention. He has since sold the homestead,
but yet owns the tree claim in Nebraska

On coming again to his native county
Mr Brayton purchased the old family homestead and although not actively engaged in
its operation superintends its cultivation
He has made a number of valuable and substantial improvements on the place and now
has one of the best farms in the township

16

Since casting his first presidential vote
for Abraham Lincoln in 1860, Mr Brayton
has supported the men and measures of the
Republican party, and is a stanch advocate
of its principles He was elected township
collector and has filled other positions of
honor and trust He belongs to the Methodist
Episcopal church of Illinois City, and is one of
its trustees As a citizen he is public-spirited
and manifests a commendable interest in
everything pertaining to the welfare of the
community and to the public good He
well deserves mention among the honored
pioneers of the county, who have not only
witnessed its growth and development, but
laid the foundation for its present prosperity
and advancement

STEPHEN H SPENCER, long an honored resident of Rock Island, was born
August 7, 1838, in Pleasant Valley, Iowa,
just across the river from the village of
Hampton, Rock Island county His paternal grandfather was Calvin Spencer, who
made his home in Vermont and served as a
soldier in the colonial wars Roswell H
Spencer, the father, was a native of the
Green Mountain state, and when a young
man settled in Scott county, Iowa, becoming one of its earliest settlers He was a
brother of Judge Spencer, an honored pioneer of Rock Island

On the old homestead farm in Scott
county, Iowa, our subject passed the days
of his boyhood and youth, and in Cornell
College at Mt. Vernon, that state, completed his education In early life he made
two overland trips to Pike's Peak, Colorado, where he spent about two years in prospecting On the outbreak of the Civil war
he was among the first to enlist, becoming

a private of Company B, Second Iowa Volunteer Infantry, and participated in the battle of Fort Donelson, where he was wounded in the calf of the leg, the ball lodging in the flesh, where it remained until his death Thus disabled for active service on the field, he was made secretary on the staff of General Grant, a position he continued to fill until the expiration of his term Later he was connected with the commissary department on the Government Island until after the close of the war He then engaged in merchandising for two years and also had charge of his cousin's interest in a store while that gentleman was away

In November, 1867, in Pleasant Valley, Iowa, was celebrated the marriage of Mr Spencer and Miss Jennie N Allen, a native of Albany, New York, who during her childhood was brought west by her father, William Allen, who engaged in agricultural pursuits in Scott county, Iowa, from 1856 until his death, August 20, 1895 He was one of the substantial farmers of the locality, was widely and favorably known, and was a stalwart supporter of the Republican party Mrs Spencer, who is a most refined and cultured lady, was provided with good school privileges, completing her education in Davenport

For a time after his marriage Mr. Spencer engaged in mercantile business with Colonel Reid in Moline, and was later a contractor for one year, but at the end of that time sold out his interests here on account of failing health and went to Colorado, spending a year and a half in Denver He then returned to Rock Island, where he lived retired until his death which occurred on the 25th of May, 1873 Thus passed to his reward a man of noble character, one who had   part in life

"wherein all honor lies," and who had gained and retained the confidence, respect and esteem of his fellow men. His acquaintanceship was an extended one and his friendships many, and such of the pioneers of Rock Island as are yet living remember him with a feeling of admiration and almost reverence

Mr and Mrs Spencer had only one child—Charles Allen, who was born in Rock Island, October 17, 1868. He began his education in the public schools of Pleasant Valley, Iowa, later attended Kemper Hall Military Academy, and also took a business course in a commercial college of Davenport In 1887 he accepted a position in the Rock Island National Bank, with which he has since been connected, now being the popular teller of that institution He was married in Rock Island, January 11, 1893, to Miss Louise Whisler, a native of Albany, Whiteside county, Illinois, and a daughter of Captain W H Whisler, now of Rock Island, where she completed her education by graduating from the high school A little daughter graces this union—Helen, who is the joy and pride of the household Both Mrs Spencer and her daughter-in-law are members of the Rock Island Methodist Episcopal church, and the family is one of prominence in social circles. Charles A Spencer is one of the leading young business men of the city, and whether in public or private life, is always a courteous, genial gentleman, well deserving the high regard in which he is held

MISS EMMA L HOLLISTER, whose home in Port Byron township, Rock Island county, is a representative of one of the oldest and most highly respected families of the east   Lieutenant John Hollister, who founded the family in the new world, was born in England in 1612, and crossed the Atlantic in 1642, becoming one of the most prominent and influential men of Weathersfield, Connecticut, where he was admitted as a freeman the year following his arrival   Many times he represented his town in the colonial legislature, and obtained his title while serving in the Indian campaigns and the colonial wars   His death occurred at Weathersfield in April, 1665   In his family were five sons and three daughters, one of whom was Joseph, whose son Joseph also had a son of that time, who became the father of Isaac Hollister, our subject's grandfather, a native of Glastonbury, Connecticut

Miss Hollister's father, Edmund Hollister, was born in Glastonbury, December 28, 1867, but was reared in Granville, New York, and obtained a good education in the Granville Academy, after which he successfully engaged in teaching for some time during early life   On the 11th of January, 1832, in Granville, he was united in marriage to Miss Emma Louisa Hall, who was born in 1807, and was a daughter of Hon Nathaniel Hall, of White Hall, New York In 1837 Mr Hollister left his eastern home and emigrated to Port Byron, Illinois, becoming one of the pioneers of Rock Island county   On first settling here he engaged in the manufacture of lumber on Mill creek, but in 1854 purchased the farm on which his daughter now resides and turned his attention to agricultural pursuits   He died upon that place in 1890, and in March, 1892, his wife also passed away, being interred by his side in Fairfield cemetery, Coe township, where a suitable monument marks their last resting place   Edmund Hollister

labored with all the strength of a great nature and all the earnestness of a true heart for the bettering of the world about him, and when he was called to the rest and reward of the higher world his best monument was found in the love and respect of the community in which he lived for so many years

To Mr and Mrs Hollister were born three sons and two daughters, as follows (1) Lucy Cornelia, a native of New York, was reared in Rock Island county, and was educated in the schools of Milan and Rock Island   On the 27th of February, 1856, she gave her hand in marriage to Hon. A. S Coe, an honored pioneer of Coe township, who was born in Monroe county, New York, in 1817, and was a son of Simeon Maltby Coe, a native of New York   On first coming to Illinois, in 1836, the Coe family located near Sterling in Whiteside county, but in 1840 took up their residence in what is now Coe township, where A S Coe successfully engaged in the nursery and horticultural business   He took quite an active and prominent part in public affairs, was for one term a member of the state legislature, and was supervisor and member of the county board for several years   He owned a valuable farm of one hundred acres set out in trees and shrubs and everything found in a complete nursery   His political support was given the men and measures of the Republican party   He died October 17, 1869, leaving a family of six children, of whom three are still living   Edmund Hollister, who is married and engaged in farming on the old homestead, Emma Louisa, now the wife of Professor Wallace H Wigam, of the West Side Commercial College of Chicago, and Simeon F , who resides with his mother   (2)   Emma Louisa Hollister is the

second of the family. Her childhood and
youth were passed in Milan and Port Byron,
and in the schools of Rock Island and Milan,
she obtained her education   In 1864 and
1865 she visited New York, and has since
traveled in Iowa, visiting friends and relatives in those states   She is a faithful member of the Congregational church of Port
Byron, and is loved and respected by all
who know her   (3) Albert F Hollister is
represented elsewhere in this volume   (4)
Edmond Nathaniel Hollister enlisted in the
Union army for three years, as a member of
the One Hundred Twenty-sixth Illinois Volunteer Infantry and after the war successfully
engaged in farming near Port Byron   He
was an active and prominent member of the
Congregational church, served as supervisor
of his township and filled a number of official
positions of honor and trust   He died in
October, 1896, leaving a wife, who was in
her maidenhood Miss Agnes J Plummer and
still resides in Port Byron   (5) Isaac Frederick Hollister, also one of the brave boys
in blue, belonged to the Twelfth Illinois
Volunteer Infantry, participated in the battles
of Fort Donelson and Shiloh, and being severely wounded was honorably discharged
He then took a commercial course in Chicago, but died on the 4th of February, 1864

JACOB L HARRIS, a representative
agriculturist of Edgington township, is
finely located on section 5, where he owns
one of the most fertile and desirable farms
in the county   His operations have been
marked with uniform success, and in addition to being a thorough and skillful farmer,
he is a business man of more than ordinary
capacities, wise and judicious in his investments, and ?? ?? ?? ?? ?? ?? ?? ?? ??

afforded at this day and age by improved
machinery and all other appliances required
by the modern tiller of the soil

St. Joseph county, Indiana, was the
earliest home of our subject, his birth occurring there September 17, 1837, but during his infancy he was brought to Rock Isl-
and county by his parents, Thomas and
Jane (Findley) Harris, the former a native
of Ohio, and the latter of Pennsylvania
His paternal grandfather, Jacob Harris, was
born in Scotland, and during childhood
started for America in company with his
parents and brother, but his father died on
the ocean   On reaching the shores of this
country he was bound out to a German living in Pennsylvania, and soon learned to
speak the German language   He became a
cabinetmaker and joiner, and, as a pioneer,
moved to St Joseph county, Indiana, locating in Harris township, which was named
in his honor   There he reared his family of
twelve children, who were all living at the
time of his death, which occurred when he
was past the age of ninety years   Andrew
Findley, our subject's maternal grandfather,
was born in Pennsylvania and was of English extraction   He also settled in Indiana
at an early day, and in 1857 emigrated to
Minnesota, carrying on farming in both
states   He was twice married and became
the father of twenty children   In 1885 he
went to California, where he died five years
later at the age of eighty years

With a wagon and ox team Thomas
Harris, father of our subject, moved west
to Missouri, about 1838, and took up his
residence in Buchanan county, where he
resided a few years and then returned to
Indiana   In about 1849 he moved to Rock
Island county where he entered two hundred and forty acres which he at once be-

gan to improve and cultivate, soon transforming the wild land into a most productive farm In 1859 he built the large and handsome house now owned and occupied by our subject, and there made his home until his death At one time he was one of the largest land owners in the county, was continually buying and selling real estate, and met with excellent success in his undertakings. The old homestead contained one hundred and twenty acres In 1859 he went to Pike's Peak on a prospecting tour, and the following year, in company with his son, Jacob, again started for the gold fields He died on the plains July 3, 1860, while on his way home, and the following day was buried at Omaha, Nebraska His wife survived him until the fall of 1865, when she, too, was called to her final rest, at the age of forty-five He was forty-four at the time of his death Originally both were members of the Lutheran church, but as there was no church of that denomination in this community, she joined the Baptists During the Mormon trouble Mr Harris raised a company and helped to drive out people from Nauvoo, Illinois, and was ever prominently identified with the interests of his adopted state His sterling worth was widely recognized, and his circle of friends and acquaintances was very extensive

Our subject is one of a family of ten children, of whom seven are still living, five sons and two daughters, the others being as follows John S , now a resident of Colorado, Henry C , of Rock Island, Samuel H , of Glenwood Springs, Colorado, Sebaldus, who lives near Sacramento, California, Adelia, wife of Mr McNeil, of Spokane Falls, Washington, and Veritas, wife of Charles Thompson, of Glenwood Springs Colorado

With the exception of eight years spent in farming in Jasper county, Iowa, Jacob L Harris has made his home in Edgington township, Rock Island county, since infancy, and in its public schools began his education, which was completed at the high school of Edgington He has always followed agricultural pursuits and has added to the old homestead of one hundred and twenty acres, until he now has four hundred and eighty-five acres of the best land to be found in the county

On the 11th of September, 1862 Mr Harris was united in marriage to Miss Ann Eliza, a daughter of Thomas and Rachel McGrew, early residents of Ohio Her paternal grandfather, Nathan McGrew, was of Scotch-Irish descent, and was a farmer by occupation, while her maternal grandfather, David Robbins, was a native of Pennsylvania, and was an early settler of Illinois City, Illinois Mrs Harris' mother was also born in the Keystone state, and at a very early day was brought by her parents to this state, where she was married Mr McGrew was never a resident of Illinois, only coming here for his wife, after which he returned to Ohio, where he died in 1855, when in middle life Four years later his widow returned to the Prairie state and took up her residence in Buffalo Prairie township, Rock Island county, where she spent seven years Since that time, however, she has been a resident of Jasper county, Iowa In her family were three sons and three daughters, namely Nathan, Elizabeth Jane, wife of George Pence, Ann Eliza, wife of our subject, Keziah, David and Thomas

Mr and Mrs Harris have become the parents of two sons, George T and Ernest L ort Business College and later took a scientific course at Hopkinton, Iowa. He married Miss Hayden, of Rock Island, and has two children, Anna and Mabel. Ernest L. first attended the Mt. Vernon College of Iowa, and afterward went to Germany, at first pursuing his studies in Berlin and later in Heidelberg, where he entered the university, and graduated in 1895 with the degrees of M. A., Ph. D. and LL. D. While in Heidelberg he was married Thursday, March 5, 1896, at the home of the bride's mother, Mrs. Minna Herbst, to Else Herbst. After a wedding tour through Switzerland, they came to America, and now reside in Rock Island. They have one child, Wilhelmina Elizabeth. While abroad Ernest L. Harris also traveled through England, Ireland, Scotland, France, and all the other countries of Europe.

Politically, Mr. Harris is a true-blue Republican, and has held a number of township offices. His estimable wife is a member of the Presbyterian church, which he supports and attends with her, and they certainly deserve honorable mention among the representative and prominent citizens of Rock Island county, none occupying a more enviable position in social circles.

ALBERT J. WHITNEY.—The subject of this history, a man of more than ordinary intelligence and business capacity, owns a fine farm of three hundred acres on section 28 Buffalo Prairie township, and is prominent among the agricultural interests of Rock Island county, contributing largely to its reputation by building up one of the most desirable homesteads within its borders. He is one the peer of life and the midst of his ... honored and esteemed

by his friends and neighbors, and enjoying, as he deserves, a generous portion of this world's goods.

Mr. Whitney is a native of Buffalo Prairie township, born April 15, 1854, a son of Flavel J. Whitney, whose birth occurred in Portage county, Ohio, May 31, 1819. The family, which is of English origin, was founded in Connecticut during early colonial days, and in that state Josiah Whitney, grandfather of our subject, was born. He became a pioneer settler of Portage county, Ohio, where in the midst of the wilderness he developed a large farm and reared his family.

On June 9, 1849, Flavel J. Whitney wedded Miss Louisa Norton, a native of Moscow, New York, and a daughter of Ansel Norton, who was also an early settler of Portage county, Ohio, and lived on a farm adjoining the Whitneys. In 1840 Mr. Whitney came to Illinois and settled in Rock Island county, taking up their residence in Buffalo Prairie township, where Mr. Whitney entered government land. He was the first to engage in teaching on the prairie, conducting a school in his own home before any school-house had been erected, and his neighbors paid the tuition of the scholars in corn and oats, or hauled rails for him. He broke and fenced his land and added to his original purchase from time to time until he had over four hundred acres of valuable land and was numbered among the thrifty and well-to-do farmers. He assisted in organizing the township, was elected the first township clerk and continued to acceptably serve in that position for eighteen consecutive years. He was also the first justice of the peace, serving about thirty years. He was also the first postmaster of Buffalo Prairie, serving sixteen years, was township treasurer for a number of years, and a member of the board of supervisors for some years, and most faithfully performed the duties of these offices, thus winning the commendation of all concerned His public and private career were alike above reproach and he was honored and esteemed by all who knew him He died February 8, 1882, upon the farm where he first located on coming to the county, but his wife is still living and makes her home with her children In their family were three sons and two daughters Herbert F, who was married and died in Buffalo Prairie township, in 1895, Albert J, of this sketch, Dr Perry N, a resident physician of Cedar Vale, Kansas, Emma L, wife of J R Wylie, of Denver, Colorado, and Eva M wife of W S Hand, of Buffalo Prairie township

Albert J Whitney acquired his early education in the common schools of Rock Island county, and later attended Lombard University, at Galesburg, Illinois, for two years Subsequently for several years he successfully engaged in teaching, making his home with his parents until 1876, when he located upon his present place, which is a portion of the old homestead After the death of his father he became the owner of two hundred and twenty acres belonging to the estate, having purchased the interests of the other heirs, and to this has added an eighty-acre tract, making it one of the best farms in the township It is improved with a large and substantial residence, good barns and outbuildings, a fine orchard and two and a half miles of hedge fence. Besides general farming he is extensively interested in the breeding of fine stock, including Percheron horses and Poland China hogs and Hereford cattle. In 1892 he began raising th

a herd, the finest to be found in this section of the state

In Mercer county, Illinois, Mr Whitney was married, January 17, 1884, the lady of his choice being Miss Rilla A Kincaid, who was born and reared in that county and educated at the Aledo Academy Her father, Frank Kincaid, is now a resident of New Windsor, Illinois Six children grace this union—Bertha L, Bessie M, Mabel R, Frank J, Blanche L and Ruth C

In politics, Mr Whitney is a stanch Democrat and was the third of that party elected township clerk in Buffalo Prairie township, a position he has now filled for about eight years with credit to himself and to the satisfaction of his constituents He has been a delegate to numerous county conventions and for several years was a most efficient member of the school board, having always taken an active interest in educational affairs Upright and honorable in all the relations of life he has gained the respect and confidence of all with whom he has come in contact and has made many friends throughout his native county

---

DANIEL HARTWELL is a leading representative of the industrial interests of Moline, and his successful life demonstrates the possibilities that lie before young men of energy and determination He is now enjoying a large trade as a plumber, gas and steam fitter, and has a well appointed establishment at No 1104 Third avenue

Mr Hartwell was born in Sullivan county, New York, August 9, 1857, and is a son of Daniel Hartwell, Sr His mother died at his birth and he was reared in another ent on a farm until sixteen years of age, when he went to New York City, where he remained for four years At the age of twenty-two he began learning the plumber's and gas fitter's trade in McKean county, Pennsylvania, and became an expert workman In 1881, he removed to Davenport, Iowa, and soon afterward secured employment in the corn planter works in Moline, where he remained for a few months He next became salesman for the Moline Pump Company, and then with a desire of reaping the profit from his own labors he embarked in business for himself as a plumber and steam and gas fitter

On the 22d of June, 1887, in Moline, Mr Hartwell was united in marriage to Mrs Sarah Hardin, née Schofer She was born in Moline and is a daughter of Jacob and Sarah Schofer. Mr and Mrs Hartwell now have one child, Irving, who was born in Moline, August 26, 1892. Their many excellencies of character have gained them a large circle of friends who esteem them highly for their sterling worth In politics Mr Hartwell has been a stalwart Republican since casting his first presidential vote for Garfield, but has never been an aspirant for political honors He belongs to the Masonic Lodge and the Knights of Pythias fraternity and is highly regarded by his brethren of those orders, who recognize his sterling worth and true manliness

It will be interesting in this connection to note something of the Schofer family, of which Mrs Hartwell is a representative, for her parents were numbered among the pioneer settlers of the county Her brother, John M Schofer, who resides at No 1203 Twelfth avenue, was born in Moline, March 5, 1855 ''   ''   ''   '   ''   ''   ''   ''
came with   ''   ''   ''   ''   ''   ''   ''

childhood and was reared to manhood in Pennsylvania, where he learned the miller's trade. In the fall of 1845, he came to Moline, where he was married Ten children were born to this union, two of whom died in childhood, while eight are still living, namely Lawrence Emerson, of Prospect Park, who has two children, John M ; Mrs Hartwell, Alvin Henry, a painter by trade, living in Rock Island, who is married and has five children, Clara A., wife of John Peterson, who is living near Moline and has two children, Mary F. wife of Swan Johnson, who resides near Moline and has three children, Frank Douglas, of Prospect Park, who has three children, and Le Roy, a molder by trade, who is married and lives in Rock Island

The father of this family supported the Democracy. He was a member of the United Brethren church, filled the office of trustee, and for a number of years served as class leader For some time he held membership in the Odd Fellows Society, but in later life did not continue his affiliations

John M Schofer spent his boyhood in Moline, attended the public schools, and when about fourteen years of age began working for the Dimmock & Gould Sawmill Company, in whose employ he remained twelve years, giving his wages to his father until after he had attained his majority Later he was employed in the corn planter works for about seventeen years He continued his residence in Rock Island until 1894, when he purchased his present home in Moline

Mr Schofer was married December 21, 1882, to Ellen C Connell, a native of Rock Island, and a daughter of John and Nancy (Connell) Connell Three children were born of this union John J, born in Rock

Island, December 11, 1883, Mary E, who died in infancy, and Frances, born in Rock Island, July 27, 1891 John M Schofer was a Democrat until 1896 when he voted with the Republican party He is a member of Camp No 38, M W A, and King Philips Tribe, No 94, Improved Order of Red Men In the last named he is filling the office of junior sagamore, and is one of the active workers in the team

WILLIAM STUHR —Among those agriculturists of Hampton township whose places manifest to the most casual observer the energy and ability of their owner in his chosen calling, is the subject of this personal history His residence, which is a very neat and comfortable one, is situated on section 24, where he owns two hundred and ninety acres of valuable land, and besides general farming is successfully engaged in stock-raising

In the township where he still continues to live, Mr Stuhr first opened his eyes to the light of day February 15, 1852, and is a son of Joseph and Anna (Comafeldt) Stuhr, who were born, reared and married in Germany, and soon after their wedding emigrated to America After a time spent in the vicinity of St Louis they came to Hampton township, Rock Island county and with the few hundred dollars which the father possessed, he purchased a small tract of thirty acres, but as he prospered in his undertaking he was able to add to this amount two forty-acre tracts In his family were seven children, but only three are now living—John, who carries on farming in Henry county, Illinois, William and Bertha, wife of Justus Heeren, of Port Byron, by whom sl

William Stuhr grew to manhood upon the home farm and acquired his education in the district schools of the neighborhood He and his two brothers, John and Henry, carried on their farming operations together until Henry died. In 1879 they had purchased sixty acres, and two years later Henry and our subject bought one hundred and ninety acres, but in October, 1881, the former died, and our subject then purchased his interest in the property He now has two hundred and ninety acres of rich and arable land, supplied with all the conveniences and accessories of a model farm of the present century

On the 1st of September, 1881, Mr Stuhr was joined in wedlock with Miss Anna Belling, a native of Hampton township, and a daughter of Andrew Belling She received a good common-school education and is a lady of cultured and refined tastes Both she and her husband hold membership in the German Lutheran church, and have the respect and esteem of all with whom they come in contact His father was a Republican in politics, but he votes independent of party ties, endeavoring to support the man best qualified for the office

JOHN DEVINNEY is one of the busiest, most energetic and most enterprising men of Hampton township, his home being on section 10, where he is successfully engaged in farming stock raising and the breeding of thoroughbred Hambletonian horses He was born on that section September 13 1837, a son of Andrew and Edith (Wainwright) Devinney, honored pioneers and highly respected citizens of Rock native of

Indiana county, Pennsylvania, born in 1806, of Irish ancestry, but the birth of the mother occurred in Lancastershire, England They were married in the Keystone state, where they continued to live for a few years, and where their two oldest children were born In 1834, however, they emigrated to Illinois, and the same year the father entered land on section 10, Hampton township, but for a short time lived on another farm Subsequently he built a house and located on his own place, and in connection with its cultivation and improvement, also engaged in lumbering and rafting logs down the river to Moline, Rock Island and Davenport He died at the age of seventy-two, having only survived his wife about three months, and both were buried in a private cemetery on the home farm on section 10, Hampton township

At the age of seventeen our subject began his career, he and his brother erecting a steam sawmill on the home farm and furnishing nearly all of the hard wood lumber that was used in Rock Island, Moline and Davenport for many years. He was interested in that business for about fifteen years, and at the age of eighteen began investing in lands, from which he would cut the timber and then sell He also devoted considerable attention to farming, and now owns three hundred and twenty acres on section 10, Hampton township, and one hundred and sixty acres of well improved land in Jasper county, Iowa

On the 28th of February, 1858, was celebrated the marriage of Mr. Devinney and Miss Fannie F Cook, of Hampton township, a daughter of Horace and Harriet E (Mears) Cook Eight children have been born t th..., . . "... - S ua..l A , a mechanic   . .) . .. wh. . . . .rn. d

and has two children, Mary, wife of Calvin Segur, of Ida county, Iowa, by whom she has five children, Hattie, wife of John Searls, of Zuma township, Rock Island county, George, a farmer of Hampton township, who is married and has two children, John, who married Inez Adams, who is now deceased They had one child He now makes his home with his father; Albert, who is married and lives in Hampton township, and Andrew, who was born August 27, 1879, and is still at home.

Mr Devinney voted for Lincoln in 1864, later supported Weaver, and in 1896 cast his ballot for Bryan Thus it can be seen that he is independent in politics, preferring not to be bound by party ties He has filled some of the offices in Alpha Lodge, No 420, A F & A M , of Port Byron, of which he is a member, and belongs to the Methodist Episcopal church at that place, of which he is now trustee Tireless energy, keen perception, honesty of purpose, a genius for devising and executing the right thing at the right time, joined to every-day common sense, guided by resistless will power, are the chief characteristics of the man, and in business affairs he is always energetic, prompt and notably reliable

SYLVESTER DAILEY, whose home is on section 4, Zuma township, is one of the most active and enterprising farmers and dairymen of Rock Island county Greater fortunes have been accumulated, but few lives furnish so striking an example of the wise application of sound principles and safe conservatism as does his The story of his success is short and simple, containing no ...ttin. .h.pt..., but in it lies one of the most valuable secrets of the great prosperity which it records, and his business and private life are pregnant with interest and incentive, no matter how lacking in dramatic action,—the record of a noble life, consistent with itself and its possibilities in every particular

On the farm where he still resides, Mr Dailey was born December 1, 1840, a son of David and Caroline M (Dow) Dailey, natives of Vermont and Massachusetts, respectively The father was born in February, 1813, and being a natural mechanic he worked at various trades, including carpentering and joining, and was employed as a stone mason on the state capitol of Vermont. On leaving the Green Mountain state he started for Illinois, coming by water to Chicago, where he purchased a yoke of oxen and drove across the country to Rock Island county, arriving here in August, 1838, when the greater part of this region was still in its primitive condition In Zuma township he took up a claim, built a log house and resided there for three years, it being the farm on which our subject now resides The father then bought land in the Rock River bottom, and moving his house to that place, made it his home for the same length of time, when he sold and purchased another tract of three hundred and eighty acres, which he transformed into a highly productive and well improved farm There he spent the last years of his life, dying in 1881, at the age of sixty-eight years His wife passed away in the spring of 1893, at the age of eighty-six and now lies by his side in Zuma cemetery For some years he served as justice of the peace and was everywhere recognized as one of the most prominent and influential citizens of the township, as well as one of its honored pioneers. He

Brethren church Of his six children five reached years of maturity but only Sylvester and Lyman are now living

Amid pioneer scenes the subject of this sketch grew to manhood, and as his school privileges were limited to a few months' attendance at the subscription schools, he is almost wholly self-educated by reading and study since reaching manhood On attaining his majority he left home and started out in life for himself His first purchase consisted of forty acres of bottom land on Rock river, in Zuma township, to which he later added a like amount, and at once commenced to develop and improve the same, making it his home for twelve years On the 21st of February, 1865, he enlisted in Company A, One Hundred and Fifty-sixth Illinois Infantry and with his regiment proceeded to Chattanooga He was on duty in the south until the close of the war, being stationed most of the time in Georgia and at Memphis, Tennessee, where he was mustered out September 29, 1865

Previous to his enlistment Mr Dailey was married, October 15 1863, to Miss Elizabeth Allen, a native of Coe township, Rock Island county, and a daughter of David Allen, whose father, David Allen, Sr, was one of the first settlers of the county, and a composer and teacher of music The children born of this union are as follows Frank a mechanic, who is engaged in business in Joslin, Rock Island county; John C, also a mechanic, who is now engaged in farming on the home place, George C, an engineer and buttermaker, who now conducts his father s creamery and feedmill, and Mary, wife of Professor Charles Argubright, who is teaching in a business college and the public schools of Woodbine Iowa

school privileges, and previous to her marriage the daughter was a stenographer in the government employ, being with Mr Wheeler, who constructed the Hennepin canal

After his return from the war, Mr Dailey returned to his first farm, but after living there for ten years he sold and purchased one hundred and ninety-three acres of partially improved land on section 4, Zuma township, which he has transformed into his present valuable farm   Later he bought eighty acres adjoining, and upon that tract lived for ten years, after which he spent two years in Port Byron for the purpose of educating his children   He then returned to his farm, which is one of the most desirable places in the county, improved with three good residences, substantial barns and outbuildings, all of which he has erected, being a practical mechanic. He not only did the carpenter work but also manufactured the brick used for foundations and chimneys   In 1895 he built a creamery upon his place, which has been in successful operation since the 4th of April of that year, and also conducts a feed mill, besides carrying on his large farm in a most thorough and profitable manner   In 1897 he bought another feed mill and creamery in Coe township, four miles from his home   Through his own unaided efforts he has won prosperity, and is to-day one of the wealthy and most substantial agriculturists of Zuma township   His paternal and maternal great-grandfathers both served seven years each in the Revolutionary war

Sylvester Dailey began for himself without a cent, going in debt for an ax to earn his first money   Bought the ax, but made the handle himself, as he felt that he could not   ,

Since   ,   Mr that

Lincoln in 1864 Mr Dailey has been an unswerving Republican in politics, and has served as a delegate to a number of conventions   He has also served his fellow citizens in the capacity of collector, road commissioner nine years, and school director for a number of years, with credit to himself and to the entire satisfaction of all concerned   He and his wife are faithful members of the United Brethren church, while his daughter belongs to the Methodist Episcopal church, and the family is one of prominence, holding an enviable position in social circles, where their sterling worth is justly appreciated

CAPTAIN DANIEL C DAGGETT —
   The history of a county, as well as that of a nation, is chiefly the chronicles of the lives and deeds of those who have conferred honor and dignity upon society   The world judges the character of a community by those of its representative citizens, and yields its tributes of admiration and respect for the genius, learning or virtues of those whose works and actions constitute the record of a state's prosperity and pride There it is proper that a just celebrity would be given to those men who are distinguished in their day and generation, that the living may enjoy the approbation of their contemporaries, as well as that of a grateful posterity   Among the most prominent men of Rock Island county is Captain Daggett, who is commanding officer of the entire naval force of the state, as well as a leading business man and influential citizen of Moline, his residence being at 920 Twelfth avenue

The Captain was born at Norwalk, Ohio, January 15, . . . and belongs to a family that is connected with some of the most distinguished people of the new world The first of the Daggetts to come to this country was John Daggett, who when a young man crossed the Atlantic in 1630 and took up his residence in Massachusetts He was a son of William Daggett, a merchant and exporter, residing in Boxford, England The family had twenty-four representatives in the Revolutionary war, including a captain, a colonel and Lieutenant Daniel Daggett, and has also been well represented in the other wars of this country It is connected by blood and marriage to Daniel Webster and other great statesmen, and by three different lines with the poet Whittier

Captain D. C Daggett, our subject's father, was a native of Taunton, Massachusetts, where he grew to manhood and married Miss Mary Elizabeth Brown, of Newburyport, who also belonged to an old family of English origin, founded in this country in 1630 In 1854 they removed to Norwalk, Ohio, where the Captain engaged in railroading as a mechanic and was made master mechanic just prior to the Civil war He assisted in organizing a company, which was mustered into service as Company D, Eighth Ohio Infantry, in 1861, and he was commissioned second lieutenant When discharged at the close of the war he held the rank of captain, and had also served as quartermaster and adjutant of his regiment After his return home, he joined his father in Milwaukee, Wisconsin, where they built the first match factory in the west, the machinery being brought from Bangor, Maine There he remained with his family and continued to make his home until called to his final rest in 1883 He was an honored member of the Loyal Legion and highly resp.......... .. ..

wife passed away in 1873 Their children are as follows George H, who is now connected with the Board of Trade of Minneapolis and is a grain commission merchant of that city, Frank S, who is living retired in Passadena, California, D C, of this review, Arthur F, junior member of the firm of George H Daggett & Company, of Minneapolis, and Lilla, wife of Charles L Burgmeyer, of New York

Captain Daggett, of this review, was reared and educated in Milwaukee, where he remained until he had attained his majority He traveled for two years through the eastern states, and also spent about three years in Colorado, principally for his health On his return to Milwaukee, he spent only a few months there, and then came to Moline, where he accepted a position in the shipping department of the Deere & Mansur Company, with which he has since been connected, being promoted from time to time until he now holds the responsible position of advertising manager and is a stockholder

Here Captain Daggett was married January 15, 1880, to Miss Lida L Bustard, a native of Illinois, who was reared and educated in Rock Island county, of which her father, John Bustard, an eastern gentleman, was one of the pioneers The children born to them are Bertha May, Frank Stacy and Lilla, who are all attending school in Moline, and one son who died in infancy

The Captain is a firm supporter of the men and measures of the Republican party and although he has never aspired to official honors, he most acceptably served as alderman for one term As a member of the State militia, in 1893, he organized the Second Battalion of Naval Militia of Illinois, which consists of four companies of seventy

men each, representing a ship's crew   Two
of the companies are located in Moline, one
in Alton and one in Quincy, the last being
mustered in by Captain Daggett, in May,
1897   He was commissioned first commanding officer by Governor Altgeld, and as
such has command of the entire naval force
of the state   The desk of the commanding
officer displayed in the battle ship, Illinois,
at the World's Fair in Chicago, was presented to the state by an act of congress,
together with the other equipments of that
vessel, and the state in turn presented it to
Captain Daggett, who numbers it among
his most valuable possessions   Socially he
is a member of the Society of Colonial
Wars, the Sons of the Revolution, and an
associate member of the United States Naval
Institute   As an honored and valued citizen of Moline, he certainly deserves honorable mention in a work of this character,
whose object it is to perpetuate the lives of
the leading and most eminent men of this
section of the state

REV LOUIS A C WINTER, pastor
of the Zion Evangelical Lutheran
church, which is situated in section 16,
Hampton township, has for twenty-six years
filled the pulpit of that church and resides
in the parsonage near by   He was born
in the province of Saxony, in the kingdom of Prussia, and is a son of August
and Frederica Winter   The mother died
when he was five years of age and the
father died five years later, leaving three
children, while three others had passed
away in childhood   Those who survived
were Louis, August and Amelia, now the
wife of William Schroether of Rock Island
When or['   .   \ at (five with (

paternal uncle who soon afterward came to
America, locating in Altenburg, Perry county, Missouri

Rev Mr Winter, who was born November 1, 1845, was about eleven years of age
when he came to America   He was reared
in the Lutheran faith, was confirmed at the
age of thirteen, and about that time determined to enter the Master's vineyard and
devote his life to the ministry   For two
years he pursued his studies in Concordia
College, and continued among its pupils for
four years after the removal of the school to
Fort Wayne.   He then returned to St
Louis, where he spent three years in a seminary, and thus by a broad and liberal education was well fitted for his chosen profession

Mr. Winter began preaching when about
twenty years of age, delivering his first ser-
mon as a student in East St Louis   He
was ordained at Boone, Iowa, when about
twenty-three years of age, and entered upon
his first pastoral work at that place   For a
year and a half he remained in Boone, and
then came to Hampton township, Rock
Island county, where he has since continued as the loved pastor of the congregation
of Zion Evangelical church   In 1877 the
parsonage was destroyed by fire and the
records were burned, but the work that Mr
Winter has accomplished is indicated in a
measure by the following   From July 31,
1874, to March 23, 1897, he baptized five
hundred and seventy-three children and confirmed two hundred and twenty-nine, all of
whom received their instructions in catechism
work under his direction   Since 1880 two
thousand, five hundred and ninety have participated in the communion service, and
from March 17, 1878, until May 20, 1897,
he married eighty-eight couples and preached

one hundred and thirty funeral sermons between January 20, 1874, and May 25, 1897

While in Boone, Iowa, Mr Winter was united in marriage April 13, 1871, to Miss Eva Beierlein, of Rock Island, a daughter of John and Margaret (Heinzel) Beierlein She was a student in the Lutheran parochial schools, and to her husband has been a most able and earnest assistant in his work Their union has been blessed with nine children, and with the exception of August, who died at the age of fourteen and was buried in the Rock Island cemetery, all are yet living These are Louis, Cecelia, William, Ernest, Anna, Albert and Clara

JOHN A. P BERG —Success in any line of occupation, in any avenue of business, is not a matter of spontaneity, but is the legitimate offspring of subjective effort in the proper utilization of the means at hand, the improvement of opportunity and the exercise of the highest functions made possible by specific ability in any case In view of this condition the study of biography becomes of value and its lessons of practical use Among the representative business men and contractors and builders of Moline is Mr Berg, who has for over a quarter of a century been identified with the development and prosperity of the city His home is at 1203 Seventh avenue

Mr Berg was born February 13, 1839, in the Province of Smalen, Sweden, where he grew to manhood and was educated in the common schools, and also became familiar with various pursuits, including carpentering, the millwright's, brick and stone mason's trades Before leaving his native land he also engaged in contracting and building He was married in Sweden, in 1865, to Miss Johanna Frederica Johnson

also a native of that country, and there their only daughter was born

With his little family, Mr Berg crossed the Atlantic in 1868, and by way of Quebec, Montreal and Chicago, went to Rockford, Winnebago county, Illinois, where he resumed contracting and building and assisted in the erection of the Swedish Lutheran church In 1880, he located in Rock Island, where for two seasons he assisted in the construction of the arsenal, the last season being foreman of one department At the end of that time he came to Moline He has erected some of the largest public buildings in the county, including Augustana College, four churches in Moline and the Grant and Lincoln school-houses, which stand as monuments to his architectural skill He also built the high school at Geneseo, Illinois, and has the contract for the court house in Fulton county, now under course of construction Besides these he has erected many of the best residences and business blocks in Moline and Rock Island He is prompt and faithful in carrying out his part of every contract, is recognized as one of the most thorough and reliable builders of the city, and his work has given universal satisfaction. On the organization of the Moline Manufacturing Company, in 1892, he became a stockholder and was elected its first president They are extensively engaged in the manufacture of brick in East Moline, their plant covering one hundred twenty acres Mr Berg is also a stockholder in the Moline Furniture Company

Mr Berg is the inventor of several useful articles, among which is an adjustable clamp hook used for the hanging of any kind of platform or scaffolding, such as is used by painters, carpenters, and other trades A very simple device but easily adjustable, and capable of sustaining great weight An improvement in heating furnaces by which more heat is obtained at less expense than with any other contrivance now known Another article is an adjustable platform to be used on roofs of houses, placed in position without the use of a nail and made as solid as the everlasting hills With this platform it is unnecessary to displace shingles to make a steady support One of the most useful of his inventions is a movable and adjustable derrick, so constructed that it can be partially closed or folded together, enabling it to be taken through an ordinary door, and yet stout enough to lift several tons weight

To our subject and his wife have been born seven sons and two daughters, of which one son, Oscar, and one daughter, Hannah, are dead The living are Anton Augusta, now the wife of Hans Bjorkman, of Moline, Anton Theodore, who is married and has two children and is with his father in business, Heening William, a mechanic, who is employed by Deere & Co, Carl August, who is with the same company, Arthur, who is engaged in clerking, and Gustafe Robert and Walter Rainhold, who are still attending school

Since casting his first presidential ballot for Rutherford B Hayes, Mr Berg has been a stanch Republican, which party his three oldest sons also support He has never cared for office, preferring to give his undivided attention to his extensive business interests, but faithfully discharges every duty of citizenship in a most commendable manner and gives his support to all worthy objects for the good of the community With the Lutheran church he and his family hold membership and are widely and favorably l

WILLIAM EDGINGTON, whose home is on section 12, Buffalo Prairie township, is accredited with the ownership of one of the best farms in the locality, it comprising two hundred and eighty acres of rich and arable land, which he has placed under a high state of cultivation, and the farm buildings and machinery upon the place are fully in keeping with the enterprise of the proprietor

Mr Edgington is living on a part of the old homestead where his birth occurred January 4, 1840, and belonged to one of the most highly respected pioneer families of the county His paternal grandfather, Asahel Edgington, was born in Pennsylvania of Scotch ancestry, and served as a soldier in some of the Indian wars of early days He was taken prisoner several times and once was held in captivity for over a year During pioneer days he emigrated to Ohio, where he died when John Edgington, our subject's father, was quite young

The father was born in Steubenville, Jefferson county, Ohio, in 1809, and for a number of years after reaching manhood engaged in merchandising in that state, where he met and married Miss Susan Crabbs, a native of Springfield, Ohio, and a daughter of Philip Crabbs, who was of German descent and was one of the pioneer settlers of Springfield It was in 1834 that John Edgington came to Rock Island county and entered six hundred and forty acres of wild land on sections 11 and 12, Buffalo Prairie township, which as time advanced he converted into an excellent farm, improved with a commodious and elegant residence and substantial outbuildings, it being one of the best stock farms in the county He added to his landed possessions and he had about six hundred acres and was numbered among the most prominent farmers and reliable business men of his community He personally assisted in building the first court house in Rock Island and cheerfully gave his support to all measures which he believed calculated to promote the moral, intellectual or material welfare of this section of the state His fellow citizens appreciating his sterling worth and ability called him to a number of important official positions including that of supervisor and he proved a most capable and trustworthy officer After the death of his wife, which occurred in 1885, he lived with his children for a time, and then removed to Reynolds, where he passed away February 16, 1897, honored and respected by all who knew him They now rest side by side in the Reynolds cemetery where a monument has been erected to their memory

In their family were nine children, two sons and seven daughters, as follows James, who was the first white child born north of Rock river in Rock Island county, and is now living retired in Reynolds, Sarah, who died at the age of twenty-two years, William E, of this review, Mrs Jane Walker, a resident of Moline, Mrs Margaret Dodge, of Galesburg, Illinois, Drucilla, wife of Rev. S H Parvin, a Presbyterian minister now located in Muscatine, Iowa, and Mrs Fred Titterington, of Rock Island

Upon the home farm William Edgington spent the days of his boyhood and youth, and in the local public schools acquired his elementary education which was supplemented by a course in Knox College of Galesburg On laying aside his text-books he returned to the farm and remained with his father until after he had attained his majority In this county he was married September 8, 1867, to Miss Emily P Beckett,

who was born, reared and educated in Williamstown, Vermont, and previous to her marriage successfully engaged in teaching Seven children have been born to them, five of whom are yet living and all have been provided with excellent school privileges, completing their educations at Knox College, or Aurora, Illinois, with the exception of the youngest They are as follows Susan B, a successful teacher of Rock Island county, Charles William, who is assisting his father on the farm, Mary J, also a teacher, Frank E, at home, and James Everett, who is still attending school

After his marriage Mr Edgington located upon a part of the old homestead where he still resides and has a large, pleasant residence where hospitality reigns supreme, the many friends of the family always being sure to find a hearty welcome Politically he follows in the footsteps of his father, having always supported the men and measures of the Democratic party since casting his first presidential ballot for Stephen A Douglas, "the little giant," in 1860 He has been a delegate to a number of county, congressional and state conventions, and was a member of the county board of supervisors at the time of the erection of the present elegant court house in Rock Island, which stands as a monument to their energy and enterprise As a member of the school board, he has for a quarter of a century been active in promoting the cause of education in his township and elevating the grade of schools While not a member of any religious organization, Mr Edgington is a liberal supporter of the Presbyterian church in Edgington, to which his wife and four children belong, and when the present house of worship was erected he was president of the building committee and as such his services were very effective in securing their neat little church He is an esteemed member of society and is held in high regard by all with whom he comes in contact, whether in business or social life

WILLIAM EDELMAN, a well-known livery man and a prominent and influential citizen of Hampton, was born March 1, 1836, in Wingershusen, Kries Schotten, Hessen-Darmstadt, Germany, and is a son of Peter and Anna (Theis) Edelman He attended the public schools of his native land until fourteen years of age, when he was confirmed in the German Lutheran church The father continued to engage in farming in that country until the son was eighteen years of age and then sold his property there and came to America on the sailing vessel, William Tell, which was thirty-two days in crossing the Atlantic, during which time they encountered a severe storm, which lasted three days They landed in New York in the fall of 1854, and the father purchased a little home at Coby's Corner, Monmouth county, New Jersey, but in the spring of 1856 came to Rock Island where he worked as a laborer

Our subject found employment on a farm, where he remained until after the outbreaking of the Civil war, when, August 12, 1862, he enlisted in Company K, One Hundred and Twenty-ninth Illinois Volunteer Infantry He was elected first corporal, but after about a year he resigned and served as private, and participated in the battle of Resaca, May 15, 1864, Cassville, Georgia, May 19, Dallas, May 25, Burned Hickory, June 15 At the last named engagement he was wounded in the right leg below the kne by a minie ball taken and until

the following morning lay on the battle field without attention, suffering untold agony When picked up by the ambulance he was taken to the field hospital, where his leg was amputated below the knee, but the following Friday he was taken to Marietta, Georgia, where with others he was put in a cattle car which conveyed them to Chattanooga While at the hospital at that place gangrene set in and a second operation was performed He next suffered from erysipelas and was sent to the ward for that disease. After two months spent in Chattanooga, he was sent to hospital No 19, Nashville, Tennessee, and in a short time afterward was granted a furlough and returned home, where the third amputation took place on account of the presence of dead bone This was performed by Dr Farral, of Rock Island In January, he went to the hospital in Quincy, where he remained until June 6, 1865, when he was honorably discharged and returned to Hampton

During that summer Mr Edelman taught a private school and the following winter pursued his studies in the public schools Going to Pleasant Valley, Iowa, he was there employed for about a year, and on his return to Hampton in the spring of 1867 was elected tax collector He had secured a team and successfully engaged in the huckstering business until 1871 He was married on the 9th of May, of that year to Miss Caroline M M. Burmeister, who had just come from Germany two weeks previous, it being a case of "love at first sight " To them were born six children, of whom one died in childhood Those living are Charles William, a fisherman living in Hampton, who is married and has one child, Anna, wife of Henry Guildenpfening, a farmer of Hampton township by whom she has three

children, Caroline M M , Sophia E , and
Irena L D

Soon after his marriage Mr Edelman
purchased the property where he now lives
and started a livery stable, which he has
since successfully conducted   He is also interested in the ice business, having a contract to furnish that commodity to the government vessels, and also does a large retail
business   He has taken quite an active
and prominent part in public affairs, has
served as collector three terms, was census
enumerator in 1880, has twice been president of the village board, is now alderman
and has served as judge of elections many
times   He is prompt and faithful in the
discharge of his official duties, and merits
and receives the confidence and esteem of
all with whom he comes in contact   After
becoming a citizen of this country, he cast
his first vote for Stephen A Douglas, but
has since been a loyal Republican, an unswerving supporter of the principles of that
party   He and his wife are consistent members of the German Lutheran church, known
as Zion church, of which he has been trustee for several years, and they are widely
and favorably known, their friends being
many throughout the county

WILLIAM H WHITESIDE —Hon-
ored and respected by all, there is no
man in Rock Island county who occupies a
more enviable position than Mr Whiteside
in mercantile and financial circles, not alone
on account of the success he has achieved,
but also on account of the honorable,
straightforward business policy he has ever
followed   He possesses untiring energy,
is quick of perception, forms his plans
readily, and   h   a   d   t   r

tion, and his close application to business
and his excellent management have brought
to him the high degree of success which to-
day is his   He is conducting a first-class
general store in Joslin, and is also a stockholder and manager of the Joslin creamery

A native son of Rock Island county, Mr.
Whiteside was born in Moline February 7,
1856, and is a son of William Whiteside, of
that city, whose sketch appears elsewhere in
this work   Our subject was reared in Zuma
township, and attended the common schools
to a limited extent, but is mainly self-educated   He remained at home until twenty-
five years of age, assisting in the operation
of the farm, and then went on the road as
a traveling salesman for harvesting machinery, being thus employed for five years,
during which time he traveled in Illinois,
Georgia, the Dakotas, and nearly all of the
wheat-growing states east of the Mississippi
On leaving the road Mr Whiteside came to
Joslin, where he embarked in general merchandising on a small scale, but has increased his stock from year to year to meet
the growing demands of his trade until he
now has a large line of everything found in
a first-class store of the kind   In 1895 he
erected his present substantial store building   Two years previous he purchased
stock in the Joslin Creamery, has been secretary, treasurer and general manager of the
company since its organization, and has
placed the business on a good paying basis

On the 3d of April, 1884, was consummated the marriage of Mr Whiteside and
Miss Mary Allen, a native of Henry county,
Illinois, who was educated in the graded
schools of Colona, and for some years previous to her marriage successfully engaged
in teaching   Three children grace this union
William E , Roy A and Florence K

Since attaining his majority, Mr Whiteside has been unwavering in his support of the principles of the Republican party, has been a member of the county central committee for the past ten years, was a delegate to a number of county, congressional and district conventions During President Harrison's administration he was postmaster of Joslin and proved a most popular official, always discharging his duties in a prompt and efficient manner In August, 1897, he was again appointed postmaster by President McKinley, and is now filling that office He is a member of the Masonic Order, and a member of the Home Forum and the Modern Woodmen Lodge of Joslin, in which he has served as clerk for three years. In 1876 he visited Europe and spent some time in England In this way he has gained a broad and comprehensive knowledge of places and events which only travel can bring As a public-spirited, progressive citizen, he gives his support to all enterprises which he believes calculated to benefit his community or advance the general welfare His wife, a most estimable lady, holds membership in the Methodist church Their elegant residence, which is the largest and finest in Joslin, has just been completed and there they delight to entertain their many friends

PHILIP KEENE —There is no element which has entered into our composite national fabric which has been of more practical strength, value and utility than that furnished by the sturdy, persevering and honorable sons of Germany, and in the progress of our Union this element has played an important part Intensely practical, and ever having ' i u j i h u i n d th

ethics of life, the German contingent has wielded a powerful influence, and this service can not be held in light estimation by those who appreciate true civilization and true advancement

Mr Keene, whose home is now at No 2116 Fifth avenue, Moline, was born in Bavaria, Germany, September 29, 1829, a son of George and Margaret Keene, who were farming people of that country, and emigrated to the new world in 1836 On landing at Baltimore, Maryland, they proceeded at once across the country to Wheeling, and there took passage on a river boat for Cincinnati They located at Newport, Kentucky, where the father engaged in agricultural pursuits until his death from an attack of cholera in 1852 The mother passed away at the same place about 1843, leaving two sons, the older of whom, John, married and settled at Newport By occupation he was a machinist. His death occurred September 2, 1897.

The educational privileges afforded our subject were very meagre, and he is almost wholly self-educated In Cincinnati he learned the machinist's trade, serving a four-years' apprenticeship, during which time he received but three dollars a week and had to board himself He continued to follow his trade in that city for two years, and then took charge of an engine in a cotton factory at Newport, where he remained for two years and a half, working in machine shops when the factory was not running Having been employed in the manufacture of steamboat engines and machinery, he came west in 1848, and for five or six years was an engineer on the Mississippi He brought the Rock Island & Davenport ferry boat from Cincinnati to Rock Island, where he located in 1855 and until 18 served as engineer on that vessel The boat was then taken south and later to Little Rock, where it was used in the government service as a transfer and ferry boat on the Arkansas river, Mr Keene serving as engineer, and and thus aiding his adopted country in her efforts to preserve the Union When hostilities had ceased he returned to Illinois in June, 1865, and for the following three years was engineer on a packet running between St Louis and St Paul Subsequently he accepted the position as engineer in the flouring-mills of R I Warner, remaining with him until the mill closed down, and in the meantime he was also employed by the city to run a fire engine Later he engaged in the flour and feed business in Rock Island for over a year, and in October, 1870, came to Moline to take charge of the engine in the big sawmill of Dimock & Gould He also has general supervision of their extensive steam plant, and for over a quarter of a century has now been one of their most valued and trusted employes

Mr Keene was married in Newport, Kentucky, May 1, 1850, to Miss Margaret K Baxter, a native of Delaware, who, during childhood, was taken by her father, William Baxter, to Newport, where he worked at his trade of cotton spinning There the mother died, but the father spent his declining years at the home of Mr Keene, in Rock Island To our subject and his estimable wife were born six children, namely Emma, now the wife of Judge Sullivan, of Grand Junction, Colorado, Annie, wife of W A Shields, of Pollock, Louisiana, Ida, wife of W C Tremper, of Providence, Rhode Island, Edward S, a man of scholarly attainments, who is now a professor in the mechanical department of the Agric it, '

Dakota; William B , a machinist by trade, who is now engaged in fruit farming in Grand Junction, Colorado, and Charles F , of the same place, who is now serving as cashier for the Denver & Rio Grande Railroad There were also three other children who died in infancy

Politically, Mr Keene has been identified with the Republican party since its organization, voting at Rock Island for John C. Fremont in 1856, but has never aspired to official positions, although he served as alderman from his ward for one term Both he and his wife are active and prominent members of the Methodist Episcopal church of Moline, with which he has been officially connected for a quarter of a century, serving as president of the board of trustees for twenty-three years Fraternally he is a Master Mason For forty-two long years he has been identified with the growth and development of Rock Island county, and his upright, honorable career has gained for him the confidence and respect of all with whom he has come in contact, either in business or social life

JOHN ALFRED JOHNSON, deceased, was born in Ostergotland, Sweden, and died in Hampton, February 2, 1896 He belonged to that class of modest, unpretending citizens, whose lives nevertheless contain many valuable lessons of devotion to duty, honesty in all relations and fidelity to principle He had the respect of all who knew him and his death was a loss to the entire community He was the eldest of a family of seven children and was about fifteen years of age when his father was drowned, leaving the family with no means of support his own resources and from that time made his own way in the world   He was reared on a farm and had a fair common-school education, but this was his only capital   His mother afterward married again, becoming the wife of August Freed, and they now reside in Moline

Mr Johnson came to America with his stepfather in 1868 and after a short time spent in Princeton, Illinois, removed to Moline, where he secured employment with the Moline Plow Company   He became a skilled polisher and was one of the trusted employes of that corporation   About this time he formed the acquaintance of Miss Hannah Josephine Anderson, who was born in southern Sweden and was only seven years of age when brought to America by her parents, John and Mary (Queenstrom) Anderson   Her father located in Watertown, where he worked for some years, after which he purchased a farm of forty acres. Mrs Johnson obtained a fair common-school education and was married at the early age of sixteen years, the wedding being celebrated October 7, 1876   The young couple resided in Moline until the following spring when they removed to her father's farm, where they remained one year, where they continued until the spring of 1879, when they took up their residence upon the farm which is now the home of Mrs Johnson   They rented the place for a time, but Mr Johnson later purchased it and transformed it into one of the finest farms of this section of the county, improved with all modern accessories and conveniences   The farm comprises one hundred acres and was acquired through the earnest and well directed efforts of our subject and the assistance of his estimable wife

Three chil ...   ... l th ... t this worthy cou, ... l i. u m who v ...

born in Hampton township, July 29, 1877, and died on the 6th of May, 1895, his remains being interred in Hampton cemetery, Carl Andrew, born in Hampton township, October 20, 1878, and Frank William Robert, born on the homestead, January 11, 1890   The two younger children are still with their mother on the farm

In his political affiliations Mr Johnson was a Republican and served as village trustee and police magistrate, filling the office with marked fidelity and ability   He was reared in the Lutheran faith, as was Mrs Johnson, and she now attends the Swedish Lutheran church in Moline   In appearance Mr Johnson was a man of slender build, hardly of medium height, with light hair and dark eyes   He made friends easily and his sterling worth enabled him to retain their friendship and regard when once gained   He was true to his duties of citizenship, faithful to every trust reposed in him, honorable in business and devoted to his family, and all who knew him entertained for him unqualified respect.   Mrs. Johnson still survives him and is living on the old homestead with her two sons, surrounded by many friends.

NELSON G ELLIOTT, an agriculturist residing on section 35, Buffalo Prairie township, is a man whose successful struggle with adverse circumstances shows what can be done by industry and economy, especially if a sensible wife second his efforts to secure a home and competence   He was obliged to make his way in life without any of the aids which are usually considered essential to success, but is now the owner of one of the most valuable farms in his section of the county

At a very early day in the history of this

country the Elliott family was founded in New England, and Ital Elliott, the grandfather of our subject, was born He became a resident of Broome county, New York, where his son, Lorenzo C, was born in 1816, and later took his family to Allegany county, that state, being one of its first settlers There the son who was our subject's father, grew to manhood and married Miss Mary Ann Davis, who was born, reared and educated there, and a daughter of Joseph Davis, also a pioneer of Allegany county, and a soldier of the war of 1812 For his service he was given a land warrant and located a tract in Rock Island county, Illinois In 1845 Mr Elliott came to this country and entered two hundred and twenty-two acres of land in Buffalo Prairie township on sections 34 and 35, which he transformed into a fine farm He took quite an active and prominent part in public affairs, serving as supervisor fifteen years and justice of the peace for a number of years, and was regarded as one of the most useful and valued citizens of his community He died here October 12, 1894, and was buried with Masonic honors, having been for a number of years an active member of that fraternity His worthy wife still resides on the old homestead at the age of seventy-four

In the family were nine children who reached the age of maturity, namely Adelia, now the wife of Marvin Freeman, of Oregon, Nelson G , of this sketch, Hattie, wife of Seth Parmanter, of Beloit, Kansas, Calista, wife of William Jennings, of Rock Island county, W D , who operates the old home place, Doctor A V , a physician of Beresford, South Dakota, Diana, wife of John Castor, of Mercer county, Illinois, Esthi i | ω ι ι Η ι, Γ ιιι

of Laurel, Iowa, Lunaette, wife of Thomas Campbell, of Coon Rapids, Iowa

Mr Elliott, whose name introduces this review, was born in Allegany county, New York, November 19, 1843, but when only two years old was brought to Rock Island county, where he has since made his home, his education being obtained in its public schools He remained on the home farm until June, 1862, when he enlisted in Company F, Sixty-ninth Illinois Volunteer Infantry, as a private, for three months service With his regiment he went to Vicksburg, and was engaged in guarding prisoners, general guard duty and in skirmishing with the guerillas until honorably discharged at Camp Douglas, Chicago, in the fall of 1862

On his return home Mr Elliott assisted in the work of the farm until he had attained his majority, and then operated rented land on his own account for about four years On the expiration of that time he purchased sixty acres of his present farm, and as his financial resources increased he bought additional tracts until he had two hundred and forty acres He has erected a large and comfortable residence and good barns and outbuildings, has placed the land under a high state of cultivation, and to-day has one of the best farms in the township, the result of his own untiring labors, perseverance and good management

In Buffalo Prairie township, April 7, 1864, was performed a wedding ceremony which united the destinies of Mr Elliott and Miss Mary E Castor, a native of Pennsylvania, who during her childhood was brought to Illinois by her father, Lewis H Castor, who located here about 1854 The children born of this union are as follows
ν ʼʼ ι ι ι ·· --d in farm-

ing in Buffalo Prairie township, Florence, wife of Daniel Hyatt, of Millersburg, Mercer county, Illinois, Sarah J, wife of Sherman Murdock of Rock Island county, Josephine, at home, Ella, wife of George Kistler, of Mercer county, Mary A, who resides at home and is successfully engaged in teaching, Alfred D, Olive and Luman C., all at home, and Cameron L and Blanche, who died in childhood

Mr Elliott cast his first vote for George B McClellan in 1864 and has since been a stanch Democrat, voting for William J Bryan and free silver in the fall of 1896 He has served as a delegate to many of the county conventions of his party and has filled the offices of school director, road commissioner, township trustee and supervisor for three terms, proving a most capable and popular official In 1883 he purchased a half interest in a store in Marston, with which he was connected for one year, and two years after selling out at that place became interested in merchandising at Buffalo Prairie Fourteen months later he disposed of his interest and has since devoted his energies wholly to his farm, in the operation of which he has met with excellent success, being numbered among the well-to-do and prosperous citizens of his community He and his wife are active members of Antioch Baptist church of Mercer county, and give a liberal support to all enterprises which they believe calculated to benefit the community or advance the welfare of their fellowmen

EDWARD F ARCULARIUS —The material advancement of the Prairie state is the wonder ' '' ll and it has been largely secu to sturdy and in-

telligent manhood of citizens from the eastern states, with their moral, intellectual and physical stamina, but their work is nearly complete, and every year sees more new graves filled by those who helped to build an empire, and soon, too soon, will the last of those sturdy pioneers be laid away, but their memory will forever remain green among those who loved them and appreciated their efforts The late Edward F Arcularius was among the honored pioneers of Rock Island county, and bore an important part in its upbuilding and progress

He was born in Albany, New York, February 15, 1803, and was of German descent, his father having been a native of the fatherland During his boyhood the family removed to New York city, where he learned the tanner's trade, and after his emigration to Pike county, Illinois, he continued to work at the same for some time He was first married in that county, and by that union had five children, two now living— Mrs Jennie Hebberd, of Galesburg, Illinois, and Mrs Lucy Lamore, of Sydney, Nebraska In 1834 he removed to Rock Island county, when most of the land was still in its primitive condition and the settlements were few and far between, and he erected the first house on the road between Rock Island and Dixon, it being a log structure in which the family lived while he cleared and developed his new farm He prospered in his undertakings and became one of the well-to-do citizens of his community

His first wife died after the removal to Rock Island county, and on the 11th of July, 1853, he wedded Miss Emily Axelson, of Rock Island county, who was born in the eastern part of Sweden and had come to America with her brother and sister in 1852. She had received a fair education in her native tongue, but on reaching this country was unable to speak a word of English She can now both speak and read the latter language Of the six children born of the second union, one died in infancy, and the others are as follows Hettie, wife of Jason Cox, of Moline, by whom she has three children, Ellen, wife of Ernest Rathburn, of Chicago, by whom she has two children, Margaret, wife of Cassius Cox, of Moline, by whom she has three children, Theresa, wife of Adelbert Abrams, of Lawrence, Michigan, by whom she has three children, and Martin L.

For many years Mr Arcularius was an active and prominent member of the Methodist Episcopal church and served as class leader, trustee, steward and Sunday-school superintendent He was also called upon to fill a number of public positions of honor and trust, including that of school director, and proved a most faithful and capable official His career was ever such as to commend him to the confidence and esteem of the entire community, and his death, which occurred October 2, 1887, was widely and deeply mourned, as he had a host of friends and acquaintances throughout the county

Martin Arcularius, the only son, was born October 6, 1871, on the old homestead in Hampton township, and remained at home until he had attained his majority, acquiring his education in the public schools of the neighborhood On starting out in life for himself he worked as a farm hand for one year, and then was in the express business in the city for the same length of time, after which he returned home and worked with his brother-in-law until 1897, when he took entire charge of the farm He is a thorough and skillful farmer and is meeting with will h l   '

operations He cast his first vote for Harrison in 1892 and four years later supported McKinley, being unwavering in his allegiance to the Republican party He is a charter member of the Home Forum at Moline and is a most progressive, enterprising young man, of industrious habits and excellent business ability

FREDERICK BEHRENDT, deceased Everywhere in our land are found men who have worked their own way from a humble position to one of prominence in the various walks of life, becoming wealthy and influential citizens It is one of the glories of our nation that it is so, and it should be a strong incentive and encouragement to the youth of the country Prominent among the self-made men of Zuma township was the subject of this sketch—a man honored and respected wherever known, and most of all where he was best known His home was on section 4

Mr Behrendt was born January 2, 1829, in the province of Brandanborg, Germany, where he was reared and educated in his native language, and at the age of twenty he entered the German army, where he served for three years, during which time he participated in two wars—Bardenben and Schleswig-Holstein He was married in his native land in 1854, to Miss Maria Hachrat, also of German birth, and engaged in farming and working by the day when not called out for military service

In 1872, with the hope of bettering his financial condition, Mr Behrendt sailed for the new world, and came at once to Rock Island county, Illinois, where he rented one hundred acres of land in Coe township for six years During his residence on that place   ' '   'red sixty acres additional for one year, and later spent three years on a hundred-and-sixty-acre farm in Coe township, which he rented, but at the end of that time purchased his late fine farm of two hundred fifty-seven acres in Zuma township He also had purchased another fine farm of two hundred and ten acres in Canoe Creek township The home place is improved with good and substantial buildings, a fine orchard and the land is under a high state of cultivation, making it one of the most desirable farms in the locality

Mr and Mrs. Behrendt became the parents of six children, namely Dora, wife of August Wilkin, of Hampton township, Minnie, wife of Christ Bartsch, of Coe township, Anna, wife of Herman Schwenecker, of Coe township, and Frederick, William and Charley, who assisted their father in the operation of the home farm, and still reside on the old homestead

After becoming an American citizen, Mr Behrendt was identified with the Democratic party, and was a loyal supporter of the institutions of his adopted country, where he found a happy home and gained a comfortable competence With the Lutheran church he and his estimable wife held membership On the 20th day of August, 1897, Mr Behrendt died, after an illness of twenty-four days, having always been prior to that a stout and healthy man

---

ROBERT C J MEYER, M D —Among the representatives of the medical profession whose skill and ability have gained them prestige in Rock Island county is this gentleman, a well-known and successful practitioner of Moline He was born on the farm in Coe township, Rock Island county, June 1, 1865, and is a son of John and Magda

whom were natives of Holstein, Germany. They were married there and their wedding journey consisted of a voyage to America For a year they resided in Chicago and then spent the following year in La Salle county, Illinois, where the father worked at anything he could get to do that would yield him an honest living About 1855 he came to Moline, spent two years in the city, and then removed to a rented farm Later he purchased forty acres of land, to which he afterward added at different times an eighty-acre tract and forty-acre tract, his attention being devoted to agricultural pursuits throughout his remaining days He had a family of seven children, two of whom died in infancy Those living are Eliza, wife of David Ash, of Des Moines, Iowa, Mary, wife of John Mason, of Des Moines, George, a farmer of Audubon county, Iowa, Robert C J , and Henry, of Audubon county

The Doctor attended the country schools and remained on the home farm until nineteen years of age, after which he spent two years at carpenter work with his brother-in-law in Des Moines Hearing a lecture on phrenology he became quite interested in it and read extensively on the subject After his return to the farm in Rock Island county, he continued his reading and in the fall of 1888 went to New York, where he entered the American Institute of Phrenology. spending two months there On leaving that institution he went on a lecture tour through southern Illinois, and in 1889 was forced to return home on account of his father's illness After his father's death he took up the study of medicine in the office of Dr George E Merriman, of Moline, and attended a course of lectures in Rush Medical College of Chicago in which institution he was graduated in 1892 He spent the summer of 1891 in Wooster University of Cleveland, Ohio, and was also granted a diploma by that school

Doctor Meyer opened his office in Moline in 1892 and on the 31st of August of that year married Miss Nellie Mumm, daughter of John H Mumm, of Moline In his practice he has met with very flattering success On the day he opened his office he had a patient, and from the beginning his practice has rapidly increased, until he now has a very lucrative patronage He is a close student of his profession and keeps constantly abreast with the times in his investigation and study. He has been two terms vice president of St Anthony's Hospital of Rock Island, and is an adjunct member of Mercy Hospital of Davenport He belongs to the Iowa and Illinois Central District Medical Association, the Association of Military Surgeons of the United States, and to the Association of Military Surgeons of Illinois He has invented several new surgical instruments that are a great help to the profession and has planned a greatly improved surgical instrument case that is a marvel of compactness It only measures twelve by four inches and two and a half inches in depth, yet contains seventy instruments He is also the originator of the Meyer X Ray Anatomical Chart, which is printed in colors and shows all of the thoracic and abdominal organs in their relative sizes and positions with relation to the ribs and external parts and with each other

It shows the arteries, veins and nerves (and their branches) of the extremities, neck and head, as well as the intercostal nerves and arteries (one side showing the deep, the other the superficial)

It shows all the bones of the extremities, ribs and sternum

It shows the lymphatics, and is a very valuable addition to medical study

The Doctor has not only invented several surgical instruments, but is also the inventor of a tire tightener, for which he has a caveat It is a little device for tightening the tires of buggies and wagons, and its practical utility at once appeals to all He joined the Second Battalion Naval Militia in the fall of 1893 as one of its original members and was immediately appointed on the staff as the assistant surgeon, and has never failed to do his duty when called

Doctor Meyer has been a stalwart Democrat since attaining his majority, is chairman of city committee, and a People's party man in local politics, of which he is chairman, and secured a majority of six hundred and thirty-two votes for his candidate (Mr. Swensson) last spring, was appointed by President Cleveland a member of the board of pension examiners He has also been overseer of the poor of Moline since 1896 He is a member of the library board and takes a deep interest in all that pertains to the educational, social, moral or material welfare of the city

As an illustration of the enterprising spirit of Dr Meyer it is only necessary to refer to the work he performed, in connection with others, in securing the location of the Northwestern Illinois Insane Hospital at Watertown Citizens of Rock Island remember the repeated efforts of its representatives in the Illinois legislature to secure the passage of an act to locate such a hospital in some one of the northwestern counties An act was finally passed that was introduced by Representative Payne, and commissioners were appointed by Governor Altgeld In the appointment of these com-in the entire northwestern part of the state wanted one of its citizens as a commissioner. Dr Meyer and others from Moline went to Springfield and secured the appointment of T S Silvis, of Rock Island, who subsequently resigned on account of ill health, and the same parties secured the appointment of T J. Medill, also of Rock Island

Warren, Knox and other counties desired the location of the hospital within their boundaries Rock Island presented two sites, the Watertown site being the favorite of Moline Galesburg offered a site worth thirty thousand dollars The board of supervisors of Rock Island voted twenty thousand dollars for the site somewhere in the county. Citizens of Moline added subscriptions to the amount of seven thousand, two hundred dollars This not being equal to that of Galesburg Dr Meyer, C H Pope and M J McEntry gave their personal bond for three thousand dollars, or two hundred dollars more than that offered by Galesburg Monmouth came into the field with a very liberal offer, and the friends of Watertown buckled down to the work, raised an additional ten thousand dollars, relieved Meyer, Pope and McEniry from their bond and pledged thirty-seven thousand, two hundred dollars This secured the site But work, hard work, was required and the credit is due to a great extent to Messrs Pope, McEniry and Dr Meyer

In August, 1892, Dr Meyer joined Moline Lodge, No 133, I O O F, the same year became a member of the Modern Woodmen of America, of which he was formerly the examiner, and is now medical examiner for the Knights and Ladies of Honor, Knights of the Globe, as well as many old law a a p tion He belongs to the Turners Society, and is a social, genial gentleman who has many friends in these fraternities He is a leader of thought and action in the medical world, and still greater success undoubtedly awaits him

HENRY DENNHARDT —Among the sturdy and stalwart citizens of Rock Island county, whose place of birth was in the far-away German fatherland, and who, with the industry and thrift so natural to the people of that country, have rapidly progressed toward the financial condition so much coveted by all, is the subject of this sketch He is now one of the leading and well-to-do farmers of Hampton township, his place consisting of one hundred and twenty-eight and a half acres on section 26, near the village of Barstow

Mr Dennhardt was born on the 28th of November, 1833, at Colbetz, Germany, a son of Andrew and Elizabeth (Stroh) Dennhardt Until fourteen years of age he attended the public schools of his native land, and then commenced learning the weaver's and butcher's trades with his father, who followed both of those occupations He was married March 24, 1856, to Miss Elizabeth Ganzer, also a native of Germany, and about six months after the marriage, with the hope of benefitting their financial condition, they started for America, sailing on the 6th of October, of that year They were six weeks upon the briny deep and experienced a storm of a week's duration when all on board thought they would be shipwrecked They finally landed safely in New York and proceeded to Hampton, Illinois, arriving there two weeks later

Mr Dennhardt was first employed at chopping cordwood, and as he had never done that kind of work his hands were soon badly blistered He was thus employed through the first winter, and the following summer secured work on a farm at sixty-five cents per day During the following three years while employed in manufacturing shingles and railroad ties, he managed to save eighty dollars, with which he purchased a yoke of oxen, and broke a ten-acre field to secure the crops from the same for two years He next bought a colt with which to plow his corn, and later traded his oxen for another horse After securing his team of horses, he rented an eighty-acre farm and the first year cleared two hundred dollars, the second eight hundred, but the third, owing to the illness of himself and wife, only cleared two hundred dollars He then purchased eighty-five acres of his present farm, paying for the same two thousand dollars cash down, and subsequently bought forty-five acres for one thousand dollars He has built a good house, set out a fine orchard and shade trees, and now has a most desirable farm, which stands as a monument to his thrift and industry He also owns two shares in a creamery.

To Mr and Mrs Dennhardt have been born nine children, namely· Henry, who is married and engaged in carpentering in Moline, Edward, a resident of Green county, Iowa, who is married and has four sons, Annie is the wife of Benjamin Deem, of Henry county, Illinois, by whom she has five children, Andrew is married and is the present telegraph operator at the crossing of the I V & N and the Chicago, Burlington & Quincy Railroads in Bureau county, Illinois, Rachel is the wife of John Mosher, of Hampton township, Rock Island county, and has two children, Bertha is at home, Christian is clerking in a bank in

Cherokee county, Iowa, Albert, born October 23, 1871, was educated in the common schools, and Frank completes the family

Since casting his first vote for Lincoln, Mr Dennhardt has been a stanch Republican, and he and his wife are members of the Lutheran church, and have contributed liberally to the building of two churches He is entirely a self-made man, having begun life here with no capital, and by his own industry, economy and good management has succeeded in accumulating a comfortable competence

---

HENRY MUELLER —No country affords greater opportunities to the poor man than our own, it is indeed the poor man's country Here an industrious, frugal man has a chance to accumulate wealth Many fail to do so, but the best of our population lay by some of their earnings, and soon find themselves in the possession of a handsome property Among them is the gentleman whose name heads this article He is now one of the most energetic and progressive farmers of Buffalo Prairie township, where he owns and operates two hundred and ninety acres of rich and arable land, pleasantly located on section 15

Mr Mueller began his earthly existence April 2, 1840, in Bavaria, Germany, of which country his parents, Charles Frederick and Elizabeth (Teressel) Mueller, were also natives In 1854 the father and son Henry took passage on a sailing vessel at Bremen, and after a long and tedious voyage of forty-seven days reached the harbor of New York They at once proceeded to Cleveland, Ohio, and thence to Detroit, Michigan, where they worked for three months and then went to La Fayette, Indiana There the father found employment in a wagon shop, while our subject worked at anything he could find to do While in that state they were joined by the mother and other children, and in June, 1855, came to Rock Island, where the father at first worked in a sawmill and afterward in a cooper shop Subsequently he purchased five acres on the bluff where he continued to make his home until called to his final rest in 1870 For a number of years, including the period of the Civil war, he successfully engaged in the hotel business, becoming quite well-to-do, and at the time of his death owned the Union House His wife survived him seventeen years, passing away in 1887

The subject of this sketch is the oldest in their family of ten children, the others being as follows Mrs Shillinger, a resident of Rock Island, Mrs Shrader, whose home is on Elm street, that city, John G , who married and located in Rock Island, where he was conducting the Union House at the time of his death, Christ, a farmer of Henry county, Illinois, Mrs Ahrhorn, who conducts the Commercial Hotel in Rock Island, Mrs John Dorras, a resident of Lone Tree, Iowa, Mrs Frink and Mrs Schasel, both of Rock Island, and Mrs Lizzie Small, of California

Henry Mueller was a lad of fifteen years when he arrived in Rock Island county, where for some years he worked as a farm hand or in a cooper shop in the city of Rock Island In 1863 he had a very severe spell of sickness and for some time his life was despaired of He had no use of his hands and feet, for two months was under the care of an eminent doctor of Davenport, and on his return to Rock Island continued tr   u   f w m nths until he

finally recovered Having partially regained his health, he accepted a position in a saloon, where he remained about three years, and then went to Johnson county, Iowa, where he operated forty acres of land for four years

In Rock Island Mr Mueller was married December 26, 1865, the lady of his choice being Miss Christiana Dorries, a native of Ohio, whose father at one time owned the farm on which our subject is now living Seven children blessed this union— Conrad, who is married and is now successfully engaged in farming in Edgington township, Rock Island county, George, who is married and follows the same occupation in Mercer county, Illinois, Lizzie, wife of Nicholas Stamn, a substantial farmer living near Iowa City, Iowa, where he owns about three hundred acres of land, Fred and Louis, who are still with their father, Emma, wife of John Katell, of Rock Island county, and Bertie, at home The wife and mother was called to her final rest February 14, 1877 Two years later Mr Mueller was again married in Rock Island county, his second union being with Mrs Minnie Wellnich, a German lady, who was reared and first married in Prussia, having by that union three children—Mary, Willie and Clara Wellnich. Two daughters grace her marriage to our subject—Lena and Katie

Returning to Rock Island county in 1870, Mr Mueller purchased one hundred and sixty acres of partially improved land, which forms a part of his present fine farm of two hundred and ninety acres of fertile and productive land, which, by the exercise of industry, energy and excellent management, he has brought to a model condition of cultivation and improved with a good set of farm buildings

Mr Mueller cast his first vote for Abraham Lincoln in 1864, but after the election of General Grant became a Democrat, and continued to support that party until the fall of 1896, when he voted for McKinley Although he has served as school director for some years, he has never sought office, preferring to devote his entire time and attention to his extensive business interests He and his family hold membership in the Lutheran church, and occupy a prominent position in social circles He has been the architect of his own fortunes and has never been afraid of putting his shoulder to the wheel whenever necessary It has been forty-two years since he came to the county, and has watched with interest the transformation that has taken place, and has been an important factor in this growth and development, always bearing his part in any enterprise for the good of the community

JOEL GROUT FRANKLIN The pioneers of a country, the founders of a business, the originators of any undertaking that will promote the material welfare or advance the educational, social and moral influence of a community, deserve the gratitude of humanity The subject of this sketch is not only one of the earliest settlers of Rock Island county, but has been prominently identified with its growth and prosperity along various avenues of business, and his name deserves an honored place in its records For many years he was actively identified with its business interests, but now in his declining days is living retired in the village of Barstow, where he is surrounded by the comforts which years of honest toil have brought him

Mr F

Windham county, Vermont, October 25, 1810, and is a son of Joel and Fannie Grout) Franklin, the former also a native of Guilford, and the latter of Stratton, Vermont Upon the home farm our subject spent the days of his boyhood and youth and was provided with a fair common school education When seventeen years of age he had the misfortune to lose his father, whose death resulted from a kick of a horse, and as he was the oldest of a family of seven children the management of affairs to a great extent devolved upon him The other children all reached years of maturity but are now deceased

Our subject had charge of the farm until he had attained his majority and then worked by the month for two years At the end of that time he accepted an agency for a circulating publication, and while thus employed traveled all over the New England states Seeing accounts of the Black Hawk war and of Rock Island county, he concluded to come west, and accordingly packed his trunk and took the stage at Brattleboro, Vermont, to Bennington, that state, thence he proceeded to Troy, New York, by the Erie canal to Buffalo, by the lakes to Chicago, and by stage to Rockford, Illinois, where he and his comrade, Lewis Weatherhead, purchased a skiff, and came down the Rock river to Rock Island, where they landed on the 4th of July, 1838 They purchased claims on sections 26 and 27, Hampton township, range 1 east of the 4th principal meridian, each securing a quarter section, and our subject taking the one on section 26, where he at once began to make a home

On the 22d of January, 1840, Mr Franklin was united in marriage to Miss Betsey Lydalia Edwards of Hampton township, whose parents, Luther and Mary (Wilcox) Edwards, had also come from Windham county, Vermont, in 1839 Six children blessed this union. Mary, wife of William Golden, of Barstow, by whom she has three children, Adaline, wife of Benjamin Golden, of Crawford county, Kansas, Sanford, a farmer and railroad man of Elk county, Kansas, who is married and has two children, Rosetta, wife of Marvin Spencer, a farmer of Osceola, Stark county, Illinois, by whom she has three children, Leslie E., who with his wife and seven children lives on the old homestead, and one who was drowned by falling in a tub of water in childhood The wife and mother died in Barstow, November 9, 1887, and was buried in Home cemetery at that place

Soon after coming to the county, Mr Franklin split white oak clapboard, and built a comfortable little house 16 x 22 feet, containing two rooms, with a fireplace of clay and sticks, the chimney being on the outside of the building For several years that continued to be the home of the family and later a more commodious frame residence was erected The former is now used as a corn crib, while the other, as a dwelling, rents for eleven dollars per month For many years Mr Franklin was actively engaged in agricultural pursuits, and still owns eighty acres of farming land adjoining the old homestead on the west, but has given his first farm to his son, Leslie E He has dealt quite extensively in real estate, platted the village of Barstow, and in 1879 erected the first house in the place, it being used by his daughter as a boarding house Being appointed the first postmaster, he continued to hold that position for fourteen years, but has now laid aside all business cares and enjoys a

Casting his first vote for Andrew Jackson Mr Franklin continued to support the Democratic party until the war, since which time he has been a pronounced Republican, and in 1868 voted for General Grant He has never been an aspirant for office, but served one term as highway commissioner He may be termed the founder of the village of Barstow, was especially instrumental in having the railroad junction located here, and the place has now become an important business center and shipping point Since its organization he has been a stockholder in the First National Bank of Moline, has been watchful of all the details of his business and of all indications pointing toward prosperity, and while advancing his own interests has never been unmindful of the rights and privileges of others He contributed liberally to the erection of the Methodist Episcopal church in Barstow, and has always cheerfully given his support to all worthy enterprises calculated to advance the moral, intellectual or material welfare of the community On the rolls of Rock Island county's honored pioneers and representative citizens his name should be found among the foremost

JOHN SCHAFER.—Among the worthy citizens of Zuma township who are of German birth, is the gentleman whose name introduces this sketch He was reared in his native land and there learned the traits of economy and frugality which have been the source of his present competency Many of the best citizens of Rock Island county are his countrymen, and they almost invariably merit and receive the esteem and respect of the community to the same degree that he does For many years he was act-

ively identified with the agricultural interests of the county, but has now laid aside
all business cares and is living retired at
the home of his son on section 5, Zuma
township

Mr Schafer was born August 5, 1819,
in Wurtemburg, Germany, where his father,
Charles Schafer, was also born, reared and
married In 1848, the latter with his
family emigrated to America and first located in Huntingdon county, Pennsylvania,
where he spent two years, but at the end of
that time, in company with our subject,
came to Rock Island county, Illinois, and
purchased adjoining farms

In the land of his nativity, John Schafer
had acquired a good education in both German and Latin, and while residing in Pennsylvania had attended the public schools,
where he became familiar with the English
language, and is to-day one of the best informed men of his locality, being a great
reader of the best literature On locating
in Rock Island county, he purchased forty
acres of wild land in Zuma township, on
which he erected a log house, and there the
family lived while he opened up and developed his little farm As his financial resources increased, however, he extended its
boundaries until he owned five hundred
acres of the best land to be found anywhere
in the county, and as his children have
started out in life for themselves, he has
given some of his property to each His
little log cabin, he replaced by a neat and
substantial frame residence, which he surrounded by good barns and outbuildings, a
fine orchard, shade and ornamental trees,
and shrubbery, making it one of most attractive and desirable places in the locality

In 1848, in Pennsylvania, occurred the
marriage of

Schlock, also a native of the Fatherland,
and they became the parents of eleven children, ten still living, and with the exception
of the youngest all are now married They
are as follows Matt, a substantial farmer
of Zuma township, John, a banker and
business man of Port Byron, Charles, a
farmer of Zuma township, Laura, wife of
Gotlieb Wiess, who is engaged in the manufacturing business in Rock Island, Henry
C, who follows agricultural pursuits on the
Rock river bottoms, Emma, wife of George
Setzer, of Zuma township, George J, a
farmer in Iowa, Samuel, an agriculturist of
Zuma township, David, who died in infancy, Frank Herman, who received a good
literary education, and is now pursuing a
theological course at Evanston, Illinois, and
William, who owns and operates one hundred and sixty acres of the old homestead

Since becoming a voter Mr. Schafer has
been identified with the Democratic party,
and has served as assessor, township trustee, and in other local offices of honor and
trust Coming to this country in limited
circumstances, he has been the architect of
his own fortunes and is deserving of the
highest commendation Possessing the esteem and respect of the entire community
he may well be ranked among the honest
and representative German-American citizens of the county His honor and integrity are unimpeachable, his word being considered as good as his bond

WILLIAM R CAREY has attained
distinctive preferment in political circles and through his official positions has
been an important factor in promoting the
best interests of his county He is now
                                         ard of

supervisors and as such has materially advanced the work of development and progress

Mr Carey was born near Monmouth, Illinois, March 24, 1847, and is a son of Richard and Nancy (Edwards) Carey When he was about six years of age his parents sold their property in Warren county and removed to Henderson county, where the father again purchased a farm, but made it his home for a year only He then sold and removed to Knoxville, and after a few years located on a farm near Watago, Knox county, where he remained five years and then removed to Mercer county. Later he engaged in hotel keeping for a few years in Oxford, Henry county, spent one year in Hampton, purchased property in Watertown, residing for a year on a farm in Pleasant Valley and then went to Carbon Cliff, where he kept hotel and owned a farm He afterward established a home in Port Byron, where his death occurred about 1886 In politics he was a Republican and was a prominent member of the Methodist Episcopal church, serving as class leader and also working in the Sunday school He had five children, the eldest of whom died in infancy William R , the second, was followed by Leonard H , who is engaged in mining in Montana, and Nelson F , who is living in Carbon Cliff and has three children

William R Carey left home when about fifteen years of age and lived for a year and a half with an aged couple in the neighborhood, after which he returned to his father s family He enlisted in Company G, One Hundred and Fortieth Illinois Infantry, in the one-hundred-days service, but remained at the front for six months, doing guard duty in M ⁻ ⁻⁻ ᵣᵣ⁻ He ⁻ˡ⁻⁻ had ⁻⁻ᵥᵉᵣᵃˡ skirmishes ⁻ ⁱ ⁱ ⁱ ᵏ ⁱ ʳᵐⁱⁿ⁻ ʰ ⁱⁱ⁻

he then attended school in Hampton for a time and on the 28th of February, 1865, re-enlisted in Company D, Ninth Illinois Cavalry, joining the regiment at Eastport, Mississippi He did service through Iuka, Tuscumbia, Montgomery, Selma, Utah and Gainesville, but not in battle, and in the fall of 1865 was mustered out at Selma, and with the regiment went to Chicago, where he was paid off

Mr Carey then returned to Watertown, where his father was living, and worked at brickmaking in that place and in Hampton until the fall of 1867, after which he rented a farm in Pleasant Valley In 1869 he removed to Carbon Cliff, where he worked for the Argillo Works for some time. In 1871 he began farming, which he continued for about five years, and then returned to his old position at the Argillo Works

On the 20th of November, 1867, Mr Carey married Mattie C Fullerton, of Hampton, a daughter of Hugh and Elizabeth (Johnson) Fullerton Six children have been born to them Alice, a graduate of the Port Byron Academy, who was engaged in teaching music, and in teaching in the public schools, died in Carbon Cliff, in the spring of 1891, Birdie Belle, also a music teacher, died shortly before her sister, both the victims of typhoid fever, Minnie, wife of Fred Ball, station agent and telegraph operator at Atkinson, Illinois, by whom she has one son, Milton, who was born in Carbon Cliff, and is now studying telegraphy, and Charles, who was born in Carbon Cliff, and completes the family The mother died in the spring of 1888, and her death was deeply mourned by a large circle of friends

Since casting his first presidential vote, Mr Carey has been an earnest and zealous

Republican. In 1875 he was elected high-way commissioner, serving three years, and from 1881 until 1895, was justice of the peace He was elected supervisor for one year in 1890, and in 1893, 1895 and 1897 was elected for terms of two years He has served on various important committees, was chairman of the finance committee in 1893, as a member of the board was identified with the building of the court house, and since 1895 has been chairman of the board Thus he is at the head of public improvement and material progress and his labors have been of great benefit to the county He has served as notary public for several years and has also been deputy sheriff In the discharge of his official duties he is prompt and faithful, displaying a loyalty to the public good that is above question

---

WILLIAM S PARKS —The subject of this personal narration is one of the most successful and progressive farmers resident within the borders of Rock Island county, and may be termed one of the pioneer citizens and representative men of the community He has made his special field of industry a success, and is highly esteemed and respected by those who know him best He is engaged in general farming, and its usual concomitant, stock-raising, on his homestead, which lies in section 15, Edgington township

Mr Parks was born May 20, 1845, in the village of Edgington, a son of Henry H and Martha (Gingles) Parks, natives of Ohio and Pennsylvania respectively, who became pioneer settlers of Rock Island county The paternal grandfather, Jonathan Parks, was born in Co

and in early life emigrated to Worthington, Ohio, when it was still on the western frontier He was a teamster in the war of 1812, and was a blacksmith by trade His death occurred in Worthington, when about sixty-two years of age, and his wife, who lived to the advanced age of eighty-seven, now sleeps by his side in the cemetery at that place In their family were ten children, but only three are now living Rodney Henry H , and Sylvia, wife of James Dickey, of Xenia Ohio

Robert Gingles, the maternal grandfather of our subject, was a native of Pennsylvania, and was of Scotch-Irish descent On his emigration to Illinois in 1840, he first located in Mercer county, whence he came to Rock Island county, living on a number of farms here Throughout life he engaged in agricultural pursuits, and died at about the age of eighty years In his family were several children

As early as 1838 Henry H Parks came to Rock Island county by wagon driving a team for George Parmenter, and has since resided in Edgington township within sight of his present home During the first three years he passed here he worked by the month, as he was in limited circumstances, possessing on his arrival only ten dollars in money and a horse valued at forty dollars, which his father had given him, but by hard work, economy and good management, he was at length able to purchase forty acres of land, to which he added from time to time as his financial resources increased until he had a fine farm of three hundred and twenty acres of well-improved and valuable land in Edgington township He has now laid aside all business cares, making his home with our subject, and is enjoying a well-

In early manhood Henry H Parks married Miss Martha Gingles, by whom he had four children—Martha A , wife of Daniel Montgomery, John H , William S , and James J The wife and mother, a most estimable woman, was called to her final rest in 1876, at the age of fifty-six years She was an earnest Christian, a faithful member of the Methodist church, to which Mr Parks also belongs For many years he served as class leader, being the first to fill that position in the church in Edgington township, and he has also acceptably served in various township offices. He was prominently identified with the growth and development of this region, and can relate many interesting experiences of pioneer days On locating in Edgington township, his nearest post office was Rock Island, then called Stephenson, and the first post office in his township was one mile and a half north of the present village of Edgington At that time the recipient of a letter had to pay twenty-five cents at the post office before it would be given him Our subject well remembers going for the mail on horseback, following an Indian trail before the roads were laid out

Mr Parks, whose name introduces this review, has spent his entire life in Edgington township, was reared to farm life, and obtained his early education in the district schools, but later attended the Aledo Collegiate Institute To a great extent members of the family have carried on business together, and as boys our subject and his brother John started out in life for themselves Although they each own a half section of land in separate farms, they continue business together as general farmers, dairymen and stock raisers he no por their place ᵗ ᵗ ᵗʰ

and hogs They first purchased one hundred sixty acres, to which they added from time to time, and then father also gave them a portion of his land, all of which he had divided among his children They are thorough, systematic farmers of more than ordinary business ability, and the success which they have achieved is certainly well deserved Upon his place our subject keeps twenty-eight cows for dairy purposes

On the 7th of October, 1875, was celebrated the marriage of William S Parks and Miss Ella J Fairchild, and to them was born one son who died at the age of three years Both hold membership in the Presbyterian church, where Mr. Parks is now serving as elder, trustee and treasurer Fraternally, he belongs to the Modern Woodmen of America, and politically is identified with the Republican party For three years he was school director in his district, and served one term as supervisor He is a man of recognized ability, and, with his amiable wife, stands high in the community where they have so long made their home Those who know them best are numbered among their warmest friends, and no citizens in Rock Island county are more honored or highly respected

PROFESSOR WILLIAM H ALLEN, —whose long and arduous service with the Union army in the Civil War well indicated his loyalty to his country, is now principal of the public schools in Carbon Cliff One of Ohio's native sons, he was born in Tuscarawas county, October 8, 1844, and is a son of John and Margaret (Little) Allen, who removed to Morrow county Ohio, in 1853 In 1857 they went to Marion county, Ill ᵗ ᵗ where the father ᵗ ᵗ ᵗ ᵗ ᵗ ᵗ acres of wild land, which he transformed into a good farm

During those years the educational privileges which Professor Allen received were very meagre   At the age of seventeen, prompted by a spirit of patriotism, he left home and on the 13th of August, 1862, as a private, joined Company K, One Hundred Eleventh Illinois Infantry   He remained at Camp Marshall until October, when the regiment was sent to Columbus, Kentucky, and did garrison duty until the spring of 1863, after which they did garrison duty at Fort Heiman   Professor Allen, on account of illness was granted a furlough and while at home his regiment went to Paducah, Kentucky, where he joined his command, remaining there until the fall of 1863   They then joined General Dodge and went to Pulaski, Tennessee, doing guard duty there until the early spring of 1864, when they moved near Decatur, Alabama, which was in possession of the rebels   Crossing the river in the dead of night with muffled oars, they landed at daylight and found that the rebels had kept their horses saddled for two days expecting the attack   From Decatur they went to Larkinsville, Alabama, and afterward joined Sherman at Chattanooga, taking part in the Atlanta campaign and the celebrated march to the sea   Professor Allen participated in the battles of Resaca, Dallas, Kenesaw Mountain, Atlanta, Ezra Chapel and Jonesboro   He followed Hood from Atlanta to Alabama, then returned to Atlanta and in November started for the sea coast   He was severely wounded in the battle of Fort McAllister by a musket ball which struck him in the head and he fell unconscious just outside the trenches   He was carried to the hospital, where the

fatal and his name was published on the dead list   After three days the Doctor inquired for him and finding that he was still alive took him in charge   For some time thereafter he had not the use of either of his legs or his right arm   He remained in the hospital at Fort McAllister until Christmas day, when he was taken to Beaufort, South Carolina, and a week later to the hospital on David Island, where he remained from January 6 to March 27, when he was sent to the hospital in Quincy, continuing there until July, when he was discharged and returned home

As soon as he had sufficiently regained his health Mr Allen began attending the country schools and later continued his studies in the Kinmundy high school   He then taught for a few months, after which he entered the Westfield College and was graduated in the commercial department   He has since successfully followed teaching, spending seven years in Coles county, eight years in Marion, one year in Edgar, and five years in Morgan county, also one year in Jasper county, Missouri, after which he joined the corps of teachers in Henry county, where he continued three years   He next became assistant in the county superintendent's office at Geneseo, where he remained six months, and in 1894 came to Carbon Cliff as principal of the schools here

Professor Allen has been a Republican since supporting Grant for the presidency in 1872   He is a prominent member of the Methodist Episcopal church, and an active worker in the Sunday-school   He also belongs to the Grand Army of the Republic, and in all life's relations is as true and faithful to his duty as he was in the days of Civil war, when he followed the starry banner on

J E VOLKEL, the well-known and popular postmaster of Buffalo Prairie, is an important factor in business circles and his popularity is well deserved, as in him are embraced the characteristics of an unbending integrity, unabated energy and industry that never flags He is a leading merchant of the village, and as a public-spirited citizen is thoroughly interested in whatever tends to promote the moral, intellectual and material welfare of the community

A native of Illinois, Mr Volkel was born February 5, 1860, in Mercer county, and is a son of George Volkel, a native of Germany, who during his childhood was brought to America by his parents, locating in Ohio, where the grandfather died About 1840 the family came to Springfield, Illinois, and the father of our subject later took up his residence in Rock Island county, becoming one of its substantial farmers He wedded Mary Platt, a native of New York, and they became the parents of two children J E, of this review, and Adeline, wife of Dr Marston, whose sketch appears elsewhere in this work On the outbreak of the Civil war, the father manifested his loyalty to his adopted land by enlisting in the One Hundred and Twenty-sixth Illinois Volunteer Infantry, faithfully serving until his death in 1862, when only twenty-five years of age His wife survived him a number of years, passing away April 5, 1886

Our subject was reared and educated in Rock Island county, and at the age of nineteen began clerking in a store in Buffalo Prairie, where he acquired a thorough and practical knowledge of business methods After filling that position for two years he bought an interest in a store at Marston, but two ye . . . . . t . .t .
his present . . . . .t .. . . . .a .

years bought out his partner, becoming sole proprietor He carries a large and complete stock of general merchandise, and having won an excellent reputation for good goods and fair dealing, he receives a liberal share of the public patronage

In this county on the 13th of January, 1885, Mr Volkel was united in marriage to Miss Jennie Burrows, who was born, reared and educated in Mercer county, and is a daughter of John Burrows, an early settler of that county residing near Millersburg Mr and Mrs Volkel now have four children—Mary M, Rudolph, Beatrice and Mervil The parents are both consistent members of the Presbyterian church, and occupy an enviable position in social circles

In April, 1890, Mr Volkel was appointed postmaster of Buffalo Prairie, and is still filling that position to the satisfaction of the many patrons of the office He is unwavering in his support of the principles of the Republican party, voting for all its presidential nominees since casting his first ballot for James G Blaine in 1884 While a resident of Mercer county he served as collector, and also as justice of the peace, and proved a most capable and trustworthy official Fraternally he is a member of the Modern Woodmen of America and the Home Forum As a business man he is prompt and reliable, and as a citizen his course has ever been such as to commend him to the confidence and high regard of the entire community

---

LEONARD F BAKER.—Men of marked ability and strong individuality leave their impress upon the world in such indeli-
l . . . . .l . . . . j will ss to ob-
.t... t the.r . . . tv ~w put trom the

minds of men   Their commendable acts live long after they have passed from the scene of their earthly careers   Mr Baker is one of the strong characters who have become an integral part of the business life of Rock Island county, and by the exercise of his powers has not only advanced his individual prosperity, but has contributed to the welfare of the county   He has filled public positions of honor and trust in the most creditable manner, and has won the utmost regard of all with whom he has come in contact

Mr Baker was born in Worcester county, Massachusetts, December 5, 1824   His father, Captain Silas Baker, was a native of the same state and a son of Silas Baker, Sr., who was also born there.   The Baker family was of English origin and was founded in Massachusetts in the seventeenth century   Mrs Silas Baker, the grandmother, was a resident of Lexington, and witnessed the opening battle of the Revolution at that place

Captain Silas Baker was reared to manhood in Massachusetts, and there married Abigail Hager, also a native of that state, and a daughter of John Hager, who belonged to one of the old families   Captain Baker owned and operated a large farm in Massachusetts, upon which he reared his family and spent his entire life   His wife died in 1850   They had three sons and four daughters who reached mature years, and one of the brothers, Silas W Baker, is now living on the old family homestead, which was settled by the grandfather about two hundred years ago

Leonard F Baker obtained his education in the common schools and in the Massachusetts Academy, where he remained as a student f   ʼ   ʼ ʼ   ʼ

engaged in teaching school for several years in Massachusetts, and in 1830 came to Rock Island county with M W Wright, by whom he was employed as a clerk for three years, receiving in that time an excellent business training   In 1853 he entered into partnership with H F Thomas, built a store and put in a large stock of mercandise, successfully continuing the business until the war, when he sold out   In the meantime he was called to public office, having been elected justice of the peace in 1852   For about thirty years thereafter he filled that position, and no higher testimonial of his faithful service can be given than the fact of his frequent re-election   In 1865 he was elected supervisor, serving on the county board for one term, and for sixteen years and nine months he held the office of postmaster of Hampton   About 1876 he again embarked in merchandising and continued in active business until 1893   For a time he was in partnership with Henry Clark, but later purchased his interest   His business affairs have ever been prosecuted with energy and with the strictest regard for the ethics of commercial life   His enterprise, good management and honorable dealing secured to him a liberal patronage and he thereby acquired a handsome competence

Mr Baker was married in Massachusetts, September 7, 1851, to Milla W Sawyer, a native of the Bay state, and a daughter of Silas Sawyer, who belonged to one of the old Massachusetts families   They now have three living children — Agnes M , wife of John L Wells, a business man of Chicago, Howard Grant, a merchant of Hampton, and Silas Sawyer, who is in business with his brother in Hampton   They also lost three children, two in infancy, and a d   ught   M   on E   who had in 1896

The mother of this family passed away in May, 1887, and was laid to rest in Hampton cemetery She was an active worker in the Congregational church, and a most estimable lady

In his political views Mr Baker was a Whig in early life and on the organization of the Republican party joined its ranks He has been a resident of Rock Island county for forty-seven years and is a public-spirited and progressive citizen, has given his support to all measures for the public good Over his life record there falls no shadow of wrong His public service was most exemplary, and his private life has been marked by the utmost fidelity to duty.

EDWIN E WARREN.—Among the well-to-do and successful farmers and fruit growers of this county, who have accumulated a competency through their own exertions and economy, and who are carrying on the business of farming in a manner which draws forth praise from every one, is the subject of this biographical notice, who resides on section 31, Hampton township

Mr Warren was born March 10, 1840, in Windsor county, Vermont, a son of Ephraim and Almira (Snell) Warren, and is a representative of the same family to which belonged Dr Warren who became so famous at the battle of Bunker Hill The father, also a native of the Green Mountain state, was both a farmer and carpenter by occupation, and also successfully engaged in veterinary surgery to some extent. When our subject was about twelve years of age, the family removed to Chautauqua county, New York, and after a few years spent there went to Caledonia county Minnesota but the follow ·   · · 1   1   ul

county, Illinois In Hampton township the father purchased one hundred twenty acres of land which is now owned by his youngest son, and there he spent his remaining days, dying January 7, 1896, at the advanced age of eighty-eight years The mother is still living and is about seventy-seven years of age

In their family were eight children, two of whom died in Vermont, one in infancy and the other in childhood Those still living are as follows Lucinda, wife of Jacob Warner, of Hampton township, Jennie D , who first married Avery Jackson, and after his death Melville C Follette, now of Chicago, Edwin E , of this sketch, Julia, wife of George Bowles, of Hampton township, by whom she has two children, Byron C , who is married and has one child, and lives on the old homestead in Hampton township, and Anna E , wife of Oliver P. Sowers, of Moline

Edwin E Warren was about eighteen years of age when he came with the family to Rock Island county He had previously attended the country schools and after locating here continued his studies for a time in the public schools At the age of twenty-one he started out in life for himself, first operating a threshing machine which he purchased In this way he saved enough to make a payment on a farm of eighty acres in Hampton township, where he lived for a few years, and then sold and bought his present farm, which is one of the most highly cultivated and improved places in the township

On the 24th of November, 1864, Mr Warren was united in marriage to Miss Rachel Cook, of Hampton township, by whom he had two children Minnie Bell is the widow of Bart Smith, who was killed on the railroad and left two children—Clara B. and Alice Derilla   Estella May, the younger daughter, is the wife of Frank L McRoberts, of Port Byron, and has two children—Warren W and Charles Edwin Mrs Warren died January 13, 1876

Mr Warren was again married June 27, 1878, the lady of his choice being Miss Derilla Smith, of Hampton township, who is a native of Whiteside county, Illinois, and a daughter of William R and Mary E (Lynn) Smith   The father was born in Tennessee and the mother in Galena, Illinois, where their marriage was celebrated Mrs Warren received a good common-school education and attended the high school of Port Byron until eighteen years of age   By her marriage to our subject she has become the mother of three children, whose names and dates of birth are as follows   Frank Leroy, October 27, 1881, Ethel Anna, October 18, 1884, and Grace Pearl, February 4, 1890

In politics, Mr Warren is an independent Democrat, casting his first vote for George B McClellan in 1864, and has constantly refused to become a candidate for office, his friends having urged him to accept the nomination for supervisor   His father, who was also a Democrat, filled various township offices and was supervisor for several years   Our subject is a charter member of the Baptist church of Watertown, helped to build the church at that place, of which he is now trustee, and has served as superintendent of the Sunday-school, in which his wife has taught a class of young ladies for many years   Both are charter members of the Riverview Home Forum, No 30, and occupy an enviable position in social circles, where their true worth and many exc

appreciated   Mr Warren is also a Master Mason, belonging to the lodge in Port Byron, and in business circles also stands deservedly high

JOHN C SWANK, a progressive and enterprising farmer, and a business man of more than ordinary capacity, is a worthy representative of the agricultural and stock-raising interests of Zuma township, his home being on section 8   Here his entire life has been passed, his birth occurring December 28, 1844, in the township where he still continues to reside, and with its development and prosperity he has been prominently identified.

Monroe Swank, the father of our subject, was born in Kentucky, October 18, 1812, but when two years old was taken to Indiana by his parents, who first settled in Harrison county, and later in Montgomery county, where they reared their family The grandfather, Joseph Swank, had served as a soldier in the war of 1812   In Montgomery county, Indiana, Monroe Swank grew to manhood and married Miss Mary A. Clevenger, who was born and reared in Ohio   In 1838 they emigrated to Illinois, and took up their residence in Zuma township, Rock Island county, where the father took up a claim and later entered one hundred and sixty acres on the Rock river bottom   Erecting a cabin, he at once began to clear and cultivate his land, but after opening up a small tract, he sold the place and removed to the farm now owned and occupied by our subject   Like many of the early settlers he and his family suffered for a time with fever and ague and were forced to endure all the hardships and privations   secure a

home on what was then the western frontier There were a few Indians still in the
neighborhood and wild game of all kinds
was found in abundance and furnished many
a meal for the early settlers Mr Swank
is still living with our subject in Zuma township, and is recognized as one of the most
honored and highly respected pioneers of
the county, being one of those who opened
up this region to civilization He has been
called upon to mourn the loss of his estimable wife, who patiently shared with him all
the discomforts of life on the frontier, her
death occurring December 24, 1890, on the
seventieth anniversary of her birth

In the public schools near his boyhood
home John C Swank began his literary education, which was supplemented by three
terms' attendance at the Western College
in Iowa, and six months in the Wesleyan
Academy, near Crawfordsville, Montgomery
county, Indiana. In early life he also visited Minnesota, Nebraska, Tennessee and
other states of the Union, gaining a thorough knowledge of men and events which
only travel can bring After completing his
studies he returned to his old home in Zuma
township and has since devoted his energies
to farming, stock dealing and shipping, with
results which cannot fail to prove satisfactory He has become one of the principal
stock dealers and shippers in his part of the
county, shipping about seventy-five car-loads
annually, and is recognized as one of the
most substantial and reliable business men
of the township

On the 26th of December, 1870, in Zuma
township, was celebrated the marriage of
Mr Swank and Miss Rebecca Shannon, who
was born in Iowa, but was reared in Rock
Island county. Her father James Shannon, is now . . . .

The children born of this union are as follows Laura E , wife of Henry F Long,
of Zuma township; John L , who is married, and is engaged in farming in the same
township, Frank E , David M , Nettie E.,
B Harrison, Mary A , Clara and Samuel,
all at home, William, who died at the age
of three years, three months and three days,
and Thomas, who died at the age of eight
months

A pronounced Republican in politics,
Mr Swank cast his first presidential vote
for General Grant in 1868, and has since
taken quite an active and prominent part in
local politics He has been a delegate to
numerous county conventions, and also to
the congressional conventions, and has
served his fellow citizens as justice of the
peace, road commissioner, assessor and
supervisor, filling all the offices four years,
with exception of assessor, which he held
for three years It is needless to say that
his duties were always promptly and faithfully discharged as his life has ever been
characterized by fairness and fidelity to
every trust reposed in him He is energetic
and persevering, with a remarkable faculty
for the conduct and dispatch of business.
Fraternally he is identified with the Independent Order of Odd Fellows, the Modern
Woodmen of America and the Knights of
the Globe.

LIEUTENANT CHARLES J ARENS-
CHIELD, a retired farmer of Watertown, Rock Island county, although of foreign birth, has served his adopted country
in two of its great wars, and in a manner to
reflect credit upon him and his native land
He was born in the principality of Hanover,
Germany February 11 1827 and is the

son of Charles and Margaret (Daling) Arenschield, natives of the same country

Charles Arenschield, Sr , was a civil engineer by profession, a well educated man, who could converse fluently in four or five different languages In his native land he served as an officer in the German army, and carried a scar on his forehead from a wound received at the battle of Waterloo While strongly attached to the fatherland, he believed that in the new world the opportunities would be greater for the future welfare of his children, and therefore determined to make this country his home Accordingly in 1835, he came with his family, consisting of wife and three children, and first located in Montgomery county, Ohio, near the present city of Dayton

After residing in that county some two or three years, he removed to Hardin county in the same state, and commenced to develop a farm He had been in that county but a short time when he was selected county surveyor, which office he filled in a highly satisfactory manner About 1838 his wife died and he subsequently again married, but by his second union had no children By the first union there were four, three of whom are yet living After living to a ripe old age he passed to his reward, leaving behind him a record of a life well spent

The mother of our subject died when he was but ten or twelve years of age, and henceforth his lot in life was a hard one during his boyhood and youth In his native land he attended school from the time he was six years of age, but on coming to America that privilege was denied him, and all told after the family located in Hardin county he attended school but twenty-one days Notwithstanding this he is however a well in

of which both himself and his descendants have reason to be proud

In Hardin county the family located in the heavy timber, which had to be cleared and planted, and young Charles was expected to do his part of that laborious work He toiled early and late at such work until he was twenty years old Whether inherited or not, he had a taste for military life, and on the 21st of January, 1847, he enlisted in Company I, First Regiment Mounted Rifles of the United States army at Urbana, Ohio, with the understanding that the regiment was to guard emigrant trains across the plains to Oregon The war with Mexico had been declared, and instead of assigning the regiment to the duty for which it was enlisted, it was sent to Mexico, and was with General Scott on his march from Vera Cruz to Mexico city With others Mr Arenschield enlisted for five years, but Congress having passed an act permitting the discharge of all soldiers enlisted for another purpose, but who were sent to Mexico, our subject availed himself of the opportunity and was duly mustered out after eighteen months of hard service He was injured on the knee while trying to mount an unbroken horse and has never fully recovered

On receiving his discharge, Mr Arenschield returned to Hardin county, Ohio, only to find his father's home broken up in consequence of the death of the latter's second wife He then worked at farm labor by the month for a time, but having received a land warrant from the general government for his services in the Mexican war, he concluded to purchase an eighty-acre farm in Hardin county, giving his land warrant, which called for one hundred sixty at one

dollar and a quarter per acre, in part payment The land purchased was covered
with heavy timber which had to be cleared
After a small portion was cleared and a log
cabin erected he leased the place and worked
out to get money to pay the balance due
on it

Time was passing and our subject realized the need of a helpmeet, so on the 28th
of December, 1852, he was united in
marriage to Miss Harriet R Toland, of
Clark county, Ohio, but then residing in
Springfield, that state, where the wedding
ceremony was performed With his young
bride he removed to his farm, and there
resided a little more than two years, when
he sold out with the intention of going to
Iowa With his wife and one child, he
started upon the journey, driving overland
with a team, and after a tedious drive of a
little over three weeks arrived at the residence of Owen Toland, his wife's father,
then residing near Moline Here he left
his wife and child to visit for a time, while
he took a trip to Iowa to secure their future
home

Making his selection of land Mr Arens-
schield returned to Moline for his wife The
weather had now become so bad that he
could not cross the river, and therefore rented a house in what is now the village of
Watertown in which to remain during the
winter But "the best laid schemes of
mice and men gang aft aglee" So Mr
Arenschield has never become a citizen of
the Hawkeye state In the spring of 1856
he rented a farm of Henry McNeal and commenced its cultivation The same year he
helped lay out the village of Watertown and
then purchased the two lots on which he now
lives, erect ' ' '   (| ,| .. |.|
1857 he be   '.   .

the road and the following year purchased
seven and a half acres adjoining From
time to time he added to his possessions until he owned one-half block in the village
and forty-six acres adjoining Watertown
In 1874 he bought one hundred and sixty
acres in Fillmore county, Nebraska, which
is now owned by one of his sons

To Mr and Mrs. Arenschield six children were born Charles Oscar is married,
has three children, and is engaged in farming, Victor L , a carpenter by trade, is married, has three children, and resides in Geneva, Nebraska, Edwin M , a graduate of
the medical department of the State University of Iowa, resides in Ottumwa, that
state, is married and has three children, W
Sherman, an engineer on the Chicago, Rock
Island & Pacific Railroad, is married and
resides at Eldon, Iowa, Luella May, born
July 22, 1858, died October 2, 1859, Earl
Ray, born February 21, 1874, died August
29, 1874 The mother of these children
was born in Canton, Starke county, Ohio,
April 24, 1833, and died March 19, 1897,
mourned not alone by the family, but by a
large circle of friends

When the war for the Union commenced,
our subject held back for a time, but his
patriotic blood was stirred within him, so
on the 6th of August, 1862, he enlisted once
more in the service of his adopted country
as a private in Company F, Eighty-ninth
Illinois Volunteer Infantry at Rock Island,
but was mustered in at Chicago a few days
later as fourth sergeant, serving as such
until the battle of Stone river, when he was
make second sergeant With that rank he
served until July, 1863, when he was appointed acting first sergeant, serving as such
until March 1 1?°, when he was commis-
· |· |l\ · .\.(((,·)·| ·-·((·(||||· lieutenant,

On September 21, 1864, he was promoted to first lieutenant and served as such until the close of the war

During his term of service Lieutenant Arenschield took part in some of the most severe engagements of the war, including Stone river Liberty Gap, Chickamauga and Mission Ridge, and was all through the Atlanta campaign With his regiment he was in East Tennessee at the time of Lee's surrender, and was still there when the news of the assassination of Lincoln was received At different times Lieutenant Arenschield commanded three different companies, and should have been commissioned captain He was mustered out June 10, 1865

Returning home, our subject settled down to his old life, and has since gone on the even tenor of his way, doing his duty as best he could and enjoying the good will of all He cast his first presidential ballot in 1852 for John P Hale, and notwithstanding he was of foreign birth voted for Fillmore and Donelson in 1856 and Bell and Everett in 1860 In 1868 he voted for Grant He has never been an office seeker, neither did he ever seek promotion while in the army, at first refusing the commission of lieutenant In 1878 he united with the Baptist church in Watertown, and has endeavored at all times to serve the Master as well and as faithfully as he served his country In presenting the life history of Mr Arenschield, the writer feels that it is impossible to do justice to a man who so nobly served his country, and so faithfully performed every duty of citizenship He has the esteem of all who know him and is well worthy of representation in the record of the leading and most prominent men of Rock Island co

ALBERT R BEAL, M D, physician and surgeon of Watertown, was born in Zuma township, Rock Island county, July 3, 1867, and is a son of Lucius W and Elizabeth S (Drum) Beal His father was a farmer and was born in the same township His grandfather, Daniel N Beal, who is about ninety years of age, makes his home in Moline He was born, reared and married in Vermont, and in 1837 located in Zuma township, since which time he has been a resident of Rock Island county The Doctor's father resided in this county until 1881, when he removed to Cherokee county, Iowa, where he was elected county auditor in 1885, serving in that capacity for ten years He is a Republican in politics, served as deputy sheriff of Rock Island county, and was supervisor and assessor of Zuma township for about ten years

The Doctor remained on the old homestead until fifteen years of age and attended the country schools He went to Iowa, and later entered the Western College in Toledo, where he pursued his studies three years Previous to this time he was also a student in Port Byron Academy for one year In 1889 he began the study of medicine in the Iowa State University of Iowa City and after two years began practice at a mining camp in the state of Chihauhua, Mexico, where he remained one year He prospered there and at the end of that time entered the Rush Medical College of Chicago, where he was graduated in 1893 He afterward spent a few months at Cripple Creek, Colorado, and then went to Washta, Iowa, where he remained for three and a half years In the fall of 1896 he came to Watertown, and is already established in a good practice

The Doctor was married in Iowa, April

2, 1895, to Miss Ida M Freeman, of Milwaukee, with whom he had become acquainted during her temporary residence in Washta She is a daughter of William W and Mary A (Wheeler) Freeman She acquired a good common-school education and is a lady of superior musical talent, having been able to play on a musical instrument since five years of age The Doctor and his wife have one child, Elizabeth, who was born in Watertown, March 16, 1897 Throughout the community they are widely and favorably known and enjoy the hospitality of the best homes of the town

The Doctor is a Republican and cast his first presidential vote for Harrison in 1888 Since 1890 he has been a member of Little Sioux Lodge, No 521, A F & A M , is a member of the Odd Fellows Lodge in Washta, Iowa, and of Watertown Camp, Modern Woodmen of America He belongs to the Presbyterian church, and is a member of the Tri-City Medical Association Deeply interested in his profession, he is a close student of medical journals and does all in his power to perfect himself in his chosen calling He is now enjoying a liberal patronage which he well merits

CHARLES OTIS NASON, who is now living retired at 1802 Third avenue, Moline, needs no special introduction to the readers of this volume, but the work would be incomplete without the record of his life No man in Rock Island county has been more prominently identified with the business history of the community or has taken a more active part in its upbuilding and progress He has ever cheerfully given his support to those enterprises that tend to public dev   t ..l. h d.ly .t

exception, he has been connected with every interest that has promoted general welfare. His name is a synonym for honorable business dealing, he is always mentioned as one of the invaluable citizens of the county, and on the rolls of its most honored pioneers his name should be found among the foremost

Mr. Nason was born in Hartford, Windsor county, Vermont, September 20, 1828, and is of English extraction His father, Horace Nason, a native of Ipswich, Massachusetts, was reared and educated in New England, where he also learned the machinist trade. Enlisting in the American army in the war of 1812, he started for Plattsmouth, but hostilities ceased before he reached his destination. He wedded Miss Mary Lamb, a native of Granville, Vermont, in which state her father was also born, and for a number of years after his marriage he worked at his trade in Hartford, Vermont, but spent his last years in Claremont, New Hampshire, where his death occurred

Charles O Nason, of this review, is one of a family of three sons and six daughters, all of whom reached years of maturity, but he and four sisters are the only ones now living In the schools of Claremont he obtained a good practical education, but at the age of seventeen he laid aside his text books to accept the position of assistant overseer of a cotton factory, and was later promoted overseer, which position he continued to acceptably fill for several years Coming west in the spring of 1857 on a visit to his uncle, John Deere, of Moline, he was prevailed upon to remain and accept a position in the Deere establishment He was first employed in the woodworking shop, and was steadily advanced until he became superintendent which is possible position he retained until 1894, when he retired from active business On the organization of the Moline Plow Works, he became one of its stockholders, was director for many years, and for a number of years was treasurer of the company. He is also a stockholder and treasurer of the People's Power Company, and has been connected with a number of Moline's most prominent manufacturing enterprises. While advancing his own interests, he has not been unmindful of the welfare of his adopted city and county, but has been actively identified with its growth and development, giving his hearty support to all measures for their advancement and progress

In Claremont, New Hampshire, August 7, 1849, was celebrated the marriage of Mr Nason and Miss Charlotte Johnston, who was born in Meriden, New Hampshire, and is a daughter of Thomas and Delia (Pierce) Johnston, also natives of the Granite state. Two children were born of this union — Clarence E , now a prominent business man of Moline, who is engaged in the oil business He married Ella Estell, a native of Illinois, who was reared and educated in Moline Ellen Frances, the younger child, began her education in the schools of Moline, and was later a student at St Mary's, Knoxville, Illinois

The family spend a few months every summer in the east, having a beautiful summer home at York Beach, Maine Mr and Mrs Nason are members of the Episcopal church, and in social circles hold an enviable position Politically, Mr Nason is a stanch Republican, always giving his support to the men and measures of that party, and while not a politician or aspirant for office, he was elected mayor of Moline in 1887, and served one term the credit to himself and satis-

faction to his constituents He has made an untarnished record and unspotted reputation as a business man In all places and under all circumstances he is loyal to truth, honor and right justly valuing his own self-respect as infinitely more profitable than wealth, fame and position

HENRY STRUSS.—A brilliant example of a self-made American citizen and a grand exemplification of the progress that an ambitious foreigner can make in this country of unbounded opportunities, is shown in the case of Mr Struss, one of the leading German-American residents of Rock Island county, and a well-known farmer residing on section 7, Zuma township His singular success is due to his own energy and the high ideal which his lofty and laudable ambition placed before him Success in any walk of life is an indication of earnest endeavor and persevering efforts characteristics which he possesses in an eminent degree

Mr Struss was born on the 8th of February, 1844, in the Grand Duchy of Oldenberg, Germany, where he attended school and continued to make his home until seventeen years of age His knowledge of English was wholly self-acquired since his arrival in the United States It was in 1861 that he crossed the broad Atlantic, arriving in New York on the 1st of July, and he first stopped at North Dover, near Cleveland, Ohio, where he worked for one month With a friend he then proceeded to La Crosse county, Wisconsin where he worked by the month for about two years and a half, and then came to Illinois, but shortly afterward went to Clinton county, Iowa where in partnership with a friend he operated a rented farm for about two years Later he worked by the month for two or three years in Clinton and Scott counties, Iowa

Coming to Rock Island county, Illinois, in 1870, he and his brother purchased one hundred twenty-seven acres of land in Zuma township, where our subject is still living They at once began to clear and improve the place, which they operated together for some time, then Henry Struss rented his brother's portion for a few years, and subsequently purchased his interest, the brother, J Diedrich Struss, removing to Rock Island, where he died December 18, 1882 To the original tract our subject has added forty acres, has added a large addition to his residence, and built a good barn, which was destroyed by fire in the fall of 1895, but with his characteristic energy he at once rebuilt He has a good orchard and the well tilled fields and neat and thrifty appearance of his place testify to industrious habits and excellent management

On the 15th of January, 1874, on the farm where he still resides, was celebrated the marriage of Mr Struss and Miss Frederica Magerkurth, a native of Hanover, Germany, where she was reared and educated She came to the new world with her father, who joined two sons here Mr and Mrs Struss have become the parents of seven children— Helena, wife of Henry Schroeder, of Hampton township, Rock Island county, Wilhelmina, at home, Frederica, who completed her education in the Port Byron Academy and is now one of the successful teachers of Rock Island county, Louisa, Conrad Henry, August Carl and Eleonora The family are all members of the Lutheran church and are highly respected by all who know

Since voting for General Hancock, Mr Struss has been a pronounced Democrat in politics, and in 1896 supported W J Bryan and the free silver platform He is one of the representative and prominent citizens of Zuma township, and is held in high regard by all who know him

ALONZO P CLAPP, deceased, was numbered among the honored pioneers of Rock Island county, who located on the Mississippi when this locality was a wild and unimproved region In the work of development Mr Clapp took an active part in the early days and aided in opening up the country to civilization As the years passed by he faithfully performed his duties of citizenship and his interest in the welfare and progress of the community never abated Becoming widely and favorably known he made many friends, and his death was a loss to the entire community

Mr Clapp was born in Massachusetts, October 16, 1808, and was there reared to manhood, acquiring a common-school education He emigrated westward at an very early day and engaged in mercantile pursuits in Tazewell county, Illinois, as early as 1836 It was while residing at that place that he formed the acquaintance of Miss Sarah Bailey, and their friendship ripening into love they were married on the 8th of June, 1839, the ceremony being performed by the Rev Nathaniel Wright She was born near Philadelphia in 1820, and when a maiden of sixteen summers accompanied her parents, Elisha and Mary (Ward) Bailey, on their removal to Tazewell county

Previous to his marriage Mr Clapp had retired from merchandising and had embarked in farming on the bluff near Hampton, and had erected two houses in Hampton Thither he brought his bride, and though he afterward purchased the farm on the bluff he continued to make his home in Hampton For some years he engaged in agricultural pursuits and met with success in his undertaking He placed his land all under a high state of cultivation, and the well-tilled fields returned to him bounteous harvests His integrity in all trade transactions, his well directed efforts, his industry and enterprise, combined to make him one of the most successful agriculturists of the community, and he became the possessor of a comfortable competence

Mr Clapp was a man of sterling worth and unswerving fidelity to principle, and commanded the respect of all who knew him, so that his death, which occurred July 20, 1885, was widely and deeply mourned He was laid to rest in Hampton cemetery, where a substantial monument marks his last resting place, but his memory is enshrined in many hearts, and especially was he dear to the early pioneers, whose experience he had shared In politics he was a Republican and served as constable, but was never an office seeker For some years he was a member of the Methodist Episcopal church of Hampton, of which his wife is the only surviving member of the number who composed the church when she united The first time she attended church in Hampton the services were held in a blacksmith shop, and one winter the church met on a steamboat which was frozen in the river at Hampton wharf When Mrs Clapp joined the church on probation, services were held in a log school house which stood near the site of the present school house, the occasion being a quarterly meeting at which Re ·····   ··   ··· ·· ···

19

Elder St Clair was the presiding elder Through all these years she has been true and faithful to her Christian vows and her well spent life has won her the love and respect of a very large circle of friends

CHARLES G WALDMAN -- While "the race is not always to the swift, nor the battle to the strong," the invariable law of destiny accords to tireless energy, industry and ability a successful career The truth of this assertion is abundantly verified in the life of Mr Waldman, senior member of the firm of Waldman & Titterington of Edgington, Illinois

A native of Rock Island county, he was born near Edgington September 13, 1867, and is a son of Andrew Waldman, in whose family were six children, four yet living Sarah, wife of Amassa Space, of Malone, Iowa, Frank, a resident of Grant City Missouri, Jacob, of Sears, Illinois, and Charles G The father, a native of Germany, crossed the broad Atlantic and became a resident of Rock Island county about 1852 In Edgington township he successfully engaged in farming and reared his family While he and his wife were returning home from a funeral October 16, 1877 they were killed by a train on a railroad crossing near Milan, he at the age of forty-nine, and she on her fiftieth birthday Both were earnest and consistent members of the German Lutheran church, and enjoyed the respect and esteem of all who knew them

On a farm in Edgington township, Charles G Waldman passed the days of his boyhood and youth, and in the district schools of the neighborhood acquired his elementary education, which was supple-·········· ···· ·· · ·· ·· ······· ··

Rock Island, the Normal school of Geneseo, Illinois, and the Davenport Business College, thus becoming well equipped for the responsible duties of business life As a boy he began clerking in an implement store in Edgington, was later in the employ of Mr. Stoddard, and in 1895, in partnership with M A Titterington, bought out his employer, the firm becoming Waldman & Titterington They now carry a large line of general merchandise, agricultural implements, wagons, buggies, etc , and from the public receive a liberal patronage, their honorable, straightforward business methods winning them the confidence of the entire community

Mr Waldman gives his political support to the men and measures of the Democratic party, and is now serving as assistant postmaster of Edgington, while socially he affiliates with Andalusia Lodge, F & A M , and the Modern Woodmen of America A man of keen perception, of unbounded enterprise, his success in life is due entirely to his own efforts, and he deserves prominent mention among the leading and representative business men of the county His genial, pleasant maner has made him quite popular in both business and social circles, and as a public-spirited, enterprising man, he is recognized as a valued citizen of the community.

FRANK E KELLEY, who resides on section 10, Buffalo Prairie township, was born in Henry county, Illinois, May 2, 1859, and is a son of Martin Kelley, a native of Ohio, who was there married and later lost his wife. He then came to Illinois in an early day, locating in Rock Island county For his second wife he married Marietta Carr, a daughter of J' t of Carr one of the

early settlers of the county. Subsequently Mr Kelley removed to Henry county, but afterward returned to Buffalo Prairie township, Rock Island county, and still later purchased the old Carr homestead of five hundred and twenty acres He built there a house and greatly improved the place, raising his family on that farm He now owns a part of the old farm

Frank E Kelley was reared to manhood in the neighborhood of his present home and acquired his education in the public schools He assisted in the cultivation and development of his father's land until he had attained his majority, when he went to Licking county, Ohio, and was married there, January 18, 1882, to Maud Hirst, a native of that county, and a daughter of Richard Hirst, who was born in Loudoun county, Virginia and who removed with his mother to Ohio, and was married there to Anna Maria Kelley, also a native of Loudoun county. In the family were three sons and two daughters, Servetus, of Licking county, Mrs Eva Stone, and Mrs Kelley being the surviving members of the family John, who was a graduate of the College of Physicians and Surgeons of Columbus, located in Brownsville, Ohio, where he soon became recognized as the leading physician of the town He died there at the age of twenty-nine Vinson followed farming for several years in Iowa, and then returned to the old family homestead in Ohio, where his death occurred After her mother's death Mrs. Kelley resided with her grandmother, Mrs. Maddox, who belonged to one of the old and prominent families of Virginia By her marriage, Mrs Kelley has three sons— Richard Hirst, Raymond Ellis and Hartsell

After his marriage, Mr Kelley rented land for about three or four years and then purchased his father's old homestead of one hundred and fifty acres, upon which he has made some valuable improvements, transforming the place into one of the fine farms of the township. His business career has been one crowned with the success that follows well directed and energetic efforts He had no capital with which to begin life, but has steadily worked his way upward and is now the possessor of a comfortable competence

In his political views Mr Kelley is a stanch Republican, exercising his right of franchise in support of the men and measures of that party, but political office has no attraction for him. The cause of education finds in him a warm friend and for three years he served as a member of the school board He takes a deep interest in all that pertains to the welfare of the community, and is a public-spirited, progressive citizen.

E WHITNEY ADAMS —The name of this lamented citizen of Rock Island county, who passed to his rest on the 13th of May, 1888, is remembered as that of one of the first settlers of Hampton township, and of a man who assisted greatly in its development and prosperity He was by nature liberal and public-spirited, and always maintained an interest in the people around him and contributed to the best of his means and ability to their improvement socially, morally and financially. No man is more worthy of representation in a work of this kind, and there is none whose name is held in more grateful remembrance

Mr Adams was born October 6, 1825, in Nicholas county, Kentucky, where he acquired a fa

and when about sixteen years of age was brought to Illinois by his parents, Ephraim and Elizabeth (Riley) Adams, who settled on the bluff of south Watertown, in Rock Island county, where the father engaged in farming About two years after his arrival here our subject went to Moline, where he served an apprenticeship to the blacksmith's trade and continued to work until his marriage, which important event of his life was celebrated November 2, 1848, Miss Ann Willis, of Hampton township, becoming his wife She was born in Maryland, a daughter of Thomas and Mary (Pope) Adams, also natives of that state, who in 1840 brought their family to Rock Island county, Illinois, and also made a home on the bluffs south of Watertown. There the father, who was a farmer by occupation, spent his remaining days

Mr and Mrs. Adams began their domestic life in Hampton, where he conducted a blacksmith shop for some time, but later turned his attention to agricultural pursuits as being more agreeable to his taste and better suited to his health He purchased a tract of two hundred and sixty-five acres which constituted nearly the whole of Campbell's Island After clearing away the timber which covered it, he placed acre after acre under the plow and soon transformed the wild tract into one of the most productive and fertile farms of Hampton township He continued to make his home in Hampton on the river bank in full view of the Mississippi and the island on which his farm was located. In politics he was an ardent Democrat but never aspired to public office, preferring to give his undivided attention to his business interests He was a man universally respected, one whose word was con-   s death the community felt that it had lost one of its most honored and useful citizens

Mrs Adams proved herself full worthy as the companion and helpmeet of this excellent man, and most satisfactorily settled the estate after his death   There were five children born to them   Emma Euella is the wife of Oscar Bysant, of Moline, and has two children Murton and Clare   Clara A married George F Holland, a native of Weedsport, New York, who was highly educated and was a bookkeeper in Chicago at the time of his death which occurred in December, 1892, when he was fifty-three years of age   Joseph W a resident of Mason City Iowa, married Alice Vincent and has two children—Joseph W and Stella Myra is the wife of Ship Silvis, of Carbon Cliff, and has one child, Marguerite   Harry B , also of Mason City, Iowa married Rena Farror and has one child

---

SIMEON E ROBERTS has demonstrated the true meaning of the word success as the full accomplishment of an honorable purpose   Energy, close application perseverance and good management—these are the elements which have entered into his business career and crowned his efforts with prosperity   He now resides on section 35 Buffalo Prairie township, where he owns three hundred and twenty acres of valuable land, and in addition to this he has other landed possessions aggregating eight hundred acres

Mr Roberts was born in Dearborn county, Indiana April 20, 1835   His grandfather, Ebenezer Roberts, was one of the heroes of the Revolution, was wounded in battle

sion by t

of Maine, and removed with his family to Dearborn county Indiana, where he made a home in the wilderness   His son, Arthur P Roberts, was born in Maine, in 1812, and was reared in the Hoosier state, where he married Mary B Freeman, a native of Indiana   By trade, Mr Roberts was a blacksmith, as was his father   In 1839 he removed to Illinois, and the grandfather came to this state the following year   The former located near Oquawka, Henderson county, where he resided until 1852, when he came to Rock Island county, and purchased two hundred and seven acres of raw land in Buffalo Prairie township   There he built a house, developed an excellent farm and planted one of the best orchards in the county   His buildings were neat and substantial structures, and he was regarded as a very progressive farmer   His land was purchased with the proceeds of a California trip   In 1850 he went to the gold mines, where he spent eighteen months, returning with twenty-eight gold pieces of fifty dollars each   His death occurred November 2, 1887   His first wife passed away some years previous, but he was survived some years by his second wife

In the family were ten children   Moses, who grew to mature years and married, but is now deceased, Simeon E , Rebecca Jane, wife of John McNutt of Audubon county, Iowa, Isaac, who died in the service while defending his country in the Civil war, Martha Ann, who married but is now deceased, Philip, deceased, Mary, widow of Michael Coon, of Kansas, Joshua, of Rock Island county, Lydia, wife of George Parmenter, of Grinnell, Iowa, Elisha B , a farmer of Rock Island county, Ernest, now   of Elmer

Mr Roberts, of this review, was a child of about five years when he came to Illinois, and a young man of eighteen when the family removed to this county He aided his father in clearing the land and opening up a farm, continuing to assist him in its further cultivation until twenty-three years of age, when with his father and brother Isaac, he started for Pikes Peak, but on reaching the Missouri river, he determined to go no further and returned to his home Here he traded his outfit for twenty acres of land which he still owns, and upon the place built a home, and planted one thousand apple trees From time to time he has added to his land until he now has something over seven hundred acres, included in three farms, and comprising some of the most valuable land in the county He is very progressive and methodical in his farming operations, is honorable in his dealings and by his enterprise and industry has accumulated a handsome competence, thus fully realizing the dreams of his youth

Mr Roberts was married in Buffalo Prairie township, November 28, 1862, to Miss Nancy A Campbell, who was born near Steubenville, Ohio, a daughter of Arthur and Elizabeth (McNutt) Campbell, also natives of that state, whence they came to Illinois in 1852 Twelve children born of this union are now living—Emeline, wife of Thomas Hayes, of this county, Priscilla wife of Otto Schutte, of Buffalo Prairie township, Charles, a farmer of this county, Arthur, who is married and follows farming in Buffalo Prairie township, Elizabeth Jane, who was formerly engaged in teaching, now at home, Alice, wife of William Robinson, of Andalusia township, Mollie, Ella, Clarence, Ira, Frank P and Myrtle, all at home Bertha

In politics Mr Roberts has been a stanch Republican since casting his first presidential vote for Fremont, and in 1896 had the pleasure of visiting and shaking hands with President McKinley in Canton, Ohio He has taken quite an active part in local politics, serving on different committees and acting as delegate to the county, judicial and congressional conventions He has filled the office of collector and other positions of honor and trust, yet has never been an office seeker He aided in organizing the school districts, served for seventeen consecutive years as school trustee, and has long labored earnestly and effectively in the interests of the cause of education His wife and children are members of the Baptist church and Mr Roberts is also an attendant on its services, and contributes liberally to its support He belongs to Andalusia Lodge, A F & A M, having been made a Mason in 1862 He and his family receive and merit the high regard of the entire community His public and private life are above reproach, for his career has ever been one characterized by the utmost fidelity to duty The part which he has taken in the development of the county has impressed his name indelibly upon its records and he well deserves mention among the honored pioneers

LARS P NELSON, who for sixteen years has been a resident of Moline, where he is now successfully engaged in the livery business, has led a life of honest toil Throughout his career of continued and far-reaching usefulness his duties have been performed with the greatest care, and business interests have been so managed as to win the confidence of the public and the prosperity which should always attend honorable effort

Mr Nelson was born in Sweden, near Hoganas, July 27, 1850, a son of Nels and Christine (Pierson) Anderson   He was reared on a farm, obtained his education in the common schools and on attaining his majority left the land of his birth for the land of the free   During the two weeks voyage to New York city a severe storm was encountered, lasting three days   From the east Mr Nelson made his way to St Louis, where he followed anything that he could get to do   He afterward went to Chicago, where he was ill in the hospital for a time   On recovering his health he secured a situation on a farm and in the following spring went to the mines in the Lake Superior region of northern Michigan, where he was employed from April until November   He then returned to the farm where he had previously worked and was engaged in picking corn for a short time   Through the winter he engaged in chopping wood in the timber regions of Michigan, and in the spring went to Geneseo, Illinois, where he soon obtained a situation as a farm hand, being employed in that capacity for eight years

In 1881 Mr Nelson came to Moline and was employed to drive an express wagon for a time   In August, 1882, he bought out his employer and successfully conducted the business until 1897, enjoying a liberal patronage, which brought to him good financial returns   In 1892 he purchased the livery stable which he now owns, being proprietor of one of the well appointed barns of the city.   His genial manner, courtesy to his patrons and honorable dealing insures him a continuance of the liberal public support which is a.. .d.d l im.

Mr Nelson has been twice married   He was married April 27, 1882, to Matilda Johnson, of Geneseo, Illinois, who was born in Princeton, Bureau county   They became parents of four children—Helen J., Eddie P , Agnes F and Alice L   The mother died December 29, 1893, and Mr Nelson was again married July 25, 1895, his second union being with Mrs Rose A Stacy, who was born in Whitewater, Wisconsin, a daughter of Allison Miller   Her first husband was Milo Stacy, by whom she had three children, two of whom died in infancy, and Vera Roberta, who died at the age of ten years

In 1876 Mr Nelson cast his first presidential vote for R B Hayes, and has since been a Republican   He has been solicited by his party and friends to become a candidate for the offices of alderman and supervisor but has steadily refused   In the spring of 1897, however, he was appointed street commissioner of Moline, and is now acceptably filling that position   He belongs to Olive Lodge, No 583, I O O F , of which he has served for three terms as treasurer, and is also a member of the Rebecca Lodge   He is a charter member of Camp, No 38, M W A , is second vice-president of the Home Forum, and is left supporter of the patriarch in Moline Encampment, No 153   His has been an industrious and well spent life, which has won him success in business and esteem in social circles

JOHN H. FOSTER, merchant and postmaster at Foster, Rock Island county, is one of the public-spirited citizens to whose energy and foresight this locality is indebted for many improvements   While he, as a prosperous business man, has given close attention to his private business affairs, he has never forgotten or ignored that bond of common interest which should unite the people of every community, and he has always been ready to promote progress in every line

In Rochester, Monroe county, New York, Mr Foster first opened his eyes to the light of day May 15, 1840, and is descended from a family of English origin which was early founded in New England, where Grandfather Foster was born His father, Jonathan Foster, was a native of Massachusetts, where he was reared upon a farm and learned the brick and stone mason's trade, at which he worked for many years in Rochester, New York He was one of the pioneer settlers of that city and was married in Pittsford, the same county, to Miss Hulda Griffin, who was born there Her father, James Griffin, was also a pioneer of Monroe county, and was a soldier in the war of 1812 For some years Mr. Foster was one of the leading contractors and builders of Rochester, where his death occurred in 1873, and his wife passed away in 1887

The first seventeen years of his life John H Foster spent in his native city, and then joined an older sister, Mrs Sarah French, in Springfield, Illinois, where he attended school for two years and a half, thus completing his literary education which was begun in Rochester, New York For about a year and a half he worked on a farm in Sangamon county, and spent the following year in the employ of Mr Bates, a farmer of Lincoln, Logan county, Illinois After spending a short time with his sister in Springfield in the fall of 1860, he went to Muscatine, Iowa, where he visited an uncle, Sewall Foster, who was one of the first settlers in th

from the government on which the present city of Muscatine now stands

About 1837, previous to the birth of our subject, his father had entered two hundred and forty acres of land in Drury township, Rock Island county, and in 1860 the son visited the place After spending a short time at his old home in Rochester he located here on the 5th of March, 1861, built a shanty, and the first year broke fifty-five acres In the fall of that year he again returned to Rochester, where he was married in October, to Miss Louise Wimble, who was born, reared and educated there He brought his bride to his new home in Rock Island county, and to the further development and improvement of his place he devoted his entire time and attention for some years, making it one of the best farms in the locality In 1871, he removed to Muscatine, Iowa, where he conducted a grocery store for five years and then returned to his farm Later he embarked in general merchandising at Foster, which he has since carried on, and has established a good country trade, and during the last year of President Cleveland's administration succeeded in establishing a post office at his place, which was named in his honor He was appointed the first postmaster and has now filled that position for nine years He is a wide-awake, progressive business man and has met with a well deserved success in his undertakings, being now one of the most prosperous citizens of Drury township

To Mr and Mrs Foster have been born five children George G , a resident of Omaha, Nebraska, where he holds a responsible position with the Milwaukee, Omaha, Minneapolis & St Paul Railroad, Fred who is married and now operates his father's f D l f F l C H ogan, of

Muscatine, Iowa, Kate, at home, and Sadie, who died at the age of five years

In politics Mr Foster is a sound Democrat, and has been honored by his fellow citizens with several important local positions including those of supervisor, trustee and school director His wife was the first lady ever elected treasurer of a school board in Illinois, and has acceptably filled that position for years, and is still the treasurer Wherever known they are held in high regard, and their circle of friends and acquaintances is indeed extensive Mr Foster is a Master Mason

MATTHEW J McENIRY, the popular postmaster of Moline, and one of its representative and prominent citizens, is a native of Rock Island county, born in Zuma township, April 9, 1858, and is a son of William and Elizabeth (Coughlin) McEniry The father, a native of County Cork, Ireland, became a resident of Moline in 1841, and remained here until after his marriage in 1846 Being a brickmaker by trade, he followed that occupation for about twelve years and then purchased a farm of seven hundred sixteen acres in Zuma township, where he successfully engaged in agricultural pursuits until called to his final rest in 1874 In connection with general farming he also became an extensive raiser and shipper of stock Although he came to the New World a poor man, by industry, perseverence and good management he steadily worked his way upward to a position of wealth and affluence, accumulating a handsome property

To the parents of our subject were born six children who in order of birth are as follows ⌐ ⌐ ⌐ , ⌐ ⌐

Dwyer, a resident of Dwyer, St Louis county, Missouri, Michael F , a grain dealer of Lenox, Iowa, John, a mail clerk living in Moline, Matthew J , of this sketch, William, who is also represented in this work, and Mollie, who is living at the family residence, No 1910 Third avenue, Moline

Upon the home farm Matthew J McEniry remained until twenty-five years of age, receiving his early education in the country schools of the neighborhood At the age of seventeen he went to Prairie du Chien, Wisconsin, where he graduated on the completion of a commercial course, and on attaining his majority entered Notre Dame University near South Bend, Indiana, where he pursued the four years scientific course, graduating with high honors in the class of 1882

His school days over Mr McEniry returned to the home farm where his mother was still living, and in 1884 was elected supervisor of Zuma township on a fusion ticket, acceptably serving in that position for one term In 1883 he was also appointed deputy sheriff of Rock Island county for a term of four years and in the meantime began reading law with his brother. He entered the law department of the University of Michigan in 1887 and graduated the following year, after which he formed a partnership with his brother in Moline, under the firm name of McEniry & McEniry

As a lawyer our subject met with excellent success, and in 1892 was the nominee of the Democratic party for state's attorney, made a thorough and systematic canvass and delivered about thirty addresses in various parts of the county, including every township He has ever taken an active and conᵗⁱⁿ... ... ... has been a delegate to nearly every state convention of his party since 1882, and has continuously served on the county central committee, being at present its secretary Mr McEnny has served nearly four years in the Illinois Naval Marines and holds the office of ensign In July, 1894, he received the appointment of postmaster of Moline, which is a second class presidential office, and served faithfully, and acceptably discharged the duties of that position until October 1, 1897 He has ever been found true to every trust reposed in him whether public or private, and the place which he occupies in the social world is a tribute to that genuine worth and true nobleness of character which are universally recognized and honored Reared in the Holy Catholic church he was confirmed by Archbishop Foley of Chicago, and is now a communicant of St Mary's church of Moline He has been a member of the executive committee of the Old Settlers' Association of Rock Island county, is now serving as its vice-president, and also belongs to the Moline Social Club

---

ALEXANDER ASHDOWN This gentleman who spent his early manhood in active business and mainly in agricultural pursuits, is now living retired on a fine farm on section 8, Canoe Creek township A man of great energy and more than ordinary business capacity, his success in life has been due to his own efforts and the sound judgment which has enabled him to make wise investments and take good advantage of his resources

Mr Ashdown was born in Kent county, England, April 21, 1824, a son of Edward and Anna

was overseer on a farm and the children were all taught to work from early childhood, thus having no chance to attend school except Sunday school, where our subject was taught to read When he was thirteen years of age, his father, with the two youngest sons, came to America and spent two or three years in New York state It was his intention of making his home there, but as he could not persuade the remainder of the family to join him, he returned to his native land with his two sons, there spending his remaining days

During his boyhood and youth Alexander Ashdown worked at whatever he could find to do He was married October 11, 1850, to Miss Charlotte Martin, who was born in Kent county, England, May 22, 1831, and is a daughter of George and Fannie Lambert) Martin For seven years he continued to work at day's labor in England, where three of his children were born, but on the 20th of June, 1857, the family sailed from the East India docks, London, and after a stormy voyage of forty-five days landed at Castle Garden, New York The following morning they started for Illinois and on arriving at Geneseo, this state, drove from there in a coal wagon to Tawkett's Ferry whence they proceeded to the home of Mr Ashdown's brothers, Mark and Henry, who had come to Rock Island county in 1850

Our subject started to bind wheat at one dollar per day but the first half day almost died from the heat as he was clad in a heavy pair of corduroy trousers From an old gunny sack his wife then made him a pair, which were considerably cooler The following year he rented a farm near his present home, and after operating rented land for seven years he was able to purchase one .... ken, but with no improvements there except a small house in which the family lived for a few years, when it was replaced by their present comfortable home Together Mr and Mrs Ashdown worked early and late, exercising the strictest economy, and are to-day numbered among the well-to-do citizens of their community To the original purchase he added another forty-acre tract, making a valuable farm of one hundred and sixty acres

Of the nine children born to this worthy couple eight are still living, three were born in England, and one six weeks after their arrival here. George, who is engaged in the livery business at Sundance, Wyoming, and is also serving as deputy sheriff, is married and has one child, Lottie Eliza is the wife of Joseph Robinson, of Wyoming, and has eight children—Charles, Kate, Fred, Clara, Myrtle, Bessie George, Archibald and Levi Fred died of croup at the age of four years Henry, who operates his father's land, married Lucy Farber and has five children—Mabel, Clyde, Alexander, Leonard and John Alfred, a resident of Mapleton, Iowa, married Cora Martin and has four children—Nettie, Blanche, Ralph and Walter. Fannie is the wife of William G McConnell, of Canoe Creek township, and has five children—Frank, Lottie, Theresa, Grace and Wallace Clara is the wife of George Lephardt, of Canoe Creek township, and has two children—Lawrence and Frances Kate is the wife of Joseph McClellan Martin, of Hillsdale, Illinois, and has two children—Fay and Sylva Emma is the wife of Stephen Wallace Woodborn, of Canoe Creek township, who is now studying for the ministry in Monmouth, Illinois They have six to be [...] there are three of th [...] grandchildren that

are now married, and there are four great-grandchildren, all in Wyoming.

After voting for Lincoln in 1864, Mr Ashdown was a Republican until 1876, when he supported Tilden, in 1880 did not vote, but the following three presidential elections cast his ballot for Cleveland, and in 1896 supported Bryan For the success that he has achieved in life Mr Ashdown deserves great credit, for he began life here without capital, and through his own efforts has become one of the substantial citizens of Canoe Creek township as well as one of its honored and valued citizens He enjoys the respect and esteem of all who know him

CHARLES G ALSENE —The world instinctively pays deference to the man who has risen above his early surroundings, overcome the obstacles in his path and reached a high position in the business world This is a progressive age, and he who does not advance is soon left far behind Mr Alsene, by the improvement of the opportunities by which all are surrounded, has steadily and honorably worked his way upward and has attained a fair degree of prosperity He is now numbered among the leading business men of Moline, where he is engaged in the grocery trade as a member of the firm of Alsene & Lundeen

Mr. Alsene was born in Sweden, November 8, 1856, his parents being John Harry and Anna Louisa (Johanson) Swanson, the former a farmer by occupation His boyhood days were spent on his father's farm and in attendance at the common schools of the neighborhood His father died when he was sixteen years of age, but he continued to work upon the home farm until coming to America with the exception of one season spent in Stockholm He was a young man of twenty-four years when he determined to try his fortune in the new world Accompanied by a sister he crossed the briny deep, reaching New York after a voyage of two weeks For two years he was employed on a farm near Woodhull, Illinois, and while thus engaged had the misfortune to break his arm, which necessitated his following some less arduous pursuit With the money that he had saved he resolved to further perfect his education and spent two years as a student at Augustana College

Mr Alsene then secured employment in a sawmill in Rock Island, where he remained through the summer months, and then accepted a clerkship in a grocery store there A year later he came to Moline, where he engaged in clerking for five years, and in 1887 embarked in business for himself, forming a partnership with Mr Lundeen They began operations on a small scale, but success attended their efforts, and they not only greatly enlarged their stock, but in 1891 also erected their substantial store building They now enjoy a liberal patronage as the result of their straightforward dealing, their industry and their earnest desire to please their customers

On the 1st of January, 1887, in Moline, was celebrated the marriage of Mr Alsene and Miss Hannah Anderson, also a native of Sweden They now have two children Anton Frederick, born in Moline, February 25, 1888, and Hazel Elvira, born in Moline, April 29, 1890 Mr Alsene exercises his right of franchise in support of the men and measures of the Republican party, and socially is connected with Camp No 38, M W A , of which he is a charter member He need never have occasion to regret his re ⋅ ⁗

he has found prosperity, a comfortable home and many friends It is but just and merited praise to say of him that as a business man he ranks with the ablest and that as a citizen he has the honor and esteem of all classes

FREDERICK S GATES Great are the changes which time and man have wrought in Rock Island county since this gentleman took up his residence in Port Byron in 1850 As the years have passed he has seen its wild lands transformed into beautiful homes and farms, its timber regions made into marketable products, its primitive homes made into substantial residences and the work of improvement carried forward until the county to-day ranks among the best in this great commonwealth Mr Gates, as one of the pioneers, participated in the work of advancement, and well deserves mention as a representative man in this volume

Born in Essex county, Vermont, January 15, 1837, he is a son of Hon George W Gates, a native of the same county, whose father, Samuel Gates, was also born in the Green Mountain state The ancestry can be traced back to Stephen G Gates of England, who located in Massachusetts in 1662 The great-grandfather, Judge Samuel Gates, was one of the heroes of the Revolution and received a pension for his services He it was who planted the family on Vermont soil The grandfather, Samuel Gates, Jr , manifested his loyalty to his country by service in the war of 1812

George W Gates was reared to manhood in Vermont, and married Sarah Todd, who was born, reared and educated in Port- ⁗ ⁗ ⁗ Todd who followed the sea   Mr Gates engaged in farming and in the manufacture of lumber and potash, and while residing in the east served as county sheriff   In 1850 he removed to Port Byron, where he built a mill and engaged in the manufacture of lumber   He also contracted and built the Milwaukee road from Port Byron to the junction, and carried on merchandising for some time, continuing in active business here until 1865, when he removed to Independence, Missouri   He was elected judge of Jackson county, Missouri, afterward represented his district for three terms in the state legislature, and became one of the most distinguished and influential men of that locality   He died in Independence in 1892, and his wife passed away the previous year   The children were Eliza, who married Doctor George Vincent, of Vermont and died at their home in Hampton, Illinois, Charles C , a graduate of Amherst College, who successfully practiced law in Chicago until his death, George P , who resided in Port Byron from 1850 until 1866, when he removed to Independence, Missouri, where he conducted a flouring mill and later engaged in the banking business, Fred S , W G , proprietor of a stock ranch in Arizona   Mrs Margaret Moulton, a widow of Independence, Judge E P Gates, who is now circuit judge of Jackson county, Missouri, residing in Independence

Frederick S Gates came to Port Byron when a lad of fourteen, and was reared in this county, and educated in the Port Byron schools, supplemented by one term of study in Mt Morris Seminary   In July, 1862, he enlisted in his country's service, joining Company E, One Hundred and Twenty-si***h *ll *** * *n*** ***   b** * * * assigned t*   * * ** * ** *

in the siege of Vicksburg, did guard duty at various points, and remained with his company until the summer of 1863, when on account of failing health he was forced to resign, and returned home   He had entered the service as a private, but was promoted to the rank of sergeant, and held a lieutenant's commission on leaving the army   It was almost two years before he regained his health

In 1865 Mr Gates embarked in merchandising, but after eight months sold out and removed to Little Rock, Arkansas, where he engaged in the hardware business for a few months, but again his health forced him to leave the south, and he once more settled in Port Byron, giving his attention to the lumber trade   In 1888 he went to Columbia county, Arkansas, where he built a steam sawmill and engaged in the manufacture of lumber until February, 1894   Before going south he had organized a stock company to deal in lumber, and served as its president until 1888   He was general manager of the American Lumber Company, and under its control built and operated the mill in Arkansas   Since his return he has again been chosen president of the Port Byron Lumber Company   He built the sawmill and at different times has erected a number of residences in this city, thus adding to its material development

Mr Gates was married in Port Byron, in November, 1861, to Emma L Moore, a native of the city, and a daughter of George S Moore, one of the pioneers of Port Byron   She was educated in Knox Seminary, and became the mother of three children   Edward W , who died in 1875, aged six months, Flora I , who died in 1885, at the *** ** ****** **** **l M I*l, who died * * * * ** *** *** * ** ***

Mr Gates is a Jeffersonian Democrat, but votes independently at local elections He has filled the offices of supervisor, school director, school trustee, and a member of the village board, discharging his duties with marked fidelity He is a member of the Masonic lodge of Port Byron, and the Modern Woodmen, and is one of the trustees and a member of the executive board of the Port Byron Academy He takes a deep interest in everything pertaining to the public welfare of the town, and withholds his support from no enterprise calculated to prove of public benefit He and his wife hold membership in the Congregational church, and enjoy the hospitality of many of the best homes in Rock Island county Mr Gates has made for himself an honorable record in business, and by his well directed efforts has acquired a handsome competence As a citizen, friend and neighbor he is true to every duty and justly merits the esteem in which he is held

---

WILLIAM R BROWN was born in Milan, September 17, 1860, and is now numbered among the progressive and enterprising business men of that place, his attention being devoted to the management of a livery barn He is a representative of a well known family, his father having maintained a home in Rock Island county for more than forty years His grandfather, Oliver Brown, was a carpenter by trade, reared a large family, and died in Milan at an advanced age His maternal grandfather was Casper Remsburg, who died in Ohio The parents of our subject are William H and Susan (Remsburg) Brown, the former a native of Pennsylvania and the latter of Maryland

state of his nativity and learned the carpenter's trade which he has made his life work In the '50s he came to Rock Island county, and has since been identified with its building interests His wife, who went to Ohio during her early girlhood, and was there reared, proved to him a faithful companion and helpmeet on life's journey She died about 1890, at the age of seventy years Like her husband, she held membership in the Methodist church

William R Brown of this review, has spent his entire life in Milan He attended its public school and on laying aside his text books secured a situation in a flouring mill, where he was employed for three years In 1884 he established a livery, which with the exception of two years he has conducted continuously since He keeps a fine line of stylish and modern turnouts and his earnest desire to please his customers combined with honorable business methods has won for him a liberal patronage Mr Brown votes with the Republican party, and is now serving his third term as tax collector of the township He takes a deep and commendable interest in all that pertained to the welfare of his native town, neglects no opportunity to advance its interests and is now serving as chief of the fire department He belongs to the Methodist church, and is a man of kindly genial disposition

---

WALTER JOHNSON, editor of the Rock Island Union and president of of the Union Printing Company, Rock Island, Illinois, was born in London, England, April 27, 1843, and is the son of John F and Harriette Augusta (Ryley) Johnson, both natives of England and reared I by three

children, Walter, Henry P and Florence,
the latter now deceased, but who became
the wife of George Kendall. Henry P.
lives in Portland, Oregon, and is engaged in
the grocery trade.

John F Johnson was a ribbon manufacturer in England He came to America in
1851, and located at Welton, Iowa, where he
engaged in general merchandising, and at the
same time ran an extensive farm In 1859
he moved to Lyons, Iowa, where he also engaged in merchandising He remained
there about three years when he removed
to Davenport, in the same state, and engaged in the grocery trade About 1867
he came to Rock Island, where he continued
to reside until his death in 1888 His
first wife died in 1856 at Maquoketa, Iowa
They were both members of the Episcopal church

The paternal grandfather of our subject
was Thomas George Johnson He was a
harness maker and saddler in Coventry,
where he lived and died He had quite a
large family The maternal grandfather,
Thomas Ryley, was a sea captain

Walter Johnson was in his ninth year
when the family came to America He remained with his father until his majority,
assisting in the store His school life was
of short duration commencing in Coventry,
England, and continuing for a brief period
in Iowa He came to Rock Island in 1867,
and the following year commenced work on
the "Union" as local editor In 1874, when
the company was formed he bought a fourth
interest In 1876 he became joint editor
with William Henry Burdett He still occupies the editorial chair, and under his
management the paper has thrived and is
recognized as a power not only in Rock
Island count   u N th dll is   The

Union is the only morning paper published
in Rock Island, and politically is strongly
and reliably Republican

On the 22d of March, 1869, Mr Johnson
was married to Miss Ellen Head, daughter
of William A and Ann Head   Three
children have been born to them—Harriette A, Marguerite and Eliot Leigh
The two daughters yet remain at home
The son was drowned when nineteen years
of age. Religiously Mr and Mrs Johnson
are Episcopalians. Fraternally he is a Modern Woodman, United Workman and Fraternal Tribune As a Republican he was
appointed by President Harrison surveyor
of customs and served three years, being the
first incumbent of the custom house, which
was established in 1891 As a citizen he
has the best interests of his adopted city
at heart, and advocates all measures that
will aid in its growth and prosperity This
is fully attested in the columns of his paper

F W RANK, an attorney at law of Moline, was born in this city in 1873, and
is a son of Joseph and Lena (Lezson) Rank
His father, who has long been prominently
identified with the business interests of the
city, was born in Wurtemburg, Germany,
September 14, 1838, and is a son of Andrew and Magdalena (Meyer) Rank   Andrew Rank died in Germany, and the following year Joseph Rank came with his
mother and one sister to America   Two
brothers of the family had already crossed
the Atlantic   Joseph Rank remained for
six months in New York City, and six
months in Trenton, New Jersey, where he
worked in a wall paper factory, after which
he came to Moline, and served an apprenticeship at the shoemaker's trade, working

two years for forty dollars He then worked as a journeyman for two years, after which he established a shop of his own on a small scale, his capital consisting of only forty dollars From time to time he increased his facilities to meet the growing demand of the trade and after about seven years purchased a store on Third avenue He bought his present store in 1886 and now carries the largest boot and shoe stock in Moline, doing an extensive and profitable business

In February, 1865, Joseph Rank married Lena Lezson, of Muscatine, Iowa, who was born in Luxembourg, Germany, and came to America during her early girlhood Five children have been born of this union— Agnes, who was graduated in a musical college, Fred W , George, Mary, a graduate of St Mary's College of Moline, Robert Walter. The father of this family was a Democrat for many years and in 1860 voted for Douglas, whom he heard deliver a political speech in Rock Island In 1896, however, he voted the Republican ticket He and his family all attend the Catholic church

F W Rank, whose name begins this article, attended the common schools in his early youth and at the age of twelve years entered St Mary's parochial school, where he was graduated afterward He later matriculated in the Iowa Commercial College of Davenport, where he was graduated in 1891. Soon afterward he entered the employ of the Santa Fe Railroad Company as stenographer for A E Taylor, of Fort Madison, and in a few months was promoted to the position of private secretary to H R Nickerson, general superintendent of the road, with whom he traveled f

vice was with the Rock Island Railroad Company as chief clerk for the master mechanic in Stewart, Iowa

Wishing, however, to make the practice of law his life work, Mr Rank began his reading in 1893 under the direction of W H Wilson, of Davenport, and in 1894 was a student in the office of Cook & Dodge, of that city He is a graduate of the law department of the Iowa State University of the class of 1896, and within five days after the completion of his course in that institution he opened a law office in Moline Here he is meeting with fair success and has already won a place among the leading young attorneys of the city

In politics Mr Rank has always been a stanch Republican and took an active part in the memorable campaign of 1896 making speeches in all parts of the county Governor Tanner, in recognition of his services, appointed him public administrator of Rock Island county Mr Rank was reared in the Roman Catholic church, and was confirmed in Moline by Bishop Spaulding when ten years of age He belongs to the Moline Social Club, and is a popular, enterprising and progressive young man

SAMUEL SHARPE DAVIS, vice-president of the Davis Company, and secretary and manager of the People's Power Company, Rock Island, Illinois, is numbered among the wide-awake business men of the city He was born in Covington, Kentucky, February 1, 1858, and is a son of John B and Anna E (Sharpe) Davis the former a native of Maysville Kentucky and the latter of Mayslick, in the same state They were the parents of three children, Thomas B Mary and Samuel S

The Davis family are of Scotch-Irish origin Thomas Bodley Davis, the paternal grandfather of our subject, was a native of Pennsylvania, who early in life moved to Kentucky For some years he served as captain of a steamer plying between Pittsburg and New Orleans, and died of yellow fever while on his way up the river at the early age of thirty-four years In his family were three children

The maternal grandfather was Samuel K Sharpe, a native of Maryland, and a practicing physician, who followed his profession principally in Maysville, Kentucky, where he spent the greater part of his life He was one of a family of eight, one brother and six sisters He located permanently in Rock Island in 1875, and here died in 1890, at the age of ninety years His wife preceded him to their heavenly home nine years, dying in 1881 at the age of seventy-six years Doctor Sharpe was a remarkably strong man physically and mentally, and religiously was a strong Presbyterian, of which body his wife was also a member Politically he was a Democrat

John B Davis, the father, followed the the river almost his entire life, principally on the Ohio and Mississippi rivers, although for a time he was in the employ of the Canadian government, having charge of the boats carrying the supplies of the Hudson Bay Fur Company, on the Saskatchewan river He was in the work from 18— to 1887

Captain Davis first moved with his family to Augusta, Ark , shortly after the close of the Civil war In 1868 they went to Memphis, Tennessee, but in 1874 settled permanently in Rock Island From the age of sixteen he was upon the river the greater part of the time i

Ohio and Mississippi rivers he knew almost their entire length When he left the employ of the Canadian government he took charge of one of the boats of the Diamond Jo line, continuing as captain until about a year before his death, which occurred in 1890, at the age of sixty-one years

Politically Captain Davis was a Democrat, and showed his loyalty to the government by enlisting in the Second Minnesota Volunteer Infantry Regiment, serving with the rank of major He was in the service nearly three years and was in the battles of Chickamauga, Mill Springs, Corinth and Tullahoma In the first named he was wounded His service was principally under Generals Buell and Thomas Religiously, he was a Presbyterian and died in the faith Fraternally, he was a Mason His widow, who now resides in a pleasant home, 547 Twenty-third street, is also a member of the Presbyterian church, and in the work of the Master takes a lively interest

Samuel S Davis, of whom we now write, accompanied his parents in their various removals, as already mentioned and was a youth of sixteen when the family permanently located in Rock Island His education was obtained in the schools of Maysville, Kentucky, Memphis, Tennessee, and Rock Island On the steamer, Montana, commanded by his father, he commenced service as clerk in 1873, and continued in that capacity for several seasons, attending school during the winter months in Rock Island In 1876 his father had a government contract for carrying supplies from Bismarck, Montana, up the Missouri, Yellowstone and Big Horn rivers to the place where Custer was massacred, and was accompanied by our subject

Returning to Rock Island Mr Davis

was employed as clerk for J H Langley, who was agent for a line of steamers plying between St Louis and St Paul On the 1st of January, 1878, he began work for Thomas Yates, who opened a branch office for plumbing and steam fitting in Moline, and continued in his employ until January, 1881, when Mr Yates died During that time he and his brother Thomas got out a number of patents of their own on steam appliances

In February, 1881, together with his brother and Jacob Riley, of Rock Island, as co-partners, under the firm name of Davis & Co, they bought out the business of the heirs of Thomas Yates in both Rock Island and Moline, and in 1882 he and his brother bought Mr Riley's interest, Thomas B running the Rock Island office and Samuel S the Moline branch This partnership was continued until 1891, when the Davis Company was incorporated and succeeded to the business

While still in partnership with his brother, Mr Davis planned and superintended the construction of the Moline water works, which were started January 1, 1884 In the spring of 1884 he installed the first electric light plant in Moline, the dynamo being operated in the water works building until 1886 That year he also constructed the Davis block, on Sixteenth street, Moline, and as secretary and manager of the Merchants Electric Light Co, lighted the streets of Moline with eighty arc lights, superseding gas

In 1887 The Peoples' Light and Fuel Manufacturing Co was organized, of which Mr Davis was made secretary and general manager He bought up the stock of the Moline Gas & Coke Co, and consolidated it with The Merchants Electric Light Co of

Moline In 1888 The Merchants' Electric Light Co, of Rock Island, was organized and a building erected on Nineteenth street in which the plant was placed to be run by steam In the fall of the same year a power plant was completed at the foot of Fourth street Moline, to be run by water power, and the machinery of the Peoples' Light and Fuel Manufacturing Co, of Moline, and the Merchants' Electric Light Co, of Rock Island, was moved into it

In 1893 the Peoples' Power Co was organized which bought up the Rock Island Brush Electric Light Co and the Rock Island Gas & Coke Co, and removed all the machinery, together with that of the old Moline Gas Co, to the large plant now at the foot of Fourth street, Moline. Mr Davis planned the organization and constructed the plants of each of them.

On the 21st of September, 1892, Mr Davis married Miss Appolonia Weyerhauser, daughter of Frederick and Sarah Weyerhauser, and they now have one child, Edwin W The family reside at No 541 Twenty-third street, Rock Island Both Mr and Mrs Davis are members of the Broadway Presbyterian church, of which he is a trustee Fraternally he is a member of Trio Lodge, No 57, A F & A M, Barrett Chapter, No 18, R A M, and Everts Commandery, No 18 K T He is also a member of the Knights of Pythias and Modern Woodmen of America Politically he is a Democrat, but never held nor desired public office

As a business man Mr Davis has made an enviable reputation His ability to please and carry forward to successful completion any enterprise in which he may be interested is unquestioned, and while his business ventures have been almost solely in connection with general machinery, he is at all times interested in any and everything calculated to build up and beautify his adopted city and county

WILLIAM McROBERTS, SR The deserved reward of a well-spent life is an honored retirement from business, in which to enjoy the fruits of former toil To-day, after a useful and beneficial career, Mr McRoberts is quietly living at his pleasant home on section 17, Coe township, surrounded by the comforts that earnest labor has brought him

He was born in County Down, Ireland, January 29, 1829, there grew to manhood, and attended school to a limited extent, but is principally self-educated by reading and observation in later years His early life was spent upon a farm, and for three years before coming to America he worked in a gristmill It was in 1850 that he crossed the broad Atlantic and joined his brother James, in Allegheny county, Pennsylvania, the latter having come to the new world the year previous For two years our subject worked at the butcher's trade, receiving ten dollars per month and board, and then with his brother engaged in gardening near Pittsburg for about five years, building up a good trade and doing a profitable business

In 1857 Mr McRoberts started westward, and after traveling some in Ohio and Illinois, finally located in Coe township, Rock Island county, where he rented land for six years and successfully engaged in farming In the meantime he traveled quite extensively in the south and west, but finding no more suitable location than Rock Island county in 1864 he purchased an improved fa   t l   i t t   nship

and in connection with its cultivation also operated rented land and engaged in raising, feeding and selling stock A few years later he sold his first purchase and bought one hundred and twenty acres where his son George is now living, and upon that place made many substantial and useful improvements, including the erection of a large residence, good barns and outbuildings He bought more land from time to time, owning one hundred and sixty acres across the road from his son's place and two hundred and fifty-seven acres in two well improved farms, besides some timbered tracts He was one of the most active, enterprising and reliable farmers in the township, and has given to each of his children one thousand dollars in cash, besides supplying his sons with stock on starting out in life for themselves Through his own unaided efforts Mr McRoberts has attained to a position of affluence, and is the owner of two valuable and well improved farms and a good home, which stand as monuments to his thrift, industry and good management

In 1850, in Allegheny county, Pennsylvania, was celebrated the marriage of Mr McRoberts and Miss Lizzie Alcot, a native of Manchester, England, who came to the United States when a child of twelve years with her father, Rev William Alcot, a Methodist Episcopal minister, who settled in Allegheny county and devoted his life to the work of the Master. He was also a very prominent Odd Fellow Mr McRoberts has been called upon to mourn the loss of his estimable wife, who passed away in 1894 The children born to them were as follows Mary, now the wife of John Fife, a farmer of Coe township, William, James H and Eddie all prominent and well-to-do farmers of the same township, Frank, a merchant of Port Byron, John and George, also agriculturists of Coe township, and Emma, who is keeping house for her father The children have all been educated, and the sons are all now married and successfully engaged in business The family is one of the highest respectability and quite prominent in social circles

For many years during early life Mr McRoberts was a Republican, but now casts his ballot for whom he considers best qualified to fill the offices, regardless of party affiliations He has never aspired to public office, but being a warm friend of our school system, he has for twenty years been a most efficient member of the school board Although reared in the Presbyterian faith, after locating here, he and his wife joined the Methodist Episcopal church, and assisted in building the Fairfield church, of which he has since been a faithful and active member His upright, honorable course in life has commended him to the confidence and esteem of all with whom he has come in contact, his actions have ever been sincere, his manner unaffected, and his example is well worthy of emulation

CHARLES LAMB, who is classed among the successful farmers and stock-raisers of Cordova township, is well worthy of notice in a work of this kind, and to be ranked among the men who have distinguished themselves as useful and enterprising citizens His home is now on section 3, Cordova township, and his entire life has been passed in Rock Island county, his birth occurring in Hampton township, December 24, 1857.

Benjamin Lamb, father of our subject, was a na'

brought to Rock Island county by a Mr Stowell, to whom he had been given, and with whom he remained until that gentleman's death, when Mr Lamb was about fourteen years of age He then started out to fight life's battle unaided and has since been dependent upon his own resources for a livelihood He had previously acquired a fair common-school education and become quite familiar with agricultural pursuits While working as a farm hand by the month he saved enough money to purchase a team, and then operated rented land on his own account for a few years His first purchase consisted of the farm near Barstow where our subject was born, but he now owns and operates a fine farm of one hundred four acres in Cordova township, and is one of the highly respected citizens of that community

In 1853 Benjamin Lamb wedded Miss Rachel Cook, and they became the parents of seven children, of whom five are still living Asenath married and died at the age of twenty-five, leaving three children Charles is next in order of birth Mary is the wife of Horace Crosby Lucinda married Will Wilsenholm and lives in Peoria Eliphalet died at the age of three years Ida and Milton are still at home.

The common schools afforded our subject good educational privileges, and he grew to manhood on the home farm On the 28th day of December, 1881, was celebrated his marriage to Miss Sarah Shninger, of Whiteside county, Illinois, who was born in Greene county, Iowa, and is a daughter of Lewis and Hannah (Rathburn) Shninger The children born to them are as follows Lillie, Clarence, who died at the age of thirteen months, Bennie, Ada and Ida twins Roy and Ora

For four years after his marriage, Mr Lamb worked with his father for one-half the crops raised, and then purchased the old homestead but in 1894 sold and bought one hundred and twenty acres where he now resides He is a wide-awake, progressive agriculturist, always abreast with the times, and is meeting with a well deserved success in his chosen calling His political support has been given the Republican party since casting his first vote for General Garfield in 1880, but he has never been a politician in the sense of office seeking, though for several years he has most capably served as school director He and his estimable wife hold membership in the Methodist Episcopal church, and are charter members of the Home Forum at Barstow, while in social circles they hold an enviable position

JOHN H MUELLER is one of the worthy citizens of Moline that the fatherland has furnished to the new world He was born in Holstein, Germany, July 16, 1852, and is a son of Frederick J and Johanna (Johansen) Mueller His father was a blacksmith by trade and also owned a small tract of land of fourteen acres in the edge of the village There our subject became familiar with farm work, and even in his early boyhood he worked in his father's smithy after school hours were over He attended school until sixteen years of age and then became a regular hand in his father's shop, not only mastering the blacksmith's trade but also learning to make spades, forks and various other kinds of tools When about eighteen years of age he became possessed of a desire to seek a home in A
study of F

The year 1871 saw the fulfillment of his hopes He landed at Castle Garden at eight o'clock on the 21st of November, and from there made his way to Davenport, Iowa, where he remained three days and then came to Moline Securing a situation in a blacksmith and wagon-making shop, he was thus employed until 1875 He came to this country not to remain a German citizen but with a strong desire to ally his interests with those of the United States, and at once took steps to secure naturalization rights On the 2nd of November, 1876 at ten A M, he was given the papers which made him a citizen of the republic, and he has since been loyal and faithful to its interests

In 1875 Mr Mueller was forced to abandon the shop, his health giving way under the strain in warm weather In May of that year he rented a building at No 1517 Second avenue, where he has since conducted extensive bottling works and also carried on business as a wholesale dealer in Pabst beer, wines and liquors He has a large trade and through his business interests has accumulated a handsome competency

Mr Mueller was married July 17, 1875, to Catherine Wriedt, of Moline, who was born in Holstein, Germany, where they became acquainted, and who emigrated to America in 1873 They have four children William C, born October 1, 1876, is a graduate of the Moline school and of the Davenport Business College, and is now holding a responsible position as collector for the Charmel Ice Company Henry F, born May 11, 1878, is a graduate of the Moline schools and the Chicago School of
d is now
M ne, born

February 16, 1880, graduated in music in Mrs Swan's school in September, 1897 Alma, born December 15 1881, completes the family Mr Mueller has a very pleasant home which he purchased in 1879, and the household is noted for its hospitality, being a favorite resort with the many friends of the family Mr Mueller is a man of excellent business ability, of great energy and determination, straightforward in his dealings and by his well directed efforts he has attained a high degree of success

---

ENOCH WARMAN, residing on section 18, Drury township, is numbered among the self-made men of Rock Island county, his accumulations being the result of his own industry, obtained by self-denial and economy, and the exercise of a naturally good judgment, both in regard to agricultural pursuits and business matters He came to the county in the fall of 1862 and since that time this has been the field of his operations and the center of his interests and hopes

Mr Warman was born in Wayne county, Indiana, November 25, 1825, a son of Enoch and Mary (Brockway) Warman, the former a native of Virginia and the latter of Maryland At an early day they emigrated to Indiana, becoming pioneer settlers of Wayne county where the father carried on farming until his death in 1836 His mother survived him a number of years and carefully reared their family of ten children, namely Eliza, who died soon after her marriage Joshua, who died after reaching manhood, Thomas, who was married and died leaving one child, Franklin, who also died leaving a family, Enoch, who is next in order of birth, Sarah Ann, wife of Malon Broderick, of Union

of Joseph Kimmel of Wayne county, Mary, wife of Collins Willitts, of Howard county, Indiana, and Catherine, wife of George Williver of Oxford, Indiana

In the county of his nativity, Mr Warman, of this review was reared, assisting in the work of the farm during the summer months and attending the public schools to a limited extent during the winter season when his services were not needed at home After attaining to man's estate he took charge of the farm and aided his mother in the care of the family He was married in Wayne county, in 1852, to Miss Elmira Reynolds, who was also born there, a daughter of Milton Reynolds, and they have become the parents of eight children Oton Omar, who is married and resides in Missouri James, who is married and lives in Drury township, Rock Island county Sherman, who is married and is engaged in the implement business at Millers Store, Buffalo Prairie township, Willard who holds a business position in Chicago Orson who is married and has one child, and assists his father on the home farm, Emma, wife of Abner Bowser, of Rock Island county, Mary, wife of J A Brown of Kansas City, Missouri, and Sarah R, deceased wife of Wilson Bowser

In the fall after his marriage, Mr Warman removed to Iowa locating at Littsville Louisa county, where he engaged in farming for eight years but since the fall of 1862 has made his home in Drury township, Rock Island county, where he purchased a tract of one hundred and twenty acres Only about twelve acres had been placed under cultivation and the only improvement upon the place consisted of a log house in which the family lived while Mr Warman turned his attention to its further development The first summer he was placed by

a substantial frame residence, good barns and outbuildings have been erected, an orchard and ornamental trees have been set out, and to-day the farm is one of the most highly improved and desirable places in the township

On attaining his majority, Mr Warman became a Democrat, but when the south threatened to secede he joined the Republican party, voting for Abraham Lincoln in 1860, and has since been one of its most ardent supporters Although he cares nothing for political office, he has served as a member of the school board for many years as he is a warm friend of the cause of public education. His uprightness, integrity and public-spiritedness have won him the confidence and esteem of his neighbors, and he is classed among the most respected representative citizens of Drury township His estimable wife holds membership in the Christian church and is beloved by all who know her.

HENRY C. CONNELLY —The gentleman whose name honors this page was born in the village of Petersburg, Somerset county, Pennsylvania, December 22, 1831, the fourth in order of birth of the eight children of James and Marie (Hugus) Connelly, the former a contractor and heavy dealer in stock, who assisted in building the great National Road Our subject's maternal ancestors on both sides were Huguenots, who fled from France at the time of the massacre. Some of their descendants, Hugus and Aukeny by name, fought with Washington His great-grandfather, Peter Aukeny, was a captain from Pennsylvania in the war of the Revolution His paternal grandfather, Bernard Connelly, came to this country from the north of Ireland, near the close of the last century and located in Philadelphia, where he met with financial success In after years he located in Somerset county, where he purchased a large tract of land and engaged extensively in raising live stock He reared three sons and four daughters. One of the points he loved to dwell upon in his old age was that he had given his children the best education the country afforded, in addition to deeding each a farm Bernard Connelly's wife was an Eggleton, of English birth, and was the first and for many years the only member of the Episcopal church in Somerset county

The early boyhood days of our subject, until the death of his father, were passed in his native village Then his mother moved to the town of Somerset with her family, thus enabling her children to enjoy the superior educational advantages afforded there After leaving the Somerset Academy he learned the trade of printing in the office of the Somerset Visitor, whose editor was General A. H Coffroth, who has since become one of Pennsylvania's distinguished sons When twenty years of age he became half owner and editor of the Beaver Star, a connection that continued two years and a half, at the expiration of which period he disposed of his interest therein, and, forming a partnership with Emanuel J Pershing, a brother of Judge Cyrus L Pershing of Pennsylvania, moved to Rock Island, in February, 1855, and purchased the Rock Islander, which was soon changed to a daily. In 1857 Messrs. Pershing and Connelly purchased The Argus and consolidated the two papers Mr Connelly's connection with the consolidated paper continued until 1859

In 1858 Mr Connelly began reading law under the instruction of Judge J W Drury, and was admitted to the bar in 1860 He at once entered upon the practice of his profession, continuing successfully in his new vocation until September 12, 1862, when he entered the army From the Chicago Inter Ocean of September 27, 1887, the following outline of Major Connelly's military career is taken "Henry Clay Connelly is a member of General John Buford Post, No 243, Rock Island, of which he was a charter member, and its first commander He was commissioned second lieutenant of Company L, Fourteenth Illinois Cavalry, January 7, 1863 In the spring the regiment went to the front, its first headquarters being Glasgow, Kentucky While here the regiment was active in scouting, and the Confederate forces at Celina and near Turkey Neck bend, on the Cumberland river, were attacked and routed The next work was the pursuit of General Morgan for twenty-eight days and nights, the battle of Buffington Island, in Ohio, and the capture of Morgan Lieutenant Connelly was present at the capture In August, under General Burnside the Union forces went to East Tennessee With the advance guard Lieutenant Connelly entered Knoxville, September 1, General Burnside taking formal possession on the 3d He heard the last toot of the last locomotive of General Buckner, commanding the Confederates, sounded in Knoxville He was at the taking of Cumberland Gap, at Bristol, and at the numerous encounters in that locality, at the defense of Knoxville and its incidents, at Bean Station, at Danbridge, Fair Garden, Walker's Ford, Strawberry Plains, and at the fight with Thomas' Cherokee Indians in North Carolina. During the East Tennessee campaign he was placed in charge of a battery of ʻʻʻʻ, On the Indian raid

after following a mountainous Indian trail, the 2nd of February the Cherokees were surprised in their camp, attacked and the Legion cut to pieces, many of them being killed or captured Lieutenant Connelly had with him a part of his battery Herculean efforts were required to take the guns and caissons over the great mountains and through the deep ravines, but the work was successfully accomplished General Grant in a special dispatch highly complimented the Fourteenth for this work. He received his commission as captain after this expedition, and did duty at brigade headquarters as assistant adjutant general and also as inspector He participated in the Atlanta campaign On the Macon raid his regiment, being in General Stoneman's command, shared the misfortunes of this officer, and after it had cut its way out in a splendid charge Being dismounted by reason of loss of horses on the Macon raid, the regiment did duty as infantry at the siege of Atlanta, and was one of the first which entered the city after its fall Being remounted and re-equipped about the 1st of November, 1864, it took a position on the right of the Union army on the Tennessee river to watch General Hood's advance From the river to Columbia, Major Connelly day and night was with the rear guard, being repeatedly surrounded With splendid courage his command charged the Confederate lines with success Near Mt Pleasant, and also at Duck river, after dark, finding himself cut off and surrounded, he placed himself at the head of his command and carried the column through the Confederate lines with success

"During the advance of General Hood's great and aggressive army, including the battle of Franklin and the advance of the

Union army to Nashville, his officers and the men of his command speak in eulogistic terms of Major Connelly's leadership and his sterling qualities as a soldier   From second lieutenant he was promoted captain over his first lieutenant, and by a vote of the officers of his regiment, who also voted the sentiment of the rank and file, he was elected major over six captains who held commissions older than his "

The Inter Ocean's article is brief and does not give in detail the events leading to Captain Connelly's promotion, which are now related   Colonel F M Davidson, of the Fourteenth, wrote two letters to Governor Oglesby recommending him for the position of major   These letters were written at Edgefield, Tennessee, the first bearing date February 7, 1865, in which Colonel Davidson says   " In recommending Captain Connelly for this position (major), it affords me much pleasure to bear witness to the gallant and successful manner in which he has conducted himself as a soldier whenever and wherever he has been called upon to face the enemy   His bearing on the Morgan raid to the day he (Morgan) was captured, his skill through the entire campaign in East Tennessee under General Burnside, and particularly on the 14th day of December, 1863, at the battle of Bean Station, fighting General Longstreet's corps, in which he handled a battery with the coolest daring and most splendid success, his energy on the North Carolina expedition in the month of February, 1864, commanded by myself, his bravery and dash during the recent campaign in Tennessee, under General Thomas, and particularly on the night of the 23d of November, 1864, when, being surrounded by C   D   E   other officers

lines, he placed himself at the head of the column, rallied the men, and charged out without the loss of a man, and also on the 15th of December (at Nashville), when he rallied his regiment after being broken under a fearful cannonade from the enemy's batteries   In short his whole career as a soldier proves him to be worthy of prompt promotion "

General Oglesby hesitated to commission a junior captain over so many seniors, and Colonel Davidson, being advised of this hesitation, on March 28, 1865, wrote again as follows   " I can only repeat what I said of Captain Connelly in my communication to Governor Oglesby dated February 7, 1865   Aside from his being an officer of the first order (particular mention of some of his acts of bravery being therein set forth), his high tone as a gentleman, and his acknowledged talent as a man, loudly call for official recognition of his services to his country   He has capacity for any position as field officer   Anything you may be able to do for him will be esteemed as a personal favor "

Upon his return from the war Major Connelly resumed his practice.   In 1866 he was elected police magistrate for a term of four years, and was city attorney of Rock Island during the years 1869, 1870 and 1871   In January, 1894, his son, Bernard D , who is a graduate of the Iowa State University and had been for five years associated with the law firm of Douthitt, Jones & Mason of Topeka, Kansas, became associated with him under the firm title of Connelly & Connelly   Their practice covers the various branches of the law, and the firm ranks as one of the leading firms of Rock Island   During his life Island &

Milan street railway Major Connelly succeeded to the presidency of the company after Mr Davenport's death

In August, 1869, the steamer Dubuque, plying on the Mississippi river between St Louis and St Paul, on an upriver trip carried a large number of harvest hands. The employes of the boat were negroes Some difficulty arose between a white man and a negro, which resulted in a riot on the boat, when near Hampton, Rock Island county About a dozen negroes lost their lives by being clubbed and then being thrown or driven into the river, in which they were drowned Michael Lynch led the assault on the defenseless blacks He and a dozen others were indicted for murder, all of them excepting Lynch taking a change of venue to Henry county Lynch was captured in Arkansas and brought back a prisoner to Rock Island, tried, convicted and sent to state's prison for ten years A most intense hatred existed against Lynch among the people Major Connelly ably defended him and procured a comparatively light verdict for him The mass of the people thought he should have been hung

Major Connelly was one of the original stockholders of both the Rock Island Buggy Company and the Rock Island Savings Bank He has always taken great interest in all matters pertaining to the advancement of the prosperity of Rock Island, and in 1861 labored many weeks with senators and members of the house at Washington to secure the passage of the bill by congress, locating the great national arsenal at Rock Island More recently he has been one of those who obtained the passage of a special bill through both branches of congress authorizing the construction of an electric r

tween Rock Island and Davenport, Iowa Major Connelly is a strong believer in and supporter of the doctrines of the Democratic party In the Buchanan campaign of 1856 and the Douglas-Lincoln campaign of 1858 he was an active worker The late Judge Jere S Black, who was a personal friend of Mr Connelly, and at that time a member of Buchanan s cabinet, gave him to understand that he could have the post-office at Rock Island This appointment he respectfully declined He was a firm friend of Senator Douglas and considered it inconsistent for him to accept office from Mr Buchanan while he used the power of his administration in the state—though unsuccessfully—to defeat Senator Douglas President Johnson appointed him to the postmastership of Rock Island, but a Republican senate failed to confirm the nomination

At the Democratic congressional convention, which met at Monmouth in 1882, the late Hon P I Cable placed Major Connelly in nomination in a strong speech. This was done in opposition to the latter's wishes The Democratic state convention which met in Peoria in 1884 honored him by making him temporary chairman of the convention His severe campaign work in the army developed heart trouble, and the excessive heat, combined with the labor he had done in the congressional convention, before taking his place in the state convention, produced an attack which prostrated him, and he was obliged to retire from the chair On the money question Major Connelly voted for President McKinley He has been an indefatigable worker for the success of the Hennepin Canal, and for nearly twenty years as a member and president of
 nd as a

member, secretary and president of the public library of the same city, has given his personal attention to their success

On the 12th of May, 1857, Mr Connelly was united in marriage to Miss Adelaide McCall, a native of New York, whose grandfather fought in the war of 1812, and other ancestors in the Revolutionary war. Of their children, Clark H has for ten years past been with the First National Bank of Sioux City, Iowa, Alvin H is a manufacturer of and wholesale dealer in hardwood lumber in Kansas City, Mabel is the wife of Dr C. W. McGavren, of Missouri Valley, Iowa, Bernard D is associated with his father, and Miss Lucia is at home

Major Connelly has been a frequent contributor to The National Tribune of articles relating to personal experiences during the war and has written several instructive and interesting papers for various law journals Following the religious faith of his ancestors, some of whom were warm adherents of John Calvin and served with distinction as soldiers under the Prince of Conde and Admiral Coligny, he is Presbyterian in sentiment His success in life may be ascribed to positive, determined pursuit of business, and to the fact that he is a man of honesty and integrity

CHARLES W NEGUS is one of Rock Island's native sons and a representative of one of her most prominent and honored families, whose identification with her history dates from an early period in the development of the county His father, Isaac Negus, was a native of New York, and of English descent Having arrived at years of maturity he married Miss Jerusha Waldo, a native of Connecticut who also

came of English ancestry In his early business career he was engaged in selling the goods of the Seth Thomas Clock Company at Watertown, and at an early period in the history of Illinois he came to this state, remaining for a time in Galena About 1844 he came to Rock Island, and the following year carried on business here as the representative of the Seth Thomas Clock Company Subsequently he engaged in the real estate business, owning a number of valuable pieces of property in Rock Island, together with large tracts of land lying between this city and Cambridge He was a prominent factor in the substantial development of the community, took a deep interest in all that pertained to its welfare, and was active in support of many measures that secured its progress and advancement He was a public-spirited and progressive citizen and may well be classed among the honored pioneers who laid the substantial foundation for the present prosperity of the city His death here occurred at the age of eighty-four years He left to his family an untarnished name and the example of a life well spent His wife passed away at the age of fifty-nine years She was a member of the old school Presbyterian church, and he also attended services there

This worthy couple were the parents of four children, three sons and a daughter, of whom Charles W. and William O are now living Born in the city which is still his home, Charles W Negus witnessed almost its entire growth and development. His preliminary education, acquired in the public schools, was supplemented by a course in the Northwestern University at Evanston. In 1863 he began freighting on the plains of the west from the Missouri river to Denver,

Colorado, and was thus engaged for three years On the expiration of that period he returned to Rock Island, and has since been largely connected with its hotel interests, being engaged in the hotel business at intervals for twenty years

On the 10th of May, 1880, Mr. Negus was united in marriage to Miss Ida M Myers, and they have one son, Charles Drake They also lost one son, Isaac Waldo, who was killed by the street cars when eight years of age Mrs Negus is a member of the Central Presbyterian church Mr Negus affiliates with the Knights of Pythias fraternity, gives his political support to the Democracy, and has served as a member of the city council as alderman from the Third ward He is public-spirited and progressive, and the interests that are calculated to advance the best interests of Rock Island never solicit his support in vain.

MARVIN H LYON, the well-known proprietor of the City Steam Laundry of Moline, is one of the most active and enterprising young men of the place, and is now doing a successful business, his plant being located at 403 Fifteenth street He was born in Freeport, Illinois, September 22, 1866, and is descended from a good old New England family of English descent, which was founded in this country by three brothers who crossed the Atlantic to escape religious persecution His grandfather, Captain Lyon, was a soldier in both the Revolution and the war of 1812, fighting valiantly for the independence of his native land

Edwin Lyon, our subject's father, was born in Connecticut, in 1815, and in early life remov

Miss Amy Meade, a relative of General Meade, a distinguished officer of the Civil war In 1866 they came to Illinois, but later spent some time in Iowa, though the father died in Moline, in 1889, and was buried here with Masonic honors, being a prominent member of that order The mother now finds a pleasant home with our subject

In the city of his birth Marvin H Lyon spent the days of his boyhood and youth, and acquired his education in the public schools Coming to Moline in 1882, he accepted a position in a laundry, where he was employed for some years, and then purchased the City Steam Laundry, which he still owns and operates with good success, receiving a liberal share of the public patronage

On the 28th of June, 1893, Mr Lyon was joined in wedlock to Miss Nellie Pierce, who was born, reared and educated in Moline, and is a daughter of Harrison P Pierce They now have a little son, Marvin H , Jr , who is the joy and pride of the household

Politically Mr. Lyon is a stanch Republican, and is an earnest advocate of the principles of protection and sound money, but has never been an aspirant for official honors In 1888 he joined the Illinois National Guards, and in 1893 was commissioned second lieutenant of his company With his command he assisted in quelling the riot in Spring Valley, and for three weeks in 1894 was stationed in Chicago during the great strike of that year, when several lives and much property were destroyed. As a soldier he is brave and fearless, as a business man is upright and honorable in all his dealings, and as a citizen deserves the high regard in

WILLIAM McROBERTS, Jr —Rock Island can boast of quite a number of enterprising and thorough-going farmers, who are devoting considerable attention to the raising of fine stock, and among that class of citizens there is probably none who takes higher rank than the subject of this narrative He has met with eminent success in his operations and is now among the prosperous agriculturists of Coe township, his home being on section 21

The birth of our subject occurred near Pittsburg, Pennsylvania, September 6, 1856, but the following year he was brought to Rock Island county by his father, William McRoberts, Sr , whose sketch appears elsewhere in this volume He remained upon the home farm in Coe township until after he had attained his majority, and conned his lessons in the district schools of the neighborhood On starting out in life for himself he rented a part of the old homestead, but after his marriage he located on a farm of eighty acres which he owned on section 11, Coe township, making his home upon that place for thirteen years He then purchased his present valuable farm of one hundred sixty acres on section 21, where he has made many useful and substantial improvements In connection with general farming he is successfully engaged in raising a good grade of horses, cattle and hogs, and is recognized as one of the most enterprising, progressive and energetic farmers of the community

On the 3d of October, 1882, Mr McRoberts led to the marriage altar Miss Lura Barrett, a native of Maine, who in 1864 accompanied the family on their removal to Illinois, and received a good education in the school- of Port By-- b-t -r---l-d -- her to suc

vious to her marriage Her father, Daniel P Barrett, is also represented on another page of this book Mr. and Mrs McRoberts have two children—Grace L and W Morris, who are both attending the home school The parents are prominent members of the Fairfield Methodist Episcopal church and Mr McRoberts affiliates with the Court of Honor of Port Byron, while politically he is identified with the Republican party, being a firm advocate of protection and sound money For three years he most acceptably served as road commissioner and has been a member of the school board for two years In all of life's relations he has been true and faithful to every trust reposed in him, and enjoys the respect and esteem of the entire community

BERNARD D CONNELLY, junior member of the well known law firm of Connelly & Connelly, whose office is in the Mitchell & Lynde block, is one of the younger members of the Rock Island bar, but his prominence is by no means measured by his years, on the contrary he had won a reputation which many an older practitioner might well envy He was born October 19, 1866, in the city which is still his home, and is a son of Henry C and Adelaide M (McCall) Connelly, natives of Pennsylvania and New York, respectively (See sketch elsewhere in this work)

The days of his boyhood and youth our subject passed in his native city and graduated from the public schools in 1883 Subsequently he attended the State University of Iowa, from which he graduated in June, 1887, with the degree of A B Going to Topeka, Kansas, he spent five years with law office of D P Abbott Law & Mason, one of the most prominent firms of that state, and being admitted to the bar April 1, 1891, he successfully engaged in practice in that city until January, 1894, when he returned to Rock Island, and has since been connected with his father in business under the firm style of Connelly & Connelly He lives at home with his parents at No 1200 Second avenue Fraternally he is a member of the Phi Delta Theta, a college society and politically is an ardent Republican, having taken an active and prominent part in the McKinley campaign in 1896 Socially he is deservedly popular, as he is affable and courteous in manner and possesses that essential qualification to success in public life, that of making friends readily and of strengthening the ties of friendship as time advances

MISS LUCY GOODRICH is a representative of one of the honored pioneer families of Rock Island county She resides on section 7, Canoe Creek township, which has long been the family home She was born in Port Byron and is a daughter of Calvin and Emily (Fisher) Goodrich Her father was born in Huntsville, New York, April 8, 1811, and was a son of Philo Goodrich, a native of Connecticut, who married Lucretia Williams, a native of the same state At the age of ten years he was left an orphan, and for four years thereafter resided in the home of a Presbyterian minister He was then apprenticed to a cabinetmaker, serving for a five years' term, during which he became an expert workman He then followed his trade in New York and Ohio until 1836, when he came to I

of which he had become the possessor He located the claim in Effingham county and then returned to New York, where in 1838 he was united in marriage to Emily Fisher, who was born in Oneida county, that state, in March, 1813 They lived in Chautauqua county until 1840, and then with teams proceeded to Warren, Pennsylvania, by rafts to Louisville, Kentucky, and thence by steamer to Port Byron, thus becoming identified with Rock Island county in the days of its early development

Mr Goodrich worked at his trade of cabinetmaking until 1853 when he purchased a farm in Canoe Creek township, and devoted his remaining days to agricultural pursuits He had received but little opportunity for acquiring an education, but he possessed a practical knowledge that made him a successful business man and was very energetic and industrious By reading and observation he also became well informed and was a man of such known integrity and honor that he was held in the highest esteem and his advice was often sought by others His known fairness caused him frequently to be solicited to accept the office of justice of the peace and finally he succumbed to the urging of his friends and entered upon the duties of that position There he labored to ameliorate all differences instead of aggravating and his fidelity to the cause of right was above question He also served as school director, road commissioner, assessor, collector and in other local offices of honor and trust

In his boyhood days Mr Goodrich became a member of the Methodist church and while speaking in one of the church meetings his wife first saw him She was converted and joined that church at the age of fifteen He was a very earnest church worker, served as superintendent of the Sunday school and was known as Deacon Goodrich, although he never held the office. His political support was given the Republican party His death occurred January 11, 1886, and his wife passed away January 21, 1896, their remains being interred in the family burying-ground on the farm All who knew them held them in the highest esteem and their loss to the community was deeply felt.

This worthy couple became the parents of nine children, but five died in childhood. Luella became the wife of Hiram Rake and removed to Iowa Later they went to Arkansas and subsequently to Texas, where she died, leaving five children, four of whom are living Mrs Katy Chapel, who has three children and resides in Deport, Texas, and Ethel, of Blossom, Texas, who is married and has four children, Allen, a farmer of Texas, and Nellie, also of the Lone Star state Arthur Goodrich, the only son living, was born at Port Byron, November 3, 1840, and lives in Canoe Creek township He married Eliza Turner and has six children Alice G is the next of the family and was born in Port Byron, and now living in Canoe Creek Lucy lives on the old homestead

Upon the father's death Miss Lucy Goodrich inherited from her father's estate a valuable farm of eighty acres lying on sections 7 and 8 Canoe Creek township, the old homestead This she still owns and has given her personal supervision to its management The land is under a high state of cultivation and yields to the owner a golden tribute She possesses superior business and executive ability, is practical, energetic and progressive and has now one of the fine farms of the county She has

added a number of substantial improvements to the place, including a good residence which was erected in 1893

FRANK P. GILLETT, who resides on section 7, Drury township, owns a valuable farm of two hundred acres, whose well tilled fields and excellent improvements indicate the progressive and enterprising spirit of the owner He was born on this farm July 23, 1854, and is descended from an old Connecticut family of French Huguenot ancestry His father, Sidney Gillett, was born in New Haven, Connecticut, May 10, 1810, and during his childhood went with the grandfather to Muskingum county, Ohio, locating near Zanesville, where he was reared to manhood He removed thence to Indiana, and a few years later drove an ox team to Scott county, Iowa, where he established a home in 1836 He made there a claim, which he afterward sold and conducted a wood-yard near Buffalo, Iowa He was married in Rock Island, to Jane McNutt, who was born near Steubenville, Ohio, November 15, 1815 Her father, Barnet McNutt, came to Illinois in 1839, reaching Andalusia on the 12th of May He located in Buffalo Prairie township, and spent his last years there He and wife and most of his children are laid to rest in the Dunlap cemetery

Upon his marriage Sidney Gillett took up his residence near Buffalo, Iowa, and later moved to Buffalo Prairie township, where he had a small tract of land, which he transformed into a good farm About 1852 he purchased three hundred and nine acres of timber land in Drury township which he at once began to clear A little log house and a few improvements had been made and these he afterward replaced with substantial buildings, adding to his farm all modern accessories and conveniences He was a self-educated man, broad minded and well-informed and possessed excellent business ability. In several township offices he manifested his loyalty as a citizen by his prompt and faithful discharge of duty He died March 4, 1875, and his wife passed away January 7, 1892, their remains being interred in Dunlap cemetery, where a monument has been erected to their memory

Frank P Gillett is the youngest child and only son in a family of three children, his sisters being Nancy Jane, wife of Mathias Releford, of Mercer county, Illinois, and Laura, wife of Charles Degraff, of Muscatine, Iowa Mr Gillett spent his youth on the old homestead midst play and work and in the common schools pursued the branches of a practical English education After attaining his majority he remained at home and assisted in carrying on the farm In 1878 he went to Rooks county, Kansas, where he took up a homestead of one hundred and sixty acres, which he still owns He operated and improved that place for five years, and then returned to the farm in Rock Island county, purchasing the interests of the other heirs therein Since coming into possession he has made some good improvements upon the farm which add to its value and attractive appearance and his rich land yields to him a golden return for his labor

Mr Gillett was married in Muscatine, Iowa, October 8, 1877, to Miss Winifred Hays, who was born in Sangamon county, Illinois, but was reared and educated in Rock Island county. Her father, James Hays, was one of the early settlers of Sangamon county and in 1856 took up his res-

idence in Rock Island county Six children have been born to Mr and Mrs Gillett — Bessie, Laura Belle, James Roy, Alice J and Agnes M, twins, and Nola They lost one son, Clarence, who died in childhood.

Mr Gillett gives an unwavering support to the Republican party, and has voted for each presidential nominee since casting his first ballot for R B Hayes He has served two terms as collector of his township, one term as assessor and for about eight years as township clerk He has also been a delegate to the county conventions of his party His wife is a member of the Baptist church, and he contributes liberally to its support Socially he is connected with the Woodmen, and his courteous manner, sterling character and well-spent life have won him the regard not only of his brethren of that fraternity but also of those with whom he has come in contact in all the relations of life

---

SAMUEL STOCUM is a leading representative of the business interests of Cordova, where he is extensively engaged in buying and shipping stock, and also conducts a livery stable and deals in agricultural implements. Of excellent business ability and broad resources, he has attained a prominent place among the substantial citizens of this part of the county, and is a recognized leader in public affairs He has won success by his well-directed energetic efforts, and the prosperity that has come to him is certainly well deserved

Mr Stocum is a native of the Empire state, his birth having occurred in Niagara county, on the 26th of March, 1845 His parents, Hiram and Priscilla Beebe Stocum, were also natives of New York, and the former was of German lineage, while the latter belonged to one of the old New England families The father died when our subject was about eight years of age, after which he and his older brother made a home and living for their mother and younger brother Soon after the father's death the family removed to Farm Ridge, La Salle county, Illinois, and in that locality Samuel Stocum secured work as a farm hand by the month, his time being thus spent until 1864, when, at the age of nineteen years, he responded to his country's call for troops Prompted by a spirit of patriotism, he joined the army and was assigned to Battery C, First Illinois Light Artillery, which was sent to the Indianapolis hospital and later to Government island, New York, where Mr Stocum remained for about eleven montsh He took part in several skirmishes, and was honorably discharged in August, 1865

After his return from the war Mr Stocum rented land and engaged in farming in La Salle county until 1877 He then removed to Cordova township, where he followed agricultural pursuits and also worked in a lime kiln In 1888 he embarked in the butchering business, and gradually worked into stock dealing, which business he is now successfully following Being an excellent judge of stock, his purchases and sales are conducted with profit, and he has acquired a fair competence In 1892 he established his livery stable, and keeps therein a fine line of horses and carriages, while his honorable dealing and courtesy to his customers has secured to him a liberal patronage He also deals in agricultural implements, which he sells on commission He is a good business man, sagacious and far-sighted enterprising and industrious and in co

In LaSalle county, Illinois, Mr Stocum was united in marriage to Miss Emma Applebee, a native of that county and a daughter of Nathan and Phebe (Halkett) Applebee They now have two children Frank W , who was born in Farm Ridge, LaSalle county, September 7, 1871, and Robert, who was born in Cordova, January 11, 1877, and married Ida Enright, November 18, 1896

Mr Stocum was reared in the faith of the Democracy and while home on a ten days' furlough cast his first presidential vote for McClellan He was not then twenty-one years of age but by reason of his service in the army had the right of franchise Since 1888 he has voted with the Republican party He has served for eight years as constable and for one term as alderman for Cordova He is a charter member of Burr Oak Camp, No. 33, M. W A , and is a member of Riverside Lodge, No 149, K P. He has ever been true and faithful in the discharge of his political, civic, military and social duties, and his well spent life commends him to the confidence and regard of all

C W HEALD, an honored early settler of Moline, is now living retired in his pleasant home at 822 Fifth avenue For many years he has resided in Rock Island county, and his name is inseparably connected with its business and industrial interests One of his leading characteristics in business affairs was his fine sense of order and complete system and the habit of giving careful attention to details, without which success in any undertaking is never an

A native of Massachusetts, Mr Heald was born in Barre, Worcester county, March 12, 1829 His ancestral history is one of close identification with New England The first of the name to come to America was John Heald, who lived at Berwick on the Tweed, whence he emigrated to the new world in the seventeenth century and was admitted as a free man of Massachusetts, June 2, 1641 From that time representatives of the family have been prominent in public affairs, several of the name holding official positions of honor and trust Captain Timothy Heald, the grandfather of our subject, was born in Massachusetts and when the colonies attempted to free themselves from the yoke of British tyranny he joined the service and valiantly aided in the struggle for independence He was a carpenter and millwright by trade and in connection with those occupations also engaged in bridge building to some extent

Stephen Heald, the father of our subject, was born in Hubbardstown, Massachusetts, September 18, 1799, and in his native state was reared to manhood and learned the millwright's trade He afterward became the owner of a foundry and machine shop and carried on an extensive business along those lines at Barre, Massachusetts He reared his family there and made Barre his home until his death, which occurred January 24, 1887, when he had reached the advanced age of eighty-seven years His wife, Mrs Mary Heald, was the daughter of Ebenezer Newton, a farmer of Worcester county, Massachusetts She survived her husband some years, passing away in 1892, at the age of eighty-eight They had a family of four sons and one daughter, but lost one child in infancy, and Mary Elizabeth

21

but is now deceased Henry Newton grew to manhood and married, but is also deceased Leander Stephen, of Barre, Massachusetts, remained at the old homestead

C W Heald, whose name begins this sketch, was reared to manhood in Barre, obtained a good education in the high school and afterward learned the machinist's trade with his father Thinking to improve his opportunities in the new and growing west, he came to Moline in 1854, and has since been an honored and valued resident of this city The firm of Williams, Heald & Co was organized and they established an iron foundry and machine shop, beginning business on a small scale This plant was equipped with machinery from the foundry of Mr Heald's father, and was operated by men who had also been in his father's employ, and to the new industry was given the appropriate name of the New England Works of the Mississippi Valley. For fifteen years the first partnership was continued, their business prospered and an extensive trade was built up Our subject then withdrew and became one of the organizers and founders of the Moline Malleable Iron Works, owned by a stock company Mr Heald was made master mechanic, and for twenty years continued his connection with that corporation, serving as its president a portion of the time. In 1894 the business was sold to C H Deere and others For forty years, Mr Heald was one of the active and enterprising business men of the city, one who did much to help the upbuilding of Moline, and is highly regarded in commercial circles He has taken out a number of important patents, among others a drive chain, known as the Heald chain now extensively used in sawmills · · · '' s industrial interests have made him known throughout the length and breadth of the land, and in trade circles his name is synonymous with honorable dealing

Mr Heald was married in Moline, August 2, 1859, to Daphne L Churchill, a native of Ellington, New York, and a daughter of Cullen C Churchill, a farmer and stock raiser of the Empire state Mrs Heald was educated in her native town and in Jamestown, New York, and before her marriage successfully engaged in teaching in Moline and Rock Island, Illinois, and Dubuque, Iowa Two children were born to our subject and his wife Mary Lizzie is now the widow of R C Bingham and formerly resided in Rootstown, Ohio, where her husband conducted a farm and large apiary until his death which occurred in 1893. Mrs Bingham and her daughter Ruth now make their home with her father Charles C, the only son of our subject, is a master mechanic and has charge of the foundry department in the Malleable Iron Works He married Mrs Ella Wetzel, of Peoria.

In politics Mr Heald, of this review, was formerly a Republican, but is now independent He has served as alderman but has never sought or desired office, preferring to give his attention to his business interests His wife holds membership in the Congregational church, while they are both active supporters of all measures calculated to advance the material, social, educational or moral welfare of the community. After forty years of great activity in business life, Mr Heald has practically retired His life has been well spent, marked by integrity in all business relations and fidelity to every duty ' ' ' ' ' character ı ' ı ' ʟ ' ʊ '

him the uniform regard of all and Moline is glad to number him among her citizens as a great industrial benefactor.

CASSIUS ELMER GENUNG —Among the sturdy, energetic and successful farmers and stockraisers of Canoe Creek township, who thoroughly understand the vocation which they follow, and are consequently enabled to carry on their calling with profit to themselves, is the subject of this sketch He is actively engaged in agricultural pursuits on section 18, where he owns one hundred and twenty acres of rich and arable land, and in connection with general farming is successfully engaged in the breeding of thoroughbred Jersey red hogs

A native of Rock Island county, Mr Genung was born in Coe township, May 27, 1862, and is a son of William and Elizabeth (Dunmire) Genung, natives of New York and Pennsylvania, respectively, who came with their parents to Illinois during pioneer days The paternal grandfather was the first white man to leave the settlement along the Mississippi and go among the Indians in Coe township The maternal grandparents located in Mercer county, where they died, after which the mother came to Coe township, where she met and married Mr Genung Later he purchased one hundred and sixty acres of land, which he improved and cultivated, and added to it, until he had a valuable tract of two hundred forty acres, on which his widow is still living His death occurred in November, 1891

In the family were twelve children, of whom three died in childhood but the others r t " \ ıı ı ı̇v. Ch ster a farmer ı \ııbıl ıı ınıtı f ıv ı nıried and has four children, Helen is the wife of Charles Armstrong, of Canoe Creek township, by whom she has five children, our subject is next in order of birth, Frank, a graduate of the College of Physicians and Surgeons of Chicago, is married and lives in Warsaw, Knox county, Nebraska, Sarah is the wife of Dayton Camp, of Coe township, and has three children, George lives on the old homestead, Emma is the wife of James Waddell, of Coe township, by whom she has one child, and Charles and Addie Rebecca, both at home with their mother

Mr Genung, of this review, received a good common-school education, and remained at home until twenty-three years of age He was then married June 30, 1885, the lady of his choice being Miss Maggie Waddell, of Canoe Creek township, who was born in Youngstown, Ohio, a daughter of David and Jane (Black) Waddell When eleven years of age she removed with her parents to Mercer county, Illinois, ten years later came to Rock Island county, and after spending the next decade here, Mr and Mrs Waddell went to Whiteside county, where they purchased two hundred and sixty acres of land and still reside Three children grace the union of Mr and Mrs Genung, namely Jennie, born in Coe township, February 9, 1887, Bessie, born in Canoe Creek township, December 17, 1888, and William, born in Canoe Creek township, January 2, 1891

For ten years after his marriage, Mr Genung continued to work for his father, and in 1887 purchased his present farm, upon which he has made many improvements which add to its value and attractive appearance He and his wife are both consistent members of the United Brethren church, wh

Modern Woodmen Lodge in Hillsdale He has been an ardent Republican since casting his first vote for James G Blaine in 1884, but has never been an office seeker, though he has served as school director to the best of his ability

LEWIS McGREER, a representative farmer of Drury township, is finely located on section 4, where he is maintaining his place among the progressive and intelligent men around him He was born in the same township on the 25th of April, 1839, and belongs to one of the oldest and most honored pioneer families of Rock Island county His parents, John R and Rebecca (Miller) McGreer, were both natives of Union county, Indiana, and the paternal grandfather Alexander McGreer, an early settler of that county, was born in Ireland The birth of the father occurred in October, 1815, and he continued to reside in his native county for a few years after his marriage, but in 1836 he and the grandfather, with their respective families, emigrated to Rock Island county, Illinois, where they entered land, cleared and fenced it, and opened up good farms Later they moved across the line into Mercer county, where they owned adjoining farms, which they operated for a number of years On selling out there John R McGreer went to Muscatine, Iowa where he resided some time, and was for several years engaged in the ferry business, owning an interest in a number of boats Subsequently he returned to Rock Island county and settled on a farm adjoining our subject's in Drury township, where he spent his remaining days, dying in 1895 at the age of eighty years His wife had died several years

1 1863

Three sons and three daughters were born to them but only two reached years of maturity, the other being Thomas R , now a business man of Lincoln, Nebraska.

Amidst the primitive scenes of frontier life, Lewis McGreer spent his boyhood and youth in Rock Island and Mercer counties, and remained with his father until he had reached man's estate, acquiring a fair common-school education. In 1861, in this county, he wedded Miss Virginia Pullen, who was born in Indiana, but was reared in Rock Island county, her father, Dennis Pullen, being one of its early settlers Two sons and one daughter were born to them— Lee, who is married and engaged in business in Omaha, Nebraska, Elbert, who is married and carries on farming in Drury township, and Hettie, wife of Dr Close, of Eliza, Mercer county, Illinois

After his marriage Mr McGreer purchased a part of the old homestead in Mercer county, which he operated for several years and then sold and bought eighty acres adjoining his present farm. That place he improved and cultivated and continued to reside there until trading it for the old homestead of three hundred and twenty acres in Mercer county A few years later he returned to Drury township and bought his father's place, opposite his present home, but subsequently purchased eighty acres in Montgomery county, Iowa, where he lived for one summer, during which time he built a house and made other improvements upon his land In the fall, on his return to Illinois, he again located in Mercer county, but three years later bought his present farm and soon afterward sold the old homestead Only about thirty acres of the one hundred and twenty-five had been cleared when he took possession February

29, 1876, but to-day it is one of the most highly cultivated and best improved places in the community. An excellent orchard has been set out, a large and comfortable residence erected and a good barn built in the spring of 1897 In connection with general farming, Mr McGreer is also successfully engaged in stock-raising, and all his undertakings have proved quite profitable, so that to-day he is numbered among the well-to-do and substantial citizens of Drury township

Since casting his first vote for Stephen A Douglas in 1860, Mr McGreer has been a stanch Democrat, and in the fall of 1896 supported Hon W J Bryan and free silver He has witnessed almost the entire development of the county, and can well remember when there were only two houses between the old McGreer homestead on the Mercer county line and the city of Rock Island, a distance of thirty-two miles In the wonderful transformation that has since taken place he has borne an important part, aiding in its development and progress, and giving his support to all measures calculated to advance the general welfare

MERRITT GOBLE, an energetic and progressive farmer residing on section 22, Black Hawk township, Rock Island county, was born April 7, 1849, and belongs to one of the most honored pioneer families of the county, his parents being Benjamin and Barbara (Vandruff) Goble, a sketch of whom is given elsewhere in this work Our subject was reared on a farm in Henry county, Illinois, and obtained a fair education in the district schools near his boyhood home

On the 20th of February 1873, Mr.

Goble led to the marriage altar Miss Clara A., daughter of Harrison M and Mary Catherine (Lantz) Coon, natives of Pennsylvania Her paternal grandfather, John Coon, was born in the same state of German ancestry, was a farmer by occupation, and died when past the age of eighty years, leaving a large family. Jacob Lantz, her maternal grandfather, was also a native of the Keystone state, was an agriculturist and died at an advanced age

When Mrs Goble was twelve years of age, her parents, accompanied by their family, left Pennsylvania, and the father for a time engaged in lumbering in Jefferson county, Pennsylvania, whence he came to Rock Island county, Illinois, in 1863 He first located at Carbon Cliff and later purchased a farm in Black Hawk township, but after operating it for some years returned to Pennsylvania, where he is now engaged in the lumber business He has now reached the ripe old age of eighty-four, but his estimable wife lost her life July 4, 1883, in a fire in a barn at Hebron, Nebraska, when seventy-two years of age Both were earnest and consistent members of the Methodist Episcopal church, and during the Civil war Mr Coon served as regimental quartmaster In their family were eleven children, eight sons and three daughters, namely John, Jacob, James, Samuel, Michael, William, Catharine, David, Clara and Caroline All are still living with the exception of William, Michael and Catharine.

Mrs Goble obtained her education mainly in the public schools of Milan and Rock Island, and is a lady of culture and refinement By her marriage she has become the mother of four children—Gememmes Le Roy, Charles Benjamin, Flora Leona and Mer

at the age of five years and ten months The oldest son married Miss Martha Herrick and lives near Watch Tower on the Rock Island bluff, where he is engaged in the dairy business

In 1869 Mr Goble returned with his father to Rock Island county and after his marriage lived on the Hewitt farm for one year The following nine years were passed on the Cheney farm, and at the end of that time he removed to his father's old homestead on Section 22, Black Hawk township, where he still continues to reside He has sold two acres to the Hennepin Canal Company, but still owns one hundred and ninety-seven acres of excellent land, and devotes his time and attention to farming and stock raising

As a Republican he takes quite an active interest in political affairs, has served as delegate to the county conventions of his party, and has filled the office of road commissioner. He and his wife hold membership in the Methodist church, of which he is now a trustee They are hospitable, intelligent and affable people, whom it is a pleasure to meet, and their friends are many throughout Rock Island county

HAMILTON WREATH, deceased, was for many years a valued representative of the agricultural interests of Rock Island county, and was a loyal, faithful citizen whose loss to the community was deeply mourned He was born in County Antrim, Ireland August 11, 1828, and was a son of Benjamin and Mary (Hamilton) Wreath He came to America with his parents in 1840, the family locating in Pennsylvania, and subsequently removing county, where the father became the owner of forty acres of land, making that farm his home throughout his remaining days

Our subject acquired a fair common-school education, and entering upon his business career, turned his attention to agricultural pursuits He purchased forty acres of land adjoining his father's farm in Coe township, and further completed his arrangements for a home by his marriage to Miss Sarah C McConnell, December 14, 1864 She was born in Westmoreland county, Pennsylvania, a daughter of William and Sidney McConnell, natives of Allegheny county, Pennsylvania, whence they removed to Rock Island county, in 1852, settling in Coe township, where her father became owner of a large tract of land, entering one hundred and sixty acres of the amount from the government

Soon after their marriage Mr Wreath sold his forty-acre farm and in the same neighborhood purchased eighty acres For eighteen years he continued the cultivation and development of that property, and then purchased one hundred and sixty acres in Canoe Creek township, where his widow still resides He made excellent improvements upon the place, erected substantial buildings, placed the land under a high state of cultivation and developed one of the best farms in the neighborhood

To Mr and Mrs Wreath were born eight children—William Walter, Clara, who married Ferdinand Taggart and has one child, Hazel, Jennie, wife of William Feaster, of Canoe Creek township, by whom she has three children, Zella, Anna and Sarah Madge, and James Hamilton, Letitia, Samuel Ross, Joseph Irwin and Wilson Findley, all at ho re

In early M W d's appeared the

Democracy, but later became a stanch Prohibitionist as he was an earnest advocate of temperance principles He was a conscientious, earnest Christian gentleman, a faithful member of the United Presbyterian church, and in 1867 was ordained a ruling elder, which position he filled up to the time of his death, which occurred January 31, 1891. His remains were interred in the Pleasant Unity cemetery. His benevolence was unostentatious and genuine, and there was nothing in the story of his life to show that he ever for a moment sought to compass a given end for the purpose of exalting himself His memory will be a sacred inheritance to his children, it will be cherished by a multitude of friends Throughout his career of continued and far-reaching usefulness, his duties were performed with the greatest care and his personal honor and integrity were without blemish.

CHARLES MEWES —In the respect that is accorded to men who have fought their way to success through unfavorable environment we find an unconscious recognition of the intrinsic worth of character which can not only endure so rough a test, but gain new strength through the discipline. The following history sets forth briefly the steps by which our subject, now one of the substantial agriculturists of Drury township, overcame the disadvantages of his early life His home is situated on section 14, where he owns one hundred and eighty acres of well improved and valuable land.

Mr Mewes was born on the 9th of January, 1832, in Prussia, Germany, where he was reared and well educated in his native language, but his knowledge of English has all been acquired through his own efforts

since coming to this country Before leaving the old world he was married in 1859 to
Miss Frederica Fuhlman, also a native of
Prussia, and they have become the parents
of seven children, five sons and two daughters, namely Ferdinand, the present supervisor of Drury township, whose sketch is
given elsewhere in this work, Charles W ,
William A , Albert H. and Edward, who
are assisting their father on the home farm,
Annie, wife of Louis Kleist, of Drury township, and Martha, who is now keeping house
for her brother Ferdinand

While still a resident of Prussia, Mr
Mewes served as a coachman for a noble-
man of high rank for six years, and spent
four years as right servant to another titled
gentleman In 1862 with his little family
he sailed for the United States and first
located in Muscatine, Iowa, where he found
employment and continued to reside for
about a year and a half He then came to
Drury township, Rock Island county, where
he worked as a farm hand for a time and
then with his hard earned savings purchased
a tract of forty acres of timber land adjoining his present farm He at once began to
clear and improve his land, placing acre
after acre under the plow, and as he prospered in his undertakings was able to buy
more land until he now has one hundred
and eighty acres under a high state of cultivation, and improved with a good set of
farm buildings, which stand as monuments
to his thrift and industry The success that
he has achieved is certainly well deserved
as he has made his own way in the world
unaided by capital or influential friends

Since becoming an American citizen,
Mr Mewes has been a firm supporter of the
men and measures of the Republican party,
casting his f   t   f   M   b   in Lincoln

in 1864. For some years he has done
effective service in the cause of education as
a member of the school board, and does all
in his power to promote the moral, educational or material welfare of the community
He and his wife and some of their children
are active and prominent members of the
Methodist Episcopal church, and for about
twenty years he served as a local preacher,
but for the past four years has given up the
work of the ministry owing to defective
hearing He is one of Rock Island county's honored and highly respected German-
American citizens and no one is more deserving of mention in a work of this character than Charles Mewes

HENRY KROEGER was for many years
one of the most highly esteemed and
valued citizens of Rock Island He was of
foreign birth, but his duties of citizenship
were performed with a loyalty equal to that
of any native son of America, and when his
nation was imperiled by the hydra-headed
monster, rebellion, he went to the defense
of the union and protected the cause of his
adopted country on many a southern battle
field

Mr Kroeger was born in Holstein, Germany, November 1, 1824, and having acquired his education in the schools of that
land he began learning the cabinet-maker s
trade, which he followed for some time
For two years he served in the Danish army
and for three years in the German army,
the period of his military service being from
1846 until 1851, and in both armies he held
the rank of sergeant part of the time In
1852 he determined to try his fortune in the
new world and crossed the Atlantic to America locating in Boston where he remained

for two years, working at the carpenter s trade In 1854 he came to Rock Island and followed the same vocation until the 1st of September, 1861

At that time Mr Kroeger offered his services to his adopted country and joined the boys in blue of Company E, Forty-third Illinois Infantry, of which he was made first lieutenant He served for three years and seven months in the army of the Mississippi under General Grant, whom he saw nearly every day for a time He participated in the battle of Shiloh, the siege of Vicksburg, the battles of Corinth and Paducah and all of the engagements of his command and was never absent from duty for a single day, being very fortunate in escaping all wounds On the 1st of September, 1862, he was promoted to the captaincy of Company I, of the Forty-third Illinois Regiment, and was attached to the Seventh Army Corps under General Steele. As an officer he had the confidence of his men and the respect of his superiors and his own bravery and faithfulness inspired and encouraged the men under him. On the surrender of Lee he resigned and was honorably discharged at Little Rock, Arkansas, April 9, 1865

Returning to Rock Island, Mr. Kroeger engaged in carpentering and was prominently connected with the building interests of this city He erected many of the substantial structures here, and prospered in his business, owing to his well-directed efforts, his skill, his fidelity to the trusts committed to his care and his honorable dealing In this way he acquired a handsome competence, which was the just reward of his labors.

While in Boston Mr Kroeger was married August 10 1852 to Miss Henrietta Meyer, a native of Hanover, Germany, who

came to America in 1847 They had three children—John, who died at the age of six months, Lizzie, wife of Rev H Brammer, of Louton, Iowa, by whom she has ten children, John, Bertha, Paul, Lizzie, Mary, Martha, Topea, Clara, Hulda and Martin; and Charles William, who died at the age of three years They have also an adopted son, Fred, who has resided in their family since two years of age He is now stationed at Springdale, Arkansas He wedded Mary Minnigan, and they have three children, Freda, Lena and an infant.

Mr Kroeger and his wife were members of the Lutheran church, and had a large circle of friends in Rock Island, where they made their home for the long period of forty-three years In politics he was a Republican, casting his first presidential vote for Abraham Lincoln He was numbered among the progressive and enterprising citizens of the community, whose sterling worth commended him to the confidence and regard of all He died May 3, 1897.

ISAAC BOWERS CROSBY, deceased, whose long identification with Rock Island county and devotion to its interests and welfare made him one of its most valued citizens, was born near Nashua, New Hampshire, on the 18th of November, 1819, and was a son of John and Mary (Bowers) Crosby His father was engaged in the lumber business in the Granite state and afterward removed to Lockport, New York, where he conducted a hotel for about twenty years

Isaac B Crosby remained with his father until about twenty-five years of age and then determined to try his fortune in the west He came to Rock Island county, locat.ng in Cordova township, where he soon afterward became acquainted with Miss Elizabeth Marshall, and their friendship ripening into love they were married March 10, 1847, at her home four miles from Cordova, by the Rev William Blanchard. Mrs Crosby was born April 5, 1824, in Mercer county, New Jersey, a daughter of John and Charity (Golden) Marshall Her father died in New Jersey, leaving the mother and nine children, three of whom had come to Illinois about 1839 In 1842 one of these returned to the east for the mother and other children and by team the family made the journey to Rock Island county Mrs Crosby was then about eighteen years of age

At the time of their marriage Mr Crosby rented land and after a year and a half made his first purchase, comprising two hundred acres constituting the present home of his widow The log cabin upon the place continued to be their home for a few years, and they endured many of the hardships and privations incident to frontier life, but as the years passed they were enabled to add many improvements and comforts to their place Having purchased property in Albany, Whiteside county, Illinois, Mr Crosby moved with his family to that village in 1857, where they remained two years He owned a number of lots in different parts of the village and also a part of Beaver Island Shortly after returning to his farm in the fall of 1859, their home, situated on Main street, Albany, Illinois, was ruined by a very destructive tornado that swept through the place and which destroyed the largest part of the village In 1867 Mr Crosby erected a pleasant residence on the farm which has since been remodeled and enlarged,

provements making the farm one of the best in the county, lacking none of the accessories and conveniences of the model farm of the nineteenth century As his financial resources increased he also extended the boundaries of his land until he owned a very large tract

The home of Mr and Mrs Crosby was blessed with a family of ten children, but three died in infancy The others are Amos Buell, who married Jennie Whitford, by whom he has two children, and lives in Chetopa, Kansas, Clara, who became the wife of Stephen Sprague, and died in Fisher, Minnesota, leaving three children, Horace Mann, who wedded Mary Lamb, by whom he has one child, Harrison Amos, Mary Ella, who became the wife of Henry W Fletcher, and died at Riverside, California, leaving three children, Isaac F, who married Lucy Mack, by whom he has one child, and is engaged in the practice of medicine in Menlo, Iowa, having graduated in the College of Physicians and Surgeons, of Chicago, in 1889, Hattie, who died in Cordova in 1888, at the age of twenty-two years, and Lottie E, at home

Mr Crosby was an extensive reader and a well-informed man of scholarly tastes In his early life he had learned the carpenter's trade with his father, and followed it to a limited extent after coming to this county, but devoted the greater part of his time to farming, which he prosecuted with such vigor that he acquired a handsome competence that leaves his widow in comfortable circumstances He was ever watchful of the happiness and welfare of his family, and did all in his power to bring to them the pleasant things of life In his political views he was a Republican, and filled the office of justice of the peace for many years

In early life he was a member of the Congregational church, but afterward united with the Baptist church and served as one of its deacons, taking an active part in its work and upbuilding For years he was superintendent of the Baptist Sunday-school in Cordova A few years before his death he investigated spiritualism and became a strong believer in it, and while his views were changed he could not give up his little country Sunday-school that he had carried on so many years in the district school-house near his home There was no one to take his place in that work, and he thought many would feel the loss of the Sunday-school, as they had there been influenced for good It was always his greatest pleasure to influence those around him to lead better and purer lives

Fraternally Mr Crosby was a Mason, and his life was ever honorable and true in all its relations His example is well worthy of emulation and his memory is enshrined in the hearts of his many friends He passed away November 29, 1873, since which time Mrs Crosby has lived with her eldest son, Horace She is an estimable lady, possessed of many excellencies of character, and, like her husband, shares in the high regard of many friends

---

FRANK A LANDEE —No foreign element has become a more important part in our American citizenship than that furnished by Sweden The emigrants from that land have brought with them to the new world the stability, enterprise and perseverance characteristic of their people and have fused these qualities with the progressiveness and indomitable spirit of the west Mr Lanc￼ ￼ ￼ ￼ ￼ ￼ ￼ ￼ ￼ ￼ ￼ ￼ ￼ this ￼ ￼

He came to America a poor boy, hoping to benefit his financial condition, and his dreams of the future have been more than realized. He now occupies a very prominent place in business circles in Moline, being general foreman of the Rock Island division of the Western Union Telegraph Company, president of the Moline Furniture Company, and a partner in a general mercantile establishment

Mr. Landee was born in Kalman, Sweden, August 11, 1852, and is a son of John M and Anna Landee His early boyhood days were spent in his native village, where he attended school His mother died when he was ten years of age, his father three years later, and when a youth of fourteen he came with his brother, George Frederick, to America, locating first in Knox county, Illinois, where he attended school and also worked for a few years At the age of eighteen he removed to Peoria, where he learned telegraphy, since which time he has been connected with that profession For a year and a half he remained in Peoria, and was then called to Chicago in 1871 to become a member of the extra force that was needed on account of the great fire of that year He made his headquarters in the western metropolis until 1883, but in the meantime traveled throughout the country as a representative of the Western Union, the Atlantic & Pacific, the Baltimore & Ohio and the Mutual Union Companies He also established telephone exchanges in different parts of Illinois and put in about thirty of the first telephones used in Chicago He established the system in Quincy, Keokuk, Springfield, Davenport, Rock Island and Moline, and had charge of all the territory for the Mutual Telegraph Company from the Allegheny mountains west to St Paul and

Kansas City and south to Louisville For two years he was office electrician for the Western Union and is now general foreman of the Rock Island division He is an expert electrician, and his fidelity to the interests of the company he has represented has won him constant advancement and gained him unqualified confidence and regard He is a man of excellent business ability and broad resources, and is now prominently connected with the commercial interests of Moline as president of the Moline Furniture Company and as a partner of the firm of Swanson & Landee, general merchants

Mr Landee was married in Knoxville, Illinois, April 9, 1879, to Hannah Johnson, who was also born in Sweden, and came to America with her parents, A N and Charlotte Johnson After their marriage they resided in Chicago until 1883, when they spent one year in Davenport, and have since made their home in Moline They have five children Effie, who was born in Chicago, June 20, 1880, died in Moline, at the age of eight years, George Edward, born in Chicago, July 19, 1882, Frank Julian, born in Moline, November 14, 1884, Marian Hannah, born in Moline, December 21, 1886, and Anna Irene M , born in Moline, February 11, 1892

Mr Landee cast his first presidential vote for Hayes in 1876, and has since been a stalwart supporter of the men and measures of the party He has never been an aspirant for political honors, but labors earnestly for others and has frequently been a delegate to county and congressional conventions He is a valued member of the Swedish Lutheran church, and a member of its board of trustees His life record is one well worthy of emulation and contains many valuable le   '   .   .   who   ng the

possibilities that are open to young men who wish to improve every opportunity for advancement

ROBERT WAGNER, one of the active, enterprising and progressive business men of Rock Island, has spent his entire life in this city It is the place of his birth, which occurred June 15, 1866, his father being George Wagner, one of the leading residents of the county He attended the public schools, the German private schools, the University of Iowa City, and the United States Brewer's Academy in New York city, graduating in the last named institution with the class of 1887 Thus thoroughly equipped for a business career he returned to his home, and for two years was employed as foreman in his father's brewery, after which he entered into business with his father, the relationship being maintained until the consolidation of the brewing interests of the city when he was elected president of the new stock company, a position which he still fills He thoroughly understands the business and his able management and untiring perseverance have made the new concern one of the leading enterprises in this line in northwestern Illinois The volume of the business is now very extensive and the trade is constantly increasing

On the 15th of November, 1894, Mr Wagner was united in marriage to Miss Thekla I Klug, of Davenport, who was born, reared and educated in that city, and is a daughter of Otto Klug, a pioneer of Davenport They hold an enviable position in social circles and have many warm friends throughout the community

Mr Wagner gives his political support

to the men and measures of the Democracy and believes firmly in its principles, but has never sought or desired political preferment for himself He belongs to the Knights of Pythias fraternity and is a well-known citizen Among his warmest friends are those who have known him from boyhood, a fact which indicates a life well spent and a fidelity to the best principles which govern conduct Like his father he occupies a place in the front ranks among the leading business men of his native city

JOHN H ZOLLNER —It has been said that biography yields to no other subject in point of interest and profit and it is especially interesting to note the progress that has been made along various lines of business by those of foreign birth who have sought homes in America—the readiness with which they adapt themselves to the different methods and customs of America, recognize advantages offered and utilize opportunities which the new world affords Among this class is Mr Zollner, now one of the wealthy and most reliable farmers of Rock Island county, his home being on section 26, Drury township, where he owns four hundred and forty acres of valuable land.

He was born August 3, 1833, in Prussia, Germany, in which country his parents, Jacob and Mary (Guern) Zollner, spent their entire lives By trade the father was a weaver. On a farm in his native land our subject spent the days of his boyhood and youth and in the public schools was educated After the death of his parents, he and his two sisters came to the United States with an un ? Ter K h wh settled in St Clair M L in where Mr Zoll-

ner remained for two years, during which time he learned the English language After he had attained his majority he spent one winter in the pineries of Wisconsin, and the following summer engaged in rafting logs down the Mississippi from Stephens Point to Muscatine, Iowa He then spent three years in Muscatine county, where he was employed on the farm of A J. Westbrook, who is now living retired in the city of Muscatine

After Fort Sumter had been fired upon, Mr Zollner in April, 1861, enlisted at the president's first call for three months troops, joining Company A, First Iowa Volunteer Infantry, and the first battle in which he took part was at Wilson creek, Missouri. On the expiration of his term, he was discharged at St Louis and returned to Muscatine, but a few days later joined Company H, Eleventh Iowa Infantry, under Captain Benjamin Beach, and again went to the front as a member of the army of the Tennessee At the battle of Shiloh he was wounded and for six months was unfit for duty, during which time he was confined in the hospitals at St Louis, Keokuk and Muscatine Rejoining his regiment at Corinth, the next day he participated in the battle of Iuka, Mississippi, which was followed by the engagement at Corinth and the siege of Vicksburg In January, 1864, he veteranized with his regiment and in April the whole brigade was granted a thirty days furlough, which Mr Zollner spent in Muscatine They were then ordered to join the command at Huntsville, Alabama, and later participated in the engagement at Kenesaw Mountain June 11, 1864, the great battle of Peach Tree Creek, July 22, 1864, where General McPherson was killed the Atlanta campaign were with Sherman on the celebrated march to the sea, and were in many hotly contested battles, including that of Bentonville, which ended the war After participating in the grand review at Washington, D. C., Mr Zollner returned to Louisville, Kentucky, where he was granted a thirty days furlough and returned home, but before the expiration of the thirty days his term of enlistment expired and he was honorably discharged with the rank of corporal.

While on a furlough Mr Zollner was married July 10, 1865, in Muscatine, to Miss Mary Kranz, who was also born and reared in Prussia They have become the parents of twelve children, eleven still living, namely Albert A , who is married and engaged in farming in Buffalo Prairie township, Rock Island county. John F , at home, Mary, wife of George Shireman, of Nicholas, Iowa, Minnie, wife of Frank Fox, of Lisbon, Iowa, Louis W , Fritz C , who is now in St John, North Dakota, Kate, wife of Charles Spickler, of Drury township, Rock Island county, Benjamin, Adam, Annie and Willie, all at home, Alice A died in infancy.

Soon after his marriage Mr Zollner came to Rock Island county and purchased forty acres of land, on which he erected a log house, where he lived while developing and improving his place, but the little cabin has long since given place to a commodious and pleasant residence Good outbuildings have also been erected, and other tracts added to the original purchase until the farm now comprises four hundred and forty acres of rich and arable land

Greatly opposed to slavery, Mr Zollner joined the Republican party on its organization, casting his first vote while at Portage, Wisconsin

and has since been an ardent supporter of that party He has served on the board of commissioners and also the school board. and the duties of both positions he most capably and satisfactorily performed He belongs to the Grand Army Post at Illinois City, and Shiloh Commandery, No 2, U V U , at Rock Island He and his wife attend the Methodist Episcopal church, of which some of their children are members, and in social circles the family hold an enviable position, their true worth being widely recognized In days of peace as well as on southern battle fields, Mr Zollner has manifested his loyalty to his adopted country by faithfully performing every duty of citizenship, and wherever known is held in high regard

A H WENDT, a well-known furniture dealer and undertaker of Port Byron, is distinctively a man of affairs and one who has wielded a wide influence A strong mentality, an invincible courage, a most determined individuality have so entered into his make-up as to render him a natural leader of men and a director of opinion The city may well accord honor to him

Mr Wendt began his earthly career in Prussia, Germany, September 8, 1853 a son of Henry and Catherine Boehm) Wendt, who were born, reared and married in that country In 1865 the father brought his family to this country, and for some years successfully engaged in the tailoring business in Moline but is now living retired in Rock Island, enjoying a well-earned rest

In his native land our subject had been provided with good school privileges, but his knowledge of English is all self-acquired He was twelve years of age when he arrived here, and for the first season worked for William Nurse, of Rock Island, in his nursery He next served a four-years' apprenticeship to the cabinetmaker's trade in a furniture manufactory, doing at first only a boy's work, but rose gradually, step by step, until he had thoroughly mastered every detail of the business In the same establishment he served as chief salesman for some five or six years Coming to Port Byron in 1880 he started in business for himself in a small way as a furniture dealer and undertaker, but has prospered in the enterprise and now carries a large and well selected stock of everything to be found in his line In 1882 he purchased a lot and erected thereon a fine double store building 46 x 80 feet, it being the best business block in the village He also has the finest residence in this part of the county, it being built of Milwaukee pressed brick in the latest style of architecture and supplied with all modern conveniences In connection with his business in Port Byron, he also has a branch store in La Clare, and also attends to the undertaking business at that place The success that he has achieved in life is due to his own unaided efforts, good management and excellent business ability

In Moline, on the 25th of August, 1880, was celebrated the marriage of Mr Wendt and Miss Lizzie Erler, also a native of Germany, who was reared and educated in the schools of Chicago and Port Byron, having made her home in those cities during her childhood and youth In 1865 her father had removed to the latter place, becoming one of its successful merchants Three children h   i u ' i u t Mr and Mrs Wendt, n   t t ' t, Willm nd Fail

The Republican party has always found in Mr Wendt a stanch supporter, and he takes a deep and commendable interest in public affairs He has served on the town board of trustees for several years, and is a trustee and secretary of the board of Port Byron Academy, which position he has held for about five years, during which time he has done much to promote the cause of public education in his community Although not members of any religious organization, he and his wife attend the Congregational church, and contribute liberally to its support as well as that of other churches Fraternally, Mr Wendt affiliates with the Knights of Pythias Lodge, of which he is past chancellor commander and treasurer, the Modern Woodmen of America, in which he has also passed all the chairs, and the Court of Honor, of which he is one of the supreme officers, and has assisted in organizing lodges of that order throughout the state Since coming to Port Byron, September, 1880, he has been numbered among its most enterprising and progressive business men, as well as one of its representative and reliable citizens, and has won the confidence and esteem of all with whom he has come in contact

P H WEIDEMANN, a well-known general merchant of Hillsdale, Illinois, is a man whose sound common sense and vigorous, able management of his affairs have been important factors in his success, and with his undoubted integrity of character have given him an honorable position among his fellow men His birth occurred in Schleswig, Germany, May 8, 1865, but when only two years old he was brought to America by his parents P H and May (Mahlstedt) Weidemann, who at once located in Rock Island county, where the father turned his attention to farming   After renting for a few years he bought one hundred twenty acres in Zuma township, where he spent his remaining days, dying January 8, 1886   His wife survived him a short time, her death occurring December 27, 1891

There were eight children born to this worthy couple, but two died in childhood The others are all living in Rock Island county, are married, and with the exception of our subject, follow agricultural pursuits In order of birth they are as follows Adolph, who has four children and lives in Hampton township, Katy, wife of John G Sauchio, of Zuma township, by whom she has six children, John, who has three children and makes his home in Zuma township, Henry, who has three children and lives in Zuma township, P H , of this sketch, and Daniel, of Coe township

When ten years old Mr Weidemann, of this sketch, left home and went to live with his mother's brother in Henry county, with whom he made his home for seven years, during which time he attended school, thus acquiring a good practical education   At the age of seventeen he returned to Zuma township, where he worked by the month, giving his wages to his father until he attained his majority   He next began learning the carpenter's trade, and during his two years' apprenticeship was paid five dollars per month for his services   His father had just died and he was forced to borrow money to buy tools, but from his meager wages saved enough to pay it all back

In the spring of 1887, Mr Weidemann went to Kansas, where for about a year he was emplo*

ing for a railroad in building depots for a part of the time, and met with a fair degree of success in that state   On his return to Illinois, he spent a short time in Rock Island and Moline, and later worked on the Catholic church in Wenona, Illinois, but spent the winter in Zuma township, after which he was employed in Rock Island until his marriage

That important event in his life was celebrated October 10, 1889, Miss Minnie Brockman, of Hillsdale, becoming his wife She was also born in Germany, and was only four years old when she came to this country with her parents, Frederick and Elizabeth (Hahn) Brockman, both of whom are now deceased, the mother dying in March, 1883, and the father October 11, 1896   Mr and Mrs Weidemann have two interesting children, Harvey Edward, born in Rock Island, December 30, 1892, and Hattie, born in Moline September 30, 1894, on her mother's thirtieth birthday

Mr Weidemann purchased a home in Rock Island, where he continued to reside until 1892, following contracting and working at his trade   During a dull season he borrowed money and purchased an interest in a mercantile establishment in Moline, with which he was profitably connected for eighteen months   On selling out in March, 1895, he came to Hillsdale and embarked in business, and now carries a large stock of general merchandise valued at four thousand dollars   By fair and honorable dealing he has built up a good trade, which is constantly increasing and has gained the confidence and respect of his many patrons His father's estate was settled in 1893 after the death of his mother, and he received five hundred and ninety dollars   He
. . . . ublican

party since casting his first vote for Harrison in 1888, and socially affiliates with the Court of Honor, while his wife is a member of the Home Forum Their sterling worth and many excellencies of character have gained for them a host of warm friends, and they have the respect and esteem of all who know them

In addition to his stock of goods, Mr Weidemann has just finished building a large store building and public hall, which is a credit to the town

JOHN M GALLAGHER, who resides on section 10, Rock Island township, has for some years lived retired on his pleasant farm just outside the city limits of the county seat, there enjoying the rest to which many years of honorable labor justly entitle him He was born in County Donegal, Ireland, in 1813 and grew to manhood there, with but limited school privileges In 1840 he took passage on a sailing vessel, which weighed anchor at Londonderry, on the 10th of May and after a voyage of six weeks reached the American harbor Going to Philadelphia he spent about three years in that city clerking for a cousin who was engaged in the grocery and dry goods business

On leaving Philadelphia Mr Gallagher went to St Louis, where he remained for about three or four years, devoting his time to merchandising In 1847 he came to Illinois and embarked in the grocery and dry goods business in Rock Island, where he carried on operations for several years He then sold his store and traded some lots which he owned in Davenport, Iowa, for eighteen acres of land upon which he now resides This was wild tract, entirely undeveloped, but he began to improve

it and had soon made it a productive and fertile piece of land He erected a pleasant and commodious brick residence, made other substantial improvements and from time to time added to his property until he now has over fifty acres just outside the city limits and two miles from the court house. He also owns Turkey Island in the Rock river, comprising forty-eight acres The task of clearing his land was a very arduous one, but with characteristic energy he continued his work until rich fields yielded to him a golden return for his labor In 1864 he went to Montana, where he engaged in cutting lumber and in raising hay through the first season. He then purchased a ranch, stocked it with cattle and for twelve years carried on business there with good success He was then joined by his nephew, Thomas H Dougherty, who assumed the management of the ranch and Mr Gallagher returned to Rock Island county, where he spent the winter The following year he returned to Montana, and sold the ranch, since which time he has resided continuously in this county

Mr Gallagher was the second in a family of four children His brother, Hugh, spent his entire life in County Donegal, Ireland His sister Mary is the deceased wife of John Williams, and Martha is now the widow of Thomas Dougherty, who died about 1893 Mr and Mrs Dougherty joined Mr Gallagher about 1850, and she has since lived with her brother, acting as his housekeeper for many years She has two children, Thomas H and Mary Jane The son has for a long time been associated with his uncle in business and is a capable, enterprising man

In his political views Mr Gallagher was long a stalwart Republican, but in 1896 supported W J Bryan and the free silver platform He has never sought or desired office, preferring to give his undivided attention to his business interests in which he has met with signal success His business interests have been conducted in the most honorable and straightforward way and his prosperity is the legitimate result of energy, enterprise and perseverance He and his sister, Mrs. Dougherty, are members of the United Presbyterian church of Rock Island, and have the respect of all who know them

WILLIAM HAINES LYFORD, M D , is engaged in the practice of medicine and surgery in Port Byron, and has that love for and devotion to his profession which has brought to him success and won him a place among the ablest representatives of the medical fraternity in this locality He was born in Port Byron, September 8, 1836, and is a son of Dr Jeremiah Hall Lyford, who was born near Concord, New Hampshire, October 19, 1808 The family is of English origin, and was founded in America by Francis Lyford, who settled in Massachusetts about the middle of the seventeenth century Among his decendants were those who fought for the independence of the country in the war of the Revolution and others who became prominent in statescraft The father of our subject grew to manhood in New Hampshire and was a graduate of Dartmouth College In 1831 he removed to Ravenna, Ohio, where he remained two years, during which time he was united in marriage to Mary Ann (Weeks) Haines, a native of New Hampshire, who was reared and educated in South Burwick Her father was secretary under Governor Clinton at the time of

22

the building of the Erie canal and was a man of much prominence

In 1836 Dr Jeremiah Lyford removed to Port Byron and was the pioneer physician of this section of Illinois, and also eastern Iowa, for his practice extended over four counties, and he would frequently be gone from home for two or three days together He traveled on horseback, fording the swollen streams and meeting with other experiences common to the pioneer physicians Charitable and benevolent by nature, his kindness won gratitude in many a home, and his memory is enshrined in many hearts He continued in active practice for over forty years, and died January 23, 1878, at the age of seventy, his remains being interred in Port Byron cemetery, where a marble monument marks his grave He was very prominent in the affairs of the county, lending his support to all measures for the public good and was active in church work His wife is still living on the old homestead at the age of eighty-four years In their family were four sons and a daughter William H , Eugene A , who was a student in the Northwestern University, enlisted July 6, 1862, in the Eighty-eighth Illinois Infantry, and was killed at the battle of Stone River, December 31, 1862, his remains brought home and interred in Port Byron cemetery, Albert E is now engaged in mining in Oregon, Frederick B is the next of the family, Mary is the wife of George L Smith, a lawyer of St Louis

Dr Lyford, whose name begins this review, was educated in the Rock River Seminary and Iowa College, of Davenport, Iowa, where he was a schoolmate of Charles H Deere He studied medicine with his father and for two years was a student in the office of Dr N S Davis of Chicago He took his first course of lectures in 1857, in Rush Medical College, and was graduated in that institution with the class of 1859, after which he began practice with his father in Port Byron He has remained here continuously since, with the exception of four years, from 1883 until 1887, which were spent as a medical practitioner in Evanston, Illinois He aided in organizing the Iowa and Illinois District Medical Society of Rock Island, Illinois, and Scott county Iowa, and belongs to the Chicago Medical Society, the Illinois Medical Society, and the American Medical Association He is examining physician for most of the old line insurance companies at this point, and is a progressive member of his profession, who keeps abreast of the latest discoveries and theories by his perusal of medical journals His skill and ability is attested by the liberal patronage he enjoys, and which ranks him as one of the leading physicians of the county. For some years the Doctor has also engaged in buying and selling farm lands and other real estate in Rock Island county, and now owns two hundred and fifty acres of land here, besides property on Staten Island, New York, and in Port Byron.

The Doctor was married in his native town, April 25, 1861, to Miss Jane, the youngest daughter of Judge Holmes She was born in Lunenburg, Vermont, came to Rock Island county during her girlhood, and was educated in Knox Seminary, at Galesburg, Illinois Fourteen children were born of this union, namely: Grace R , wife of Frank Skelton, of Port Byron Charlotte Ellen, a graduate of the Northwestern University, of the class of 1889, and now the wife of James Boyd, editor of the Galva Standard, Mary Annette wife of Dr Charles W Hunter Victor Illinois Edward

Hall, a farmer of this county; Clarence H., assistant secretary of the Mulford Heater Works, of Galva, Florence C , a student in the Northwestern University, Francis E , who is on the farm with his brother, Lucy and Bessie, students in Port Byron Academy, Ernest J and Edna C , who are students in the public schools

Dr Lyford cast his first presidential vote for Lincoln in 1860, and for many years supported the Republican party, but now casts his ballot with the Prohibition party. He was one of the first members of Port Byron Lodge, I O O F , is past grand, and has filled all the chairs He attends the Congregational church, to which his wife belongs, has been a liberal contributer to its support, and takes an active part in its work and upbuilding He completed the Chautauqua course and was graduated in 1891 A man of scholarly attainments and broad general culture, of courteous, affable manner and sterling worth, he has the unqualified confidence and regard of the community in which his entire life has been passed

MRS JULIA BUELL BRYANT is one of the most prominent and highly esteemed ladies of Moline, her home being at 322 Seventeenth street She is a native of Albany, New York, and is a representative of one of the most distinguished families of the east, which was of English origin and founded in Connecticut during early colonial days. Her great-grandfather, Major Elias Buell, was a noted officer of the Revolutionary war, serving under General Putnam. Judge Jesse Buell, her grandfather, one of the most prominent men of his day in New York, was born in Bennington, Vermont, but was reared in the Empire state, his home at first being at Kingston and later in Albany, where he built a residence of brick imported from Holland. He became one of the leading editors and publishers of the latter city, and was for a time connected with the Albany Argus, of which he was the founder

William Pierce Buell, father of Mrs Bryant, was born in the city of Albany, where he spent the days of his boyhood and youth, and was married there to Miss Margaret Scace, an English lady, who was reared and educated in her native land She departed this life in 1871, but Mr Buell is still living at the age of seventy-four at the old home in Albany where his birth occurred He is quite wealthy and has traveled extensively both in this country and Europe In his family were three children, two sons and one daughter, the former being William Pierce, Jr, a prominent business man of Albany, who occupies the old homestead, and Charles Major, who as a drummer boy joined the Union army and never recovered from the hardships and exposures endured while in the service, dying in 1878

Mrs Bryant was also born in the ancestral home erected by her grandfather, and was educated in the Albany Young Ladies' Academy In September, 1864, she gave her hand in marriage to C H Boschen, a native of Germany and a prominent merchant of New York city, where he successfully engaged in the wholesale grocery business until his death in 1866 Of this union was born a son, William C Boschen, who is married and is now engaged in the banking and brokerage business on Broadway, New York

After the death of her husband Mrs Boschen left the metropolis and returned to the old home in Albany, making her home

with her parents and educating her son in that city On the death of her mother in 1871, however, she again went to New York, where she continued to reside some years. In the meantime her son had learned civil engineering, and in that capacity spent some time in Denver, Colorado, where she resided with him for five years There she became acquainted with Alfred R Bryant, one of the leading business men of Moline, Illinois, and on the 14th of July, 1887, they were united in marriage at her home in Albany

Mr Bryant was born June 6, 1844, in Indianola, Illinois, and was the son of Adam H and Mary (Goodman) Bryant, both of whom were natives of Virginia and came to Illinois about 1839 At that time they had never met, but soon becoming acquainted at Grand View, Illinois, they were there married and soon afterward moved to Indianola, where their family of nine children were born, five of whom are now living Adam H Bryant was for many years an active member of the Methodist Episcopal church and died in the faith in 1889 His widow is yet living and makes her home in Indianola Alfred R Bryant grew to manhood in his native village and attended its public schools He also took a course in Bryant & Stratton Commercial College, and in early life successfully followed the teacher's profession Later, after studying law, he was admitted to the bar and engaged in practice for a time in Danville, Illinois, but on coming to Moline became connected with the Moline Plow Company, first as traveling man and collector, and later as purchasing agent, secretary and finally general manager of the company. He sold his interest in the business in 1892, and the following year purchased a half interest in the Moline

Pump Company, of which he was subsequently elected president   In connection with J N Warr he established the Building, Loan & Savings Association, and being a public-spirited, progressive citizen, became connected with numerous enterprises for the building up of the business interests of the city, among which was the street railway running to the bluff.   He was an active and prominent member of the Episcopal church, and it was mainly through his efforts that the house of worship was erected in Moline, he contributing liberally of his means to its support at all times   He was a stanch Democrat and took a deep and commendable interest in political affairs, but would never accept office, preferring to devote his attention wholly to his extensive business As a Knight Templar Mason he was a prominent member of that old and honored fraternity, and his life was ever in harmony with its teachings   In his death, which occurred May 2, 1896, the community felt that it had lost one of its most valued and useful citizens, one who faithfully performed every duty which devolved upon him and cheerfully gave his support to all measures calculated to prove of public benefit   His remains were interred in Riverside cemetery

Since the death of her husband Mrs Bryant has continued to reside in Moline, but spends considerable time in visiting in New York and Albany. She, too, is an active member of the Episcopal church, in which faith she was reared, her mother being an English lady and a member of the established church of her native land   She receives the warmest respect and esteem of all who have the pleasure of her acquaintance, and is much beloved by those with whom she come in contact for her gentle ways and kind manner

GEORGE WAGNER comes from the fatherland and the strongest and most creditable characteristics of the Teutonic race have been marked elements in his life and have enabled him to win success in the face of opposing circumstances   He possesses the energy and determination which mark the people of Germany and by the exercise of his powers he has steadily progressed, and has not only won a handsome competence but has commanded universal respect by his straightforward business methods   Such in brief is the history of his career, but a more detailed account cannot fail to prove of interest to the readers of this volume for during more than forty years he has been a resident of Rock Island county

Mr. Wagner was born in Wurtemberg, Germany, January 13, 1832, and there acquired a fair common-school education, after which he learned the baker s trade, serving an apprenticeship of several years   In 1853 he crossed the Atlantic to the new world, and located in New York, where he followed his trade for two years   With a cousin he then came to the west and located in Rock Island among its early settlers   Here he established a bakery, which he carried on for two years, when he sold out to his cousin, removing to Moline, where he again established a bakery, carrying on the business with good success for eight years or until 1865.   During that period he also started a steam cracker bakery, the first in this part of the country, and a good trade brought to him a liberal income.   He sold his interests with the intention of returning to Germany, but changing his plans he purchased the brewery of Mr Smidt in Rock Island and engaged in the operation of that enterprise on a small scale, but as his patronage increased, he enlarged his facilities and soon built one of the most extensive brewing industries in this part of the state He successfully carried on the business for about thirty years, at the end of which time, in connection with the other home brewers, he organized a stock company, of which his son, Robert Wagner, was elected president, while Otto Huber became secretary and treasurer, thus leaving to younger men the more active management of the business With other interests of the city Mr Wagner has been prominently connected, his foresight and sound judgment proving an important feature in their prosperity He is now a stockholder and director in the People's National Bank and has invested largely in real estate in Moline and Rock Island, part of which is improved with substantial business houses

In 1853 was celebrated the marriage which united the destinies of Mr Wagner and Miss Frederica Epinger, who was born in Wurtemberg, Germany To them were born six children, three of whom are living Robert, before mentioned, Ernest, a prominent business man of St Louis, and George, who is also in that city They lost one infant, while George died in Moline in 1865, at the age of two years, and Caroline, who grew to womanhood and was married, passed away in 1878

Mr Wagner is a member of the Odd Fellows society and the Order of Druids In politics he was a staunch Democrat for many years, but in 1896 voted for William McKinley and the party which advocated sound money He has been a resident of Rock Island for forty-two years and has therefore witnessed the greater part of its growth and development In its progress he has m.

ever taken his part in support of those measures calculated to prove of public good His strict integrity and honorable dealing in business commend him to the confidence of all, his pleasant manner wins him friends and he is one of the popular and honored citizens of Rock Island

WILLIAM GOLDSWORTHY, proprietor of the Hillsdale creamery and feed mills at Hillsdale, was born at Mineral Point, Iowa county, Wisconsin, February 3, 1852, and is a son of Colin and Johanna (Polglase) Goldsworthy, both natives of County Cornwall, England, in which country they were married In 1838 they came to America, and the father followed his trade of marble dressing in New York for about a year They removed then to Wisconsin, where the father engaged in contracting in the stonemason's trade, spending his remaining days in the Badger state

During his boyhood our subject assisted his father, receiving but limited educational privileges He attended school only three months after he was nine years of age, and was a self-educated as well as a self-made man, but experience, observation and reading have made him well-informed At the age of seventeen he started out in life for himself, going to northwestern Iowa, where he worked by the month until he had attained his majority

While in Palo Alto county, Iowa, he was married March 28, 1873, to Miss Luella Richardson, of that county, a native of Erie county, Pennsylvania, and a daughter of David Richardson In 1875 Mr Goldsworthy removed to Moline, and for eighteen years was employed by the Barnard & Leas   : their service as a man of all work and rising to the position of superintendent of the iron department On severing his connection with that enterprise he removed to Hillsdale and purchased an interest in the creamery, of which he soon afterward became sole proprietor From the time of his first connection therewith the business has greatly increased The plant was equipped with poor machinery, and only about four hundred pounds of milk was received every other day Mr Goldsworthy at once infused his enterprising, progressive spirit into the concern, and within a few months it was very evident that a master mind was in control The old machinery was replaced by that of the most improved and perfect pattern He made a personal canvass among the best farmers of the neighborhood and soon convinced them that the most honorable methods should be pursued in his dealings and that the enterprise would be conducted in a progressive way Thus gaining their confidence, they were willing to do business with him, so that within six months he was receiving about seven thousand pounds of milk daily, from about one hundred farmers, thus not only benefiting himself but materially advancing the prosperity of the community by furnishing a market for his neighbors This enterprise has been of especial benefit during the stringent times when the production of grain is not very profitable

Mr Goldsworthy was called upon to mourn the loss of his first wife while they were living in Moline She had three children, two of whom are now living William C and Luella. Mr Goldsworthy was again married March 27. 1883. his second union being with Martha Richardson. a sister of his first wife They had three

children, but Walter W., now attending Hedding College, Abingdon, Illinois, is the only one now living The deceased were Mattie and Lloyd. Mrs Goldsworthy is a most able assistant to her husband, acts as his bookkeeper, and does all in her power to add to the success which is now crowning his efforts, and which he so richly deserves

In politics Mr. Goldsworthy was formerly a Republican, but is now a Prohibitionist While residing in Moline, he was appointed notary public and filled that office, for five years. In the spring of 1895 he was elected justice of the peace of Hillsdale, and is now acceptably serving in that office He and his wife belong to the Home Forum, of which he served as president for two years When fourteen years of age he became a member of Emory Lodge, No 311, I O G T, and has always been an earnest advocate of temperance principles Since nine years of age he has been a member of the Methodist Episcopal church, has long served as a teacher in the Sunday schools, and as the first president of the Epworth League of Hillsdale He gives his support to every interest that is calculated to elevate humanity, and his own life has been one of unbending integrity and honorable purpose He has justly won the proud American title of a self-made man, for he entered upon his business career without capital, and by perseverance, energy and straightforward dealing has achieved success.

HENRY SADDORIS.— The gentleman whose name stands at the head of this sketch is one of the pioneers of Rock Island county dating his residence here from November, 1842, and by developing a good farm from the wild land, he has materially aided in its growth and prosperity   He has met with a well-deserved success in his calling, and his fine, well-ordered farm, which is pleasantly situated on section 16, Coe township, with its carefully cultured fields, its neat buildings, and all their surroundings, denote the skillful management, industry and well-directed labors of the owner

George Saddoris, father of our subject, was born in Pennsylvania, of German parentage, was there reared, and married Sarah Evans, a native of England   In 1812 they removed to Ohio, being numbered among the first settlers of Holmes county, where in the midst of the wilderness the father developed a good farm and spent his remaining days, dying in 1843   His wife had passed away about five years previous

Henry Saddoris first opened his eyes to the light July 23, 1819, in Holmes county, Ohio, and amid the primitive scenes of pioneer life grew to manhood   He assisted his father in the arduous task of clearing and developing a new farm, remaining at home until nearly grown, and then learned the wagonmaker's trade in Berlin, Ohio, where he served a three years' apprenticeship and then worked as a journeyman for two years

In November, 1842, Mr Saddoris came to Rock Island, where he worked for Mr Blythe at fifteen dollars per month for one year and then took up his residence in Port Byron, where he also worked for others for a time and later conducted a shop of his own for about fourteen years   At the end of that period he purchased a tract of land on section 18, Coe township, and to its improvement and cultivation devoted his time and attention until 1864, when he sold and bought ol

he now resides   He has purchased more land from time to time, at one time having five hundred acres in Coe township, and still owns one hundred and sixty acres in his present farm   He has erected thereon a commodious and substantial residence, two good barns, sheds, cribs, etc., has a fine orchard, a beautiful maple grove of ten acres, an acre and a half of European larch, and a great quantity of small fruit upon his place, so that it is one of the most desirable farms in the county

Mr Saddoris was married in Port Byron in 1847 to Miss Nancy Trent, who was born and reared in Kentucky, and died here in 1871   The children born of this union were as follows   Arista, who is married and engaged in farming in Coe township, Dell Woodard, Nettie, wife of Charles Ashdown, Frank, who is married and carries on farming in Dodge county, Nebraska, Rose, wife of Dr Peterson, of Clinton, Iowa, Fred, who resides in York county, Nebraska, and Jessie, wife of Will Grove, of Coe township   In Coe township Mr Saddoris was again married in February, 1872, his second union being with Miss Emma Flickinger, a native of the township, and a daughter of Samuel Flickinger   Four children grace the second union, namely   Kate, now the wife of George Hollister, a farmer of Coe township, and Albert, Clarence and Walter, all at home

In his political affiliations Mr Saddoris was formerly an old-line Whig, supporting "Tippecanoe and Tyler, too," in 1840, but joined the Republican party on its organization in 1856, and was one of its most earnest advocates until 1876, when he joined the Democracy   In early life he took quite an active and prominent part in politics,
.   .   ..   '   pervisor

of his township, and justice of the peace in Port Byron for four years, but never sought official positions and refused all further honors Since 1840 he has been a member of the Masonic fraternity, belonging to the blue lodge of Port Byron, and at one time was connected with the chapter and commandery of Rock Island He served as master of the lodge of La Clair, while holding membership there For fifty-five years Mr Saddoris has now been a resident of Rock Island county, and has witnessed almost its entire development and progress He has seen deer cross his own fields, but great are the changes that have since taken place. The wild lands have been transformed into beautiful homes and farms, where now live a happy and contented people, who are surrounded by all the comforts of civilized life

JOHN HASSON, proprietor of a livery stable at Port Byron, was born in Philadelphia, Pennsylvania, October 23, 1853, but when only four years old was brought to Rock Island county by his parents, Alexander and Elizabeth (Cartwright) Hasson, who located in Coe township The father, a native of Ireland, on coming to America when a young man, first located in the Quaker City He was there married and continued to live for a few years, but finally emigrated to Illinois After renting land for a time in Coe township, he became the owner of a good farm there, which he successfully operated for a few years, but spent his last days in Port Byron, where his death occurred March 17, 1895 All of his eight children reached man and womanhood and seven are still living

Amid [...] John Hasson spent the days of his boyhood and youth and acquired a fair education in the country schools near his home. At the age of twenty-three he left the parental roof and began life for himself After spending a few weeks in Minnesota he returned to Rock Island county and in 1881 entered the Moline Plow Company's shops, where he was employed for four years He then purchased eighty acres of land in Coe township, which he operated for five years, but in March, 1890, came to Port Byron, where he has since successfully engaged in the livery business

While at work in Moline, Mr Hasson was married April 24, 1883, the lady of his choice being Miss Nellie Bovard, of Coe township, who was born in Port Byron, but at the time of her marriage her parents, James and Margaret Bovard, were living in that township. They were natives of the north of Ireland, had come to America single and were here married Mr. and Mrs Hasson have two children. Harry Bovard, born in Coe township, March 6, 1886, and Raymond F , born April 24, 1890 Mr. Hasson usually gives his allegiance to the Democratic party, but at local elections votes independently, supporting the man whom he considers best qualified to fill the office He is a straightforward, honorable business man, and wherever known is held in high regard

JULIUS G JUNGE —In past ages the history of a country was the record of wars and conquests, to-day it is the record of commercial activity, and those whose names are foremost in its annals are the leaders in business circles The conquests now made are those of mind over matter, not of man over man, and the victor is he who can successfully establish, control and operate extensive commerical interests Mr Junge is unquestionably one of the leading and influential business men of Rock Island, being vice-president of the Rock Island Brewing Company, and makes his home at 519 Twenty-third street

A native of Prussia, he was born March 23, 1848, and is a son of Joseph and Johanna (Herschel) Junge, who were also of German birth, and for some years the father served as a soldier in the Prussian army In 1854 he brought his family to America, and first located on a farm near Fort Madison, Iowa, where he successfully engaged in agricultural pursuits and wine growing There he spent his remaining days, dying at the advanced age of eighty-one, and his wife, who survived him for six years, passed away at the age of seventy-nine

Our subject is the youngest in the family of seven children, and was reared at Fort Madison, but his education was mostly obtained in the schools of Burlington, Iowa. On starting out in life for himself he went to Jollyville, that state, where he conducted a general store and also served as postmaster for three years Since 1871, however, he has made his home in Rock Island, where for about eight years he served as bookkeeper for a firm, and then established a general bottling establishment, which he conducted for a year In 1893 he became a stockholder in the brewery association, with which he has since been connected, and was elected vice-president and general supervisor, which responsible positions he is still filling to the entire satisfaction of the company He is also a stockholder in the Peoples Bank of Rock Island and is interested in other business enterprises in

In Rock Island, September 3, 1878, was celebrated the marriage of Mr Junge and Miss Amelia M Frice, a native of Leland, Illinois, who was reared in Oledo, and educated in the Sisters Academy of Davenport Three daughters grace their union—Olga, a young lady of excellent musical talent, who was educated at Sacred Heart Convent of Omaha, Nebraska, Frieda, who is attending the Rock Island high school, and Lillie, who is also a student in the public schools of the city

For some years Mr Junge has been interested as a dealer in pacing horses, and has owned two noted horses—Bulmont, whose record was 2 09¼, and Scal, four years old, whose record was 2 08¼. In business affairs he is energetic, prompt and notably reliable, and has met with excellent success in all his undertakings, being now numbered among the substantial and prosperous men of the city He has never taken a very active part in political affairs and usually votes independent of party lines, endeavoring to support the best men.

FERDINAND MEWES The fine farm of two hundred acres belonging to this gentleman on sections 14, 22 and 23, Drury township, invariably attracts the eye of the passing traveler as being under the supervision of a thorough and skillful agriculturist and a man otherwise of good business qualifications He dates his residence in the county from the fall of 1863, and since attaining to man's estate he has been actively identified with its farming interests

Mr Mewes comes from across the sea, his birth occurring in Prussia, Germany, October 21, 1859 His father, Charles county where he continued to make his home until his emigration to the new world in 1862 After about a year and a half spent in Muscatine, Iowa, he came to Drury township, Rock Island county, where he still continues to reside   Here Ferdinand Mewes grew to manhood, but his opportunities for securing an education were very limited and the knowledge he has acquired has been mostly obtained since he reached years of maturity   He remained with his father until he had attained his majority, assisting in the work of the home farm

On the 6th of May, 1885, Mr Mewes led to the marriage altar Miss Mary Krueger, a native of Rock Island county, whose father, William Krueger, had come from Germany to America on the same vessel with the Mewes family   She died June 17, 1894, leaving four children: Elizabeth, Edward, Elmer and Ella, who are now cared for by Mr. Mewes' sister Martha, who acts as his housekeeper

The fall previous to his marriage, Mr Mewes purchased a tract of one hundred and twenty acres of partially improved land on which a small house had been erected, and there he began his domestic life   To its further development and cultivation he at once turned his attention, and has extended its boundaries until it now comprises two hundred acres of rich and valuable land   The well-tilled fields and neat and thrifty appearance of the place testify to the skill and ability of the owner in his chosen calling

Since casting his first vote for Hon James A Garfield, Mr Mewes has been an uncompromising Republican, and is recognized as one of the most influential members of hi- party in Drury township   In 1893 he .... township assessor the

following year was collector, and in 1895 and 1896 was again elected assessor   The next year he was elected supervisor, and is now one of the most popular and capable members of the county board   He is also serving as school director in his district, and has been a delegate to a number of conventions   His straightforward, honorable course commends him to the confidence of all who know him, and his circle of friends is only limited by his circle of acquaintances

CAPTAIN JOHN O'CONNOR, the jovial and well-known captain of the steamer Inverness, plying between Stillwater and St Louis, has for the past fourteen years been one of the highly respected citizens of Rock Island, where in 1895 he erected his handsome residence at No. 1417 Fourth avenue, which is built in a modern style of architecture and supplied with all the latest conveniences.

The Captain was born in Buffalo, New York, February 5, 1853, a son of John and Ann (Greenan) O'Connor, natives of Ireland, in whose family were only two children, the younger being Ellen, who died April 11, 1885   The grandparents of our subject spent their entire lives in Ireland, where both grandfathers died at a ripe old age   The father, who was a ship carpenter by trade, located at Buffalo on his arrival in America, making his home there for some years   Subsequently he spent a short time in Chicago and then moved to Houston county, Minnesota, where he followed agricultural pursuits, but returning to Chicago he died in the great fire which nearly blotted out that city in 1871   He was twice married and by the first union had one daughter—Mary, who died in Buffalo when quite young The mother of our subject lived to the ripe old age of eighty-five years, her death occurring in St Louis, May 10, 1887 Both parents held membership in the Catholic church.

Captain O'Connor was but three years old when he accompanied his parents on their removal to Minnesota, where he spent fifteen years upon a farm, receiving his early education in the district schools of that state, which he attended during the winter season Later he pursued his studies in the public schools of St Louis, and completed his literary course in Rice's College of that city There he continued to reside until coming to Rock Island When quite small he began to make his own way in the world, and the success that he has achieved has been due entirely to his own industry, perseverance and well-directed efforts

On leaving home Captain O'Connor began steamboating on the Mississippi river, which occupation he has since followed, and has been master of a number of vessels, including the steamers—J G Chapman, Peter Kerns, Inverness and Dexter, plying principally between Stillwater and St Louis

In 1877 was celebrated the marriage of the Captain and Miss Catharine Fitzgerald, a daughter of Michael and Johanna Fitzgerald, and one child has blessed their union, a daughter—Ellen The parents are both communicants of the Catholic church, and are people of the highest respectability and sterling worth Politically, Captain O'Connor is identified with the Republican party, and socially is a member of the Modern Woodmen of America and the Pilot Association Genial and pleasant in disposition

has the happy faculty of easily retaining them Success is not measured by the heights which one may chance to occupy, but by the distance between the starting point and the altitude he has reached, therefore the Captain has gained a most brilliant success—a just reward of meritorious, honorable effort, which commands the respect and admiration of all

ALBERT F HOLLISTER, who resides on section 18, Coe township, owns and operates there a valuable farm of two hundred and ten acres, whose neat and thrifty appearance well indicates his careful supervision Substantial improvements are surrounded by well tilled fields, and all the accessories and conveniences of a model farm are there found

Mr Hollister was born in Washington county, New York, June 1, 1836 His father, Edmund Hollister, was born in Connecticut, and with the grandfather, Isaac Hollister, removed to Washington county, New York The latter was a ship carpenter and in early life worked in the East Indies Our subject now has in his possession a handsaw which was owned by the grandfather while thus engaged Edmund Hollister grew to manhood in New York and there married Emma Louisa Hall, a native of Vermont, who was reared and educated in Washington county, a daughter of Nathan Hall, who died during the early girlhood of Mrs Hollister The father of our subject continued farming in the Empire state until 1837, when he came to Rock Island county, casting his lot with its pioneer settlers He secured a claim in Coe township, and later one in Zuma township chased a saw-mill and engaged in the manufacture of lumber, also operating a small farm In 1853 he removed to Coe township, where he purchased a farm, upon which he reared his family and spent his remaining days, dying at the advanced age of eighty-three years His wife departed this life in 1891, and was buried by his side in Fairfield cemetery

Albert F Hollister was reared amid the wild scenes of the frontier He was familiar with Rock Island county when the majority of its homes were log cabins, when its forests were uncut and its prairies uncultivated He assisted his father and received but limited educational privileges In 1857 he went to Kansas, remaining there two years, during which time the state was in great excitement over the slavery question Returning home he remained only a short time when he went to Colorado, where he spent one year, and three years in Nebraska engaged in railroad construction In 1888 he returned to Rock Island county, and located upon the farm which he now makes his home He had purchased the place some years previous and erected thereon a good set of buildings He has a neat, substantial residence, a good barn and other necessary outbuildings and an air of thrift and enterprise pervades the place

Mr Hollister was married in Rock Island county, October 12, 1860, to Rebecca Reed, a native of Pennsylvania, who came to Illinois during her childhood, in company with her father, David Reed, who settled in Coe township Five children have been born to Mr. and Mrs Hollister, namely Eva G , wife of Dr L A Golden, of Smith county, Kansas, Emma L., wife of George ⌐ .... (.. township, G. . \ . b .f Lol Barrett .it

New Boston, Illinois, Frederick A and Edmund J , at home The family is one of prominence in the community, widely and favorably known, and their circle of friends is very extensive

Mr Hollister is a stalwart advocate of the principles of the Republican party, and does all in his power to promote its growth and insure its success He has served as a delegate to numerous county conventions, was elected and served as supervisor for several terms, and was school treasurer for a number of years Socially he is connected with the Knights of Pythias and the Ancient Order of United Workmen He is a man of exemplary habits, commendable purpose and unbending integrity, and in all life's relations merits the confidence which is so freely accorded him His residence in Rock Island county covers the greater part of sixty years, during which he has ever borne his part in the work of development and progress, and is therefore deserving of honorable mention among the pioneers

---

CAPTAIN LUKE E HEMENWAY, now living retired in the city of Moline, at his pleasant home at 1213 Fifteenth street, has as large a circle of friends and acquaintances as probably any man in Rock Island county He dates his residence here from August 7th, 1855

The Hemenways are of English descent, the first of the name to locate in America being Ralph Hemenway, who came in 1830 from Gloucester, England, and located at Roxbury, Massachusetts At Shewsbury, that state, was born Francis S Hemenway, the father four -object and Samuel Hemenway, his grandfather while his great-grandfather,

Daniel Hemenway, was born in Farmingham, Massachusetts The last named served as a soldier in the Revolutionary war, commencing at the battle of Bunker Hill and continuing until the close of the struggle

Francis S Hemenway removed with his parents to Shoreham, Vermont, in 1792, where his father opened up a farm, and our subject has in possession the original deed for the land, dated March 6, 1792 Here he grew to manhood and married Clara Turrill, a native of Massachusetts, daughter of Ebenezer Turrill, of Grafton, Massachusetts, and granddaughter of Captain James Turrill At Shoreham he learned the carpenter's and joiners trades, which occupations he followed in connection with farming until his removal to Ogle county, Illinois, in 1853 Farming was his principal pursuit in Ogle county, where his death occurred in 1858 His wife survived him some five or six years

Luke Hemenway was born in Whoreham, Vermont, August 7, 1816, and there received a common school education At the age of thirteen years he left home and lived with an uncle until after he attained his majority, in the meantime receiving a thorough business training in the mercantile trade In 1838, at the age of twenty-two years, he came west and located at Grand Detour, Ogle county, where he engaged in mercantile business, in which line he continued with fair success until 1855, when he came to Moline to take charge of the office of John Deere, who at that time had built up quite an extensive business as a manufacturer of plows With Mr Deere he continued until 1860, when he formed a partnership with Messrs Wyckoff & Barnard, under the firm name of Hemenway, Wyckoff & B——— and engaged in the manu-

facture of chairs, and later in mill machinery supplies

The war for the Union was now in progress and in the summer of 1864 Mr Hemenway assisted in raising a company for the one-hundred-day service and was commissioned as captain of the same, it becoming Company H, One Hundred and Thirty-second Illinois Volunteer Infantry With headquarters at Paducah, Kentucky, the regiment did guard duty at various places, thus relieving the old and tried soldiers who were sent to the front On being mustered out October 17, 1864, at the close of the period of enlistment, Captain Hemenway returned to Moline and entered the employ of the Moline Plow Company, a new concern, and took charge of its general office. He remained with this company until 1875, when he was compelled to retire on account of ill health Two years later he was appointed postmaster by President Hayes and re-appointed by President Garfield, in all serving nine years That he made an efficient official goes without saying

Captain Hemenway was married in Ogle county, Illinois, June 23, 1842, to Miss Jane E Marsh, a native of Bethel, Vermont, and a daughter of Peleg S Marsh, and granddaughter of Colonel Joel Marsh, of Revolutionary fame There are three living children of this union, the oldest being Fred C Hemenway, the present sheriff of Rock Island county The next in order of birth is Ellen M , now the wife of Joseph M Christy, a coal operator residing in Des Moines, Iowa Charles F , the youngest of the family, is the cashier of the Moline National Bank Mrs Hemenway, a woman of excellent character, a faithful wife and loving mother, passed away in December, 1883

In early life Captain Hemenway was a

Whig, and cast his first presidential ballot for William Henry Harrison His last ballot for a Whig candidate was in 1852, when he voted for General Scott On the organization of the Republican party he allied himself with that organization, and in 1856 voted for General John C Fremont, the "great pathfinder," and has voted for each nominee of that party for president up to and including William McKinley. Religiously, the Captain is a Congregationalist, and fraternally, a charter member of Doric Lodge, A F & A M , and the only charter member now living He was the second worshipful master of the lodge

Since the death of his wife, Captain Hemenway has made his home with his children, at whose firesides he is ever welcome While past his four score years, he is quite active and as he goes in and out among his old friends and associates, he knows that he enjoys the esteem and good will of all

IGNATZ HUBER —Forty-six years have passed since this gentleman took up his residence in Rock Island, years in which he has wrested from the hands of fate a handsome competence for himself, while at the same time he has in many ways promoted the best interests of the city by his support of measures calculated to prove of public good and by his advancement of business enterprises which, promoting the commercial activity, have added to the general prosperity

Mr Huber is a native of Bavaria Germany, born on the 1st day of February, 1826 He grew to manhood in his native land and was educated in the German, English and l— —— —— —— He then learned the brewer's trade under the direction of his father, and in 1849 sailed for America, believing that he would find better opportunities for advancement in the new world At Rotterdam, he boarded a westward-bound sailing vessel and after a voyage of forty-two days landed at New York on the 16th of June, 1849 Going westward to Canton, Ohio, he spent the winter there, working as a farm hand, after which he removed to Columbus, where he was employed in a brewery for a time His next location was Cincinnati, where he was engaged in the same line of business until 1851 — the year of his arrival in Rock Island

On coming to this city Mr Huber began working in a brewery by the month, but on the expiration of the first month he purchased an interest in the enterprise and after three years became sole proprietor. He has since been alone, and from small beginnings has increased his business until it has now reached extensive proportions. In 1893 he consolidated his business with others in the formation of a stock company, he and his son Otto being the principal stockholders He is now one of the directors, while his son is secretary and treasurer of the company Mr Huber is also a stockholder and director in the People's Bank and owns considerable valuable real estate in Rock Island, Moline, Geneseo, Illinois, and Davenport, Iowa, including both business and residence property He is very successful in all that he undertakes for he has the essential qualifications of the prosperous business man, being energetic, careful, earnest and determined He came to Rock Island with very limited means, but has steadily worked his way upward, overcoming all the difficulties and obstacles in his path until to-day he stands on the plane of affluence

In October, 1854, Mr Huber was united in marriage to Miss Catherine Koeler, a native of Germany, born and reared in Hessen Castle She came to America when a young lady, and by her marriage she has become the mother of three children Amelia and Lillie, at home, and Otto All have been provided with good educational advantages and share in the esteem in which their parents are universally held They also lost three children, two in early childhood and one at the age of nine years

Mr Huber is a member of the Catholic church, while his wife is an adherent of the Lutheran faith In politics he is a stanch Democrat and warmly advocates the principles of his party He has never sought or desired public office, but was elected alderman and so acceptably filled the position that he was twice re-elected During his long residence in Rock Island his history has been familiar with the majority of its citizens and his honorable record commends him to their confidence and regard His life has been well spent in the faithful performance of the duties of public and private life, and his name is a synonym of all that is honorable in business pursuits

B YRON KENDALL devotes his time and energies to farming and stock-raising on section 30, Canoe Creek township, and the industry which characterizes his business career has brought him a fair measure of success He was born in the township which is now his home, November 5, 1849, a son of George and Rebecca (Levin) Kendall His father was born in Maine, near Kendall's Mills The grandfather prob-

ably a native of Massachusetts, was of English descent George Kendall entered upon the scene of life's activity in November, 1811, and spent his boyhood days in Maine where at an early age he began work in the lumber woods He afterward spent the winter season for some years in the neighborhood of Halifax engaged in lumbering, and about 1835 made his way westward to Greene county, Illinois, where he worked in a flouring mill, continuing his residence there until 1844 During that time he became acquainted with and married Rebecca Levin, who was born in Calhoun county, November 5, 1821 Soon after their marriage they removed to Rock Island county, and secured a squatter's claim on the bluff, but believing that the bottom lands were better, Mr Kendall sold his first claim and secured land on sections 31 and 32, Canoe Creek township, now owned by Edward McMurphy. In 1858 he sold that property and located on section 30, becoming owner of forty acres there In 1868 he bought eighty acres on section 29, which he also improved. In his political faith he was a Democrat until 1846 when he became a Whig, and in 1856 he joined the new Republican party He filled various township offices, such as clerk, assessor and collector, and for two terms was supervisor His sterling worth and strength of character made him a leading and influential citizen, and he was widely and favorably known throughout the county He died April 8, 1891, and his son, Lewis N, died on the same day Both were victims of la grippe and were buried in Bethesda cemetery

In the Kendall family were seven children, but only two are now living Three died in infancy, and Sarah A died when past thirty-nine years of age being buried in Bethesda cemetery   John F , living on the old homestead, and our subject are the only ones now living

Byron Kendall spent his boyhood days on the farm and acquired a fair education in the common schools   When about twenty years of age he went to Greene county, Illinois, where he remained with his uncle, Nat Kendall, for eight months   In 1871 he removed to Woodson county, Kansas, where he remained for three months, and then, on account of ill health, went to Minnesota, where he remained for three years, securing a claim in Rock county   This he partially improved, but, on account of the grasshoppers, was forced to abandon it   He worked in a flouring mill for a time, and then went to Janesville, Wisconsin, spending the winter of 1875 in the School of Telegraphy at that place   In May 1876, he went to Chicago, where he accepted a position with the Western Union Telegraph Company, continuing there until 1882, after which he was station agent and operator on the St Paul, Minneapolis & Manitoba Road at various places in Minnesota   He remained with the company until November, 1887, after which he spent two years as a traveling salesman and then returned to the home farm   He visited the World's Columbian Exposition in 1893, and his travels have made him a well-informed man   He now gives his time and attention to his farm, and his enterprising, progressive methods have won him a place among the leading agriculturists of the county.

In 1872 Mr Kendall supported General Grant for the presidency and has since been a pronounced Republican in politics   He was elected supervisor in 1896, and as such was instrumental in securing the new court house at I........................ and ...... on

the committees of roads and bridges, poor and cruelty to animals   He is a progressive, public-spirited citizen, doing all in his power to advance the general interests, and wherever known is held in high regard

D T BARRETT —In studying the lives and character of prominent business men, we are naturally led to inquire into the secret of their success and the motives that have prompted their actions   Success is not a question of genius as held by man, but it is rather a matter of experience and sound judgment, for when we trace the career of those who stand high in public esteem, we find in nearly every case that they are those who have risen gradually, fighting their way in the face of all opposition   Self-reliance, conscientiousness, energy, honesty—these are the traits of character that insure the highest emoluments and greatest success   To these may we attribute the success that has crowned the efforts of our subject

Mr Barrett was born July 22, 1824, in Camden, Maine, six miles above Rockland, and belongs to an old and honored Massachusetts family of English origin, which was founded in this country by Thomas Barrett, and his three sons, who settled in the old Bay state, were commissioned officers in the Revolutionary war and took a prominent part in colonial affairs   The great-grandfather of our subject also bore the name of Thomas, and was a native of Massachusetts, as was also the grandfather, Daniel Barrett, Sr , who at an early day emigrated to Maine and built many miles of turnpike in that state, which was a most difficult task, as the road many times had to be cut out of solid granite and required years with a gang of men steadily at work   He constructed the road from Lincolnville to Camden

Daniel Barrett, Jr , father of our subject, was born and reared in the Pine Tree state, became a farmer of Camden, and was a soldier in the war of 1812   He spent the last eleven years of his life in Northport, Maine, where he had purchased a farm   By the governor he was appointed general inspector of lime and had several deputies under him   In early life he married Miss Bethiah Jordan, also a native of Maine, and a daughter of Robert Jordan   They became the parents of ten children, of whom nine are still living, namely Bethiah, wife of William Frohock, of Searsmont, Maine, D. T , who is next in order of birth, Hannah, widow of William Barnes, of Camden, Maine, Margaret, who died at the age of eighteen years, Harriet, wife of Franklin Rhodes, of Reno, Nevada, Robert J , who was accidentally killed in a granite quarry, and left a wife and one child, Arathusia, wife of Richard Crane, an extensive farmer residing near Topeka, Kansas, Edward H , who was for a number of years extensively engaged in the lumber business in California, and being taken ill in camp, where he could receive no medical attention, died soon afterward, and Nelson, a ranchman of Reno, Nevada

Mr Barrett, of this review, spent his early life upon his father's farms at Camden and Northport, Maine, and was provided with fair school advantages   After his father's death he took charge of the old homestead and cared for the family for several years   With his father he had learned the stone mason's trade, and at the age of twenty-seven went to Rockland, Maine, where he worked at that trade, principally being emp

also learned the art of manufacturing lime, and for a number of years was employed in building lime kilns principally

In 1864 Mr Barrett came to Rock Island county, Illinois, and first located in Rural township, where his five uncles, the Jordan brothers, were living   They were among the first settlers of the county and were prominent and influential men   After about a year spent at that place, in the fall of 1865 Mr Barrett came to Port Byron, where in connection with his brother-in-law, Henry Sidlinger, he built a lime kiln and engaged in the manufacture of lime   Some years later he formed the Port Byron Lime Company, and has since been actively engaged in the manufacture of that product, it being one of the largest industries in the state   He also deals quite extensively in cement and hard coal, and has a branch office in Rock Island

In Rockland, Maine, on the 26th of July, 1864, Mr. Barrett was united in marriage to Mrs Lucy Cushman, a native of that state and a daughter of a Mr Sidlinger, a substantial farmer, of Union, Maine   Six children have been born to them, namely Ida, who was well educated and successfully engaged in teaching in both the public schools and an academy, is now the wife of Abraham Freeburg, a prosperous farmer of Preemption, Illinois   Walter was first engaged in the mercantile business with Simonson & Schafer for a number of years, and was later head clerk for the mercantile firm of McCabe Brothers, in Rock Island   He died in that city in December, 1895, at the age of thirty-eight years, leaving a wife and child   Lura is the wife of William McRoberts, Jr , a farmer of Coe township, whose sketch appears elsewhere in this work

lents in

23

the Port Byron Academy, died at the age of eighteen years   E E , a civil engineer, graduated at the Illinois University at Champaign, was in the employ of the government for several years, and is now inspector for the government, having charge of the levee that is being built from New Boston to Burlington, Iowa   He married Grace Hollister, daughter of A F Hollister, of Coe township

Mr. Barrett is a staunch Republican in politics, was a member of the village board for several years, and has filled other local positions of honor and trust   He spent one year in Minneapolis, where he had charge of a lime business   Both he and his wife are active and prominent members of the Methodist Episcopal church, with which he has been connected since eighteen years of age, and is now serving as steward and trustee.   His life has been one of industry and perseverance, and the systematic and honorable business methods which he has followed have won him the support and confidence of many, and wherever known he is held in the highest regard

THOMAS E COLE, one of the prominent and substantial farmers and extensive stockraisers of Rock Island county, first opened his eyes to the light of day December 27, 1863, on his present farm, which is pleasantly located on section 33, Buffalo Prairie township.   His father, George M Cole, was a native of Pennsylvania, where he continued to reside until thirteen years of age, when he left home and started out to make his own way in the world   He traveled extensively over the United States and spent a time in the south but at an early day located permanently in Rock Island county, becoming one of its honored pioneer and influential citizens   His first purchase consisted of an eighty-acre tract, which he placed under cultivation and it now forms a part of the present farm of our subject   Here the father reared his family and continued to make his home until called to his final rest in 1875, at the age of sixty-three years   He was one of the leading men of his neighborhood and was elected to various official positions of honor and trust, discharging the duties of the same with marked fidelity   His wife, who is still living, now makes her home in Illinois City   The children born to them who grew to mature years are George W ; Eliza, who died unmarried, Vania, wife of J S Mills, of Harlan, Iowa, and Thomas E

Amid rural scenes Mr Cole, of this sketch, grew to manhood, and remained with his father until the latter's death, since which time he has purchased the interest of the other heirs in the old homestead and now owns and operates four hundred acres of valuable land   In connection with general farming, he has for the past five years, been interested in the breeding of fine stock, and has established an enviable reputation as a breeder and dealer.   He has upon his place a large drove of Poland China hogs, a herd of polled Angus cattle, and several head of standard bred trotting horses, including a four-year-old, which has a fine record

In Edgington township, on the 4th of March, 1884, Mr Cole led to the marriage altar Miss Elsie L Titterington, whose father, James Titterington, now deceased, was one of the honored pioneers of the county   Six children have been born to them namely Lonnie E · George W , who died in infancy, Florence M , Alpha L , James Foy, and Helen Gertrude

On the 20th of May, 1895, Mr Cole met with a very unpleasant experience While he and his family were at supper, three robbers entered the house, bound and and blindfolded them and deliberately took everything they wanted after first eating their supper They were disappointed in their search for money, finding only about ten dollars and a half, but among other things took Mr. Cole's watch After they were gone our subject managed to get loose and snatching his revolver started in pursuit but was unsuccessful in getting his neighbors to join him in the hunt Nothing daunted, however, and failing to get the help of his neighbors, he went to Muscatine, Iowa, and telephoned up and down the railroad and river and then took a train for Burlington the next evening After a long and thorough search, he himself captured one of the robbers and police officers took another, both of whom were tried, convicted and sent to prison The county court afterward gave him a reward of one hundred and fifty dollars, and his friends and neighbors added to the amount, thus showing their appreciation of his bravery and sympathy for him in his misfortune He is a stanch Democrat in politics and although he has never been an aspirant for office would undoubtedly make a most efficient sheriff, as his fearlessness at the time of his own trouble would indicate

MARK ASHDOWN --While there is much truth in the strictures made upon the modern scramblers for the almighty dollar who seek to accumulate vast fortunes by selfish

nothing more worthy of praise than the quiet and steady pursuit of some honest calling and the determined exercise of the industry, economy and sagacity which enable a man to acquire a home and a competence The subject of this biography, now a prosperous citizen of Port Byron, is a man whose brave struggle with early adversity has brought him a competence without the sacrifice of principle For many years he was actively identified with the agricultural and business interests of Rock Island county, but is now living retired, having acquired a sufficient amount of this world's goods to enable him to pass his declining years in ease and comfort

Mr Ashdown was born in Kent county, England, June 3, 1831, of which country his parents, Edward and Ann (Bakurst) Ashdown, were also natives The father, who was born in Sussex, came to America in 1842, accompanied by his two sons, Henry and Mark, but after spending about thirteen months in Macedon, Wayne county, New York, they returned to England, where he died In the fall of 1850, the sons again came to this country and located in Wayne county, New York, where our subject worked on a farm for five years He was there married, December 23, 1852, to Miss Mary Ann Beale, also a native of Kent county, England, who in 1850 had come to America with her father, Henry Edward Beale, who also settled in Wayne county, New York

In 1855 Mr Ashdown emigrated to Illinois, and after spending one summer in Port Byron he went to Canoe Creek township, where he operated rented land for seven years, the place comprising three hundred acres In connection with general farming he
using In

1861 he purchased a tract of eighty acers, the following year another forty-acre tract, and in 1863 eighty acres, all in Coe township, and upon his farm erected a fine large residence, good barns and other outbuildings He continued to engage in agricultural pursuits until selling his place in 1881 to his son, removing to Port Byron in October of that year Here he purchased residence property, and for some four or five years engaged in the manufacture of lumber and also dealt in agricultural implements, but in 1895 disposed of his business and has since lived retired, enjoying the firuits of his former toil He owns two valuable farms in Coe township, aggregating four hundred acres of productive and well improved land, and besides his own residence he has other houses in Port Byron which he rents

Mr and Mrs Ashdown have two sons and one daughter, namely. William Henry, born in Wayne county, New York, who is married and is now one of the substantial farmers of Coe township, Rock Island county, Charles Edward, born in Rock Island county, is married and owns and operates a valuable farm in Coe township, and Ella E is the wife of Luther S Pearsell, a merchant of Port Byron They lost one son in infancy

In early life Mr Ashdown was identified with the Democratic party, but now is an ardent Prohibitionist For eight years he most acceptably served as justice of the peace in Coe township, for thirteen years was a member of the school board, and has also been a member of the town board in Port Byron In summing up the events of his life, it can most truly be stated that there never was a resident of Port Byron who was . . . . teemed t . . . .

active business life he was looked upon as a model of honor and an example of a truly honest business man.

JESSE SIMPSON, one of the representative farmers and prominent citizens of Coe township, is the subject of this personal narrative, whose farm is pleasantly located on section 8 Believing that '' from labor, health and contentment springs,'' he has bent every energy toward perfecting his agricultural projects, and has proved himself eminently one of the best citizens of Rock Island county

Mr. Simpson was born December 19, 1847, in Westmoreland county, Pennsylvania, where the birth of his parents, Thomas and Eliza (Fisher) Simpson, also occurred The grandfather, James Simpson, who was a soldier in the early wars of this country, became a pioneer of the Keystone state The father of our subject was a second cousin of General Grant Until 1856 he carried on agricultural pursuits in the county of his nativity, and then came to Illinois, arriving in Rock Island county in November Three of his brothers had located in Moline some years previous After renting land for about five years, he purchased two hundred and forty acres of fairly well improved land in Coe township, and to its further development and cultivation devoted his energies until his death in 1873, becoming one of the most successful farmers of the neighborhood He was elected to several positions of honor and trust, the duties of which he most faithfully performed After his death his wife and sons carried on the place for several years, their Jesse and Wesley rented it for a time, and later bought the interests of the other heirs

In the family were five sons and three daughters, namely Sarah, who became the wife of Joseph Reynolds and died December 25, 1895, James, a farmer of Cordova township, Rock Island county, Eliza, widow of Dr Fleming, of Port Byron, now residing with her brother in Laporte City, Iowa, John, a farmer of New Mexico, Hannah, who died at the age of one year, Jesse, of this review, Wesley, who owns and operates a part of the old homestead, and Erastus, a business man, station agent and telegraph operator in Laporte City, Iowa All are married with the exception of Wesley

Our subject was a lad of nine years when he was brought by his parents to Rock Island county, where he has since made his home, while his education was acquired in the local schools He never left the parental roof and now he and his brother own the old farm, which comprises two hundred and twenty acres of valuable and well improved land There is a fine orchard upon the place, together with shade and ornamental trees, and a comfortable and commodious residence has been erected, so that it is now one of the most desirable farms in Coe township

In Rapids City, Illinois, on the 25th of January, 1877, was consummated the marriage of Mr Simpson and Miss Matilda J Smith, a native of Guernsey county, Ohio, who during her childhood was brought to Illinois by her father, James Smith He settled on a farm in Coe township, where his daughter was reared and educated, and here he spent his remaining days, dying January 1, 1865 Three children blessed the union of Mr and Mrs Simpson—Charles, who ass

home farm, Elsie, who with her brother is attending the home school, and Maudie, who died at the age of three years The parents are both consistent members of the Methodist Episcopal church and also belong to the Court of Honor

Since casting his first presidential vote for General U S Grant in 1872, Mr Simpson has been unswerving in his allegiance to the Republican party, and takes an active and commendable interest in public affairs For six years he has been a member of the school board, and during that time has done much to promote the cause of education in his locality He is one of the reliable and most esteemed citizens of Coe township, and is looked up to as one of its most influential men His adherence to the dictates of honor in all his business transactions, his spotless private life and his public-spiritedness in all matters for the benefit of the community, have elevated him to a high pinnacle in the minds of his fellow-citizens

JOHN BORUFF —If one desires to gain a vivid realization of the rapid advance in civilization which the last half century has brought about, he can listen to the stories that men who are still living can tell of their boyhood The log cabin in the clearing, the still ruder schoolhouse with its rough seats made of slabs its limited range of studies and its brief terms arranged on the subscription plan, the routine of work at home unrelieved by any of the modern devices by which machinery is made to do in a short time what formerly occupied the entire year,—these and many similar descriptions will bring up in sharp contrast the advantages of to-day The subject of this respected citizen of Drury township, whose home is on section 34, has many reminiscences of this sort

Mr. Boruff was born October 4, 1818, in Claiborne county, Tennessee, a son of Valentine Boruff, a native of Pennsylvania, where he was reared and married. For some time he made his home in Tennessee, and on leaving that state removed to Montgomery county, Indiana, where he spent a few years. In 1833 he brought his family to Mercer county, Illinois, where he entered land, improved a farm and continued to reside until called to his final rest

Thus amid pioneer scenes John Boruff spent the days of his boyhood and youth, and until attaining his majority remained under the parental roof, assisting his father in the arduous task of clearing and developing a new farm In Mercer county he was married in 1841, to Miss Mary McGreer, a native of Union county, Indiana, and a daughter of William McGreer, also an early settler of Mercer county They began their domestic life upon a farm adjoining his father's and there continued to reside until their removal to Drury township, Rock Island county, in 1847 Here Mr Boruff purchased two hundred and eight acres of wild land, and as time advanced he placed acre after acre under the plow until to-day he has one of the most highly cultivated and valuable farms in the locality He first built a little log cabin, but this has long since given place to a commodious and comfortable frame residence, which is surrounded by good barns and substantial outbuildings To his original purchase he added until he owned five hundred acres of rich and productive land lying in Mercer and Rock Island counties His property has all been acquired through his own individual efforts

as he started out in life for himself empty-handed and has made his own way in the world unaided

Mr Boruff lost his first wife, who died March 15, 1866, leaving three sons, namely: William Mc , an agriculturist of Mercer county, who is married and has two sons, Jackson, a farmer of Pottawattomie county, Iowa, who is married and has two sons and one daughter, and Alexander, a farmer of Mercer county, who is married and has two daughters In Cedar county, Iowa, Mr Boruff was again married March 15, 1868, his second union being with Mrs. Mary A. Doty, who was born in Indiana, but was reared and educated in Cedar county, Iowa Her father, Samuel Stephenson Smith, was a native of Ohio, where he wedded Mary Steel, and later removed to Park county, Indiana, spending his last years there Her mother later became the wife of Joseph Lindsay, of Cedar county, Iowa, by whom she had three children Mrs Boruff was first married in Cedar county, and by that union had two sons, Dow Douglas Doty, a ranchman of Wyoming, who is married and has one daughter, and J R Doty, who is also married and has one daughter, and is living with his brother in the west One son has been born of the second marriage, Samuel H. Boruff, who now operates the old home place for his father He is married and has one son, Charles S

Mr Boruff has been a lifelong supporter of the Democratic party, but has never cared for the honors or emoluments of public office, preferring to give his undivided attention to his business interests He attends the Presbyterian church, of which his wife is a member, and contributes to its support, and as a public-spirited citizen has borne his part in promoting those enterprises for the good of the community along various lines   For a half century he has been numbered among the valued and useful man of the county, and has the respect and esteem of all who know him

JOHN W MAXWELL, a wide-awake, enterprising business man of Port Byron, where he has made his home since November, 1854, was born in Westmoreland county, Pennsylvania, February 11, 1832, a son of James and Christina (Albright) Maxwell, also natives of the Keystone state Their marriage was celebrated in Westmoreland county, where they reared their family, and where the father carried on farming until his death

In the county of his nativity, Mr Maxwell grew to manhood, but his opportunities for attending school were limited, and his education has principally been obtained by reading and study in later years   In Greensburg, Westmoreland county, he learned the carpenter's and joiner's trade, serving a three years' apprenticeship, and later worked as a journeyman for about three years   In 1854 he came west to Port Byron, Illinois, joining an uncle, Jesse Maxwell, who had resided here for some years, and in partnership they engaged in contracting and building until the war   There are still standing a great many residences, houses and barns, in Port Byron and vicinity, which show the artistic skill and handiwork of our subject

In July, 1862, Mr Maxwell enlisted in Company E, One Hundred and Twenty-sixth Illinois Volunteer Infantry, and with his regiment went to Jackson, Tennessee, and from there to Vicksburg, where he participated in the siege and capture of that stronghold   They later went to La Grange, Mississippi, and with Steele's division took part in the battle of Little Rock, which was followed by a number of skirmishes and lesser fights   With his command, Mr Maxwell was stationed at Duvall's Bluff for about a year but was mostly engaged in active duty until mustered out in August, 1865   On his return to Port Byron he embarked in the manufacture of lime, and has succeeded in building up a large and profitable business, making from eighty to ninety thousand barrels per year

Returning to Westmoreland county, Pennsylvania, Mr Maxwell was married there on the 1st of January, 1856, to Miss Sarah Allshouse who was born in the same neighborhood as her husband, and is a daughter of Samuel Allshouse, a pioneer of that county   To them have been born four children, as follows. S J , is a well educated man, who was for some years engaged in business in Port Byron, but now resides in Colorado   Alma is the wife of Rev J W Edwards, a Methodist Episcopal minister, now located in Tonica, Illinois   Marcellus died during the war, in 1863, and Gracie was accidentally drowned in the Mississippi, August 4, 1892, when twenty years of age

Since voting for John C Fremont in 1856, Mr Maxwell has upheld the principles of the Republican party, and has taken an active and commendable interest in political affairs   He has been a delegate to a number of county conventions, has served on the town board of road commissioners, and has also been a member of the school board for some years   As a Mason he is a member of the blue lodge of Port Byron, while religiously, both he and his wife are consistent members of the Methodist Episcopal church In 1860 Mr Maxwell went to Colorado, where until the fall of that year he engaged in the butchering business, and the following year again returned to that state on a prospecting tour, but with that exception he has spent his time in Port Byron since coming west in 1854, and is numbered among its honored and most valued and useful citizens He has uniformly given his encouragement to the enterprises tending to the general welfare of the people around him, is a supporter of all measures for the public good, and is deserving of honorable mention in a work of this character, whose duty it is to preserve a record of the leading and representative citizens of Rock Island county

CAPTAIN ALPHEUS MILES BLAKE-SLEY, of the Rock Island Stove Company, Rock Island, Illinois, is a native of Kingsville, Ashtabula county, Ohio He was born April 28, 1835, and is the son of Alpheus and Almira (Webster) Blakesley, the latter being the daughter of Clark Webster, a strong Abolitionist whose home was for years a station on the "underground railroad" and who lived to a ripe old age His father, Michael Webster, was in the war of 1812 and lived to the remarkable age of one hundred and two years.

Alpheus Blakesley was a machinist by trade and showed great ability as an inventor, which talent is plainly inherited by his son as evinced by his numerous patents His parents were of New England stock and English descent He died when the son was but a few weeks old, leaving his widow and three children, George O, Celia and Alpheus M The sister lived but two years and the widow died in 1845 when the subject of our story was but ten years old

Left homeless by the death of his mother, Alpheus removed to Wisconsin to reside with an aunt, but the arrangement not being satisfactory he left to fight his battles alone

After a few years at farm work he secured a position at Rockford, Illinois. Realizing keenly his lack of early advantages, he set out to secure a better education and entered Kimball's Academy at Rockford, finishing his course finally at Kingsville Academy, Ohio, when twenty-one years of age In the interim he learned the tinner's trade with the old firm of Blinn & Emerson, at Rockford, and soon after, with his brother, helped establish the first hardware store at Sterling, Illinois. At first the firm was Hall & Blakesley, then Manahan & Blakesley After about three years his brother sold out and removed to Rockford, where he continued with him in the same line of business under the name of Blakesley & Moffat

At the first call for troops in April, 1861, he enlisted for three months' service in the Rockford Zouaves, a company made up mostly of Colonel Ellsworth's first company, and commanded by Captain G L. Nevius Mr Blakesley served out his term but on account of ill health did not re-enlist However, he assisted Captain Bross to raise and drill a company at Sterling, Illinois, and on August 13, 1862, again enlisted as a private at Rockford, where he was mustered in Company E, Seventy-fourth Illinois Volunteers At the organization of his company and regiment soon after, he was elected second lieutenant. He was in most of the battles of the Army of the Cumberland and saw much hard service, being soon promoted to first lieutenant and a little later to captain of his company He was in over

A. M. BLAKESLEY.

forty engagements, and with the exception of a few days, was continually on duty in command of his company or of the regiment until the close of the war

After his final discharge the captain took up his residence in Beloit, Wisconsin, where he embarked in the hardware and stove trade On the 19th of July, 1865, he married Mary Ann Avery of Belvidere, Illinois, daughter of Egbert Hamilton and Sarah (Coggeshall) Avery Four children have been born to to them— Ella Avery, George Webster, Charles Alpheus and Theodore Seward Ella A married G C Blakslee, of Rock Island, George W married Alice Avery, of Chicago, and is at present bookkeeper for the Rock Island Stove Company, Charles A died in childhood, while Theodore S is now in college

In 1868 Captain Blakesley removed to Hiawatha, Kansas, where he continued in the hardware business until drouth, the grasshopper plague and the loss of his stock by fire caused his return to Illinois, where he engaged with Cribben & Sexton, of Chicago, as traveling salesman In 1877 he engaged with the old Rock Island Stove Company, in the same capacity, continuing with them until December, 1880, when, with Messrs Frank Mixter and Phil Mitchell, he formed a co-partnership under the name of Rock Island Stove Company, for the manufacture of stoves and ranges, an industry that has grown to be one of the most prominent in the city and of which Captain Blakesley and Mr Mixter are the managing partners He is also a director in the Rock Island Buggy Company, and in the Rock Island Plow Company While he is always deeply interested in public affairs, he has never aspired to political honors In politics he is a Republican In

religious preference, a Presbyterian, and in social life he prizes highly his membership in the Loyal Legion of the United States He is also a member of the G A R and of the Society of the Army of the Cumberland He has always been as active in church work as he is enterprising in business, serving as chairman of the building committee of the local Y M C A from start to finish, and taking prominent part in various moral and temperance movements He is at present an elder and trustee of the Broadway Presbyterian church, to the work of which he gives much thought and time It is worthy of mention here that his parents and grandparents and his kindred as far as known, as well as those of his wife, were all religious people, zealous in christian work

Mrs Blakesley is an active member of the Daughters of the American Revolution, thirteen of her ancestors having been massacred by the English at Fort Griswold, in Groton, Connecticut She is also president of the Ladies' Relief Society of Rock Island, and has ever been active in her work among the poor of the city She has held several prominent offices in the ladies' societies of the church and has in every way been a true helpmeet to her husband

BENJAMIN GOBLE —No state in the Union can boast of a more heroic band of pioneers than Illinois In their intelligence, capability and genius they are far above the pioneers of the eastern states, and in their daring and heroism are equal to the Missouri and California argonauts Their privations, hardships and earnest labors have resulted in establishing one of the foremost commonwealths in America, the possibilities of which are greater than those possessed by any of her sister states In Mr. Goble we find not only a pioneer of Rock Island county, but also a native son of Illinois, his birth having occurred at Fort Compton, Wabash county, October 17, 1813

The parents of our subject were George and Nancy (Arnold) Goble, natives of Kentucky and Illinois, respectively, who were married at Fort Compton The paternal grandfather, Benjamin Goble, was born in Ireland and as a young man came to America, where he was twice married, having by the first wife four sons and by the second three children. He was a farmer by occupation and died in Indiana As a Continental soldier he took an active part in the Revolutionary war Stephen A and Sallie Arnold were the maternal grandparents of our subject The former was born in Kentucky and became one of the earliest settlers of Illinois, raising the first crop of wheat in this state He was also a Revolutionary hero, being captain of a company which valiantly aided in the struggle for independence His death occurred in Wabash county, Illinois

Our subject is one of a family of eight children, seven sons and one daughter, but with the exception of himself all are now deceased The father, who was a farmer by occupation, came to Illinois in 1810, was married at Fort Compton, and died October 25, 1829, at the age of forty-five years, being laid to rest in a cemetery at Rock Island His wife, who was a devout member of the Methodist church, long survived him and spent her last days in Oregon, where she died January 6, 1870, at the age of seventy-six

In the year of his birth Mr Goble, of this review, was taken by his parents to Clay county, Ill

can Bottom, and the year following to Missouri, locating five miles north of St Louis In 1828 he went to Merrimac, and on the 26th of May, 1829, located in Rock Island county, with the development and progress of which he has since been prominently identified He at first worked at whatever he could find to do, receiving a salary of fifty cents per day, and has made as many as thirty-five thousand rails He was often employed by Mr Davenport, working on the site of the present city of that name, and helped hew the logs and erect the log house for Colonel Davenport in 1832 In those early days he also spent considerable time in hunting, has killed over three hundred deer, and has captured one hundred and fifteen swarms of wild bees

On the 22d of August, 1833, Justice Joel Wells performed a wedding ceremony which united the destinies of Mr Goble and Miss Barbara Vandruff, a daughter of Joshua and Betsy (Weiscover) Vandruff, it being the second marriage in Rock Island county. Eleven children blessed their union, namely Emeline, Jesse, Vester; Louisa, wife of Jasper Woods, Benjamin, Sylvester, Barbara Ann, wife of David Dilts, Merritt, Emma, wife of Lee Hiserodt, Ferrell, and Angeline, wife of Frederick H Cook, of Tiskilwa, Illinois The wife and mother was called to her final rest in 1893, at the age of seventy-six years, after sixty years of happy married life

Mr Goble was a soldier in the Black Hawk war and has been actively identified with every movement calculated to advance the general welfare or promote the prosperity of his native state In 1852 he removed to Henry county, where he purchased land, and became the owner of four valuable farms, aggregating five hundred acres of rich and arable land In connection with general farming, he also dealt extensively in cattle and hogs, which proved quite profitable, especially during the Civil war. when he sold one drove of one hundred head of hogs at eleven dollars and a half per hundred pounds and another lot at twelve dollars and forty cents In April, 1869, he sold his property in Henry county and went to Council Bluffs, Iowa, where he spent the summer and then returned to Rock Island county, living near Sears, on the island, until 1882, when he moved to Milan After the death of his wife he lived for a time with a daughter in Tiskilwa, but now makes his home with his son Merritt on section 22, Black Hawk township He has given all of his children a good start in life

Being the oldest living resident of the county, Mr Goble was honored by being chosen to lay the corner stone of the elegant new court house just completed in Rock Island He has seen the country develop from an unbroken wilderness and has ever borne his part in the wonderful transformation that has taken place He is noted for his remarkable memory, having the faculty of remembering facts and dates and associating them accurately His honesty and integrity are proverbial, and he has the respect and esteem of young and old, rich and poor In early life he was a Democrat, but since the outbreak of the Civil war has been an ardent Republican, and has ever proved one of the most loyal, patriotic and valued citizens of this great commonwealth

---

MAHLON J YOUNG Fortunate is he who has back of him an ancestry honorable and distinguished, and happy is he if his lines of life are cast in harmony therewith Our subject is blessed in this respect, for he springs from a prominent family, which was early founded in Ohio His paternal grandfather, a native of Pennsylvania, became a successful farmer of the Buckeye state, where he died at the extreme age of one hundred years, while his wife lived to be ninety-seven

In the family of this worthy couple were seven children, one of whom was Mahlon Young, the father of our subject He was also born in Pennsylvania, but spent most of his life in Ohio, where he followed agricultural pursuits He faithfully served his country in the Mexican war and was a consistent member of the Methodist church, to which his wife also belonged She bore the maiden name of Orrilla Young and was a native of Vermont By her marriage she became the mother of seven children, of whom six are still living Noah is the oldest, Sylvia, a resident of Norwalk, Ohio, is the widow of George Mead, who was a member of the Union army during the Civil war and now fills a soldier's grave, John B, who was lieutenant of Company F, Third Ohio Cavalry, and was drowned in the Ocmulgee river in Georgia just prior to starting for home at the close of the war, Mary A is the wife of O L Mullen, of Jerseyville, Illinois, Martha E is the wife of Alfred Noyes, of Norwalk, Ohio, Mahlon J is next in order of birth, and Orrilla J is the wife of W L Lucas, of Cleveland, Ohio The father of this family departed this life in 1887, at the age of seventy-five, but the mother is still living.

Mr Young, of this review, was born in Townsend, Ohio, March 22, 1852, was reared in Huron county, that state, and pursued his studies in the schools of Townsend Monroeville and Norwalk completing his education by a collegiate course Thus well fitted for teaching, in 1869 he had charge of a district school for one term, but with that exception throughout his entire business career he has been connected with railroad service

On resigning his school, Mr Young accepted the position of assistant cashier in the freight office at Sandusky, Ohio, of the Lake Shore & Michigan Southern Railroad Company, was soon afterward promoted billing clerk, later chief clerk, and in 1872, when the company extended its line from Sandusky to Toledo, making that division its through line, a fine passenger station was erected at a cost of eighteen thousand dollars, and Mr Young was placed in charge, Sandusky being the largest and most important point on the division In August, 1874, he was promoted to the agency at Oberlin, Ohio, which position he held until September, 1884, when he was offered a position in the auditor's office of the Denver & Rio Grande Western Railroad at Denver, Colorado

While on his way west Mr Young met W C Brown, now general manager of the Chicago, Burlington and Quincy road, who offered him a clerkship at East St Louis or the agency at East Alton With such encouragement for the future he concluded to remain, thinking his prospects for advancement would be better here, and in October 1884, began working for the Burlington as agent at East Alton About three months later he was transferred to the agency at Astoria, Illinois, and six months later to the agency at Beardstown, the division and superintendent's headquarters In December, 1886, he was promoted to the agency at Rock Island, and has since had charge of the freight and

ticket departments here His long retention attests the capable discharge of the duties of that responsible position and the faithfulness with which he promotes the company's interest

While residing in Ohio, Mr Young was quite extensively interested in the telephone business In 1879 he received from the American Bell Telephone Company the franchise for Lorain county with a fifteen-year lease, and soon after put in exchanges at Oberlin, Elyria, Lorain and Wellington, and constructed trunk lines connecting the four cities In 1883 he sold out to the Midland Telephone Company, of Chicago For several years he was engaged in the grain and coal business under the firm name of Young & Arnold, and was for three years president and one of the proprietors of the Oberlin Telegraph College at Oberlin, Ohio

On the 24th of September, 1874, at Sandusky, Ohio, Mr Young was united in marriage to Miss Mary A Hudson, a daughter of William and Mary (Lloyd) Hudson, and they have become the parents of four children, namely Edward H , a graduate of St Stephen's College, of Annandale, New York, May O , who graduated at the Rock Island high school, and is now attending the Leland Stanford University of California, and Mahlon J , Jr , and Maude E., at home The family, which is one of social prominence, occupies a pleasant home at No 712 Seventeenth street, Rock Island, where the latchstring is always out to their many friends Mrs Young holds membership in the Episcopal church

In social relations Mr Young is identified with the Knights of the Globe of Rock Island, and is a Knight Templar Mason, belonging to the Norwalk Ohio Commandery,

No 18 His political support is given the men and measures of the Republican party, and as a public-spirited, progressive citizen he takes a deep interest in the welfare of his adopted city and county, and does all in his power to promote its interests

B WINTER, a wholesale liquor dealer engaged in business at 1512 Third avenue, Rock Island, is a self-made man who, without extraordinary family or pecuniary advantages at the commencement of life, has battled earnestly and energetically, and by indomitable courage and integrity has achieved both character and fortune By sheer force of will and untiring effort he has worked himself upward

Mr Winter was born on the river Rhine, in Germany, July 28, 1849, and is a son of Joseph and Mary S (Dauber) Winter, also natives of that country, who emigrated to America in 1853 and located first in Henry county, Illinois Later they removed to a farm near Milan in Rock Island county, where the father died in 1893, at the age of seventy-five years Our subject was only three years old when he crossed the Atlantic, and was a lad of seventeen when he took up his residence in Rock Island county His early educational privileges being somewhat meagre, he has become a self-educated as well as a self-made man

On starting out in life for himself, Mr Winter secured a position in a wholesale liquor house and has since been connected with the liquor business in one capacity or another In June, 1880, he embarked in business for himself, forming a partnership with James E Mott one of the old settlers a

of the city, and at the end of five years he purchased his partner's interest and has since been alone Although he started out in life for himself empty-handed, he is now at the head of a large and profitable business, the result of his own industry, enterprise and good management

In Davenport in December, 1871, Mr Winter was joined in wedlock to Miss Lizzie Bartermeier, who was born, reared and educated in that city They became the parents of four children Agnes, at home, Louis J, who is now acting as his father's bookkeeper, Robert, who holds a responsible business position in Rock Island, and Mamie, who died at the age of three years The wife and mother died in 1882, and two years later Mr Winter married her sister, Miss Johanna Bartermeier, who also spent her early life in Davenport – her native city The four children born of this union are Cora, Basilius, Jr, Florence, and George P

In politics Mr Winter has been a lifelong Democrat, but at local elections generally votes independent of party ties He has ever taken an active and prominent part in political affairs, and is now serving his third term as a member of the city council, being first elected in 1887 He is an influential and popular member of that body and the duties of his office he has most faithfully and capably performed, winning the commendation of all concerned He and his family are all communicants of the Catholic church

P ETER NELSON is one of the leading and influential citizens of Moline, who has taken an active part in promoting its [illegible] rial development   An adopted son of America, his loyalty is above question and his labors in the interests of the city have been most effective and beneficial

Mr Nelson was born in the province of Skone, Sweden, May 12, 1846, and is a son of Nels and Magnel (Nelson) Swenson   His boyhood days were spent on the home farm and in the common schools he pursued his studies until sixteen years of age, when he was apprenticed to a shoemaker for a four years' term, during which time he received no compensation for his services save his board   When his apprenticeship was ended he worked in different towns as a journeyman for a year, but feeling that he might better his financial condition in America he left the land of his nativity on attaining his majority   Sailing from Gottenberg, after a stormy voyage of twelve days he landed at New York, whence he came to Moline, where he had a married sister living   Securing a situation as a farm hand in Henry county, he there remained for three and a half years, after which he went to Texas to work on a railroad, but the climate did not agree with him and in a few months he went to New Orleans, where he was employed as a street car driver for three months   Returning then to Moline he was employed as a teamster until 1873, when he entered the service of the Moline Plow Company as a man of all work   After a time, however, he was given charge of a machine and is now one of the oldest wood workers in the factory, his connection therewith covering almost a quarter of a century.   His long continued service is the highest possible testimonial of his efficiency and fidelity to duty and indicates the confidence reposed in him by the company.

Mr Nelson was married in Moline Jan-uary 4, 1877, the lady of his choice being Miss Augusta Johnson, who was born in the province of Smoland, Sweden   She came to America when seventeen years of age, and after two years spent in Oregon, Illinois, removed to Moline   Mr and Mrs Nelson have five children—Myrtle Theresa, born January 9, 1878, Edith Ophelia, born January 8, 1880, and died at the age of seven years, George Henry, born September 24, 1882, Gustav Ryno, born October 31, 1885, and Fridolph Leroy, born July 30, 1889

Mr Nelson has been active in his advocacy of the principles of the Republican party since casting his first presidential vote for Grant in 1872   In 1890 he was elected alderman from the fifth ward, and has held that office continuously since   In the first year he served on the committee on sewers and bridges, in the second and third years was chairman of the police committee, the next year was chairman of the park committee and has since been a member of the committee on streets and alleys, serving as its chairman in 1896   During his first term in office Third avenue was paved and the sewers and water mains were extended   In the third year Thirteenth, Fourteenth, Fifteenth, Sixteenth, Seventeenth and Eighteenth streets were paved up to Fourth avenue   In the fourth year the Nineteenth street storm drain was constructed from Twelfth avenue to the river, and many other improvements have been made   In 1896 considerable relief to those out of employment was furnished by the city in the improvement of Third street and Twelfth avenue   In the present year Mr Nelson is chairman of the committee on grounds and buildings, and a member of the fire, water and light committee.   He is very progressive and has taken a most active part in promoting the city's interests and substantial improvement

Mr Nelson and his family attend the Swedish Methodist church, of which his daughter is a devoted member He is a charter member of Swedish Olive Lodge, No 583, I O O F, which was established January 9, 1875 He served as its its first treasurer, was its third vice-grand, has been noble grand and has filled all the other offices. He is one of the most valued citizens that Sweden has furnished to the new world, is a man of sterling worth in all the relations of life, and his name is honorably and inseparably connected with the history of his adopted city

---

REV WILLIAM STEVENSON MARQUIS, D D —Only the history of the good and great comes down to us through the ages The true religion has been the strongest influence known to man through all time, while the many false doctrines that have sprung up have flourished only for a day and then vanished More potent at the present than at any period in the world's history are the work and influence of Christianity, and among those who are devoting their lives to its inculcation among men is Dr Marquis, the honored pastor of the Broadway Presbyterian church, of Rock Island He is one of the leading ministers of that denomination in Illinois, and his life is a source of inspiration and encouragement to all who know him

The Doctor was born in Kenton, Ohio, October 2, 1853 His great-grandfather, Rev Thomas Marquis, who was known as the Silver-tongued Marquis, was born near Winchester Virginia in 1753, the fourth

son of a large family, and was of Irish descent William Marquis, the grandfather, devoted his life to farming, and always resided in Pennsylvania Rev James E Marquis, father of our subject, was born in Washington county, Pennsylvania, became a minister of the Presbyterian church, and had charge of congregations in Kenton, Shelby, Mansfield and Ontario, Ohio He afterward removed to Illinois, and became superintendent of the synod of central Illinois His last charge was at Elmwood, this state, where he died February 22, 1863 He married Mary Du Bois, a daughter of Daniel Du Bois. Her father was a cabinet maker in early life, but in pioneer days removed from New Jersey, his native state, to Carlisle, Ohio, where he owned and operated a large farm He had a family of ten children, and died when about seventy years of age Mary Du Bois was first married to a gentleman of the same family name, and by that union had one son, Stanley Du Bois She was born in Carlisle, Ohio, April 9, 1827, and is still living in Bloomington, Illinois By her second marriage she had five children, of whom three are now living—Rev William, Frank, who is cashier in the People's Bank, of Bloomington, Illinois, and Chalmers C superintendent of the Pantagraph, of Bloomington.

Dr Marquis of this review, was a child of only five years when brought by his parents to Illinois He acquired his early education at Elmwood, and was graduated at the high school in Bloomington in the class of 1872 He afterward entered the Illinois Wesleyan University, of that city, where he was graduated in 1876, and by graduation he completed the course in the Princeton Theological Seminary in 1879 His first pastorate was at Minonk, being called to that church after completing his theological course. Since June, 1884, he has been pastor of the Broadway Presbyterian church of Rock Island, which now has about three hundred and fifty active members.

The first meeting looking toward the organization of this church was held October 7, 1874. Later in the year other meetings were held, indicating a steadily increasing interest in the work. A canvass for subscriptions was started and plans were proposed for the building of the church on the corner of Broadway and Spencer streets, now known as Seventh avenue and Twenty-third street. Commissioners were sent to the Rock River Presbytery, which met at Princeton April 13, 1875, bearing a petition for an organization. The prayer was granted, and April 27 a committee from the Presbytery arrived to complete the organization, which occurred April 29, 1875. For a few months the pulpit was filled by supplies and the 1st of November Rev T H Hench was installed as the regular pastor and served until June 23, 1878, when he resigned. The corner stone of the new church building was laid May 2, 1876. Rev J. R. Miller, D. D., now editor of the Presbyterian Board of Publication, Philadelphia, the second pastor, resigned June 16, 1880, and on the 25th of August was succeeded by Rev J. C Holiday, who resigned February 3, 1884. On the 31st of March of the same year, Rev W S Marquis was chosen to fill the same office, and for thirteen years has efficiently labored with the people of this church. Under his able supervision the church is now in excellent working order, the various societies are in a thriving condition and are accomplishing a good work in the city. A large Sunday-school is conducted, ...

the South Park Mission. It is impossible to estimate the influence of this church organization, but in the years of its existence it has become a power in the community whose force is broadly felt, and not a little of this is due to Dr Marquis, whose devotion to and sympathy with the church and the people has endeared him to all hearts.

On the 21st of December, 1881, was celebrated the marriage of Doctor Marquis and Miss Adelaide M Bell, daughter of Reuben P and Lydia A (Edwards) Bell, of Minonk. Four children blessed this union —Helen A, who died at the age of five years, Laura Betta, William B; and Stewart D.

In politics Doctor Marquis has usually affiliated with the Republican party. He is a man of scholarly attainments and broad general information, and in 1879 the degree of A M was conferred upon him by the Wesleyan University of Bloomington, while in 1895 the degree of D. D was conferred upon him by Knox College of Galesburg. He has been three times a delegate to the general assembly of the church, and it is a peculiar coincidence that on all three occasions the sessions were held in Saratoga, New York. He is a man of thoughtful, earnest purpose, of strong intellectual endowments, of broad charity and kindly nature, and by all denominations, as well as his own people, is held in the highest regard.

HEMAN A BARNARD —The city of Moline boasts of quite a number of men of inventive genius, men who have done much, by reason of superior ability in this line, to advance the interests of the place, but none are held in higher regard, or deserve greater recognition than the sub-ject of this sketch, who has been so closely identified with its material prosperity for nearly half a century Like so many others who have attained fame and wealth in the great state of Illinois, he is a native of the Green Mountain State, and in common with those born upon its rugged hills, he has that strong force of character and steadfast determination that is sure to win

H A Barnard was born at Hyde Park, Vermont, January 13, 1826, and is a son of Asa and Deborah (Taylor) Barnard, both of whom were natives of New England The father was a farmer by occupation and engaged in that calling almost his entire life He served as a soldier in the war of 1812, and was in the battle of Plattsburg From Hyde Park, he removed to Burling-ton, Vermont, in 1836, and there his last days were spent

When the family removed to Burlington our subject was but ten years of age. His education, begun in the public schools of Hyde Park, was completed in Burlington The farm to him had no special attractions and early in life he evinced a taste for me-chanics, therefore it was determined that his taste in this direction should be culti-vated For five years he served an appren-ticeship at Winooski Falls to learn the trade of millwright, at the end of which time he engaged with his employers, Ed-wards & White, as a journeyman, and for the succeeding two years was engaged in constructing mills for that firm in New England and Canada He then formed a partnership with William Warner and en-gaged in the manufacture of furniture at Cowensville, Canada, under the firm name of Warner & Barnard In connection with the manufacture of furniture they ran a saw
24

and planing mill The business was carried on successfully for two years, when the plant was destroyed by fire

Concluding that they would not rebuild, the partnership was dissolved, and Mr Bar-nard decided to come west with a view of engaging in agricultural pursuits somewhere in Iowa Arriving in Rock Island he deter-mined there to spend the winter Moline, at that time, was coming into prominence as a manufacturing center, and in the spring of 1855 he removed to that city, where he worked at his trade as a journeyman for about four years He then formed a part-nership with L E Hemingway and engaged in the manufacture of chairs Two years later J B Wyckoff was admitted as a part-ner, and soon afterward J S Leas In 1870 a stock company was formed and the business incorporated under the name of the Barnard & Leas Manufacturing Company The capital stock of the company was fixed at three hundred thousand dollars, and Mr Barnard was elected president, Mr Leas vice-president, and William Bennett, secre-tary The manufacture of mill machinery was now the principal product of the factory, and in this it has a world-wide reputation

On the organization of the Barnard & Leas Manufacturing Company, Mr Barnard turned his attention mainly to the improve-ment of all mill machinery, and in the past thirty years has invented and patented many improvements in the same, including roller mills, bolting machines, flour packers, wheat separators, purifiers and dust collectors By reason of the practical utility of each of these inventions, the company has built up an immense trade, and has become one of the first of the many important manufactur-ing concerns of Moline In addition to his interest in the Barnard & Leas Manufacturing Company, Mr. Barnard is a stockholder and vice-president of the Salt Lake Mill & Elevator Company, of Salt Lake, Utah, and is also a stockholder and director in the First National Bank of Moline

Mr. Barnard has been twice married, his first union being with Miss Della Boright, of Canada, in 1849 She died in Moline in 1856, leaving one son, Charles A., now secretary of the Barnard & Leas Manufacturing Company, a man of good business and executive ability. Four years later Mr Barnard was again married at Ypsilanti, Michigan, to Miss Emily Sober By this union five children have been born. Stella is now the wife of B F. Towndrow, of Idaho Frank is married and is engaged in the factory Agnes is now the wife of Thomas Cassady, of Council Bluffs, Iowa Harry died when sixteen years of age, and Ruth yet remains at home

Politically Mr Barnard has always been a stanch Republican and has never differed with the majority of his party save upon the question of the free coinage of silver He believes that it would be for the best interests of the country to engage in free coinage regardless of other nations He has never had any aspirations for political honors, but has served his municipality, first as chairman of the old town board, and since the organization of the city as a member of the board of aldermen In other ways he has served his party as delegate to various county and state conventions, in which he has wielded considerable influence, by reason of his strong individuality and conscientious discharge of duty

Fraternally, Mr Barnard is a Mason, holding membership with the blue lodge at Moline and with the council and commandery of I C I-I avl In the area assumed he has filled all the chairs and is now past master of the lodge As a citizen he ever stands ready to discharge every duty devolving upon him, and the best years of his life have been given to the building up and advancement of his adopted city and county. Few men are better known throughout the state and nation, especially in the west, and among business men, than Heman A Barnard, the subject of this sketch, who is honored for his sterling worth and exalted character

---

ANDREW WILLIAMSON, Ph D , professor of mathematics and astronomy in Augustana College, has devoted almost his entire life to educational work, and his name occupies a leading place on the roll of Illinois' most successful teachers He was born at Lacquiparle, Minnesota, January 31, 1838, while his father, Dr Thomas S Williamson, was serving as missionary to the Dakotas His early educational privileges were supplemented by study in Knox College of Galesburg, Illinois, where he matriculated in 1853 He was graduated at Marietta, Ohio, in 1857, and studied natural sciences for a year as a resident graduate of Yale University He has at various times spent in the aggregate about two years in visiting public schools, normal schools, colleges, teachers' institutes and educational associations in order to observe and study different methods of instruction

Professor Williamson has been most successful as an educator He is not only a man of broad mental culture, but has the faculty of imparting clearly, intelligibly and readily to others the knowledge that he has acquired In 1860 and 1861 he was engaged in teaching at Zumbrota and Preston,

Minnesota, but in the latter year put aside all personal considerations to enter his country's service and aid in the preservation of the union He followed the starry banner on many a hotly contested battle field and was promoted successively to lieutenant, regimental quartermaster and acting assistant adjutant-general

When the war was over Professor Williamson returned to his educational duties and from 1866 until 1870 was principal of Center College Academy of Ohio, where he educated about two hundred public school teachers He was afterward principal of graded schools at Manterville and Spring Valley, Minnesota, for a year was principal of a mission boarding school for the Chippewa Indians at Odanah, Wisconsin, and for four months was instructor in history and physics in the University of Minnesota His nervous condition making it impossible for him longer to engage in teaching, he then turned his attention to merchandising and also served as notary public and postmaster at Sleepy Eye, Minnesota, from 1873 until 1876 In the latter year he resumed his profession as principal of a graded school in Blue Earth City, Minnesota, and from January, 1877, until May, 1880, he was a member of the faculty of Gustavus Adolphus College of St Peter, Minnesota On the 1st of September, 1880, he accepted the professorship of mathematics and astronomy in Augustana College of Rock Island and has since occupied that place

JAMES G BLYTHE —An honored retirement from labor is a fitting reward of a well spent life and after years of active identificat n w th th business interests of

Rock Island Mr Blythe is now enjoying the rest which his former labor made possible For fifty-seven years he has been a resident of this city and has therefore witnessed almost its entire growth and development He belongs to that class of citizens whose interest in their community is manifested in a substantial way and throughout his life he has been a leading factor in the promotion of enterprises that have led to the best advancement of the city

Mr Blythe was born in County Antrim, Ireland, October 3, 1810, of Scotch parentage He is a son of John and Susan (Gilmer) Blythe, the former a native of Scotland, and the latter of Ireland They had a family of six sons, but our subject is now the only surviving one The father was a cooper by trade and for a few years sailed the high seas In 1811 he came to America, taking up his residence in Columbiana county, Ohio, where he worked at coopering and farming His death occurred there in 1852 at the age of seventy-two years, and his wife died in 1874 when nearly ninety-one years of age They were both members of the old Seceders Church, now called the United Presbyterian

The paternal grandfather of James Blythe was Thomas Blythe, a native of Perthshire, Scotland, in which place he spent his entire life, dying at an advanced age He was a cooper by trade and had two sons and one daughter The maternal grandfather, James Gilmer, was a native of Ireland, and made farming his life work. He also was quite old at the time of his demise

The father of our subject was a well educated man and it was his great regret that he could not give his children excellent advantages in that direction, as there were no public schools in Ohio at the time and the few private schools were very unproficient. James G. Blythe, of this review, obtained his education therein, supplemented by the broad general knowledge that reading, experience and observation have brought to him. He remained upon his father's farm in Ohio until sixteen years of age, and then began learning the wagon maker's trade. At that time all the parts of a wagon were made in the shop from the crude materials. He also learned buggy making and engaged in that business until 1871. He came to Illinois in 1836, and in 1840 took up his residence in Rock Island, where he has since made his home, having come to this place from Quincy, where he had resided for three years. He established a little wagon making shop in a rented building which stood on a part of the ground now occupied by the Commercial Hotel. His operations were necessarily carried on on a small scale at first, but with the increasing population of the city he built up a very extensive business and in 1851 admitted to partnership Simon B. Stoddard, now deceased. For twenty years that connection was continued and in 1871 they sold out, Mr. Blythe retiring to private life. His business methods were above question, the work which was turned out from his shop was always satisfactory and his straightforward dealing and courtesy to his patrons secured to him an extensive trade which yielded him a good income.

On the 20th of October, 1840, Mr. Blythe was united in marriage to Miss Rebecca Hamilton, a native of Kentucky, and a daughter of James and Susan Hamilton. They never had any children of their own but reared an adopted son, Charles, whom they received into their home when quite young. He is still living in Rock Island.

He married Miss Kat have three children.

Mr. Blythe was f byterian and his wife Methodist church. S he is now living at the where fifty-five years a himself and wife. D he has resided at thi valued member of th and in politics was a V tion of the party, sinc been a Republican. of industry and usefu in business and his fi an example which is w tion. Rock Island nu honored pioneers and county would be inc record of his life.

LEVI F. CRALLE Rink livery of Mo ney, Illinois, July 16, Edward M. and Sarah parents were married their home in Olney u entered the United St Civil war. He serve pated in several battle to Rock Island arser river to do guard duty tioned there he remove in 1864, where he f after the war until his

The subject of thi the heroes who aided i the Union, He was and nine months old a listment in May, 18 Company G, One Hu

Illinois Infantry For six months he remained in the service, doing guard duty at the fort in Columbus, Kentucky, and was mustered out in October, 1864

After his return from the war Mr Cralle began earning his own living and his wages were given his father until he had attained his majority In 1873 he began running an express line in Moline and followed that business until 1882, when he purchased a half interest in a livery stable on Third avenue, doing business at that point until 1888, when he sold out and purchased a barn on Sixteenth street He was there in business until 1895, when he formed a partnership with C F Heminway, with whom he is still associated They have a large and well-appointed livery stable, supplied with a fine line of carriages and horses and are most accommodating and straightforward in their treatment of their patrons, so that they are now enjoying a large and profitable business Mr Cralle also owns a livery stable at No 1909 Second avenue, Rock Island, which he has operated since April, 1896

On the 30th of January, 1873, Mr Cralle married Miss Mary Witherspoon, of Moline, who was born in Maryland They have three children Maude, a graduate of the high school of Moline, who has also been a student in the State Normal of Normal, Illinois, Arthur and Chester, at home

Giving his support to the Republican party, Mr Cralle has been elected supervisor of Moline on that ticket, filling the office for five years from 1889 He served on the finance committee, was chairman of the poor farm committee one year, and did efficient service in the interest of the public on several other important committees He is a prominent member of civic societies and

popular with his brethren of the fraternities He belongs to Moline Lodge, No 133, I O O F , served as its secretary for some time, and in 1889 was elected treasurer, which office he held for eight consecutive years He belongs to Doric Lodge, No 319, A F & A M , Barrett Chapter, No 18, R A M , of Rock Island, is senior warden of Everts Commandery, No 18, K T , of Rock Island, and is second ceremonial officer of Kaaba Temple of the Mystic Shrine in Davenport He and his wife and daughter all belong to the Order of the Eastern Star He is a charter member of Camp No 38, M W A , and of St George's Lodge, No 28, K P , in which he has been trustee and manager from the beginning He renews his association with his old army comrades through his membership in Graham Post, G A R , and has attended a number of reunions of the veterans His nature is genial and generous and his circle of friends is very extensive

GENERAL WILLIAM CLENDENEN, who has attained distinctive preferment in military circles, and is one of the enterprising and representative business men of Moline, was born in Whiteside county, Illinois, April 12, 1845 His father, Robert G Clendenen, was a native of Lancaster county, Pennsylvania, and a son of David Ramsey Clendenen, who was also born in the Keystone state, his ancestors, of Scotch lineage, being among the early settlers of Pennsylvania Reared in the state of his nativity, Robert G Clendenen, emigrated to Illinois in 1835, and became one of the pioneers of Whiteside county, where he entered land and developed a farm He married Hannah Clark, who

who was born and reared in New York, and accompanied her father, William Clark, to Whiteside county, about 1835. Mr Clendenen became a prominent citizen of that county and held numerous positions of honor and trust   He served for some time as deputy sheriff and for four years filled the office of sheriff   In politics he was a staunch Republican and served as a delegate to various party conventions   In business he was successful, and he reared a family who are an honor to his name.   His death occurred in Whiteside county in 1867, and his widow is now living with her oldest son, Frank, who is a leading business man of Joliet, Illinois   The youngest son is C. C Clendenen, now of Georgia

General Clendenen, of this review, is the second in order of birth, and was reared in his native county, acquiring a good education in the common and high schools there   He enlisted in 1864 as a member of the One Hundred and Fortieth Illinois Infantry, which was assigned to the army of the Tennessee, and with his regiment participated in many skirmishes and raids, protecting the railroads and doing guard duty. He enlisted as a private, but was promoted to the rank of first sergeant and then to sergeant major, in which capacity he served until honorably discharged at the expiration of his term in October, 1864 He re-enlisted in the One Hundred and Eighth United States Regiment, formed of colored troops, was promoted to second lieutenant and commissioned first lieutenant, serving until March, 1866. After the close of hostilities the regiment was engaged in guard duty in Mississippi until the following spring

With an honorable war record, Lieutenant Clendenen returned to his home in

Whiteside county, and in 1867 entered a drug store to learn the business   The following year he purchased an interest in a drug store in Morrison, and continued operations at that point until 1873, when the firm established a branch store at Moline, and Mr Clendenen assumed charge of the same In 1877 the partnership was dissolved and he succeeded to the ownership of the Moline store, building up an extensive trade The liberal patronage which is now accorded him is justly merited and he ranks among the leading druggists of the city

General Clendenen was married in Morrison, Illinois, April 16, 1867, to Rachel E Gridley, a native of New York, and a daughter of James G Gridley, a pioneer settler of Whiteside county   She came to the west with her father when a maiden of ten summers and was reared and educated in Morrison   She died in Moline in 1887, leaving three children   Robert G , the eldest, is a graduate of the Moline high school, and was his father's assistant in the drug store until twenty-one years of age   He is now married and follows farming near Cedar Rapids, Iowa   Frank J , a graduate of the Moline high school, is with his father in business. Mabel H is now a successful teacher of Moline.   The General was again married in Whiteside county, May 20, 1879, his second union being with Mrs Laura E Mayo, who was born near Buffalo, New York, and came to the west during her childhood   By her first marriage she had a daughter, Cecelia T., who is now employed in the store of D M. Sechlar, of Moline

In politics General Clendenen is a stalwart Republican.   His interest in military affairs has never abated, and in 1877 he joined the Illinois National Guards as second lieutenant   He was promoted to the rank of first lieutenant, January 4, 1878, to the captaincy in November of the same year, became major May 30, 1879, lieutenant-colonel July 30, 1880, colonel of the Sixth Regiment, May 17, 1882, and brigadier general March 28, 1892, serving in the last named office until removed by Governor Altgeld for political reasons He served in the state militia for sixteen years and his military record is without a blemish He and his family are prominent members of the Congregational church, and he belongs to the blue lodge and chapter of the Masonic fraternity in Moline He has served three years as commander of the Grand Army Post, belongs to the Modern Woodmen of America, and is now recorder of the Home Forum of Moline, in which his wife is serving as treasurer, while his son Frank also holds membership therein The son is also a member of the National Guards with the rank of captain of Company F, Sixth Regiment General Clendenen is a man of exemplary habits, who has attained to high rank in social and military circles as the result of his merit and sterling worth

---

PROFESSOR JAMES C JACOBS, principal of the Rock Island Business University, and one of the most successful educators of Illinois, was born in Stark county, this state, near Toulon, November 16 1850, and is a son of Reuben Henry and Matilda (Fisher) Jacobs, natives of Ohio Reuben H Jacobs lost his father when a year and a half old. He was reared in Ohio, learned the trade of a carpenter and builder and afterwards engaged in contracting When a young man he came to Illinois, locating near Canton, where he married Miss Fisher, whose father died near

Canton when more than eighty years of age He had a large family of twelve children Mr Jacobs removed from that place to Toulon, where for a time he followed the tailoring trade, which he had learned in his boyhood Soon afterward, however, he located upon a farm and about 1855 removed to Galva, Illinois, becoming one of its pioneer settlers Making his home there until 1868 he then located on a farm near Shelbina, Missouri, and engaged in contracting and building, making his home in that locality until his death, which occurred in February, 1896, at the age of seventy-eight years His wife still survives him and is living on a farm in Missouri, at the age of seventy-three years Both were faithful members of the Methodist Episcopal church

They had a family of ten children, eight of whom are now living, namely David E , Jennie, wife of Thomas Byers, of Shelbina, Missouri, Henry Franklin, Frederick Welker, James C ; John Wesley, Edith Freelove, wife of James McNeeley, and William Alonzo, both deceased, Elizabeth Seeley, wife of Robert Byers, of Shelbina, Missouri, and Lew Wallace, of Fayette, Missouri

Professor Jacobs, of this review, spent the first eighteen years of his life in Galva, Illinois, and attended its public schools He afterward pursued his studies in the Gem City Business College of Quincy, and the Normal Institute, which was then connected with that school During his boyhood he learned the carpenter's trade and worked with his father for some years, also engaged in contracting on his own account. When he had completed his education he began teaching in a district school in Shelby county, Missouri, and later became principal of the graded schools in Liberty, Missouri, and in Quincy, Illinois He was also principal of the Iowa Commercial College of Davenport, and in 1893 established the Rock Island Business University, located at the corner of Nineteenth street and Second avenue This school has met with remarkable success in the short period of its existence, having now an average attendance of one hundred pupils Professor Jacobs is a most successful educator, possessing the happy faculty of imparting readily and clearly to others the knowledge that he has acquired The courses taught in his school are full and comprehensive and embrace the most practical methods for fitting the students for life's responsible duties

On the 18th of February, 1876, Mr, Jacobs was united in marriage to Miss Mary Mae Wedge, of Kewanee, Illinois They have two children—Virgil LeRoy and Marguerite Mae Mrs Jacobs is a daughter of Homer L and Mary L (Lance) Wedge, the former born in Litchfield, Connecticut, the latter in Pennsylvania He became one of the pioneer settlers of Burlington, Iowa, and until within a few years of his death was actively and prominently connected with its business interests He died in 1882, at the age of seventy-seven years, and his wife passed away in 1868 Both were devout members of the Methodist church and had the high regard of all with whom they came in contact The paternal grandfather of Mrs Jacobs was Abijah Wedge, who was of English descent, and connected with the Wedges of the Bank of England He served as a captain in the American army in the war of 1812, and came to the west, dying in Wethersfield, Illinois, when more than eighty years of age He had three sons and two daughters His wife

one hundred years Both held membership in the Methodist church and Mr Wedge was a minister of that denomination The maternal grandfather of Mrs Jacobs was Peter Lance, who died during her infancy, and his wife's father reached the remarkable age of one hundred and four years

Mrs Jacobs is a lady of superior culture and has proved not only a companion to her husband but has indeed been to him a helpmeet When only sixteen years of age she obtained a teacher's certificate, and for the past eighteen years has been very successful in educational work Since the establishment of the Rock Island Business University she has been her husband's able assistant Her reputation as a teacher of elocution is exceptionally high, and her work as a public reader is of a superior order She gives many entertainments, where her interpretation of character, her pleasing voice and clear presentation of the thoughts of the author make her readings very attractive Her son, Virgil, eight years of age, is called the Boy Orator of the Mississippi Valley He has inherited his mother's talent, and reads many very difficult selections, being especially fine as an impersonator

Professor Jacobs and his wife hold membership in the Methodist church, and are favorites in high social circles, where true worth and intelligence are accepted as the passports into good society He is a member of the Knights of the Globe and the Court of Honor, and gives his political support to the measures promulgated by the Republican party

The following information concerning Mrs Jacobs' ancestors was gleaned from a little historical Orville P Wedge, of

Galva, Illinois "I was on the farm where my father was raised and where your father was born It is still in the Wedge family A cousin of mine, Charles Wedge, owns it and lives there The Wedge family is of English extraction One Wedge (given name supposed to be Thomas) settled in Washington, Litchfield county, Connecticut, died of small-pox and was buried beside a large rock Charles Wedge says the spot has been pointed out to him This man left three sons named Isaac, Asahel and Stephen, who settled in Warren, Litchfield county, Connecticut All three were soldiers in the Revolutionary war We belong to the tribe of Isaac W, who was my grandfather and your great-grandfather His wife's maiden name was Ruth Parmley They had a family of eleven children—eight boys and three girls Your grandfather, Abijah W, was the seventh son, and married Lucinda Holloway, January 5, 1809 He emigrated to Ohio in 1817 He served in a Connecticut regiment through the war of 1812 At the memorable battle of Lundy's Lane, fought near Niagara Falls, July 25, 1814, General Brown being in command of the American forces and General Rial in command of the British, Colonel Winfield Scott, the real hero of the day, was sent with 1,200 men to make a demonstration, and about sunset came upon the whole British force, well posted on an eminence and defended by a battery of artillery Scott at once determined to attack and sent Major Jessup (in whose regiment Orderly Sergeant Abijah Wedge commanded a company) to turn the British left, under cover of night This movement was entirely successful, and Sergeant Wedge had the honor of capturing General Rial and his orderly, who, riding through the bushes mistook the Sergeant's

company for his own men As already stated, your grandmother's name was Lucinda Holloway Her father, John Holloway was one of those German soldiers whom the king of England hired from a German prince to help his hosts subdue his revolting colonies He was a Hessian Like many of his comrades he did not like the position of a mercenary whose life and services had been sold for British gold, and like many more he ran away from the Hessian army and joined the Washington forces, and thus became in the best sense an American After the war he settled in Washington, Litchfield county, Connecticut He married Elizabeth Kinsley, whose father lived to be one hundred and seven years old They had a family of nine children—eight girls and one boy Your grandmother was the third girl of this number On my trip I visited the cemetery in Warren, where many of our ancestors are buried Isaac and Asahel Wedge of the old stock were Baptists, deacons in the church The old church in which they used to worship is still standing in a dilapidated condition, not used "

EZRA SMITH —The title of general of finance has been aptly bestowed upon those men, who, marshalling the peaceful hosts of industry, conquer new realms of commerce and widen the reach of business activity Of this class the subject of this sketch is a notable representative, his financial operations assuming breadth and scope, which indicate the determination, persistence, sound judgment and power of combination which distinguish the born leader of men Coming to Moline in very moderate circumstances, he has made his way to the front rank in business affairs and this success is made still more emphatic by the broad and generous interest that he shows in all that concerns good citizenship For years he was identified with the building interests of the city, but now gives his attention principally to the real estate business

Mr. Smith was born June 12, 1822, in the town of Half Moon, Saratoga county, New York, and of the same state both his grandfather, John Smith, and his father, William Smith, were also natives, belonging to an old family of English origin that was founded there at an early day in the history of this country William Smith served as corporal in a Light Horse Brigade during the war of 1812, and was ever a loyal and patriotic citizen Upon the old homestead in Saratoga county he grew to manhood, and married a native of the same county, Miss Sarah Vincent, a daughter of John Vincent The father of our subject became one of the substantial farmers of his native county, where he reared his family and spent his entire life, dying in 1878 at the ripe old age of eighty-four years His estimable wife had passed away in 1870

In the family of this worthy couple were seven children, five sons and two daughters, all of whom reached years of maturity Lydia died unmarried, Amanda became the wife of Nelson Overacker, of Saratoga county, New York, John W was also single at the time of his death, Ezra is next in order of birth, Augustus is a resident of Saratoga county, Albert remains on the old homestead there, and Giles B also makes his home in Saratoga county

In the county of his nativity, Ezra Smith passed the days of his boyhood and youth, receiving a fair common-school education and was reared at his father's home Learnin the carpenter and joiners trade

in early life, he successfully engaged in contracting and building for many years On the 27th of December, 1848, in Saratoga county, he was united in marriage to Miss Elizabeth Van Danburg, who was born January 7, 1824, a daughter of Nicholas and Sallie Van Danburg, also natives of Saratoga county, where her father in Clifton Park followed agricultural pursuits for many years Subsequently both parents came to make their home in Moline, where the mother died in 1866, at the age of fifty-five years, but the father returned to Saratoga, New York, in 1867, making his home with a son until he, too, was called to his final rest May 24 1884, at the age of seventy-seven. His remains, however, were laid beside those of his wife in Riverside cemetery, Moline, where a neat and substantial monument marks their last resting place On coming to the new world from Holland the paternal great-great-grandfather of Mrs Smith located on the Mohawk river in the Empire state, in whose development and progress the family bore an important part Her great-grandfather Van Danburg was a soldier of the Revolutionary war She is the oldest in a family of three children Peter Van Danburg is married and still lives in Saratoga county Mahala, the sister, became the wife of David T Smith, no relative of the subject of this sketch, and they also became early settlers of Moline, where she died February 19, 1864, her remains being taken back to Clifton Park, Saratoga county, New York, and buried She left two children, a son and daughter, who were reared by their aunt, Mrs Ezra Smith. David T Smith died two years later and was buried by her side and a nice monument marks the place Sarah M, the older, is now the wife of Robert C Boyd, who holds a responsible business position in the wholesale establishment of J V Farwell & Co , Chicago, and Abel P is engaged in the manufacturing business in Rockford, Illinois

After his marriage Ezra Smith located in Clifton Park, Saratoga county, New York, where he engaged in contracting and building until his emigration to Illinois in January, 1856, when he took up his residence in Moline, where he followed the same occupation for fourteen years, erecting many of the public school buildings, churches, banks, business houses and residences of that place, which to-day stand as monuments to his architectural handiwork In 1857 he took the contract for building ten houses at Dennison, Iowa, and there built the first residences and the court house He took his wagons and men and drove from Moline. He completed all of them and returned to Moline in November of that same year In 1870 he purchased a third interest in the Moline Pump Company, with which he was connected for five years, and for the following decade was successfully engaged in the hardware business He then removed to his present home in Park Ridge, where, in 1868, he had purchased forty acres of land, which, in 1891, he laid out in town lots, making an addition to Moline now known as Park Ridge He has since given his attention to the real estate business

Mr and Mrs Smith have only one daughter, —Sarah Elizabeth, now the wife of Addison F Pomeroy, of Chicago, who holds an important position with the Illinois Central Railroad Company They were married December 8, 1886 Mrs Smith is a consistent member of the Congregational church, which her husband also attends and to which he contributes liberally, although not a member

In his political affiliations Mr Smith is a Jacksonian Democrat and cast his first presidential ballot for James K Polk, since which time he has taken quite an active interest in political affairs, and has served as a delegate to a number of conventions In 1876 he was elected county supervisor, and for three years also acceptably served as a member of the Moline school board For forty-one years he has been prominently identified with the business interests of Rock Island county and has done much to advance the welfare of the community, being one of its most progressive and public-spirited citizens, to whose energy and foresight it is indebted for many improvements In advancing his own interest he has never overlooked the general welfare, and has thus gained the respect and esteem of all who know him

On Mrs Smith's mother's side the family were English and the first settlers at Kinder Hook, New York, being among the founders of that village, which is now a handsome residence city The family were very wealthy and influential

A H ARP, M D —The attainment of a leading position in the medical profession is a difficult matter and must depend upon individual merit for it results from the mental mastery of known principles in the medical science By close application, earnest study and untiring devotion, Dr. Arp has become known as a leader in his chosen calling, and now enjoys a most luxurious practice in Moline and Rock Island county.

The Doctor was born in Davenport, Iowa, December 4, 1861, and is a son of C M and Catherine M (Wessel) Arp His father died when the D tor was only three and a half years of age and the mother removed to Moline with her family, making her home with her brother, Dr P H Wessel

Our subject attended the public schools of this city and at the age of sixteen began the study of law in the office of William A Meese, city attorney, but not finding that profession to his taste he abandoned it for the study of medicine, which he began under the direction of his uncle, Dr P H Wessel   In the fall of 1879 he entered the Iowa State University, where he graduated in 1882, being one of the first to complete the three years' course in medicine in that institution   He then began practice in Moline in his uncle's office, but did not form a partnership with him until 1888   The firm of Wessel & Arp then continued in active practice until May 1, 1895, since which time our subject has been alone   He has made a specialty of surgery and in this branch has achieved distinction, possessing superior skill and ability   He has employed electricity to a considerable extent in his practice and with excellent results   From his boyhood he has studied and experimented with electricity and after entering the medical profession began investigating its use in his calling   He used the induction currents for some time and in December, 1895, when the Roentgen methods were made known he adopted the same   In February, 1896, however, he put in an Edison outfit, which he used in his practice and gave two public exhibitions of his work in Moline   That apparatus, however, was replaced November 5, 1896, by Professor Nicola Tesla's alternating coils, the latter instrument being more convenient and always ready for use By the means of his electrical appliances he has been ⸱   ⸱ ⸱⸱ ⸱⸱⸱⸱⸱⸱ ⸱⸱⸱⸱⸱

in all parts of the body, the most recent of which the following is an account taken from a local paper in the summer of 1897

Seventeen months ago, the little son of William Smith of Davenport, then six years and three months of age, while playing with a closet key in his ·mouth, coughed and swallowed the key, which was two and one-quarter inches long and from a fifth to a fourth of an inch thick

Physicians advised that nothing should be done about it till it should begin to give the boy trouble   The lad experienced little or no pain from it for over a year   But about three months ago, abdominal pains began, and there was trouble after eating The boy lost his appetite, became emaciated and had several mysterious hemorrhages

Finally arrangements were made with Dr Arp, and the boy was brought to his office Saturday evening   The Doctor had prepared himself for a previously unheard-of operation, the removing of the key by the introduction into the boy's stomach through the throat of a small pair of forceps incased in a flexible tube, fitted with a sliding lock at the handle of the tube.

The X-Ray apparatus was brought into requisition, and by the use of the flouroscope the key was readily located   The boy was then placed under an anæsthetic, his body inclined and head downward

By means of a Crookes tube, under the operating table, the key was outlined, then the forceps were introduced through the throat   The Crookes tube located the forceps also   Some difficulty was experienced in bringing forceps and key together, but by the working of the operator's hands on the outside of the boy's body, and assisted by the position of the body, the result was soon achieved the mouth of the forceps was opened by working the sliding handle of the pliable tube, the key dropped into the correct position, and was withdrawn with the tube and forceps

The boy experienced no bad result from the operation, except a temporary difficulty in swallowing liquids, he could swallow solid foods as well as ever.

The key had corroded, and this corrosion had caused the boy's trouble In places the key had by corrosion been reduced to the thickness of a sheet of paper Its angles had become sharp, and it was greatly changed from its original shape

His investigations have been carried out along original lines and he has discovered many scientific truths of great value to the profession He belongs to the Illinois State Homeopathic Society and the Iowa State Medical Society In 1883 he was appointed city physician of Moline, holding the office continuously until 1887, and after a period of five years he was re-appointed in 1892, and again in 1896 He was appointed the first member of the hospital board under the state law, was its secretary for some years, and for two years has been its president

Dr Arp cast his first presidential vote for Blaine in 1884, and has taken quite an active part in local politics In 1896 he supported the silver platform, and in 1897 voted with the Citizens' party in local election. He is a member and examining physician of the McLean Legion of Honor at Moline and the Select Knights, also belongs to the Modern Woodmen of America, and was physician of Camp No 38 for eight years He is a charter member of King Philips Tribe of Improved Order of Red Men The cause of temperance finds in him a staunch advocate

On the 24th of December, 1889 Dr Arp was married in Rock Island, to Miss Mattie Hardy, a native of Wisconsin, and a daughter of Joseph Hardy. She is a graduate of the Rock Island high school, was graduated in music under Professor Kramer, of Davenport, and for two years engaged in teaching music in Chicago The Doctor and his wife have two children A Henry, born in Moline, September 22 1893, and Louis C , born February 10, 1896

PETER LANGBEHN —Many of the most enterprising and prosperous business men of Moline have come from the land beyond the sea, and especially is this true of the many who have left their homes in the German Empire and sought in this land of freedom a refuge from the military despotism and the penury and poverty that so rule their native land Among these quite a prominent figure is the gentleman whose name heads this sketch, and who is now successfully engaged in the bakery and confectionery business at No 516 Fifteenth street, Moline.

Mr. Langbehn was born June 4, 1849, in Holstein, Germany, and is a son of Hans Frederick and Engel Langbehn, the former a shoemaker by trade Our subject attended the schools of his native land until sixteen years of age, and then served a three years' apprenticeship to the bakery and confectionery business, receiving no compensation for his labors with the exception of his board Like all able bodied young men of that country he was forced to enter the army, in which he served for three years during which time he participated in the Franco-German war and was in several severe and hard fought battles of that campaign, among them being the battle of Gravelotte, August 18, 1870, siege and surrender of Metz, September 7-10, 1870, battle of Orleans, December 3-4, 1870, battle of Keaugenayau, December 8, 1870, battle of Epuishayau, January 7, 1871, battle of Lemans, January 11-12, 1871.

For three months after leaving the army Mr Langbehn remained in the fatherland, but on securing his discharge papers he sailed at once for the new world, arriving here in 1873 The first two years were spent in work at his trade in Chicago, where he was able to save much of his wages, and in 1875 he came to Moline, where he continued to follow his chosen calling In 1880 he was able to embark in business for himself in a small way and purchased a lot, whereon he erected a building Having prospered in this venture, in 1897 he built a handsome brick block two stories in height, and one hundred eleven by forty feet in dimensions

In Moline, Mr Langbehn was married in 1878, the lady of his choice being Miss Mary Kroning, also a native of Germany, who died in December, 1892, leaving three children—Henry William, who graduated from Augustana College with the class of 1897, Peter and Frank

In his political affiliations, Mr Langbehn was first a Democrat, but is now a Republican, and religiously he is a member of the Lutheran church of Rock Island He belongs to Doric Lodge, No 319, F & A M, Schiller Lodge, No 11, A O U W, in which he has filled all the chairs, and the Turner Society of Moline, in which he has served in every office, with the exception of president As a representative and prominent citizen of Moline, he should find a place in the history of men of business and enterpris n th t t v wh for c f

character, sterling integrity and control of circumstances have contributed in such an eminent degree to the solidity and progress of the country

CONRAD SCHNEIDER, the oldest grocery merchant in continuous business in Rock Island, now conducts a store at the corner of Twentieth street and Third avenue, and is recognized as one of the busiest, most energetic and most enterprising men of the city By honesty and fair dealing he has secured a liberal share of the public patronage, and to-day enjoys an excellent trade

Mr Schneider was born November 26, 1848, in St Louis, Missouri, and is one of a family of seven children born to Frederick and Margaret (Steininger) Schneider, both natives of Germany, but only two are now living, the other being Maggie, wife of Frederick Schuck The paternal grandfather, who was a farmer by occupation, spent his entire life in Germany, but the maternal grandfather came to the new world and engaged in contracting in St Louis, and afterwards moved to Rock Island and there died at an old age The father of our subject followed the cooper's trade and also carried on farming On crossing the Atlantic he first located in St Louis, but previous to the Civil war he brought his family to Rock Island, where he followed agricultural pursuits He died in 1885 at the age of seventy-three years, but his estimable wife is still living, now making her home with her daughter, Mrs. Schuck Both held membership in the Lutheran church and were highly respected by all who knew them

Our subject obtained his education principally in the schools of Rock Island, and in early life learned the cooper's trade, which he followed for some years For fifteen years he then clerked in the grocery store of Charles Hansgen, where he acquired an excellent knowledge of the business, and after one year spent in the employ of the city undertaker, he opened a grocery store of his own in 1883, since which time he has done a successful business along that line

On the 2d of June, 1873, Mr Schneider was joined in wedlock to Miss Annie Falkenberg, and they now have four children, namely Annie, Eddie, Clara and Waldo The parents are both active and prominent members of the German Lutheran church, in which Mr Schneider is now serving as assistant treasurer Their home is at 2502 Fourth avenue In politics he is a Republican, and he has creditably served his fellow citizens in the capacity of supervisor for eight years

His career proves that the only true success in life is that which is accomplished by personal effort and consecutive industry It proves that the road to success is open to all young men who have the courage to tread its pathway, and the life record of such a man should serve as an inspiration to the young of this and future generations, and teach by incontrovertible facts that success is ambition's answer.

ELMORE W HURST, one of the most able and successful attorneys practicing at the Rock Island county bar, is the junior member of the well-known firm of Jackson & Hurst, whose office is located in the Masonic Temple It is said that the poet is born, not made, but the successful lawyer has to be both born and made—made by close application earnest effort, by perseverance and resolute purpose The abilities with which nature has endowed him must be strengthened and developed by use, and only by merit can the lawyer gain a pre-eminent position such as Mr Hurst has attained

A native of Rock Island, he was born December 6, 1851, and is a son of William and Anna (Hurlock) Hurst, both natives of Delaware, where his grandparents spent their entire lives. The father, who was of English descent, came to Rock Island in 1837, and was prominently identified with its development and prosperity For many years he was one of the leading merchants of the city, where he died in 1892 at the age of eighty-three years, having survived his wife only one month, her death occurring at the age of seventy-six Both were faithful members of the Methodist church and enjoyed the respect and esteem of all who knew them Of their five children three are still living Mary, Julia, wife of M T Stafford, and Elmore W One son, William, was a member of the First Colorado Regiment during the Civil war, and was killed in battle

Mr Hurst, of this review, acquired his literary education in the public schools of Rock Island, and on laying aside his text books entered upon his business career as bookkeeper and later as assistant cashier in the Rock Island National Bank, where he remained for eight years. He then began reading law with W H Gest, and on his admission to the bar in 1883 began practice here, where he has still continued, forming his present partnership with William Jackson in 1891 He has met with excellent success both professionally and financial, and is now a director in the Rock Island

Savings Bank as well as attorney for the same

On the 29th of May, 1873, Mr Hurst was united in marriage to Miss Harriet M Field   They are both active and prominent members of the Methodist church, in which he is serving as trustee, and fraternally he is identified with the Knights of Pythias, the Modern Woodmen of America, and the Ancient Order of United Workmen. As an ardent Democrat, he has taken quite a prominent part in political affairs, on that ticket was elected to the legislature in 1888, and two years later was re-nominated, but declined to again become a candidate   In the fall of 1896 he was an elector on the Bryan and Sewall ticket   Upright, reliable and honorable, his strict adherence to principle commands the respect of all   The place he has won in the legal profession is accorded him in recognition of his skill and ability, and the place which he occupies in the social world is a tribute to that genuine worth and true nobleness of character which are universally recognized and honored   His home is at the corner of Sixth avenue and Nineteenth street

JOHN DEERE CADY, secretary of the Sylvan Steel Works, Moline, was born in New York city, January 26, 1866, and is a son of Merton Y and Alice (Deere) Cady, whose sketch appears elsewhere in this volume   When but six years of age he was taken by his parents to Chicago, where the succeeding five years were spent   In that city he began his education in the public schools, and on the removal of the family to Moline in 1877, he entered the public schools of that city   When sixteen years of age h   l (il)   \ d ms   Aud

over, Massachusetts, from which he graduated two years later

In 1896 he was engaged with the Sylvan Steel Company as time keeper, and went through various promotions till he was made secretary of the company, a position which he now acceptably fills   He is a stockholder in the Davis Company, plumbers of Moline and Rock Island, and was formerly a stockholder in the Moline Elevator Company

At Louisville, Kentucky, April 30, 1896, Mr Cady was united in marriage with Miss Clara Gilmore, a daughter of Emily Ward Gilmore, of that city   They now make their home at No 1213 Eleventh avenue

Politically he is a Republican by birth and inclination   While at Andover he was a member of the K O A, a fraternal society connected with the academy   In the social circles of Moline and Rock Island both occupy a prominent place, and have many warm friends

ANSON MILETUS HUBBARD —Years of quiet usefulness and a life in which the old-fashioned virtues of sincerity, industry and integrity are exemplified have a simple beauty that no word can portray   Youth has its charms, but an honorable and honored old age, to which the lengthening years have added dignity and sweetness, has a brighter radiance, as if some ray from the life beyond rested upon it

Mr Hubbard is a man who makes old age seem the better portion of life   He is now living retired at 1928 Seventh avenue, Moline, Illinois, enjoying the rest which should always follow a long and useful career

He is descended from an old and prominent family only that was early founded in the new world, he having been the third son of Rufus Hubbard, who was the third son of David Hubbard, who was in the Revolutionary war and who was the son of Jonathan Hubbard, who was the son of Ephriam Hubbard, who was the son of John Hubbard, who was the son of John Hubbard, who was the son of George Hubbard, who was born in England in 1595, and landed at Watertown (now within the limits of Boston, Mass) in 1633, with his wife and two sons, George and John, the first named being about thirteen years of age Tradition says he was from Glastonbury in Somersetshire, and again from Surrey, with some slight preponderance in favor of the latter place

Anson M. Hubbard is then the eighth in line from George Hubbard the American emigrant, who was the progenitor of a large part of the New England Hubbards, and who traces his connection more or less distinctly to "Hubba the Dane," a "Norse sea king, who with his brother, Hingua, landed with an immense fleet and twenty thousand warriors on the coast of East Anglia, or Kent (England), to avenge the death of their father, who had been killed in a former incursion of the Danes" They fortified their camp strongly and awaited reinforcements from the Baltic, spending the winter in procuring horses and corrupting the loyalty of some of the Northumbrian chieftains toward their own king, Ethelred In February, 867, they left their camp on the coast and marched landward and seized York Kings Osbert and Ælla patched up a truce between themselves, united their forces and engaged Hingua and Hubba outside of the city, and eventually drove them back within its walls

The Northumbrians battered breaches in
25

the walls, rushed through and fell upon Hingua's and Hubba's forces with great vigor and fury, but the ferocious Norsemen in their savage desperation finally turned and dispelled their relentless foes Osbert was killed and Ælla was taken prisoner This last victory gave to Hingua and Hubba undisputed possession of all that dominion south of the Tyne and north of Nottingham The native inhabitants were constrained to purchase the friendship of Hingua and Hubba, who immediately began to prepare for a southern invasion

Leaving a small force in possession of York, to cultivate the country and retain possession of it, they proceeded against Ethelred and Alfred (afterwards Alfred the Great). They crossed the Humber into Lincolnshire, burned the rich monastery of Bardenay and put its occupants to the sword. A small army of Saxons in the district of Kestevan stopped their progress for one day, but soon the victorious invaders were sweeping on to the monastery of Croyland Having pillaged and burned the monastery they marched to Medeshampsted, where the inhabitants resisted them stoutly and wounded Hingua. From the ashes of Medeshamsted they proceeded on to Huntington, destroying it, then took the Isle of Ely They met Ethelred and Alfred the Great at Excesdune [Aston] and after a terrific battle were routed and in confusion fled as far as Reading A solitary thorn tree marks the spot on which the Danes were defeated

Other battles were fought at Basing and Morton, in which the Danes were victorious, they having received fresh reinforcements from the Baltic Ethelred was killed and then the invaders returned to Reading to divide their spoils, and rejoice in the glory of their conquests In 8-8 Hingua and

Hubba, with a fleet of twenty-three ships, ravaged the coast of Demetia or South Wales, and crossing to the northern coast of Devonshire, the sanguinous Hubba landed his troops in the vicinity of Apledore It appears as if the two brothers had previously agreed to crush the king (Alfred) between the pressure of their respective armies

At the castle of Kynwoith, built upon an almost impregnable rock, Odun, the Saxon leader, took his position The Danish leader (Hubba) was too wary to hazard an assault, and calmly pitched his tents at the foot of the mountain, in the confident expectation that the want of water would force the garrison to surrender But Odun, gathering courage from despair, silently left his entrenchments at the dawn of morning, burst into Hubba's camp, slew him with twelve hundred of his followers, and then drove the remnant of the routed army to their fleet

Thus perished Hubba, and also for a long time the martial fire that burned in the breasts of the adventurous Danes, though Hingua afterward invaded Ireland, but was killed there, while Halfdene and Gothrun, the successors of Hingua and Hubba, made very creditable stands against Alfred the Great, at Ethandune Gothrun was captured by King Alfred, but was permitted to live, on the condition of his embracing Christianity, which he accepted, and with thirty of his followers was baptized at Aulre, Alfred being Gothrun's godfather. They jointly signed a compact, wherein it was declared that "the lives of Englishmen and Danes were of equal value." The "Hinguas," the "Gothruns" and the "Hubbas," then in the main, adopted the names of their kings with the habits of civilization, and acq   , soil helped

the Britains to protect it against subsequent marauding invaders, and sometimes these unwelcome visitors were their own erstwhile countrymen, but their allegiance to their adopted country was true, and they became during Britain's rapid advancement toward commercial and agricultural supremacy, her most skilled and reliable husbandmen

The rapid and extensive movements of Hubba over the territory now England and Wales, and his penchant for encamping upon and fortifying high places has been of great value to the historical and archeological student, leaving as he did indubitable traces of his remarkable marches

Throughout England and Wales have existed seven historic eminences, that have borne the name of "Hubba's Hill."

Francis Grose, F A. S , in his Antiquities of England and Wales, thus refers to a spot known as Hubba's Stone Priory (also Hubberston or Hubbaston). "The ruin stands in Pembrokeshire, not far from Milford Haven, and is called by the inhabitants the priory; but whether for monks or nuns, or what order, and when and by whom founded are particulars not handed down by tradition, or at least not known by the generality of the neighboring people —[See Grose's Antiquities of England and Wales, also H P Hubbard's One Thousand Years of Hubbard History]

After the death of King Hubba by Odun in 878 Hubba's descendants populated Eastern and Southeastern England from the River Humber down to the English channel, comprising mainly Lincolnshire, Rutland, Cambridge, Norfolk, Suffolk, Essex and Kent

They engaged principally in agriculture, horticulture and floriculture and their doings to the historical terret remain hidden up to about the thirteenth century, since which time, some of them at least, have come more prominently into public notice, as shown by the various grants of arms awarded to "Hibbards," "Hubbarts," "Hobarts," "Hubberts," "Huberts," "Hubarts," and "Hubberds," being grants made at different times, to the Hubbard tree trunk, according to registered data, in the Herald's College, London, a universally acknowledged authority Two or three of earlier and later names may be mentioned

"John Hubbard was born about 1235, and lived in Tye, Norfolk " No record of his death. "Thomas Hubbard, a descendant and heir of John, was born about 1400, and lived at Leyham, Norfolk " No record of his death He left sons, James and William Sir James Hubbard was the youngest son of Thomas Hubbard, of Leyham, Norfolk, and was born about 1425 He represented in Parliament in 1467 and 1478 Ipswich Norfolk, after having become a member of the bar at Lincoln's Inn, during the time of King Henry VII He was one of the governors of this famed law school from 1479 to 1503 November 1, 1486, he was created attorney-general of England, by King Henry VII, and soon thereafter sworn of the privy council He rendered good service to his sovereign during the coast fisheries difficulty, in November of 1487, and was knighted February 18, 1502-3 Sir James died in 1507, and was buried in Norwich Cathedral.

Right Hon. John Gellibrand Hubbard, eldest son of John, of Stratford Grove, Essex (who died in 1847), was born March 21, 1805. He was educated at Bordeaux, France, was a well-known Russian merchant, as was his father, and represented the shire of Buckingham from 1859 to 1868

in the House of Commons, where he was recognized as a rare authority upon finance, and for many years was one of the directors of the Bank of England, of which he afterward became Governor-General. From 1874 to 1887 he represented the city of London in Parliament He built and endowed St Alban's church, Holborn, which was consecrated February 26, 1863 July 22, 1887, he was raised to the Peerage, and made Lord Addington, of Addington Manor, Surrey The Baron married May 19, 1837, the Hon Maria Margaret Napier, now Dowager Lady Addington, eldest daughter of William John, the eighth Lord Napier To them were born sons and daughters His death occurred at Addington Manor, August 28, 1889, and he was buried in the parish churchyard.

Anson Melitus Hubbard was born October 10, 1818, at Bergen, Genesee county, New York. His ancestor, George Hubbard, the progenitor of this branch of the family, after remaining two years in Watertown settled in 1635 upon a tract of land fronting upon the Connecticut river, six miles below Hartford, which he, with others, purchased of the Indians These lands were called the "Naubuc Farms," and extended three "large miles" back from the river His portion of this land has remained continuously in the possession of his descendants since that time, Rufus Hubbard, the father of Anson M, having been born in 1789 on this same farm, which is in the present township of Glastonbury, Hartford county, Connecticut

Anson M Hubbard came west to Illinois with his father in 1836, stopping at Fairfield (now Mendon), Adams county, one year, and removing in 1837 to Geneseo, Henry county, in the same state In the

east he had received excellent educational advantages, and had become quite proficient in
music   He was about eighteen years of
age at the time of the removal to Illinois
and for some time assisted his father in developing and improving the home farm
After locating at Geneseo, he resumed the
study of music under the instruction of Professor Samuel R Bacon, of that place, and
afterward with Professor Thomas Hastings,
of New York city, and later with Doctor
Lowell Mason, of Boston, Massachusetts
In 1840 he began teaching both vocal and
instrumental music, and continued teaching and dealing in musical merchandise for
many years, the principal fields of his operations being Henry, Whiteside and Rock
Island counties

In 1843 he married Miss Marietta M
Moore, of Ellisville, Fulton county, Illinois,
and in 1844 removed to Moline, Rock Isl-
and county, in the same state   Mrs Hubbard is a daughter of John and Mary (Lyon)
Moore, the former a native of Riverhead,
Long Island, and the latter of Newburg,
New York   Her maternal grandfather,
Moses Lyon, was a general in the Revolutionary war, and was an intimate friend
of General Washington   General Lyon of
the Civil war belonged to the same family

To Mr and Mrs Hubbard were born
four children   Charles E , who died in
1878, at the age of thirty-four years, leaving a wife and one child, a daughter   He
was for many years organist in the First
Congregational church of Moline, beginning
at the age of nineteen, and playing almost
continuously until his death   His daughter,
Mrs. Florence Hubbard Joslin, now fills the
same position   Georgiana M , now the
widow of ⁿ   I Γ Γ al i   ith lei - ni
Roy Cha   l   with fii parent-

William H , a master mechanic in a large
smelting works in Pueblo, Colorado, is
married and has three children   Horace S ,
the youngest, is married and engaged in
business in Chicago

Mr Hubbard became a fine bass singer,
an excellent choir leader and singing teacher,
teaching the old-fashioned " singing school "
for many years, traveling from place to
place in his own conveyance   In 1844 he
became the leader of the choir of the First
Congregational church of Moline, leading it
continuously for thirty-five years, with the
exception of eight years spent upon a farm
near Geneseo, Henry county, Illinois, to
which place he removed in 1854, and during
which time he performed a similar service
there, for about two years   For the first
few months of his stay upon the farm he returned each week to lead the choir in Moline, thus finishing his engagement for the
year

At one time in 1892 there were seven
Hubbards in this choir, the leader, his wife
and a son and daughter, singers, another son
as organist, and a younger brother and sister
of his own, singers.   During the winter of
1863-4 he was the conductor of a musical
allegory, called " The Great Rebellion, "
which was played in Moline, Rock Island,
Davenport, and Geneseo, at which perform-
ances nearly two thousand dollars were
raised for the aid societies of these places,
for the benefit of sick and disabled soldiers
of the Civil war, which the allegory represented   From seventy-five to eighty per-
formers took part in this allegory, including
a lieutenant and eleven soldiers from Rock
Island Arsenal, kindly granted by General
Rodman, commandant   A younger brother
and sister (twins) of the leader and his three
sons and daughter took part

In 1844 he organized the first brass band in Moline, which at that time was the only one within a radius of one hundred miles and it was playing for the first time at a public celebration on July 4, 1845, in Rock Island, the day of the murder of Colonel George Davenport, on the Government Island   He led this band for ten years, playing on all public occasions and celebrations both on land and river throughout the surrounding counties   This band played on the occasion of the arrival of the first passenger train over the Chicago & Rock Island road in 1853, and later at a banquet in Rock Island, February 22, 1854, in honor of the new road   Three of the original members of this band are still living the leader, and two brothers, Thomas Merryman, in Moline, and Joseph Merryman, in Denver, Colorado

Mr Hubbard united with the Congregational church of his native place at twelve years of age, thereafter identifying himself with the Congregational church of each place of residence   He was one of the earliest members of the First Congregational church of Moline, beginning his work with it in the same year of its organization   He has served officially as trustee, clerk and deacon for many years and still holds the latter office

Mr Hubbard, who is numbered among the pioneers, was president of the Rock Island County Old Settlers' Association in 1888   He was instrumental, with others, in the organization of the Central Illinois Musical Association, which met at various times in Quincy, Alton, Springfield, Jacksonville, Peoria, and Galesburg, holding musical festivals, which were conducted by William B Bradbury and George F Root   Of this association Mr Hubbard also served as president

He cast his first presidential ballot in 1840 voting for William Henry Harrison, or "Tippecanoe and Tyler, too," but since 1856 has been a strong Republican   He was one of eight old gentlemen, who, having worked and voted for William Henry Harrison, the grandfather, in 1840, formed themselves into a "Tippecanoe Club," and worked and voted for Benjamin Harrison, the grandson, in 1888, riding in several processions, during that campaign

In 1862 he purchased the interest of E S Waterman in the hotel known as the old Moline House, and besides the public, entertained many Union soldiers, and many Confederate prisoners, as they were paroled, and discharged from the government prison on Rock Island, these last-named men being in great demand during corn-picking, especially on the surrounding farms, some of the farmers coming fifty miles to secure such help   Continuing in this house until the close of the war in 1865, he removed to and opened another hotel, naming it the Central House, which he successfully conducted four years, thus making seven years in the hotel business

During the year 1862 he was appointed police magistrate, by Governor Yates, to fill a vacancy of three years, caused by the resignation of Mr Waterman, who was leaving the state   At the close of this term, he was elected for, and served another term of four years, making seven years of capable service in this office   Declining a further nomination, he then gave his attention to his profession, and the tuning of organs and pianos, still doing something at the latter, for the accommodation of his friends

Mr and Mrs Hubbard celebrated their silver wedding, March 31, 1868, with all their children at home   In 1893, they celebrated their golden wedding, with their daughter and her son, and their youngest son and his wife at home   Fifty or more of their friends surprised them during the evening, bringing with them as a gift, a full set of twenty-five volumes of the " Encyclopaedia Brittanica," than which nothing could have suited better, or be more valued by all the family

Mr Hubbard is a firm believer in a Divine Providence,

'There's a divinity that shapes our ends,
Rough hew them how we will

The evidence upon which this belief is founded is, his own experience in choosing his profession, when the partial plan he had formed for his life-work seemed to be "hedged in;" and the door leading in the opposite direction, he was, by invitation, aptness, circumstances and surroundings impelled to enter. And now he accepts the situation, and looking back over the field, says: "It is well "

For fifty-three years he has been identified with the interests of Moline, has watched with interest its growth and progress, and deserves to be numbered among its honored pioneers and valued citizens   His long and useful career has gained for him the respect and esteem of all with whom he has come in contact and his friends are many throughout this section of the state

JOHN W. STEWART, M D , is one of the most prominent business men of Rock Island   Young men in the past have often been deterred from devoting themselves to a business life because of the widespread impression that such a life yields no opportunity for the display of genius   The time, how   "   to which other

things being equal, the business man must take a secondary place to the lawyer, the doctor, the minister or the editor   In fact, as a rule, let the business man be equally equipped by education and natural endowment and you will find him to-day in every community exerting a wider influence and wielding a larger power than a man of equal capacity treading other walks of life   The " men of affairs " have come to be in a large degree the men upon whom the country leans   The subject of this sketch is pre-eminently a " man of affairs," and is now conducting a wholesale business, dealing in shelf and heavy hardware, blacksmith's and machinist's supplies

Dr Stewart was born in Frederick county, Maryland, January 21, 1844, and is a representative of an old and honored family of that state   His grandfather, John Stewart, was born there and was identified with its business interests as a farmer and merchant   In the days of slavery he owned a number of negroes, but when twenty-eight years of age he set them at liberty   He was of Scotch-Irish descent, and died at the age of eighty-eight   Six of his children reached mature years, one of whom was Dr Alexander Stewart, of Shippensburg, Pennsylvania   Our subject is also a cousin of Judge Stewart, a prominent jurist of Chambersburg, Pennsylvania. His father, John S. Stewart, was born in Maryland and married Margaret B Witherow, a daughter of John Witherow, of Scotch-Irish ancestry   He was born in Maryland, and made farming his life work   The parents of our subject had but two children. The elder is Rosa J., widow of James C Annan, of Emmitsburg, Maryland, who is a son of Dr Andrew Annan a prominent abolitionist, who on the morning of the battle of Gettysburg drove over the scene of the conflict with General Reynolds, who was killed later in the day, and whose monument now stands at the entrance of the Gettysburg cemetery Dr Annan died in Emmitsburg, Maryland, at the advanced age of ninety-two The father of our subject died in 1852, aged forty years For many years he was a member of the Presbyterian church and died in the faith Mrs Stewart afterward became the wife of Rev Robert S Grier, who served as pastor of one church for fifty-two years She is now a widow for the second time. A devoted member of the Presbyterian church, she has spent a long life in the Master's service

Dr Stewart, of this review, was reared in his native county, and after attending the schools of Emmitsburg pursued his studies in Tuscarora Academy of Pennsylvania, and was graduated at LaFayette College, of Easton, Pennsylvania He then studied medicine, was graduated at the University of Pennsylvania with the class of 1867, and engaged in practice in Dayton, Ohio, and at the Soldiers' Home He was the physician at the latter place until September, 1869, when he came to Rock Island, and succeeded to the hardware business formerly owned by Harper & Co _ His time and attention has since then been devoted to mercantile pursuits For eighteen years he was associated in partnership with Captain James M. Montgomery, but since 1892 has been alone in business He is in the wholesale trade and carries a large stock of shelf and heavy hardware, blacksmith's and machinist's supplies, and takes large contracts for furnishing goods in his line The house is represented by several traveling salesmen and his business has assumed extensive proportions Dr. Stewart is a man of keen

discrimination, sound judgment and great enterprise and his business methods commend him to the confidence and support of all He is also a director in the Rock Island Building & Loan Association, and has been an active factor in many interests that have advanced the welfare of his adopted city

On the 5th of December, 1867, Dr Stewart married Miss Rosa B McLean, daughter of William and Nancy (Johnston) McLean, natives of Pennsylvania, the former born in Adams county, near Gettysburg, the latter near Shippensburg, Cumberland county. James McLean, the paternal grandfather, was born in Adams county, of Scotch-Irish parentage, and was a descendant of William McLean, who located in that locality in 1832, the first of the name to establish a home there. He wedded Margaret Reid, and had four children He died in middle life, his wife surviving him a number of years He was a relative of the McLean who surveyed the Mason and Dixon Line, and other representatives of his family were prominent in the war of the Revolution George Johnson, the maternal grandfather of Mrs Stewart, was also born in Pennsylvania, and was of Scotch-Irish descent. He made farming his life work and accumulated a handsome property He married Margaret Maxwell, and they had twelve children

Mr McLean, father of Mrs Stewart, engaged in the manufacture of leather at various points in eastern Pennsylvania and was an extensive land owner He and his wife held membership with the Presbyterian church at Shippensburg, and he served as its treasurer for many years His death occurred in Shippensburg December 22, 1892, in his eighty-fifth year, and his wife passed away in 1880, aged seventy-three years. They had eight children, of whom three are now living—Margaret Reid, wife of J R McCalister, of Pittsburg, Rosa B , wife of our subject, and Florence Edith, wife of George C. Coughlin, of Norristown, Pennsylvania. Those deceased are Nancy, wife of Lieutenant William Harper, who served in the late war, Mary C , wife of George H Stewart, of Shippensburg, Pennsylvania, James E., a graduate of Princeton College, who was collector at the port of Chicago during the time of the great fire there, and at one time a partner of Orville Grant, of Chicago, in the leather business He was a man of much prominence and superior ability, and at the time of his death was president of a bank in Shippensburg George, a corporal of the One Hundred and Thirtieth Pennsylvania Infantry, was wounded at the battle of Fredricksburg in in 1862, and died in Harewood Hospital, Washington, nine days later, but was buried at Shippensburg Sarah E died in infancy

Mrs Stewart is a graduate of Oakland Institute of Pennsylvania By her marriage she has become the mother of four sons and four daughters· Florence A is a graduate of the art department in Wilson College, Pennsylvania William McLean is a graduate of Augustana College and is now traveling in the interests of the house Alexander is a graduate of the law department of Michigan University, Ann Arbor, Michigan Margaret completed the regular course and was graduated from Wilson College, Pennsylvania John S , a graduate of the Rock Island High School, is now associated with his father in business Nancy J., who is a graduate of the Rock Island High School, Rosabel and James E , are at home Dr and Mrs Stewart have provid-

ed their children with excellent educational advantages and their home is the center of a cultured society circle They reside in a commodious residence, which was erected by the Doctor in 1872, at the corner of Nineteenth street and Eighth avenue He is president of the Augustana University Association, and he and his wife are prominent members of the Broadway Presbyterian church, in which he has served as elder and Sunday-school superintendent since the organization of the church. By his ballot he supports the Republican party, but otherwise is not actively interested in political affairs Mrs Stewart advocates the principles of the Prohibition party He is a man of broad general information and culture, and of superior intellectual endowments, of much force of character, and possesses in a large degree those qualities which indicate the high minded man and which throughout the world command respect and regard

JOHN EDGAR POOLE, of Moline, was born in Yarmouth, in the province of Nova Scotia, February 18, 1840

"The ancient family of Poole, of Poole Hall, took its surname from the lordship of Poole in Cheshire, England Sir William Poole was sheriff of Cheshire the sixteenth year of Henry VIII, 1525 A D Sir Francis Poole, member of parliament for Lewis, in 1743 married Frances, daughter of Henry Pelham, Esq , of Lewis, Sussex, and their daughter, Frances, married Henry, second viscount Palmerston in 1767 " Squire Poole, the progenitor of the Yarmouth branch of the family, was descended in the sixth generation from John Poole, the earliest record of whom in America is that he was an inhabitant of

Cambridge, then Newtown, Massachusetts, in 1632 His name is found with that of Thomas Dudley, Symon Bradstreet and five others as being among the earliest settlers of that place. It is thought that he is one of those who came over with Governor Winthrop, of whom a considerable number having landed at Salem, proceeded to the present site of Cambridge and established a permanent settlement there About 1635 John Poole removed to Lynn, which then embraced the towns of Reading, Wakefield, Lynnfield and parts of Woburn, Saugus and Chelsea There he owned two hundred acres of land, and was the wealthiest settler in Reading township at the time it was set apart from Lynn in 1639 He lived in that section which subsequently became Wakefield and the original Poole homestead occupied the site of the Wakefield rattan factory. John Poole built the first grist and fuller mill in Wakefield in 1664, and in addition owned a large tract of land at the north end of the "great pond," where he built the first sawmill in the town He also had a farm at Lynnfield He died February 1, 1667, and his wife, Margaret, passed away April 19, 1662 In his will, dated February 14, 1662, he divided his property between his only son, Jonathan, and his grandson, John.

Captain Jonathan Poole was born in Cambridge in 1634, and inherited from his father the old homestead and large tracts of land at the north end of the "great pond " He was the second man to serve as captain of the Reading Militia, and according to the historian Savage, his services in King Philip's war were much prized In October, 1671, he was appointed quartermaster, and in May, 1674, cornet to the Three County Troop, a leading military company of those days, and was holding the latter office at the time of King Philip's war in 1675 In the summer he saw active service under Lieutenant Hasey In the campaign under Major Appleton in the fall he held important positions He commanded the garrison forces and Quaboog in September and in October moved his troops to Hadley, being assigned to the defense of Hatfield When that place was attacked by the Indians on the 19th of October he was in command of a company and successfully defended the north side of the town. When Major Appleton had the command of the army of the west suddenly thrust upon him he felt his great responsibility and sought to strengthen his position by calling to his aid efficient officers He promoted Cornet Poole to a captaincy, not having time to consult the council, to whom he afterward sent word of his action They replied that it was his place to recommend and theirs to promote Major Appleton then sent Mr Poole with letters to the council and his demeanor was such as to win their approval and his promotion was confirmed He then had command of Connecticut towns until April 7, 1676 He was married in 1665 to Judith Whittingham, by whom he had ten children One daughter, Sarah, became the wife of Deacon Thomas Bancroft, an ancestor of George Bancroft, the historian

One son, Jonathan Poole, married Bridget Fitch, and among his many descendants are those noted for rare literary attainment These include Fitch Poole, who founded in South Danvers, now Peabody, Massachusetts, the first temperance society in America His son, Fitch, was the first librarian of Peabody Institute and the author of several humorous sketches

Charles Henry Poole, of Washington, D C , was the author of several topographical and engineering reports and had almost completed a genealogical history of the Poole family at the time of his death in 1880 Dr William Frederick Poole was the librarian of the Chicago Public Library and afterward of the Newbury Library of that city, was considered the most eminent librarian of his time and was the author of Poole's index to periodical literature   Henry Ward Poole, A M., professor of modern languages in the National College of Mines in Mexico, was an authority on mathematics and the nature of musical sounds, was the inventor of Poole's enharmonic organ and a noted collector of rare books and curios

Captain Jonathan Poole was a justice of the peace, a selectman for twelve years, president of the council of war from 1675 until 1676, and a representative to the general court in 1677   He died December 24, 1678   His eldest son, Lieutenant John Poole, was born at the old homestead, September 20, 1665, and inherited from his grandfather a large tract of land at the northern end of "great pond.'   He was an officer in the Indian wars   He wedded Mary Goodwin and had twelve children, the eldest of whom, also named John, was born at Reading, January 20, 1689, and succeeded to the ownership of the homestead   He married Sarah Eaton. Of their six children, Jonathan Poole was born at Reading, January 20, 1720   He was twice married   He wedded Mary Leman, and after her death, Mary Sheldon. By the second union he had four children, including Samuel Sheldon Poole, who was born March 25, 1751, in Reading, Massachusetts He was a   '   t the   of

1770, and at the breaking out of hostilities he refused to renounce his allegiance to the King and removed to Yarmouth, Nova Scotia, in 1774   He was married there October 19, 1775, to Elizabeth, daughter of Captain Seth Barnes, who was born in Plymouth, Massachusetts, and descended from the Mayflower stock   Mr Poole was elected justice of the peace in 1785, and the same year elected a member of the provincial parliament at Halifax. He was re-elected for fifty years thereafter with the exception of the years 1800, 1804, 1811 and 1814   He died October 7, 1835, and was buried at Yarmouth   He taught school while in Nova Scotia, and some times officiated as a minister in the absence of the regular preacher in districts where the people were too poor to employ a pastor. For thirty years he was *Custos Rotulorum* for the county, was probate judge for a few years and also a school commissioner in 1809   He was an original shareholder in the Yarmouth Marine Insurance Association and in 1809 was the owner of the largest vessel in the country, the brig Falkirk, of one hundred and eighty-one tons   His grandson, Captain John Poole, the father of our subject, was born in Yarmouth in 1812, went to sea at the age of fifteen and when twenty years of age was captain of a ship   He never lost but one vessel, of which he was master, in forty years of experience   This was in midocean and after eight days of untold suffering from hunger and thirst, he and his crew were taken off of what remained of the wreck above water (by an Austrian war ship, having on board the personal effects of the late Emperor Maximilian, of Mexico, after that unfortunate adventurer had been executed 'y the victorious General Juerez) and was landed at Gibraltar He married Harriet Dane, and their son John Edgar is the immediate subject of this review

Mr Poole, now a leading citizen of Moline, obtained his education in the common schools, and after making several voyages to the West Indies with his father, commenced life at the age of sixteen as clerk in a general merchandise store in Yarmouth In 1858 he accepted a position as bookkeeper with the firm of Kenny, Hawkins & Co , in St John, New Brunswick, doing an extensive ship commission business From here he went to Indianapolis in 1863, accepting a like position in a wholesale drug store From this city he went to Chicago in 1862, where he resided until 1877, when he accepted the position of bookkeeper for the extensive plow manufacturing company of Deere & Co , which position he has held continuously up to the present time In 1864 Mr Poole was married to Annie Humphries, of St John, New Brunswick His residence is at 1920 Fifth avenue.

MERTON YALE CADY, the well-known architect and decorator of Moline, Illinois, comes of a family noted for its inventive genius, and which is of English descent, being founded in this country prior to the Revolutionary war His father, Ira L Cady, was a native of Connecticut, but grew to manhood in New York He married Miss Clotilda Yale, daughter of Linus Yale, the inventor of the famous Yale lock, and a direct descendant of Elihu Yale, of New Haven, Connecticut, the founder of Yale College Few men are better known in the scientific world than Linus Yale, who not only invented the celebrated lock which bears his name, but other inventions, among

which was a threshing machine, which was afterward patented and manufactured by his son

Ira L Cady was by profession a bank lock expert, and was engaged in the manufacture and sale of burglar proof safes and safe locks the greater part of his life He made his home in Newport for many years, and there reared his family In 1857 he removed to New York city where he spent his remaining days, dying in 1886 His wife survived him five years, dying in 1891 Their remains were interred in the beautiful Greenwood cemetery, in Brooklyn

The subject of this sketch is the oldest in the family of four children, all of whom grew to mature years, but one is now deceased His boyhood and youth were spent in Newport, New York, and in the public schools he received his primary education Later he attended the Cooper Institute at Cooperstown, New York, until seventeen years of age, when he went with his parents to New York City and for the next five years was engaged in learning the trade of iron architecture Being possessed of a natural genius for mechanics, a characteristic which he undoubtedly inherited from his grandfather Yale, he turned his attention to various pursuits, and finally became a bank lock expert, with a thorough knowledge of all the mechanical details of his calling Until 1872 he followed his profession in New York City, and then removed to Chicago, where he continued in the same line until 1877, when he removed to Moline

On coming to Moline Mr Cady turned his attention to architectural work, and furnished plans and specifications for many of the public and private buildings of Moline and Rock Island, among which are the postoffice and nearly all the buildings of the great manufactory of the John Deere Company In 1882 he visited many of the principal cities of Europe, with the view of studying interior decorations After spending some months abroad, especially in Italy, where great attention is given that art, he returned home, and has since combined interior decoration with his architectural profession In both lines he is acknowledged as authority, and in all that he does is shown the skill of the natural mechanic and the natural artist

In 1865 Mr Cady was united in marriage with Miss Alice Deere, the youngest daughter of the Hon John Deere, the well-known inventor whose fame is world-wide, and a sketch of whom appears elsewhere in this work. By this union two children have been born, John Deere Cady, now secretary of the Sylvan Steel Works of Moline, Alice Mabel, graduating at Miss Annie Brown s school 715 Fifth avenue, New York, in 1891 She married Charles Porter Skinner, of Davis county, Rhode Island, June 4, 1894 The family reside in the old home of John Deere, which was inherited by Mrs Cady, on the death of her father in 1887. It is situated upon the summit of the bluff overlooking the Mississippi river, and commands a view of unsurpassed beauty of scenery

Politically, Mr. Cady is a stanch Republican, having an abiding faith in the principles of that party His zeal for party does not run, however, to office seeking, but only in that quiet advocacy of its principles and the casting of his ballot for its nominees in all general elections His business interests and love of art have a stronger hold upon him than all things of a political nature He is essentially a home man, and because his profession as a lock expert called him   it

up and turned his attention exclusively to architecture and decorative art

Religiously Mr Cady and family are Congregationalists, holding membership in the First Congregational church, Moline In the various lines of church work they contribute of their time and means, and in all philanthropic work in their midst join heart and hand As a citizen, Mr Cady is esteemed by all, and is a gentleman in the highest sense of the term. His wife has here spent almost her entire life and is respected for her many excellent traits of character For some years they have spent their summer in the mountains, but are always glad to return to their beautiful home on the banks of the Father of Waters, where they know that they are surrounded by many warm friends, who will always wish them long life with much joy and happiness.

CHARLES J SEARLE —Whatever may be said of the legal fraternity, it cannot be denied that members of the bar have been more prominent actors in public affairs than any other class of the community. This is but the natural result of causes which are manifest and require no explanation The ability and training which qualify one to practice law also qualify him in many respects for duties which lie outside the strict path of his profession and which touch the general interests of society Holding marked precedence among the members of the bar of Rock Island county, and retaining a clientele of so representative a character as to alone stand in evidence of his professional ability and personal popularity, Mr. Searle must assuredly be accorded a place in this volume He is not only at the the head of a large general practice, but is also serving his second term as state's attorney with office in the Mitchell & Lynde building, Rock Island

Mr Searle, was born in Fort Smith, Arkansas, May 16, 1865, and is a son of Elhanan J and Cassie R (Pierce) Searle, the former a native of Ohio and the latter of Illinois Of the six children born to them, only two are now living,—Charles J and Blanche. The paternal grandfather, James Searle, was born in Ohio, of English ancestry, and in 1837 became a pioneer settler of Rock Island county, where he followed agricultural pursuits throughout the remainder of his life He reared a large family and died in 1876 at about the age of seventy-five years Charles R Pierce, the maternal grandfather of our subject, was also of English origin, and was a native of Kentucky, when he emigrated to Sangamon county, Illinois, in 1825, making his early home in the same neighborhood with Abraham Lincoln He remained there until a few years before his death, when he removed to Leavenworth, Kansas, where he passed away at the ripe old age of eighty-four years During the Black Hawk war he was a member of a company from Macon county and was prominently identified with the early development of that state By occupation he was a farmer and stock raiser.

At an early date Elhanan Searle, our subject's father, became a resident of Rock Island county, and on attaining his majority entered the Northwestern University at Evanston A short time previous to the outbreak of the Civil war he began the study of law in the office of Lincoln & Herndon, but when the south took up arms against the general government he responded to the president's call for troops, enlisting in the Tenth Illinois Cavalry Later

he became colonel of an Arkansas regiment, and for four years and one month faithfully fought for the old flag and the cause it represented Subsequently he successfully engaged in the practice of law at Fort Smith, Arkansas, for some time served as district judge, and was later appointed to fill a vacancy on the supreme bench On the expiration of that term he was elected to the same position, but at the end of two years resigned and returned north After practicing for some years in Chicago he removed to St Louis, where he continued to prosecute his profession for about three years, but since that time has lived retired, making his home in Rock Island for the past seven years The family occupy the old homestead of General Rodman at 2601 Eight and a half avenue Mrs Searle is a consistent member of the Christian church.

Charles J Searle was about three years old when he accompanied his parents on their removal to Arkadelphia, Arkansas, and later went with them to Little Rock, where he attended the common schools After coming north he pursued his studies in the common schools of Chicago and the high school of Pana, Illinois, after which he went to Marshall county, Kansas, where he improved a farm and engaged in teaching for one term For one year he was a student in the Campbell Normal University at Holton, that state, where he carried off all the honors of his class, and then taught another term of school in Brown county, Kansas He then entered the Iowa State University at Iowa City, where he completed the two-years' law course, and at that institution took all the honors of both the junior and senior classes, and was also prominent in the athletic exercises.

After looking around for a location, Mr

Searle finally decided on Rock Island, where he opened an office August 12, 1889, becoming the youngest member of the Rock Island county bar. His skill and ability soon winning recognition, he is now at the head of a large and lucrative practice. In 1890 he stumped his congressional district in the interest of the Republican party, and has since taken quite an active and prominent part in political affairs. In 1892 he was elected state's attorney, running more than five hundred votes ahead of his ticket, was nominated by acclamation four years later, and re-elected by a majority of nearly three thousand—a fact which plainly indicates his popularity and the high position he occupies among his professional brethren. As a fluent, earnest and convincing advocate he has but few equals. Always dignified and courteous, he commands alike the respect of the court and the esteem of his associates at the bar. He has always taken an active interest in all public matters, being particularly instrumental in securing the new court house and the location of the Northern Hospital for the Insane. Socially he is a member of the Knights of Pythias and Sons of Veterans.

GEORGE E. BAILEY, subject of this sketch, has for many years been identified with the business interests of Rock Island. Upon the commercial activity of a community depends its prosperity, and the men who are now recognized as leading citizens are those who are at the head of extensive business enterprises. He is a man of broad capabilities, who carries forward to a successful completion whatever he undertakes. He is one of the leading grocers of Rock Island, member of the firm of

George E. Bailey & Co., located at 1611 and 1613 Second avenue.

Mr. Bailey was born in Troy, Vermont, June 18, 1840, the fourth child and third son of James P. and Mary A. (Hall) Bailey, also natives of the Green Mountain state, in whose family were ten children: Saloma, a widow of A. H. Pierce, of Lewis, Iowa, Hosford H., Colwell L., deceased, George E., Charles O., William A., John B., Sarah A., wife of D. P. Van Horn, of Cotter, Iowa, James Edgar, deceased, and Oscar P., deceased. In early life the father was colonel in the state militia of Vermont, and was called out to settle a difficulty with the Canadians in 1837. In 1852 he removed to Columbus City, Iowa, where he followed the occupation of farming, until called to his final rest in 1891, at the age of eighty-two years. His wife still survives at the age of eighty-two. In the east they held membership in the Baptist church, but in Iowa joined the Methodist church, of which they became active and prominent members. The father greatly assisted Governor Kirkwood in organizing troops for the late war.

The paternal grandfather of our subject, Samuel Bailey, was also a native of Vermont, and was a soldier in the war of 1812. In early life he followed the carpenter's trade, and engaged in bridge building and contracting. He died at the advanced age of ninety years, while the maternal grandfather, James Hall, a native of Vermont, died in Canada at the age of eighty-seven.

At the age of twelve years George E. Bailey accompanied his parents on their removal to Iowa with the rest of the family, and at that early day in Iowa could not get a common-school education, a few months in winter is all the time that could be spared from the farm for schooling, and that with limited teachers, and at the age of seventeen started out to make his own way in the world, working as a farm hand by the month Subsequently he rented a farm at Ainsworth, Iowa, where he lived until 1861, when feeling his country needed his services, he laid aside all personal interests and disposed of his farm lease and enlisted in the Fifth Iowa Infantry During his four years and nine months of constant service he did what he could with his limited knowledge to serve his country well, without a murmur, participating in many important engagements, including the following: New Mardid, Champion Halls, Vicksburg, Fort Blakely, Mobile, and many others, and was in a part of Fremont's campaign in Missouri, and in 1863 was commissioned second lieutenant and transferred to the Fiftieth United States Colored Infantry. He served under a number of noted commanders, among whom were Pope, McPherson, Slocum, Canby, Hawkins and Force, and in 1865 resigned his commission, being then assistant provost marshal of the District of Northern Mississippi

On receiving his discharge, Mr. Bailey returned home and January, 1866, came to Rock Island and embarked in his present business, which he has since conducted with success He is now numbered among the most substantial men of the city, holding an enviable place in business circles

On the 8th of October, 1861, was celebrated the marriage of Mr Bailey and Miss Eliza C., daughter of Lewis G and Mary Harding. They have two daughters, Dollie, now the wife of D B. Shaw, his present partner, of Rock Island, by whom she has one son, George B , and Lelah, wife of W. T Drips, by whom she has three children,

William, Arthur and Lewis Mrs Bailey is a member of the Methodist church, as also are the two daughters, and with her husband enjoys the high regard of all who know them In his political affiliations, Mr Bailey is an ardent Republican and at one time was a member of the board of aldermen from the Second ward, now the Fourth ward, of Rock Island His social, genial nature has gained him many friends and he has the respect and confidence of all with whom he comes in contact, either in business or social life Aside from his political affiliations Mr. Bailey has the distinction of not being connected with any church, any insurance or other organization, not even drawing a pension from the government

HENRY E BIGGS, proprietor of a restaurant in Prospect Park, was born April 9, 1848, in Ohio county, West Virginia, and is a grandson of General Benjamin Biggs, a noted officer in the Revolutionary and Indian wars He was a native of England and came to the new world with four brothers, one of whom settled in Ohio, another in Maryland and two in West Virginia The General took up his residence in West Liberty, West Virginia, where he had a tomahawk right to four hundred acres He became very prominent and wealthy and reared a family of nine children

Benjamin Biggs, our subject's father, was born at West Liberty, in 1800, where he spent his entire life, following the occupation of contracting and building. He married Lydia Carney, a daughter of Edward Carney, and a native of Delaware, where there are three farms to-day which the records show belonged to the maternal grandfather To Mr and Mrs Biggs were born nine children, five sons and four daughters, of whom eight are still living Mrs M L Bradford, of Stewartsville, Rock Island county, George, of Ohio, Allen, of West Liberty, West Virginia, Mrs M A Gilbreath, of Wheeling, that state, James H , of West Liberty, Mrs S J Thornton, of Stewartsville, Illinois, Daniel E , who reresideson the old homestead at West Liberty, and Henry E , of this sketch

In West Liberty, West Virginia, Henry E Biggs grew to manhood, and completed his education in the State Normal School. He then learned the painter's trade, which he followed in Wheeling for a few years In West Liberty he was married November 27, 1873, to Miss Lizzie Durbin, who was born, reared and educated there, and is also a graduate of the State Normal For five years she successfully engaged in teaching Having no children of their own, Mr and Mrs Biggs have adopted two, Lillie, a proficient music teacher, who now holds a position in the central telephone office at Moline, and Lena, who is now a student in the Moline schools

In August, 1881, Mr Biggs came to Moline, Illinois, joining his two sisters, who had located here some years previously. For one year he worked in the shops of Deere & Company, then clerked in a grocery store for three years, and later established a grocery store in Stewartsville, which he conducted for five years At the end of that time he opened his present restaurant in Prospect Park and now enjoys a liberal patronage He is also interested in the raising of fine poultry and has about sixteen varieties, including the buff leghorn, Indian game, buff cochin and black leghorn At times he also works at painting and paper hanging.

Politically, Mr Biggs is independent, endeavoring to support the best man regardless of party He was elected and served for four years as justice of the peace in South Moline township Fraternally he is a member of the Modern Woodmen of America and the Home Forum, in the work of which he has taken an active and prominent part, and has filled all the chairs in the Odd Fellows society. Since 1891 he has served as solicitor and collector for the Equitable Building & Loan Association of Peoria, Illinois, and he faithfully performs every duty which falls to his lot, whether public or private.

INDEX.

CPSIA information can be obtained
at www.ICGtesting.com
Printed in the USA
LVHW050155170723
752652LV00005B/93